Assessment, Evaluation, and Programming System for Infants and Children

AEPS

Edited by **Diane Bricker, Ph.D.**

VOLUME 2

AEPS Curriculum
for Birth to Three Years

Also in this Series: _____

AEPS

Assessment, Evaluation, and Programming System for Infants and Children

VOLUME 2

AEPS Curriculum for Birth to Three Years

Edited by

Juliann Cripe, Ph.D.
University of Kansas
University Affiliated Program at Parsons

Kristine Slentz, Ph.D.
Department of Educational Curriculum and Instruction
Western Washington University

and

Diane Bricker, Ph.D.
Center on Human Development
University of Oregon

·P A U L ·H·
BROOKES
PUBLISHING Co

Baltimore • London • Toronto • Sydney

Paul H. Brookes Publishing Co.
P.O. Box 10624
Baltimore, Maryland 21285-0624

Typeset by Brushwood Graphics, Inc., Baltimore, Maryland.
Manufactured in the United States of America by
Versa Press, East Peoria, Illinois.

Third printing, January 1997.

The following AEPS forms can be purchased separately; these separate packages are printed in different colors:

AEPS Data Recording Forms, Birth to Three Years (printed in black; sold in
   package of 10)
AEPS Family Report, Birth to Three Years (printed in brown; sold in package of 10)
AEPS Family Interest Survey, Birth to Three Years (printed in blue; sold in
   package of 30)
AEPS Child Progress Record, Birth to Three Years (printed in green; sold in
   package of 30)

To order, contact Paul H. Brookes Publishing Co., P.O. Box 10624, Baltimore, Maryland,
21285-0624 (1-800-638-3775).

Please see page ii for information about other volumes in the AEPS series, all available from
Paul H. Brookes Publishing Co.

The Assessment, Evaluation, and Programming System for Infants and Children was developed in part with support from Grants #G008400661 and #H024C80001 from the U.S. Office of Education and Grant #09DD0019 from the Department of Health and Human Services to the Center on Human Development, University of Oregon. The content, however, does not necessarily reflect the position or policy of DOE or the University of Oregon and no official endorsement of these materials should be inferred.

Library of Congress Cataloging-in-Publication Data
(Revised for vol. 2)

Assessment, Evaluation, and Programming System for infants and children.
   Includes bibliographical references and index.
   Contents: v. 1. AEPS measurement for birth to three years—v. 2. Assessment, Evaluation,
   and Programming System curriculum for birth to three years.
   1. Assessment, Evaluation, and Programming System.   2. Child development—Testing.
3. Child development deviations—Diagnosis. I. Bricker, Diane D.   II. Title.
RJ51.D48A87   1992   305.23'1'0287   92-6690
   ISBN 1-55766-096-4   CIP

British Library Cataloguing-in-Publication data are available from the British Library.

CONTENTS

CONTRIBUTORS

THE EDITORS

Juliann Cripe, Ph.D., Southeast Kansas Birth to Three Program, University of Kansas, University Affiliated Program at Parsons, 2601 Gabriel, Parsons, Kansas 67357-0738. Dr. Cripe is an assistant scientist with the University of Kansas Univesity Affiliated Program at Parsons. Specializing in early intervention and communication skills and disorders, she has helped develop inservice training materials for families and direct service personnel to assist them in improving the communication skills of their children. She also has co-directed or coordinated a number of United States Department of Education–funded demonstration, inservice, and outreach projects focused on family participation, assessment and intervention, staff development, and rural service delivery options.

Kristine Slentz, Ph.D., Western Washington University, Mail Stop 9090, Bellingham, Washington 98225. Dr. Slentz is a professor of elementary education and special education in the department of educational and curriculum instruction at Western Washington University, specializing in early childhood. She provides consultation in the areas of integrated training for early childhood teachers, early development, and activity-based approaches to assessment and intervention. Dr. Slentz actively participates in inservice training and service delivery innovation in early childhood special education by authoring and coordinating local, state, and national grants.

Diane Bricker, Ph.D., Center on Human Development, University of Oregon, 901 E. 18th Street, Eugene, Oregon 97403-1211. Dr. Bricker is a professor of special education and a highly respected, well-known authority in the field of early intervention. She has directed a number of national demonstration projects and research efforts focused on examining the efficacy of early intervention; the development of a linked assessment, intervention, and evaluation system; and the study of a comprehensive, parent-focused screening tool. She presently directs the Early Intervention Area of the Center on Human Development, University of Oregon.

THE CONTRIBUTING AUTHORS

Tsai-Hsing Hsia, M.S., doctoral student, University of Oregon, Center on Human Development, 901 E. 18th Avenue, Eugene, Oregon 97403

Susan Janko, Ph.D., Child Development and Mental Retardation Center, University of Washington, CD413 CTU-CDMRC, WJ10, Seattle, Washington 98195

Angela Losardo, Ph.D., assistant professor, University of Oregon, Center on Human Development, 901 E. 18th Avenue, Eugene, Oregon 97403

Angela Notari, Project Director, University of Washington, Child Development and Mental Retardation Center, Experimental Education Unit WJ-10, Seattle, Washington 98195

Nancy Reid, M.S., toddler teacher, Olympia School District, 706 South Rogers Street, Olympia, Washington 98502

Betsy Ryan-Seth, M.S., teacher of students with moderate and severe mental retardation, Shasta Middle School, 4656 Barger Drive, Eugene, Oregon 97402

Margaret Veltman, Ph.D., assistant professor, University of Oregon, Center on Human Development, 901 E. 18th Avenue, Eugene, Oregon 97403

ACKNOWLEDGMENTS

The *AEPS Curriculum for Birth to Three Years* and its companion volume, *AEPS Measurement for Birth to Three Years,* have taken years to complete. Numerous people participated in developing some aspect of the curriculum contained in this volume. Some did library research, some wrote items, some reviewed items, some rewrote items, some used items with children, some reworked the format, some proofread, some edited, and importantly, some kept reminding us that this project was worth doing. Each contributor provided leadership, content, or enthusiasm that was needed to finish the project or a phase of the project.

As indicated above, many people assisted in developing this curriculum. Those who deserve special mention because of their help in developing items are Angela Losardo, Sarah Drinkwater, Tsai-Hsing Hsia, Susan Janko, Ruth Kaminski, Chris Marvin, Pat Morris, Angela Notari, Nancy Reid, and Margaret Veltman. Misti Waddell provided valuable assistance with her able coordination of the many activities necessary for the completion of the curriculum. Brenda Kameenui spent long hours editing the work and did an excellent job. Casie Givens typed the thousands of words that make up the curriculum and did it with good cheer and great competence. Other people contributed as well, and if their particular contributions have not been singled out it is because the passage of time makes memory increasingly faulty. To those individuals we extend our gratitude and our apology for failing to mention their specific effort.

Finally, we recognize the many parents and interventionists who bravely kept trying the suggested curriculum content and activities and providing constructive feedback. If this document is useful, it is because of their feedback and their commitment to improving services for young children with disabilities.

PREFACE

Development of the *Assessment, Evaluation, and Programming System for Infants and Children* began in the mid-1970s, as we have described in the Preface to Volume 1, *AEPS Measurement for Birth to Three Years*. As with the AEPS Test (included in Volume 1), the development of the companion AEPS Curriculum contained in this volume has taken years longer than we originally expected. Rather than developing along a singular path, this curriculum evolved through a series of stages and changes to its present form. This evolutionary process was driven by two forces.

First, although the conceptual goal of assisting interventionists and parents in using "naturalistic" activities as a teaching vehicle has never changed, the strategy for presentation changed considerably as we became better able to articulate ways in which activity-based intervention could be employed across a range of children, settings, conditions, and goals. Our growing sophistication over the years resulted in reformulations that, we hope, have contributed to the quality and usefulness of the curriculum.

The second force that spurred continued change in the curriculum was personnel. Except for Diane Bricker, the group of individuals who initiated work on the curriculum are entirely different from those who put the finishing touches on the version contained in Volume 2 of the AEPS. Across the years, individuals working on the curriculum have represented a broad range of perspectives and disciplines. The ongoing involvement of new personnel has, we believe, brought a richness and depth not otherwise obtainable.

At times, the benefits garnered from many researchers, interventionists, and caregivers participating in development of the curriculum have even grown from professional differences of opinion. For example, when current personnel did not agree with content or format proposed by previous individuals, resolution of such dilemmas lengthened the developmental period for our work but also enriched the curriculum. The blending of diverse perspectives has made the AEPS Curriculum better able to support and assist the work of interventionists and caregivers today.

One basic dilemma, with us throughout the evolution of the curriculum, perhaps warrants particular mention: How were we to ensure an evenness in the level of material presentation so that the information was specific enough to guide practice, yet general enough to allow users to adapt it to their programs and populations? It has been difficult to arrive at a balance in which adequate guidance is offered but relevant application to individual children and settings remains possible. We hope that balance has been obtained, but we ask the user to judge.

As with Volume 1, *AEPS Measurement for Birth to Three Years*, the profits from the sale of this second volume will be directed to a fund to provide support for the curriculum's revision and refinement. Future work will be focused on improving the content and format to better meet the needs of young children with disabilities and their families.

Juliann Cripe
Kristine Slentz
Diane Bricker

Introduction

The importance of early experience for young children has long been recognized and has been the foundation for early intervention programs designed for young children who have disabilities or are at risk. Beginning with unclear expectations and a narrow focus, early intervention programs have evolved into comprehensive approaches that produce positive change in the lives of participating children and their families. In large measure, the increasingly positive outcomes engendered by early intervention programs have occurred because of the growing sophistication of personnel, curricular materials, and assessment/evaluation tools. The assessment, intervention, and evaluation system described in this volume is an example of this growing sophistication, which will, in turn, enhance future intervention efforts with young children in need of services.

Accompanying this enhancement in quality has been the growth in the number of early intervention programs. This growth has been systematically spurred on by the passage of important federal legislation beginning with the Education for All Handicapped Children Act, PL 94-142, which was signed into law in 1975. This landmark legislation required public schools to accept all school-age children no matter how severe their disability, and it introduced the concept of the individualized education program (IEP). (In 1990, PL 101-476 reauthorized the Education for All Handicapped Children Act and changed the name to the Individuals with Disabilities Education Act, or IDEA.) Eleven years after the original enactment of PL 94-142 PL 99-457 (Education of the Handicapped Act Amendments of 1986), extended the mandate for public school programs to 3-, 4- and 5-year-old children with disabilities, and offered states incentives to serve infants and toddlers. PL 99-457 strongly urges the inclusion of families as partners in the development of intervention plans, known as individualized family service plans (IFSPs) and in the delivery of services to their children. The most recent amendment, PL 102-119 (Individuals with Disabilities Education Act Amendments of 1991), further encourages family participation, permits states to move away from the use of categorical labels for preschoolers, and strongly urges the inclusion of children at risk in intervention programs. Accompanying this series of important federal enactments have been an increasing number of state mandates to provide services to infants and young children who have disabilities and their families.

As noted, accompanying the growth of early intervention programs has been an increasing sophistication in the delivery of services. Personnel are better prepared, curricular content is improved, intervention techniques are more effective, and assessment and evaluation approaches are more appropriate and useful. Importantly, there has been a move to develop approaches that are cohesive, coordinated, and comprehensive. Approaches that treat program components as isolated and unrelated units are being replaced by to approaches that systematically link the major components of assessment, intervention, and evaluation. The Assessment, Evaluation, and Program-

1

ming System, as presented in this volume, is one such linked approach. The components of this system are displayed in Figure 1.

WHAT IS THE ASSESSMENT, EVALUATION, AND PROGRAMMING SYSTEM?

AEPS is an assessment and evaluation system that has an associated curriculum. The AEPS is more than an assessment measure; it is a comprehensive and linked system that includes assessment/evaluation, curricular, and family participation components. The material contained in Volume 1 describes the measurement component of the system for the developmental range from birth to 3 years; Volume 2 presents the associated curriculum.

Volume 1, *AEPS Measurement for Birth to Three Years*, is divided into three sections. Section I provides a comprehensive description of the Assessment, Evaluation, and Programming System. Section II presents the AEPS Test items composed of the six domains that cover the developmental period from 1 month to 3 years. Section III describes how to involve families in the assessment and evaluation process as well as how to provide specific strategies and forms for doing so.

Volume 1 also provides useful appendices to assist in the implementation of the AEPS. Appendix A contains summarized psychometric information on the AEPS Test that has been collected since the early 1980s. Readers requiring more detail are referred to specific published articles. Appendix B contains a series of IEP/IFSP goals and objectives specifically related to each item on the AEPS Test. Appendix C contains a set of Assessment Activity Plans. Appendix D contains examples of the AEPS Test Data Recording Forms, the Family Report, the Family Interest Survey, and the Child Progress Record.

Volume 2, *AEPS Curriculum for Birth to Three Years*, is composed of three sections. Section I describes the relationship between the AEPS Test described in Volume 1 and the Curriculum. The numbering system for the AEPS Test and Curriculum permits efficient movement between the two. Procedures for general use of the AEPS Curriculum are also described in Section I. Section II explains in detail how to use the AEPS Curriculum separately or in conjunction with the AEPS Test. Section III presents the AEPS curricular activities covering the fine motor, gross motor, adaptive, cognitive, social-communication, and social domains. For each item on the AEPS Test, an associ-

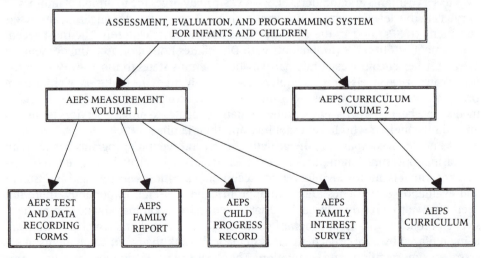

Figure 1.   Components of the Assessment, Evaluation, and Programming System (AEPS) for Infants and Children.

ated set of curricular activities is described including cross-references to the AEPS Test; the item's importance to a child's development; procedures for using an activity-based intervention approach, as well as more structured approaches; cautions; and teaching suggestions.

Volumes 1 and 2 have been designed to be of practical use to early interventionists. Used either separately or together, the philosophy, material, and procedures contained in these volumes should enhance intervention efforts with a range of children and their families.

INTRODUCTION TO VOLUME 2

Volume 2, *AEPS Curriculum for Birth to Three Years*, is the curricular component of the Assessment, Evaluation, and Programming System for Infants and Children and was developed to meet two purposes. First, the AEPS Curriculum provides interventionists (e.g., teachers, child development specialists, occupational therapists, physical therapists, psychologists, communication specialists) and caregivers with a range of activities that can be used to facilitate children's acquisition of functional and generic skills. Second, the AEPS Curriculum provides a direct link between assessment, intervention, and evaluation. The AEPS Test and AEPS Curriculum were developed to provide a direct and ongoing correspondence between initial assessment, IEP/IFSP development, program planning, intervention activities, and subsequent evaluation.

The developers of the Curriculum were interested in creating a tool that targets intervention on important and generic behaviors in the child's daily play and routine activities rather than in teacher-directed activities. They were interested in laying out the Curriculum following an activity-based approach, encouraging the use of the least intrusive interventions necessary for the child to make progress. Finally, they were interested in developing a tool that linked directly to previous assessment efforts and progress monitoring. None of these important goals has been lost in the evolution of the AEPS Curriculum. In addition, other important goals, such as family involvement, adaptations for specific disabilities, and teaching considerations have come to be a part of the system.

The content in Volume 2 is focused on assisting interventionists and caregivers in developing intervention plans based on Volume 1 *AEPS Measurement for Birth to Three Years*. Section I discusses how the AEPS Curriculum was designed to accommodate an activity-based approach to early intervention. It also describes the relationship between the AEPS Test in Volume 1 and the Curriculum. Section II contains the Curriculum Administration Guide, and Section III presents the curricular activities.

Understanding the purpose of the curricular system and how it operates is fundamental to its appropriate use. Reading and understanding Section I of Volume 1 is highly recommended if the material in Volume 2 is to be maximally useful to interventionists, caregivers, and, ultimately, children.

REFERENCES

Education for All Handicapped Children Act of 1975, PL 94-142. (August 23, 1977). 20 U.S.C. 1401 et seq: *Federal Register,* 42(163), 42474–42518.

Education of the Handicapped Act Amendments of 1986, PL 99-457. (October 8, 1986). Title 20, U.S.C. 1400 et seq: *U.S. Statutes at large, 100,* 1145–1177.

Individuals with Disabilities Education Act of 1990 (IDEA), PL 101-476. (October 30, 1990). Title 20, U.S.C. 1400–1485: *U.S. Statutes at large, 104,* 1103–1151.

Individuals with Disabilities Education Act Amendments of 1991, PL 102-119. (October 7, 1991). Title 20, U.S.C. 1400 et seq: *U.S. Statutes at large, 105,* 587–608.

Understanding the AEPS Curriculum

AN ACTIVITY-BASED APPROACH

The AEPS Curriculum was designed to accommodate an approach to early intervention known as activity-based intervention. The AEPS Curriculum provides information to interventionists that encourages the integration of goals and objectives into a child's daily activities and life experiences. The format of the AEPS Curriculum emphasizes the use of routine and planned activities to work on the child's selected goals and objectives. That is, for each goal and objective, a number of activities are suggested that interventionists or caregivers can readily use to enhance the development of the target skill. The AEPS Curriculum recommends more structured, individual intervention programs only when activity-based intervention proves unsuccessful or progress is unacceptable.

The activity-based intervention approach was designed to take advantage, in an objective and measurable way, of natural instruction that parents use with their young children.

> Activity-based intervention is a child-directed, transactional approach that embeds intervention on children's individual goals and objectives in routine, planned, or child-initiated activities, and uses logically occurring antecedents and consequences to develop functional and generative skills. (Bricker & Cripe, 1992, p. 40)

Two features of this approach should be emphasized. First, multiple targets (e.g., motor, communication, social, cognitive, adaptive) can be addressed in single activities. For example, a water activity in which children are washing baby dolls can be used to promote communication ("I need soap"), social skills (taking turns with the washcloth and soap), adaptive skills (washing hands), motor skills (reaching and grasping), and cognitive skills (finding a towel to dry the baby). A second feature of activity-based intervention is the built-in rewards for children who are participating in fun and interesting activities. If the activities are well chosen or child selected, they will provide

5

ample motivation for the child, and artificial contingencies may be eliminated. The AEPS Curriculum provides a description of routine and planned activities for each AEPS Test objective and goal. Activities were selected because they can be used to work on multiple targets and because most children find them interesting.

An activity-based approach teaches skills by embedding children's target objectives into functional, routine activities that are of interest to children. For example, rather than establishing special sessions for teaching labeling of objects, items are named in the context of a relevant activity. Naming body parts might be stressed during bathtime, items of clothing can be named when dressing or during doll play, and labeling foods and eating utensils can be naturally worked into snack or mealtimes. If the pincer grasp is a target skill, the child can practice this grasp during snack time with a raisin, apple slice, or Cheerios, or during an art activity with pieces of tape or small wooden beads.

The advantages of using an activity-based format with infants and young children are many. First, the notion of providing relevant antecedents and consequences within an activity is incorporated into teaching functional skills in the child's usual environment. When the antecedents and consequences are relevant or part of an activity, motivation and attention problems tend to be less frequent. Second, activity-based intervention addresses the issues of generalization and maintenance. Teaching a particular skill is not limited to only one activity, but it is taught by a variety of interventionists, family members, and caregivers across different materials and settings. Third, an activity-based approach helps keep targeted objectives functional for the child. If the skills targeted for intervention are those used in daily activities, they are likely to be useful to the child in coping with environmental demands. A fourth advantage is that when skill teaching is embedded in daily activities, other people, such as caregivers and peers, can be used as change agents and teaching resources. Fifth, activity-based intervention can be used with a heterogeneous group of young children. Children can act as peer models for one another and be involved in presenting antecedents and consequences. For example, in a painting activity, each child is given a different color of paint and must request various colors from other children to complete his or her painting. Sally's request for red paint, for example, may act as an antecedent event to which Paula responds. Paula's response (e.g., looking, smiling, verbalizing, offering paint) may act as a positive consequence to Sally. Such activities tend to enhance children's active participation, and are less teacher-directed and controlled.

AEPS Curriculum users who would like more information on how to employ activity-based intervention are referred to *An Activity-Based Approach to Early Intervention* (Bricker & Cripe, 1992).

LINKING ASSESSMENT, INTERVENTION, AND EVALUATION[1]

The AEPS Curriculum provides a direct link between assessment, intervention, and evaluation. Assessment refers to the process of establishing a baseline or entry-level measurement of the child's skills and desired family outcomes. The assessment process should produce the necessary information to select appropriate and relevant intervention goals and objectives and family outcomes. Figure 1 illustrates the relationship of

---

[1]Adapted from Bricker, D., Janko, S., Cripe, J., Bailey, E., & Kaminski, R. (1989). *Evaluation and programming system: For infants and young children.* Eugene: University of Oregon, Center on Human Development.

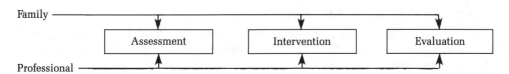

Figure 1.   A schematic of a linked assessment-intervention-evaluation approach including professional and family participation.

these three processes as well as the desired participation of professionals and family members in each process. The assessment-intervention-evaluation system can be divided into six phases:[2]

Phase One: Initial assessment
Phase Two: Formulation of the individualized education programs (IEPs) or individualized family services plans (IFSPs)
Phase Three: Intervention
Phase Four: Ongoing monitoring for immediate feedback on individualized intervention procedures
Phase Five: Quarterly evaluation of children and families
Phase Six: Annual or semi-annual evaluation of individual child and family progress and program effectiveness for total groups and subgroups of children such as those at risk or with disabilities

Phase One: Initial Assessment

The link between assessment, intervention, and evaluation begins with the entry of children into an intervention program. The major objective of the initial assessment is to formulate a useful and appropriate IEP/IFSP.

In the initial assessment, a program-relevant (i.e., curriculum-based) assessment is administered to determine the content of the IEP/IFSP. This content provides the road map for moving children from their beginning skill repertoires to the acquisition of skills specified as annual goals in their IEP/IFSP. For the family, this initial assessment should help determine priority interests that can be developed into family outcomes. The formulation of a useful IEP/IFSP is crucially dependent upon an accurate assessment of a child's beginning skill level so that an intervention plan can be developed to improve areas where a deficit exists. An assessment that measures functional skills and is sensitive to the conditions in which a child is most likely to perform the skill will facilitate the development of appropriate and useful IEPs/IFSPs.

Formulation of an IFSP allows opportunities for family outcomes as well as child goals. Family assessment should yield program-relevant information that will aid in developing functional outcome statements, but the process and tools should not be intrusive to family members.

---

[2]A more detailed description of the six phases of linked assessment, intervention, and evaluation is contained in Bricker, D. (Ed.). (1993). *AEPS measurement for birth to three years.* Baltimore: Paul H. Brookes Publishing Co.

Phase Two: Formulation of the IEP/IFSP[3]

The IEP/IFSP should be based primarily on information accumulated during the initial assessment period. (This testing should be validated at the first quarterly evaluation.) Relevant information is obtained from the caregiver's knowledge of his or her child as well as from professional observation and testing. This initial information is used to develop a plan of action for the interventionists and caregivers to identify the specific content areas that the IEP/IFSP will address. The IEP/IFSP should be straightforward so that it can be used as a guide for interventionists and caregivers. It can also be used as a criterion against which the success of the intervention is evaluated.

The child's portion of the IEP/IFSP itemizes goals, objectives, and a time frame for meeting the selected goals. The family's portion of the IFSP contains a statement of family resources, concerns, and priorities related to enhancing the child's development, based upon the family's identification of their interests and needs. Priorities are established collaboratively during a discussion with appropriate family members. A set of outcome statements evolves from these priorities, and activities and resources necessary for reaching outcomes, as well as a timeline, are specified.

Phase Three: Intervention

Once the IEP/IFSP has been formulated by caregivers and interventionists, the actual intervention activities can be initiated. The child's performance on the program assessment indicates where intervention should begin. Items that the child is unable to perform become the intervention goals and objectives. Often, the goals and objectives require prioritization. If the assessment tool links directly to a curriculum, such as the AEPS, interventionists can easily locate the intervention activities that were developed to facilitate acquisition of specific goals and objectives. There is a direct correspondence between the assessment items (skills) identified as goals or objectives and the intervention content and strategies specified in the associated curriculum. Following is an example of the link between the program assessment and intervention.

To illustrate the correspondence between items on the AEPS Test and Curriculum, a completed Data Recording Form from the Adaptive Domain of the AEPS Test is shown in Figure 2. Juan's performance on Strand A: Feeding, indicates he reached criteria for Goal 1 (Uses tongue/lips to take in and swallow solid foods and liquids), but did not meet the specified criteria for Goals 2, 3, 4, and 5.

For Goal 2 (Bites *and* chews hard and chewy foods), Juan met the criteria for Objective 2.2 (Munches soft and crisp foods), but not for Objective 2.1 (Bites *and* chews soft and crisp foods). For Goal 3 (Drinks from cup/glass), the child met the criteria for Objective 3.2 (Drinks from cup and/or glass held by adult), but did not meet criteria for Objective 3.1 (Drinks from cup and/or glass with some spilling). Juan met the criteria for Goal 4 , Objective 4.3 (Accepts food on spoon), but did not meet criteria for Objective 4.2 and Objective 4.1. He did not meet criteria for any of the objecti
ed with Goal 5 (Transfers food and liquid).

Results from the completion of the AEPS Family Report are similar to the interventionist's assessment using the AEPS Test. After discussing the results, the early intervention staff and Juan's family select Objectives 2.1, 3.1, and 4.2 as priority targets. The next step is to move directly to the Adaptive Domain of the AEPS Curriculum. The AEPS Curriculum Adaptive Domain is cross-referenced to the Adaptive Domain of the AEPS Test as shown in Figure 3. Figure 3 contains the appropriate cross-referenced

---

[3]Further information on the development of IEPs/IFSPs can be found in Chapter 5 of Bricker, D. (Ed.). (1993). *AEPS measurement for birth to three years.* Baltimore: Paul H. Brookes Publishing Co.

AEPS

Adaptive Domain

S = Scoring Key	Q = Qualifying Notes
2 = Pass consistently	A = Assistance provided
1 = Inconsistent	B = Behavior interfered
performance	R = Reported assessment
0 = Does not pass	M = Modification/adaptation
	D = Direct test

Name: **Juan**

Test Period: **1st**
Test Date: **6 / 92**
Examiner: **Tobias**

	IEP	S	Q	S	Q	S	Q	S	Q
A. Feeding									
1. Uses tongue/lips to take in and swallow solid foods and liquids		2							
1.1 Uses lips to take liquids from cup/glass		2							
1.2 Uses lips to take food off spoon/fork		2							
1.3 Swallows solid and semisolid foods		2							
1.4 Swallows liquids		2							
2. Bites *and* chews hard and chewy foods		0							
2.1 Bites *and* chews soft and crisp foods	✓	0							
2.2 Munches soft and crisp foods		2							
3. Drinks from cup/glass		0							
3.1 Drinks with some spilling	✓	1							
3.2 Drinks from cup or glass held by adult		2							
4. Eats with fork/spoon		0							
4.1 Brings food to mouth with utensil		0							
4.2 Eats with fingers	✓	0							
4.3 Accepts food on spoon		2							
5. Transfers food and liquid		0							
5.1 Pours liquid		0							
5.2 Transfers food		0							
B. Personal hygiene									
1. Initiates toileting									

Figure 2. Portion of a completed AEPS Test Data Recording Form for the Adaptive Domain, Strand A.

Objective 2.1   Bites *and* chews soft and crisp foods

DEVELOPMENTAL PROGRAMMING STEPS

PS2.1a   The child chews soft and crisp foods.
PS2.1b   The child bites soft and crisp foods.

IMPORTANCE OF SKILL

Biting and chewing are necessary to the transition from pureed foods to solid foods and may affect the ability of the growing child to receive adequate nutrition. As the child develops teeth, the munching pattern is replaced by the more powerful and effective rotary jaw movements of chewing. The ability to bite and chew foods expands the variety of tasteful meals and snacks and reduces the risk of choking.

PRECEDING OBJECTIVE

Adap A:2.2   Munches soft and crisp foods

CONCURRENT GOAL AND OBJECTIVES

FM A:3.1   Grasps hand-size object with either hand using the palm, with object placed toward the thumb and index finger
Adap A:4.2   Eats with fingers
Cog B:1.0   Visually follows object and/or person to point of disappearance
Cog D:1.1   Imitates motor action that is commonly used
Cog E:1.2   Retains object . . . [*continues*]

TEACHING SUGGESTIONS
Activity-Based

- Provide regular opportunities for the child to eat soft and crisp foods during snack and mealtimes, while adults and peers are eating the same foods.
- Present soft and crisp foods, such as bread, saltine crackers, bananas, cheese slices, and dry cereal.
- Allow the child to handle soft and crisp foods freely at meal and snack times, without always requiring that the food be eaten. The child may be less hesitant to bite and chew soft and crisp foods if he or she becomes familiar with the texture of the foods by handling them.
- Make eating a relaxed and pleasant experience for the child. Use the child's preferences of foods and favorite mealtimes to introduce soft and crisp foods.

(continued)

Environmental Arrangements

- There are many kinds of crisp foods that vary in the degree of difficulty to bite and chew. Saltine crackers, rice cakes, celery sticks, apples, and Cheerios are crisp. More crisp are melba toast, potato chips, raw carrots, and corn chips. Begin with easier foods and systematically introduce crisper foods as the child begins to bite and chew.
- The size of the food should be appropriate for finger feeding. The child may be more interested in trying a more solid, crisp food if finger feeding than if fed by an adult.
- Initially introduce only a small amount of one soft or crisp food at each meal. Alternate soft and crisp foods with other foods and liquids that the child manages easily. Gradually introduce more soft and crisp foods as the child begins to bite and chew them.
- Begin by using foods that the child prefers to eat. Cook a small amount of a fruit, vegetable, or pasta to make it very soft. Gradually cook the same food less and less to encourage the child to bite through the same food in a crisper form. Carrots, green beans, and zucchini are examples of vegetables that can be eaten fully cooked or partially cooked. . . . [*continues*]

Instructional Sequence

- Model biting and chewing by biting through hard and chewy foods and moving the jaw up, down, and in a rotary motion. Encourage the child to imitate, using a mirror if necessary.
- Verbally encourage the child to bite through hard and chewy foods and chew each bite ("Bite hard," "One bite at a time," "Keep chewing"). . . . [*continues*]

Figure 3. Sample portions from Adaptive Domain, Strand A, Goal 2, Objective 2.1 of the AEPS Curriculum.

page from the AEPS Curriculum. One can link the assessment findings to intervention targets by using the AEPS Curriculum Adaptive Domain, Strand A: Feeding, Goal 2 and Objective 2.1. Following Objective 2.1 is a series of developmental programming steps leading to the acquisition of Objective 2.1. Objective 4.2 is included as a concurrent objective. This means that this objective can be taught simultaneously, using many of the activities suggested in the Curriculum under Objective 2.1. Specific environmental arrangements and instructional sequences are described for the objective.

Phase Four: Ongoing Monitoring

A useful IEP/IFSP specifies both the tasks to be conducted and the manner in which the success of the program is to be evaluated. A variety of strategies may be used for daily or weekly monitoring of child progress (e.g., trial-by-trial data, brief probes during or after intervention activities). The strategies selected should be determined by specific goals or objectives, program resources, and the need for daily or weekly monitoring as a source of feedback to keep intervention efforts on track.

Phase Five: Quarterly Evaluation

Quarterly evaluations should focus on determining the effect of intervention efforts on children's quarterly objectives specified in the IEP/IFSP. This can be done by using the initial assessment measures in conjunction with the weekly data. Quarterly evaluations should be used to compare the child's progress with some standard or expectation for progress. Without assigning an expected date of completion for objectives and goals, it is difficult to determine if the progress made by the child is acceptable.

Phase Six: Annual or Semi- annual Evaluation

Annual or semi-annual evaluations are used to evaluate the progress of individual children and families, as well as the overall effectiveness of the program (i.e., subgroup analysis). Without subgroup comparisons, it is difficult to know how to improve intervention strategies for subpopulations of children and families. Methodological design and measurement problems facing the field of early intervention make subgroup evaluations difficult; however, analyses of subgroups yield important findings on generalization of outcomes for selected groups of children and families.

SUMMARY

The AEPS Curriculum follows an activity-based approach to early intervention. The Curriculum emphasizes the use of routine and planned activities to develop children's selected goals and objectives. An understanding of activity-based intervention is useful to Curriculum users.

  The six phases of the linked system outline the importance of directly relating the processes of assessment, intervention, and evaluation. Employing this system allows efficient effort and use of resources, accountability in terms of program impact over time, and individualization through the design of programs specific to the needs of children and their families. Fundamental to such a system is an appropriate assessment/evaluation tool and an associated curriculum such as the AEPS Test and AEPS Curriculum.

REFERENCES

Bricker, D. (Ed.). (1993). *AEPS measurement for birth to three years.* Baltimore: Paul H. Brookes Publishing Co.

Bricker, D., Janko, S., Cripe, J., Bailey, E., & Kaminski, R. (1989). *Evaluation and programming system: For infants and young children.* Eugene: University of Oregon, Center on Human Development.

Bricker, D., & Cripe, J.J. (1992). *An activity-based approach to early intervention.* Baltimore: Paul H. Brookes Publishing Co.

AEPS Curriculum Administration Guide

The AEPS Curriculum contains intervention activities and strategies for each of the AEPS Test goals and objectives. The numbering system used in the AEPS Test and Curriculum permits the user to move directly from assessment and/or evaluation outcomes to appropriate and relevant intervention activities. For each AEPS Test assessment and/or evaluation goal and objective, the AEPS Curriculum describes relevant intervention content and a variety of intervention strategies from naturalistic to adult guided. Prior to using the AEPS Curriculum it is essential to read the administrative procedures contained in this section, which describe the Curriculum's format and procedures for its use.

The AEPS Curriculum has several important features that make it compatible with the AEPS Test. First, the Curriculum provides intervention content that is directly tied to the IEP/IFSP goals developed from the AEPS Test results. Second, efficiency of program staff is enhanced by providing programming information that is tied directly to assessment outcomes. Third, the curricular content is focused on assisting program staff to target functional and useful skills. Finally, the information provided in the AEPS Curriculum assists interventionists in implementing an activity-based intervention approach, which encourages generalization of learned skills through the integration of teaching in daily activities.

Although the AEPS Curriculum contains considerable information on intervention activities and procedures, it does not provide information that may be necessary in two areas—behavior management and task analysis. Effective child management techniques are essential to maximize intervention efforts whether at home or in a center setting. Interventionists who need assistance in managing a child's behavior or in helping parents manage their child can utilize the resources listed at the end of this section.

For children with severe disabilities or significant difficulty acquiring a skill, interventionists and caregivers may need to reduce a skill into simpler components. Task analysis is an effective procedure for dividing objectives or developmental programming steps into simpler and more discrete response units. If assistance is needed to task analyze skills, the resources listed at the end of this section may be useful.

AEPS CURRICULUM FORMAT

As indicated earlier, the AEPS Curriculum is designed to work in conjunction with the AEPS Test. The content of the AEPS Test covers domains of behavior and specific skills considered essential for infants and young children developmentally birth to 3 years to gain independent functioning and cope with environmental demands. Six broad areas of development called domains are used in the AEPS Test and Curriculum: Fine Motor, Gross Motor, Adaptive, Cognitive, Social-Communication, and Social. Each of the domains encompasses a set of skills or behaviors traditionally seen as related developmental phenomena.

The six domains are divided into a series of strands, which organize related groups of behaviors under a common category. Every strand contains a series of items called goals. The goals were developed to be used as annual goals on a child's IEP/IFSP. Associated with each goal is an accompanying set of objectives that represents more discrete skills. The objectives enable the examiner to accurately pinpoint a child's level within a specific skill sequence.

The identification system associated with the strands (e.g., A, B), goals (e.g., 1, 2), and objectives (e.g., 1.1, 1.2) reflects the sequential arrangement of the test items on the AEPS Test. In addition, the numbering system helps AEPS Test users locate and refer to items.

The AEPS Curriculum follows the same format as the AEPS Test, which provides a direct correspondence between the assessment and the curriculum. The cross-referencing system in the AEPS Curriculum utilizes an abbreviated term for the name of the domain (e.g., SC for social-communication) and then identifiers indicate the strand, goal, and objective. For example, Soc A:1.3 refers to the Social Domain, Strand A, Objective 1.3; GM B:2.0 refers to the Gross Motor Domain, Strand B, Goal 2. Goals are identified by a single digit and objectives are identified by the number of the goal, a period, and then the number of the objective. The names of each domain are abbreviated as follows:

Fine Motor Domain: FM
Gross Motor Domain: GM
Adaptive Domain: Adap
Cognitive Domain: Cog
Social-Communication Domain: SC
Social Domain: Soc

Each AEPS Curriculum item is associated with a particular AEPS Test domain, strand, goal, and objective, as shown in Figure 1.

Each AEPS Curriculum domain contains an introduction that describes the domain content, relevant general considerations, and associated curricular activities for each goal and objective on the AEPS Test. Whereas each goal and objective contains information specific to the skill, some information is necessarily redundant in the Developmental Programming Steps and Teaching Suggestions sections throughout the curriculum. To avoid repetition, the first item of each strand indicates with a checked box (☑) the information applicable to subsequent items. The following items do not repeat the information, but, if necessary, the user can refer to the checked box con-

AEPS Test and AEPS Curriculum structure	Example
Domain	Social
Strand	A: Interaction with Adults
Goal (G)	1: Initiates an affectionate response toward familiar adult.
Objective (O)	1.1: Responds appropriately to familiar adult's affective tone.

Figure 1.   An example from the Social Domain to show the corresponding structure of the AEPS Test and the AEPS Curriculum.

tained in the earlier item. The format for the curricular activities includes the following items: developmental programming steps, importance of skill, preceding objective, concurrent objective, teaching suggestions, and teaching considerations.

Developmental Programming Steps   The developmental programming steps either offer steps to develop more basic or discrete skills than appear in the AEPS Test objective, or they offer general guidelines to develop simpler, more basic skills as possible prerequisites to the AEPS Test objective and goal. These developmental programming steps directly correspond to a goal or objective of the AEPS Test. For example, the two developmental programming steps for the Fine Motor Domain, Strand A , Objective 3.3 are identified as PS3.3a and PS3.3b. For some objectives, specific developmental programming steps are not included because the objective already represents a basic, discrete skill. In this case, the user can refer to the *instructional sequence* for suggestions if a child needs a more discrete or specific target.

Importance of Skill   The importance of skill section provides a brief explanation of the importance of the targeted skills to the independent functioning of a child. The hierarchy of the skills and their relationship to other important objectives is explained. This section also offers information that may help family and team members understand the importance of the objective.

Preceding Objective   The preceding objective section lists the AEPS Test objective that precedes the targeted objective and its developmental programming steps to ensure that the most appropriate objective for the child has been chosen.

Concurrent Objective   The concurrent objective section lists the AEPS Test objectives that can generally be targeted at the same time that the child works on the objective being discussed and its associated developmental programming steps. This section helps identify targets that can be easily combined into activities, rather than developing an activity for each specific target. This section is particularly relevant to development of group activity plans and to assisting in the development of an activity-based intervention approach.

Teaching Suggestions   The teaching suggestions section contains appropriate activities for implementing the developmental programming steps and the associated objective. First, procedures for employing an *activity-based* intervention approach are specified. These are routine or planned activities that are likely to occur throughout the day. These activities are the least intrusive form of intervention and maximize the use of naturalistic teaching techniques. Activity-based intervention can be used in home, daycare, and mainstream sites, as well as in classroom programs. Second, *environmental arrangements* to enhance the child's acquisition of the skill are listed. These offer ideas for increasing the number of teaching opportunities within activities and for increasing the likelihood of the child's success. An *instructional sequence* is provided at the end. This form of intervention is the least preferred, but perhaps necessary for skill acquisition with some children. *Instructional sequences* are also arranged hierarchically to help the interventionist choose the least intrusive method.

Teaching Considerations   The teaching considerations section lists precautions for consideration while working with a child on the targeted skill. Adaptations for sensory and motor impairments are recommended when appropriate. The interventionist should always read this section prior to working with the child on the targeted skill.

AEPS CURRICULUM PROCEDURES

The first step in assessing a child is to administer the AEPS Test and examine the child's performance domain by domain. All goals on which the child has met criterion are noted, and remaining goals on which the child has not met criterion are prioritized in terms of intervention emphasis. The objectives of the selected goals should then be examined to choose the appropriate teaching target. For example, if Goal 1 (Uses 50 single words) from Strand D of the Social-Communication Domain has been chosen, the next step is to examine the child's performance on the five associated objectives (1.1: Uses five descriptive words, 1.2: Uses five action words, 1.3: Uses two pronouns, 1.4: Uses 15 object and/or event labels, and 1.5: Uses three proper names). If, for example, the child has met criterion for Objectives 1.5 and 1.4, then further work on Objectives 1.3, 1.2, and 1.1 is appropriate. Depending on a number of variables (e.g., caregiver preference, child's disability, program resources), any or all of these objectives might be selected as teaching targets.

Once the objectives are selected, the interventionist can move to the AEPS Curriculum. If Objective 1.3 is a chosen objective, the associated curricular activities will be listed under Objective 1.3. Location is straightforward because the AEPS Curriculum uses the same numbering system as the AEPS Test. Therefore, to locate the associated curricular activities for Objective 1.3, the interventionist turns to the Social-Communication Domain of the AEPS Curriculum, then to Strand D, Goal 1, and Objective 1.3.

SUMMARY

The introductory material, as well as the information contained in the Administration Guide, is included to set the stage for the efficient and effective use of the AEPS Curriculum in conjunction with the AEPS Test. The user is urged to carefully read this material prior to employing the curriculum. In addition, we strongly recommend that the AEPS Curriculum be used in association with the AEPS Test. Without accurate, in-depth knowledge of children's behavioral repertoires, selecting appropriate intervention activities is guesswork; so too is monitoring progress. The field of early intervention has become, through legal, legislative, professional, and parental efforts, a legitimate enterprise that can no longer tolerate less than quality outcomes. Producing quality outcomes for children and families is dependent upon careful and comprehensive assessments that lead to appropriate intervention accompanied by ongoing evaluation. Use of the AEPS Test and AEPS Curriculum will help interventionists attain this quality.

RESOURCES

Behavior Management and Task Analysis

Alberto, P., & Troutman, A. (1982). *Applied behavior analysis for teachers.* Columbus, OH: Charles E. Merrill.
Bailey, D., & Wolery, M. (1992). *Teaching infants and preschoolers with disabilities* (2nd ed.). Columbus, OH: Charles E. Merrill.

Kaplan, J., (1991). *Beyond behavior modification* (2nd ed.). Austin, TX: PRO-ED.

Orelove, F.P., & Sobsey, D. (1991). *Educating children with multiple disabilities: A transdisciplinary approach* (2nd ed.). Baltimore: Paul H. Brookes Publishing Co.

Sulzer-Azaroff, B., & Mayer, R. (1977). *Applying behavior-analysis procedures with children and youth.* New York: Holt, Rinehart & Winston.

Wolery, M., Bailey, D., & Sugai, G. (1988). *Effective teaching: Principles and procedures of applied behavior analysis with exceptional students.* Newton: Allyn & Bacon.

Assessment, Evaluation, and Programming System Curriculum

AEPS

FINE MOTOR DOMAIN

Margaret Veltman, Betsy Ryan-Seth, Kristine Slentz, and Juliann Cripe

The Fine Motor Domain addresses a major accomplishment in the infant and toddler years—the use of the hands for precise reaching, grasping, and manipulation. These skills serve the child well throughout life, enabling the child to hold a fork or chopsticks, to insert keys in doors, and to sketch drawings or write stories. To manage these sophisticated motor actions, the child begins with the basic fine motor skills contained in this section of the Curriculum. The Fine Motor Domain is divided into two strands: Strand A: Reach, Grasp, and Release; and Strand B: Functional Use of Fine Motor Skills. The first strand delineates the sequence of voluntary development of sophisticated hand and finger movements. The second strand focuses on functionally using these new skills to turn, assemble, or activate objects, and to copy written shapes.

Much of a child's knowledge of the world is facilitated through the development of fine motor skills. For example, a young child extends a hand to a bright-colored rattle, grasps it, and brings it toward his or her face. In the process, the child shakes the rattle and hears a noise. The child waves the rattle back and forth, watches it, and puts it in his or her mouth and sucks on it. The fine motor skills of reaching and grasping provided this young child opportunities to develop visual, auditory, and oral skills. As fine motor skills develop, opportunities to explore and manipulate the environment increase as well. The child who can intentionally release objects can gain a great deal of attention from caregivers by dropping food, eating utensils, or toys to the floor while smiling and waiting for the caregiver to bend over and pick them up.

The infant has plenty of time and interest in practicing fine motor skills while lying in the crib, sitting in a swing or stroller, or while being carried. Early fine motor practice includes swiping at objects, grasping objects, playing with fingers, and mouthing objects. However, opportunities need to be available. One of the easiest, yet most important, activities is to provide different objects for the infant to watch, touch, taste, smell, and hear. These toys do not need to be expensive; children often prefer common household objects for play. The toys or objects simply must be accessible and safe; it is never too early to check the safety of toys and materials used by an infant. It is also important to consider safety as the child becomes more mobile and capable of manipulating objects.

Reflexes are important in both fine and gross motor development. Reflexes are predictable motor responses that follow a specific sensory input; they develop automatically with the maturation of the central nervous system during infancy. Reflexes affect early movements in most positions. For example, when the infant is lying on his or her back and the head is turned to the side, the infant may go into a "fencing posture" where the arm and leg on the turned side are extended and the other arm and leg are flexed. This reflex, known as the asymmetrical tonic neck reflex (ATNR), can interfere with the infant's ability to bring the hands to the mouth, bring the hands together, or roll over.

Caregivers are often impressed with a newborn's ability to "squeeze" a finger. This ability to tightly grasp a stimulus is a reflex called the palmar grasp. It is important for the interventionist to be knowledgeable about reflex development and inhibition in order to explain skills to caregivers and design activities for individual children. Motor abilities develop as a result of the interaction between innate abilities and experience gained in the environment. The AEPS Curriculum is based upon this transactional model.

Infants and young children with motor problems form a heterogeneous group. Some children have a disability in which a relatively precise description can be made, such as cerebral palsy. Other children have disabilities that are described more generally as mild, moderate, or severe. Motor variations may be transient and disappear over time or they may evolve into a more serious disability. It is often difficult for interventionists to make accurate predictions of development; therefore, they should monitor progress carefully. It is also important for caregivers and interventionists to maintain close contact with specialists (e.g., physical and occupational therapists) because their guidance is critical to meeting the needs of some children with motor disabilities. The AEPS Curriculum was not written specifically for children with motor disabilities, and adaptations will need to be made when engaging in activities to develop fine motor skills.

Strand A

Reach, Grasp, and Release

GOAL 1 Simultaneously brings hands to midline

DEVELOPMENTAL PROGRAMMING STEPS

☑ This goal is the most basic step for the skill to be taught. Most children will benefit from the activities outlined here that emphasize this goal. For children who need more structure, consider designing programming steps from the *environmental arrangements* suggestions or from the *instructional sequence* outlined for this goal.

IMPORTANCE OF SKILL

This skill provides the child with opportunities to explore his or her own body and the external environment. The child begins to actively explore and to visually regard fingers and hands. The child is able to explore with one hand objects placed in the other hand. Simultaneously bringing hands to midline aids the development of self-awareness, eye–hand coordination, and the use of the hands to attain desired ends. It is a skill that will be used by the child to hold an object (e.g., a bottle) with both hands.

PRECEDING OBJECTIVE

FM A:1.1   Makes directed batting and/or swiping movements with each hand

CONCURRENT GOAL AND OBJECTIVES

Cog A:1.0   Orients to auditory, visual, and tactile events
Cog B:1.1   Visually follows object moving in horizontal, vertical, and circular directions
Cog C:1.3   Indicates interest in simple and/or mechanical toy
Cog G:1.4   Uses sensory examination with objects
SC A:1.2   Turns and looks toward noise-producing object
SC A:2.2   Looks toward an object
Soc A:1.1   Responds appropriately to familiar adult's affective tone

TEACHING SUGGESTIONS

Activity-Based

- When offering objects to the child, be sure to present the object from the front, to encourage reaching with both hands toward midline.
- Encourage the child to hold the breast or the mother's hand as the child feeds. The child's shoulders should be encircled with the mother's arm, while she holds the child close and secure. This will help the hands come to the midline.
- For the child who holds his or her head erect and bears weight on forearms in prone position (on stomach), present small toys on the floor at midline to encourage manipulation with two hands.
- When the child is nursing, drinking from a bottle, or sucking a pacifier, gently take the nipple from the child's mouth and wait for a response.
- When the child is lying on his or her back for diapering, activate a squeeze-toy or musical toy, holding it within arm's reach on or above the child's chest. Wait for a response.
- Encourage the child to play with hands and objects in the sidelying position. Encourage the child to mouth both hands and objects if this response is age-appropriate.
- Place an object (e.g., block, rattle, squeeze-toy) in the child's hand during face-to-face play, feeding, and bathing.
- When the child is lying on his or her back or in a supported sitting position (in crib, infant carrier), activate the mobile or crib gym.
- When changing diapers, bathing, or picking up the child from the crib, present your face within the child's visual field and talk to the child. Wait for a response.

☑ If your data indicate the child is not making progress toward the goal, provide additional structure within the suggested activities by incorporating the following *environmental arrangements and/or materials:*

Environmental Arrangements

- Position the child to provide increased opportunities for hands to reach toward midline. For example, holding the child with neck and shoulders supported or sitting the child in the corner of the couch both provide easier opportunities for the child than lying flat on the back.
- Hang or dangle objects or toys (e.g., bells, rattle, crib gym, mobile) within the child's visual field and at the child's midline. Pay special attention to safety with hanging objects.
- When the child grasps an adult's finger while feeding, have the adult hold the child's fingers a moment, then release. Repeat as often as the child initiates the behavior.
- Arrange soft support for the child's shoulders or elbows when lying or sitting to encourage hands toward midline. For example, position rolled-up towels behind the elbows when the child sits. Gradually remove support as the child begins to bring his or her hands together at midline.

☑ If this goal is particularly difficult for a child, it may be necessary, within activities, to use an *instructional sequence*.

Instructional Sequence

- Place an adult's index fingers in the child's palms and allow the child to grasp the fingers. Slowly move the child's hands to midline while securing the grasp on the adult's fingers.

- As the child grasps the fingers, say, "There you go," and move the child's hands to midline. Gently tug and raise the child's shoulders off the surface.
- Physically assist the child to bring his or her hands to midline by touching the child's arms or shoulders.

☑ Combining or pairing different levels of instructions may be helpful when beginning to teach a new and difficult skill. Fade to less intrusive instructions as soon as possible, to encourage a more independent performance.

TEACHING CONSIDERATIONS

1. The child should be in a quiet or active alert state.
2. Position the child so that his or her head, trunk, and shoulders are stable and symmetrical.
3. Approach the child straight on and to the middle of the body.
4. Free the environment of objects or events that compete with the toy or object presented to the child.
5. Objects should be used that provide cues to which the child with a sensory impairment can respond. For example, use noise-producing toys for a child with a visual impairment.
6. Allow adequate time for the child to respond.
7. Activation of objects should be continued or facilitated to reinforce the child's interest.
8. Consider safety with all objects that the child handles. Never leave the child unattended with potentially hazardous objects.

> **Objective 1.1** **Makes directed batting and/or swiping movements with each hand**

IMPORTANCE OF SKILL

The ability to make directed movements toward objects indicates the beginning of coordination between motor and visual responses. The child who coordinates looking with hand movements begins to learn the relationship between the position of objects in space and his or her own body movements. The child learns the relationships of objects with one another as well. The child develops initial cause and effect relationships and increases his or her attention span as objects move and are transformed by the child's own activity. Memory also develops as the child repeats movements with his or her arms to obtain effects.

PRECEDING OBJECTIVE

FM A:1.2   Makes nondirected movements with each arm

CONCURRENT GOAL AND OBJECTIVES

GM B:1.6   Holds head in midline when in supported sitting position
Cog A:1.0   Orients to auditory, visual, and tactile events
Cog B:1.1   Visually follows object moving in horizontal, vertical, and circular directions
Cog C:1.3   Indicates interest in simple and/or mechanical toy

Cog G:1.4   Uses sensory examination with objects
SC A:1.2   Turns and looks toward noise-producing object
SC A:2.2   Looks toward an object

TEACHING SUGGESTIONS
Activity-Based

- Activate a variety of interesting simple or mechanical toys (e.g., rattles, bells, squeeze-toys, wind-up toys). Wait for the child's response.
- Activate mobile within the child's reach when the child is lying on his or her back or in a supported sitting position (in crib, infant carrier).
- When holding the child for feeding, look at and talk to the child.
- Indicate interest by exclaiming surprise while activating the toy.
- In face-to-face interactions, pause, then stick out and wiggle your tongue. Wait for the child to bat or swipe, and then wiggle your tongue again. Use your voice, eyes, and head to encourage the child to bat at your face.
- During bathing, hold the child in a secure sitting position. Float an object near the child and encourage batting or swiping.
- Introduce toys within face-to-face interactions when the child is manifesting interest in the adult's behavior.
- Have siblings or older children play face-to-face with the child and see if the child will bat or swipe at their faces.

Environmental Arrangements

- In order to stimulate the child's interest, present familiar objects in novel ways (make toy dance or fly about room, use hand puppet to present toy, make funny noises and exaggerated facial expressions).
- Hang or dangle toys or objects within the child's reach (bells, rattle, crib gym). Batting and swiping are more likely to occur if the object catches the child's attention and is easily activated by the child's movements. Pay special attention to safety with hanging objects.
- Present toys or objects (stuffed animal, mirror, rattle) within the child's reach. Slowly move the toy or object in a horizontal, vertical, or circular direction, keeping it within the child's visual field.
- Present talking toys that move to stimulate attention and directed movement of the child's arms.
- Alternate speed and movement pattern of an object to maintain the child's interest.
- Use objects that are likely to attract the child's attention, such as large, bright-colored, or noise-making toys.
- Tie a soft yarn "bracelet" to the child's wrist and to an easily activated toy or mobile. Once the child begins to associate movement of the arm with activation, remove the yarn and encourage the child to activate the toy directly.
- Dangle or wave a pocket mirror near the child's hands. Make sure the child can see the reflective part. Touch it to the child's hand, then remove it slightly. Wait for the child to bat or swipe.

Instructional Sequence

- Model stretching an arm to touch a dangling toy.
- Provide tactile cues by touching or tickling the child with toy or object.

- Pair presentation of a toy or object with auditory or verbal cues (e.g., tapping or shaking objects, making exaggerated sounds, exaggerating the pitch and volume in an adult's voice).
- Physically assist the child by touching the child's arms or shoulders to help the child swipe at an object.

TEACHING CONSIDERATIONS

1. The child should be in a quiet or active alert state.
2. Position the child so that the head, trunk, and shoulders are stable and symmetrical.
3. The environment should be free of objects or events that compete with the toy or object presented to the child.
4. Objects should be used that provide cues to which the child with a sensory impairment can respond. For example, use noise-producing toys for a child with a visual impairment.
5. Allow adequate time for the child to respond.
6. Activation or exploration of objects should be continued or facilitated to reinforce the child's interest.
7. Objects should be within reach of the child so that the child's batting or swiping movements cause objects to move.
8. Consider safety with all objects that the child handles. Never leave the child unattended with potentially hazardous objects.

Objective 1.2   Makes nondirected movements with each arm

IMPORTANCE OF SKILL

Making nondirected movements with the arm when an object is present allows sensory exploration to occur as the child accidentally contacts and transforms the object. The child's random movements with his or her arms will lead to directed movements as the repeated, nondirected movements contact objects. Eventually, the child will learn to purposefully reach and grasp for objects, which allows the child greater independence in exploration and play.

PRECEDING OBJECTIVES

No objectives precede Fine Motor A:1.2 in this curriculum. Developmentally primitive reflexive patterns largely dominate movement before the nondirected arm movements emerge.

CONCURRENT OBJECTIVES

GM A:1.1	Turns head past 45° to the right and left from midline position
Adap A:1.4	Swallows liquids
Cog A:1.4	Responds to auditory, visual, and tactile events
Cog B:1.2	Focuses on object and/or person
SC A:1.2	Turns and looks toward noise-producing object
SC A:2.2	Looks toward an object

FM A

TEACHING SUGGESTIONS
Activity-Based

- When the child is on his or her back in an environment that is relatively quiet, talk to and engage the child in "conversation," allowing the child to take "turns." Respond to the child's movement with more "conversation."
- When the child is on his or her back in a crib or playpen, or sitting in an infant carrier or car seat, activate the crib gym or mobile. Wait for the child to respond by quieting, looking, or moving, and then activate the toy again.
- When bathing the child, place the child on his or her back on a large sponge in the bathtub. Fill the tub with water so that the child's arm movements will cause splashing, but do not use so much water that the child's ears, mouth, or nose will be submerged.
- When the child is moving his or her arms and legs, synchronize your voice to the movement. Stop talking when the child stops moving; begin again when the child moves again.
- When the child looks at toys or objects, activate them within the child's visual field (e.g., rattle, squeak-toy, bells).

Environmental Arrangements

- Help the child differentiate between sounds and silence. Speak and pause, introduce and activate a toy, remove the toy and wait for the child's response. When the child responds, use your voice to show your pleasure.
- Attach noise-producing objects to loose elastic bands and put them around the child's arms or legs so that the child's movement produces an immediate auditory event. For example, put jingle-bells on shoe strings or mittens.
- Slightly elevate the child's head and shoulders or the child's hips with a diaper or towel. Observe to see if the change in position facilitates arm waving.
- Attach interesting toys or objects to the sides of the child's crib (e.g., mirror, bright-colored object, stuffed animal).
- Secure a plexiglass or metal mirror in the crib or near the child's chair so that movement of the arms provides an immediate visual event.

Instructional Sequence

- Provide tactile cues by gently touching or tickling the child's arms with the toy, kissing or making "raspberries" on the child's hands.
- Pair presentation of a toy or object with auditory or verbal cues by tapping or shaking the object, making exaggerated sounds, or altering the pitch and volume of your voice.
- Physically assist the child by stroking or touching the child's arms or hands.

TEACHING CONSIDERATIONS

1. The child should be in a quiet or active alert state.
2. Position the child so that the child's head, trunk, and shoulders are stable and symmetrical.
3. The environment should be free of objects or events that compete with the toy or object presented to the child.
4. Objects should be used that provide cues to which the child with a sensory impair-

ment can respond. For example, use noise-producing toys for a child with a visual impairment.

5. Allow adequate time for the child to respond.
6. Activation of objects should be continued or facilitated to reinforce the child's interest.
7. Consider safety with all objects that the child handles. Never leave the child unattended with potentially hazardous objects.

GOAL 2   Brings two objects together at or near midline

IMPORTANCE OF SKILL

The ability to bring objects together at the midline provides new opportunities to combine movements using actions and objects. This skill is also important because the hands begin to work independently. The child begins to explore and develop new schemes for acting upon objects in the environment, such as banging objects together. This allows the child to learn more about objects, and the relationship of objects to each other and to self as the child gains sensory input through visual, auditory, and tactile means.

PRECEDING GOAL AND OBJECTIVES

FM A:1.0	Simultaneously brings hands to midline
FM A2.2	Holds an object in each hand
Cog E1.1	Retains one object when second object is obtained

CONCURRENT OBJECTIVES

FM A:3.2	Grasps cylindrical object with either hand by closing fingers around it
GM B:1.6	Holds head in midline when in supported sitting position
Adap A:1.4	Swallows liquids
Cog B:1.1	Visually follows object moving in horizontal, vertical, and circular directions
Cog C:1.2	Acts on mechanical and/or simple toy in some way
Cog G:1.3	Uses simple motor actions on different objects
SC A:3.1	Engages in vocal exchanges by cooing
Soc A:2.2	Responds to familiar adult's social behavior

TEACHING SUGGESTIONS
Activity-Based

- Throughout daily activities, provide the child with an object to hold in each hand, such as a spoon, block, rattle, sock, toy people, or toy animals. Name the objects for the child.
- At changing time, put powder or lotion in one or both of the child's hands. Encourage the child to rub hands together.
- During bathtime, encourage the child to put the washcloth and soap together.

- Play social games like "Pat-a-Cake" with objects that will give the child practice in bringing his or her hands together.
- Sing nursery songs such as "Clap, Clap, Clap, Your Hands" while the child is holding an object in each hand.
- After changing diapers or dressing or undressing the child, encourage the child to hold a foot in each hand.
- Introduce the child to "rhythm band" instruments that produce exciting auditory and tactile experiences when banged together at midline (cymbals, sticks, blocks, tamborines).

Environmental Arrangements

- Find two objects to hold, one in each hand, similar to the objects held by the child. Imitate the child's actions to start, then introduce novel actions by putting the objects together.
- Hold the objects (e.g., maracas, bell rings) in each hand and face the child. Activate the toys by banging them together at midline to gain the child's interest. Hold the objects out to the child's hands simultaneously. As the child touches the objects, bring them together once more to activate them. Give the objects to the child.
- Use objects that produce visual as well as auditory effects when brought to the midline, such as clear rattles with objects inside.
- When the child is holding one object in each hand, clap your hands and say, "Bang, bang, bang!" or "Clap, clap, clap!" Encourage the child to imitate.
- If grasping and holding onto objects is difficult for the child, use toys that can be safely attached to the child's hands and allow the child to practice bringing them together.
- Give the child objects that make a noise when they are brought together (blocks, bells).
- When the child is holding an object in one hand, present another object at midline for the child to grasp and hold.
- Vary the size and shape of objects. Objects with different properties of texture, sound, or color will offer interest and variety.
- Use materials such as clay or Play-Doh that the child can initially pull apart and then stick back together.
- Have the child hold a container at midline and drop small objects inside or remove small objects.

Instructional Sequence

- Model banging two blocks together and say, "Bang, bang, bang!"
- When the child is holding one object in each hand, face the child and grasp a part of each object without touching the child's hands. Guide the two objects to midline. Pair the action with a verbal statement (e.g., "Bang, bang, bang!" or "Boom, boom, boom!").
- When the child is holding one object in each hand, tap or support the child's arms behind the elbow.
- When the child is holding one object in each hand, hold the child's shoulders in a stable, slightly forward position and guide the hands to midline from the shoulder.

TEACHING CONSIDERATIONS

1. The child should be in a quiet or active alert state.
2. Position the child so that the child's head, trunk, and shoulders are stable and symmetrical.

3. Use objects that can be easily held (e.g., squeeze-toys, rattles) and cannot be swallowed.
4. The environment should be free of objects or events that compete with the toy or object presented to the child.
5. Objects should be used that provide cues to which the child with a sensory impairment can respond. For example, use noise-producing toys for a child with a visual impairment.
6. Allow adequate time for the child to respond.
7. Activation or exploration of objects should be continued or facilitated to reinforce the child's interest.
8. Consider safety with all objects that the child handles. Never leave the child unattended with potentially hazardous objects.

Objective 2.1   Transfers object from one hand to the other

DEVELOPMENTAL PROGRAMMING STEP

PS2.1a   The child brings hands together and touches an object with one hand while holding an object in the other hand.

IMPORTANCE OF SKILL

The transfer of objects from one hand to the other indicates that the child has increased wrist mobility. This facilitates motor activities such as banging objects in an up and down vertical pattern and shaking objects from side to side. Also, when transferring objects from one hand to the other, the child learns that the hands are distinct from one another and can be used together to attain desired ends. The development of eye–hand coordination, grasping, and releasing are enhanced as the child transfers an object from one hand to another. This skill allows the child increased independence in exploration and play.

PRECEDING GOAL AND OBJECTIVES

FM A:1.0   Simultaneously brings hands to midline
Cog B:1.2   Focuses on object and/or person
Cog E:1.2   Retains object

CONCURRENT OBJECTIVES

FM A:3.3   Grasps hand-size object with either hand using whole hand
FM A:5.2   Releases hand-held object with each hand
GM B:1.6   Holds head in midline when in supported sitting position
Adap A:1.4   Swallows liquids
Cog B:1.1   Visually follows object moving in horizontal, vertical, and circular directions
Cog C:1.2   Acts on mechanical and/or simple toy in some way
Cog E:1.1   Retains one object when second object is obtained
SC A:1.1   Turns and looks toward object and person speaking
Soc A:2.2   Responds to familiar adult's social behavior

TEACHING SUGGESTIONS

Activity-Based

- When the child is holding large, light objects (e.g., diaper, stuffed animal, foam block) with both hands, present another object to encourage letting go with one hand.
- Throughout daily routines, give the child objects to hold (e.g., spoon during feeding, washcloth during bathing, powder during diapering).
- When playing with the child, provide him or her with an object to hold in one hand (e.g., block, rattle, squeak-toy). Encourage the child to transfer the object from one hand to the other.
- When using toys such as a steering wheel or a drum, encourage the child to practice using both hands together at midline.

Environmental Arrangements

- Provide the child with toys or objects that have surfaces that both hands can touch or hold at the same time (e.g., stacking ring, rattle, diaper, big spoon).
- Provide the child with toys or objects that predictably activate or produce noise when transferred (e.g., bells, rattle, squeak-toy).
- When the child is holding an object, offer a more desirable object to the occupied hand.
- Put a bin of objects (e.g., small balls, bean bags, Rack-a-Stack) to one side of the child as he or she is sitting. Give the child objects to put away in the bin, offering objects on the child's side that is not next to the bin.

Instructional Sequence

- Model transferring a small ball from one hand to the other. Use exaggerated vocal and gestural cues to engage the child's interest.
- Provide the child with verbal cues to transfer an object to the other hand.
- Provide tactile cues by touching, tickling, or nudging the occupied hand with a second object.
- Physically assist the child to transfer an object from one hand to the other by gently guiding the occupied hand toward the empty hand. Fade assistance as child becomes more proficient.

TEACHING CONSIDERATIONS

1. The child should be in a quiet or active alert state.
2. Position the child so that his or her head, trunk, and shoulders are stable and symmetrical.
3. The environment should be free of objects or events that compete with the toy or object presented to the child.
4. Objects should be used that provide cues to which the child with a sensory impairment can respond. For example, use noise-producing toys for a child with a visual impairment.
5. Use objects that can be easily grasped (e.g., small squeeze-toys, rattles).
6. Allow adequate time for the child to respond.
7. Activation or exploration of objects should be continued or facilitated to reinforce the child's interest.

8. Consider safety with all objects that the child handles. Never leave the child unattended with potentially hazardous objects.

Objective 2.2   Holds an object in each hand

DEVELOPMENTAL PROGRAMMING STEP

PS2.2a   The child holds an object in one hand.

IMPORTANCE OF SKILL

Holding an object in each hand indicates that the child's grasp is now voluntary. The child begins to perform actions upon objects held in each hand. This skill is important because it helps the child learn about objects in the environment by looking at, touching, and mouthing objects held in the hands. This sensory input contributes to the child's exploration of the environment.

PRECEDING OBJECTIVE

Cog E:1.2   Retains object

CONCURRENT OBJECTIVES

FM A:3.3   Grasps hand-size object with either hand using whole hand
GM B:1.6   Holds head in midline when in supported sitting position
Cog C:1.3   Indicates interest in simple and/or mechanical toy
Cog E:1.1   Retains one object when second object is obtained
Cog G:1.3   Uses simple motor actions on different objects
SC A:3.1   Engages in vocal exchanges by cooing
Soc A:2.2   Responds to familiar adult's social behavior

TEACHING SUGGESTIONS
Activity-Based

- Engage the child in "giving" games in which the adult gives the child objects to hold in each hand (e.g., blocks, pop beads, squeak-toys).
- At mealtimes, present food that the child can hold and feed to him- or herself (e.g., crackers, slices of soft fruit).
- Engage the child in peekaboo in which the adult's or child's eyes are covered by hands or a cloth. Wait for the child to pull off the hands or cloth.
- When the child grasps one finger of your hand, place another finger in the other hand.
- Throughout daily routines, give the child objects to hold in each hand (e.g., two spoons during feeding, bath toys during bathing, socks during dressing).
- Place adult's finger in the palms of both the child's hands. Let the child grasp fingers.

Environmental Arrangements

- Use paper, clay, or Play-Doh to encourage the child to pull one large object apart and hold one piece in each hand.

- Present objects to the left of the child's midline for grasping with the left hand and to the right of the child's midline for grasping with the right hand.
- Hold out one object so that the child must extend his or her arm to obtain it; offer a second object close to the child's free hand so that it can be obtained easily.
- Introduce objects to the child's hands when arms are positioned close to the body.
- Provide two of the same object or toy for the child to hold in each hand (e.g., blocks, pop beads, rattles).
- Use objects of different textures and firmness for the child to hold, such as a sponge and a plastic rattle.

Instructional Sequence

- Model reaching toward an especially inviting toy (e.g., Koosh Ball) with each hand.
- Initially use objects that the child can most successfully hold and slowly introduce slightly more difficult objects.
- Verbally instruct the child to "Get the Koosh Ball."
- Hold your hand over the child's hand when the child is grasping the object to provide additional sensory input. Gradually fade assistance as the child becomes more proficient.

TEACHING CONSIDERATIONS

1. The child should be in a quiet or active alert state.
2. Initially, the grasping behavior will be most successful when the child's hands are positioned with the palms downward.
3. Position child so that the child's head, trunk, and shoulders are stable and symmetrical.
4. The environment should be free of objects or events that compete with the toy or object presented to the child.
5. Objects should be used that provide cues to which the child with a sensory impairment can respond. For example, use noise-producing toys for a child with a visual impairment.
6. Use objects that can be easily grasped (small squeeze-toys, rattles).
7. Allow adequate time for the child to respond.
8. Activation or exploration of objects should be continued or facilitated to reinforce the child's interest.
9. Consider safety with all objects that the child handles. Never leave the child unattended with potentially hazardous objects.

Objective 2.3   Reaches toward and touches object with each hand

---

IMPORTANCE OF SKILL

This skill is important because the child accomplishes a means to an end by directing a reach toward an object and touching it. The child's actions are purposeful. This skill also fosters eye–hand coordination and visual control, as the child uses the eyes to assist directing the hand toward the object. Being able to reach toward and touch an object offers opportunities to explore and learn about objects in the environment. By touching objects, the child begins to learn about the properties of objects and to separate him- or herself from the environment.

PRECEDING OBJECTIVES

FM A:1.1   Makes directed batting and/or swiping movements with each hand
Cog B:1.2   Focuses on object and/or person

CONCURRENT GOALS AND OBJECTIVES

GM A:1.0   Turns head, moves arms, and kicks legs independently of each other
Cog A:1.0   Orients to auditory, visual, and tactile events
Cog B:1.1   Visually follows object moving in horizontal, vertical, and circular directions
Cog G:1.4   Uses sensory examination with objects
SC A:1.2   Turns and looks toward noise-producing object
SC A:2.2   Looks toward an object
Soc A:2.2   Responds to familiar adult's social behavior

TEACHING SUGGESTIONS
Activity-Based

- While in a face-to-face position with the child (e.g., at changing time and during play), encourage the child to reach for an adult's face or hair. Talk to the child with exaggerated facial expressions. Shake head and hair.
- During bathtime, encourage the child to touch bubbles or tepid water as it flows into the tub. Provide sponges and toys that float for the child to reach for and touch.
- Kiss the child's hands or make "raspberries" on them. Release the child's hands and make kissing sounds or clicks with the mouth, encouraging the child to reach for your mouth. Wait for the child's response.
- Encourage the child to stroke the fur of a household pet or a stuffed animal.
- Activate a mobile within the child's reach when the child is lying on his or her back or is in a supported sitting position (e.g., in crib, infant carrier).
- Throughout daily routines, present objects or toys for the child to reach and touch (e.g., foot when changing diapers, spoon or bottle when feeding, shoe when dressing).

Environmental Arrangements

- Initially, present objects to the child at chest height and at midline where reaching is easiest.
- Blow large bubbles with nontoxic bubble solution. Catch the bubble with the bubble wand and touch it to the child's hand. Pair the activity with the verbal exclamation, "Pop!"
- Hang or dangle objects in front of the child to reach and touch (crib gym, rattles, bells). Attach toys to the highchair, walker, or table.
- Provide the child with objects that produce noise or activate when touched (e.g., bells, rattle, crib gyms).
- Provide objects with varied visual, auditory, and tactile input (e.g., soft blocks, bright-colored toys, bells).

FM A

Instructional Sequence

- Model reaching toward and touching an object with each hand.
- Pair presentation of a toy or object with auditory or verbal cues (e.g., tapping or shaking object, making exaggerated sounds, altering voice pitch and volume).
- Verbally direct the child to reach for and touch an object.
- Provide tactile cues by touching or tickling the child with a toy or object.
- Physically assist the child's reaching by holding his or her shoulders or elbow in a stable, slightly forward position, and guiding the arm to the object. Gradually fade assistance as the child becomes more proficient.

TEACHING CONSIDERATIONS

1. The child should be in a quiet or active alert state.
2. Position the child so that his or her head, trunk, and shoulders are stable and symmetrical.
3. The environment should be free of objects or events that compete with the toys or objects presented to the child.
4. Use objects that provide cues to which the child with a sensory impairment can respond. For example, use noise-producing toys for a child with a visual impairment.
5. Allow adequate time for the child to respond.
6. Activation or exploration of objects should be continued or facilitated to reinforce the child's interest.
7. Place objects within reach of the child to prevent frustration.
8. Consider safety with all objects that the child handles. Never leave the child unattended with potentially hazardous objects.

Goal 3 Grasps hand-size object with either hand using ends of thumb, index, and second fingers

---

IMPORTANCE OF SKILL

Grasping objects allows the hand to explore, manipulate, and control objects of different textures, shapes, sizes, and weights. Manual exploration of people and objects stimulates learning. Using the ends of the thumb, index, and second fingers to grasp demonstrates control and refinement of the grasp skill, which provides the child with greater manual dexterity to hold and manipulate objects. This is an important skill for later activities, such as holding a crayon to color and a spoon to eat.

PRECEDING OBJECTIVE

FM A:3.1   Grasps hand-size object with either hand using the palm, with object placed toward the thumb and index finger

CONCURRENT GOALS AND OBJECTIVES

FM A:5.0   Places and releases object balanced on top of another object with either hand

FM B:1.0   Rotates either wrist on horizontal plane

FM B:2.2	Fits object into defined space
FM B:3.0	Uses either index finger to activate objects
GM B:1.2	Regains balanced, upright sitting position after *reaching* across the body to the right and to the left
GM B:2.2	Maintains a sitting position in chair
GM C:2.3	Pulls to kneeling position
Adap A:4.2	Eats with fingers
Cog C:1.0	Correctly activates mechanical toy
Cog D:1.1	Imitates motor action that is commonly used
Cog F:1.2	Stacks objects
Cog G:1.2	Uses functionally appropriate actions with objects
SC B:2.2	Uses nonspecific consonant–vowel combinations and/or jargon
Soc C:1.5	Entertains self by playing appropriately with toys

TEACHING SUGGESTIONS
Activity-Based

- Allow the child to explore objects that pull apart (e.g., pop beads, Legos, Tinkertoys, Mr. Potato Head).
- Allow the child to finger feed hand-size bits of food (e.g., crackers, slices of soft food, cheese sticks).
- Encourage the child to hold his or her own bottle or cup.
- Activate a variety of interesting or mechanical toys (e.g., rattle, wind-up toy, squeeze-toy) in which the child indicates interest. Wait for the child's response.
- Encourage the child to pull up droopy diaper or pants by grabbing material at waist.
- During playtime, provide the child with hand-size toys (e.g., small balls, blocks).
- When passing a toy to the child, offer the part that is easiest to grasp (ear of teddy bear, ring of key ring, wide end of rattle).
- Encourage the child to take hand-size objects (e.g., blocks in a basket, cars in a can) out of a container.

Environmental Arrangements

- Provide the child with toys or objects that activate or produce noise when grasped (e.g., rattle, bells, squeeze-toy).
- Offer the child a hand-size object at chest level toward the center of his or her body.
- Provide objects that pull apart (e.g., pop beads, Legos, Tinkertoys, Mr. Potato Head) with pieces partially pulled out.
- Put a bead or block on the end of pull toys (e.g., See-N-Say, Farmer Says) to facilitate pulling.
- Use a variety of hand-size objects or toys (e.g., small cars, balls, blocks).

Instructional Sequence

- Model picking up blocks one at a time.
- Verbally direct the child to pick up the Tinkertoys.
- When presenting an object to the child, continue to hold the object until the child approximates grasping the object with the ends of his or her thumb, index, and second fingers.
- Place an object in the child's hand in a position that gives him or her the sensation of the response. Close the child's hand around the object.

FM A

TEACHING CONSIDERATIONS

1. The environment should be free of objects or events that compete with the toy or object presented to the child.
2. Objects should be used that provide cues to which the child with a sensory impairment can respond. For example, use noise-producing toys for a child with a visual impairment.
3. Use objects that can be easily grasped (e.g., small squeeze-toys, rattles).
4. Allow adequate time for the child to respond.
5. Activation or exploration of objects should be continued or facilitated to reinforce the child's interest.
6. Place objects directly in front of the child so that he or she can grasp objects with either hand.
7. Consider safety with all objects that the child handles. Never leave the child unattended with potentially hazardous objects.

Objective 3.1   Grasps hand-size object with either hand using the palm, with object placed toward the thumb and index finger

---

IMPORTANCE OF SKILL

Using the palm to grasp with the object held toward the thumb and index finger is a step in the refinement of the grasping response. This refined grasp allows the child greater control to hold onto and manipulate objects. The child becomes aware that the object is separate from self and can be transformed by the child's actions.

PRECEDING OBJECTIVE

FM A:3.3   Grasps hand-size object with either hand using whole hand

CONCURRENT GOAL AND OBJECTIVES

FM A:2.1   Transfers object from one hand to the other
FM A:5.2   Releases hand-held object with each hand
FM B:1.1   Turns object over using wrist and arm rotation with each hand
GM B:1.3   Regains balanced, upright sitting position after *leaning* to the left, to the right, and forward
GM B:2.2   Maintains a sitting position in chair
Adap A:4.2   Eats with fingers
Cog C:1.1   Correctly activates simple toy
Cog E:1.1   Retains one object when second object is obtained
Cog G:1.3   Uses simple motor actions on different objects
SC A:3.0   Engages in vocal exchanges by babbling
Soc A:2.2   Responds to familiar adult's social behavior

TEACHING SUGGESTIONS
Activity-Based

- Allow the child to explore objects that pull apart (e.g., pop beads, Legos, Tinkertoys, Mr. Potato Head).
- Allow the child to finger feed hand-size bits of food (e.g., crackers, slices of soft food, cheese sticks).
- Encourage the child to hold own bottle or cup.
- Activate a variety of interesting or mechanical toys (e.g., rattles, squeeze-toys). Wait for the child's response.
- Set hand-size objects or toys (e.g., blocks, beads, small balls) in front of the child whenever the child indicates an interest. Encourage the child to grasp them.
- When passing a toy to the child, offer the part that is easiest to grasp (e.g., ear of teddy bear, ring of key ring, wide end of rattle).

Environmental Arrangements

- Offer the child a hand-size object at chest level toward the center of the child's body.
- Provide objects that pull apart (e.g., pop beads, Legos, Tinkertoys, Mr. Potato Head) with pieces partially pulled out.
- Put a bead or block on end of pull toys (e.g., See-N-Say, Farmer Says) to facilitate pulling.
- Use a variety of hand-size objects or toys (e.g., small cars, pop beads, blocks).

Instructional Sequence

- Model grasping a block with the palm with the block placed toward the thumb and index finger.
- When presenting an object to the child, continue to hold onto the object until the child approximates grasping the object using the palm with the object placed toward the thumb and index fingers.
- Place an object in the child's hand in a position that gives him or her the sensation of the response. Close the child's hand around the object.

TEACHING CONSIDERATIONS

1. The environment should be free of objects or events that compete with the toy or object presented to the child.
2. Objects should be used that provide cues to which the child with a sensory impairment can respond. For example, use noise-producing toys for a child with a visual impairment.
3. Use objects that can be easily grasped (e.g., small squeeze-toys, rattles).
4. Allow adequate time for the child to respond.
5. Activation or exploration of objects should be continued or facilitated to reinforce the child's interest.
6. Place objects directly in front of the child so that he or she can grasp objects with either hand.
7. Consider safety with all objects that the child handles. Never leave the child unattended with potentially hazardous objects.

Objective 3.2 Grasps cylindrical object with either hand by closing fingers around it

---

IMPORTANCE OF SKILL

This skill allows the child opportunities to grasp more varied objects and to manipulate and look at objects in different ways. The child begins to discriminate between objects and selects movements to use on different ones. This skill helps the child become more discriminating in perception and motor skills and allows the child more interesting exploration and play.

PRECEDING OBJECTIVE

FM A:3.3   Grasps hand-size object with either hand using whole hand

CONCURRENT OBJECTIVES

FM A:2.1   Transfers object from one hand to the other
FM B:1.1   Turns object over using wrist and arm rotation with each hand
GM B:1.4   Sits balanced without support
Adap A:4.1 Brings food to mouth using utensil
Cog C:1.2   Acts on mechanical and/or simple toy in some way
Cog E:2.1   Uses part of object and/or support to obtain another object
Cog G:1.3   Uses simple motor actions on different objects
SC A:1.1   Turns and looks toward object and person speaking
SC A:3.1   Engages in vocal exchanges by cooing
Soc A:2.2   Responds to familiar adult's social behavior

TEACHING SUGGESTIONS
Activity-Based

- Encourage the child to grasp, hold, and explore adult's fingers.
- Encourage the child to activate and explore with cylindrical rattles.
- Encourage the child to wrap fingers around the bottle when drinking.
- Allow the child to grasp the spoon handle when being fed.
- Encourage the child to activate musical toys with a cylindrical object or stick (e.g., xylophone, drum, wood blocks).
- During daily routines, provide the child with cylindrical objects to grasp (e.g., hairbrush with handle when dressing, spoon when feeding, tube of ointment when changing diapers).
- Present cylindrical bits of finger food (e.g., cheese sticks, bread sticks) at snack and mealtime.
- Hold the child's hand briefly when he or she grasps your fingers.

Environmental Arrangements

- Introduce a variety of objects of different textures and hardness. Find the preferred grasping object and change gradually to less-preferred objects.
- Set cylindrical objects or toys in front of the child (rattle with handle, cylindrical

block, stick). Encourage him or her to grasp the toy or object by closing his or her fingers around it.

- Provide toys that activate or produce noise when grasped (e.g., squeeze-toys, rattles).
- Hold a toy to the child's mouth and allow oral exploration. Let the object fall to the child's chin and wait for his or her response.
- Use a variety of cylindrical objects or toys (e.g., objects with handles, rattle, cylindrical blocks).
- For a child still drinking from a bottle, provide a bottle with two side chambers and a space in the middle to facilitate grasp.

Instructional Sequence

- Model holding a cylindrical block with your fingers.
- Verbally direct the child to pick up a bottle.
- When presenting an object to the child, continue to hold onto the object until he or she approximates grasping it by closing his or her fingers around it.
- Assist the child's fingers to close around an object by tapping the child's palm. (Be sure the wrist is in a neutral position, neither extended nor flexed.)
- Put the cylindrical object in the child's grasp and hold your hand over the child's hand to give him or her extra input and sensation of response.

TEACHING CONSIDERATIONS

1. The environment should be free of objects or events that compete with the toy or object presented to the child.
2. Objects should be used that provide cues to which the child with a sensory impairment can respond. For example, use noise-producing toys for a child with a visual impairment.
3. Use objects that can be easily grasped (e.g., small squeeze-toys, rattles).
4. Allow adequate time for the child to respond.
5. Activation or exploration of objects should be continued or facilitated to reinforce the child's interest.
6. Place objects directly in front of the child so that he or she can grasp them with either hand.
7. Consider safety with all objects that the child handles. Never leave the child unattended with potentially hazardous objects.

Objective 3.3   Grasps hand-size object with either hand using whole hand

---

DEVELOPMENTAL PROGRAMMING STEPS

PS3.3a   The child grasps hand-size object with either hand, holding the object on the little finger side of hand and against the palm. The thumb is not holding the object (ulnar palmar grasp).

PS3.3b   The child briefly holds an object placed in either hand.

IMPORTANCE OF SKILL

Grasping a hand-size object with the whole hand marks the beginning of the grasp progression in which repetition and modification produce more sophisticated responses. This skill is also the first voluntary grasp and aids the development of eye–hand coordination and self-awareness. As the child grasps and manipulates objects, the child learns about properties of objects.

PRECEDING OBJECTIVES

FM A:2.3   Reaches toward and touches object with each hand
Cog B:1.2   Focuses on object and/or person
SC A:2.2   Looks toward an object

CONCURRENT OBJECTIVES

FM A:2.2   Holds an object in each hand
GM A:3.5   Bears weight on one hand and/or arm while reaching with opposite hand
GM B:1.6   Holds head in midline when in supported sitting position
Cog B:1.1   Visually follows object moving in horizontal, vertical, and circular directions
Cog C:1.3   Indicates interest in simple and/or mechanical toy
Cog E:1.2   Retains object
Cog G:1.4   Uses sensory examination with objects
SC A:1.2   Turns and looks toward noise-producing object

TEACHING SUGGESTIONS

Activity-Based

- Allow the child to grasp the spoon or bottle when he or she is being fed.
- Provide hand-size objects to play with during bathtime (e.g., floating animals, small ball, squeeze-toy).
- Encourage the child to grasp knees and feet while lying on back.
- Encourage the child to finger feed bits of hand-size food (e.g., crackers, slices of soft fruit).
- During playtime, provide the child with hand-size toys (e.g., small cars, wooden beads).

Environmental Arrangements

- Introduce a variety of objects with different textures and hardness. Find the preferred objects to grasp and change gradually to less-preferred objects.
- Lower crib gym so that the child can grasp toys while lying on his or her back and bring them to the mouth.
- Provide toys that activate or produce a noise predictably when grasped (e.g., squeeze-toys, rattles).
- Hold a toy to the child's mouth and allow oral exploration. Let the object fall to the child's chin or chest and wait for his or her response.
- Use a variety of hand-size toys or objects (e.g., blocks, beads, small cars). Pay special attention to safety with small objects.

Instructional Sequence

- Place an object in the child's grasp. Allow the child to explore it, then model grasping the object to remove it. Reintroduce the object in a slightly different position. This action should result in the child's involuntary orienting, groping, and finally grasping.
- When presenting an object to the child, continue to hold onto the object until the child grasps it using his or her whole hand.
- Hold an object to the right of the child and say, "Here you go." Touch the child's hand with the object.
- Prompt the child's fingers to close around an object by tapping or stroking the child's palm or hand with the object or your hand.
- Put a hand-size object in the child's grasp and hold your hand over the child's hand to give him or her extra input and sensation of response.

TEACHING CONSIDERATIONS

1. The environment should be free of objects or events that compete with the toy or object presented to the child.
2. Objects should be used that provide cues to which the child with a sensory impairment can respond. For example, use noise-producing toys for a child with a visual impairment.
3. Use objects that can be easily grasped (e.g., small squeeze-toys, rattles).
4. Allow adequate time for the child to respond.
5. Activation or exploration of objects should be continued or facilitated to reinforce the child's interest.
6. Place objects directly in front of the child so that he or she can grasp objects with either hand.
7. Consider safety with all objects that the child handles. Never leave the child unattended with potentially hazardous objects.

GOAL 4   Grasps pea-size object with either hand using tip of the index finger and thumb with hand and/or arm *not* resting on surface for support

---

IMPORTANCE OF SKILL

Grasping objects allows the hand to explore, manipulate, and control objects of various textures, shapes, sizes, and weights. Manual exploration of people and objects stimulates learning in social contexts. Grasping pea-size objects using the tip of the index finger and thumb (pincer grasp) without using the support of a surface for additional stability demonstrates increased dexterity of the fingers. The child is able to use the thumb and index finger separately from the rest of the hand, allowing the child to efficiently pick up tiny objects.

PRECEDING OBJECTIVE

FM A:4.1   Grasps pea-size object with either hand using tip of the index finger and thumb with hand and/or arm resting on surface for support

CONCURRENT GOALS AND OBJECTIVES

FM B:3.0	Uses either index finger to activate objects
GM B:1.2	Regains balanced, upright sitting position after *reaching* across the body to the right and to the left
Adap A:4.2	Eats with fingers
Cog C:1.0	Correctly activates mechanical toy
Cog E:2.1	Uses part of object and/or support to obtain another object
Cog G:1.2	Uses functionally appropriate actions with objects
SC B:2.2	Uses nonspecific consonant–vowel combinations and/or jargon
SC C:2.3	Carries out one-step direction *with* contextual cues
Soc A:3.2	Responds to communication from familiar adult
Soc C:1.5	Entertains self by playing appropriately with toys

TEACHING SUGGESTIONS

Activity-Based

- Allow the child to finger feed small bits of food from a tray or flat surface (e.g., peas, diced cooked carrots, Cheerios).
- Encourage and model pointing and poking with the index finger extended (e.g., pop bubbles, poke at holes punched in paper, poke at holes in clay, point at pictures in books, dial play telephone).
- Engage the child in play with mechanical toys with levers that can be grasped with the thumb and index finger (e.g., Busy Box, pop-up toy, jack-in-the-box).
- Give the child pull-toys, extending the toy to the child with the string first. (Remove ring or handle from string so that the child must manipulate the string to activate the pull-toy.)
- Encourage the child to play toy keyboard instruments (e.g., Cookie Monster Piano, Soft Sounds) with his or her index finger.

Environmental Arrangements

- Present a pea-size object in your hand for the child to grasp.
- Place a pea-size object near the edge of a surface so that the child is less likely to use the surface for additional support while grasping.
- Provide the child with small toys or objects (e.g., pegs, toy people). Pay special attention to safety with small objects.
- Offer the child pea-size objects at chest height and toward the middle of the child's body.
- Place pea-size objects on a surface that provides high contrast background (e.g., raisins on white table top, oyster crackers on colored plate).
- Offer the child one pea-size object at a time.
- Use a variety of pea-size objects (e.g., Cheerios, small pegs, strings). Pay special attention to safety with small objects.
- Put pea-size objects into egg cartons so that the child must reach inside with thumb and forefinger to grasp the object.
- Begin by presenting larger objects and fade to smaller objects when the child demonstrates competence in obtaining an object using the tip of the index finger and thumb with the hand and/or arm *not* resting on a surface for support.

Instructional Sequence

- Model grasping a Cheerio on the child's highchair tray.
- Present a Cheerio on a plate held high for the child to reach for and grasp. Gesture and verbally prompt the child to get it.
- Provide visual or auditory cues by pointing or tapping a surface on which there is a pea-size object.
- Hold a pea-size object in own pincer grasp until the child grasps the object using the tip of the index finger and thumb with the hands and/or arm *not* resting on a surface for support.
- Assist the child's grasp by providing support or stability behind the child's elbow. Gradually fade assistance as the child becomes more proficient.

TEACHING CONSIDERATIONS

1. The environment should be free of objects or events that compete with the toy or object presented to the child.
2. Objects should be used that provide cues to which the child with a sensory impairment can respond. For example, use noise-producing toys for a child with a visual impairment.
3. Allow adequate time for the child to respond.
4. Activation or exploration of objects should be continued or facilitated to reinforce the child's interest.
5. Place objects directly in front of the child so that he or she can grasp the objects with either hand.
6. Be sure an adult is nearby to supervise the child's manipulation of pea-size objects. Consider safety with all objects that the child handles. Never leave the child unattended with potentially hazardous objects.

Objective 4.1   Grasps pea-size object with either hand using tip of the index finger and thumb with hand and/or arm resting on surface for support

---

DEVELOPMENTAL PROGRAMMING STEP

PS4.1a   The child grasps a pea-size object with either hand using the tip of the index finger and thumb with the hand and/or arm resting on a surface for support. The thumb is to the side of the index finger (inferior pincer grasp).

IMPORTANCE OF SKILL

As the grasping of pea-size objects becomes more refined, the development of eye–hand coordination and greater manual dexterity are enhanced. By using the tip of the index finger and thumb, the child can more readily grasp and pick up flat objects such as paper and coins. The child becomes more efficient at picking up small objects, which contributes to the child's independence in eating and in play.

PRECEDING OBJECTIVE

FM A:4.2   Grasps pea-size object with either hand using side of the index finger and thumb

CONCURRENT GOALS AND OBJECTIVES

FM B:3.0   Uses either index finger to activate objects
GM B:1.2   Regains balanced, upright sitting position after *reaching* across the body to the right and to the left
Adap A:4.2   Eats with fingers
Cog C:1.0   Correctly activates mechanical toy
SC A:3.0   Engages in vocal exchanges by babbling
Soc A:2.1   Initiates simple social game with familiar adult
Soc C:1.5   Entertains self by playing appropriately with toys

TEACHING SUGGESTIONS
Activity-Based

- Allow the child to finger feed small bits of food from a tray or flat surface (e.g., peas, oyster crackers, raisins).
- Encourage pointing and poking with the index finger extended (e.g., pop bubbles, poke at holes punched in paper, poke at holes in clay, point at pictures in books, dial play telephones).
- Give the child pull-toys, extending the toy to the child with the string first (remove ring or handle from string so that the child must manipulate the string to activate the pull-toy).
- Encourage the child to play toy keyboard instruments (e.g., Cookie Monster Piano, Soft Sounds) with his or her index fingers.
- Present the child with flat objects to grasp (e.g., coins, paper, plastic chip).

Environmental Arrangements

- Place a pea-size object in the middle of a flat surface so that the child must reach for it. The child may rest his or her arm on a surface to assist the grasp.
- Offer the child a pea-size object at chest height and toward the middle of the child's body.
- Place pea-size objects on a surface that provides high contrast background (raisins on white table top, oyster crackers on colored plate).
- Use pea-size objects that are easily molded to the finger and thumb tips, such as Play-Doh or marshmallows.
- Offer the child one pea-size object at a time.
- Use a variety of pea-size objects (peas, beads, string). Pay special attention to safety with small objects.
- Begin by presenting larger objects and fade to smaller objects when the child demonstrates competence in obtaining an object using the tip of the index finger and thumb.

Instructional Sequence

- Model grasping a Cheerio on the child's highchair tray.
- Verbally prompt the child to get a Cheerio off the highchair tray.

- Provide visual or auditory cues by pointing or tapping a surface on which there is a pea-size object.
- Hold a pea-size object in your pincer grasp until the child grasps the object using the tip of the index finger and thumb.
- Guide the child's arms to the surface before presenting an object so that the child has adequate support to stabilize arms and grasp successfully. Provide additional support or stability behind the child's elbow. Gradually fade assistance as the child becomes more proficient.

TEACHING CONSIDERATIONS

1. The environment should be free of objects or events that compete with the toy or object presented to the child.
2. Objects should be used that provide cues to which the child with a sensory impairment can respond. For example, use noise-producing toys for a child with a visual impairment.
3. Allow adequate time for the child to respond.
4. Activation or exploration of objects should be continued or facilitated to reinforce a child's interest.
5. Place objects directly in front of the child so that the child can grasp objects with either hand.
6. Be sure an adult is nearby to supervise the child's manipulation of pea-size objects. Consider safety with all objects that the child handles. Never leave the child unattended with potentially hazardous objects.

Objective 4.2 Grasps pea-size object with either hand using side of the index finger and thumb

---

IMPORTANCE OF SKILL

The grasping of a small object using the side of the index finger and thumb indicates that the child is beginning to differentiate finger use. The child demonstrates more control of the finger and thumb and depends less on the other fingers and the palm of the hand. This grasp facilitates the development of the more refined pincer grasp, which is important to independent eating and play.

PRECEDING OBJECTIVE

FM A:4.3   Grasps pea-size object with either hand using fingers in a raking and/or scratching movement

CONCURRENT GOAL AND OBJECTIVES

GM B:1.3   Regains balanced, upright sitting position after *leaning* to the left, to the right, and forward
GM B:2.2   Maintains a sitting position in chair
Adap A:4.2   Eats with fingers
Cog E:1.1   Retains one object when second object is obtained

SC A:3.0   Engages in vocal exchanges by babbling
Soc A:2.2   Responds to familiar adult's social behavior

TEACHING SUGGESTIONS
Activity-Based

- Allow the child to finger feed small bits of food from a tray or flat surface (peas, Cheerios, cracker pieces).
- Give the child pull-toys, extending the toy to the child with the string first (remove ring or handle from string so that the child must manipulate the string to activate the pull-toy).
- Provide the child with picture books. Encourage the child to turn the pages of the book.
- Present the child with mechanical toys with levers that can be grasped with the side of the index finger and thumb (e.g., Busy Box, pop-up toy, jack-in-the-box).
- Allow the child to turn on or off a light switch.

Environmental Arrangements

- Offer the child a pea-size object at chest height and toward the middle of the child's body.
- Place pea-size objects on surfaces that provide a high contrast background (e.g., raisins on white table top, oyster crackers on colored plate).
- Offer the child one pea-size object at a time.
- Use a variety of pea-size objects (e.g., beads, Cheerios, Legos). Pay special attention to safety with small objects.
- Begin by presenting larger objects and fade to smaller objects when the child demonstrates competence in obtaining an object using the side of the index finger and thumb.

Instructional Sequence

- Model grasping a Lego, using the side of the index finger and thumb.
- Verbally prompt the child to pick up a Lego from the floor.
- Provide visual or auditory cues by pointing or tapping a surface on which there is a pea-size object.
- Hold a pea-size object in own pincer grasp until the child grasps the object using the side of the index finger and thumb.
- Provide support or stability behind the child's elbow and gently guide his or her arm to the surface. Gradually fade assistance as the child becomes more proficient.

TEACHING CONSIDERATIONS

1. The environment should be free of objects or events that compete with the toy or object presented to the child.
2. Objects should be used that provide cues to which the child with a sensory impairment can respond. For example, use noise-producing toys for a child with a visual impairment.
3. Allow adequate time for the child to respond.
4. Activation or exploration of objects should be continued or facilitated to reinforce the child's interest.
5. Place objects directly in front of the child so that he or she can grasp the objects with either hand.

6. Be sure an adult is nearby to supervise the child's manipulation of pea-size objects. Consider safety with all objects that the child handles. Never leave the child unattended with potentially hazardous objects.

Objective 4.3 Grasps pea-size object with either hand using fingers in a raking and/or scratching movement

---

IMPORTANCE OF SKILL

The child now attempts to involve the fingers in securing pea-size objects rather than use the whole hand. The use of fingers in a raking or scratching movement develops coordination and strength in the fingers and hands. The adjustment and control of the fingers will evolve from this more primitive response, which is an important precursor to use of the pincer grasp.

PRECEDING OBJECTIVE

FM A:3.3   Grasps hand-size object with either hand using whole hand

CONCURRENT OBJECTIVES

GM B:2.2   Maintains a sitting position in chair
Adap A:4.2   Eats with fingers
Cog E:1.2   Retains object
Cog E:4.1   Uses more than one strategy in attempt to solve common problem
Cog G:1.4   Uses sensory examination with objects
SC A:3.1   Engages in vocal exchanges by cooing
Soc A:2.2   Responds to familiar adult's social behavior

TEACHING SUGGESTIONS
Activity-Based

- Allow the child to finger feed small bits of food from a tray or flat surface (e.g., Cheerios, cracker pieces, diced cooked carrots).
- Give the child pull-toys, extending the toy to the child with the string first (remove ring or handle from string so that the child must manipulate the string to activate the pull-toy).
- Engage the child in play with small toys or objects (e.g., pegs, toy people).
- Allow the child to turn on or off a light switch.
- Encourage the child to pick up thin books and papers from a flat surface.

Environmental Arrangements

- Present a pea-size object in your hand for the child to grasp.
- Offer the child a pea-size object at chest height and toward the middle of the child's body.
- Place pea-size objects on a surface that provides a high contrast background (e.g., raisins on white table top, oyster crackers on colored plate).
- Offer the child one pea-size object at a time.

FM A

- Use a variety of pea-size objects (e.g., Cheerios, small beads, Legos). Pay special attention to safety with small objects.

Instructional Sequence

- Model grasping Legos from a flat surface, using a raking motion.
- Verbally prompt the child to pick up Legos from a flat surface.
- Begin by presenting larger objects and fade to smaller objects when the child demonstrates competence in obtaining an object using fingers in a raking or scratching movement.
- Provide visual or auditory cues by pointing or tapping a surface on which there is a pea-size object.
- Assist the child's grasp by providing support or stability behind the child's elbow. Gradually fade assistance as the child becomes more proficient.

TEACHING CONSIDERATIONS

1. The environment should be free of objects or events that compete with the toy or object presented to the child.
2. Objects should be used that provide cues to which the child with a sensory impairment can respond. For example, use noise-producing toys for a child with a visual impairment.
3. Allow adequate time for the child to respond.
4. Activation or exploration of objects should be continued or facilitated to reinforce the child's interest.
5. Place objects directly in front of the child so that he or she can grasp objects with either hand.
6. Be sure an adult is nearby to supervise the child's manipulation of pea-size objects. Consider safety with all objects that the child handles. Never leave the child unattended with potentially hazardous objects.

GOAL 5   Places and releases object balanced on top of another object with either hand

---

DEVELOPMENTAL PROGRAMMING STEPS

PS5.0a   The child places a small object onto a small target (with either the left or right hand), aligning and releasing; the object falls over.

PS5.0b   The child places a small object onto a small object without releasing the object.

IMPORTANCE OF SKILL

The ability to place and release one object balanced on top of another indicates that the child is able to combine several movements to produce a desired outcome. It also indicates an understanding of the relationship between two objects in space. The child demonstrates improved eye–hand coordination and manual dexterity and becomes aware of cognitive concepts such as objects in a series and quantity.

PRECEDING OBJECTIVE

FM A:5.1   Releases hand-held object onto and/or into a larger target with either hand

CONCURRENT GOALS AND OBJECTIVES

FM A:2.0   Brings two objects together at or near midline
FM A:3.0   Grasps hand-size object with either hand using ends of thumb, index, and
            second fingers
GM B:1.2   Regains balanced, upright sitting position after *reaching* across the body to
            the right and to the left
Cog C:2.0   Reproduces part of interactive game and/or action in order to continue
            game and/or action
Cog D:1.1   Imitates motor action that is commonly used
Cog E:1.0   Retains objects when new object is obtained
Cog E:4.1   Uses more than one strategy in attempt to solve common problem
Cog F:1.2   Stacks objects
Cog G:1.2   Uses functionally appropriate actions with objects
SC B:2.1   Uses consistent consonant-vowel combinations
SC C:2.3   Carries out one-step direction *with* contextual cues
Soc A:3.1   Initiates communication with familiar adult
Soc C:1.5   Entertains self by playing appropriately with toys

TEACHING SUGGESTIONS
Activity-Based

- Engage the child in play with objects to place and release on top of other objects (e.g.,
  toy man on block, car on block).
- During play time, provide the child with toys or objects that stack (e.g., nesting cups,
  blocks, cans).
- Make a city, fort, or tower with the child by building and stacking blocks.
- Encourage the child to help clear dishes from the table by stacking them.
- Play a game with the child in which you each take a turn to stack a block. Allow the
  child to knock over the blocks and stack them again.

Environmental Arrangements

- Use magnetic objects to ensure success in balancing one object on another.
- Stabilize the lower object to ensure the child's success in balancing the second object
  on top.
- Use objects for balancing that are graded in size from larger to smaller (e.g., nesting
  cups).
- Use a variety of toys or objects to place and release (e.g., different kinds of blocks,
  spools, empty boxes, jar lids).
- Encourage the child to build or stack objects against a wall.

Instructional Sequence

- Model placing and releasing objects balanced on top of one another for the child.
- Verbally direct the child to stack the nesting cups.
- Provide the child with visual or auditory cues (e.g., tap surface of object, point to
  object, verbally direct child).

FM A

- Provide physical assistance by stabilizing and supporting the child's shoulder or elbow. Fade assistance as the child becomes more proficient.

TEACHING CONSIDERATIONS

1. The environment should be free of objects or events that compete with the toy or object presented to the child.
2. Objects should be used that provide cues to which the child with a sensory impairment can respond. For example, use noise-producing toys for a child with a visual impairment.
3. Use objects that can be easily grasped (e.g., blocks, cups).
4. Allow adequate time for the child to respond.
5. Activation or exploration of objects should be continued or facilitated to reinforce the child's interest.
6. Place objects directly in front of the child so that he or she can grasp objects with either hand.
7. Consider safety with all objects that the child handles. Never leave the child unattended with potentially hazardous objects.

Objective 5.1   Releases hand-held object onto and/or into a larger target with either hand

---

DEVELOPMENTAL PROGRAMMING STEP

PS5.1a   The child releases a hand-held object onto or into a large target with either hand while resting his or her hand on the edge.

IMPORTANCE OF SKILL

The ability to release a hand-held object onto or into a large target indicates some knowledge of the relationship between two objects in space. This skill fosters the development of eye–hand coordination and manual control. It provides the child with a new means of play and increased opportunities to interact with the environment. Cognitive development is enhanced as the child learns about concepts such as empty or full and in or out.

PRECEDING OBJECTIVE

FM A:5.2   Releases hand-held object with each hand

CONCURRENT GOALS AND OBJECTIVES

FM A:2.1   Transfers object from one hand to the other
FM A:3.1   Grasps hand-size object with either hand using the palm, with object placed toward the thumb and index finger
FM B:1.1   Turns object over using wrist and arm rotation with each hand
GM B:1.2   Regains balanced, upright sitting position after *reaching* across the body to the right and to the left
Cog B:1.0   Visually follows object and/or person to point of disappearance

Cog B:2.1   Locates object and/or person who hides while child is watching
Cog C:2.0   Reproduces part of interactive game and/or action in order to continue
             game and/or action
Cog D:1.1   Imitates motor action that is commonly used
SC B:1.0   Gains person's attention and refers to an object, person, and/or event
SC C:2.3   Carries out one-step direction *with* contextual cues
Soc A:2.0   Initiates and maintains interaction with familiar adult

TEACHING SUGGESTIONS
Activity-Based

- Put toys away together, dropping toys into plastic bags, boxes, drawstring bags, or toy chests.
- Allow the child to play in the garden, putting rocks in pots, soil in pots, or shovels in pots.
- Encourage the child to practice taking objects out and putting them back into containers (e.g., take raisins out of a raisin box and put them into a cereal bowl, remove crayons from a box and put them into a cup).
- Allow the child to finger feed. Give the bowl or cup to the child to practice dropping the spoon and food into it.
- Encourage the child to drop paper into a wastebasket.
- When doing laundry, encourage the child to drop clothes into the basket.
- Encourage the child to release hand-held objects (e.g., blocks, small cars, ball) into a dump truck. Dump the contents from the truck and fill the truck again.

Environmental Arrangements

- Use objects and containers that will produce a loud sound when combined (e.g., blocks and coffee cans, beads and tin containers).
- Release objects onto or into targets that produce interesting effects (e.g., sticks off a bridge or piggy bank into the water), or that have interesting trajectories (e.g., clothing down chutes or slides, a ball or wagon down a curvy incline).
- Provide the child with containers to drop toys into (e.g., basket, box, bucket).
- Offer objects to the child in rapid succession so that the child must release one object to get another.
- Use a variety of hand-held objects and targets.
- Begin with very large targets and small objects (e.g., socks in a laundry basket). Fade to objects and targets closer to the same size (e.g., spoon in silverware slot, doll in bed) as the child becomes more proficient.

Instructional Sequence

- Model releasing a hand-held object onto or into a larger target for the child.
- Verbally direct the child to put the clothing into the laundry basket.
- Provide visual or auditory cues (e.g., tap object against a target, point to a container, verbally direct the child).
- Position the child so that the hands are directly over the target. Encourage the child to hit or tap an object against the inside edge of a container. This will sometimes elicit a release.
- Encourage the child to release an object by gently pulling an object from the child's grasp.

TEACHING CONSIDERATIONS

1. The environment should be free of objects or events that compete with the toy or object presented to the child.
2. Objects should be used that provide cues to which the child with a sensory impairment can respond. For example, use noise-producing toys for a child with a visual impairment.
3. Use objects that can be easily grasped (e.g., blocks, cups).
4. Allow adequate time for the child to respond.
5. Activation or exploration of objects should be continued or facilitated to reinforce the child's interest.
6. Place objects directly in front of the child so that he or she can grasp the objects with either hand.
7. Consider safety with all objects that the child handles. Never leave the child unattended with potentially hazardous objects.

Objective 5.2 Releases hand-held object with each hand

DEVELOPMENTAL PROGRAMMING STEP

PS5.2a The child releases hand-held object with the left and right hand by pushing or pulling the object against a surface.

IMPORTANCE OF SKILL

The ability to release hand-held objects indicates increased manual strength, control of wrist (extension), and differentiated use of fingers. This skill increases independence as the child lets go of a toy when he or she desires. The skill increases the child's awareness that the child is separate from the environment and develops the child's knowledge of cause and effect. Releasing and throwing objects is a sign of emerging differentiated play and provides the child with the opportunity to expand the repertoire of manipulative behaviors. This is important to independent play.

PRECEDING OBJECTIVE

FM A:2.2   Holds an object in each hand

CONCURRENT GOALS AND OBJECTIVES

FM A:2.1   Transfers object from one hand to the other
FM A:3.3   Grasps hand-size object with either hand using whole hand
GM B:1.4   Sits balanced without support
Adap A:4.2   Eats with fingers
Cog B:1.0   Visually follows object and/or person to point of disappearance
Cog B:2.3   Reacts when object and/or person hides from view
Cog C:2.1   Indicates desire to continue familiar game and/or action
Cog E:1.1   Retains one object when second object is obtained
SC A:3.0   Engages in vocal exchanges by babbling
Soc A:2.1   Initiates simple social game with familiar adult

TEACHING SUGGESTIONS
Activity-Based

- Dangle toys tied to a cord or ribbon from a highchair. Activate the toy in the child's visual field, then drop it over the side. Allow part of the toy to show if the child loses interest immediately after the toy disappears. Pay special attention to safety with dangling objects.
- Allow the child to drop toys into the bathtub before taking a bath.
- When playing outside, encourage the child to release pebbles or rocks onto the pavement.
- Play ball with the child, rolling the ball back and forth.
- Release balls or play cars and trucks down the slide at the playground.
- Knock down towers made of blocks by rolling or throwing the ball at them.
- When the child is holding one object, present another object and encourage him or her to release the object already in hand.
- Encourage the child to release a hand-held object. Play a game by retrieving the object for the child and presenting the object to him or her again.
- At snack time, encourage the child to release garbage into the wastebasket.
- Encourage the child to hang his or her coat on a hook.

Environmental Arrangements

- Give objects to the child in a highchair to drop onto the floor (e.g., blocks, beads). Encourage the child to look over the side of the chair to see the dropped objects.
- Play with a balloon, holding it and batting it to the child. Encourage the child to return it. Pay special attention to safety with balloons.
- Provide the child with a variety of hand-held objects or toys and encourage the child to release them (e.g., blocks, cars, pop beads).
- Hold out your hand to the child and encourage the child to release the object into your hand.
- Roll a ball, truck, or chime ball to position just barely within reach of the child. The child's touch with his or her fingers should propel the object away.

Instructional Sequence

- Model dropping a ball that bounces back to your grasp.
- Verbally direct the child to throw you the ball.
- Provide the child with visual or auditory cues (e.g., tap object in child's hand, point to object, verbally direct child).
- Assist the child to release object by gently guiding the child to straighten flexed wrist or by stroking child's hand. Gradually fade assistance as the child becomes more proficient.

TEACHING CONSIDERATIONS

1. The environment should be free of objects or events that compete with the toy or object presented to the child.
2. Objects should be used that provide cues to which the child with a sensory impairment can respond. For example, use noise-producing toys for a child with a visual impairment.
3. Use objects that can be easily grasped (e.g., blocks, cups).
4. Allow adequate time for the child to respond.

5. Activation or exploration of objects should be continued or facilitated to reinforce the child's interest.
6. Place objects directly in front of the child so that he or she can grasp the objects with either hand.
7. Consider safety with all objects that the child handles. Never leave the child unattended with potentially hazardous objects.

Strand B

Functional Use of Fine Motor Skills

| GOAL 1 | Rotates either wrist on horizontal plane |

DEVELOPMENTAL PROGRAMMING STEP

PS1.0a   The child rotates either wrist on a vertical plane.

IMPORTANCE OF SKILL

A child who rotates either wrist on a horizontal plane demonstrates independent movement of the wrist and the forearm. This skill allows the child the independence to perform many functional skills, such as turning on a faucet. It also affords the child the independence to perform more complex manipulation of objects in the environment.

PRECEDING OBJECTIVES

FM B:1.1   Turns object over using wrist and arm rotation with each hand
Cog G:1.2   Uses functionally appropriate actions with objects

CONCURRENT GOAL AND OBJECTIVES

GM C:3.2   Moves up and down stairs
GM D:2.1   Pushes riding toy with feet while steering
Adap A:5.1   Pours liquid
Adap B:2.1   Washes hands
Cog C:1.0   Correctly activates mechanical toy
SC D:1.4   Uses 15 object and/or event labels
Soc C:1.3   Plays near one or two peers

TEACHING SUGGESTIONS
Activity-Based

- Encourage the child to play with toys such as a Busy Box that have knobs that can be turned by rotating the wrist. Make sure the action of turning the knob produces an effect such as dinging a bell, moving a picture around on the Busy Box, raising the ladder on a firetruck, or opening the door to a toy house.
- Encourage the child to use horizontal wrist rotation to open doors and remove lids on jars.

- Allow the child to make juice by twisting an orange half on a squeezer.
- Encourage the child to participate in cleaning activities with you, such as washing the table with a sponge after a meal or messy activity, or emptying water from cups into the sink.
- Encourage the child to manipulate the handle of a drinking fountain independently. The child may drink from the fountain or simply watch the effect.

☑ If your data indicate that the child is not making progress toward the goal, provide additional structure within the suggested activities by incorporating the following *environmental arrangements:*

Environmental Arrangements

- Play games with cards. Show the child how to deal cards and turn them face up.
- Provide jars with the lids already loosened. Gradually make the task more challenging by screwing the lid a quarter turn.
- Close doors to encourage the child to turn door knobs when entering or leaving a room.
- Provide toys with large, easy-to-manage wind-up mechanisms (e.g., alarm clock, toy train, toy radio). Systematically introduce smaller mechanisms as the child begins to develop wrist rotation.
- Allow the child to manipulate a bubble gum machine filled with cereal.

☑ If this goal is particularly difficult for a child, it may be necessary to use an *instructional sequence* within activities.

Instructional Sequence

- Model twisting common items. Use exaggerated facial and vocal expressions.
- Remind the child to "twist" the container lid, door knob, or orange half on the squeezer.
- Create a result from minimal wrist-rotation effort by the child (e.g., complete turn of water fountain handle so water is dispensed, crank toys to point where minimal effort by child will result in toy being activated). Systematically decrease the amount of assistance given.
- Use minimal physical assistance as necessary.

☑ Combining or pairing different levels of instructions may be helpful when beginning to teach a new and difficult skill. Fade to less intrusive instructions as soon as possible to encourage a more independent performance.

TEACHING CONSIDERATIONS

1. Use objects or events to elicit responses that provide cues to which the child with a sensory impairment can respond. For example, use noise-producing toys for a child with a visual impairment.
2. Use objects that can be easily activated (e.g., squeeze-toys, switches) initially for a child with a motor impairment.
3. Allow adequate time for the child to respond to toys.
4. Activation or exploration of objects should be continued or facilitated to reinforce the child's engagement in the activity.
5. Consider safety with all objects that the child handles. Never leave the child unattended with potentially hazardous objects.

Objective 1.1   Turns object over using wrist and arm rotation with each hand

DEVELOPMENTAL PROGRAMMING STEPS

PS1.1a   The child turns his or her hand and arm from palm-side down (prone) to facing midline while holding an object. For example, holds two blocks with hands palm-side down and turns them toward each other.

PS1.1b   The child turns his or her wrist and arm over when not holding an object (clasps fingers together and turns wrists and hand; turns one arm and hand while examining fingers).

IMPORTANCE OF SKILL

A child who turns an object over using wrist and arm rotation is preparing to use only one hand to complete some manipulative tasks. This skill offers the child the opportunity to explore objects more completely and to control their movement.

PRECEDING GOALS

FM A:3.0   Grasps hand-size object with either hand using ends of thumb, index, and second fingers

FM A:4.0   Grasps pea-size object with either hand using tip of the index finger and thumb with hand and/or arm *not* resting on surface for support

CONCURRENT GOALS AND OBJECTIVES

GM B:2.0   Sits down in and gets out of chair
GM C:1.0   Walks avoiding obstacles
Adap A:3.0   Drinks from cup and/or glass
Adap A:4.0   Eats with fork and/or spoon
Adap C:1.0   Undresses self
Cog C:1.2   Acts on mechanical and/or simple toy in some way
Cog G:1.2   Uses functionally appropriate actions with objects

TEACHING SUGGESTIONS

Activity-Based

- Allow and encourage the child to feed him- or herself with a spoon. Play at feeding dolls, stuffed animals, and peers "pretend" food.
- Allow the child to play with containers in sand, water, dirt, or cornmeal. Encourage the child to dump the contents of one container into another.
- Encourage the child to wash and dry his or her own hands, turning the hands back and forth under the water and rubbing soap on the palms and backs of hands.
- Allow the child to drink from a cup. Play at giving "pretend" drinks to dolls, stuffed animals, and peers.
- During preparation for activities, have the child dump crayons, stickers, brushes, blocks, or peg people out of storage containers.

- Encourage the child to turn pages of a book when reading a story with an adult.
- Allow the child to shake and dump the contents of a container into a bowl during baking activities.

Environmental Arrangements

- Turn the child's arms and hands over when drying, lotioning, or powdering the child after a bath or shower.
- When giving the child a requested object, place the object in the child's hand in such a way that pronating hands (palms down) or supinating hands (palms up) will enable him or her to move the object (e.g., pronation to push toy grocery cart, supination to carry large ball).
- Provide small objects in containers and show the child how to "dump" the contents.

Instructional Sequence

- Model turning your hand over to receive lotion.
- Give verbal directions to "Turn your hand over" as you try to give the child an item.
- Get the child to supinate or pronate his or her hand by gently touching the child's hand with the requested object. For instance, if the child requests powder, pretend to start pouring powder on his or her hand while simultaneously nudging the hand to a supinated position.
- Fully guide the child's hand over to receive an object by turning the wrist and hand simultaneously.

TEACHING CONSIDERATIONS

1. Use objects or events to elicit responses that provide cues to which the child with a sensory impairment can respond. For example, use noise-producing toys for a child with a visual impairment.
2. Use objects that can be easily activated (e.g., squeeze-toys, switches) initially for a child with a motor impairment.
3. Allow adequate time for the child to respond to toys.
4. Activation or exploration of objects should be continued or facilitated to reinforce the child's engagement in the activity.
5. Consider safety with all objects that the child handles. Never leave the child unattended with potentially hazardous objects.

GOAL 2 Assembles toy and/or object that require(s) putting pieces together

---

DEVELOPMENTAL PROGRAMMING STEP

PS2.0a   The child takes apart a toy or object that has pieces.

IMPORTANCE OF SKILL

Successful assembly of objects with many different pieces demonstrates the child's ability to translate a visual understanding of a process into motor output. This perceptual motor skill is comprised of finely coordinated bilateral hand activity, the ability to cope with different or changing spatial orientations, greater wrist control, and finger differentiation. The child utilizes problem-solving skills when assembling objects. This skill provides the child with play opportunities with a variety of toys or objects and fosters creativity as the child designs and builds objects.

PRECEDING OBJECTIVES

FM B:2.1   Fits variety of shapes into corresponding spaces
Cog D:1.1   Imitates motor action that is commonly used
Cog G:1.2   Uses functionally appropriate actions with objects

CONCURRENT GOALS AND OBJECTIVES

FM A:5.0   Places and releases object balanced on top of another object with either hand
Adap B:2.0   Washes and dries hands
Adap B:3.0   Brushes teeth
Adap C:1.0   Undresses self
Cog E:4.0   Solves common problems
Cog F:2.1   Groups functionally related objects
SC C:2.3   Carries out one-step direction *with* contextual cues

TEACHING SUGGESTIONS
Activity-Based

- Establish a routine for the child to put objects away in containers after play. For example, put crayons in a box, peg people in a bus, plastic eggs in egg cartons, toy milk bottles in a carrier, or soap in a soap dish.
- Encourage the child to play with simple puzzles that have few interlocking pieces.
- Engage the child in games with toys that need to be assembled (e.g., Mr. Potato Head, Cootie Bug, Tinkertoys).
- Demonstrate for the child how Magic Marker caps fit on the ends of the markers for storage after using. Have the child help put the markers away.
- Encourage the child to play with "sets" of related toys where multiple pieces can be assembled into various combinations during play (e.g., farm, airport, garage, train, Legos).

Environmental Arrangements

- Have the child complete the assembly of a toy with the last piece. For example, show the child how to put the harness on a Fisher-Price horse and attach the wagon, and then have the child put the toy person in the wagon for a ride. Or put all of the peg children in the bus and have the child put the driver in and drive away. Systematically increase the number of pieces the child contributes.
- Use bristle blocks or Duplos that easily stay together.
- Start with toys that have only two or three pieces and gradually work up to more.
- Use puzzles that have shapes of pieces drawn underneath or draw the shapes yourself.

Instructional Sequence

- Model assembling a toy such as a Cootie Bug. Hand the child the final piece.
- Provide the child with a verbal or visual (pointing) cue of what comes next in assembling a toy.

- Give the child one piece at a time to assemble in the proper order.
- Place a piece loosely in position and physically guide the child to complete the task.

TEACHING CONSIDERATIONS

1. Use objects or events to elicit responses that provide cues to which the child with a sensory impairment can respond. For example, use noise-producing toys for a child with a visual impairment.
2. Use objects (e.g., large puzzle pieces, puzzle pieces with knobs) that can be easily manipulated by a child with a motor impairment.
3. Allow adequate time for the child to respond to toys.
4. Activation or exploration of objects should be continued or facilitated to reinforce the child's engagement in the activity.
5. Consider safety with all objects that the child handles. Never leave the child unattended with potentially hazardous objects.

Objective 2.1 Fits variety of shapes into corresponding spaces

---

DEVELOPMENTAL PROGRAMMING STEPS

PS2.1a The child places round objects into corresponding spaces. For example, the child puts the plug in a drain, a cup in a holder, or peg people in vehicles.

PS2.1b The child removes a variety of shapes from corresponding spaces. For example, the child takes out pieces from puzzles or form boards, a plug out of the tub, or the cup and toothbrush out of their holders.

IMPORTANCE OF SKILL

Putting shapes into corresponding spaces demonstrates the child's understanding of concepts such as size, form, and position in space. It is indicative of the child's increased ability to express spatial relationships among objects. This skill helps the child coordinate, place, and release objects within a well-defined space. The skill also aids in the development of perceptual motor and cognitive skills.

PRECEDING OBJECTIVE

FM B:2.2 Fits object into defined space

CONCURRENT GOAL AND OBJECTIVES

GM B:1.0 Assumes balanced sitting position
Adap A:4.2 Eats with fingers
Cog D:1.1 Imitates motor action that is commonly used
Cog F:2.1 Groups functionally related objects
Cog G:1.2 Uses functionally appropriate actions with objects
SC C:2.3 Carries out one-step direction *with* contextual cues
Soc A:3.2 Responds to communication from familiar adult

FM B

TEACHING SUGGESTIONS
Activity-Based

- Talk about things that fit together or into one another as you cook (e.g., lids on pots, bread in toaster), as you dress the child (e.g., button in hole, shoe on foot), and as you bathe the child (e.g., plug in drain, peg man in bath toy).
- Encourage the child to put objects in containers designed for their fit (e.g., crayons in the box, peg people in a bus, plastic eggs in egg cartons, toy milk bottles in a carrier, soap in a soap dish).
- Demonstrate for the child how Magic Marker caps fit on the ends of the markers for storage and have the child help put them away.
- Give the child coins to put in his or her own piggy bank.
- Provide simple puzzles or form boards with fitting pieces. Pieces do not need to interlock.
- Provide the child with games such as pegs and pegboards, clothespins and jar, toy people and vehicles, or Nerf basketball and hoop.
- Provide two or three different sizes of pots with fitting lids. Provide Tupperware containers of different shapes and sizes with lids. Encourage the child to fit lids to corresponding containers.

Environmental Arrangements

- Use thick puzzle pieces that are easy to hold and manipulate on a shallow form board.
- Use puzzles with handles on pieces or attach handles (e.g., thread spools).
- Begin with hand-size pieces and gradually choose smaller items. For example, first have the child put a cup back in the holder after brushing his or her teeth, then have the child put away the cup *and* the toothbrush in their places on the holder.
- Begin fitting circles only into corresponding holes, then progress to shapes that will fit into corresponding holes in more than one way (e.g., square, triangle, cross).
- Use color cues to help the child distinguish shape differences (e.g., circles are red on the board, squares are blue).
- Use objects that can be easily activated (e.g., shapes for shape sorters, forms with knobs for form boards, plastic eggs for egg cartons).
- When introducing shapes and shape sorters or form boards, present them in completed form and let the child remove and replace pieces to explore.

Instructional Sequence

- Model the placement of a shape and then let the child try.
- Give the child a verbal or gestural cue, such as, "That circle block goes here."
- Place pieces near their corresponding space and have the child complete the placement.
- Use pieces smaller than the corresponding spaces and systematically increase the closeness of fit.
- Use minimal physical assistance to guide the child's hand and object.

TEACHING CONSIDERATIONS

1. Use objects or events to elicit responses that provide cues to which the child with a sensory impairment can respond. For example, use noise-producing toys for a child with a visual impairment.

2. Use objects that can be easily grasped (e.g., large puzzle pieces, puzzle pieces with knobs).
3. Allow adequate time for the child to respond to toys.
4. Activation or exploration of objects should be continued or facilitated to reinforce the child's engagement in the activity.
5. Consider safety with all objects that the child handles. Never leave the child unattended with potentially hazardous objects.

Objective 2.2   Fits object into defined space

DEVELOPMENTAL PROGRAMMING STEPS

PS2.2a   The child puts an object into a defined space in such a way that the object does not fit completely into the space.
PS2.2b   The child takes an object out of a defined space. For example, he or she removes a block from a dump truck, or takes a car out of a toy garage.

IMPORTANCE OF SKILL

Fitting objects into defined spaces indicates the child's functional coordination of a number of sophisticated fine motor movements of arms, hands, and fingers. This skill also represents the child's ability to combine and manipulate related objects together in different spatial configurations. It provides the child with varied means of play and interaction with objects.

PRECEDING OBJECTIVES

FM A:5.1   Releases hand-held object onto and/or into a larger target with either hand
Cog E:1.2   Retains object

CONCURRENT GOALS AND OBJECTIVES

GM C:1.5   Cruises
Cog C:1.2   Acts on mechanical and/or simple toy in some way
Cog E:4.0   Solves common problems
Cog G:1.2   Uses functionally appropriate actions with objects
SC C:2.3   Carries out one-step direction *with* contextual cues
Soc B:2.0   Responds to established social routine
Soc C:1.5   Entertains self by playing appropriately with toys

TEACHING SUGGESTIONS
Activity-Based

■ During the daily routine, talk about and point out objects that fit into defined spaces. For example, food belongs on a plate, soap in a soap dish, sock on foot, or toy car in a toy garage.
■ Encourage the child to assist with activities that put objects into defined spaces, such as mail in a mailbox, dirt in planter pots, or utensils in drawers.

- Provide numerous containers for the child to play with in functional ways. For example, have separate containers for cars, dolls, balls, or blocks.
- Play dump trucks, buckets, wagons, or toy shopping carts that can be filled with small objects.
- Encourage the child to put objects away in their correct storage areas (e.g., crayons in a box, books in a book rack, laundry in a basket, toys in a toy box or on a shelf, groceries in a cupboard).
- Serve appealing finger food at snack and mealtime. Encourage the child to put the food into his or her mouth.
- When introducing objects to the child, present them so that the object is already *in* a defined space; the child must remove the object to explore it and then return it to its space.

Environmental Arrangements

- Arrange objects to produce an effect when one object is activated. For example, a bell rings when a ball hits a target, or water splashes when an object is dropped into a bucket of water.
- Use large receptacles for objects, such as blocks in a shoe box. Decrease the size of the receptacle systematically to a drinking cup size.
- Offer the child a second and third object while he or she is still grasping the first object and holding it over an open container. This will encourage the child to drop an object to obtain another.
- Begin with two objects that can fit together only one way (e.g., two nesting blocks, baby and cradle, toy car and garage, telephone and receiver). Systematically introduce more and varied combinations as the child begins to fit objects into spaces.
- Use objects that can be easily manipulated (e.g., hand-size pieces that fit only one or two ways).

Instructional Sequence

- Model putting the baby on her bed so that she can "take a nap."
- Give a verbal and gestural cue for your request. "See the baby's bed? It's right here (point). Put the baby on her bed so she can take a nap."
- Give the child materials one at a time. "Here's the baby's bed (child receives bed) and here's the baby (child receives doll). Put the baby on her bed so she can take a nap."
- Gently assist the child to place an object in a defined space.

TEACHING CONSIDERATIONS

1. Use objects or events to elicit responses that provide cues to which the child with a sensory impairment can respond. For example, use noise-producing toys for a child with a visual impairment.
2. Use objects that can be easily manipulated (e.g., large puzzle pieces, puzzle pieces with knobs) by a child with a motor impairment.
3. Allow adequate time for the child to respond to toys.
4. Activation or exploration of objects should be continued or facilitated to reinforce the child's engagement in the activity.
5. Consider safety with all objects that the child handles. Never leave the child unattended with potentially hazardous objects.

FM B

| GOAL 3   Uses either index finger to activate objects |

DEVELOPMENTAL PROGRAMMING STEPS

PS3.0a   The child isolates his or her index finger by pointing (not necessarily with intent).

PS3.0b   The child uses his or her thumb or fingers to poke.

IMPORTANCE OF SKILL

A child using an index finger to activate objects is demonstrating the ability to organize fine motor behavior in a goal-directed manner. The use of an index finger versus the whole hand indicates that the child's fingers are becoming differentiated and can be used for tasks independent of the whole hand. This skill aids in the development of eye-finger coordination, cause-and-effect relationships, and problem-solving skills.

PRECEDING OBJECTIVE

FM B:3.1   Uses either hand to activate objects

CONCURRENT GOAL AND OBJECTIVES

GM B:1.0   Assumes balanced sitting position
GM C:1.5   Cruises
Adap A:4.2   Eats with fingers
Cog G:1.2   Uses functionally appropriate actions with objects
SC B:1.2   Points to an object, person, and/or event
Soc A:3.2   Responds to communication from familiar adult
Soc B:2.1   Responds to routine event

TEACHING SUGGESTIONS

Activity-Based

- Have the child poke at holes punched in paper, poke holes into clay, point at pictures in books, or dial a play telephone with the index finger extended.
- Show the child how to wash his or her belly button and between toes using the index finger during a bath.
- While bathing or playing outside, show the child how to pop bubbles with his or her index finger.
- When the child pats pictures or mirror images, model pointing in return and encourage the child to point, too.
- Give the child the opportunity to activate familiar objects in the environment with an index finger. For example, encourage the child to turn on and off lights, press elevator buttons, turn the television or radio off, or press doorbells.
- Engage the child in play with a Busy Box or other toy with buttons to poke to produce an effect.

Environmental Arrangements

- Provide various toys for the child to explore that provide highly salient feedback in response to fine motor movement. Use toy pianos and other musical toys that require touch.
- Give the child pull-toys that are extended with the string first. (Remove the ring or handle from the string so that the child must manipulate the string to activate the object.)
- Put finger food, small blocks, or toys into egg cartons or other small containers so that items can only be accessed using the index finger.
- Provide finger paints and show the child how to "write" with the index finger. Put shiny or interesting toy rings or finger puppets on the child's index fingers and encourage the child to wiggle the fingers to make them move.

Instructional Sequence

- Model activating the object for the child, then give the child a turn.
- Give the child a verbal cue to activate the object, such as, "Push the button."
- Have the child point to an object, then brush the object against the child's finger to activate it.
- Use minimal physical assistance to guide the index fingers to an object.

TEACHING CONSIDERATIONS

1. Use objects or events to elicit responses that provide cues to which the child with a sensory impairment can respond. For example, use noise-producing toys for a child with a visual impairment.
2. Use objects that can be easily activated (e.g., switches, squeeze-toys).
3. Allow adequate time for the child to respond to toys.
4. Activation or exploration of objects should be continued or facilitated to reinforce the child's engagement in the activity.
5. Consider safety with all objects that the child handles. Never leave the child unattended with potentially hazardous objects.

Objective 3.1 Uses either hand to activate objects

DEVELOPMENTAL PROGRAMMING STEPS

☑ This objective is the most basic step for the skill to be taught. Most children will benefit from the activities outlined here that emphasize this skill. For children who need more structure, consider designing programming steps from the *environmental arrangements* suggestions or from the *instructional sequence*.

IMPORTANCE OF SKILL

A child using a hand to activate objects is demonstrating the ability to use hands in a goal-directed way that will lead to reinforcement. The use of the whole hand versus the use of an isolated index finger indicates that finger differentiation has not yet occurred or is insufficient to successfully activate an object. With this skill, the child utilizes manual dexterity and a variety of fine motor skills to activate different objects, such as turning knobs. The child learns cause-and-effect relationships and practices problem solving skills.

PRECEDING OBJECTIVE

FM A:2.3   Reaches toward and touches object with each hand

CONCURRENT GOAL AND OBJECTIVES

GM B:1.0   Assumes balanced sitting position
Adap A:4.2   Eats with fingers
Cog C:1.1   Correctly activates simple toy
Cog D:1.1   Imitates motor action that is commonly used
Cog G:1.2   Uses functionally appropriate actions with objects
Soc A:3.2   Responds to communication from familiar adult
Soc B:2.1   Responds to routine event

TEACHING SUGGESTIONS

Activity-Based

- Engage in interactive play with blocks, vehicles, balls, and other hand-size objects.
- Provide opportunities for the child to explore various toys that provide highly salient feedback when activated. Have a Busy Box, musical toys such as a tambourine or jingle-bells, or a Happy Apple toy available. Show the child how to activate them.
- Give the child many opportunities to activate familiar objects in the environment. Encourage the child to push open doors and cupboards and pull open drawers.
- Let the child activate appliances such as the vacuum, toaster, or sink that require use of the entire hand.

Environmental Arrangements

- Use pump dispensers for soap and lotion and let the child do the pumping.
- Provide materials that lend themselves well to patting, slapping, pushing, and pulling. For example, show the child how to pop bubbles, flatten clay, finger paint, or push floating toys.
- Allow the child to push the large buttons on vending machines to receive food or a drink.
- Create an entertaining effect that the child's hand can easily activate. Build a tower of blocks and have the child knock it down; pile up bubbles in the bath and have the child smash them; or make a sand tower and have the child flatten it.
- Make special switches to activate toys for children who have a light touch or who lack coordination (e.g., joysticks, pressure plates).

Instructional Sequence

- Model activation of the object for the child, then give the child a turn.
- Give the child a verbal cue to activate the object, such as "push the car."
- While holding the child, gently brush the child's hand against an object, activating it.
- Use minimal physical assistance to guide the child's hand to an object.

TEACHING CONSIDERATIONS

1. Use objects or events to elicit responses that provide cues to which the child with a sensory impairment can respond. For example, use noise-producing toys for a child with a visual impairment.
2. Use objects that can be easily activated (e.g., musical toys, squeeze-toys, switches).
3. Allow adequate time for the child to respond to toys.
4. Activation or exploration of objects should be continued or facilitated to reinforce the child's engagement in the activity.
5. Consider safety with all objects that the child handles. Never leave the child unattended with potentially hazardous objects.

GOAL 4   Copies simple written shapes after demonstration

DEVELOPMENTAL PROGRAMMING STEP

PS4.0a   The child traces simple shapes.

IMPORTANCE OF SKILL

Copying simple written shapes encourages greater control with a writing implement such as a crayon or pencil. This skill also aids the development of eye–hand coordination and perceptual motor skills. By reproducing simple shapes, the child practices concepts such as straightness, curves, slants, continuity, enclosure, and intersection. This skill also fosters visual discrimination—a skill important to reading and writing. The child practices tracing shapes that are the basis of letters and numbers. Copying shapes is a precursor to drawing representational pictures.

PRECEDING OBJECTIVE

FM B:4.1   Draws circles and lines

CONCURRENT GOALS AND OBJECTIVE

GM B:2.0   Sits down in and gets out of chair
Cog C:1.0   Correctly activates mechanical toy
Cog G:1.4   Uses sensory examination with objects
SC B:1.0   Gains person's attention and refers to an object, person, and/or event
SC C:2.0   Carries out two-step direction *without* contextual cues
Soc A:2.0   Initiates and maintains interaction with familiar adult

TEACHING SUGGESTIONS
Activity-Based

■ Point out shapes in the natural environment (wheels are circles, clocks are circles, windows are rectangles) and trace the shapes with your finger.

- Make pudding prints or whipped cream art on the table top and copy each other's designs.
- Take turns drawing pictures with shapes on magic slates, chalkboard, or paper. Use circles for faces, squares for houses, or triangles for pizza slices.
- Use shapes in flannel board play or art activities, giving the child an opportunity to feel, copy, and match them.
- Encourage the child to make circles, crosses, and triangles with his or her index finger in sand, flour, dirt, or finger paint.
- Hang the child's work on display to encourage the activity.

Environmental Arrangements

- Give the child a template or piece of cutout cardboard that will guide the writing implement around the desired shape.
- Give the child pre-cut shapes to paste using glue sticks, or give the child bottles to trace the outline of their shape.
- Draw dot-to-dots of shapes for the child to trace.
- Engage the child's attention to the activity by making dots on the writing surface. The auditory component (tapping) of this action usually captures the child's interest.
- Begin with large exaggerations of desired shapes and gradually diminish the size.

Instructional Sequence

- Model copying a shape with a pencil on paper.
- Use gestures and verbal instructions, such as, "Go 'round and 'round," or "One line here, another here."
- Hold the end part of the child's writing implement as the child makes marks on the writing surface. Gently guide the tool through the desired motion, pairing the action with an auditory cue (e.g., zoom, 'round and 'round, zip).
- Allow the child to hold an adult's hand or end of a writing implement as the adult makes marks on the writing surface. Guide the tool through the desired motion, pairing the action with an auditory cue (zoom, 'round and 'round, zip).
- Use minimal physical assistance to guide the child's hand in copying shapes.

TEACHING CONSIDERATIONS

1. Use objects or events to elicit responses that provide cues to which the child with a sensory impairment can respond. For example, use noise-producing toys for a child with a visual impairment.
2. Use writing implements that can be easily managed by the child; use necessary adaptive implements for a child with a motor impairment.
3. Allow adequate time for the child to respond to toys.
4. Activation or exploration of the materials should be continued or facilitated to reinforce the child's engagement in the activity.
5. Consider safety with all objects that the child handles. Never leave the child unattended with potentially hazardous objects.

Objective 4.1   Draws circles and lines

DEVELOPMENTAL PROGRAMMING STEPS

PS4.1a   The child draws a circular shape.
PS4.1b   The child makes a horizontal stroke with a writing utensil.
PS4.1c   The child makes a vertical stroke with a writing utensil.

IMPORTANCE OF SKILL

With this skill, the child gains greater control at maneuvering the writing utensil and making intentional strokes. Circles and lines are the basic elements of numerals and letters. This skill is a precursor to writing and to drawing pictures.

PRECEDING OBJECTIVE

FM B:4.2   Scribbles

CONCURRENT GOALS AND OBJECTIVE

GM B:2.0   Sits down in and gets out of chair
GM C:1.0   Walks avoiding obstacles
Adap A:4.0   Eats with fork and/or spoon
Adap B:3.0   Brushes teeth
Cog C:2.0   Reproduces part of interactive game and/or action in order to continue game and/or action
Soc C:1.1   Initiates social behavior toward peer

TEACHING SUGGESTIONS
Activity-Based

- While playing outside, encourage the child to make lines and circles with his or her index finger or with sticks in the sand, dirt, or mud.
- Use soap crayons in the bath and take turns drawing lines and dots.
- Point out shapes in the environment (e.g., wheels are circles, clocks are circles, plates are circles) and trace around them with your finger.
- "Paint" with water on the sidewalk, making long lines and big circles.
- Draw "happy faces" together.
- Provide crayons or markers for drawing. Take turns drawing lines and circles with different colors.
- Hang the child's work on display to reinforce the activity.

Environmental Arrangements

- Make lines and circles in clay or cookie dough and "feel" the configuration.
- Provide auditory component to the child's activity as the child marks the surface (e.g., zip, zoom, 'round and 'round).

- Give the child a template or piece of cutout cardboard that will guide the writing implement around the desired shape.
- Begin with large exaggerations of lines and circles and gradually diminish the size.
- Engage the child's attention to the activity by making dots on the writing surface. The auditory component (i.e., tapping) of this action usually captures the child's interest.

Instructional Sequence

- Model drawing circles and lines on paper.
- Use verbal cues and gestures to cue the child. For example, say, "Make a line *this* way," or "Go 'round and 'round."
- Hold the end of the child's writing implement as the child makes marks on the writing surface. Gently guide the tool through the desired motion, pairing the action with an auditory cue (e.g., zoom, 'round and 'round, zip).
- Allow the child to hold an adult's hand or the end of the writing implement as the adult makes marks on the writing surface. Guide the tool through the desired motion, pairing the action with an auditory cue (e.g., zoom, 'round and 'round, zip).
- Use minimal physical assistance to guide the child's hand in drawing lines and circles.

TEACHING CONSIDERATIONS

1. Use objects that provide cues to which the child with a sensory impairment can respond. For example, use clay, sand, or other textured surfaces for a child with a visual impairment.
2. Use writing implements that can be easily managed by the child; use necessary adaptive implements for a child with a motor impairment.
3. Allow adequate time for the child to respond to toys.
4. Activation or exploration of the materials should be continued or facilitated to reinforce the child's engagement in the activity.
5. Consider safety with all objects that the child handles. Never leave the child unattended with potentially hazardous objects.

Objective 4.2 Scribbles

DEVELOPMENTAL PROGRAMMING STEP

PS4.2a   The child makes marks on paper.

IMPORTANCE OF SKILL

Spontaneous scribbling provides the child with the opportunity to learn the relationship between finger movements that guide the tool and the resulting visual feedback. This skill also aids in the development of fine motor control and eye–hand coordination. Scribbling provides the child with a means of expression and an opportunity to be creative.

PRECEDING OBJECTIVES

FM A:3.2   Grasps cylindrical object with either hand by closing fingers around it
Cog G:1.2   Uses functionally appropriate actions with objects

CONCURRENT GOALS AND OBJECTIVES

GM B:2.0   Sits down in and gets out of chair
GM C:1.0   Walks avoiding obstacles
Adap A:4.1 Brings food to mouth using utensil
Adap B:3.1 Cooperates with teeth brushing
Cog C:1.1   Correctly activates simple toy
Cog D:1.1   Imitates motor action that is commonly used
SC C:2.3   Carries out one-step direction *with* contextual cues

TEACHING SUGGESTIONS

Activity-Based

- Encourage the child to engage in activities with marking tools, such as painting with paint brushes, or drawing in dirt with sticks.
- While you write letters or pay bills, give the child paper and crayons to use to imitate your activity.
- Color together on plain paper or in coloring books without attention to "staying in the lines."
- Hang large sheets of paper on a wall for the child to color on (e.g., paper grocery sacks cut open work well).
- Wrap toys in paper and allow the child to "decorate" the packages.
- Hang the child's work on display to reinforce the activity.

Environmental Arrangements

- Provide the child with a large space to write on; gradually decrease the space to the size of writing paper.
- Offer the child a picture of his or her favorite object to point to with a writing implement.
- Move the paper around beneath the child's poised writing implement to create a mark. Call attention to the mark, then wait for the child's response.
- Engage the child's attention to the activity by making dots on the writing surface. The auditory component (tapping) of this action usually captures the child's interest.

Instructional Sequence

- Model scribbling on paper.
- Verbally encourage the child to scribble on paper.
- Hold the end part of the child's writing implement as the child touches it to the writing surface. Gently guide the tool to give the child the idea, pairing the action with an auditory component (e.g., zip, 'round and 'round). Release and wait for the child's response.
- Physically assist the child in drawing lines and circles on paper.

TEACHING CONSIDERATIONS

1. Use objects that provide cues to which the child with a sensory impairment can respond. For example, use clay, sand, or other textured surfaces for a child with a visual impairment.
2. Use writing implements that can be easily managed by the child; use necessary adaptive implements for a child with a motor impairment.

FM B

FM B

3. Allow adequate time for the child to respond to toys.
4. Activation or exploration of the materials should be continued or facilitated to rein-
    force the child's engagement in the activity.
5. Consider safety with all objects that the child handles. Never leave the child unat-
    tended with potentially hazardous objects.

GROSS MOTOR DOMAIN

*Margaret Veltman, Betsy Ryan-Seth,
Kristine Slentz, and Juliann Cripe*

The Gross Motor Domain consists of four strands tracing the development of the infant from the earliest movements in the supine and prone positions to sitting and walking and functional use of motor skills in play. Many of a child's efforts in the first year of life are concentrated on acquiring new and more complex motor skills. Often caregiver and infant interactions center upon the acquisition of these motor actions, and the actions themselves become important to the child's development in other domains. For example, children use movement to communicate wants and needs when they crawl to the refrigerator and touch the door or reach with extended arms toward a toy that is out of reach. When these movements are combined with vocalizations and interpreted successfully by the caregiver, the basis for communication is advanced. Development of motor skills builds the child's confidence and increases interest in and opportunities for exploring. The child is able to make choices through movement and exercise some control over the environment by crawling from one room to another, climbing on and off a riding toy, or sitting on the couch. The child who moves about with increased independence faces new challenges and frustrations.

The first strand in the Gross Motor Domain examines the infant's ability to move body parts independently of each other and to position the body in supine (on back) and prone (on stomach) to facilitate movement and locomotion. Gross motor development follows a predictable sequence, progressing in a cephalocaudal (head to toe) and proximal-distal (from midline away) direction. This means development proceeds from the head down to the feet and from the chest out to the fingers. The infant learns to control the head before the trunk, control arms before fingers, and move the eyes in a controlled manner before stabilizing and turning the head. The infant learns to control his or her body in a horizontal position before a vertical position. Head control is evident while the infant lies on the stomach or back before sitting or standing upright. These body control sequences are predictable but not invariable. Each infant's development may vary widely from others of comparable age but still be normal. It is important to acknowledge normal variations in style and ability when designing developmental activities.

The newborn infant's motor responses are jerky and uncoordinated. Moving or making contact appear to be accidental occurrences of which the infant has little or no control. While the infant is learning to move in new ways, concentration on the action is critical. The child may appear to be moving in slow motion, focusing every ounce of energy on learning a new motor skill. Once the skill is learned, the child will practice it over and over again with obvious enjoyment. Continual use of arms, legs, trunk, head, fingers, and other body parts produces increased control. While prone, the child will use his or her forearms momentarily and will prop higher and for longer periods of time until able to reach for objects with one arm. At the same time the child is developing skills in the prone position, he or she is also exploring with the hands and eyes.

Trunk control is evident when the infant begins to roll and squirm. Movements become skillful and purposeful as the infant becomes adept at exploring the environment through simple locomotion such as pivoting, creeping, rocking, and crawling. The infant may combine many different types of locomotion to gain access to a desired person or object, even relinquishing a new, more sophisticated pattern for a primitive but faster mode.

The second strand in the Gross Motor Domain of the AEPS Curriculum focuses on balance in sitting. Sitting skills are very functional and greatly increase the child's freedom of movement and comfort. Sitting requires the infant to balance the head and trunk, initially with support, then independently. When placed in a sitting position, the newborn may lift his or her head and even extend the trunk momentarily before slumping. As body control develops in prone and supine positions, and as head righting, equilibrium, and protective responses mature, the infant can not only lift the head and extend the trunk, but also sit without support of the hands. The young child becomes increasingly facile at regaining and maintaining balance in sitting while reaching for and interacting with objects. The infant learns to shift in and out of sitting and into other positions to increase access to the environment. The infant's ability to sit down in and get out of a chair also increases the child's socialization and independence.

The young child learning to sit independently may frequently topple over or slump. However, back muscles develop strength over time and with use, resulting in increased stability. It is important with sitting, as with all motor activities, to allow the child's ability to emerge without providing too much adult support. When the child is slow, clumsy, or unsure, the caregiver is easily tempted to provide maximum support that preempts the child's learning of the skill. This curriculum emphasizes the use of the least intrusive support necessary for the child to accomplish the skill independently. Using opportunities throughout the day and arranging the environment to ensure safety is the preferred way for the child to learn skills such as sitting. A few minutes practicing sitting after a diaper change or while propped with towels in a laundry basket helps develop strength for most young children just as well as a 20-minute exercise regimen.

Balance and mobility in standing and walking are the culmination of muscle development throughout the body and of months of practice on increasingly sophisticated motor actions. This marks a major milestone for caregivers as the child's ability to walk independently eliminates the task of carrying, supporting, or wheeling the child everywhere. Stairs become the ultimate challenge and a frontier that provides many fears for caregivers.

The development of gross motor skills in the infant and young child is generally carefully watched and proudly acclaimed by the family and caregivers. The gross motor milestones are recorded in baby books and used as comparative measures between generations within the family. Knowing that the father and all of his siblings walked at 9 months places the expectation for early walking upon the child. The combination of this environmental expectation and the possibility of a genetic propensity for early development of gross motor skills may actually contribute to the development of walking at an early age, but then again it may not. High expectations can also lead to discouragement for the child and inhibition in experimenting with motor actions. The child wants to please and is sensitive to the caregiver's impatience and anxiety. A child who has normal movement, tone, and strength, but is still not walking alone when the caregiver thinks he or she should, usually needs more time rather than coaxing or special shoes.

The AEPS Curriculum includes play skills within the Gross Motor Domain. A tricycle and a ball provide opportunities to gain balance and control, as well as to have fun with playmates. These activities combine motor actions of different levels of complexity, providing the child with practice on new skills while gaining proficiency in old ones. Some activities combine unusual motor expectations such as pushing a riding toy with alternating feet. The sitting position is not a natural way to learn to alternate the feet in motion; therefore, even though sitting is a prerequisite skill for a riding toy, it does not guarantee success. Pushing with legs is very different from walking with legs. Even for the young child with well-developed walking skills, a riding toy poses new challenges.

Infants and young children with motor problems form a heterogeneous group. Children with cerebral palsy have a clearly defined set of motor problems; other children are described simply as delayed or atypical. Motor impairments may be transient and disappear over time or may become more serious. It is often difficult for the interventionist to make accurate predictions about development; he or she must monitor progress carefully. It is also important to maintain close contact with specialists, such as physical and occupational therapists—their guidance will be critical to meeting the needs of children with motor impairments. The AEPS Curriculum was not written specifically for children with severe motor impairments, and adaptations will need to be made for these children when engaging in activities to develop gross motor skills.

GM

Strand A

Movement and Locomotion in Supine and Prone Position

GOAL 1 Turns head, moves arms, and kicks legs independently of each other

DEVELOPMENTAL PROGRAMMING STEPS

In order to achieve this goal, a child must perform Objectives 1.1–1.3 to criteria. Refer to the developmental programming steps for each objective to develop the skills.

IMPORTANCE OF SKILL

A child's first posture when lying on his or her back (supine) is characterized by the complete flexion experienced in utero. From this position, the child begins to bend and stretch the limbs and turn the head, increasing the range of movement in the legs, arms, and head. This permits the child to practice the antigravity extension movement that will allow an upright posture within the first year of life. The ability to move body parts independently of one another is basic to all other gross motor skills, such as crawling, sitting, and walking.

CONCURRENT GOALS AND OBJECTIVES

FM A:1.2   Makes nondirected movements with each arm
Cog A:1.0   Orients to auditory, visual, and tactile events
Cog B:1.0   Visually follows object and/or person to point of disappearance
SC A:1.0   Turns and looks toward person speaking
Soc A:1.1   Responds appropriately to familiar adult's affective tone

TEACHING SUGGESTIONS
Activity-Based

- When the child is engaged with another familiar adult in an interactive game, observe the child for voluntary independent head, arm, and leg movements.
- Give the child opportunities to be held or to lie naked on smooth, soft blankets to encourage pleasurable tactile sensations for body movements. Make sure the child remains warm if lying undressed.
- Talk to the child in gentle tones while the child is lying on his or her back in a crib or enclosed space. Pause periodically for the child's response.

- While doing daily chores such as washing dishes and cooking, seat the child in close proximity and talk to and touch him or her occasionally. This encourages the child to attend and respond.
- Encourage the child to use arms and legs to splash water when in the bathtub.

☑ If your data indicate the child is not making progress toward the goal, provide additional structure within the suggested activities by incorporating the following *environmental arrangements:*

Environmental Arrangements

- Safely affix an easily activated mobile to the crib in the child's visual field. Change the location of the mobile to encourage the child to visually explore a larger area.
- Sing nursery songs and touch different body parts as a signal for the child to move those limbs or his or her head.
- If the child has difficulty keeping his or her head from turning to the side or moving out of an asymmetrical tonic neck reflex (ATNR fencing) once in that position, assist the child's head to midline by shaping a rolled blanket around his or her head, extending it from ear to ear.
- Place the child gently over your knee and bounce him or her. Watch for leg and arm movements as well as head turning. Do not maintain this position for prolonged periods or if the child expresses displeasure.
- When bathing, drying, or putting lotion on the child, stroke one leg, one arm, and one side of the face at a time, encouraging separate responses.
- Slightly elevate (with folded blanket or cloth diaper) the child's head and shoulders or hips when the child is lying on his or her back.
- Put jingle-bells on the child's booties, mittens, or hat, so that he or she can control the sounds.
- Give the child opportunities to move in less demanding positions, such as on stomach supported at chest or in a sidelying posture. Practice independent movements in all positions.

☑ If this goal is particularly difficult for a child, it may be necessary, within activities, to use an *instructional sequence.*

Instructional Sequence

- When the child is lying on his or her back, gently stroke or blow on the bottom of one foot and then the other, one hand and then the other, one ear and then the other, while encouraging single disassociated movements.
- If the child enjoys "raspberries" (putting mouth against skin and blowing), begin by blowing a "raspberry" on the child's stomach and then back away. After a signal from the child (smile, slight movement, vocalization), repeat the action, moving slowly toward the child's body. Remain there until the child's hands or feet move toward or touch your head or face.
- When holding the child in a face-to-face position, hold his or her hand to your mouth and kiss, then gently release. Wait for a response from the child (smile, slight movement, vocalization), then repeat the action.

☑ Combining or pairing different levels of instructional sequences may be helpful when beginning to teach a new and difficult skill. Fade to less intrusive instructional sequences as soon as possible to encourage more independent performance.

TEACHING CONSIDERATIONS

1. If the child has a motor impairment or abnormal muscle tone, consult a physical therapist about the appropriateness of this skill and about related programming issues.
2. Provide a quiet and safe space for the child to practice this skill in a comfortable manner.
3. Consider safety with all objects that the child handles. Never leave the child unattended with potentially hazardous objects.

Objective 1.1 Turns head past 45° to the right and left from midline position

---

DEVELOPMENTAL PROGRAMMING STEP

PS1.1a   The child turns his or her head 45° to the right and left from midline position.

IMPORTANCE OF SKILL

The development of controlled movement progresses from head to foot. Initially, the infant looks at objects and follows them with the eyes and head for brief periods. Development progresses to allow the child to turn the head past 45° to a stimulus, demonstrating control of head-turning on a horizontal plane. This controlled movement builds strength necessary for the child to hold the head in an upright position. Turning the head allows the child more visual exploration of the environment.

CONCURRENT GOALS AND OBJECTIVES

FM A:1.2   Makes nondirected movements with each arm
Adap A:1.4   Swallows liquids
Cog A:1.0   Orients to auditory, visual, and tactile events
Cog B:1.0   Visually follows object and/or person to point of disappearance
SC A:1.0   Turns and looks toward person speaking
Soc A:1.1   Responds appropriately to familiar adult's affective tone

TEACHING SUGGESTIONS
Activity-Based

- Talk to the child in gentle tones while the child is on his or her back in a crib or an enclosed space or when the child is held in a face-to-face position. Once the child focuses on your face, move slowly from one side to the other while continuing to speak to him or her.
- When coming into the child's immediate environment, speak gently to the child from one side and wait for the child to turn toward you.
- When feeding the child at the breast, with a bottle, or with a spoon, give the child visual or tactile cues indicating the direction of nourishment. Require head-turning response toward food.
- Encourage head-turning when novel and interesting events occur, such as a pet walking past or a mother, father, or sibling entering the room.

Environmental Arrangements

- Hang bold, colorful pictures on both sides of the child's visual field in the crib or next to a chair or infant seat to encourage head turning for visual exploration.
- If the child cannot maintain head in midline, shape a rolled blanket or small towel around the child's head from ear to ear, or use commercial head supports.
- Hold the child close to your body or provide him or her with large, soft barriers in the crib (stuffed animals, blankets, towels) so that the child receives tactile sensations for movements of the head.
- Pair your own voice with stronger visual cues, sounds from favorite toys, or vocal clicks and other noises until he or she focuses on your face. Recapture the child's waning or disengaged attention by using slightly different pairings.
- Dim lights in the child's immediate environment and reintroduce them in locations where the child will have to turn to see them (open blinds in the child's room after a nap; plug in Christmas tree lights).
- Move a push toy in front of the child to encourage the child to follow with his or her eyes and head.
- Encourage the child to "track" you either auditorily or visually as you sing or as you play peekaboo around corners of the crib.
- Place a mirror to one side of the child's crib, play area, or changing table. Position the child so that the mirror is sometimes on the left and sometimes on the right.

Instructional Sequence

- Position the child so that his or her head and shoulders are slightly forward and are not held in a stiff, elevated, or retracted fashion. If the child can control his or her own posture, make the presentation of activities contingent on the child's successful attempt at optimal positioning.
- Systematically increase the distance the child must turn his or her head to see a favorite toy or event (e.g., musical bear, jack-in-the-box). Verbally direct the child to look.
- Touch the child's cheek gently with nipple, spoon, or pacifier. This should elicit a rooting response in a very young child who will then turn his or her head to find the food source with the mouth.
- Gently guide the child's head in the direction of a favorite toy or activity.

TEACHING CONSIDERATIONS

1. If the child has a motor impairment or abnormal muscle tone, consult a physical therapist about the appropriateness of this skill and about related programming issues.
2. Turning the head to one side may obligate some children to engage in an asymmetrical tonic neck reflex (ATNR).
3. Make sure that the child is turning his or her head voluntarily and not in response to gravity. The child's head should turn, not drop, to each side.
4. Have the child turn his or her head in both directions and not favor one side.
5. For a child with a visual or hearing impairment, stronger or more varied cues may be necessary to elicit responses.
6. Consider safety with all objects that the child handles. Never leave the child unattended with potentially hazardous objects.

GM A

Objective 1.2 Kicks legs

DEVELOPMENTAL PROGRAMMING STEP

PS1.2a   The child kicks both legs together.

IMPORTANCE OF SKILL

Initially, an infant's legs are postured in full flexion. Development progresses to allow the child to kick legs alternately, which builds strength necessary for other gross motor skills such as crawling and walking. As the child kicks the legs, he or she gains sensory input and learns about the environment. This skill fosters self-awareness necessary for the child to learn that he or she is separate from the environment.

CONCURRENT GOALS AND OBJECTIVE

FM A:1.0   Simultaneously brings hands to midline
Cog A:1.0   Orients to auditory, visual, and tactile events
SC A:1.0   Turns and looks toward person speaking
Soc A:1.1   Responds appropriately to familiar adult's affective tone

TEACHING SUGGESTIONS
Activity-Based

- Talk to the child in gentle tones while the child is lying on his or her back in a crib, enclosed space, or when held in a face-to-face position. Pause periodically and wait for the child's response.
- While putting pants or socks on the child, gently drop the child's legs or feet onto a soft surface, allowing them to "bounce."
- Dress the child in tights or soft, loose-fitting pants to encourage freedom of movement. Do not overdress the child as movement may be hampered by too much clothing.
- Encourage the child to kick when in the bathtub.
- Kiss or blow on the child's feet when changing diapers. Wait for the child to respond by kicking.
- Place your hands close to the child's feet so that when the child kicks, his or her feet will touch your hands. Play a "Gonna get you" game. Push gently to offer resistance and increase strength.

Environmental Arrangements

- Safely affix an easily activated mobile or crib gym to the child's crib so that it will move when the child kicks his or her legs.
- Hold the child close to your body or provide him or her with large, soft barriers in the crib (e.g., stuffed animals, blankets, towels) so that the child receives tactile sensations for movements of legs.
- Place a baby mirror in the crib, on the floor, or on the changing table so that the child can see his or her legs kicking.

- Place tissue paper under the child's feet to produce a crinkly, rattling sound when the child kicks. A squeak-toy or Happy Apple also works well.
- Use a soft piece of cloth or yarn to connect the child's ankle to a mobile so that a leg movement will activate the mobile. Gradually make the yarn longer and looser to require stronger kicking. Never leave the child unattended with ties connected to the body.
- Put jingle-bells on the child's socks or shoes.
- Slightly elevate the child's hips with a folded blanket or cloth diaper.
- Hang a beach ball over the child's feet so that gentle kicks move the ball. Gradually make the kicking more demanding by placing the ball higher.
- Provide opportunities to move legs in more supported positions, such as sidelying or supported recline in the bathtub.

Instructional Sequence

- Position the child so that head and shoulders are slightly forward and symmetrical and are not held in a stiff, elevated, or retracted fashion. If the child can control his or her own posture, make the presentation of activities contingent on the child's successful attempt at optimal positioning.
- If the child enjoys "raspberries" on his or her feet, begin by giving the child's feet a "raspberry" and then back away. After a signal from the child (e.g., smile, slight movement, vocalization), repeat the action, moving slowly toward the child's body. Remain there until the child's feet move toward or touch your head or face. Gradually require stronger kicking movements to continue the game.
- When holding the child in face-to-face position, hold the child's foot to your mouth and kiss, then gently release. Wait for some response from the child (e.g., smile, slight movement, vocalization), then repeat the action.

TEACHING CONSIDERATIONS

1. If the child has a motor impairment or abnormal muscle tone, consult a physical therapist about the appropriateness of this skill and about related programming issues.
2. For a child with a visual or hearing impairment, use cues adapted to the impairment to elicit responses. For example, a child with a severe hearing impairment will not respond to "louder" kicks of an object that makes noise. This child will more likely respond to tactile stimulation of the feet and legs.
3. If the child with a severe visual impairment is active in the crib and suddenly becomes still, it may mean the child is listening carefully to the sounds around him or her. This is a good time to help the child associate sounds with people and objects. Direct the child's legs to move the mobile or musical toy.
4. Consider safety with all objects that the child handles. Never leave the child unattended with potentially hazardous objects.

Objective 1.3 Waves arms

DEVELOPMENTAL PROGRAMMING STEP

PS1.3a The child waves both arms together.

IMPORTANCE OF SKILL

Initially, an infant's arms are positioned in full flexion. Development progresses to allow the child to wave his or her arms freely in all directions. This builds strength for future reaching and grasping skills, and the child gains sensory input from the environment. This skill fosters self-awareness and the child's knowledge that he or she is separate from the environment.

CONCURRENT GOAL AND OBJECTIVES

Cog A:1.0   Orients to auditory, visual, and tactile events
Cog B:1.2   Focuses on object and/or person
SC A:1.2   Turns and looks toward noise-producing object
Soc A:1.1   Responds appropriately to familiar adult's affective tone

TEACHING SUGGESTIONS

Activity-Based

- Talk to the child in gentle tones while the child is lying on his or her back in a crib or enclosed space, or when held in a face-to-face position. Pause periodically for the child's response.
- When undressing, let the child's arms gently drop out of each sleeve in a coat or shirt.
- Dress the child in loose-fitting shirts and sweaters to encourage freedom of movement. Do not overdress the child, as movement may be hampered by too many layers of clothing.
- Encourage the child to splash water with his arms when in the bathtub.
- Play the child's favorite face-to-face games, encouraging the child's active participation. These early excited movements of the whole body offer many opportunities to wave the arms.
- While rocking and singing, gently wave the child's arms or assist the child to clap with the rhythm of the music.

Environmental Arrangements

- Safely affix an easily activated mobile or crib gym to the child's crib so that it will move when the child waves his or her arms.
- Hold the child close to your body or provide the child with large, soft barriers in the crib (e.g., stuffed animals, blankets, towels) so that the child receives tactile sensations for movements of the arms.
- Place a baby mirror in the crib, on the floor, or near the changing table, so that the child can see his or her arms moving.
- Dangle a bright yarn ball close to the child's face. Tickle the arms with the yarn. Pay special attention to the safety of dangling objects.
- Place your face close to the child and encourage the child to reach and touch.
- Long hair, glasses, and jewelry can be interesting to children and provide reason to wave their arms or reach for the object.
- Put jingle-bells on the child's wrists or mittens.
- Use a soft piece of cloth or yarn to connect the child's wrist to a mobile so that arm movement will activate the mobile. Gradually make the yarn longer and looser to require stronger waving. Never leave the child unattended with ties connected to the body.

- Slightly elevate the child's head and shoulders (with folded blanket or cloth diaper) to make it easier for the child to move his or her arms freely.
- Give the child opportunities to reach for objects in more supported positions, such as on the stomach supported at chest, or in a sidelying posture.

Instructional Sequence

- Position the child so that the child's head and shoulders are slightly forward and not held in a stiff, elevated, or retracted fashion. If the child can control her own posture, make the presentation of activities contingent upon the child's successful attempt at optimal positioning.
- If the child enjoys "raspberries," begin by giving the child's hand a "raspberry" and then back away. After a signal from the child (e.g., smile, slight movement, vocalization), repeat the action moving slowly toward the child's body. Verbally direct the child to touch your face. Remain there until the child's hands move toward or touch your head or face. Gradually require stronger arm-waving movements to continue the game.
- When the child is lying on his or her back or is held in a face-to-face position, hold the child's hand to your mouth and kiss or give a "raspberry" and gently release. Wait for a signal from the child (e.g., smile, slight movement, vocalization) and repeat the action.

TEACHING CONSIDERATIONS

1. If the child has a motor impairment or abnormal muscle tone, consult a physical therapist about the appropriateness of this skill and about related programming issues.
2. For a child with a hearing impairment, use cues adapted to the particular impairment to elicit responses such as visual or touch cues.
3. If a child with a severe visual impairment is active in the crib and suddenly becomes still, it may mean the child is listening carefully to the sounds around him or her. This is a good time to help the child associate sounds with people and objects. Direct the child's arms to move the mobile or musical toy.
4. Consider safety with all objects that the child handles. Never leave the child unattended with potentially hazardous objects.

GOAL 2   **Rolls by turning segmentally from stomach to back and from back to stomach**

DEVELOPMENTAL PROGRAMMING STEPS

In order to achieve this goal, a child must perform the skills for Objectives 2.1–2.2 to criteria. Refer to the specific objectives for developmental programming steps to develop each skill.

IMPORTANCE OF SKILL

This goal marks the first time the child independently changes positions and it fosters curiosity and exploration of the environment. The trunk rotation used in rolling over is important for future movements against gravity, such as assuming sitting, creeping, and standing positions. The child masters a form of movement that allows him or her to move a distance, obtain toys, and escape uncomfortable positions.

PRECEDING OBJECTIVE

GM A:2.1   Rolls from back to stomach

CONCURRENT GOALS AND OBJECTIVES

FM A:2.3   Reaches toward and touches object with each hand
GM A:3.5   Bears weight on one hand and/or arm while reaching with opposite hand
Cog A:1.0   Orients to auditory, visual, and tactile events
Cog B:1.1   Visually follows object moving in horizontal, vertical, and circular directions
Cog G:1.4   Uses sensory examination with objects
SC A:1.2   Turns and looks toward noise-producing object
SC A:2.0   Follows person's gaze to establish joint attention
Soc A:3.2   Responds to communication from familiar adult

TEACHING SUGGESTIONS
Activity-Based

- When the child is lying on his or her back or stomach, approach from a position of 2–3 feet away and talk. Present your face to the child in such a way that the child is encouraged to roll 180° to engage in face-to-face interaction.
- Dress the child in clothes that will not twist or otherwise constrict rolling.
- Give the child many opportunities to play with toys or objects on the floor on both the stomach and back. Provide ample space for the child to roll freely without encountering obstacles.
- Lie on the floor a short distance from the child and engage the child by talking and touching. Encourage the child to move toward you by rolling.
- Occasionally place toys out of reach but within the child's visual field instead of giving them directly to the child.
- While the child is playing with a favorite toy, move it out of reach but within the child's visual field.

Environmental Arrangements

- Place a mirror a slight distance to the side of the child to encourage rolling for a closer look.
- Place the child on a large, partially inflated ball on either his stomach or back. Secure the child's body in a slightly upright position by holding the child's trunk against the ball with one hand. With the free hand, slowly move the ball either right or left until the child rolls.
- Position the child on a bed, waterbed, air mattress, or beanbag surface. Rolling is sometimes easier on these surfaces.
- When presenting the child with a favorite toy, allow the child to focus on it visually, then move it slowly in an arc so that following it will require the child to turn his or her head. Continue moving the toy until it is out of the child's visual range; encourage a rolling response.

Instructional Sequence

- Use toys or a peer to encourage the child to roll over.
- Verbally encourage the child to "Come here" to reach a toy; use a noise-producing toy.
- If the child initiates rolling but cannot complete it, assist the child by gently guiding the shoulders and hips in direction of the roll.
- Before the child begins to roll, assist by extending the arm on the side on which the child will roll above the child's head so the arm and shoulder do not block the rolling movement. Get the child to extend an arm out and above the head by encouraging the child to reach for an object or toy while lying on his or her stomach or back.

TEACHING CONSIDERATIONS

1. If the child has a motor impairment or abnormal muscle tone, consult a physical therapist about the appropriateness of this skill and about related programming issues.
2. Make sure the child's intended rolling path is clear of obstacles.
3. The rolling surface should be warm, clean, slightly padded, and free of floorboard heating devices or radiators.
4. If the child has abnormal muscle tone, present toys so that following them will not result in abnormal posture (head and neck extension).
5. The child may find the extraneous movement afforded by some surfaces aversive. If the child shows fearful reactions (e.g., increased muscle tone, clinging to parent, gripping surface), introduce different surfaces gradually.
6. For a child with a visual impairment, use cues adapted to the impairment to elicit responses. For example, a child with a severe visual impairment will not be attracted to a bright object; however, this child may roll toward a familiar adult in response to touch or sound cues.
7. Use visually appealing objects or touch cues with a child who has a hearing impairment.
8. Consider safety as the child learns to roll and has the potential of rolling off a surface.

Objective 2.1 Rolls from back to stomach

DEVELOPMENTAL PROGRAMMING STEP

PS2.1a The child turns from back to side.

IMPORTANCE OF SKILL

This skill marks one of the first times the child is able to independently change positions. In addition to gaining independence in changing body position, the child is able to escape uncomfortable situations. Rolling also fosters curiosity and exploration of the environment. Rolling from back to stomach is a basis for future, more advanced movements, such as creeping and standing.

GM A

PRECEDING OBJECTIVE

GM A:1.1   Turns head past 45° to the right and left from midline position

CONCURRENT GOALS AND OBJECTIVES

FM A:1.1   Makes directed batting and/or swiping movements with each hand
FM A:2.3   Reaches toward and touches object with each hand
GM A:3.5   Bears weight on one hand and/or arm while reaching with opposite hand
Cog A:1.0   Orients to auditory, visual, and tactile events
Cog B:1.1   Visually follows object moving in horizontal, vertical, and circular directions
Cog G:1.4   Uses sensory examination with objects
SC A:1.2   Turns and looks toward noise-producing object
SC A:2.0   Follows person's gaze to establish joint attention
Soc A:3.2   Responds to communication from familiar adult

TEACHING SUGGESTIONS
Activity-Based

- When the child is lying on his or her back, approach from a distance of 2–3 feet and talk. Encourage the child to roll 180° to engage in face-to-face interaction.
- Give the child many opportunities to play on his or her back on the floor with toys or objects that may fall to the child's side during exploration and manipulation with hands.
- When the child is playing with a favorite toy, move it out of reach but within the child's visual field.
- Occasionally place toys out of reach but within the child's visual field instead of giving them directly to the child. Provide ample space for rolling without encountering obstacles.
- Lie on the floor and play next to the child. Roll from your back to your stomach and encourage the child to do the same.

Environmental Arrangements

- Place the child on a large, partially inflated ball on his or her back. Secure the child's body in a slightly upright position by holding the trunk against the ball with one hand. With the free hand, move the ball slowly either right or left until the child rolls.
- Position the child on his or her back on a bed, waterbed, air mattress, or beanbag surface. Rolling is sometimes easier on these surfaces.
- When presenting the child with a favorite toy, allow the child to focus on it visually, then move it slowly in an arc so that following it will require the child to turn his or her head. Continue moving the toy until it is out of the child's visual range. Wait for a response.

Instructional Sequence

- Verbally encourage the child to "Come here" to reach a toy; use a noise-producing toy.
- If the child initiates rolling but cannot complete it, assist the child by gently guiding the shoulders and hips in the direction of the roll. Make sure the child's head is leading the movement.

■ Before the child begins to roll, assist by extending the arm on the side on which child will roll above the child's head so the arm and shoulder will not block the rolling movement. Get the child to extend an arm out and above the head by encouraging the child to reach for an object or toy placed on the floor above his or her head.

TEACHING CONSIDERATIONS

1. If the child has a motor impairment or abnormal muscle tone, consult a physical therapist about the appropriateness of this skill and about related programming issues.
2. Make sure the child's intended rolling path is clear of obstacles.
3. The rolling surface should be warm, clean, slightly padded, and free of floorboard heating devices or radiators.
4. If the child has abnormal muscle tone, do not present toys in a manner that will result in abnormal posture (head and neck extension) by the child.
5. Some children find the extraneous movement afforded by some surfaces aversive. If the child shows fearful reactions (e.g., increased muscle tone, clinging to parent, or gripping surface), introduce different surfaces gradually.
6. For a child with a visual impairment, use cues adapted to the impairment to elicit responses, such as bright objects or sound cues.
7. Use visual or touch cues with the child who has a hearing impairment.
8. Consider safety as the child learns to roll and has the potential of rolling off a surface.

Objective 2.2 Rolls from stomach to back

DEVELOPMENTAL PROGRAMMING STEPS

PS2.2a The child turns from side to back.
PS2.2b The child positions self on the verge of rolling with one arm extended and the face turned toward the extended arm.

IMPORTANCE OF SKILL

With this skill, the child gains initial control of independently changing body position and moving from one location to another. This skill fosters curiosity and exploration of the environment.

PRECEDING GOAL AND OBJECTIVE

GM A:1.1 Turns head past 45° to the right and left from midline position
Cog A:1.0 Orients to auditory, visual, and tactile events

CONCURRENT GOAL AND OBJECTIVES

FM A:1.1 Makes directed batting and/or swiping movements with each hand
FM A:2.3 Reaches toward and touches object with each hand
GM A:3.5 Bears weight on one hand and/or arm while reaching with opposite hand

GM A

Cog B:1.1   Visually follows object moving in horizontal, vertical, and circular directions
Cog G:1.4   Uses sensory examination with objects
SC A:1.2   Turns and looks toward noise-producing object
SC A:2.0   Follows person's gaze to establish joint attention
Soc A:3.2   Responds to communication from familiar adult

TEACHING SUGGESTIONS
Activity-Based

- Give the child many opportunities to play on his or her stomach on the floor with toys or objects.
- When the child is lying on his or her stomach, approach from a position of 2–3 feet away and talk. Present your face to the child in such a way that the child is encouraged to roll 180° to engage in face-to-face interaction.
- While the child is playing with a favorite toy, move it to a distance out of reach but within the child's visual field.
- Lie on the floor and play next to the child. Roll from your stomach to your back and encourage the child to do the same.
- Place a mirror to the side of the child to encourage the child to raise an arm and turn his or her head to see.

Environmental Arrangements

- Place the child on his or her stomach on a large, partially inflated ball. Secure the child's body in a slightly upright position by holding the trunk against the ball with one hand. With the free hand, move the ball slowly to either the right or left until the child rolls.
- Occasionally place toys out of reach but within child's visual field, instead of giving them directly to the child. Provide ample space for rolling without encountering obstacles.
- Position the child on his or her stomach on a bed, waterbed, air mattress, or beanbag surface. Rolling is sometimes easier on these surfaces.
- At bath or changing time, use a towel or diaper to gently lift one side of the child to assist in beginning a roll.
- Place the child on his or her stomach on a slight incline. Gravity will help get the child started. Be sure the movements are not fast or frightening to the child.

Instructional Sequence

- Verbally encourage the child to "Come here" to reach a toy; use a noise-producing toy.
- If the child initiates rolling but cannot complete it, assist the child by gently guiding the shoulders in the direction of the roll. Make sure the child's head is leading the movement.
- Before the child begins to roll, assist by extending the arm on the side on which child will roll above the child's head so the arm and shoulder won't block the rolling movement. Get the child to extend an arm out and forward by encouraging the child to reach for an object placed on the floor beyond his or her head.

GM A

TEACHING CONSIDERATIONS

1. If the child has a motor impairment or abnormal muscle tone, consult a physical therapist about the appropriateness of this skill and about related programming issues.
2. Make sure the child's intended rolling path is clear of obstacles.
3. The rolling surface should be warm, clean, slightly padded, and free of floorboard heating devices or radiators.
4. If the child has abnormal muscle tone, present toys in a manner that will not result in abnormal posture (head and neck extension) by the child.
5. Some children find the extraneous movement afforded by some surfaces aversive. If the child shows fearful reactions (e.g., increased muscle tone, clinging to parent, or gripping surface), introduce different surfaces gradually.
6. Use visually appealing objects or touch cues with a child who has a hearing impairment.
7. Consider safety as the child learns to roll and has the potential of rolling off a surface.

GOAL 3 Creeps forward using alternating arm and leg movements

---

DEVELOPMENTAL PROGRAMMING STEP

PS3.0a Child reaches with one arm while maintaining weight on the other hand and both knees.

IMPORTANCE OF SKILL

When creeping, the child practices reciprocal movements and maintains balance while shifting weight. These skills are necessary for walking and running. Creeping is the child's first efficient means of locomotion, allowing the child to cover some distance. This leads to increased independence and further exploration of the environment.

PRECEDING OBJECTIVE

GM A:3.1 Rocks while in a creeping position

CONCURRENT GOAL AND OBJECTIVES

FM A:2.3 Reaches toward and touches object with each hand
Cog B:3.1 Looks for object in usual location
Cog C:1.1 Correctly activates simple toy
Cog E:3.1 Moves barrier or goes around barrier to obtain object
Cog G:1.3 Uses simple motor actions on different objects
SC A:2.0 Follows person's gaze to establish joint attention
SC C:2.3 Carries out one-step direction *with* contextual cues
Soc A:2.2 Responds to familiar adult's social behavior

GM A

TEACHING SUGGESTIONS
Activity-Based

- Provide soft rugs and mats for the child's creeping activities.
- Creep around the child who is in a creeping position. Chase the child and let the child move after you.
- Occasionally place toys out of reach but within the child's visual field instead of giving them directly to the child. Do not place the toys too far away or the child may resort to an earlier means of locomotion (rolling) to get to them.
- Instead of playing with the child's favorite objects or toys on the floor, encourage play on low but elevated surfaces.
- Dress the child in clothes that will not ride up or constrict during creeping.
- If the child indicates a desire to get down when being held, place the child in a creeping position facing interesting objects or toys or whatever item just engaged the child's interest.
- Allow the child to move in sand, where creeping will be the most efficient means of locomotion.

Environmental Arrangements

- Set up a "mini" obstacle course with the child creeping through a tunnel or under a table to reach a favorite toy or person.
- Slowly move a pull toy in front of the child to encourage him or her to follow it.
- Give the child the opportunity to move on a scooter board that supports the trunk. Make sure the device allows the child's shoulders and hips to move freely and that the child can touch the ground with hands and knees.
- Allow the child to play on surfaces that have varied heights (e.g., low graduated stairs, large foam wedges, large blocks obstructing access to play areas).
- Set up barriers and obstacles to play areas to encourage the child to maneuver self over or around them.
- Place the child over a bolster, making sure that the child's shoulders and hips can move freely and that the child can touch the ground with hands and knees. Present toys to the right or left, so that the child will maintain weight on three limbs while reaching with the fourth.

Instructional Sequence

- Allow the child to play with a favorite object or toy and then move it to a distance of several feet away while the child is watching. When the child rolls to his or her stomach and assumes a creeping position, play with the toy to encourage the child to creep toward it.
- Allow the child to play with a favorite object or toy and then move it to a distance of several feet away while the child is watching. Wait until the child rolls to his or her stomach and assumes a creeping position. Slip a lightweight sheet or cloth diaper under the child's stomach and hold both ends up. Move forward as the child pursues the object, supporting the child's trunk and encouraging reciprocal movements of the arms and legs. Verbally encourage the child to move toward the desired object.
- Physically assist the child to move forward toward an object by pressing against the soles of his or her feet when the child is in a hands and knees position.

TEACHING CONSIDERATIONS

1. If the child has a motor impairment or abnormal muscle tone, consult a physical therapist about the appropriateness of this skill and about related programming issues.
2. If the child has abnormal muscle tone, present toys in a way that reaching for them will not result in abnormal posture or movement (head and neck extension, asymmetrical tonic neck reflex).
3. The area in which the creeping is practiced should be warm, clean, and free of floorboard heating devices or radiators.
4. Some children find highly textured surfaces aversive. If the child reacts negatively to surface textures (e.g., increased muscle tone, clinging to parent, withdrawing limbs, fussing), introduce unfamiliar textures gradually.
5. For a child with a visual impairment, use cues adapted to the impairment to elicit responses. Skills that require self-initiated mobility are significantly delayed in a child with a visual impairment. This child is more likely to respond to touch cues to move forward.
6. Use visual or touch cues to encourage a child who has a hearing impairment.
7. Consider safety as the child creeps about the environment and handles various objects. Never leave the child unattended with potentially hazardous objects.

Objective 3.1 Rocks while in a creeping position

IMPORTANCE OF SKILL

The child's rocking movement represents experimentation with the hands and knees position. In rocking, the child develops balance while shifting weight, which is necessary in creeping and eventually in walking and running. Rocking also provides a fun and soothing activity within the child's independent control.

PRECEDING OBJECTIVE

GM A:3.2   Assumes creeping position

CONCURRENT OBJECTIVES

Cog B:1.1   Visually follows object moving in horizontal, vertical, and circular directions
Cog C:1.3   Indicates interest in simple and/or mechanical toy
SC A:1.2   Turns and looks toward noise-producing object
SC A:2.2   Looks toward an object
Soc A:3.2   Responds to communication from familiar adult

TEACHING SUGGESTIONS
Activity-Based

- Play games of imitating family pets by assuming an all fours position.
- Get on the floor with the child, who is in a hands and knees position. Rock back and forth and encourage the child to do the same.

GM A

- If the child indicates a desire to get down when being held, place the child in a creeping position facing interesting objects or toys or whatever item engages the child's interest.
- Encourage the child to play on surfaces of varied heights (e.g., low graduated stairs, large foam wedges, large blocks obstructing access to play areas).

Environmental Arrangements

- Give the child the opportunity to rock while using a scooter board to support the trunk. The scooter board will enable the child to rock a greater distance with less effort. Make sure the device allows the child's shoulders and hips to move freely, and ensure that the child can touch the ground with hands and knees.
- Set up barriers and obstacles to play areas to encourage the child to momentarily assume and maintain the creeping position.
- Occasionally place the child over a bolster, making sure that the child's shoulders and hips can move freely and that the child can touch the ground with his or her hands and knees.
- Present toys on elevated surfaces so that the child must get on his or her hands and knees to obtain them.
- Instead of playing with the child's favorite objects or toys on the floor, encourage play on low but elevated surfaces.
- Put a mirror on the floor so that the child can see him- or herself rocking.

Instructional Sequence

- Allow the child to play with a favorite object or toy while lying on his or her stomach. Move the object to an elevated surface several feet away while the child is watching. After the child assumes a creeping position to look at the object, gently guide the child's hips backward and release. Look repeatedly at the object and move toward it.
- Gently guide the child's hips and verbally encourage rocking.
- After the child's bath, place the child on his or her hands and knees on a towel and dry the child in this position. When drying the child's trunk, use strokes that run the length of the trunk (from shoulders to hips), applying enough pressure to rock the child's body back and forth.

TEACHING CONSIDERATIONS

1. If the child has a motor impairment or abnormal muscle tone, consult a physical therapist about the appropriateness of this skill and about related programming issues.
2. If the child has abnormal muscle tone, present toys in a way that following them visually will not result in abnormal posture or movement (head and neck extension).
3. The child may find certain textured surfaces aversive. If the child reacts negatively to surface textures (e.g., increased muscle tone, clinging to parent, withdrawing limbs, fussing), use another surface and introduce unfamiliar textures gradually.
4. Some surfaces will afford the child better traction and movement. Begin teaching on surfaces where the child's efforts will result in greater success.
5. For a child with a visual or auditory impairment, stronger or more varied cues may be necessary to elicit responses.
6. For a child with a visual impairment, use cues adapted to the impairment to elicit responses. Skills that require self-initiated mobility are significantly delayed in a

child with a visual impairment; this child is more likely to rock while in a creeping position in response to touch cues.

7. Use visual or touch cues to encourage a child with a hearing impairment.
8. Consider safety as the child moves about the environment and with all objects that the child handles. Never leave the child unattended with potentially hazardous objects.

Objective 3.2   Assumes creeping position

IMPORTANCE OF SKILL

In assuming the creeping position, the child achieves a new position in space, which fosters self-awareness and allows the child to view the world from a new orientation. This skill further develops the equilibrium and balance needed for creeping and eventually for upright positions.

PRECEDING OBJECTIVE

GM A:3.6   Lifts head and chest off surface with weight on arms

CONCURRENT OBJECTIVES

Cog B:1.1   Visually follows object moving in horizontal, vertical, and circular directions
Cog C:1.3   Indicates interest in simple and/or mechanical toy
SC A:1.2   Turns and looks toward noise-producing object
SC A:2.2   Looks toward an object
Soc A:3.2   Responds to communication from familiar adult

TEACHING SUGGESTIONS

Activity-Based

- Instead of playing with the child's favorite objects or toys on the floor, encourage play on low but elevated surfaces.
- If the child indicates a desire to get down when being held, lower the child, stomach down, toward the floor and wait for the child to extend his or her arms to the floor. Position the child facing whatever interests him or her, with the upper body supported on extended arms.
- Roll balls, toys on wheels, or cylindrical objects between the child's arms while the child is lying on his or her stomach. See if the child will momentarily assume a creeping position to obtain the object.
- Encourage the child to play on surfaces that have varied heights (low graduated stairs, large foam wedges, large blocks obstructing access to play areas).

Environmental Arrangements

- Put the child on the floor, arms extended, to play with a favorite pet. Invite the child to come see the pet and to imitate the pet's movements.

GM A

- Set up barriers and obstacles to play areas to encourage the child to maneuver over or around them.
- Occasionally place the child over a bolster, making sure that the child's shoulders and hips can move freely and that the child can touch the ground with hands and knees.
- Encourage the child to bear weight on limbs by presenting toys on an elevated surface that would otherwise be out of the child's visual field.

Instructional Sequence

- Model or have a peer model the creeping position. Play games with the child in this position.
- Place the child on his or her hands and knees. Hold out a toy and invite the child to "Come on."
- Allow the child to play with a favorite object or toy while lying on his or her stomach. Move it to an elevated surface several feet away while the child is watching. Slip a lightweight sheet or cloth diaper under the child's abdomen and hold both ends up. Move forward with the child as the child crawls to the object. As the child attempts to raise his or her body to look at the toy, pull up on the cloth. This strategy will assist the child in completing an action (assuming a creeping position) that he or she has initiated.

TEACHING CONSIDERATIONS

1. If the child has a motor impairment or abnormal muscle tone, consult a physical therapist about the appropriateness of this skill and about related programming issues.
2. If the child has abnormal muscle tone, present toys in a way that following them visually will not result in abnormal posture or movement (head and neck extension).
3. The child may find certain textured surfaces aversive. If the child reacts negatively to surface textures (e.g., increased muscle tone, clinging to parent, withdrawing limbs, fussing), use another surface and introduce unfamiliar textures gradually.
4. Some surfaces will afford the child better traction and movement. Begin teaching on surfaces where the child's efforts will result in greater success.
5. For a child with a visual impairment, use cues adapted to the impairment to elicit responses. For example, a child with a severe visual impairment will not assume a creeping position in response to a bright-colored toy. This child may, however, respond to touch cues to assume a creeping position.
6. Use visual or touch cues with a child who has a hearing impairment.
7. Consider safety as the child moves about the environment and handles various objects. Never leave the child unattended with potentially hazardous objects.

Objective 3.3   Crawls forward on stomach

DEVELOPMENTAL PROGRAMMING STEP

PS3.3a   The child uses arms to propel self backward when lying on stomach.

IMPORTANCE OF SKILL

"Belly" crawling contributes to the child's control of the upper back and shoulders, provides the child with new sensory stimulation and body awareness, and builds stability in the shoulders, back, and pelvis. This skill is helpful for further antigravity movement, such as creeping and walking. It also provides a more efficient means of moving than rolling because it fosters balance and coordination through shifting weight. This allows the child a more active means of exploring and accessing the environment.

PRECEDING OBJECTIVE

GM A:3.4   Pivots on stomach

CONCURRENT GOAL AND OBJECTIVES

FM A:2.3   Reaches toward and touches object with each hand
Cog B:3.1   Looks for object in usual location
Cog C:1.1   Correctly activates simple toy
Cog E:3.2   Moves around barrier to change location
Cog G:1.3   Uses simple motor actions on different objects
SC A:2.0   Follows person's gaze to establish joint attention
Soc A:2.2   Responds to familiar adult's social behavior

TEACHING SUGGESTIONS
Activity-Based

- Place the child on his or her stomach in a very shallow bath and encourage movement toward toys.
- Occasionally place toys out of reach but within the child's visual field instead of giving them directly to the child. Do not place toys too far away because the child may resort to the earlier means of rolling to reach the toys.
- Play mirror games in front of the child and encourage crawling for a closer look.
- When the child has almost reached a desired object, move it back a couple of inches. Do not do this more than once or the child may become frustrated and abandon the effort altogether.

Environmental Arrangements

- Let the child pursue an object moving downward on a large wedge.
- Position the child so that the child can push off a barrier such as a wall or adult's body to propel forward and initiate the crawling movement.
- Give the child the opportunity to move on a variety of surfaces to determine which is the most manageable. Begin instruction on the "easiest" surface.
- Give the child the opportunity to move on a scooter board to support the trunk. Make sure that the device allows the child's shoulders and hips to move freely, and that the child can touch the ground with hands, forearms, thighs, and feet.
- When the child is positioned on his or her stomach, offer an object that is too large to be grasped with one hand and that will roll away when touched (ball, toy vehicle, rolling mirror). If the child becomes frustrated, hold the object stationary or help the child change position to play with it.

Instructional Sequence

- Allow the child to play with a favorite object or toy while lying on his or her stomach. Move the toy several feet away while the child is watching. Verbally encourage the child to move forward to obtain the toy.
- If the child is moving toward an object by pulling forward with the arms, gently stroke the bottom of one foot, then the other, to stimulate movement of the lower limbs.

TEACHING CONSIDERATIONS

1. If the child has a motor impairment or abnormal muscle tone, consult a physical therapist about the appropriateness of this skill and about related programming issues.
2. If the child has abnormal muscle tone (as in most types of cerebral palsy), present toys in a way that reaching them visually will not result in abnormal posture or movement (head and neck extension, asymmetrical tonic neck reflex).
3. The area in which crawling is practiced should be warm, clean, and free of floor-board heating devices or radiators.
4. The child may find certain textured surfaces aversive. If the child reacts negatively to surface textures (increased muscle tone, clinging to parent, withdrawing limbs, fussing), use another surface and introduce unfamiliar textures gradually.
5. For a child with a visual or auditory impairment, use cues adapted to the impairment to elicit responses. For example, use a bolster or large pillow to encourage a child with a severe visual impairment to sit on his or her heels. This position is a good first step to learning to crawl. Use the bolster to support the child's chest and arms while the legs are folded under the child with the buttocks resting on the heels. Gently roll the bolster forward and backward.
6. Consider safety as the child moves about the environment and handles objects. Never leave the child unattended with potentially hazardous objects.

Objective 3.4   Pivots on stomach

IMPORTANCE OF SKILL

The skill of pivoting on the stomach gives the child mobility in the prone position and permits the child to explore the environment. When pivoting, the child shifts weight and develops balance, which is necessary for creeping.

PRECEDING OBJECTIVE

GM A:3.5   Bears weight on one hand and/or arm while reaching with opposite hand

CONCURRENT GOAL AND OBJECTIVES

FM A:2.3   Reaches toward and touches object with each hand
Cog C:1.1   Correctly activates simple toy
Cog E:2.1   Uses part of object and/or support to obtain another object

Cog G:1.3   Uses simple motor actions on different objects
SC A:2.0   Follows person's gaze to establish joint attention
Soc A:2.2   Responds to familiar adult's social behavior

TEACHING SUGGESTIONS
Activity-Based

- Lie on the floor to the side of the child. Encourage the child with your voice and toys to pivot toward you.
- Play with toys to the left and right out of the child's reach but within the child's visual field, instead of giving them directly to the child. Do not place the toys too far away or the child may resort to the earlier means of rolling to reach them.
- Engage the child who is lying on his or her stomach in a face-to-face interaction. Then move to the child's right or left while continuing to speak to the child. Wait for the child's response.
- Approach the child (lying on his or her stomach) from different directions during the day and verbally encourage the child to find the source of your voice before you pick him or her up.

Environmental Arrangements

- Give the child the opportunity to move on a variety of surfaces to determine which is the most manageable. Begin instruction on the easiest surface (often a smooth one).
- Hang toys within the child's reach, but to the child's side, so that the child must pivot to reach them. Pay special attention to potential dangers with hanging toys.
- Place the child on his or her stomach for a period of play each day. Provide interesting, bold pictures or a mirror to either side of the child to encourage pivoting.
- Begin by requiring very slight pivotal movements from the child and systematically increase the movements by placing toys at greater distances. Increase distances as the child successfully reaches each one.

Instructional Sequence

- Allow the child to play with a favorite object or toy while lying on his or her stomach. Remove the toy to a distance several inches from midline to the left or right while the child is watching. Continue to call attention to the toy by verbally encouraging the child and activating the toy.
- When the child is positioned on his or her stomach, offer an object to either hand. After the child has had a chance to manipulate the object, move it to the outside of the child's hand. If the child does not change positions to obtain the object, touch the child's hand with the object and wait again for a response.
- Physically guide the child's hips and shoulders in a pivoting movement to reach a toy.

TEACHING CONSIDERATIONS

1. If the child has a motor impairment or abnormal muscle tone, consult a physical therapist about the appropriateness of this skill and about related programming issues.
2. If the child has abnormal muscle tone, present toys so that reaching for them will not result in abnormal posture or movement (head and neck extension).

GM A

3.   The area in which pivoting is practiced should be warm, clean, and free of floor-board heating devices or radiators.
4.   The child may find certain textured surfaces aversive. If the child reacts negatively to surface textures (e.g., increased muscle tone, clinging to parent, withdrawing limbs, fussing), use another surface and introduce unfamiliar textures gradually.
5.   Some surfaces will afford the child better movement. Begin teaching on surfaces where the child's efforts will result in greater success.
6.   For a child with a visual impairment, use cues adapted to the impairment to elicit responses. For example, place a child with a severe visual impairment on your lap face down with the child's head over your knees. A soft piece of fur or sheepskin on your lap may help the child feel secure and comfortable. Stroke the child's neck and spine and softly blow on the child's back. This will encourage the child to lift his or her head while lying on his or her stomach, which is a precursor to pivoting on the stomach.
7.   Use visual or touch cues to encourage the child who has a hearing impairment.
8.   Consider safety as the child moves in the environment and handles objects. Never leave the child unattended with potentially hazardous objects.

Objective 3.5 **Bears weight on one hand and/or arm while reaching with opposite hand**

DEVELOPMENTAL PROGRAMMING STEP

PS3.5a   The child assumes a "swimming" posture with weight primarily on abdomen and with arms and legs stretched out above weight-bearing surface.

IMPORTANCE OF SKILL

The achievement of weight bearing on one side while reaching with the other in a prone position represents the development of the "rotary" trunk component. This development fosters balance and coordination that are eventually necessary for sitting and walking. This skill permits the child to reach for and manipulate objects while lying on the stomach, thus increasing exploration of the environment.

PRECEDING OBJECTIVE

GM A:3.6   Lifts head and chest off surface with weight on arms

CONCURRENT GOAL AND OBJECTIVES

FM A:2.3   Reaches toward and touches object with each hand
Cog C:1.1   Correctly activates simple toy
Cog D:1.1   Imitates motor action that is commonly used
Cog E:2.1   Uses part of object and/or support to obtain another object
Cog G:1.3   Uses simple motor actions on different objects
SC A:2.0   Follows person's gaze to establish joint attention
Soc A:2.2   Responds to familiar adult's social behavior

TEACHING SUGGESTIONS

Activity-Based

- Place the child on his or her stomach for a period of play each day. Position toys or self so that the child will make contact by reaching.
- Encourage a reaching behavior in all positions by providing toys and objects at arm's length while the child is lying on his or her back or is in a sidelying or supported sitting position.
- Vary objects to maintain or engage the child's interest. If the child is more interested in people than objects, allow the child to reach toward and explore the faces of family members. Family pets, if tolerant of handling by children, are also of great interest.

Environmental Arrangements

- Use toys that make noise when the child touches them by reaching from a stomach position (e.g., Happy Apple).
- Occasionally place a bolster, small wedge, or folded cloth under the child's chest for additional support during reaching. Make sure the child's shoulders are free to move and that forearms can touch the ground.
- Roll or place a soft toy between the child's arms and under one side of the child's chest while the child is lying on his or her stomach.
- Hold the child on his or her stomach on a large ball facing a mirror. Make sure the child can see him- or herself in the mirror and then roll the ball to one side until the child can reach for and touch the mirror image with one hand.
- Block one of the child's shoulders with a rolled-up blanket or towel positioned along one side of the child's body. The roll should be placed behind the child's shoulder and extend part way down the child's trunk.
- Hang toys at shoulder height and within reach to encourage the child to rise up and reach. (Pay special attention to potential dangers with hanging toys.)

Instructional Sequence

- When the child is positioned on his or her stomach, offer an object that can be grasped with both hands but is too large to be secured with one. Let the child touch the object with outreached hand(s), then back it away and present it again to one hand.
- Allow the child to reach and grasp objects while in a sidelying position, then gently turn the child onto his or her stomach and encourage the child to continue to explore. Move the object to one side within reach of either the left or right hand. Verbally encourage the child to reach.
- If the child fails to bear weight on the opposite hand while reaching with the other, assist maintenance of the position by holding the child's weight-bearing forearm in position before and during reaching. The child should be lying on his or her stomach, bearing weight equally on each arm before an object is presented.
- When the child is up on his or her arms, gently rock the child back and forth to help shift weight from one arm to the other.

TEACHING CONSIDERATIONS

1. If the child has a motor impairment or abnormal muscle tone, consult a physical therapist about the appropriateness of this skill and about related programming issues.

GM A

2. If the child has abnormal muscle tone, present toys in a way that reaching for them will not result in abnormal posture or movement (head and neck extension, asymmetrical tonic neck reflex).
3. The child may find certain textured surfaces aversive. If the child reacts negatively to surface textures (e.g., increased muscle tone, clinging to parent, withdrawing limbs, fussing), use another surface and introduce unfamiliar textures gradually.
4. For a child with a visual impairment, use cues adapted to the impairment to elicit responses. For example, a child with a visual impairment may respond by reaching when prompted with bright colored or textured toys.
5. Use visual or touch cues to encourage a child who has a hearing impairment to reach.
6. Consider safety as the child moves in the environment and handles objects. Never leave the child unattended with potentially hazardous objects.

Objective 3.6 Lifts head and chest off surface with weight on arms

---

DEVELOPMENTAL PROGRAMMING STEPS

PS3.6a   The child lifts head and shoulders off a surface.
PS3.6b   The child lifts head off of a surface.

IMPORTANCE OF SKILL

Lifting the head and chest off the supporting surface while bearing weight on the arms demonstrates advancements in head and shoulder control. This control will be essential in future gross motor activities such as creeping, sitting, and walking. From the position of head and chest off the surface, the child develops upper back extension, a greater awareness of the upper body and arms, and the ability to look at his or her own hands while lying on the stomach. The child is able to view the world from a different angle, which increases exploration of the environment.

PRECEDING GOAL

Cog A:1.0   Orients to auditory, visual, and tactile events

CONCURRENT GOALS AND OBJECTIVES

FM A:3.3   Grasps hand-size object with either hand using whole hand
Cog B:1.0   Visually follows object and/or person to point of disappearance
Cog B:2.3   Reacts when object and/or person hides from view
SC A:2.0   Follows person's gaze to establish joint attention
SC C:2.3   Carries out one-step direction *with* contextual cues
Soc A:2.2   Responds to familiar adult's social behavior

TEACHING SUGGESTIONS
Activity-Based

- Encourage the child to play on his or her stomach with favorite objects and toys. Move toys up and down in front of the child.
- Give the child opportunities to lift his or her head in other positions, such as when the child is picked up or carried on an adult's shoulder.
- Provide a mirror at floor level for the child to look at him- or herself.
- Lie on the floor, stomach down, facing the child who is in the same position. Engage the child in face-to-face interaction. Move your face up and down.
- Sing and talk while the child is lying prone against your stomach and chest.
- Encourage head and shoulder lifting.
- Many small pets are a perfect height for children to rise up and watch. Watching fish in an aquarium on the floor or a low surface is a great way to practice this skill.

Environmental Arrangements

- Place a small, rolled up towel or diaper under the child's arms so that the chest is supported. Make sure the child's forearms can reach and rest on the surface.
- Allow the child to play with a favorite object or toy in a supported upright position and then lower the child to the floor on his or her stomach while the child is still attending.
- Introduce a toy on the floor within the visual field of the child lying on his or her stomach. Slowly raise the toy so that the child raises his or her head to follow it visually.
- Block the child's shoulders on both sides with rolled-up blankets closely bordering both sides of the child to stabilize the body. The rolls should be placed behind each shoulder and extend part way down the child's trunk.

Instructional Sequence

- Place the child in a prone position with arms bearing weight. Interact with the child while in this position, causing the child to lift his or her head and chest off the surface.
- Position the child on his or her stomach with arms forward. Present a favorite toy so that the child can see it, then move it up out of range. Activate the toy and verbally encourage the child to lift his or her head to view it.
- Position the child on his or her stomach. When the child lifts and turns his or her head to clear airway, interact with the child. (If the child is incapable of clearing airway by lifting or turning head, or if the response is weak, do *not* position the child on the stomach.)
- Gently grasp and lift the child's shoulders. This will encourage head lifting.

TEACHING CONSIDERATIONS

1. If the child has a motor impairment or abnormal muscle tone, consult a physical therapist about the appropriateness of this skill and about related programming issues.
2. If the child has abnormal muscle tone, present toys in a way that reaching for them will not result in abnormal posture or movement (head and neck extension).
3. The child may find certain textured surfaces aversive. If the child reacts negatively

GM A

to surface textures (increased muscle tone, clinging to parent, withdrawing limbs, fussing), use another surface and introduce unfamiliar textures gradually.

4. For the child with a visual or auditory impairment, use cues adapted to the impairment to elicit responses. For example, for the child with a severe visual impairment, place a piece of fur or soft quilt on the floor. Lie on the floor facing the child. Gently rub the child's lips and mouth with your finger or a pacifier; gradually change the position of the finger or pacifier. This will encourage the child to lift the head and move it from side to side. This is a precursor to the child lifting both head and chest off of a surface.

5. Consider safety as the child moves within the environment and handles objects. Never leave the child unattended with potentially hazardous objects.

Strand B

Balance in Sitting

GOAL 1   Assumes balanced sitting position

DEVELOPMENTAL PROGRAMMING STEPS

PS1.0a   When standing, the child lowers body, bends knees, and shifts weight back to a sitting position.

PS1.0b   When on hands and knees, the child rotates the body while extending and pushing with arms and shifts weight to a sitting position.

PS1.0c   When in a sidelying position, the child moves to sit by bending at the waist while extending and pushing with arms and bearing weight on the hips to raise the body off the ground.

PS1.0d   When on hands and knees, the child shifts weight to lean back and sit on legs; then extends legs out in front to sit on buttocks.

IMPORTANCE OF SKILL

The ability to assume a sitting position increases balance and motor coordination. The child integrates more complex motor actions into controlled patterns of movement. This skill enables the child to gain greater mobility and freedom to change positions. It increases the child's interaction with the environment as the child moves to a new stable position that frees the hands for exploring, reaching, and playing.

PRECEDING OBJECTIVE

GM B:1.1   Assumes hands and knees position from sitting

CONCURRENT GOALS AND OBJECTIVES

FM A:2.0   Brings two objects together at or near midline

FM A:3.0   Grasps hand-size object with either hand using ends of thumb, index, and second fingers

Adap A:4.2   Eats with fingers

Cog E:4.1   Uses more than one strategy in attempt to solve common problem

Cog G:1.3   Uses simple motor actions on different objects

SC C:2.3   Carries out one-step direction *with* contextual cues

Soc C:1.4   Observes peers

GM B

TEACHING SUGGESTIONS
Activity-Based

- When child is standing or lying in a crib, encourage the child to use crib rails to help move to a sitting position.
- Encourage the child to assume a sitting position by offering the child a favorite toy or snack at a height above the child's head.
- As the child crawls toward you, offer the child toys that must be manipulated with two hands to be activated.
- Offer the child interesting floating toys while the child is semi-reclined in the bathtub.
- Place toys on low shelves that the child can reach when either crawling or standing. Encourage the child to sit to manipulate the toys.
- Place favorite toys and objects near walls or corners of rooms. The walls will function as barriers and assist the child to change position or direction after obtaining the object.

☑ If your data indicate the child is not making progress toward the goal, provide additional structure within the suggested activities by incorporating the following *environmental arrangements:*

Environmental Arrangements

- Place pillows under the child as the child practices moving to sitting from standing.
- Allow the child to play with a favorite object or toy, then move it to a low surface or table several feet away and activate it. Encourage the child to obtain it.
- Offer a favorite toy or snack on the floor several feet away from the child. After the child moves toward the toy or snack, lift it to a height that will necessitate a change in the child's position to obtain it.
- Hold one end of a blanket while another adult holds the opposite end. Swing the child back and forth inside the blanket. Lift the end of the blanket closest to the child's back until the child assumes a sitting position.
- Show the child how to go from a stand to a squat, or to go down on one knee to assume a sitting position from a standing position when playing.

☑ If this goal is particularly difficult for a child, it may be necessary, within activities, to use an *instructional sequence.*

Instructional Sequence

- Model sitting on the floor from a standing position.
- Verbally direct the child to sit down beside you on the floor.
- Hold the child's hands and gently guide the child to sitting from standing, adding a little bounce on the pillows or mattress.
- Physically assist the child by gently guiding the child's hip or shoulder. Gradually reduce the amount of assistance.

☑ Combining or pairing different levels of instructions may be helpful when beginning to teach a new and difficult skill. Fade to less intrusive instructions as soon as possible to encourage more independent performance.

TEACHING CONSIDERATIONS

1. If the child has a motor impairment or abnormal muscle tone, consult a physical therapist about the appropriateness of this skill, the use of equipment to elicit motor responses (e.g., adapted chairs, balls), and related programming issues.
2. If the child has a visual impairment, increase the intensity and variety of cues (e.g., auditory cues, toys that produce noise, bright-colored objects). Be aware that the child may be fearful of changing positions.
3. Allow the child to practice this skill on a variety of surfaces (e.g., floor, carpet, grass).
4. If the child has a severe visual impairment, the child may need to be encouraged to use hands for balance because functional use of hands is often delayed in this child. Gently pull the child up to sitting by pulling on one arm a little more than the other. When pulled by one arm, the child will have to find and maintain his or her own balance, as when sitting alone.
5. If the child has a hearing impairment, increase the intensity and variety of cues (e.g., louder verbal cues, exaggerated facial expressions and gestures, toys or objects that can be activated).
6. Consider safety as the child moves about the environment and handles objects. Never leave the child unattended with potentially hazardous objects.

GM B

Objective 1.1   Assumes hands and knees position from sitting

---

DEVELOPMENTAL PROGRAMMING STEP

PS1.1a   From a sitting position, the child leans forward, bears weight on hands, and shifts weight from buttocks to knees.

IMPORTANCE OF SKILL

The ability to move out of a sitting to a creeping position represents control over a variety of movements (e.g., rotating trunk, shifting weight, bearing weight on hands and knees). These movements are coordinated into a complex behavior pattern, producing a smooth, balanced, and functional movement. This skill increases the child's freedom of movement and independence. Exploration increases as the child moves to the hands and knees position and interacts with the environment.

PRECEDING OBJECTIVE

GM B:1.2   Regains balanced, upright sitting position after *reaching* across the body to the right and to the left

CONCURRENT GOAL AND OBJECTIVES

GM A:3.0   Creeps forward using alternating arm and leg movements
Cog B:2.1   Locates object and/or person who hides while child is watching
Cog E:2.1   Uses part of object and/or support to obtain another object
Cog E:4.1   Uses more than one strategy in attempt to solve common problem

SC A:2.1   Follows person's pointing gesture to establish joint attention
SC C:2.3   Carries out one-step direction *with* contextual cues
Soc C:1.4   Observes peers

TEACHING SUGGESTIONS

Activity-Based

- When the child is sitting, stand or squat close by and wait for the child to move out of a sitting position onto hands and knees. Let the child use your body as a support to change position before picking up the child.
- Play with toys when sitting that will move or roll away when dropped (e.g., balls, balloons, bubbles).
- While the child is sitting, offer favorite toys or snacks from a distance so that the child will have to change position to obtain them.
- Play with the child in a sitting position on beds, sofas, or rugs so that unsuccessful attempts to change position will be cushioned.
- When bathing the child in a shallow tub, encourage him or her to reach for the plug, bubbles, or toys that are under the water and out of reach. Water will support the transition to hands and knees.

Environmental Arrangements

- Allow the child to play with a favorite object or toy (e.g., pull toy, wind-up toy) while in a sitting position, then move the toy away from the child while the child watches. Activate the toy if the child does not spontaneously assume a hands and knees position.
- Place favorite objects or toys on stair steps and encourage the child to obtain them.
- Hold the child in a sitting position on your stomach as you lie on your back. Play "Row, Row, Row Your Boat" holding the child's hands; play another game that will encourage the child to come forward on hands.
- Sit the child facing inward on adult's lap; support the child at the hips. Lean slowly backward into a reclining position to encourage the child to lean forward and bear weight on extended arms.
- Place the child in a sitting position at a low table for feeding or play. The table will provide a barrier and encourage the child to rotate to the side to change position when leaving the table.
- When drying the child after a bath with the child in a sidesitting position, put upward pressure on the child's weight-bearing side. Never force the movement; the pressure should be the same as used in normal towel drying.

Instructional Sequence

- Model "chase" games and encourage the child to join in.
- Verbally encourage the child to "come and get" the adult, a peer, or a toy as the adult, peer, or toy slowly moves away from the sitting child.
- Roll a large, partially inflated beach ball to the child while the child is sitting. When the child raises his or her arms to secure the ball, roll the child on top of the ball and allow the child to rock back and forth before resuming a sitting position.
- Physically assist the child at shoulders and hips to move from sitting to hands and knees position.

TEACHING CONSIDERATIONS:

1. If the child has a motor impairment or abnormal muscle tone, consult a physical therapist about the appropriateness of this skill, the use of equipment to elicit motor responses (e.g., adapted chairs, balls), and related programming issues.
2. If the child has a visual impairment, increase the intensity and variety of cues (e.g., auditory cues, toys that produce noise, bright-colored objects). Be aware that the child may be fearful of changing positions. Allow the child to practice this skill on a variety of surfaces (e.g., floor, carpet, grass).
3. If the child has a severe visual impairment, the child may need to be encouraged to use hands for balance because functional use of hands is often delayed in this child. Gently pull the child up to sitting by pulling on one arm a little more than the other. When pulled by one arm, the child will have to find and maintain his or her own balance, as when sitting alone.
4. If the child has a hearing impairment, increase the intensity and variety of cues (e.g., louder verbal cues, exaggerated facial expressions and gestures, toys or objects that can be activated).
5. Consider safety as the child moves about the environment and handles objects. Never leave the child unattended with potentially hazardous objects.

Objective 1.2 Regains balanced, upright sitting position after *reaching* across the body to the right and to the left

---

DEVELOPMENTAL PROGRAMMING STEPS

☑ The objective above is the most basic step for the skill to be taught. Most children will benefit from the activities outlined here that emphasize this skill. For children who need more instruction, consider designing programming steps from the *environmental arrangements* or from the *instructional sequence*.

IMPORTANCE OF SKILL

By rotating the trunk, the child's body moves segmentally rather than as a single unit. Instead of moving in line with the body, the arms can move across the body. Across body arm movement enables the child to explore and interact with more of the environment and is critical to one method of getting into and out of the sitting position. This skill also improves the child's ability to reach for and grasp objects.

PRECEDING OBJECTIVE

GM B:1.3 Regains balanced, upright sitting position after *leaning* to the left, to the right, and forward

CONCURRENT GOAL AND OBJECTIVES

FM A:2.1 Transfers object from one hand to the other
FM A:3.2 Grasps cylindrical object with either hand by closing fingers around it
FM A:5.1 Releases hand-held object onto and/or into a larger target with either hand

GM B

FM B:1.1	Turns object over using wrist and arm rotation with each hand
FM B:3.1	Uses either hand to activate objects
Adap A:4.2	Eats with fingers
Cog C:1.1	Correctly activates simple toy
Cog C:2.0	Reproduces part of interactive game and/or action in order to continue game and/or action
Cog E:1.1	Retains one object when second object is obtained
Cog E:4.1	Uses more than one strategy in attempt to solve common problem
Cog G:1.3	Uses simple motor actions on different objects
SC C:2.3	Carries out one-step direction *with* contextual cues
Soc C:1.5	Entertains self by playing appropriately with toys

TEACHING SUGGESTIONS

Activity-Based

- When the child is holding a toy or snack in one hand, offer another to the same side so that the child must reach across the body with the free hand.
- Activate favorite objects and toys to the child's side while the child is in a sitting position.
- Sit facing each other and play "Peas, Porridge, Hot" or other games that require crossover clapping motions.
- Roll a large ball back and forth with the child.
- Play peekaboo or gotcha from positions in which the child must reach across to get you.

Environmental Arrangements

- As the child sits, offer large objects that the child must lift with two hands to secure. Present them either to the left or right side of the child.
- Play beanbag toss with large targets placed all around the child.
- Place a pull toy with a string just slightly out of reach of the child and systematically move the toy farther from the child.
- Place the child sitting in front of a mirror or on an adult's lap with the child's legs straddling the adult's legs. Provide objects (e.g., blocks, chips, beanbags) on one side of the child's body and a container on the other side. When the child reaches for an object, elevate the knee opposite the direction the child is leaning. The child will shift his or her weight to catch him- or herself with arm (on side of reach).
- Give the child a set of small objects (e.g., beads, shapes, pegs) and a container to put them in. Put the objects on one side of the seated child and the container on the other side. If possible, the container should be unstable or unwieldy so that the child feels the need to stabilize it with the nearest hand. The child must then reach for an object and reach across the body to deposit the object.

Instructional Sequence

- Sit on the floor and model reaching across your body to get a toy. Then reach across your body with the other hand and move the toy to its original location. Repeat.
- While the child is sitting on the floor, hold the child's hand that is nearest a toy; verbally prompt the child to get the toy.
- When the child is in a sitting position, give the child an object to hold in one hand and then place another toy (preferably a toy that can be combined with the first toy) in

close proximity to the occupied hand. If the child does not have a spontaneous response, guide the child's free hand from behind the elbow toward the object.

■ Physically assist the child to reach across his or her body to get a toy.

TEACHING CONSIDERATIONS

1. If the child has a motor impairment or abnormal muscle tone, consult a physical therapist about the appropriateness of this skill, the use of equipment to elicit motor responses (e.g., adapted chairs, balls), and related programming issues.
2. If the child has a visual impairment, increase the intensity and variety of cues (e.g., auditory cues, toys that produce noise, bright-colored objects). Be aware that the child may be fearful of changing positions. Allow the child to practice this skill on a variety of surfaces (e.g., floor, carpet, grass).
3. If the child has a severe visual impairment, encourage the child to reach across the body for a toy by guiding the child's hand. Gently hold the arm and hand nearest the toy on the floor to ensure that the child reaches with the opposite hand. This movement encourages weight shifting.
4. If the child has a hearing impairment, increase the intensity and variety of cues (e.g., louder verbal cues, exaggerated facial expressions and gestures, toys or objects that can be activated).
5. Consider safety as the child sits and handles objects. Never leave the sitting child unattended with potentially hazardous objects.

Objective 1.3 Regains balanced, upright sitting position after *leaning* to the left, to the right, and forward

---

DEVELOPMENTAL PROGRAMMING STEPS

PS1.3a When sitting, the child *leans to the left and right* and then regains a balanced, upright sitting position.

PS1.3b When sitting, the child *leans forward* and then regains a balanced, upright sitting position.

IMPORTANCE OF SKILL

The ability to regain the sitting position after leaning improves back strength, balance, and trunk control. This skill is important to the increased freedom of the arms and hands for more active exploration. Leaning enables the child to reach for and pick up objects.

PRECEDING OBJECTIVE

GM B:1.4   Sits balanced without support

CONCURRENT GOALS AND OBJECTIVES

FM A:2.3   Reaches toward and touches object with each hand
FM A:3.3   Grasps hand-size object with either hand using whole hand
FM A:5.2   Releases hand-held object with each hand

FM B:1.1   Turns object over using wrist and arm rotation with each hand
FM B:3.1   Uses either hand to activate objects
Adap A:4.2   Eats with fingers
Cog B:2.1   Locates object and/or person who hides while child is watching
Cog C:1.1   Correctly activates simple toy
Cog C:2.0   Reproduces part of interactive game and/or action in order to continue game and/or action
Cog E:1.1   Retains one object when second object is obtained
Cog G:1.3   Uses simple motor actions on different objects
SC A:3.0   Engages in vocal exchanges by babbling
Soc A:2.1   Initiates simple social game with familiar adult
Soc C:1.5   Entertains self by playing appropriately with toys

TEACHING SUGGESTIONS

Activity-Based

- Sit in front of the child and play peekaboo by placing a cloth over your face. Encourage the child to lean forward to pull the cloth away, then encourage the child to place the cloth over his or her own face and regain an upright position. Repeat the game, sitting on each side of the child so that the child leans to the left or right to pull the cloth from your face.
- Sing songs or play games with the child that involve swaying motions. Hold the child on your lap or on your knee. Sway the child from side to side as you sing "Row, Row, Row Your Boat," for example.
- Sit the child in front of a mirror so that the child can reach for his or her image in the mirror.
- Roll a large ball back and forth to the child.
- Engage the child with favorite objects or toys that roll or move away from the child's body when the child plays with them (e.g., balls, balloons, bubbles).
- Put the child on a pillow or bolster. Play "horsy" and pretend to gallop.

Environmental Arrangements

- When carrying the child, hold the child away from your body, facing outward in a sitting position. Allow the child to lean forward and secure desired objects and toys.
- Sit in front, to the right, and to the left of the child while holding a familiar book. Encourage the child to point to pictures from a distance; this makes the child reach.
- Hand the child toys or objects from each direction or dangle them in front, to the right, and to the left of the child, forcing the child to lean to reach and grasp the objects.
- Present favorite objects and toys on the floor to the right, to the left, and in front of the child just within reach, but far enough that the child must lean to reach them.
- Provide a container to drop objects into; place objects at a distance so that the child must lean to obtain them.

Instructional Sequence

- Place the child in a sitting position facing a mirror or an interesting toy on the floor. Verbally encourage the child to lean forward to pat the mirror image by tapping and patting mirror. Activate a toy to encourage the child to reach for it. Begin by placing the child very near the mirror or toy and systematically move the child farther away from it as the child successfully leans and recovers.

- Place the child in a sitting position on your knees, facing you. Hold the child's hands and move one knee slowly up, allowing child to teeter. Then move knee back and allow child to regain balance. Repeat with other knee. Increase the amount the knees are moved as the child successfully leans and regains an upright sitting position.

TEACHING CONSIDERATIONS

1. If the child has a motor impairment or abnormal muscle tone, consult a physical therapist about the appropriateness of this skill, the use of equipment to elicit motor responses (e.g., adapted chairs, balls), and related programming issues.
2. If the child has a visual impairment, increase the intensity and variety of cues (e.g., auditory cues, toys that produce noise, bright-colored objects). Be aware that the child may be fearful of changing positions. Allow the child to practice this skill on a variety of surfaces (e.g., floor, carpet, grass).
3. If the child has a severe visual impairment, the child may need to be encouraged to use hands for balance because functional use of hands is often delayed in this child. Gently pull the child up to sitting by pulling on one arm a little more than the other. When pulled by one arm, the child will have to find and maintain his or her own balance, as when sitting alone.
4. If the child has a severe visual impairment, encourage steady sitting by varying the child's placement. For example, once the child is steady on the floor, place the child on a low stool or step. The child will have to work harder to regain balance after leaning to the right and left.
5. If the child has a hearing impairment, increase the intensity and variety of cues (e.g., louder verbal cues, exaggerated facial expressions and gestures, toys or objects that can be activated).
6. Consider safety as the child sits and handles objects. Never leave the child sitting unattended with potentially hazardous objects.

Objective 1.4 Sits balanced without support

IMPORTANCE OF SKILL

Sitting balanced without support increases the strength and control of the muscles in the upper and lower back. The firm back that results from the downward extension of muscular control is necessary for balance in standing and walking, as well as for controlled movement in the sitting position. Sitting without support enables the child to hold and explore objects with the hands. This increased interaction with the environment facilitates cognitive development.

PRECEDING OBJECTIVE

GM B:1.5   Sits balanced using hands for support

CONCURRENT GOALS AND OBJECTIVES

FM A:3.3   Grasps hand-size object with either hand using whole hand
Adap A:4.2 Eats with fingers
Cog B:1.0   Visually follows object and/or person to point of disappearance
Cog B:2.3   Reacts when object and/or person hides from view
Cog C:1.1   Correctly activates simple toy
Cog C:2.1   Indicates desire to continue familiar game and/or action
Cog E:1.1   Retains one object when second object is obtained
Cog G:1.3   Uses simple motor actions on different objects
SC A:1.0   Turns and looks toward person speaking
SC A:3.0   Engages in vocal exchanges by babbling
SC B:1.3   Gestures and/or vocalizes to greet others
Soc A:2.1   Initiates simple social game with familiar adult
Soc A:3.2   Responds to communication from familiar adult
Soc C:1.4   Observes peers

TEACHING SUGGESTIONS
Activity-Based

- While the child sits on the floor, provide opportunities for the child to free his or her hands from support and reach and grasp (hand toys to child, place objects on floor in front of the child, roll small ball toward child).
- Sit on the floor facing the child and play with favorite toys.
- During the day, provide opportunities for the child to practice independent sitting on various surfaces (e.g., floor, carpet, couch, crib) to gain stability.
- At snack time, sit the child on a table or counter and encourage child to finger feed.

Environmental Arrangements

- Put large pillows behind and to each side of the child.
- Give the child opportunities to sit in a car seat, in the corner of a sofa, propped in a chair with pillows, or in an infant carrier in the most upright position possible.
- When sitting behind the child, move back so that the child independently maintains balance for brief periods.
- Gently stroke the back of the child's neck to help child keep head erect.

Instructional Sequence

- Sit the child so that the upper legs are far apart and the feet meet to form a circle.
- Sit the child on the floor between your legs facing away from you. If the child begins to lean backward, quickly lean forward to bring the child's trunk forward, then lean back beyond the initial point of support. If the child attempts to lean on your legs, move legs away. Verbally encourage child to sit up.
- Position the child sideways between your legs so that one of your legs is behind the child's back and the other is over the child's legs.

TEACHING CONSIDERATIONS

1. If the child has a motor impairment or abnormal muscle tone, consult a physical therapist about the appropriateness of this skill, the use of equipment to elicit motor responses (e.g., adapted chairs, balls), and related programming issues.

2. If the child has a visual impairment, increase the intensity and variety of cues (e.g., auditory cues, toys that produce noise, bright-colored objects). Be aware that the child may be fearful of changing positions. Allow the child to practice this skill on a variety of surfaces (e.g., floor, carpet, grass).

3. If the child has a severe visual impairment, encourage confidence in sitting through use of a large body ball. Sit the child on top of the body ball and hold the child securely at the waist in the beginning. As the child becomes more comfortable and begins to find own balance, gradually decrease support by holding the child's legs. Gently move the child back and forth on the ball.

4. If the child has a hearing impairment, increase the intensity and variety of cues (e.g., louder verbal cues, exaggerated facial expressions and gestures, toys or objects that can be activated).

5. Consider safety as the child sits and handles objects. Never leave the child sitting with potentially hazardous objects.

Objective 1.5 Sits balanced using hands for support

DEVELOPMENTAL PROGRAMMING STEP

PS1.5a   When placed in a supported sitting position, the child holds his or her upper back straight.

IMPORTANCE OF SKILL

The child who sits using hands for support has enough head, neck, and back control to maintain this upright position, despite the pull of gravity. The child will practice increased control and equilibrium reactions to maintain balance in this position. This enables the child to eventually sit and move in a sitting position without the help of arms.

PRECEDING OBJECTIVE

GM B:1.6   Holds head in midline when in supported sitting position

CONCURRENT GOAL AND OBJECTIVES

Cog B:1.1   Visually follows object moving in horizontal, vertical, and circular directions

Cog B:2.3   Reacts when object and/or person hides from view

Cog C:1.3   Indicates interest in simple and/or mechanical toy

Cog C:2.1   Indicates desire to continue familiar game and/or action

SC A:1.2   Turns and looks toward noise-producing object

SC A:2.0   Follows person's gaze to establish joint attention

Soc A:1.2   Smiles in response to familiar adult

Soc A:3.2   Responds to communication from familiar adult

Soc C:1.4   Observes peers

TEACHING SUGGESTIONS
Activity-Based

- While folding laundry, sit the child in a laundry basket.
- While the child is sitting on your lap, position the child to use hands for support. Provide additional support with your own body to prevent falling, if necessary.
- Sit the child on the floor to play. Place toys that can be activated (e.g., wind-up toy, chime ball) on the floor in front of the child to maintain the child's interest.
- If the child indicates a desire to be put down when being carried, position the child directly in a sitting position.

Environmental Arrangements

- Lie on the floor facing the child to encourage the child to sit up and face you.
- Sit the child in a cardboard box or in a swimming ring to provide support. Cover the surrounding area with pillows.
- Sit on the floor with the child between your legs facing away from you. Dangle toys or interesting objects in front of the child's face to encourage the child to hold self upright. If the child falls back, your body will block the fall.
- Place the child in a sandbox, using sand to support the body.

Instructional Sequence

- Sit the child on the floor and place his or her hands out to the sides for support.
- Sit the child on the floor and hold him or her by the lower back. Verbally encourage the child to use his or her hands for support. Gradually move your support downward to the child's hips, upper legs, and lower legs while holding lightly.
- Support the child between your legs. Gradually move your legs away and place the child's hands on the floor as support.

TEACHING CONSIDERATIONS

1. If the child has a motor impairment or abnormal muscle tone, consult a physical therapist about the appropriateness of this skill, the use of equipment to elicit motor responses (e.g., adapted chairs, balls), and related programming issues.
2. If the child has a visual impairment, increase the intensity and variety of cues (e.g., auditory cues, toys that produce noise, bright-colored objects). Be aware that the child may be fearful of changing positions. Allow the child to practice this skill on a variety of surfaces (e.g., floor, carpet, grass).
3. If the child has a severe visual impairment, the child may need to be encouraged to use hands for balance because functional use of hands is often delayed in this child. Gently pull the child up to sitting by pulling on one arm a little more than the other. When pulled by one arm, the child will have to find and maintain his or her balance, as when sitting alone. Provide moderate support for the sitting child at the waist, then place the child's hands on the floor and gently hold them there for support.
4. If the child has a hearing impairment, increase the intensity and variety of cues (e.g., louder verbal cues, exaggerated facial expressions and gestures, toys or objects that can be activated).
5. Consider safety as the child begins to sit and handles objects. Never leave the child sitting unattended.

Objective 1.6   Holds head in midline when in supported sitting position

DEVELOPMENTAL PROGRAMMING STEP

PS1.6a   The child lifts his or her head momentarily when in a supported sitting position.

IMPORTANCE OF SKILL

The ability to sit and stand requires the child to control the muscles in the neck and back that allow the child to balance and remain upright. The development of this muscular control proceeds from the head down to the lower back. The ability to hold the head in midline when in a supported sitting position is the first step in this downward progression of muscular control. In addition, this skill enhances the child's visual exploration of the environment. The child perceives the world from an upright orientation and views a wider range of events.

PRECEDING OBJECTIVE

GM A:3.6   Lifts head and chest off surface with weight on arms

CONCURRENT OBJECTIVES

FM A:1.2   Makes nondirected movements with each arm
FM A:2.2   Holds an object in each hand
Cog B:1.2   Focuses on object and/or person
Cog C:1.3   Indicates interest in simple and/or mechanical toy
Cog C:2.1   Indicates desire to continue familiar game and/or action
Cog E:1.2   Retains object
Cog G:1.4   Uses sensory examination with objects
SC A:2.2   Looks toward an object
SC A:3.1   Engages in vocal exchanges by cooing
Soc A:1.2   Smiles in response to familiar adult
Soc A:2.2   Responds to familiar adult's social behavior
Soc A:3.2   Responds to communication from familiar adult
Soc C:1.4   Observes peers

TEACHING SUGGESTIONS

Activity-Based

- Take the child on an outing in a backpack and point out cars, animals, trees, and other objects of interest.
- When carrying the child, hold the child away from your body facing outward in a sitting position. Allow the child to lean backward for support of the head and trunk. Point out pictures, mirrors, and other wall hangings for the child to focus on.
- Give the child opportunities to view the world when held upright at the shoulders, to lift the head when lying on stomach, and to raise the head when gently pulled to a sitting position from lying on his or her back.

GM B

- Offer visual displays to hold the child's attention when the child is positioned in a carrier, propped in the corner of a sofa or seated in a car seat.
- Set the child's carrier on a table or work space. Talk to the child while you are working.
- Sit and hold the child on your lap. Talk to the child, smile, and exaggerate expressions, keeping your face near the child's face.

Environmental Arrangements

- Use a variety of chairs or seats to encourage the child to hold his or her head in midline (e.g., car seat, infant carrier, front pack, stroller, infant swing, corner of sofa).
- Use an object such as foam, cloth ring, towel, or blanket to hold the child's head in midline position when sitting in a car seat, stroller, or infant swing.
- Engage the child with your face at the child's level or with a favorite toy hanging from a support several inches in front of the child's face. Allow the child to maintain attention while in a supported sitting position.
- Dim lights in a room and use a small flashlight to illuminate objects to gain the child's attention as the child sits supported.
- Hold the child at shoulder level and have another person talk to the child over your shoulder.

Instructional Sequence

- Engage the child with your face or a favorite toy hanging from a support several inches in front of the child's face. Allow the child to maintain attention while in a supported sitting position.
- Hold the child in a supported position and engage the child's interest in a dangling toy. Tap or activate the toy; verbally gain the child's attention if the child begins to turn away.
- When carrying the child, hold him or her away from your body, facing outward in a sitting position. Allow the child to lean backward to support the trunk and head. Use your body to guide the child's head and maintain it in midline.

TEACHING CONSIDERATIONS

1. If the child has a motor impairment or abnormal muscle tone, consult a physical therapist about the appropriateness of this skill, the use of equipment to elicit motor responses (e.g., adapted chairs, balls), and related programming issues.
2. If the child has a visual impairment, increase the intensity and variety of cues (e.g., auditory cues, toys that produce noise, bright-colored objects). Be aware that the child may be fearful of changing positions. Allow the child to practice this skill on a variety of surfaces (e.g., floor, carpet, grass).
3. If the child has a severe visual impairment, help the child feel secure in a supported sitting position by holding the child just below the chest as the child sits on your lap facing you. As the child becomes steadier and is able to hold his or her head in midline, hold the child less tightly so that the child begins to find his or her balance.
4. If the child has a hearing impairment, increase the intensity and variety of cues (e.g., louder verbal cues, exaggerated facial expressions and gestures, toys or objects that can be activated).
5. Consider safety as the child begins to sit and handles objects. Never leave the child unattended with potentially hazardous objects.

GOAL 2 Sits down in and gets out of chair

IMPORTANCE OF SKILL

This skill is important for increased independence; it allows more interaction with the environment as the child changes position to sit down in or get out of a chair. Balance and coordination are enhanced as movements are combined into an elaborate pattern.

PRECEDING OBJECTIVES

GM B:2.1   Sits down in chair
GM C:3.3   Gets up and down from low structure

CONCURRENT GOALS AND OBJECTIVES

FM B:2.1   Fits variety of shapes into corresponding spaces
FM B:4.1   Draws circles and lines
Adap A:3.0   Drinks from cup and/or glass
Adap A:4.0   Eats with fork and/or spoon
Adap C:1.2   Takes off pants
Cog E:3.2   Moves around barrier to change location
Cog E:4.0   Solves common problems
SC A:2.1   Follows person's pointing gesture to establish joint attention
SC C:1.3   Locates common objects, people, and/or events *with* contextual cues
SC C:2.3   Carries out one-step direction *with* contextual cues
Soc B:2.1   Responds to routine event

TEACHING SUGGESTIONS

Activity-Based

- Provide a child-size chair at the snack table and in front of the television and a "potty" chair in the bathroom.
- Encourage the child to sit in the chair for assistance with putting on and taking off shoes and socks, or to have pants pulled on up to the knees. Then have the child get out of the chair to pull pants up to his or her waist.
- Allow the child to climb into the car seat before traveling in the car and to climb out when the car is parked.
- Provide a child-size rocking chair for story time.
- If the child requests a drink or snack, have the child sit at the table to receive it.

Environmental Arrangements

- Play musical chairs or line up chairs in a row and play "choo-choo-train."
- Provide a tub of water on a low table for water play. Encourage the child to stand up to get desired toys and sit down to play.
- When the child is sitting in a chair, allow the child to get out of the chair independently.
- At the playground, encourage the child to get in and out of child-size swings.

GM B

- Before asking the child to sit down or get out of a chair, move the chair out from under a table or turn the seat toward the child.
- Play "going to the movies"—line up chairs to watch "Sesame Street" or a favorite videotape.
- Use a chair with arms so the child can use the arms to lower into or raise out of the chair.

Instructional Sequence

- Model sitting in a chair and getting out several times.
- Pat the seat of the chair after asking the child to sit down. Hold arms out toward the child after asking the child to climb out of the chair.
- Crouch down close to the chair and allow the child to use your shoulder or arms to pull out of the chair.
- Position the child to sit in the chair by pushing the hips against the back of the seat; hold hips until the child extends back to attain a fully upright position. Pull the child's hips forward to the edge of the seat to encourage the child to get out of the chair. Gradually reduce the amount of assistance.

TEACHING CONSIDERATIONS

1. If the child has a motor impairment or abnormal muscle tone, consult a physical therapist about the appropriateness of this skill, the use of equipment to elicit motor responses (e.g., adapted chairs, balls), and related programming issues.
2. If the child has a visual impairment, increase the intensity and variety of cues (e.g., wider chairs, auditory or verbal cues). Initially, lead the child into and out of the chair and allow tactile exploration of the chair. Be aware that the child may be fearful of moving about freely.
3. Self-initiated mobility is often delayed in the child with a severe visual impairment; therefore, this child may need encouragement and support to move in and out of a chair. The child will reach out to grasp a sound cue before he or she will move out in space on hands and knees or feet.
4. If the child has a hearing impairment, increase the intensity and variety of cues (e.g., colorful chairs, louder verbal cues).
5. Be sure that the chair is sturdy and stable; remain nearby as the child sits down in and gets out of the chair.
6. Use adapted chairs for a child with a motor impairment or abnormal muscle tone (e.g., corner chair, bolster, beanbag chair).
7. Consider safety as the child sits and handles objects. Never leave the child unattended in a chair.

Objective 2.1   Sits down in chair

DEVELOPMENTAL PROGRAMMING STEPS

No standard developmental sequence appears to exist for the development of independent movement into a chair. Careful observation of the child will help determine the child's preferred mode of movement. Begin programming at the child's skill level.

IMPORTANCE OF SKILL

The ability to sit down and maintain an unsupported sitting position in a chair is a smooth movement progression that develops coordination and control over combined movements. This skill increases the child's independence by allowing the child to get into a chair without assistance and demonstrates motor planning skills.

PRECEDING OBJECTIVES

GM B:2.2   Maintains a sitting position in chair
GM C:3.3   Gets up and down from low structure

CONCURRENT GOALS AND OBJECTIVES

FM B:4.2   Scribbles
Adap A:3.0 Drinks from cup and/or glass
Adap A:4.0 Eats with fork and/or spoon
Cog D:1.0   Imitates motor action that is not commonly used
Cog E:3.2   Moves around barrier to change location
Cog E:4.0   Solves common problems
SC A:2.1   Follows person's pointing gesture to establish joint attention
SC C:1.3   Locates common objects, people, and/or events *with* contextual cues
SC C:2.3   Carries out one-step direction *with* contextual cues
Soc B:2.1   Responds to routine event

TEACHING SUGGESTIONS
Activity-Based

- Provide a child-size chair at the snack table and in front of the television and a "potty" chair in the bathroom.
- Encourage the child to sit in the chair for assistance with putting on and taking off shoes and socks or to have pants pulled on up to the knees.
- Allow the child to climb into the car seat before traveling in the car.
- If the child requests a drink or snack, have the child sit down at the table to receive it.
- Provide a child-size rocking chair for story time.
- Have the child sit down in a chair to color.
- If the child watches "Sesame Street" or a similar television program, have the child sit down in a chair to watch.

Environmental Arrangements

- Before asking the child to sit down, move the child's chair out from under the table or turn the seat toward the child.
- Place the chair firmly on the floor to prevent tipping.
- Use a chair with arms so the child can use the arms to lower into the chair.
- Sit in chairs at circle or sharing time, rather than on the floor.
- Use a variety of chairs (e.g., chair without sides, rocking chair, cube chair).

Instructional Sequence

- Model sitting in a chair.
- Pat the seat of the chair and verbally direct the child to sit down.

GM B

- Use a child-size table or other support to help the child climb into the chair.
- Sit the child down on a straight chair and offer support as the child adjusts position.
- Position the child to sit in the chair by pushing the hips against the back of the seat; hold the hips until the child extends back to attain a fully upright position. Gradually reduce the amount of assistance.

TEACHING CONSIDERATIONS

1. If the child has a motor impairment or abnormal muscle tone, consult a physical therapist about the appropriateness of this skill, the use of equipment to elicit motor responses (e.g., adapted chairs, balls), and related programming issues.
2. If the child has a visual impairment, increase the intensity and variety of cues (e.g., wider chairs, auditory or verbal cues). Initially lead the child into and out of the chair and allow tactile exploration of the chair. Be aware that the child may be fearful of moving about freely.
3. Self-initiated mobility is often delayed in the child with a severe visual impairment; therefore, this child may need encouragement and support to move in and out of a chair. The child will reach out to grasp a sound cue before the child will move out in space on hands and knees or feet.
4. If the child has a hearing impairment, increase the intensity and variety of cues (e.g., colorful chairs, louder verbal cues).
5. Be sure that the chair is sturdy and stable; remain nearby as the child sits down in and gets out of the chair.
6. Use adapted chairs with a child who has a motor impairment or abnormal muscle tone (e.g., corner chair, bolster, beanbag chair).
7. Consider safety as the child sits and handles objects. Never leave the child unattended in a chair.

Objective 2.2   Maintains a sitting position in chair

DEVELOPMENTAL PROGRAMMING STEP

PS2.2a   The child maintains a supported sitting position in a chair.

IMPORTANCE OF SKILL

The ability to maintain an unsupported sitting position in a chair fosters balance and head and trunk control. Sitting in a chair enables the child to move forward at the hips and shoulders in order to bring the arms forward and use hands for reaching and grasping. This skill will be used throughout life in a variety of settings, such as driving, eating, and reading.

PRECEDING OBJECTIVE

GM B:1.4   Sits balanced without support

CONCURRENT GOALS AND OBJECTIVES

FM A:3.1 Grasps hand-size object with either hand using the palm, with object placed toward the thumb and index finger

FM A:4.0 Grasps pea-size object with either hand using tip of the index finger and thumb with hand and/or arm *not* resting on surface for support

FM A:5.0 Places and releases object balanced on top of another object with either hand

FM B:1.0 Rotates either wrist on horizontal plane

FM B:2.1 Fits variety of shapes into corresponding spaces

FM B:3.0 Uses either index finger to activate objects

FM B:4.2 Scribbles

Adap A:3.0 Drinks from cup and/or glass

Adap A:4.0 Eats with fork and/or spoon

Cog C:1.0 Correctly activates mechanical toy

Cog D:1.0 Imitates motor action that is not commonly used

Cog E:4.0 Solves common problems

Cog F:1.0 Aligns and stacks objects

Cog G:1.2 Uses functionally appropriate actions with objects

SC B:1.0 Gains person's attention and refers to an object, person, and/or event

SC C:2.3 Carries out one-step direction *with* contextual cues

Soc A:3.0 Initiates and maintains communicative exchange with familiar adult

TEACHING SUGGESTIONS

Activity-Based

- Place the child in a chair for dressing and toileting. Use a safety seat while traveling in a car.
- Place the child in a highchair for meals.
- Sit the child in a child-size chair at a low table to play with or manipulate toys or objects.
- When shopping, place the child in a sitting position in the shopping cart.
- Place the child in an adult-size chair, couch, or rocker.
- Take the child for walks in a stroller with the seat adjusted to a sitting position.

Environmental Arrangements

- Use a chair that has arms or sides so the child has extra support if feeling insecure.
- Hold the child in a sitting position when you carry him or her. The child's back should be toward the adult's body and the child should sit supported on the adult's arms.
- Provide a surface on which the child can rest his or her feet. The child's feet should be a few inches apart and rest flatly on the foot support.
- Present objects to the child at chest level or on a table surface in front of the child while the child is in a sitting position.
- Use a variety of chairs (e.g., cube chair, stroller, highchair, car seat).
- Place the child on a riding toy that has back support; push the child on the riding toy, supporting sides if necessary.
- When the child is seated in a chair before a table, activate toys on the table's surface to maintain the child's attention.

GM B

Instructional Sequence

- Verbally encourage the child to remain seated in a chair for snacks.
- Use safety belts to hold the child's hips stable and help the child maintain a sitting position.
- Provide support at the child's hips when the child sits in a chair. Gradually reduce the amount of support.

TEACHING CONSIDERATIONS

1. If the child has a motor impairment or abnormal muscle tone, consult a physical therapist about the appropriateness of this skill, the use of equipment to elicit motor responses (e.g., adapted chairs, balls), and related programming issues.
2. If the child has a visual impairment, increase the intensity and variety of cues (e.g., wider chairs, auditory or verbal cues). Initially lead the child into and out of the chair and allow tactile exploration of the chair. Be aware that the child may be fearful of moving about freely.
3. Self-initiated mobility is often delayed in the child with a severe visual impairment; therefore, this child may need encouragement and support to move in and out of a chair. The child will reach out to grasp a sound cue before the child will move out in space on his or her hands and knees or feet.
4. If the child has a severe visual impairment, the child may enjoy gaining security in the sitting position by sitting on a body ball with your support. As the child finds his or her balance, decrease your support.
5. If the child has a hearing impairment, increase the intensity and variety of cues (e.g., colorful chairs, louder verbal cues).
6. Be sure that the chair is sturdy and stable; remain nearby as the child sits down in and gets out of the chair.
7. Use adapted chairs with a child who has a motor impairment or abnormal muscle tone (e.g., corner chair, bolster, beanbag chair).
8. Consider safety as the child sits and handles objects. Never leave the child unattended in a chair.

GM B

Strand C

Balance and Mobility in Standing and Walking

GOAL 1 Walks avoiding obstacles

DEVELOPMENTAL PROGRAMMING STEPS

PS1.0a   When walking unsupported, the child changes direction without falling.
PS1.0b   The child walks unsupported without falling.

IMPORTANCE OF SKILL

The ability to walk around objects, people, and activities without falling allows the child to negotiate the environment independently. The child can move through many settings without assistance and explore with increasing confidence. In addition, this skill is valuable in play because the child is able to follow peers.

PRECEDING OBJECTIVE

GM C:1.1   Walks without support

CONCURRENT GOALS AND OBJECTIVES

GM C:2.0   Stoops and regains balanced standing position without support
Cog B:3.1   Looks for object in usual location
Cog E:2.1   Uses part of object and/or support to obtain another object
Cog E:3.0   Navigates large object around barriers
Cog E:4.0   Solves common problems
Cog G:1.2   Uses functionally appropriate actions with objects
SC B:1.0   Gains person's attention and refers to object, person, and/or event
SC C:1.0   Locates objects, people, and/or events *without* contextual cues
SC C:2.2   Carries out one-step direction *without* contextual cues
Soc B:1.1   Meets physical needs of hunger and thirst
Soc B:2.0   Responds to established social routine

TEACHING SUGGESTIONS
Activity-Based

- Encourage the child to negotiate garden pathways, grocery store aisles, classrooms crowded with activities, and other environments without disturbing them.

125

GM C

- Face the child and move backward slowly, changing directions to avoid objects, people, and activities. Encourage the child to follow or chase you.
- Ask the child to move a familiar object located in its usual place to another room, or to return the object to its usual place in another room.
- Encourage the child to maneuver around people or pets in the environment.
- Ask the child to transport object(s) to a specified location (dirty dishes to the sink, trash in the trash can, laundry in a hamper).
- Encourage the child to push a toy (e.g., toy corn popper, lawn mower, cart) through a setting.
- Play an imitation game (e.g., "Simon says") while leading the child around obstacles.

☑ If your data indicate the child is not making progress toward the goal, provide additional structure within the suggested activities by incorporating the following *environmental arrangements:*

Environmental Arrangements

- Call the child's attention to his or her own body parts (e.g., feet, arms) as the child negotiates around obstacles.
- Encourage the child to move slowly on initial excursions through a setting.
- Create an obstacle course of boxes, baskets, large toys, or pillows. Require the child to walk around the obstacles.
- Place a favorite toy a short distance in front of the child in an area that has obstacles (e.g., people, furniture, trees). Encourage the child to walk, avoiding obstacles, to obtain the toy.
- Arrange the environment so the child can access both moving and stable objects.
- Have the child walk around obstacles on a variety of surfaces (e.g., carpet, grass, floor).

☑ If this goal is particularly difficult for a child, it may be necessary, within activities, to use an *instructional sequence.*

Instructional Sequence

- Model walking around a few "planted" obstacles.
- Follow as the child walks through a cluttered room. Give verbal cues as the child approaches obstacles that he or she will have to maneuver around (e.g., "Go around the chair," "Walk around the dog; he's sleeping.").
- Begin by requiring the child to walk short distances. Gradually increase the distance as the child becomes more proficient at avoiding obstacles while walking.
- Make moving in the environment increasingly challenging, depending upon the child's success. Start by introducing a few large obstacles far away from each other and then increase the number and proximity of obstacles while decreasing their size.
- Have the child hold onto a rope to form a chain; lead the child around obstacles.

☑ Combining or pairing different levels of instructions may be helpful when beginning to teach a new and difficult skill. Fade to less intrusive instructions as soon as possible to encourage more independent performance.

TEACHING CONSIDERATIONS

1. If the child has a motor impairment or abnormal muscle tone, consult a physical therapist about the appropriateness of this skill, the use of equipment to elicit motor responses (e.g., adapted chairs, balls), and related programming issues.

2. If the child has a visual impairment, increase the intensity and variety of environmental support and cues (e.g., tactile cues, bells and other auditory cues, verbal cues). Initially lead the child through the environment and around the obstacles. Be aware that the child may be fearful of moving about freely.
3. Gently encourage the child with a severe visual impairment to walk. Before initiating walking alone, the child may first attempt to localize (e.g., reach toward you as you speak).
4. If the child has a hearing impairment, increase the intensity and variety of cues (e.g., exaggerated movements and gestures, louder verbal cues, bright and colorful objects).
5. Avoid slippery surfaces and shoes or socks that do not have good traction.
6. Consider safety as the child moves about the environment and handles objects. Never leave the child unattended with potentially hazardous objects.

Objective 1.1 Walks without support

DEVELOPMENTAL PROGRAMMING STEPS

☑ The objective above is the most basic step toward the goal, "Walks avoiding obstacles," to be taught. Most children will benefit from the activities outlined here that emphasize this skill. For children who need more instruction, consider designing programming steps from the *environmental arrangements* or from the *instructional sequence* outlined.

IMPORTANCE OF SKILL

Walking without support is of obvious importance because it enables the child to move independently in an upright posture. Caregivers are no longer required to carry the child as the primary means of moving from one place to another. The child's visual field is expanded, and the hands are free to carry or manipulate two objects. This is an advantage over a creeping posture. Walking is also faster and less tiring than creeping.

PRECEDING OBJECTIVE

GM C:1.2   Walks with one-hand support

CONCURRENT GOALS AND OBJECTIVES

GM C:2.0   Stoops and regains balanced standing position without support
GM D:4.3   Throws ball or similar object at target
Cog B:3.0   Maintains search for object that is not in its usual location
Cog E:2.1   Uses part of object and/or support to obtain another object
Cog E:4.0   Solves common problems
Cog G:1.2   Uses functionally appropriate actions with objects
SC B:1.0   Gains person's attention and refers to an object, person, and/or event
SC C:1.0   Locates objects, people, and/or events *without* contextual cues
SC C:2.2   Carries out one-step direction *without* contextual cues

GM C

Soc B:1.1   Meets physical needs of hunger and thirst
Soc B:2.0   Responds to established social routine
Soc C:1.1   Initiates social behavior toward peer

TEACHING SUGGESTIONS
Activity-Based

■ When walking with the child and holding one hand, stop a short distance from an obvious destination (e.g., toy shelf, couch, drawer) and wait for the child to take a few steps without support.
■ Have parents greet, but not directly approach, the child after an absence. Encourage the child to walk to parents.
■ Encourage the child verbally or with enticement of toys to change location when standing.
■ Ask the child to do simple errands that require carrying objects, such as bringing a diaper and washcloth or throwing things in the trash.
■ Provide the child pull-toys with strings that produce novel effects or push-toys such as corn poppers and lawn mowers.

Environmental Arrangements

■ Play "Follow the leader" using peers to walk around objects or people in the room.
■ Place toys that are typically used together (e.g., doll, bottle, cradle, car, driver, trailer) in different locations but within the child's visual field.
■ Place stable objects (e.g., cube seat, low table) in a row across a room, leaving approximately 2 feet between each object. Place interesting toys on the object's surface to lure the child across open spaces from one stable object to another.
■ Provide extra security for the child by encouraging steps between two familiar adults.
■ Have the child walk without support on a variety of surfaces (e.g., floor, carpet, grass).

Instructional Sequence

■ Have a peer model walking to an adult for an appealing snack or toy.
■ Begin by requiring the child to walk short distances. Gradually increase the distance as the child becomes more proficient at walking.
■ Verbally encourage the child to "Come here" for an appealing snack or toy.
■ Allow the child to grasp a loose portion of your clothing (e.g., coat belt, apron, purse strap) as the child attempts to walk unsupported.
■ Interest the child in an object or event across the room and then physically direct the child toward it.

TEACHING CONSIDERATIONS

1. If the child has a motor impairment or abnormal muscle tone, consult a physical therapist about the appropriateness of this skill and related programming issues.
2. If the child has a visual impairment, increase the intensity and variety of cues (e.g., tactile cues, bells and other auditory cues, verbal cues). Initially lead the child through the environment and around the obstacles. Be aware that the child may be fearful of moving about freely.
3. Gently encourage the child with a severe visual impairment to walk. Before initiat-

ing walking alone, the child may first attempt to localize (e.g., reach toward you as you speak).

4. If the child has a hearing impairment, increase the intensity and variety of cues (e.g., exaggerated movements and gestures, louder verbal cues, bright and colorful objects).

5. Avoid slippery surfaces and shoes or socks that do not have adequate traction.

6. Clear the environment of objects that could hurt the child if the child falls. The area should be padded to cushion falls when first teaching this skill.

7. Consider safety as the child moves about the environment and handles objects. Never leave the child unattended with potentially hazardous objects.

Objective 1.2 Walks with one-hand support

IMPORTANCE OF SKILL

Walking with only one hand for support demonstrates increased balance as the child moves in an upright posture. At the same time, one hand is free to carry or manipulate objects, allowing more independence and exploration. The child who walks with one-hand support requires less carrying by caregivers and enjoys the benefits of upright locomotion.

PRECEDING OBJECTIVE

GM C:1.3   Walks with two-hand support

CONCURRENT GOAL AND OBJECTIVES

Cog B:3.1   Looks for object in usual location
Cog E:2.1   Uses part of object and/or support to obtain another object
Cog E:3.2   Moves around barrier to change location
SC A:2.1   Follows person's pointing gesture to establish joint attention
SC B:1.0   Gains person's attention and refers to an object, person, and/or event
SC C:1.3   Locates common objects, people, and/or events *with* contextual cues
Soc A:3.2   Responds to communication from familiar adult

TEACHING SUGGESTIONS
Activity-Based

- In outings with the child, walk together and hold the child's hand.
- Plan short adventures between daily activities, such as a walk from the bedroom to the bathtub at bathtime or from the play area to the highchair for a snack.
- Allow the child to walk and use a wall for support.
- Encourage the child to walk down a hallway and use a wall for one-hand support.
- Walk backward and lead the child with one hand to give encouragement and reinforcement.
- When the child indicates a desire for a toy when being held, stand the child on the floor and take one of the child's hands to lead the way to a desired toy.

GM C

- Provide the child opportunities to pull a pull-toy or hold a favorite object while the other hand is supported in walking.
- Take one hand and let the child walk around you in circles while you sing, "Ring Around the Rosey." Make falling down part of the game!
- When pushing the child in a stroller, periodically have the child get out and walk along the side of the stroller, holding onto it with one hand.

Environmental Arrangements

- Create opportunities for the child to be assisted between two support surfaces while cruising.
- Walk a short distance with the child and then rest and play before walking to the next location.
- If the child requests an object or toy that is out of reach, hold one of the child's hands and let the child reach with the opposite hand. Let the child lead with the free side of his or her body, but control the degree of the child's lean.
- Encourage the child to cruise from a low table to one of your outstretched hands.
- When walking the child with two-hand support, replace the support of one hand with an object for the child to hold, such as a small ball, block, or the child's bottle. If necessary, help position the object in the child's grasp or against the child's body to secure it.
- Use both stationary and moving support for the child to hold onto with one hand.

Instructional Sequence

- Have a peer model walking with one-hand support to obtain an appealing snack or toy.
- Begin by requiring the child to walk with one-hand support for short distances. Gradually increase the distance as the child becomes more proficient.
- Verbally encourage the child to obtain an appealing snack or toy by walking with one-hand support.
- Physically prompt the child by providing support at the hips or shoulders while the child holds onto another person with one hand. Gradually decrease the amount of assistance.

TEACHING CONSIDERATIONS

1. If the child has a motor impairment or abnormal muscle tone, consult a physical therapist about the appropriateness of this skill and related programming issues.
2. If the child has a visual impairment, increase the intensity and variety of cues (e.g., tactile cues, bells and other auditory cues, verbal cues). Initially lead the child through the environment. Be aware that the child may be fearful of moving about freely.
3. Gently encourage the child with a severe visual impairment to walk. The support of your hand, paired with a verbal cue, will be important to develop the child's confidence in walking alone.
4. If the child has a hearing impairment, increase the intensity and variety of cues (e.g., exaggerated movements and gestures, louder verbal cues, bright and colorful objects).
5. Avoid slippery surfaces and shoes or socks that do not have adequate traction.
6. Ensure that the support is sturdy and stable.

7. Consider safety as the child moves about the environment and handles objects. Never leave the child unattended with potentially hazardous objects.

Objective 1.3   Walks with two-hand support

IMPORTANCE OF SKILL

This skill is important because the child begins to take alternating steps (as opposed to side-steps used in cruising), which are necessary for walking without support. Walking with two-hand support allows the child increased mobility in an upright position. The child no longer requires stationary support, but demonstrates the necessary balance to use a moving support when taking steps. This allows more exploration of the environment.

PRECEDING OBJECTIVE

GM C:1.4   Stands unsupported

CONCURRENT GOALS AND OBJECTIVES

GM C:1.5   Cruises
Cog C:2.0   Reproduces part of interactive game and/or action in order to continue game and/or action
SC A:3.0   Engages in vocal exchanges by babbling
Soc A:2.1   Initiates simple social game with familiar adult
Soc A:3.2   Responds to communication from familiar adult
Soc C:1.1   Initiates social behavior toward peer

TEACHING SUGGESTIONS

Activity-Based

- When moving between locations, allow the child to practice walking with two-hand support.
- When the child indicates a desire for a toy when being held, stand the child on the floor and take each of the child's hands to lead the way to the desired toy.
- Provide the child with a shopping cart or doll buggy to push.
- Encourage the child to cross the platform at the top of a low slide while holding onto both rails and slide down while you watch.
- Encourage the child to push his or her chair to the next activity.
- Encourage the child to participate in games in which the child stands and moves with both hands held (e.g., "London Bridge").

Environmental Arrangements

- After the child indicates a desire to be in a different location, provide a cart, box, walker, or other object that will give the child support when the child pushes or holds onto it with two hands. Control the speed of the object by placing it on a carpet, weighing it down with heavy objects, or by holding onto the front.

- Use both stationary and moving support for the child to hold onto with both hands.
- Place the child on your feet and walk together, holding onto the child's hands. This is a fun way to "dance" to music. Provide the child with an opportunity to move on his or her feet also.
- Place a peer on a riding toy and encourage the child to push the toy.
- Remove the seat from the infant walker and let the child push the walker while holding it with both hands.

Instructional Sequence

- Have a peer model walking with two-hand support to obtain an appealing snack or toy.
- Begin by requiring the child to walk with two-hand support for short distances. Gradually increase the distance as the child becomes more proficient.
- Verbally encourage the child to walk with two-hand support to obtain an appealing snack or toy.
- Physically prompt the child by providing support at hips, shoulders, or hands. Gradually decrease the amount of assistance.

TEACHING CONSIDERATIONS

1. If the child has a motor impairment or abnormal muscle tone, consult a physical therapist about the appropriateness of this skill and related programming issues.
2. If the child has a visual impairment, increase the intensity and variety of cues (e.g., tactile cues, bells and other auditory cues, verbal cues). Initially lead the child through the environment. Be aware that the child may be fearful of moving about freely.
3. Gently encourage the child with a severe visual impairment to take both of your hands and walk. Pairing of verbal cues and your support is very important to the child's ear–hand coordination.
4. If the child has a hearing impairment, increase the intensity and variety of cues (e.g., exaggerated movements and gestures, louder verbal cues, bright and colorful objects).
5. Avoid slippery surfaces and shoes or socks that do not have adequate traction.
6. Ensure that the support is sturdy and stable.
7. Consider safety as the child moves about the environment and handles objects. Never leave the child unattended with potentially hazardous objects.

Objective 1.4   Stands unsupported

DEVELOPMENTAL PROGRAMMING STEP

PS1.4a   The child supports him- or herself with one hand while standing.

IMPORTANCE OF SKILL

Standing unsupported increases the strength and control of the muscles in the back and legs and develops balance in an upright position. These are all necessary components of walking. This new position frees the hands to hold and manipulate objects, allowing greater exploration of the environment.

PRECEDING OBJECTIVE

GM C:2.2   Pulls to standing position

CONCURRENT GOALS AND OBJECTIVES

FM A:3.0   Grasps hand-size object with either hand using ends of thumb, index, and second fingers
FM B:1.1   Turns object over using wrist and arm rotation with each hand
Cog B:1.0   Visually follows object and/or person to point of disappearance
Cog D:1.1   Imitates motor action that is commonly used
Cog G:1.2   Uses functionally appropriate actions with objects
SC B:1.0   Gains person's attention and refers to an object, person, and/or event
SC C:2.3   Carries out one-step direction *with* contextual cues
Soc A:3.1   Initiates communication with familiar adult
Soc C:1.5   Entertains self by playing appropriately with toys

TEACHING SUGGESTIONS
Activity-Based

- Place the child in a standing position facing you so that you can remove the child's coat. Hold the coat, but not the child's body.
- After a bath, place the child in a standing position and dry the child with a towel. Do not hold or grasp the child, but allow the child to spontaneously lean for support.
- When the child indicates a desire to be put down when being held, stand the child on the floor without support nearby.
- Blow large bubbles for the child to pop as he or she stands holding one hand on a support. Offer a bubble to the hand holding onto the support.
- Play face-to-face clapping games while the child is standing.
- Provide the child with several toys or objects to manipulate while the child is leaning against a support (e.g., couch, table).
- When holding the child in a standing position, remove your hold so that the child is standing unsupported.

Environmental Arrangements

- When the child is leaning against a support while standing, offer the child a large object to hold in both hands.
- When the child is standing holding onto a support, offer the child a large object to hold and simultaneously remove the support.
- Position a mirror so that the child can see him- or herself standing upright. Talk about different body parts and look for them in the mirror. Decrease adult's body support as the child becomes interested in the mirror image.
- Provide engaging activities that require two-hand manipulation with peers at a low table.
- When the child is standing and holding onto support, offer the child a toy or object to hold in one hand. Then offer another toy or object to the other hand.

Instructional Sequence

- Have a peer model standing unsupported holding a favorite toy.
- Begin by requiring the child to stand unsupported for short periods of time. Gradually increase the amount of time as the child becomes more proficient at standing.
- Verbally encourage the child to hold a favorite toy with both hands.
- Physically assist the child to stand by supporting the child at the hips or shoulders. Gradually decrease the amount of assistance.

TEACHING CONSIDERATIONS

1. If the child has a motor impairment or abnormal muscle tone, consult a physical therapist about the appropriateness of this skill and related programming issues.
2. If the child has a visual impairment, increase the intensity and variety of environmental support and cues (e.g., tactile cues, bells and other auditory cues, verbal cues). Be aware that the child may be fearful of moving about freely.
3. If the child has a hearing impairment, increase the intensity and variety of cues (e.g., exaggerated movements and gestures, louder verbal cues, bright and colorful objects).
4. Avoid slippery surfaces and shoes or socks that do not have adequate traction.
5. Clear the environment of objects that could hurt the child if the child falls. The area should be padded to cushion falls when first teaching this skill.
6. Consider safety as the child stands and handles objects. Never leave the child unattended with potentially hazardous objects.

Objective 1.5   Cruises

DEVELOPMENTAL PROGRAMMING STEP

PS1.5a   The child stands bearing his or her full weight with support.

IMPORTANCE OF SKILL

This skill is important because the child now moves in an upright position without the assistance of another person. The child gains a new visual perspective of the world while moving about and experiences increased interaction with the environment. Cruising fosters balance, coordination, and strength, all necessary skills for walking.

PRECEDING OBJECTIVE

GM B:1.4   Sits balanced without support

CONCURRENT GOALS AND OBJECTIVES

FM A:3.1   Grasps hand-size object with either hand using the palm, with object placed toward the thumb and index finger
FM B:3.1   Uses either hand to activate objects
GM C:2.2   Pulls to standing position
Adap A:4.2   Eats with fingers

Cog B:1.0 Visually follows object and/or person to point of disappearance

Cog C:1.2 Acts on mechanical and/or simple toy in some way

Cog E:2.1 Uses part of object and/or support to obtain another object

Cog E:4.1 Uses more than one strategy in attempt to solve common problem

SC B:1.0 Gains person's attention and refers to an object, person, and/or event

SC C:2.3 Carries out one-step direction *with* contextual cues

Soc A:3.1 Initiates communication with familiar adult

Soc C:1.5 Entertains self by playing appropriately with toys

TEACHING SUGGESTIONS

Activity-Based

- Allow the child to cruise along the rail of a crib or playpen.
- Play with a ball or another object that moves when touched at one end of a table where the child can reach it.
- Move together with music, encouraging the child to cruise around you.
- When the child is standing at a low, stable support (e.g., table, couch), put the child's bottle or favorite toy out of reach near the edge of the support.
- Encourage the child to participate in circle games (e.g., "Ring Around the Rosey") in which children hold hands and move to the right or left.
- Crouch down at one end of a stable support (e.g., couch, low table) while the child is standing at the other end. Encourage the child to side-step the length of the support to be picked up.
- Place a snack at the opposite end of a table from where the child is standing.

Environmental Arrangements

- Hang a Busy Box on the wall and encourage the child to walk along the wall to reach the toy.
- Place a pull-toy at the child's end of a low table. Let the child touch the toy, then pull it just out of the child's reach.
- Place the child's favorite objects or toys out of reach along the edge of a waist-high, stable support (e.g., table, low shelf, window ledge), while the child stands at the support and watches.

Instructional Sequence

- Have a peer model cruising along a support to obtain a favorite toy.
- Begin by requiring the child to cruise short distances. Gradually increase the distance as the child becomes more proficient in cruising.
- Crouch down facing the child and slowly move backward along a support, verbally encouraging the child to follow.
- Physically assist the child to side-step by providing gentle pressure or guidance to the hips or shoulders. Gradually decrease the amount of assistance.

TEACHING CONSIDERATIONS

1. If the child has a motor impairment or abnormal muscle tone, consult a physical therapist about the appropriateness of this skill and related programming issues.
2. If the child has a visual impairment, increase the intensity and variety of environmental support and cues (e.g., tactile cues, bells and other auditory cues, verbal cues). Initially lead the child along the supported object. Use textured support.

GM C

3. If the child has a severe visual impairment, have the child practice cruising barefoot to provide additional information about the environment.
4. If the child has a hearing impairment, increase the intensity and variety of cues (e.g., exaggerated movements and gestures, louder verbal cues, bright and colorful objects).
5. Avoid slippery surfaces and shoes or socks that do not have adequate traction.
6. Be aware that the child initially may need to be placed in a standing position.
7. Ensure that the support is sturdy and stable.
8. Consider safety as the child moves about the environment and handles objects. Never leave the child unattended with potentially hazardous objects.

GOAL 2   Stoops and regains balanced standing position without support

---

DEVELOPMENTAL PROGRAMMING STEP

PS2.0a   The child uses a support (e.g., furniture, wall, person) to regain a standing position after squatting or stooping.

IMPORTANCE OF SKILL

The ability to independently stoop and then recover indicates that the child can control balance well enough to move in and out of a standing position. This skill provides a practical advantage for obtaining objects from the floor without having to crawl. The child gains another means to independently change positions and can explore the environment with less chance of falling.

PRECEDING OBJECTIVE

GM C:2.1   Rises from sitting position to standing position

CONCURRENT GOALS AND OBJECTIVES

FM A:3.0   Grasps hand-size object with either hand using ends of thumb, index, and second fingers
GM D:4.3   Throws ball or similar object at target
Cog C:1.0   Correctly activates mechanical toy
Cog E:1.0   Retains objects when new object is obtained
Cog E:2.1   Uses part of object and/or support to obtain another object
Cog E:4.0   Solves common problems
Cog G:1.2   Uses functionally appropriate actions with objects
SC B:1.0   Gains person's attention and refers to an object, person, and/or event
SC B:2.2   Uses nonspecific consonant–vowel combinations and/or jargon
SC C:2.3   Carries out one-step direction *with* contextual cues
Soc A:3.1   Initiates communication with familiar adult
Soc C:2.2   Responds to communication from peer

TEACHING SUGGESTIONS
Activity-Based

- At home, let the child play with pots and pans in low cupboards.
- Offer the child many items to hold. If the child drops something, encourage the child to pick it up.
- Ask the child to retrieve something from a drawer close to the floor.
- Play ball games with the child by rolling the ball to the child on the floor while the child is standing.
- Pick flowers from the garden. Gather "treasures" on nature walks, squatting and stooping periodically to pick up bugs, leaves, and sticks before walking farther.
- Encourage the child to bend and straighten while gathering sticks or toy boats to float in puddles and shallow pools.
- Call the child's attention to his or her feet, shoes, and socks; ask the child to identify them.
- Encourage the child to pull shoestrings or Velcro straps to unfasten shoes.

Environmental Arrangements

- Occasionally place the child's favorite objects or toys on the floor instead of giving them directly to the child. Keep play things in containers at ground level.
- Play games such as "Drop the Hanky" and encourage the child to participate with assistance.
- Begin by occasionally placing tall objects on the floor for the child to pick up; systematically present smaller objects for the child to secure.
- Drop an object as you walk across a room in front of the child. Ask the child to pick it up.
- Tug at the child's shoestrings or Velcro fasteners. Encourage the child to imitate the action.
- Fill a drawer near the floor with unbreakable toys. Encourage the child to open the special drawer and play.

Instructional Sequence

- Model squatting to reach a favorite toy. Comment on it and then drop the toy again.
- Verbally direct the child to get the toy on the floor.
- Let the child sit on a stool and bend forward to feel the "squatting" position from a more secure position closer to the ground.
- Hold one side of a large object (e.g., ball, truck, doll) the child is stooping to obtain. Initially hold the object slightly above the floor so that the child does not have to stoop all the way down. Guide the child back into a standing position with the object.
- Hold and stabilize the child's hips, helping the child lower into a stoop and rise back to standing. Gradually reduce the amount of assistance.

TEACHING CONSIDERATIONS

1. If the child has a motor impairment or abnormal muscle tone, consult a physical therapist about the appropriateness of this skill, the use of equipment to elicit motor responses (e.g., adapted chairs, balls), and related programming issues.
2. If the child has a visual impairment, increase the intensity and variety of environ-

GM C

mental support and cues (e.g., tactile cues, toys that activate and make noise, verbal cues). Be aware that the child may be fearful of changing positions.

3. Verbally encourage the child with a severe visual impairment to stoop to get a toy. The child may need prompting to achieve ear–hand (your voice–the toy) coordination.

4. If the child has a hearing impairment, increase the intensity and variety of cues (e.g., exaggerated movements and gestures, louder verbal cues, bright and colorful objects, toys that activate).

5. Clear the environment of objects that could hurt the child if the child loses balance. The area around the child should be padded to cushion falls when first teaching this skill.

6. Avoid slippery surfaces and shoes or socks that do not have adequate traction.

7. Consider safety as the child stands, squats, and handles objects. Never leave the child unattended with potentially hazardous objects.

Objective 2.1   Rises from sitting position to standing position

---

DEVELOPMENTAL PROGRAMMING STEP

PS2.1a   The child rises from a sitting to standing position with support.

IMPORTANCE OF SKILL

Rising from sitting to standing without support increases the child's independence and freedom to explore the environment. This skill also increases the child's interaction with peers, as the child does not have to rely on support to change positions from sitting to standing.

PRECEDING OBJECTIVE

GM C:2.2   Pulls to standing position

CONCURRENT GOALS AND OBJECTIVES

FM A:3.0   Grasps hand-size object with either hand using ends of thumb, index, and second fingers
GM D:4.3   Throws ball or similar object at target
Cog C:1.0   Correctly activates mechanical toy
Cog C:2.0   Reproduces part of interactive game and/or action in order to continue game and/or action
Cog E:4.0   Solves common problems
Cog G:1.2   Uses functionally appropriate actions with objects
SC B:1.0   Gains person's attention and refers to an object, person, and/or event
SC C:2.3   Carries out one-step direction *with* contextual cues
Soc A:3.2   Responds to communication from familiar adult
Soc C:2.2   Responds to communication from peer

TEACHING SUGGESTIONS

Activity-Based

- When the child is dressing, assist the child to put on pants. Pull the pants up to the knees as the child sits, then have the child stand to complete dressing.
- When the child is sitting, call his or her attention to a toy or to something outside the window; encourage the child to rise to a standing position to see.
- When the child is in a sitting position, ask if the child wants to be picked up. Wait until the child attempts to stand before you pick him or her up.
- As the child sits, hold a jacket open for the child to put on. Wait for the child to stand to put on the jacket.
- When the child is finished at the table, have the child stand to stack dirty dishes on a tray or in a bin.

Environmental Arrangements

- Place an object that the child cannot manipulate without standing on a table before the seated child (e.g., top, Play-Doh factory, pounding toy).
- Encourage the child while seated at a table to stack objects (e.g., blocks, rings on a post, stacking pegs) so high that the child must stand to finish. Sturdy blocks help provide support for the child.
- When the child is sitting, ask if he or she wants to be picked up; extend your arms down toward the child, bending only slightly. Allow the child to use you for support if necessary.
- While the child is sitting, hold out a favorite toy above the child's head so that the child must rise to obtain it.

Instructional Sequence

- Have a peer model rising from sitting to standing to obtain a favorite toy.
- If the child does not readily rise from sitting to a standing position, verbally direct the child (e.g., "You can do it"). Provide specific instructions to the child (e.g., "Stand up") if necessary.
- Hold one side of a large object (e.g., ball, truck, doll) the child is playing with while sitting on the floor. Tell the child to put the ball, truck, or doll in a different location or on an elevated surface, then guide the child's movements until the child assumes a standing position. Gradually reduce the amount of assistance.
- Hold and stabilize the child's hips, helping the child move from sitting to standing. Gradually reduce the amount of assistance.

TEACHING CONSIDERATIONS

1. If the child has a motor impairment or abnormal muscle tone, consult a physical therapist about the appropriateness of this skill and related programming issues.
2. If the child has a visual impairment, increase the intensity and variety of environmental support and cues (e.g., tactile cues, toys that activate and make noise, verbal cues). Be aware that the child may be fearful of changing positions.
3. If the child has a severe visual impairment, offer your hand as support for the child to stand. Pair this with verbal encouragement.
4. Verbally encourage a child with a severe visual impairment to stand to get a toy.

GM C

The child may need prompting to achieve ear–hand (your voice–the toy) coordination.

5. If the child has a hearing impairment, increase the intensity and variety of cues (e.g., exaggerated movements and gestures, louder verbal cues, bright and colorful objects, toys that activate).

6. Clear the environment of objects that could hurt the child if the child loses balance. The area around the child should be padded to cushion falls when first teaching this skill.

7. Avoid slippery surfaces and shoes or socks that do not have adequate traction.

8. Ensure that the support is sturdy and stable.

9. Consider safety as the child stands and handles objects. Never leave the child unattended with potentially hazardous objects.

Objective 2.2 Pulls to standing position

DEVELOPMENTAL PROGRAMMING STEP

PS2.2a The child uses support to pull up one foot to a kneeling position with his or her weight resting on one foot and one knee.

IMPORTANCE OF SKILL

By pulling to stand, the child uses his or her own power to get into a standing position. This skill develops strength, coordination, and balance as the child integrates more complex motor activities into controlled patterns of movement. It affords increased interaction with the environment as the child independently changes to a new position.

PRECEDING OBJECTIVE

GM C:2.3 Pulls to kneeling position

CONCURRENT GOALS AND OBJECTIVES

FM B:3.1   Uses either hand to activate objects
Cog C:2.1   Indicates desire to continue familiar game and/or action
Cog E:2.1   Uses part of object and/or support to obtain another object
SC A:3.0   Engages in vocal exchanges by babbling
SC B:1.0   Gains person's attention and refers to an object, person, and/or event
SC C:2.3   Carries out one-step direction *with* contextual cues
Soc A:3.2   Responds to communication from familiar adult
Soc C:2.2   Responds to communication from peer

TEACHING SUGGESTIONS
Activity-Based

■ Play with or activate a favorite object or toy on a low table or couch while the child watches. The table or couch should be high enough that the child must pull to stand to obtain the object.

- Encourage the child to pull up on your body to engage in face-to-face interaction while sitting on an adult's lap.
- Talk to and interact with the child while sitting on a chair on which the child can pull to stand to reach you.
- Encourage the child to use stable objects (e.g., windowsill, wall, shelf) to pull to a standing position to look out the window, look in the mirror, or reach a shelf.
- Play games with refrigerator magnets placed at different heights on the refrigerator.
- When the child attempts to pull up on your body to engage in face-to-face interaction, hold out your hands so the child can grasp them.
- When the child wants to be picked up, hold out your arms above the child's head and encourage the child to pull up on your body to stand and be picked up.
- Encourage the child to pull up on the sides of the crib to stand and be picked up.

Environmental Arrangements

- Allow the child to play with part of an object. Pull the free piece of the object onto a low table while the child is still grasping the other part. Use a stuffed animal, pull-toy, or child's blanket.
- Tape pictures of the child's family or interesting objects on the wall at a height where the child must pull to stand to look at them.
- Keep interesting objects or toys on low shelves, stairs, or the couch so that the child must pull to a standing position to reach them.
- Attach toys or objects to the crib railing so that the child must pull to stand to manipulate them.
- Serve a snack at a low table or shelf.

Instructional Sequence

- Have a peer model pulling to stand for a favorite snack or toy.
- Verbally direct the child to stand up to get a snack or toy.
- Call attention (e.g., tap, point) to a support the child can use to hoist his or her body. If this does not elicit a response, hold the child's hands stable when the child pulls to stand.
- Place the child's hands on the support the child will use to hoist his or her body. Stand behind the child and gently lift the child's hips to achieve a standing position.
- Bend to the child and ask if he or she wants up. If the child does want to get up, stabilize the child's hips and wait until the child places his or her arms around you. Then gently lift the child's hips, letting the child assist by pulling with his or her arms.

TEACHING CONSIDERATIONS

1. If the child has a motor impairment or abnormal muscle tone, consult a physical therapist about the appropriateness of this skill and related programming issues.
2. If the child has a visual impairment, increase the intensity and variety of environmental support and cues (e.g., tactile cues, toys that activate and make noise, verbal cues). Be aware that the child may be fearful of changing positions.
3. If the child has a severe visual impairment, he or she may not initiate mobility (pull to a stand) without first reaching out to grasp a sound cue (your arm and your voice). Verbally encourage the child.
4. Verbally encourage the child with a severe visual impairment to pull to stand to get a toy. The child may need prompting to achieve ear–hand (your voice–the toy) coordination.

GM C

5. If the child has a hearing impairment, increase the intensity and variety of cues (e.g., exaggerated movements and gestures, louder verbal cues, bright and colorful objects, toys that activate).
6. Clear the environment of objects that could hurt the child if the child loses balance. The area around the child should be padded to cushion falls when first teaching this skill.
7. Avoid slippery surfaces and shoes or socks that do not have adequate traction.
8. Ensure that the support is sturdy and stable.
9. Consider safety as the child pulls to stand and handles objects. Never leave the child unattended with potentially hazardous objects.

Objective 2.3 Pulls to kneeling position

IMPORTANCE OF SKILL

Pulling to a kneeling position indicates that the child has greater trunk control. The semi-upright position is a stepping stone to standing. The strength, coordination, and balance developed in this skill are necessary for standing. Pulling to a kneeling position is also important because of the increased interaction with the environment as the child changes positions and views the world from a new perspective.

PRECEDING OBJECTIVE

GM A:3.2   Assumes creeping position

CONCURRENT GOAL AND OBJECTIVES

FM B:3.1   Uses either hand to activate objects
Cog C:1.2   Acts on mechanical and/or simple toy in some way
Cog C:2.1   Indicates desire to continue familiar game and/or action
Cog E:2.1   Uses part of object and/or support to obtain another object
SC A:3.0   Engages in vocal exchanges by babbling
SC C:2.3   Carries out one-step direction *with* contextual cues
Soc A:3.2   Responds to communication from familiar adult
Soc C:2.2   Responds to communication from peer

TEACHING SUGGESTIONS
Activity-Based

- Play with or activate a favorite object or toy on a low surface (e.g., couch, shelf, table) while the child watches. The surface should be high enough that the child must pull to a kneeling position to obtain the object, but *not* so high that the child cannot reach the object when kneeling.
- Encourage the child to engage in face-to-face interaction by pulling to a kneeling position, using your body when you are kneeling or sitting on the floor.
- Encourage the child to use a stable object (e.g., windowsill, wall, shelf) to pull to a

kneeling position in order to look out the window, look in the mirror, reach a shelf, or pat pictures on the wall.

- Play with refrigerator magnets placed at different heights on the refrigerator.
- When the child attempts to pull up on your body to engage in face-to-face interaction, hold out your hands so the child can grasp them.
- Serve a snack at a low table.

Environmental Arrangements

- Allow the child to play with part of an object. Pull the free piece of the object onto a low surface while the child is still grasping the other part. Use a stuffed animal, pull-toy, or child's blanket.
- Tape pictures of familiar or interesting objects on the wall at a height where the child must pull to a kneeling position to look at them.
- Hang a Busy Box outside of the crib at kneeling height.
- Put interesting objects or toys on low shelves, stairs, or the couch so that the child must pull to a kneeling position to reach them.

Instructional Sequence

- Have a peer model pulling to a kneeling position to see something.
- Verbally direct the child to pull to kneel to look at something.
- Call attention (e.g., tap, point) to a support the child can use to hoist his or her body. If this does not elicit a response, hold the child's hands stable while he or she pulls to kneel.
- Place the child's hands on the support the child will use to hoist his or her body. Stand behind the child and gently lift the child's hips to achieve a kneeling position.
- Bend to the child and ask if the child wants up. When the child indicates that he or she wants to get up, stabilize the child's hips and wait until the child places his or her arms around you. Then gently lift the child's hips, letting the child assist by pulling with his or her arms.

TEACHING CONSIDERATIONS

1. If the child has a motor impairment or abnormal muscle tone, consult a physical therapist about the appropriateness of this skill and related programming issues.
2. If the child has a visual impairment, increase the intensity and variety of environmental support and cues (e.g., tactile cues, toys that activate and make noise, verbal cues). Be aware that the child may be fearful of changing positions.
3. If the child has a severe visual impairment, the child may not initiate mobility (pull to a kneel) without first reaching out to where a sound came from (your arm and your voice). Verbally encourage the child.
4. Verbally encourage a child with a severe visual impairment to kneel to get a toy. The child may need prompting to achieve ear–hand (your voice–the toy) coordination.
5. If the child has a hearing impairment, increase the intensity and variety of cues (e.g., exaggerated movements and gestures, louder verbal cues, bright and colorful objects, toys that activate).
6. Clear the environment of objects that could hurt the child if the child loses balance. The area around the child should be padded to cushion falls when first teaching this skill.

GM C

7. Avoid slippery surfaces and shoes or socks that do not have adequate traction.
8. Ensure that the support is sturdy and stable.
9. Consider safety as the child kneels and handles objects. Never leave the child unattended with potentially hazardous objects.

GOAL 3   Walks up and down stairs

DEVELOPMENTAL PROGRAMMING STEP

PS3.0a   The child walks up stairs holding the rail or wall with one hand.

IMPORTANCE OF SKILL

The ability to independently negotiate stairs demonstrates the child's ability to alternately shift weight from one side of the body to the other and maintain balance. This skill is also used when climbing jungle gyms or ladders, running, and riding a tricycle. By using one hand for support, if needed, the free hand is available to carry objects and to protect self when falling.

PRECEDING OBJECTIVE

GM C:3.1   Walks up and down stairs using two-hand support

CONCURRENT GOALS AND OBJECTIVES

GM D:5.0 Climbs up and down play equipment
Cog B:3.1 Looks for object in usual location
SC B:2.0 Uses consistent word approximations
SC C:2.2 Carries out one-step direction *without* contextual cues
Soc A:3.1 Initiates communication with familiar adult
Soc C:2.2 Responds to communication from peer

TEACHING SUGGESTIONS

Activity-Based

- Play with a Slinky on the stairs.
- Activate toys out of the child's reach but within the visual field on a stairway, rather than giving them directly to the child.
- Encourage the child to independently negotiate stairs leading to and from the house, church, and daycare.
- Place a step stool by the bathroom sink, near a drinking fountain, near a coat rack, or any other facility the child frequents.
- Rather than carry the child up or down short flights of stairs, put the child down and proceed.
- Play "Follow the leader" using stairs. Guide the child to lead going up and follow going down.

Environmental Arrangements

- Replace ladder on a slide with a three- or four-step staircase for the child to climb.
- Lead the child to the banister or handrail of stairs leading to and from the house, church, or daycare.
- Arrange obstacle courses or treasure hunts that involve stairs.
- Make "mini" stairs by placing a thick catalog or book in front of a step stool. Place along the wall for support.
- Carry the child halfway up or down a short flight of stairs with railings and then put the child down on the stairs. Proceed and encourage the child to follow, remaining close enough to prevent falls.
- Place the child's favorite objects or toys on a stair landing.
- Pull a pull-toy up or down stairs as the child reaches for it.
- Use carpeted stairs to reduce slipping and increase confidence.

Instructional Sequence

- Model walking up stairs to obtain a favorite toy. Comment on it and set it down again.
- Use gestures and verbally encourage the child to climb stairs.
- Begin by having the child walk up and down a few stairs. Increase the number as the child successfully negotiates stairs.
- Walk up and down stairs behind or to the side of the child. Support the child's arm just below the shoulder joint. Gradually decrease the amount of assistance.
- Walk up and down stairs with the child, initially giving two-hand support. Release support with one hand and allow child to continue to walk up and down the stairs with one-hand support.
- Walk up and down stairs behind the child, stabilizing the child's hips as needed. Gradually decrease assistance.

TEACHING CONSIDERATIONS

1. If the child has a motor impairment or abnormal muscle tone, consult a physical therapist about the appropriateness of this skill and related programming issues.
2. If the child has a visual impairment, increase the intensity and variety of cues (e.g., verbal cues, tactile cues, toys that activate and make noise, bells attached to child). Be aware that the child may be fearful of moving about. Initially lead the child up and down the stairs.
3. If the child has a severe visual impairment, pair verbal encouragement with a helping hand when the child walks up and down the stairs. Stairs may be frightening until the child builds confidence and ear–hand coordination.
4. If the child has a hearing impairment, increase the intensity and variety of cues (e.g., exaggerated movements and gestures, bright-colored stairs, louder verbal cues).
5. Avoid slippery surfaces and shoes or socks that do not have adequate traction.
6. Remain near as the child walks up and down stairs.
7. Consider safety as the child moves about the environment and handles objects. Never leave the child unattended on the stairs.

GM C

Objective 3.1 Walks up and down stairs using two-hand support

DEVELOPMENTAL PROGRAMMING STEP

PS3.1a   The child walks up stairs using two-hand support.

IMPORTANCE OF SKILL

The child who achieves walking up and down stairs with two-hand support demonstrates the ability to alternately shift balance from one side of the body to the other. However, the child is merely practicing the movement at this point and does not yet demonstrate upper body stability while negotiating because he or she is using both hands for support.

PRECEDING OBJECTIVES

GM C:1.3   Walks with two-hand support
GM C:3.2   Moves up and down stairs

CONCURRENT GOALS AND OBJECTIVES

GM D:5.0   Climbs up and down play equipment
SC B:2.0   Uses consistent word approximations
SC C:2.3   Carries out one-step direction *with* contextual cues
Soc A:3.2 Responds to communication from familiar adult
Soc C:2.1 Initiates communication with peer

TEACHING SUGGESTIONS
Activity-Based

- Walk up and down stairs with the child to enter a home or school.
- If the child indicates a desire to go up and down stairs, let the child find the wall or rail; then stand near enough for the child to grasp your hand for assistance when beginning to walk up and down the stairs.
- Rather than carry the child up and down short flights of stairs, put the child down near the banister or handrail. Hold the hand that is away from the handrail and do not begin to walk up and down until the child grasps the support.
- Allow the child to walk up and down stairs while holding the rail or the wall.
- Place a toy out of the child's reach but within the visual field on a stairway. Encourage the child to obtain the toy.
- Step up and down street curbs when on a walk with the child.
- Rather than carry the child up and down short flights of stairs, put the child down and have an adult on each side of the child take a hand. Allow the child to initiate the stepping action.

Environmental Arrangements

- Guide the child to step up on and then off of a solid box while you hold both hands.
- Present a toy a few steps up or down from the child. Encourage the child to obtain the toy.
- Begin stair climbing by using slides or ramps for descending.

Instructional Sequence

- Model walking a peer up stairs with two-hand support.
- Use gestures and verbally encourage the child to climb up and down stairs with two-hand support.
- Begin by having the child walk up and down a few stairs. Increase the number of stairs as the child becomes more proficient.
- Walk down the stairs backward, facing the child. The child's hands should be on your shoulders, and your hands should stabilize the child's hips. Gradually decrease assistance.

TEACHING CONSIDERATIONS

1. If the child has a motor impairment or abnormal muscle tone, consult a physical therapist about the appropriateness of this skill and related programming issues.
2. If the child has a visual impairment, increase the intensity and variety of cues (e.g., verbal cues, tactile cues, toys that activate and make noise, bells attached to child). Be aware that the child may be fearful of moving about. Initially lead the child up and down the stairs.
3. If the child has a severe visual impairment, pair verbal encouragement with two helping hands as the child walks up and down stairs.
4. If the child has a hearing impairment, increase the intensity and variety of cues (e.g., exaggerated movements and gestures, bright-colored stairs, louder verbal cues).
5. Avoid slippery surfaces and shoes or socks that do not have adequate traction.
6. Remain near as the child walks up and down stairs.
7. Consider safety as the child moves up and down stairs and handles objects. Never leave the child unattended on the stairs.

Objective 3.2   Moves up and down stairs

DEVELOPMENTAL PROGRAMMING STEP

PS3.2a   The child moves up stairs.

IMPORTANCE OF SKILL

The child who can move up and down stairs using any movement pattern (e.g., creep, crawl) demonstrates body awareness and the ability to coordinate a variety of movement patterns to achieve a desired result. This skill increases the child's independence

GM C

and interaction with the environment as the child moves to change locations and re-verse directions. The child develops strength and balance while moving up and down stairs.

PRECEDING OBJECTIVE

GM C:3.3　Gets up and down from low structure

CONCURRENT OBJECTIVES

GM D:5.1　Moves up and down inclines
Cog E:3.2　Moves around barrier to change location
SC B:2.1　Uses consistent consonant–vowel combinations
SC C:2.3　Carries out one-step direction *with* contextual cues
Soc A:3.2　Responds to communication from familiar adult
Soc C:2.2　Responds to communication from peer

TEACHING SUGGESTIONS

Activity-Based

- Activate toys out of reach but within the child's visual field on a stairway rather than give them directly to the child.
- If the child indicates a desire to be put down while you are walking up or down stairs, place the child on a step and supervise closely.
- Encourage the child to independently negotiate stairs leading to and from the house, church, or daycare.
- Place a step stool by the bathroom sink, near a drinking fountain, near a coat rack, or any other facility the child frequents.
- Play peekaboo with the child over a set of stairs (similar to being on a small slide at the playground).
- Pull a pull-toy up and down the stairs as the child reaches for it.

Environmental Arrangements

- Carry the child halfway up and down a short flight of stairs and then put the child down on the stairs. Proceed and encourage the child to follow, remaining close enough to prevent falls.
- Place the child's favorite objects or toys on a stair landing.
- Replace a ladder on a slide with a three- or four-step staircase for the child to climb.
- Use carpeted stairs to reduce slipping and increase confidence and comfort.

Instructional Sequence

- Have a peer model crawling or climbing up stairs.
- Provide verbal cues and gestures to encourage the child to move up and down stairs.
- Begin by having the child move up and down a few stairs. Gradually increase the number of stairs as the child becomes more proficient.
- Provide support to the child's hips as the child moves up and down stairs. Gradually decrease assistance.

TEACHING CONSIDERATIONS

1. If the child has a motor impairment or abnormal muscle tone, consult a physical therapist about the appropriateness of this skill and related programming issues.
2. If the child has a visual impairment, increase the intensity and variety of cues (e.g., verbal cues, tactile cues, toys that activate and make noise, bells attached to the child). Be aware that the child may be fearful of moving about. Initially lead the child up and down the stairs.
3. If the child has a severe visual impairment, pair verbal encouragement with holding both the child's hands as the child walks up and down the stairs.
4. If the child has a hearing impairment, increase the intensity and variety of cues (e.g., exaggerated movements and gestures, bright-colored stairs, louder verbal cues).
5. Avoid slippery surfaces and shoes or socks that do not have adequate traction.
6. Remain near as the child walks up and down stairs.
7. Consider safety as the child moves up and down stairs and handles objects. Never leave the child unattended on the stairs.

GM C

Objective 3.3   Gets up and down from low structure

DEVELOPMENTAL PROGRAMMING STEP

PS3.3a   The child climbs onto a low, stable structure (e.g., low step, raised platform).

IMPORTANCE OF SKILL

The child who can get up and down from a low structure using any movement pattern demonstrates body awareness and the ability to coordinate movement patterns to achieve a desired event. The child practices skills necessary to climb stairs, enhancing strength and balance.

PRECEDING OBJECTIVE

GM A:3.3   Crawls forward on stomach

CONCURRENT GOAL AND OBJECTIVES

GM D:5.2   Moves under, over, and through obstacles
Cog E:3.2   Moves around barrier to change location
SC A:3.0   Engages in vocal exchanges by babbling
SC C:2.3   Carries out one-step direction *with* contextual cues
Soc A:3.2   Responds to communication from familiar adult

TEACHING SUGGESTIONS
Activity-Based

- Provide the child with cushions, large pillows, or large stuffed animals on the floor during play.

- Encourage the child to climb up and down a low bed or Futon.
- Allow the child to play with large cardboard blocks.
- Encourage the child to build and play in forts. Use blankets, pillows, cushions, large stuffed toys, and other soft, bulky objects as building materials.
- Build barriers around the child with cushions, large pillows, or large stuffed animals on the floor, requiring the child to get up and over the barrier to reach you.
- Play tumbling games on thick mats. Guide the child to get up and down.

Environmental Arrangements

- Build barriers around the child's favorite objects or toys (with cushions, large pillows, large stuffed toys) and encourage the child to obtain them. Activate the objects or toys if the child does not respond.
- Set the child on the lowest step or on a stool to put on shoes and socks. Encourage the child to get up and down independently.
- Play a "Follow the toy" or "Come and get me" game by pulling a pull-toy over a cushion, pillow, or stuffed toy as the child reaches for it.
- Put a favorite toy or bottle up on a low platform and encourage the child to get it.
- Place a mirror up on a low platform and draw the child's attention to his or her reflection.

Instructional Sequence

- Model getting on and off a low surface.
- Give verbal directions and gestural cues to the child to get up on a low surface.
- Begin a climbing activity with a low structure that is only slightly higher than the floor. Increase the height of the structure as the child becomes more proficient.
- Provide support at the child's hips as the child gets up and down from a low structure. Gradually decrease the amount of assistance.

TEACHING CONSIDERATIONS

1. If the child has a motor impairment or abnormal muscle tone, consult a physical therapist about the appropriateness of this skill and related programming issues.
2. If the child has a visual impairment, increase the intensity and variety of cues (e.g., verbal cues, tactile cues, toys that activate and make noise, bells attached to child). Be aware that the child may be fearful of moving about freely. Initially lead the child up and down low surfaces.
3. If the child has a severe visual impairment, pair verbal encouragement with gentle physical prompting as the child moves up and down the low structure. The child may need this ear–hand coordination prompting (your voice–physical touch) before the child feels confident to move out into space independently.
4. If the child has a hearing impairment, increase the intensity and variety of cues (e.g., exaggerated movements and gestures, bright-colored objects, louder verbal cues).
5. Be sure that the low structure is sturdy and stable. An adult should be near as the child moves up and down a low structure.
6. Avoid slippery surfaces and shoes or socks that do not have adequate traction.
7. Consider safety as the child moves about the environment and handles objects. Never leave the child unattended with potentially hazardous objects.

Strand D

Play Skills

GOAL 1 Jumps forward

DEVELOPMENTAL PROGRAMMING STEP

PS 1.0a The child jumps forward with one foot landing at a time.

IMPORTANCE OF SKILL

Jumping forward is a means of play for the child. While the child is entertaining self by jumping forward, balance (shifting weight and landing upright) and strength (protecting the body against gravity) are enhanced. Improved control over body movements is also required.

PRECEDING OBJECTIVE

GM D:1.1 Jumps up

CONCURRENT OBJECTIVES

Cog D:1.1 Imitates motor action that is commonly used
SC C:2.1 Carries out two-step direction *with* contextual cues
SC D:2.3 Uses two-word utterances to express location
Soc C:1.1 Initiates social behavior toward peer

TEACHING SUGGESTIONS

Activity-Based

- Play motor games such as "Mother may I" and "Simon says"; include jumping forward.
- Sing songs or nursery rhymes and encourage the child to jump to the songs ("Jack Be Nimble," "Bunny Hop").
- Play a game with the child and pretend to be an animal. Create a story or scene that has the animal jumping; act it out. For example, pretend to be kangaroos, rabbits, or frogs.
- At the playground or park, encourage the child to jump into the hopscotch squares. Jump over the cracks in the sidewalk.

151

☑ If your data indicate the child is not making progress toward the goal, provide additional structure within the suggested activities by incorporating the following *environmental arrangements:*

Environmental Arrangements

- Make a shape (e.g., square, circle) with chalk or a string on the floor or ground; have the child jump into the shape.
- Do exercises or actions to music. (Some videotapes and television programs model parent–child aerobic exercises.)
- Place an object on the floor or ground for the child to jump over. For example, draw a line with chalk or put a stick or rope on the ground.
- Create an obstacle course of boxes, baskets, and ropes. Within the obstacle course, set up a few opportunities for the child to jump over (e.g., a small box, a rope). Allow peers to participate with the child in the obstacle course. Have the child and peers take turns being the leader through the obstacle course.

☑ If this goal is particularly difficult for a child, it may be necessary, within activities, to use an *instructional sequence.*

Instructional Sequence

- Model jumping forward or have a peer demonstrate.
- If the child does not readily jump, verbally prompt the child to jump (e.g., "You can do it"). Provide specific instructions to the child (e.g., "Bend your knees," "Lift up from your toes").
- Physically assist the child by holding both hands while the child jumps forward.

☑ Combining or pairing different levels of instructions may be helpful when beginning to teach a new and difficult skill. Fade to less intrusive instructions as soon as possible to encourage more independent performance.

TEACHING CONSIDERATIONS

1. If the child has a motor impairment or abnormal muscle tone, consult a physical therapist about the appropriateness of this skill and about related programming issues.
2. If the child has a visual impairment, increase the intensity and variety of environmental support and cues (e.g., verbal cues and tactile cues, bells attached to the child). Be aware that the child may be fearful of moving about freely.
3. If the child has a severe visual impairment, offer gentle verbal and physical encouragement to the child to jump forward. The child may need to reach out and grasp a sound cue (your voice) before moving out independently to jump forward.
4. If the child has a hearing impairment, increase the intensity and variety of cues (e.g., louder verbal cues, exaggerated facial expressions and gestures).
5. Avoid slippery surfaces and shoes or socks that do not have adequate traction.
6. Be aware that the child may tire easily while learning this skill.
7. Consider safety as the child jumps. Never leave the child unattended in potentially hazardous situations.

Objective 1.1   Jumps up

DEVELOPMENTAL PROGRAMMING STEPS

PS1.1a   The child bends at the knees, raises up on his or her feet or toes, and jumps up with one foot at a time.

PS1.1b   The child bends at the knees and raises up on his or her toes while feet remain on the ground (i.e., child "jumps up" without his or her feet leaving the ground).

IMPORTANCE OF SKILL

Jumping up develops balancing skills and strength in the legs. Aside from its importance as a play skill, jumping up becomes a problem-solving strategy for obtaining objects out of reach. The child continues to develop self-awareness as he or she learns a new way to move the body through space and control motions to accomplish this. Jumping up is a skill used throughout life in many games and sports.

PRECEDING OBJECTIVE

GM D:1.2   Jumps from low structure

CONCURRENT GOALS AND OBJECTIVES

GM C:2.0   Stoops and regains balanced standing position without support
Cog D:1.1   Imitates motor action that is commonly used
SC C:2.1   Carries out two-step direction *with* contextual cues
SC D:1.2   Uses five action words
Soc A:2.0   Initiates and maintains interaction with familiar adult

TEACHING SUGGESTIONS

Activity-Based

- Stand in front of a full-length mirror and encourage the child to jump.
- Sing songs or nursery rhymes and encourage the child to jump to the songs.
- Play a game of jumping in patterns or to directions. For example, jump two times fast and two times slowly. Demonstrate for the child if necessary.
- Blow bubbles high into the air. Encourage the child to jump up to reach them.
- Play "Simon says" or "Mother may I" and include jumping in place.

Environmental Arrangements

- Provide a trampoline, mattress, or mat for jumping games.
- Hang objects (e.g., balloons, streamers) above the child's head so that the child must jump up to touch the objects. Use caution with balloons and hanging objects.
- Play music on a radio or record player and encourage the child to jump. Vary the tempo of the music.
- Attach a noise-producing object (e.g., bells on a string) to the child's ankle so that a noise is produced when the child jumps.

Instructional Sequence

- Model jumping or have a peer demonstrate.
- If the child does not readily jump, verbally prompt the child ("You do it"). Provide specific instructions to the child (e.g., "Bend your knees," "Lift up from your toes").
- Extend an object for the child to grasp (e.g., hula hoop, stick, rod).
- Physically prompt the child by holding the child's hands.

TEACHING CONSIDERATIONS

1. If the child has a motor impairment or abnormal muscle tone, consult a physical therapist about the appropriateness of this skill and about related programming issues.
2. If the child has a visual impairment, increase the intensity and variety of environmental support and cues (e.g., verbal cues and tactile cues, bells attached to the child). Be aware that the child may be fearful of moving about freely.
3. If the child has a severe visual impairment, offer gentle verbal and physical encouragement to the child to jump up. The child may need to reach out to where a sound came from before moving out independently to jump up.
4. If the child has a hearing impairment, increase the intensity and variety of cues (e.g., louder verbal cues, exaggerated facial expressions and gestures).
5. Avoid slippery surfaces and shoes or socks that do not have adequate traction.
6. Be aware that the child may tire easily while learning this skill.
7. Consider safety as the child jumps. Never leave the child unattended in potentially hazardous situations.

Objective 1.2   Jumps from low structure

DEVELOPMENTAL PROGRAMMING STEP

PS1.2a   The child step-jumps or hops (leads with one foot) from a low, stable structure to a supporting surface.

IMPORTANCE OF SKILL

Jumping from a low structure is important for its play value and for the development of leg muscles and body awareness. Active physical play allows the child to release energy and is an enjoyable way to interact with peers. Leg muscles are developed as the child practices balancing skills (shifting weight and landing upright) and gains strength (projecting the body against gravity). The child learns how to move the body through space and how to control the motions associated with jumping.

PRECEDING OBJECTIVE

GM C:3.3   Gets up and down from low structure

CONCURRENT GOALS AND OBJECTIVES

GM C:2.0   Stoops and regains balanced standing position without support
GM C:3.0   Walks up and down stairs
Cog D:1.1   Imitates motor action that is commonly used
SC C:2.3   Carries out one-step direction *with* contextual cues
Soc A:2.1   Initiates simple social game with familiar adult

TEACHING SUGGESTIONS

Activity-Based

- When walking down stairs or off a curb, encourage the child to jump from the bottom step or curb.
- When at the park or playground, jump from low, stable structures such as rocks, railroad ties, or a low platform.
- Encourage the child to jump into sand from the sturdy edge of a sandbox.
- Play a game with the child and pretend to be an animal. Create a story or scene that has an animal jumping; act it out. For example, pretend to be a frog jumping into a pond or a cat leaping from a tree.

Environmental Arrangements

- Place objects on the floor or ground beside a low, stable structure so that the child jumps onto the objects (e.g., pillows, mat).
- Make a shape (e.g., square, circle) with chalk or yarn on the floor or ground beside the structure into which the child can jump.
- Present different objects such as a sturdy box or a large building block from which the child can jump.

Instructional Sequence

- Model jumping from a structure or have a peer demonstrate.
- If the child does not readily jump, verbally prompt the child to jump ("You do it"). Provide specific instructions to the child ("Bend your knees," "Lift up from your toes").
- Physically prompt the child by holding both hands while the child jumps. Reduce assistance as the child gains skill.

TEACHING CONSIDERATIONS

1. If the child has a motor impairment or abnormal muscle tone, consult a physical therapist about the appropriateness of this skill and about related programming issues.
2. If the child has a visual impairment, increase the intensity and variety of environmental support and cues. Allow tactile exploration of the structure. Provide the child with verbal and other auditory cues. Be aware that the child may be fearful of moving about freely.
3. If the child has a severe visual impairment, pair your verbal encouragement with gentle physical prompting as the child jumps from a low structure. The child may need to reach out to where a sound came from (you) before moving out into space and jumping independently from a low structure.

GM D

4. If the child has a hearing impairment, increase the intensity and variety of cues (e.g., louder verbal cues, exaggerated facial expressions and gestures). Make the structure visually appealing (e.g., bright colors).
5. Ensure that the structure is sturdy and stable; remain near the child.
6. Avoid slippery surfaces and shoes or socks that do not have adequate traction.
7. Consider safety as the child jumps. Never leave the child unattended in potentially hazardous situations.

GOAL 2   Pedals and steers tricycle

DEVELOPMENTAL PROGRAMMING STEPS

PS2.0a   When sitting on a tricycle with feet on the pedals, the child pedals the tricycle forward.

PS2.0b   When sitting on a tricycle with feet on the pedals, the child pedals the tricycle backward.

IMPORTANCE OF SKILL

Pedaling and steering a tricycle are important for the development of balance and coordination and for play and recreation. Sitting upright and remaining on the seat of the tricycle develop balance. Coordination is enhanced through the reciprocal motion of pedaling, steering (eye–hand coordination), and simultaneous pedaling and steering. Pedaling and steering a tricycle provide amusement, active play, and transportation, as well as some skills necessary for riding a bicycle.

PRECEDING OBJECTIVE

GM D:2.1   Pushes riding toy with feet while steering

CONCURRENT GOALS AND OBJECTIVES

Cog D:1.0   Imitates motor action that is not commonly used
Cog E:3.0   Navigates large object around barriers
Cog E:4.0   Solves common problems
Cog G:1.2   Uses functionally appropriate actions with objects
SC D:3.3   Uses three-word action–object–location utterances
Soc C:2.1   Initiates communication with peer

TEACHING SUGGESTIONS
Activity-Based

- When playing outdoors, encourage the child to pedal and steer a tricycle.
- Allow the child to pedal and steer a tricycle when going for a walk.
- Take the tricycle to a playground or park and encourage the child to ride and steer the tricycle.
- Encourage the child to ride and steer the tricycle up and down a path, driveway, or sidewalk.

- Use the tricycle as transportation when traveling reasonable distances.
- Take a "trike hike" in the neighborhood. Allow the child to choose the direction to go.
- Encourage the child to play "Follow the leader" or "Copycat" with a few peers while riding tricycles. Allow the child and peers to take turns being the leader.
- Play a game with the child and a few peers and pretend that the tricycles are cars. Create a gas pump (i.e., use a box and garden hose) where the "cars" can fill up with gas.

Environmental Arrangements

- Begin on a very slight incline so that pedaling is assisted by gravity and the child can concentrate on steering.
- Place a few obstacles in a configuration and encourage the child to pedal and steer the tricycle in and out and around the obstacles. Use cones, large blocks, or boxes to make a circle, triangle, or square.
- Decorate the tricycle with streamers, crepe paper, and balloons. Attach a bell or horn to the tricycle. Encourage the child to pedal and steer the decorated tricycle with peers in a parade through the neighborhood, playground, or park.
- Begin by having the child pedal and steer the tricycle short distances. Gradually increase the distance as the child becomes more proficient.

Instructional Sequence

- Have a peer model riding a tricycle.
- Provide verbal instructions (e.g., "Push the pedals with your feet").
- To initially get the child moving, push the pedal for the child.
- Push the tricycle or pull it with a rope while the child has his or her feet on the pedals and hands on the handlebars.

TEACHING CONSIDERATIONS

1. If the child has a motor impairment or abnormal muscle tone, consult a physical therapist about the appropriateness of this skill and about related programming issues.
2. If the child has a visual impairment, increase the intensity and variety of environmental support and cues (e.g., horn on tricycle, bright colors, larger seat). Allow tactile exploration of the tricycle.
3. If the child has a severe visual impairment, place the child on the tricycle as you hold the child's hands on the handlebars and gently pull the tricycle forward. Then hold the child's waist and encourage the child to pedal. Continue verbal and physical prompting until the child develops steady balance and a sense of direction on the tricycle.
4. If the child has a hearing impairment, increase the intensity and variety of cues (e.g., louder verbal cues, colorful attachments to tricycle, exaggerated facial expressions and gestures).
5. A tricycle that is low to the ground is easier to pedal. Attach blocks to the pedals for a child who cannot reach the pedals. Strap the child's feet to the pedals to assist the child.
6. Use an adaptive tricycle (e.g., pedal with hands or arms) with a child who has limited use of the legs.
7. Teach this skill in a wide-open space.

GM D

8. Consider safety as the child moves about the environment and handles objects. Never leave the child unattended on the riding toy.

Objective 2.1   Pushes riding toy with feet while steering

DEVELOPMENTAL PROGRAMMING STEPS

PS2.1a   When sitting on a riding toy with his or her feet on a surface, the child pushes forward with feet.

PS2.1b   When sitting on a riding toy with his or her feet on a surface, the child pushes backward with feet.

IMPORTANCE OF SKILL

This skill promotes eye–hand coordination through steering and prepares the child for pedaling a tricycle. The coordination necessary for pedaling is not fully developed, but similar skills are practiced as the child pushes the riding toy along with his or her feet. Balance develops as the child sits upright and remains seated without support. The child also attains new coordination skills through pushing with feet and steering at the same time.

PRECEDING OBJECTIVE

GM D:2.2   Sits on riding toy or in wagon while adult pushes

CONCURRENT GOALS AND OBJECTIVE

Cog E:3.0   Navigates large object around barriers
Cog E:4.0   Solves common problems
Cog G:1.2   Uses functionally appropriate actions with objects

TEACHING SUGGESTIONS
Activity-Based

- When playing outdoors, encourage the child to sit on a riding toy and push with his or her feet while steering. Take the riding toy to a playground or park with the child.
- When on a walk, allow the child to ride the riding toy.
- Encourage the child to ride the riding toy up and down a path, driveway, or sidewalk.
- Use the riding toy as transportation when traveling reasonable distances.
- Encourage the child in imaginary play with the riding toy (e.g., play race car driver, cowgirl, police).
- Use a variety of riding toys (e.g., tricycle, tyke bike, Big Wheel, stick horse).

Environmental Arrangements

- Make a road with tape or blocks on the ground for the riding toy to follow.
- Place a few obstacles in a configuration and encourage the child to steer the riding toy in and out and around the obstacles. For example, use cones, large blocks, or boxes to make a circle, triangle, or square.

- Begin by having the child ride short distances. Gradually increase the distance as the child becomes more proficient at pushing with his or her feet while steering.
- Give the child a favorite doll or stuffed animal to take for a ride.

Instructional Sequence

- Have a peer model pushing a riding toy with his or her feet while steering.
- Provide verbal instructions (e.g., "Turn the handle bar," "Push with your feet").
- Physically assist the child by pushing the toy while the child steers.

TEACHING CONSIDERATIONS

1. If the child has a motor impairment or abnormal muscle tone, consult a physical therapist about the appropriateness of this skill and about related programming issues.
2. If the child has a visual impairment, increase the intensity and variety of environmental support and cues (e.g., horn on riding toy, verbal cues, colorful tape on handlebars). Allow tactile exploration of the riding toy.
3. If the child has a severe visual impairment, steer the riding toy as you hold the child's hands on the handlebars. Encourage the child to push the toy with his or her feet. Physically help the child establish balance and direction on the toy as you verbally encourage the child.
4. If the child has a hearing impairment, increase the intensity and variety of cues (e.g., louder verbal cues, bright colors, exaggerated facial expressions and gestures).
5. Teach this skill in a wide-open space.
6. Consider safety as the child moves about the environment. Never leave the child unattended on the riding toy.

GM D

Objective 2.2   Sits on riding toy or in wagon while adult pushes

---

DEVELOPMENTAL PROGRAMMING STEPS

☑ The objective above is the most basic step for the goal, "pedals and steers a tricycle," to be taught. Most children will benefit from the activities outlined here that emphasize this skill. For children who need more instruction, consider designing programming steps from the *environmental arrangements* or from the *instructional sequence* outlined.

IMPORTANCE OF SKILL

This skill promotes social exchange between the child and adult through play as the adult pushes the child. It aids in the development of balance as the child sits upright and maintains this position while moving. This position allows the child a new perspective on the environment.

PRECEDING GOAL

GM B:1.0   Assumes balanced sitting position

CONCURRENT OBJECTIVES

GM B:1.3   Regains balanced, upright sitting position after *leaning* to the left, to the right, and forward
GM B:2.1   Sits down in chair
Cog C:2.1   Indicates desire to continue familiar game and/or action
SC B:1.1   Responds with a vocalization and gesture to simple questions
Soc A:3.1   Initiates communication with familiar adult

TEACHING SUGGESTIONS
Activity-Based

- Push the child on a riding toy when playing outdoors.
- Go for a walk and pull the child in a wagon.
- Push the child on a riding toy at the playground or park.
- Play a game with the child and pretend that the riding toy is some other vehicle (e.g., train, boat, truck). Take an imaginary trip (e.g., pretend the riding toy is a train and go visit Grandma).
- Ask the child to indicate (verbally or by pointing) which direction to go.

Environmental Arrangements

- Make a road with tape or blocks on the ground for the riding toy to follow.
- Place a peer in the wagon with the child.
- Give the child a favorite doll or stuffed animal to take for a ride.
- Pull the child from room to room in the laundry basket.
- Use a variety of riding toys (e.g., tyke bike, tricycle, Big Wheel, wagon).
- Have the child ride in a grocery cart when grocery shopping.

Instructional Sequence

- Have a peer model sitting on a riding toy or in a wagon.
- Verbally prompt the child to sit on a riding toy ("Come sit on your bike"). Provide specific instructions to the child, if necessary ("Put your hands on the bar").
- Provide a physical prompt by holding the child on the riding toy (i.e., place a hand on the child's back and guide the child's hands to the handle bar).

TEACHING CONSIDERATIONS

1. If the child has a motor impairment or abnormal muscle tone, consult a physical therapist about the appropriateness of this skill and about related programming issues. This skill is basic to using adaptive means of locomotion (e.g., wheelchair).
2. If the child has a visual impairment, increase the intensity and variety of environmental support and cues (e.g., noisemaker on riding toy, verbal cues). Allow tactile exploration of the tricycle, riding toys, wagon.
3. Verbally encourage the child with a severe visual impairment and do not startle the child with quick, jerky movements.
4. If the child has a hearing impairment, increase the intensity and variety of cues (e.g., louder verbal cues, colorful riding toy).
5. Use a seat belt or padding (e.g., towels, blanket) to support the child in a wagon.
6. Teach this skill in a wide-open space.
7. Consider safety as the child moves about the environment. Never leave the child unattended on a riding toy or wagon.

GOAL 3   Runs avoiding obstacles

DEVELOPMENTAL PROGRAMMING STEPS

PS3.0a   The child turns a corner when running.
PS3.0b   The child stops and starts again when running.

IMPORTANCE OF SKILL

Running and avoiding obstacles helps develop balance and coordination as the child remains upright while running around obstacles and changing directions and speeds. This skill is important for its play value and for developing self-awareness. The child experiences freedom of motion and learns about moving through space and about the relationship of his or her body to obstacles in the environment. This skill increases the safety of the child during play.

PRECEDING OBJECTIVE

GM D:3.1   Runs

CONCURRENT GOALS AND OBJECTIVES

GM D:4.2   Kicks ball or similar object
Cog E:3.2   Moves around barrier to change location
Cog E:4.0   Solves common problems
SC C:2.1   Carries out two-step direction *with* contextual cues
SC D:2.3   Uses two-word utterances to express location
Soc A:2.0   Initiates and maintains interaction with familiar adult
Soc C:1.1   Initiates social behavior toward peer

TEACHING SUGGESTIONS

Activity-Based

- When on a walk, encourage the child to run around trees, rocks, and shrubs.
- Encourage the child to run around the play equipment, trees, or other obstacles at the playground or park.
- Play a game of "Follow the leader." Begin by having the adult lead the child around obstacles in the environment (e.g., between two trees, around a tricycle, around a bench). Then allow the child to be the leader.
- Encourage the child to play soccer or other games in which peers must be avoided while running.
- Organize a game of tag in a setting where children must run around obstacles (e.g., trees, large rocks, peers).

Environmental Arrangements

- Create an obstacle course using boxes, baskets, large toys, pillows, or other obstacles. Require the child to run by and around the obstacles. To assist the child, place tape or a chalk line on the ground for the child to follow.

- Play a game of tag with the child and a few peers. Encourage the child to run by and around peers and other obstacles in the environment (e.g., trees, benches, playground equipment, tricycles).
- Place a favorite toy a short distance in front of the child in an area that has obstacles (e.g., trees, rocks, people). Encourage the child to run, avoiding obstacles, to obtain the toy. As the child becomes more proficient, increase the distance between the child and the toy.

Instructional Sequence

- Model running around obstacles in the environment.
- Verbally encourage the child to follow you as you run around obstacles.
- Have the child walk quickly or run slowly. As the child becomes more proficient at avoiding obstacles while running, have the child run faster.
- Begin by having the child run short distances. Gradually increase the distance as the child is able to avoid obstacles while running.
- Introduce a few large obstacles that are far apart. Gradually increase the number of obstacles, decrease the distance between the obstacles, or reduce the size of the obstacles.
- Physically prompt the child by holding one hand or by leading the child with a rope, scarf, or other object the child holds.

TEACHING CONSIDERATIONS

1. If the child has a motor impairment or abnormal muscle tone, consult a physical therapist about the appropriateness of this skill and about related programming issues.
2. If the child has a visual impairment, increase the intensity and variety of environmental support and cues (e.g., verbal cues, tactile cues, bells attached to child). Initially lead the child through the environment and around obstacles. Be aware that the child may be fearful of moving about freely.
3. If the child has a severe visual impairment, hold the child's hand as you run. Verbally encourage the child and tell the child of the obstacles you are avoiding.
4. If the child has a hearing impairment, increase the intensity and variety of cues (e.g., exaggerated movements, arrows on the ground, louder verbal cues).
5. Practice this skill in a wide-open space.
6. Avoid slippery surfaces and shoes or socks that do not have adequate traction.
7. Be aware that the child may tire easily.
8. Consider safety as the child runs about the environment. Never leave the child unattended in potentially hazardous situations.

Objective 3.1   Runs

IMPORTANCE OF SKILL

Running is important for building coordination and for recreation and safety. The alternating action of the arms and legs becomes coordinated through running. Besides the pleasure of running, many later recreational activities utilize this skill. Running also

GM D

provides the child a sense of independence and a quick means of escape in times of danger.

PRECEDING OBJECTIVE

GM D:3.2   Walks fast

CONCURRENT GOAL AND OBJECTIVES

GM D:4.2   Kicks ball or similar object
SC C:2.3   Carries out one-step direction *with* contextual cues
SC D:2.4   Uses two-word utterances to describe objects, people, and/or events
Soc A:2.0   Initiates and maintains interaction with familiar adult

TEACHING SUGGESTIONS
Activity-Based

- Play games that require running (e.g., tag, T-ball, "Duck, duck, goose," "Red Rover").
- Encourage the child to run when playing outdoors (in the yard, on a walk, at the playground or park).
- Play a game of chase with the child ("You can't get me," or "I'm going to get you").
- When on a walk, stay slightly ahead of the child and encourage the child to catch up by running.
- Play a game and run like different animals (run fast like a horse, sway like an elephant). Make the sounds the animals make.
- With your arms open, encourage the child to run to you; then pick up and hug the child.

Environmental Arrangements

- Throw a ball or other object in front of the child and encourage the child to run after it.
- Place a favorite toy on the ground a short distance in front of the child. Encourage the child to run to get it. As the child becomes more proficient at running, increase the distance between the toy and the child.
- Give the child a pull-toy or a push-toy to use while running.
- Make a line on the ground with tape or chalk for the child to follow while running.
- Begin by having the child run short distances. Gradually increase the distance as the child becomes more proficient at running.

Instructional Sequence

- Model running or have a peer run at the playground or park.
- Verbally encourage the child to run to the play equipment at the playground.
- Have the child walk quickly or run slowly. As the child becomes more proficient at running, have the child run faster.
- Physically prompt the child by holding one hand or by leading the child with a rope, scarf, or other object the child holds.

TEACHING CONSIDERATIONS

1. If the child has a motor impairment or abnormal muscle tone, consult a physical therapist about the appropriateness of this skill and about related programming issues.

GM D

2. If the child has a visual impairment, increase the intensity and variety of environmental support and cues (e.g., verbal cues, tactile cues, bells attached to child). Initially lead the child through the environment and around obstacles. Be aware that the child may be fearful of moving about freely.

3. If the child has a severe visual impairment, hold the child's hand as you run. Pair verbal encouragement with your support and withdraw support as the child gains confidence that he or she will not run into an obstacle. Encourage the child to run to you.

4. If the child has a hearing impairment, increase the intensity and variety of cues (e.g., exaggerated movements, arrows on the ground, louder verbal cues).

5. Practice this skill in a wide-open space.

6. Avoid slippery surfaces and shoes or socks that do not have adequate traction.

7. Be aware that the child may tire easily.

8. Consider safety as the child runs about the environment. Never leave the child unattended in potentially hazardous situations.

Objective 3.2   Walks fast

IMPORTANCE OF SKILL

Walking fast fosters coordination through the motor actions of the arms and legs while the child maintains balance at increased speeds. Walking fast is active play to the child. While finding amusement in walking fast, the child also learns what the body can do and how it moves.

PRECEDING OBJECTIVE

GM C:1.1   Walks without support

CONCURRENT GOALS AND OBJECTIVES

GM D:4.2   Kicks ball or similar object
Cog B:2.1   Locates object and/or person who hides while child is watching
Cog E:3.0   Navigates large object around barriers
SC D:1.1   Uses five descriptive words
Soc A:2.0   Initiates and maintains interaction with familiar adult

TEACHING SUGGESTIONS
Activity-Based

- Play games such as "Red light, green light" to encourage fast walking.
- Encourage the child to walk fast when playing outdoors (in the yard, on a walk, at the playground or park) or when you are in a hurry.

- When on a walk, stay slightly ahead of the child and encourage the child to catch up by walking fast.
- Alternate walking slowly and walking fast.
- Play a game of chase with the child ("You can't get me," or "I'm going to get you"). Allow the child both to be chased and to chase.
- Encourage the child to walk fast toward you.

Environmental Arrangements

- Throw a ball or other object in front of the child and encourage the child to go after it.
- To provide some support, offer the child a push-toy such as a doll stroller, toy shopping cart, wheelbarrow, or lawn mower. Have the child hold onto the toy and push it fast.
- Play "Follow the leader" or "Simon says" with the child and walk fast.
- Walk fast to special events and encourage the child to follow.

Instructional Sequence

- Model walking fast for the child or have another child demonstrate.
- Verbally direct the child to walk fast to "catch" you.
- Have the child walk at a moderate pace. As the child becomes more proficient, have the child walk fast.
- Begin by requiring the child to walk fast for short distances. Gradually increase the distance as the child becomes more proficient at walking fast.
- Physically prompt the child by holding one hand or by gently prodding the child from behind.

TEACHING CONSIDERATIONS

1. If the child has a motor impairment or abnormal muscle tone, consult a physical therapist about the appropriateness of this skill and about related programming issues.
2. If the child has a visual impairment, increase the intensity and variety of environmental support and cues (e.g., verbal cues, tactile cues, bells attached to child). Initially lead the child through the environment or around obstacles. Be aware that the child may be fearful of moving about freely.
3. If the child has a severe visual impairment, hold the child's hand as you walk fast. Pair verbal encouragement with your support and withdraw support as the child gains steady balance and confidence that he or she will not run into an obstacle. Encourage the child to walk fast to you.
4. If the child has a hearing impairment, increase the intensity and variety of cues (e.g., exaggerated movements, arrows on the ground, louder verbal cues).
5. Practice this skill in a wide-open space, preferably outside.
6. Avoid slippery surfaces and shoes or socks that do not have adequate traction.
7. Be aware that the child may tire easily.
8. Consider safety as the child walks about the environment and handles objects. Never leave the child unattended with potentially hazardous objects.

GM D

GOAL 4   Catches, kicks, throws, and rolls ball or similar object

DEVELOPMENTAL PROGRAMMING STEPS

In order to achieve this goal, a child must perform the skills for Objectives 4.1–4.4 to criteria. Refer to the specific objectives for developmental programming steps to develop each skill.

IMPORTANCE OF SKILL

These ball playing skills are important for enhancing strength, coordination, and balance; for creating chances for social interactions; and for providing recreational opportunities. The skills can be combined to allow the child to participate in ball games with other children.

PRECEDING OBJECTIVES

FM A:5.1   Releases hand-held object onto and/or into a larger target with either hand
GM C:1.1   Walks without support

CONCURRENT GOALS AND OBJECTIVES

GM D:3.0   Runs avoiding obstacles
Cog C:2.0   Reproduces part of interactive game and/or action in order to continue game and/or action
Cog D:1.0   Imitates motor action that is not commonly used
Cog E:3.1   Moves barrier or goes around barrier to obtain object
Cog G:1.2   Uses functionally appropriate actions with objects
SC C:2.1   Carries out two-step direction *with* contextual cues
SC D:3.0   Uses three-word utterances
Soc A:2.0   Initiates and maintains interaction with familiar adult
Soc A:3.0   Initiates and maintains communicative exchange with familiar adult
Soc C:1.0   Initiates and maintains interaction with peer
Soc C:2.0   Initiates and maintains communicative exchange with peer

TEACHING SUGGESTIONS

In order to achieve this goal, a child must perform the skills for Objectives 4.1–4.4 to criteria. Refer to the specific objective for teaching suggestions and teaching considerations to develop each skill.

Objective 4.1   Catches ball or similar object

DEVELOPMENTAL PROGRAMMING STEP

PS4.1a   When a large object is tossed to the child, he or she stretches out two arms in front.

IMPORTANCE OF SKILL

This skill is an avenue for social interactions with peers. Catching a ball is necessary for many leisure activities (e.g., basketball, baseball) and helps develop eye–hand coordination.

PRECEDING OBJECTIVE

Cog E:1.2   Retains object

CONCURRENT GOALS AND OBJECTIVES

GM C:2.0   Stoops and regains balanced standing position without support
GM D:3.1   Runs
GM D:4.2   Kicks ball or similar object
Cog C:2.0   Reproduces part of interactive game and/or action in order to continue game and/or action
Cog D:1.0   Imitates motor action that is not commonly used
SC C:2.1   Carries out two-step direction *with* contextual cues
SC D:2.4   Uses two-word utterances to describe objects, people, and/or events
SC D:3.4   Uses three-word agent–action–object utterances
Soc A:3.1   Initiates communication with familiar adult
Soc C:2.1   Initiates communication with peer

TEACHING SUGGESTIONS

Activity-Based

- When playing with a ball inside or outside, encourage the child to catch the ball in midair as well as when it is rolled.
- Toss and catch balloons. (Use caution when playing with balloons.)
- Play a game of catch in which the child and adult take turns throwing and catching the ball.
- When playing outside, throw the ball against a wall (e.g., the side of a house or garage). Encourage the child to catch the ball as it bounces back. Bounce the ball toward the child and encourage the child to catch it.

Environmental Arrangements

- Use a variety of balls or similar objects that can be caught (e.g., Nerf balls, beach balls, Koosh balls, soft blocks, small stuffed animals, balls of yarn).
- Have the child sit on the couch and catch pillows as you toss them.
- Use helium-filled balloons with weights attached (e.g., pieces of candy); these move slowly and are colorful and fun to play with. (Use caution when playing with balloons.)
- Assist the child and a few peers to stand in a circle. Encourage the child to throw and catch the ball with peers.
- Allow the child to sit in a stable position before throwing the ball.
- Begin by using a ball that can easily be caught (e.g., a larger and lighter ball). Use a smaller and heavier ball as the child becomes more proficient.

Instructional Sequence

- Model catching a ball or have peers demonstrate.
- Verbally direct the child to catch the ball as you throw; tell him or her to "hold arms out."
- Initially have the child stand a short distance from the person throwing the ball. Gradually increase the distance as the child becomes proficient.
- Physically prompt the child by standing behind the child and guiding the child's hands or arms.

TEACHING CONSIDERATIONS

1. If the child has a motor impairment or abnormal muscle tone, consult a physical therapist about the appropriateness of this skill and about related programming issues.
2. If the child has a visual impairment, increase the intensity and variety of environmental support and cues (e.g., large balls, bells in ball, textured objects). Use balls or objects that can be easily grasped (e.g., clutch ball, beach ball, soft blocks). Allow tactile exploration of the ball or object.
3. If the child has a severe visual impairment, use verbal encouragement and large, soft balls or objects with bells. Help the child learn to be "ready" to catch the large object.
4. If the child has a hearing impairment, increase the intensity and variety of cues (e.g., bright-colored or textured ball, louder verbal cues, exaggerated motions).
5. Practice this skill in a wide-open space.
6. Supervise ball play carefully.
7. Consider safety with all objects that the child handles. Never leave the child unattended with potentially hazardous objects.

Objective 4.2   Kicks ball or similar object

DEVELOPMENTAL PROGRAMMING STEPS

PS4.2a   Kicks a ball or similar object while holding onto support (e.g., adult's leg, wall, railing).

PS4.2b   When an object is in front of the child's feet, the child walks into the object and moves object forward.

IMPORTANCE OF SKILL

Kicking a ball develops leg muscles and balance, coordination, and strength. The child gains balance and strength by lifting and moving the leg forward to strike the ball. For a few seconds, the child balances on one foot. Eye–foot coordination is also enhanced by kicking. The child learns additional cause-and-effect relationships as the child discovers a new way to move the ball forward. Some recreational activities require kicking (e.g., soccer) and kicking objects can be a functional means of moving objects from one location to another.

PRECEDING OBJECTIVE

GM C:1.1   Walks without support

CONCURRENT GOALS AND OBJECTIVES

GM C:2.0   Stoops and regains balanced standing position without support
GM D:3.1   Runs
GM D:4.1   Catches ball or similar object
Cog D:1.0   Imitates motor action that is not commonly used
Cog E:3.1   Moves barrier or goes around barrier to obtain object
SC C:2.3   Carries out one-step direction *with* contextual cues
SC D:3.3   Uses three-word action–object–location utterances
Soc A:2.0   Initiates and maintains interaction with familiar adult
Soc C:1.0   Initiates and maintains interaction with peer

TEACHING SUGGESTIONS

Activity-Based

- Play games such as kick ball and soccer that require kicking.
- When playing with a ball inside or outside, place the ball on the floor or ground and encourage the child to kick it.
- Kick the ball back and forth between the child and adult.
- Encourage the child to kick the ball up and down an incline (e.g., hill, driveway).

Environmental Arrangements

- Use a variety of balls or similar objects that can be kicked (e.g., Nerf ball, beach ball, gym ball, soft blocks).
- Line up or stack objects that can be knocked down when the ball is kicked. For example, line up cans or stack blocks on the ground.
- Place an object on the ground and encourage the child to kick the ball so that the ball goes over the object. It may be necessary to demonstrate for the child.
- Turn a basket or a box on its side and encourage the child to kick the ball into it.
- Make a goal using two cones, large blocks, or boxes placed a short distance apart. Encourage the child and a few peers to kick the ball between the two objects.
- Kick heavy balloons and watch the result! (Use caution when playing with balloons.)

Instructional Sequence

- Model kicking a ball or have peers demonstrate.
- Verbally direct the child to kick the ball to you.
- Begin by using a ball that can easily be kicked by the child (e.g., a larger and lighter ball). Use a smaller and heavier ball as the child becomes more proficient.
- Initially have the child kick the ball a short distance. Gradually increase the distance as the child becomes more proficient.
- Initially allow the child to use some support when kicking. For example, the child holds onto your arm, a railing, the wall, or some other stable object with one hand while kicking.

GM D

TEACHING CONSIDERATIONS

1. If the child has a motor impairment or abnormal muscle tone, consult a physical therapist about the appropriateness of this skill and about related programming issues.
2. If the child has a visual impairment, increase the intensity and variety of environmental support and cues (e.g., large or bright-colored ball, noise-producing ball). Assist the child to feel where the ball or object is located on the ground; allow tactile exploration of it.
3. If the child has a severe visual impairment, use verbal encouragement and minimal physical assistance to help the child kick the ball. Gradually reduce the physical assistance as the child becomes oriented to the ball's placement.
4. If the child has a hearing impairment, increase the intensity and variety of cues (e.g., bright-colored ball, louder verbal cues, exaggerated motions).
5. Practice this skill in a wide-open space.
6. Avoid slippery surfaces and shoes or socks that do not have adequate traction.
7. Make sure the ball stays still on the floor or ground. It is easier for the child to kick the ball when it is not moving.
8. Supervise ball play carefully.
9. Consider safety with all objects that the child handles. Never leave the child unattended with potentially hazardous objects.

Objective 4.3   Throws ball or similar object at target

DEVELOPMENTAL PROGRAMMING STEPS

PS4.3a   The child throws an object forward with one or two hands.
PS4.3b   The child flings an object with one hand.

IMPORTANCE OF SKILL

Lifting up the arm and moving the arm and object through space develops arm strength, eye–hand coordination, and cause-and-effect relationships. This skill is also important for its social and recreational value. The child enjoys social interactions when playing ball with a peer or adult. Throwing a ball is a basic skill in some recreational activities (e.g., baseball, basketball). Similar movements are required in such adult skills as hammering nails.

PRECEDING OBJECTIVES

GM D:4.4   Rolls ball at target
Cog E:1.2   Retains object

CONCURRENT GOALS AND OBJECTIVES

FM A:3.3   Grasps hand-size object with either hand using whole hand
GM C:1.1   Walks without support
GM D:3.1   Runs

GM D:4.1   Catches ball or similar object
Cog B:2.1   Locates object and/or person who hides while child is watching
Cog D:1.0   Imitates motor action that is not commonly used
Cog E:3.1   Moves barrier or goes around barrier to obtain object
Cog G:1.2   Uses functionally appropriate actions with objects
SC C:2.3   Carries out one-step direction *with* contextual cues
SC D:2.5   Uses two-word utterances to express recurrence
SC D:3.3   Uses three-word action–object–location utterances
Soc A:2.0   Initiates and maintains interaction with familiar adult
Soc C:1.0   Initiates and maintains interaction with peer

TEACHING SUGGESTIONS
Activity-Based

- When folding laundry, roll up socks for the child to throw in the laundry basket.
- When playing outside, encourage the child to throw a ball against a wall (e.g., side of a house or garage) and retrieve the ball as it bounces back.
- Provide numerous opportunities for throwing balls, bean bags, or soft toys, such as playing catch, throwing at targets, or throwing into different containers.
- When playing with a ball inside or outside, throw the ball back and forth between the child and yourself.
- Choose a target such as a tree in the environment. Take turns throwing the ball at the target; keep a record of how many times each person hits the target.
- Play "Hot Potato," throwing a "hot" stuffed sock or Nerf ball to the child and a peer.

Environmental Arrangements

- Present different objects (e.g., box, laundry basket) into which the child throws the ball.
- Use a variety of balls or objects that can be thrown (e.g., ball of yarn, beanbag, Nerf ball, small stuffed animal, soft blocks).
- Attach a hoop (e.g., coat hanger, Nerf basketball hoop) onto the wall so that it is slightly lower than the child's height. Encourage the child to throw the ball through the hoop.
- Place a large target such as a circle or square on the wall or ground (use chalk or masking tape). Encourage the child to hit the target with the ball.
- Line up or stack objects that can be knocked down when the ball is thrown. For example, place cans along a low wall or stack blocks on the ground.

Instructional Sequence

- Model throwing a ball or similar object at a target; have a peer demonstrate.
- Verbally direct the child to throw a ball at a target.
- Begin by using a ball that can be easily thrown by the child (e.g., a large and light ball). Use a smaller and heavier ball as the child becomes more proficient.
- Begin by having the child throw the ball close to the target. Gradually increase the distance between the child and the target as the child becomes more proficient.
- Offer minimal physical assistance to the child by holding the child's hands and throwing the ball together.

GM D

TEACHING CONSIDERATIONS

1. If the child has a motor impairment or abnormal muscle tone, consult a physical therapist about the appropriateness of this skill and about related programming issues.
2. If the child has a visual impairment, increase the intensity and variety of environmental support and cues (e.g., bright-colored ball, ball with bells inside, contrasting target). Use balls or objects that can be easily grasped (e.g., clutch ball, Koosh ball, soft blocks). Allow tactile exploration of the ball or object.
3. If the child has a severe visual impairment, pair verbal encouragement with physical assistance to throw a ball at a target. Use a target that makes a sound when the ball or object hits. For example, throw a ping-pong ball in a basket of many ping-pong balls. Throw a rock in a pond or river. Withdraw the physical assistance as the child orients to the target. Offer verbal encouragement when the target is hit!
4. If the child has a hearing impairment, increase the intensity and variety of cues (e.g., bright-colored or textured ball, louder verbal cues, contrasting target).
5. Practice this skill in a wide-open space.
6. Supervise ball play carefully.
7. Consider safety with all objects that the child handles. Never leave the child unattended with potentially hazardous objects.

Objective 4.4   Rolls ball at target

DEVELOPMENTAL PROGRAMMING STEPS

PS4.4a   The child rolls a ball.
PS4.4b   The child moves a ball forward (e.g., bats it, kicks it).

IMPORTANCE OF SKILL

The development of arm and hand muscles, eye–hand coordination, and cause-and-effect relationships is enhanced when the child rolls a ball. This skill provides the child a means for social interactions with peers and adults through rolling a ball back and forth. Rolling a ball is a skill component of some recreational activities (e.g., kicking a ball, bowling).

PRECEDING OBJECTIVE

FM A:5.2   Releases hand-held object with each hand

CONCURRENT GOALS AND OBJECTIVES

FM A:3.3   Grasps hand-size object with either hand using whole hand
GM C:2.0   Stoops and regains balanced standing position without support
GM D:4.1   Catches ball or similar object
Cog G:1.2   Uses functionally appropriate actions with objects
SC D:2.1   Uses two-word utterances to express agent–action, action–object, and agent–object
Soc A:2.0   Initiates and maintains interaction with familiar adult
Soc C:1.0   Initiates and maintains interaction with peer

TEACHING SUGGESTIONS
Activity-Based

- When playing with a ball inside or outside, roll the ball back and forth between the child and the adult.
- Take the ball to the playground or park and roll the ball on the grass, on the cement, or up and down the slide.
- Have the child and peers sit in a large circle. Spread the children's feet and make a star by placing their feet together (adjacent feet touch). Encourge the child to roll the ball back and forth to peers, keeping the ball within the star.
- Encourage the child to roll the ball up and down an incline (e.g., hill, driveway).
- Sit facing the child with your and the child's feet touching and your legs several inches apart. Roll the ball between you and the child, keeping it between your extended legs.

Environmental Arrangements

- Set up bowling pins (e.g., milk cartons, soda cans). Encourage the child to roll the ball to knock down the pins.
- Line up several chairs, one in front of another, so that the child rolls the ball through the legs of the chairs.
- Build roads and tunnels with blocks so that the child rolls the ball on the road and through the tunnels.
- Present an object (e.g., laundry basket or box on its side) into which the child rolls the ball.
- Use a variety of balls or objects that can be rolled, such as a ball of yarn, a gym ball, and a Nerf ball.

Instructional Sequence

- Model rolling the ball for the child or have peers demonstrate the action.
- Verbally direct the child to roll a ball at a target.
- Begin by using a ball that can be easily rolled by the child (e.g., large and light ball). Use a smaller and heavier ball as the child becomes more proficient.
- Initially have the child roll the ball a short distance from the target. Gradually increase the distance between the child and the target as the child becomes more proficient at rolling a ball at a target.
- Offer minimal physical assistance to the child by holding the child's hands and rolling the ball together.

TEACHING CONSIDERATIONS

1. If the child has a motor impairment or abnormal muscle tone, consult a physical therapist about the appropriateness of this skill and about related programming issues.
2. If the child has a visual impairment, increase the intensity and variety of environmental support and cues (e.g., bright-colored ball, ball with bells inside, contrasting target). Use balls or objects that can be easily grasped (e.g., clutch ball, Koosh ball, soft blocks). Allow tactile exploration of the ball or object.
3. If the child has a severe visual impairment, pair verbal encouragement with physical assistance to roll a ball at a target. Use another person as the target and have the

person give an audible response as the ball hits the target. Withdraw the physical assistance as the child becomes oriented to the target.
4. If the child has a hearing impairment, increase the intensity and variety of cues (e.g., bright-colored or textured ball, louder verbal cues, contrasting target).
5. Practice this skill in a wide-open space.
6. Supervise ball play carefully.
7. Consider safety with all objects that the child handles. Never leave the child unattended with potentially hazardous objects.

GOAL 5 Climbs up and down play equipment

DEVELOPMENTAL PROGRAMMING STEPS

PS5.0a   The child climbs up ladders.
PS5.0b   The child climbs down from adult-size furniture (e.g., chair, couch, bed).
PS5.0c   The child climbs onto adult-size furniture (e.g., chair, couch, bed).

IMPORTANCE OF SKILL

Climbing up and down play equipment is important for its play value and is a functional skill. The skill is fun for the child. The child develops self-awareness of how to move and control the body through space while interacting with objects and exploring the environment. Strength, balance, and coordination are developed as the child uses reciprocal motor actions in new ways to climb up and down play equipment.

PRECEDING OBJECTIVE

GM D:5.1   Moves up and down inclines

CONCURRENT GOALS AND OBJECTIVES

GM D:1.2   Jumps from low structure
Cog E:3.2   Moves around barrier to change location
Cog E:4.0   Solves common problems
SC D:1.2   Uses five action words
SC D:2.1   Uses two-word utterances to express agent–action, action–object, and agent–object
Soc C:1.0   Initiates and maintains interaction with peer

TEACHING SUGGESTIONS
Activity-Based

- Provide opportunities and equipment for climbing (e.g., structures, ladders, slides, furniture, stairs).
- When encountering ladders in the environment (e.g., stepladder, bunk-bed ladder, slide ladder), encourage the child to climb up and down.
- At the playground or park, encourage the child to climb up and down the play equipment (e.g., jungle gym, slide ladder, climbing bars).

- Play a game and pretend to be firefighters. Climb up and down a ladder to put out the "fire" in a house. Wear fire hats and use a hose and buckets as props.

Environmental Arrangements

- Use a variety of play equipment (e.g., jungle gym, ladders, climbing structures) of varying difficulty.
- Create an obstacle course in which there are a few obstacles for the child to climb up and down (e.g., stepladder, slide). Allow peers to participate with the child in the obstacle course; have the children take turns as the leader.
- To provide support in case of falls, place the climbing structure or slide in a sandbox.
- Begin with play equipment that is low to the ground. As the child becomes more proficient at climbing, use play equipment that requires the child to climb higher.

Instructional Sequence

- Model climbing up and down play equipment or have peers model.
- If the child does not readily climb up and down play equipment, verbally prompt the child ("You do it"). Provide specific instructions ("Put your hand on this bar," "Step up with this foot").
- Physically prompt the child by providing light support at the hips.

TEACHING CONSIDERATIONS

1. If the child has a motor impairment or abnormal muscle tone, consult a physical therapist about the appropriateness of this skill and about related programming issues.
2. If the child has a visual impairment, increase the intensity and variety of environmental support and cues (e.g., bright colors, large objects, verbal cues). Initially lead the child up and down the play equipment and allow tactile exploration of play equipment. Be aware that the child may be fearful of moving about freely.
3. If the child has a severe visual impairment, pair verbal encouragement with physical support to climb up and down play equipment. Withdraw physical support as the child gains confidence and becomes oriented to the equipment. Supervise carefully.
4. If the child has a hearing impairment, increase the intensity and variety of cues (e.g., exaggerated movements, louder verbal cues).
5. Ensure that the play equipment is sturdy and stable. Stay near and supervise carefully as the child climbs on play equipment.
6. Avoid slippery surfaces and shoes or socks that do not have adequate traction.
7. Consider safety with all climbing equipment. Never leave the child unattended when climbing.

Objective 5.1   Moves up and down inclines

DEVELOPMENTAL PROGRAMMING STEPS

PS5.1a   The child moves down inclines.
PS5.1b   The child moves up inclines.

GM D

IMPORTANCE OF SKILL

Moving up and down inclines is another means of discovering what the body can do and how to control the body movements necessary to accomplish the skill. Moving up and down inclines is also important in providing the child another way to play, explore, and interact with the environment.

PRECEDING OBJECTIVE

GM D:5.2   Moves under, over, and through obstacles

CONCURRENT OBJECTIVES

GM C:2.2   Pulls to standing position
GM C:3.2   Moves up and down stairs
GM D:4.4   Rolls ball at target
Cog E:3.2   Moves around barrier to change location
SC D:2.1   Uses two-word utterances to express agent–action, action–object, and agent–object
Soc A:3.1   Initiates communication with familiar adult

TEACHING SUGGESTIONS

Activity-Based

- Provide opportunities and materials for the child to go up and down inclines.
- When encountering inclines in the environment (e.g., ramps, slides), encourage the child to move up and down on them.
- At the playground or park, encourage the child to move up and down the slide.
- Engage in dramatic play (e.g., mountain climbing, hiking) and use ramps and slides.

Environmental Arrangements

- Make a ramp with a board and encourage the child to move up and down the ramp.
- Turn stairways into ramps by placing pillows on the steps; have the child slide down.
- Place a favorite toy at the top or bottom of the incline. Encourage the child to move up or down the incline to obtain the toy.
- Make a "train" on the slide by assisting the child and one or two peers to line up one after another. Have the children move together down the slide.
- Begin with inclines in which the grade is low. As the child becomes more proficient, use steeper inclines.

Instructional Sequence

- Model moving up and down an incline or have a peer model.
- If the child does not readily move up and down an incline, verbally prompt the child (e.g., say, "You do it"). Provide specific instructions to the child (e.g., say, "Get on your hands and knees") if necessary.
- Offer minimal physical assistance to the child by providing light support at the hips.

TEACHING CONSIDERATIONS

1. If the child has a motor impairment or abnormal muscle tone, consult a physical therapist about the appropriateness of this skill and about related programming issues.
2. If the child has a visual impairment, increase the intensity and variety of environmental support and cues (e.g., bright colors, tactile inclines, verbal cues). Initially lead the child up and down the incline and allow tactile exploration. Be aware that the child may be fearful of moving about freely.
3. If the child has a severe visual impairment, pair verbal encouragement with physical assistance to move up and down an incline. Gradually withdraw the physical assistance as the child becomes confident of the incline. Use your voice to help the child establish direction on the incline.
4. If the child has a hearing impairment, increase the intensity and variety of cues (e.g., exaggerated movements, louder verbal cues, tactile cues).
5. Ensure that the incline is sturdy and stable. Stay near to supervise as the child climbs up and down the incline.
6. Avoid slippery surfaces and shoes or socks that do not have adequate traction.
7. Consider safety whenever the child climbs. Never leave the child unattended when climbing.

GM D

Objective 5.2   Moves under, over, and through obstacles

DEVELOPMENTAL PROGRAMMING STEPS

PS 5.2a   The child moves over obstacles.
PS 5.2b   The child moves through obstacles.
PS 5.2c   The child moves under obstacles.

IMPORTANCE OF SKILL

Moving under, over, and through obstacles is active physical play that is both fun for the child and a good way to release energy. The child becomes aware of what the body can do, how the body moves, and what the relationship is between self and obstacles in the environment. This skill affords the child more mobility and independence in play.

PRECEDING GOAL

GM A:3.0   Creeps forward using alternating arm and leg movements

CONCURRENT OBJECTIVES

GM C:2.2   Pulls to standing position
GM D:1.2   Jumps from low structure
GM D:5.1   Moves up and down inclines
Cog E:3.2   Moves around barrier to change location
Cog E:4.1   Uses more than one strategy in attempt to solve common problem

SC C:2.3   Carries out one-step direction *with* contextual cues
SC D:1.2   Uses five action words
Soc A:3.2 Responds to communication from familiar adult

TEACHING SUGGESTIONS

Activity-Based

- Provide a variety of large toys and equipment (e.g., tunnel, cube chair, playhouse, slide, pillows, boxes).
- At the playground or park, use the playground equipment for the child to move under, over, and through obstacles. For example, have the child climb under and over jungle gym bars, crawl through and over a barrel, or move over a low platform.
- When playing in a sandbox, encourage the child to crawl in and out of the sandbox.
- Allow the child to move under dining and coffee tables and between and through chairs.

Environmental Arrangements

- Set up objects so that the child crawls through the objects (e.g., a line of chairs, a box with open ends).
- Present objects such as a sturdy box for the child to climb in and over.
- Hold up a rope or large stick and encourage the child to move under it.
- Place a favorite toy on the other side of an obstacle. Encourage the child to obtain the toy by moving over, under, or through the obstacle.
- Place a sheet over a card table to make a tent. Encourage the child to go in, move under, and move through.

Instructional Sequence

- Model or have peers model moving under, over, and through obstacles.
- If the child does not readily move under, over, and through obstacles, verbally direct the child (e.g., say, "You do it"). Provide specific instructions (e.g., say, "Duck your head," "Get on your hands and knees").
- Physically assist the child by holding his or her hand or providing light support at the hips.

TEACHING CONSIDERATIONS

1. If the child has a motor impairment or abnormal muscle tone, consult a physical therapist about the appropriateness of this skill and about related programming issues.
2. If the child has a visual impairment, increase the intensity and variety of environmental support and cues (e.g., contrasting objects, noise-producing objects, tactile cues). Initially lead the child over, under, and through obstacles, and allow tactile exploration of the obstacles. Be aware that the child may be fearful of moving about freely.
3. If the child has a severe visual impairment, pair verbal encouragement with physical assistance as the child moves around obstacles. Withdraw physical assistance as the child becomes confident about feeling his or her way around obstacles. Physically receive the child or provide a verbal reward when the child reaches a destination.

4. If the child has a hearing impairment, increase the intensity and variety of cues (e.g., exaggerated movements, louder verbal cues).
5. Ensure that the obstacles are sturdy and stable. Stay near to supervise as the child moves under, over, and through obstacles.
6. Avoid slippery surfaces and shoes or socks that do not have adequate traction.
7. Consider safety as the child moves through the environment. Never leave the child unattended with potentially hazardous objects.

GM D

ADAPTIVE DOMAIN

Kristine Slentz, Juliann Cripe, Betsy Ryan-Seth, Nancy Reid, and Tsai-Hsing Hsia

The Adaptive Domain includes goals and objectives in the areas of feeding, personal hygiene, and undressing. The skills mastered in these areas exemplify the child's growing independence, perhaps more than in any other domain. The ability to meet personal needs allows the child to feel good about what he or she can do independently, fostering self-esteem.

As the child acquires abilities in eating, drinking, toileting, hand washing, teethbrushing, and undressing, the role of adults in caregiving activities is gradually reduced. For most adaptive activities, the caregiver initially performs the entire skill for the child. Adults hold the bottle, hold a baby to nurse, hold the cup for drinking, or manipulate the spoon for semisolid foods. Likewise, toileting, bathing, dressing, and teethbrushing are completed with only minimal assistance from the child at first.

As each adaptive routine becomes familiar, the infant or young child learns to cooperate. For example, the child opens his or her mouth for food or pulls an arm out of a sleeve. Caregivers build upon these cooperative behaviors to teach new skills and promote independence.

The balance between facilitating development of a new skill and providing ongoing assistance can be difficult to strike, especially for the child who acquires adaptive skills more slowly than peers. Both the adult and child can become accustomed to an efficient, adult-completed routine, and experience difficulty affording the child time to learn the skill independently. However, with each developing skill, the caregiver gradually decreases the amount of assistance provided, yet still provides enough support for the child to successfully complete the task.

Soon after birth, reflexive feeding behaviors develop into the basic skills required to close lips around a nipple, suck, and swallow liquids. Although sucking and swallowing seem simple, infants are sustained by liquid nourishment for many months, and this demands a number of coordinated skills.

The introduction of solid foods is an important new experience, and a child may be initially ambivalent about both the spoon and the texture of the food. The infant initially continues to use the sucking motion that efficiently takes liquid from a nipple, only to push pureed food back out of the mouth. The infant may then overreact and develop a tendency to bite down on the spoon. With practice, most young children learn to efficiently use their lips to remove semisolid foods from the spoon and swallow.

181

The child who grasps at the spoon or puts hands on the bottle or breast may be indicating a readiness for finger feeding. Initial attempts may be awkward because the child uses the whole hand to pick up food, and the food falls from the fist before it reaches the mouth. With practice, the child learns to coordinate picking up the food and putting it in the mouth. Sucking finger food to make it soft is eventually replaced by munching and then biting and chewing.

The infant may tend to suck or munch on the cup when it is first introduced, having successfully sucked from nipples and munched on finger foods. The child may initially pull back from the cup or inhale liquid, surprised at how easily it enters the mouth. Coughing, sputtering, and spilling are common at first, and more liquid may spill than enters the mouth. In time, sputtering and spilling decrease as the child learns to close his or her lips around the rim of the cup to prevent spilling, to regulate the amount of liquid taken in, and to swallow without dribbling. Spilling returns when the child begins to hold the cup, bring it to the mouth, and tip it to drink independently. Eventually, the child coordinates picking up and setting down the cup without spilling.

Most children master spoon feeding before learning to use a fork because the spoon is familiar, and scooping requires a less precise movement than stabbing with a fork. The child's first attempts to bring the loaded spoon to the mouth may result in most of the food falling off the spoon, but with experience the child learns to coordinate scooping and bringing the food to the mouth.

It is typical for the child who is learning to use utensils to continue to use the fingers. Similarly, when introduced to the fork, the child attempts to use it like a spoon. As more refined skills develop, the child realizes the increased advantages of using the correct utensils.

The oral-motor abilities of the infant with a neuromuscular impairment require careful evaluation by a specialist prior to the development of mealtime intervention plans. Certain reflexive patterns and high, low, or fluctuating muscle tone may interfere with the development of typical sucking, chewing, and swallowing skills. In addition, individualized prosthetic utensils and positioning aides may be necessary to support the development of self-feeding. It is critical that the child with a neuromuscular impairment receive support in learning new adaptive skills so that the experience is positive and promotes maximum independence.

Mealtime is a valuable learning time for the child and a typical social setting for families and peers. It is important for the young child to happily anticipate mealtimes and be a social participant at the table. Many of the specific suggestions in the feeding strand are aimed at creating a relaxing and positive atmosphere when teaching new feeding and eating skills. Most children will experiment with new foods and make a mess in the process. Allowing an acceptable amount of food play helps the child learn about qualities of the new foods. The nonproductive playing with food should decrease as the foods and the skills become more familiar to the child.

Toilet training requires a number of complex skills, and success relates to the child's physical and social maturity. Muscle control is necessary to regulate elimination; as the child matures, the time between eliminations increases to a couple of hours. The child gradually develops the control to stay dry or unsoiled between adult-initiated trips to the toilet.

Subtle internal signals indicating the need to go to the toilet must be recognized if the child is to "hold it" between trips. Occasional accidents are common. Eventually, the child indicates the need to eliminate and relies less upon adult-initiated trips. Finally, the child independently initiates toileting and remains dry and unsoiled between trips. Remaining dry through the night is usually the last skill to develop.

Toilet training is a sensitive area for teaching and learning new skills, and sometimes it creates a struggle between the adult and the child. It is important not to pressure children about toilet training and to avoid a punishing situation for the child. Follow the child's interest and plan variations in the training schedule if the child becomes resistant.

Even after a child is toilet trained, relapses and accidents often occur. Stress, fatigue, exciting play, or new surroundings can all disrupt the toileting routine or the child's ability to read internal cues. A supportive and neutral adult attitude throughout toilet training has a positive impact on the child's success.

Hand washing is usually the child's first attempt to keep clean independently. It is helpful to teach the child the importance of clean hands for hygiene and social acceptability. A regular hand washing routine prior to meals and after toileting is critical, and adult and peer models are powerful teaching tools. When hand washing is first attempted, playing with soap and water are more common than getting the hands clean. Adult assistance should be encouraging and ensure cleanliness. The child will gradually develop the component skills and motivation to perform hand washing and drying routines independently.

Brushing teeth develops in the same manner as other adaptive skills because the child initially holds the mouth open for the adult. Care of the baby teeth can affect the permanent teeth, and a regular brushing routine helps establish a lifelong pattern of dental hygiene. Even after a child has mastered the basics of teethbrushing, an adult should assist to make sure all teeth are clean. The fine motor control required to brush all teeth thoroughly is beyond most 3-year-old children, and dentists recommend adult assistance until at least age 4.

The child learns undressing skills by first having the caregiver remove clothing. As the child becomes aware of the routine, he or she cooperates by raising and pulling arms and legs for clothing to be removed. The child also experiments with independently removing a hat, socks, and shoes. Eventually, the skills to manipulate shirts, pants, coats, and jackets enable the child to undress. Caregivers may be responsible for undoing fasteners, however, long after the child learns to remove clothing.

Undressing is included in this curriculum because the skills required to pull clothes off are less complicated than those required to put them on. Adults can foster undressing skills by approaching the task as a partnership, allowing the young child to do as much as possible and decreasing assistance to match emerging skills.

As with feeding, the consultation of a specialist is critical to the successful mastery of hygiene and undressing skills by the child with a neuromuscular impairment. Specially designed toothbrushes, soap dispensers, sinks, and clothing can promote more efficient acquisition of adaptive skills for this child, and prevent unnecessary frustration for teachers, family, and the child.

Teaching skills in the Adaptive Domain is fun. Many functional and motivating opportunities for the child to eat, wash, toilet, and undress occur throughout the day. Mastery of adaptive skills provides an early start to independence in home, school, and community, and increases the degree to which the young child socializes and learns with peers.

Adap

Strand A
Feeding

GOAL 1 Uses tongue and lips to take in and swallow solid foods and liquids

DEVELOPMENTAL PROGRAMMING STEPS

To achieve this goal, a child must perform Objectives 1.1–1.4 to criteria. Refer to the specific objectives for developmental programming steps for each objective to develop the skills.

IMPORTANCE OF SKILL

The use of the tongue and lips permits the child to obtain and retain food and liquids. This allows the child to eat a variety of foods and liquids. The use of the lips and tongue promotes oral motor development, which is important for the production of speech. In addition, the ability to take in solid foods and liquids is central to participation in social interactions with family and friends at mealtime. This skill provides the opportunity for many communicative, social, adaptive, cognitive, and fine motor skills to be practiced in a frequent and highly motivating routine.

PRECEDING OBJECTIVE

Adap A:1.1　Uses lips to take in liquids from a cup and/or glass

CONCURRENT OBJECTIVES

FM A:3.3　　Grasps hand-size object with either hand using whole hand
Adap A:3.2　Drinks from cup and/or glass held by adult
Adap A:4.3　Accepts food presented on spoon
Cog D:1.1　　Imitates motor action that is commonly used
Soc B:1.1　　Meets physical needs of hunger and thirst

TEACHING SUGGESTIONS

To achieve this goal, a child must perform Objectives 1.1–1.4 to criteria. Refer to the specific objective for Teaching Suggestions and Teaching Considerations to develop each skill.

Objective 1.1   Uses lips to take in liquids from a cup and/or glass

IMPORTANCE OF SKILL

The use of the lips when drinking allows the child to obtain and maintain liquid in the mouth. Using lips to drink from cups and glasses is an important step toward independent eating and drinking. The child receives liquid nourishment without dependence on the breast or bottle, allowing more social interaction. Coordination and control of lip movement is also vital to speech production.

PRECEDING OBJECTIVE

Adap A:1.4   Swallows liquids

CONCURRENT OBJECTIVES

FM A:3.3   Grasps hand-size object with either hand using whole hand
Adap A:2.2   Munches soft and crisp foods
Adap A:3.2   Drinks from cup and/or glass held by adult
Cog B:1.1   Visually follows object moving in horizontal, vertical, and circular directions
Cog D:1.1   Imitates motor action that is commonly used
Cog E:1.2   Retains object
Soc A:1.2   Smiles in response to familiar adult
Soc A:2.2   Responds to familiar adult's social behavior
Soc A:3.1   Initiates communication with familiar adult
Soc B:1.1   Meets physical needs of hunger and thirst
Soc B:2.1   Responds to routine event

TEACHING SUGGESTIONS
Activity-Based

- Present liquids in a cup or glass during regular snack and mealtimes. Put the child's favorite drink in a cup rather than a bottle.
- Provide liquids at regular intervals during the meal, alternating between food and drinks. Take care to offer liquids more often when the child is eating salty or sticky foods.
- Have tea parties using toy dishes and small amounts of drinks.
- Give the child opportunities to play with empty plastic cups and glasses and engage in imaginary drinking. Practice smacking lips on cup when "drinking" liquids.

☑ If your data indicate the child is not making progress toward the objective, provide additional structure within the suggested activities by incorporating the following *environmental arrangements:*

Environmental Arrangements

- Establish the child's attention to the cup in anticipation of drinking. Wait for the child to open lips before bringing the cup or glass to the mouth.

Adap A

- Try different types of chairs (car seat, highchair, adaptive chair) to find the upright position most comfortable for drinking.
- Present the liquid in "fun" glasses that motivate the child. Try to find glasses of favorite sizes, colors, or characters.
- Use a cup with a built-in straw to encourage sucking and swallowing at the same time.
- Use thickened liquids for easier control. Provide milkshakes, nectars, yogurt thinned with juice or milk, milk thickened with pudding or cereal, juice blended with fruit or cereal. Gradually thin drinks to normal consistency.
- Try a small, short cup that fits comfortably next to the child's lips. Soft plastic can be bent by the adult to help the child control liquid intake.
- Use cups that have been cut out on one side to allow the cup to be drained without the child tipping back the head. These cups also give the adult a clearer view of the child's lip movements.
- Start with a small amount of liquid in the cup so that the child does not have to control too much liquid too quickly. Gradually increase the amount as the child learns to drink.
- Consult a qualified speech, occupational, or physical therapist for advice about adaptive devices for lip control.

☑ If this objective is particularly difficult for a child, it may be necessary, within activities, to use an *instructional sequence.*

Instructional Sequence

- The cup or glass should initially be relatively full, so that the child can drink easily without tipping the head back. Gradually decrease the amount of liquid offered and assist the child in taking in more liquid at each opportunity.
- Demonstrate drinking from the cup, then give the cup to the child.
- Verbally encourage the child to drink from a cup or glass, giving specific directions like, "Take a small sip," "Tip your head back to get to the bottom of the glass," "Keep your lips together when you swallow."
- Physically assist the child to place the cup between the lips, tip a small amount of liquid into the mouth, and withdraw the cup.

☑ Combining or pairing different levels of instructions may be helpful when beginning to teach a new and difficult skill. Fade to less intrusive instructions as soon as possible, to encourage more independent performance.

TEACHING CONSIDERATIONS

1. Seat the child in an upright position to avoid choking.
2. Avoid hot liquids.
3. Child may prefer plastic cups and glasses that do not conduct the temperature of the liquid (and will not break if dropped!).
4. Child may initially refuse milk from a cup or glass if accustomed to drinking it only from the bottle or breast.
5. For the child with an oral-motor problem, consult a qualified specialist for teaching ideas.
6. The child who is fed by gastrostomy or nasogastric tubes may also benefit from oral stimulation. Have a qualified specialist assess the child and program for appropriate oral activities.
7. Consider safety with straws and other utensils.

Objective 1.2   Uses lips to take food off spoon and/or fork

IMPORTANCE OF SKILL

Controlled lip movement is important for functional eating skills and is a step toward independent eating. Using the lips helps the child actively remove foods from eating utensils, and closing the lips makes swallowing easier. The ability to take food from utensils allows the child to participate more comfortably in social eating activities at home and in the community. In addition, utensils can be used to eat many foods that are difficult to manage with fingers, hands, or a bottle.

PRECEDING OBJECTIVE

Adap A:1.3   Swallows solid and semisolid foods

CONCURRENT GOAL AND OBJECTIVES

FM A:3.3   Grasps hand-size object with either hand using whole hand
Adap A:2.2   Munches soft and crisp foods
Cog B:1.0   Visually follows object and/or person to point of disappearance
Cog B:2.3   Reacts when object and/or person hides from view
Cog D:1.1   Imitates motor action that is commonly used
Soc A:1.2   Smiles in response to familiar adult
Soc A:2.2   Responds to familiar adult's social behavior
Soc A:3.1   Initiates communication with familiar adult
Soc B:2.1   Responds to routine event

TEACHING SUGGESTIONS
Activity-Based

- Gain the child's attention before putting the filled spoon into the mouth. Help the child anticipate the utensil by playing lip smacking games while bringing the food to the mouth. Encourage the child to imitate.
- Offer the child opportunities to play with spoons and forks during mealtimes. Use child-size utensils and wait to introduce them until the child's initial hunger is satisfied.
- Fill the spoon or fork and place it at the center of the child's mouth. Wait to see if the child will use lips to remove the food, rather than pull the utensil directly out of the child's mouth.
- Give the child fruit popsicles to practice lip and tongue movements. Use foods and liquids with attractive colors to motivate the child. Present foods of appropriate size so the child can manage easily.
- Wait for the child to attempt to use lips and tongue to remove food that accumulates around the mouth during feeding, rather than wipe the child's face after each bite. The presence of food on the mouth may encourage the child to close lips around the food.

Adap A

Environmental Arrangements

- Try different types of chairs (car seat, highchair, adaptive chair) to find the upright position most comfortable for using utensils.
- Begin practicing this skill with only favorite foods. Choose a snack or mealtime with few distractions, ample time allotted, and multiple opportunities in a familiar and comfortable environment. Soft lights or music may be helpful.
- Put a dab of peanut butter on child's lips and encourage the child to close lips and taste it. Once the child has begun to use lips, put the dab on your finger and wait for the child to remove it with lips. Systematically move from presenting food on your finger to presenting it on a spoon and then a fork.
- Present on forks and spoons highly reinforcing foods that are difficult to eat efficiently with hands, fingers, or bottle. Try applesauce, mashed bananas, pudding, yogurt, mashed potatoes, and ice cream to find the child's preferences. As the child begins to use lips to take these foods, gradually introduce more lumpy foods.
- Consult a qualified speech, occupational, or physical therapist for advice about lip control.

Instructional Sequence

- Demonstrate the lip movements. Sitting with the child in front of a mirror may be helpful.
- If the child does not close lips when food is placed in the mouth, verbally encourage the child to do so.
- Once food is placed in the child's mouth, touch the lips gently as a reminder to the child. Avoid "scraping" the food off the utensil with the child's gum ridge, teeth, or upper lip.
- Watch for the child to move the upper lip slightly toward the spoon or fork, then move the utensil gradually to the child's mouth. Require more lip movement before bringing each successive spoonful to the child's mouth.
- Place the food in the child's mouth, pressing down firmly on the middle of the tongue with the utensil. Wait for the child to use the upper lip to help remove food.

TEACHING CONSIDERATIONS

1. Keep the child in an upright position to avoid choking.
2. Use plastic-coated utensils for a child who tends to bite during feeding.
3. The child may prefer hardened plastic or plastic-coated utensils that do not conduct the temperature of the food and are less harsh to the sensitive areas of the lips and tongue.
4. The child may initially refuse food from utensils if accustomed to eating only from a bottle, breast, or with fingers.
5. For the child with an oral-motor problem, consult a qualified specialist for teaching ideas.
6. A child who is fed by gastrostomy or nasogastric tubes may also benefit from oral stimulation. Have a qualified specialist assess the child and program for appropriate oral activities.
7. Consider safety with eating utensils and foods.

Objective 1.3   Swallows solid and semisolid foods

DEVELOPMENTAL PROGRAMMING STEPS

PS1.3a   The child swallows solid foods.
PS1.3b   The child swallows semisolid foods.

IMPORTANCE OF SKILL

Swallowing solid and semisolid foods enables a child to feel a wider variety of different textures in the mouth. Swallowing these foods is a step toward independent eating. It expands the number of ways to provide nutritious meals, and eating becomes more efficient, exploratory, and interesting!

PRECEDING OBJECTIVE

Adap A:1.4   Swallows liquids

CONCURRENT GOAL AND OBJECTIVES

Cog A:1.0   Orients to auditory, visual, and tactile events
Cog B:1.1   Visually follows object moving in horizontal, vertical, and circular directions
Cog B:2.3   Reacts when object and/or person hides from view
Soc A:1.2   Smiles in response to familiar adult

TEACHING SUGGESTIONS
Activity-Based

- Introduce solid and semisolid foods to the child during regular snack and mealtimes. When solids are first given, the child may use a sucking movement, similar to sucking from a bottle or breast.
- Present solid and semisolid foods on child-size utensils, using small bites to decrease gagging and choking. Most children initially prefer warm, but not hot, food.
- Follow diet recommendations from family and physician to ensure that developmentally appropriate foods are used.
- Whenever possible, puree or grind for the child the same foods that are served to others at the meal. Introduce only one new food at any given meal.

Environmental Arrangements

- A warm, calm, unhurried environment at mealtimes may reduce a child's tension and facilitate acceptance of new foods.
- Combining new foods with old favorites may be useful initially in getting the child to try new tastes and textures. At first, combine a small amount of the new food with a bite of familiar foods. Gradually reduce the amount of familiar food until the child is eating the new food alone.
- Gradually increase the thickness of liquid foods by adding cereal or fruit. Smooth semisolid foods such as yogurt and applesauce can be easily thickened.

Adap A

- If the child is initially resistant to both the feeding utensil and new textures, consider use of a bottle with a juice nipple to present thickened liquids.
- Alternate solid and liquid foods during feeding. Initially, present small amounts of more solid foods toward the middle of a feeding, when the child is slightly, but not terribly, hungry. Gradually increase the amount of solid nourishment offered at each feeding.
- Foods can be ground, chopped, or blended to allow easier swallowing. Juice, milk, or gravy can be used instead of water to thin foods without diluting taste.
- Consult a qualified speech, occupational, or physical therapist for advice about adaptive devices for utensils.

Instructional Sequence

- Model swallowing food and comment about it, as in "mmm, good."
- Place food toward the back of the child's mouth to induce the child to swallow. Systematically move the food forward as the child becomes more proficient.
- Verbally encourage the child to swallow the food.
- Gently stroke the child's lower jaw and neck to facilitate swallowing.

TEACHING CONSIDERATIONS

1. Seat the child in upright position to avoid choking.
2. Use plastic-coated utensils for a child who tends to bite during feeding. Insert the spoon only partially into the mouth to avoid gagging.
3. The child may prefer plastic utensils that do not conduct the temperature of the food and are less harsh than metal to the sensitive areas of the lips and tongue.
4. The child may initially refuse food from utensils if accustomed to eating only from a bottle, breast, or with fingers.
5. For the child with an oral-motor problem, consult a qualified specialist for teaching ideas.
6. The child who is fed by gastrostomy or nasogastric tubes may also benefit from oral stimulation. Have a qualified specialist assess the child and program for appropriate oral activities.
7. Consider safety with eating utensils and foods.

Objective 1.4 Swallows liquids

IMPORTANCE OF SKILL

The child's ability to voluntarily swallow liquids is both life-sustaining and an important step toward independent eating. The suck-swallow reflex present at birth is usually inhibited at about 2 months of age and replaced by a voluntary swallowing pattern.

CONCURRENT GOALS AND OBJECTIVES

FM A:1.0 Simultaneously brings hands to midline
Cog A:1.0 Orients to auditory, visual, and tactile events
Cog B:1.1 Visually follows object moving in horizontal, vertical, and circular directions

Adap A

SC A:1.1   Turns and looks toward object and person speaking
Soc A:1.2   Smiles in response to familiar adult

TEACHING SUGGESTIONS
Activity-Based

- Be sure the child is provided frequent opportunities to drink. Infants and young children should be offered liquids routinely throughout the day, even if they are not giving clear signals that they wish to eat or drink.
- Respond consistently to the child's cues for hunger/thirst. Present the bottle or breast on demand or according to the child's schedule of feedings. A relaxed, consistent feeding routine may facilitate swallowing in a smooth suck-swallow-breath sequence.
- Present a variety of liquids appropriate to the child's developmental age, such as milk, juice, or water. Use the liquids the child likes most to encourage swallowing. Smile and talk softly to the child while feeding to establish feeding as an enjoyable part of the daily routine.

Environmental Arrangements

- Soft lights and music may be relaxing for some children, to facilitate swallowing abilities.
- Positioning is important to facilitate swallowing. Be careful not to recline the child too far, or choking may occur. Put the child in his or her favorite position to facilitate swallowing.
- Thicker liquids may be easier for some children to swallow. Vary the consistency of liquids to find the consistency most easily swallowed. Then systematically thin liquids as the child becomes comfortable swallowing.
- Try a variety of nipple sizes, materials, and shapes (e.g., orthodontic, preemie, rubber, latex) or breast shields for retracted or difficult-to-grasp nipples.
- Bottle nipples with regular-size holes, in combination with thickened liquids, are helpful to control the amount of liquid taken with each suck.
- Consult a qualified speech, occupational, or physical therapist for advice about adaptive sucking/swallowing procedures for children with cleft lips or pallate.

Instructional Sequence

- Model swallowing liquid and comment about it, as in "mmm, good."
- Verbally encourage the child to swallow when drinking.
- Touch the child's lips and gently stroke the child's lower jaw and neck to facilitate swallowing.

Swallowing as addressed in this skill should be an automatic process. For this reason, any instructions used to develop the skill should be eliminated as quickly as possible.

TEACHING CONSIDERATIONS

1. Seat the child in an upright position to avoid choking.
2. Drooling is often associated with poor swallowing ability.
3. The child may initially refuse to swallow liquids from a bottle if accustomed to drinking only from the breast, and vice versa.
4. For the child with an oral-motor problem, consult a qualified specialist for teaching ideas.

Adap A

5. The child who is fed by gastrostomy or nasogastric tubes may also benefit from oral stimulation. Have a qualified specialist assess the child and program for appropriate oral activities.
6. Consider safety with bottles and liquids.

GOAL 2   Bites *and* chews hard and chewy foods

DEVELOPMENTAL PROGRAMMING STEPS

PS2.0a   The child chews hard and chewy foods.
PS2.0b   The child bites hard and chewy foods.

IMPORTANCE OF SKILL

Biting and chewing are necessary to make the transition from pureed foods to solid foods and may affect the ability of the growing child to receive adequate nutrition. The ability to bite and chew foods expands the variety of tasteful meals and snacks to include fruits, meats, and vegetables. Controlled rotary chewing also reduces the risk of choking because food is moved between the teeth and around the mouth in one mass.

PRECEDING OBJECTIVE

Adap A:2.1   Bites *and* chews soft and crisp foods

CONCURRENT GOALS AND OBJECTIVES

FM A:3.1   Grasps hand-size object with either hand using the palm, with object placed toward the thumb and index finger
Adap A:4.2   Eats with fingers
Cog B:1.0   Visually follows object and/or person to point of disappearance
Cog B:2.3   Reacts when object and/or person hides from view
Cog D:1.1   Imitates motor action that is commonly used
Cog E:1.2   Retains object
SC A:2.0   Follows person's gaze to establish joint attention
Soc A:2.2   Responds to familiar adult's social behavior
Soc A:3.1   Initiates communication with familiar adult
Soc B:2.1   Responds to routine event

TEACHING SUGGESTIONS
Activity-Based

- Provide regular opportunities for the child to eat hard and chewy foods during snack and mealtimes, while adults and peers are eating the same foods.
- Present hard and chewy foods, such as carrot slices, bread sticks, raw vegetables, fruit rolls, and meats.
- Allow the child to handle hard and chewy foods freely at meal and snack times, without always requiring that the food be eaten. The child may be less hesitant to bite and

Adap A

chew hard foods if he or she becomes familiar with the texture of the foods by handling them.

- Make eating a relaxed and pleasant experience for the child. Use the child's preferences of foods and favorite mealtimes to introduce hard and chewy foods.

Environmental Arrangements

- There are many kinds of chewy foods that vary in the degree of difficulty to bite and chew. Hot dogs, ham, hard-boiled eggs, chicken, ground beef, whole grain bread, and fish are chewy. More chewy are steak, pork chops, roast beef, and bread sticks. Begin with easier foods and systematically introduce chewier and harder foods as the child begins to bite and chew.
- The size of the food should be appropriate for finger feeding. The child may be more interested in trying a new and harder to eat food if finger feeding than if fed by an adult.
- Initially introduce only a small amount of one hard or chewy food at each meal. Alternate hard and chewy foods with other foods and liquids that the child manages easily. Gradually introduce more hard and chewy foods as the child learns to bite and chew them.
- Begin by using foods that the child prefers to eat. Cook a small amount of a fruit, vegetable, or meat to make it soft. Gradually cook the same food less and less (with the exception of meat) to encourage the child to bite through the same food in a harder form. Apples, carrots, broccoli, celery, and zucchini are examples of foods that can be eaten fully cooked, raw, or partially cooked.
- Once a child has begun to manage some hard and chewy foods, snacks like dried fruit, bread sticks, string cheese, fruit rolls, and chewy granola bars are tasty choices for encouraging the child to practice biting and chewing. After the child takes a bite, encourage him or her to move food from side to side in the mouth with the tongue.

Instructional Sequence

- Model biting and chewing by biting through hard and chewy foods and moving the jaw up, down, and in a rotary motion. Encourage the child to imitate, using a mirror if necessary.
- Verbally encourage the child to bite through hard and chewy foods and chew each bite ("Bite hard," "One bite at a time," "Keep chewing").
- Physically assist the child to bite by placing food between child's side teeth and applying gentle pressure on the chin.

TEACHING CONSIDERATIONS

1. Seat the child in an upright position to avoid choking.
2. When biting hard and chewy food, make sure the child chews thoroughly and swallows before taking another bite.
3. The child may initially refuse to eat hard and chewy foods if accustomed to eating only liquid, soft, or crisp foods.
4. For the child with an oral-motor problem, consult a qualified specialist for teaching ideas.
5. The child who is fed by gastrostomy or nasogastric tubes may also benefit from oral stimulation. Have a qualified specialist assess the child and program for appropriate oral activities.

Adap A

6. Have the child with a visual impairment touch the hard and chewy foods as you describe them.
7. Consider safety with the selection and preparation of all foods.

Objective 2.1   Bites *and* chews soft and crisp foods

DEVELOPMENTAL PROGRAMMING STEPS

PS2.1a   The child chews soft and crisp foods.
PS2.1b   The child bites soft and crisp foods.

IMPORTANCE OF SKILL

Biting and chewing are necessary to the transition from pureed foods to solid foods and may affect the ability of the growing child to receive adequate nutrition. As the child develops teeth, the munching pattern is replaced by the more powerful and effective rotary jaw movements of chewing. The ability to bite and chew foods expands the variety of tasteful meals and snacks and reduces the risk of choking.

PRECEDING OBJECTIVE

Adap A:2.2   Munches soft and crisp foods

CONCURRENT GOAL AND OBJECTIVES

FM A:3.1   Grasps hand-size object with either hand using the palm, with object placed toward the thumb and index finger
Adap A:4.2   Eats with fingers
Cog B:1.0   Visually follows object and/or person to point of disappearance
Cog D:1.1   Imitates motor action that is commonly used
Cog E:1.2   Retains object
SC A:2.1   Follows person's pointing gesture to establish joint attention
Soc A:1.2   Smiles in response to familiar adult
Soc A:2.2   Responds to familiar adult's social behavior
Soc A:3.1   Initiates communication with familiar adult
Soc B:2.1   Responds to routine event

TEACHING SUGGESTIONS

Activity-Based

- Provide regular opportunities for the child to eat soft and crisp foods during snack and mealtimes, while adults and peers are eating the same foods.
- Present soft and crisp foods, such as bread, saltine crackers, bananas, cheese slices, and dry cereal.
- Allow the child to handle soft and crisp foods freely at meal and snack times, without always requiring that the food be eaten. The child may be less hesitant to bite and chew soft and crisp foods if he or she becomes familiar with the texture of the foods by handling them.

■ Make eating a relaxed and pleasant experience for the child. Use the child's preferences of foods and favorite mealtimes to introduce soft and crisp foods.

Environmental Arrangements

■ There are many kinds of crisp foods that vary in the degree of difficulty to bite and chew. Saltine crackers, rice cakes, celery sticks, apples, and Cheerios are crisp. More crisp are melba toast, potato chips, raw carrots, and corn chips. Begin with easier foods and systematically introduce crisper foods as the child begins to bite and chew.

■ The size of the food should be appropriate for finger feeding. The child may be more interested in trying a more solid, crisp food if finger feeding than if fed by an adult.

■ Initially introduce only a small amount of one soft or crisp food at each meal. Alternate soft and crisp foods with other foods and liquids that the child manages easily. Gradually introduce more soft and crisp foods as the child begins to bite and chew them.

■ Begin by using foods that the child prefers to eat. Cook a small amount of a fruit, vegetable, or pasta to make it very soft. Gradually cook the same food less and less to encourage the child to bite through the same food in a crisper form. Carrots, green beans, and zucchini are examples of vegetables that can be eaten fully cooked or partially cooked.

■ Initially soak bread or cereal in milk or juice to make it semisolid. Once the child can manage the semisolid food easily, gradually reduce the amount of soaking, until the child is eating regular slices of bread or dry, crisp cereal.

■ Gradually begin to toast bread to introduce a crisp texture, toasting longer and longer until the child can eat a piece of crisp toast.

■ Once a child has begun to manage some soft and crisp foods, snacks like peeled and pitted peaches, melons, berries, peanut butter crackers, and occasional pie, cake, and cookies are tasty choices for encouraging the child to practice biting and chewing. After the child takes a bite, encourage him or her to move food from side to side in the mouth with the tongue.

Instructional Sequence

■ Model biting and chewing by biting through soft and crisp foods and moving jaw up, down, and in a rotary motion. Encourage the child to imitate, using a mirror if necessary.

■ Verbally encourage the child to bite through soft and crisp foods and chew each bite ("Bite hard," "One bite at a time," "Keep chewing").

■ Physically assist the child to bite by placing food between child's front teeth and applying gentle pressure on chin.

TEACHING CONSIDERATIONS

1. Seat the child in an upright position to avoid choking.
2. The child may initially refuse to eat soft and crisp foods if accustomed to eating only liquids and semisoft foods.
3. For the child with an oral-motor problem, consult a qualified specialist for teaching ideas.
4. The child who is fed by gastrostomy or nasogastric tubes may also benefit from oral stimulation. Have a qualified specialist assess the child and program for appropriate oral activities.

Adap A

5. Have the child with a visual impairment touch the soft and crisp foods as you describe them.
6. Consider safety with the selection and preparation of all finger foods.

Objective 2.2 Munches soft and crisp foods

DEVELOPMENTAL PROGRAMMING STEPS

PS2.2a   The child munches crisp foods.
PS2.2b   The child munches soft foods.

IMPORTANCE OF SKILL

Before teeth emerge, a munching pattern appears, which is a precursor to chewing behavior. Munching enables the child to eat nonpureed foods and obtain nutrition from a variety of sources, making meals and snacks more tasty and interesting.

PRECEDING GOAL

Adap A:1.0   Uses tongue and lips to take in and swallow solid foods and liquids

CONCURRENT OBJECTIVES

FM A:3.3   Grasps hand-size object with either hand using whole hand
Adap A:4.2   Eats with fingers
Cog B:1.1   Visually follows object moving in horizontal, vertical, and circular directions
Cog B:2.3   Reacts when object and/or person hides from view
Cog D:1.1   Imitates motor action that is commonly used
Cog E:1.2   Retains object
Soc A:1.2   Smiles in response to familiar adult
Soc A:2.2   Responds to familiar adult's social behavior
Soc A:3.1   Initiates communication with familiar adult
Soc B:2.1   Responds to routine event

TEACHING SUGGESTIONS

Activity-Based

- Provide regular opportunities for the child to eat soft and crisp foods during snack and mealtimes, while adults and peers are eating the same foods.
- Present soft and crisp foods, such as bread, saltine crackers, bananas, cheese slices, and dry cereal.
- Feed each other bites of cracker or cookie during snack times.
- Allow the child to handle soft and crisp foods freely at snack and mealtimes, without always requiring that the food be eaten. The child may be less hesitant to bite and chew soft and crisp foods if he or she becomes familiar with the texture of the foods by handling them.

■ Make eating a relaxed and pleasant experience for the child. Use the child's preferences of foods and favorite mealtimes to introduce soft and crisp foods.

Environmental Arrangements

■ Provide foods that melt, crumble, or disintegrate easily, such as teething cookies, zwieback, or graham crackers, to give the child the feel of soft and crisp foods without having to take a large mass into the mouth at once.
■ Provide foods that are appropriate for finger feeding. The child may be more interested in munching crisp and soft foods if finger feeding than if fed by an adult.
■ The transition to soft and crisp foods that require munching can begin with the addition of "lumps" to pureed foods. Fruit pieces in yogurt, macaroni in cooked, mashed vegetables, or commercial "junior" baby foods are easy to introduce at regular mealtimes.
■ Initially introduce only a small amount of one soft or crisp food at each meal. Alternate soft and crisp foods with semisolid foods and liquids that the child manages easily. Gradually introduce more soft and crisp foods as the child begins to munch when eating.
■ Once a child has begun to munch while eating soft and crisp foods, snacks like graham crackers, melba toast, zwieback, teething cookies, berries, peanut butter balls, and bananas are tasty choices for encouraging the child to practice munching. As the child sucks and smacks on these foods, encourage child to remove bits of food from the snack with lips and tongue.

Instructional Sequence

■ Model munching soft and crisp foods.
■ Gain the child's attention before putting the soft or crisp food into the child's mouth. Help the child anticipate the food by playing lip smacking games while bringing the food to mouth.
■ Verbally encourage the child to imitate munching motion ("Keep munching," "Up and down with your teeth").
■ Gently stroke the child's lips and chin to facilitate munching.

TEACHING CONSIDERATIONS

1. Seat the child in upright position to avoid choking.
2. Use plastic-coated utensils for child who tends to bite during feeding. Insert spoon only partially into the mouth to avoid gagging.
3. The child may prefer plastic utensils that do not conduct the temperature of the food and are less harsh than metal to the sensitive areas of the lips and tongue.
4. The child may initially refuse food with texture (lumps) if accustomed to eating only pureed, strained, or liquid foods.
5. For the child with an oral-motor problem, consult a qualified specialist for teaching ideas.
6. A child who is fed by gastrostomy or nasogastric tubes may also benefit from oral stimulation. Have a qualified specialist assess the child and program for appropriate oral activities.
7. Have the child with a visual impairment touch the soft and crispy foods as you describe them.
8. Consider safety as the child munches foods.

Adap A

GOAL 3   Drinks from cup and/or glass

DEVELOPMENTAL PROGRAMMING STEP

PS3.0a   The child drinks from a cup or glass by bringing it up to the mouth without spilling. The child may release the cup before returning it to the surface.

IMPORTANCE OF SKILL

The ability to drink from a cup allows the child greater independence in managing physical needs. The child learns to manage the amount of liquid intake by coordinating lip movements with tipping the cup while holding it. Eye–hand coordination is also developed as the child picks up the cup, brings it to the mouth, and returns the cup to the surface without spilling. Drinking from a cup without spilling is a desirable skill for eating meals and snacks in social situations (restaurants, school, friends' and relatives' homes).

PRECEDING OBJECTIVE

Adap A:3.1   Drinks from cup and/or glass with some spilling

CONCURRENT GOALS AND OBJECTIVES

FM A:3.2   Grasps cylindrical object with either hand by closing fingers around it
FM A:5.1   Releases hand-held object onto and/or into a larger target with either hand
Adap A:5.1 Pours liquid
SC B:1.0   Gains person's attention and refers to an object, person, and/or event
Soc A:3.0   Initiates and maintains communicative exchange with familiar adult

TEACHING SUGGESTIONS
Activity-Based

- Offer drinks from a cup when the child indicates thirst or at times when the child usually nurses. Provide repeated opportunities to drink from a cup or glass at snack and mealtimes.
- Provide drinks in cups at regular intervals when children are playing outside, especially during physical activities like tumbling, running, swimming, and riding tricycles.
- Have a tea party for the child and peers, dolls, and stuffed animals to encourage drinking from cups and glasses. A picnic is also a fun activity that can feature special drinks.
- Practice drinking from a cup when brushing teeth.
- Make a game of copying each other and taking turns as you sip juice, milk, or water.

Environmental Arrangements

- Positioning is important to allow the child to grasp, tip, and return the cup to the table without spilling. Use table and chairs or highchair with tray to provide comfortable support in an upright position while the child's forearms rest on the table or tray.
- Select cups or glasses that are an appropriate size and weight for the child.

- Present liquid in "fun" cups of interesting designs and colors or familiar characters.
- Cups with handles are easier for the child to grasp. Weighted cups ("tippee cups") are easier to release without spilling. Begin by using weighted cups with handles and move to regular glasses as the child becomes more proficient. Avoid plastic glasses that tip easily.
- Experiment with the optimal amount of liquid for each child. Try filling the cup only one-third full to give the child less liquid to control and less weight to manage.
- Try a cup that is relatively full so that the child can drink easily without tipping head back. Gradually decrease the amount of liquid so that the child learns to drink all of the liquid from the glass without spilling.
- Transparent cups help the child anticipate the changing level of liquid while drinking.
- Use cups that have been cut out on one side to allow the cup to be drained without the child tipping head back. These cups also give the adult a clearer view of the child's lip movements.
- Consult a qualified speech, occupational, or physical therapist for advice about adaptive devices and procedures for drinking.

Instructional Sequence

- Model drinking from a cup or have peers and siblings demonstrate cup drinking at snack and mealtimes.
- Verbally encourage the child to bring the cup up to the mouth, drink, and put the cup back on the table.
- Stand behind the child. Let the child see the liquid in the cup first. Physically guide the child's hand to lift the cup toward the mouth, drink from the cup, and put it down on the table.

TEACHING CONSIDERATIONS

1. Seat the child in an upright position to avoid choking.
2. The child may initially refuse to drink liquids from a cup or glass if accustomed to drinking only from the breast or bottle.
3. For the child with an oral-motor problem, consult a qualified specialist for teaching ideas.
4. A child who is fed by gastrostomy or nasogastric tubes may also benefit from oral stimulation. Have a qualified specialist assess the child and program for appropriate oral activities.
5. Have the child with a visual impairment feel the cup or glass as you assist in drinking.
6. Consider safety with the selection and preparation of all liquids for drinking.

Adap A

Objective 3.1 Drinks from cup and/or glass with some spilling

IMPORTANCE OF SKILL

Drinking from a cup provides opportunities to improve self-feeding and eye–hand coordination skills. It incorporates the fine motor skills of grasp and release into a functional behavior. The child will be able to participate more independently at snack and mealtimes, which provide numerous opportunities to gain social skills.

PRECEDING OBJECTIVE

Adap A:3.2   Drinks from cup and/or glass held by adult

CONCURRENT GOAL AND OBJECTIVES

FM A:3.2   Grasps cylindrical object with either hand by closing fingers around it
FM A:5.2   Releases hand-held object with each hand
Adap A:2.1   Bites *and* chews soft and crisp foods
Cog B:1.0   Visually follows object and/or person to point of disappearance
Cog B:2.3   Reacts when object and/or person disappears from view
Cog D:1.1   Imitates motor action that is commonly used
SC B:1.1   Responds with a vocalization and gesture to simple questions
Soc A:1.2   Smiles in response to familiar adult
Soc A:3.1   Initiates communication with familiar adult
Soc B:2.1   Responds to routine event

TEACHING SUGGESTIONS

Activity-Based

- Put child's favorite liquid in a cup or glass. If the child is thirsty, encourage the child to drink from the cup independently. Expect some spilling at first.
- Offer drinks from a cup when the child indicates thirst or at times when the child usually nurses. Provide repeated opportunities to drink from a cup or glass at snack and mealtimes.
- Have a tea party for the child and peers, dolls, and stuffed animals to encourage drinking from cups and glasses.
- Practice drinking from a cup when brushing teeth.
- Let the child play with cups and clear water in a sink, tub, or water table. Model cup drinking and let the child practice where spilling is okay.

Environmental Arrangements

- Positioning is important to allow the child to grasp, tip, and return the cup to the table. Use table and chairs or a highchair with a tray to provide comfortable support in an upright position while the child's forearms rest on the table or tray.
- Select cups or glasses that are an appropriate size for the child.
- Present liquids in "fun" cups of interesting designs and colors or familiar characters.
- Cups with handles are easier for the child to grasp. Weighted cups ("tippee cups") are easier to release. Begin by using weighted cups with handles and move to regular plastic glasses as the child becomes more proficient. Avoid plastic glasses that tip easily.
- Provide a large, smooth surface for the cup to be released onto, to decrease tipping and spilling.
- Use cups that have been cut out on one side to allow the cup to be drained without the child tipping head back. These cups also give the adult a clearer view of the child's lip movements.
- Use cups with lids to limit the flow of liquid when the child first begins to drink independently.
- Start with small amounts of liquid in the cup to prevent the child from feeling threatened by having to control too much liquid too quickly. Gradually increase the amount as the child learns to drink.

Adap A

- Experiment with the optimal amount of liquid for each child. Try filling the cup only one-third full to give the child less liquid to control and less weight to manage.
- Try a cup that is relatively full so that the child can drink easily without tipping the head back. Gradually decrease the amount of liquid so that child learns to drink all of the liquid from the glass without spilling.
- Transparent cups help the child anticipate the changing level of liquid while drinking.
- Consult a qualified speech, occupational, or physical therapist for advice about the use of adaptive devices for drinking.

Instructional Sequence

- Model drinking from a cup or have peers and siblings demonstrate cup drinking at snack and mealtimes.
- Verbally encourage the child to bring the cup up to the mouth, drink, and put the cup back on the table.
- Stand behind the child. Let the child see the liquid in the cup first. Physically guide the child's hand to lift the cup toward the mouth, drink from the cup, and put it down on the table.

TEACHING CONSIDERATIONS

1. Seat the child in an upright position to avoid choking.
2. The child may initially refuse to drink liquids from a cup or glass if accustomed to drinking only from the breast or bottle.
3. Be prepared for frequent spills. Use bibs or towels and have a mop handy!
4. For the child with an oral-motor problem, consult a qualified specialist for teaching ideas.
5. A child who is fed by gastrostomy or nasogastric tubes may also benefit from oral stimulation. Have a qualified specialist assess the child and program for appropriate oral activities.
6. Have the child with a visual impairment feel the cup or glass as you assist in drinking.
7. Consider safety with the selection and preparation of all liquids for drinking.

Objective 3.2   Drinks from cup and/or glass held by adult

DEVELOPMENTAL PROGRAMMING STEP

PS3.2a   The child sucks and swallows from bottle or breast.

IMPORTANCE OF SKILL

Drinking from a cup is an important step toward independent feeding. This skill permits functional use of fine motor skills. Drinking from a cup held by an adult allows the child to take liquid from a cup or glass without having to hold and tip the cup at the same time.

PRECEDING OBJECTIVE

Adap A:1.4   Swallows liquids

Adap A

CONCURRENT GOAL AND OBJECTIVES

FM A:3.3   Grasps hand-size object with either hand using whole hand
FM A:5.2   Releases hand-held object with each hand
Adap A:1.1 Uses lips to take in liquids from a cup and/or glass
Adap A:2.1 Bites *and* chews soft and crisp foods
Cog B:1.0   Visually follows object and/or person to point of disappearance
Cog B:2.3   Reacts when object and/or person hides from view
Cog D:1.1   Imitates motor action that is commonly used
Cog G:1.2   Uses functionally appropriate actions with objects
SC B:1.1   Responds with a vocalization and gesture to simple questions
Soc A:1.2   Smiles in response to familiar adult
Soc A:3.1   Initiates communication with familiar adult
Soc B:2.1   Responds to routine event

TEACHING SUGGESTIONS

Activity-Based

- At snack and mealtimes, and whenever the child is thirsty, offer drinks from a glass or cup held by an adult. Offer the cup repeatedly during each snack or meal, alternating with solid foods.
- Have a tea party for the child and peers, dolls, and stuffed animals to encourage drinking from a cup. Have the child pretend to drink before actually offering liquids in the cup.
- Provide the child opportunities to observe other people drinking from cups and glasses. As the child becomes interested, offer a sip from your drink. Make a game of taking sips from an adult's cup or glass.

Environmental Arrangements

- Begin by using preferred liquids or "special" drink like a milkshake from a restaurant. Gradually introduce a variety of liquids in the glass or cup.
- Establish the child's attention to the cup before bringing it to the child's mouth. Use encouraging facial expressions and vocalizations to prepare the child to drink from the cup as you hold it. Raise your eyebrows, purse or smack your lips, and say, "mmm" or "yummy."
- Alternate drink with food to make the child more thirsty. Stop offering the cup if the child resists or loses interest.
- Experiment with the optimal amount of liquid for each child. Try a cup that is relatively full so the child can drink easily without tipping the head back. Gradually decrease the amount of liquid so the child learns to drink all of the liquid from the cup.
- Thick liquids may be easier for the child to drink from a cup because they flow slowly. Start cup drinking by offering milkshakes, smoothies, or eggnog; gradually dilute to a thinner consistency.
- Use cups that have been cut out on one side to allow the cup to be drained without the child tipping the head back. These cups also give the adult a clearer view of the child's lip movements.
- Consult a qualified speech, occupational, or physical therapist for advice about the use of adaptive devices and procedures for drinking.

Adap A

Instructional Sequence

- Model drinking or have peers and siblings demonstrate cup drinking at snack and mealtimes.
- Place the rim of the cup on the child's lower lip. Verbally instruct the child to drink the liquid from the cup as you tip it upward. Be careful not to cause the child to lean backward.
- Place the rim of the cup on the child's lower lip. Slightly tip the cup and allow the child to take liquid into the mouth. Allow the child to close lips and encourage the child to swallow.
- Stroke the child's throat gently to facilitate swallowing after the child takes in liquid from a cup held to the lips.

TEACHING CONSIDERATIONS

1. Seat the child in an upright position to avoid choking.
2. The child may initially refuse to swallow liquids from a cup if accustomed to drinking only from the breast or bottle.
3. For the child with an oral-motor problem, consult a qualified specialist for teaching ideas.
4. The child who is fed by gastrostomy or nasogastric tubes may also benefit from oral stimulation. Have a qualified specialist assess the child and program for appropriate oral activities.
5. Have the child with a visual impairment feel the cup or glass as you assist in drinking.

GOAL 4   Eats with fork and/or spoon

DEVELOPMENTAL PROGRAMMING STEPS

PS4.0a   The child eats by stabbing food with a fork.
PS4.0b   The child eats by scooping with a spoon or fork.

IMPORTANCE OF SKILL

The ability to eat with a fork and spoon will allow the child to feel grown-up and competent. The child gains further independence in eating by using a fork or spoon to eat foods that are difficult to eat with fingers. This skill involves combining and coordinating many complex motor behaviors. The child can be involved formally in mealtimes at home and in the community, and these provide excellent opportunities to learn table manners and socialize.

PRECEDING OBJECTIVE

Adap A:4.1   Brings food to mouth using utensil

CONCURRENT GOAL AND OBJECTIVES

FM B:1.1   Turns object over using wrist and arm rotation with each hand
Cog G:1.2   Uses functionally appropriate actions with objects

Soc B:2.0   Responds to established social routine
Soc C:1.4   Observes peers

TEACHING SUGGESTIONS

Activity-Based

- Provide postural support to allow the child to concentrate on eating skills. Make sure the child's feet, back, and hips are well supported so that balance is stable and arms are free for eating.
- Provide opportunities for the child to use eating utensils during play. Have the child pretend to cook, serve, and eat food when playing with Play-Doh, water, cornmeal, and sand.
- Take turns feeding each other by offering bites of food from utensils. Offer a bite to the child and then have child offer one to you. Include pretend bites to dolls or stuffed animals.
- Provide numerous opportunities for the child to eat with utensils. Set the child's place with utensils, plate, and bowl and encourage the child to use them.
- Include the child in family meals and snacks. Have child observe others using utensils.
- Specific eating skills should be included as part of an enjoyable mealtime experience. Making meals a regular time of information sharing and social interaction facilitates development of socially appropriate eating behaviors.
- Once the use of utensils has been introduced, practice using spoons with applesauce, yogurt, pudding, and ice cream, which are reinforcing snacks. Chunks of meat, fruit, or vegetables are best for stabbing.

Environmental Arrangements

- To practice eating with utensils, use sticky foods like oatmeal and mashed potatoes that easily stay on spoon or fork. Gradually introduce more difficult foods to scoop and spear, to provide practice and variety for the child.
- Stabbing chunks of food may be easier for some children than scooping with a spoon.
- Give the child small portions to help reduce spills. Have the child ask for more and practice using larger utensils to transfer food from serving bowls to eating bowls.
- Plates with special features, such as suction cup bases and high rims, may facilitate scooping. Bowls may be easier than plates to manipulate.
- Try utensils of various materials, sizes, and designs (built-up or bent handles) to find those that work best for the child.
- Consult a qualified speech, occupational, or physical therapist for advice about adaptive utensils.

Instructional Sequence

- Model scooping or stabbing foods.
- Verbally instruct the child to scoop or stab food and bring it to mouth.
- Stand behind the child and put child's hand on handle of utensil. Scoop the food and guide it to the child's mouth.

TEACHING CONSIDERATIONS

1. Seat the child in an upright position to avoid choking.
2. Use plastic-coated utensils for the child who tends to bite during feeding.

Adap A

3. The child may initially refuse to use utensils if accustomed to eating/drinking only from the breast, bottle, or with fingers.
4. The child may prefer plastic or plastic-coated utensils that do not conduct the temperature of the food and are less harsh to the sensitive areas of the lips and tongue.
5. For the child with an oral-motor problem, consult a qualified specialist for teaching ideas.
6. A child who is fed by gastrostomy or nasogastric tubes may also benefit from oral stimulation. Have a qualified specialist assess the child and program for appropriate oral activities.
7. Have the child with a visual impairment feel the utensils before using them with food. Describe what the child is feeling.
8. Consider safety with the selection and preparation of all foods and utensils.

Objective 4.1   Brings food to mouth using utensil

IMPORTANCE OF SKILL

This skill enables the child to use an object to achieve a purpose and to take a more active role in the feeding process. By bringing the utensil to the mouth, the child develops eye–hand coordination and fine motor control. This skill is an important step toward independent eating and opens new avenues to socialization with family and friends.

PRECEDING OBJECTIVE

Adap A:4.3   Accepts food presented on spoon

CONCURRENT OBJECTIVES

FM A:3.2   Grasps cylindrical object with either hand by closing fingers around it
Cog G:1.2   Uses functionally appropriate actions with objects
Soc A:3.2   Responds to communication from familiar adult
Soc B:2.1   Responds to routine event
Soc C:1.4   Observes peers

TEACHING SUGGESTIONS
Activity-Based

- Allow the child to explore spoons of all sizes as toys before using them as eating tools. Mouthing is a predominant form of early exploration. Dip the spoon in food and let the child suck on the spoon in the course of manipulation and exploration.
- Give the child a spoon to hold while you feed the child. Allow the child to play with and manipulate the spoon; encourage a few independent bites. Be prepared for some mess!
- Provide a fork or spoon with food that can be scooped during snack and mealtimes. It may be necessary to scoop the food for the child. Encourage the child to bring a filled spoon to the mouth and eat. Use favorite foods to motivate the behavior.

- Include the child in family snacks and meals. Have the child observe others using utensils.
- Specific eating skills should be included as part of an enjoyable mealtime experience. Making meals a regular time of information sharing and social interaction facilitates the development of socially appropriate eating behaviors.

Environmental Arrangements

- Use sticky foods that easily stay on a spoon or fork; expect some spilling.
- Alternate use of utensils with finger feeding or being fed by an adult. Introduce utensils toward the middle of a meal when the child is still hungry but less likely to be frustrated by the slowness of using a spoon.
- Try utensils of various materials, sizes, and designs (built-up or bent handles) to find those that work best for the child.
- Consult a qualified speech, occupational, or physical therapist for advice about the use of adaptive utensils.

Instructional Sequence

- Model using a utensil to eat.
- Verbally instruct the child to pick up the filled spoon or fork and bring it to the mouth.
- Stand behind the child. Put the child's hand on the handle and guide the spoon to the child's mouth.

TEACHING CONSIDERATIONS

1. Provide postural support to allow the child to concentrate on eating skills. Make sure the child's feet, back, and hips are well supported so that balance is stable and arms are free for eating.
2. Seat the child in an upright position to avoid choking.
3. Use plastic-coated utensils for the child who tends to bite during feeding.
4. The child may initially refuse to use utensils if accustomed to eating/drinking only from the breast, bottle, or with fingers.
5. The child may prefer plastic or plastic-coated utensils that do not conduct the temperature of the food and are less harsh to the sensitive areas of the lips and tongue.
6. For the child with an oral-motor problem, consult a qualified specialist for teaching ideas.
7. The child who is fed by gastrostomy or nasogastric tubes may also benefit from oral stimulation. Have a qualified specialist assess the child and program for appropriate oral activities.
8. Have the child with a visual impairment feel the utensils before using them with food. Describe what the child is feeling.
9. Consider safety with foods and utensils.

Objective 4.2   Eats with fingers

IMPORTANCE OF SKILL

Eating with fingers is an independent eating skill that is used for a lifetime. It facilitates the development of the pincer grasp and chewing skills, and it offers opportunities for practice in eye–hand coordination tasks.

Adap A

PRECEDING OBJECTIVES

FM A:3.3   Grasps hand-size object with either hand using whole hand
Adap A:2.1 Bites *and* chews soft and crisp foods

CONCURRENT GOALS AND OBJECTIVES

FM A:3.1   Grasps hand-size object with either hand using the palm, with object placed toward the thumb and index finger
FM A:4.2   Grasps pea-size object with either hand using side of the index finger and thumb
Adap A:2.0 Bites *and* chews hard and chewy foods
SC A:2.1   Follows person's pointing gesture to establish joint attention
SC A:3.0   Engages in vocal exchanges by babbling
Soc A:3.2   Responds to communication from familiar adult

TEACHING SUGGESTIONS

Activity-Based

- Provide various finger foods during snack and mealtimes. Encourage the child to grasp food and eat. Use easy-to-grasp foods like bread sticks, crackers, or string beans.
- Include the child at family mealtimes by offering pieces of table food for finger feeding. Put pieces of dry cereal on a table or tray to practice fine motor skills and feeding.
- Introduce finger feeding by letting the child lick fingers and hands after dipping them in favorite foods.
- Take turns feeding the child finger food and having the child feed you. Include giving bites to dolls or stuffed animals.

Environmental Arrangements

- The size of food should facilitate grasping and require less chewing. Foods like raw vegetables should be presented after crackers, bread pieces, cereal, cheese, and bananas have been mastered.
- Sticky foods like soft cheese, peanut butter on toast, and pasta with cheese allow the child to maintain a grasp until the food gets to the mouth.
- Play hide-and-seek games with small cookies, crackers, or cereal. Place them under cups or napkins and have the child find and eat them before you hide other pieces.

Instructional Sequence

- Model eating with fingers
- Present the food and verbally instruct the child to pick it up, put it in mouth, and eat.
- Place finger food in the child's hand and guide it toward the mouth as you encourage the child.

TEACHING CONSIDERATIONS

1. Seat the child in an upright position to avoid choking.
2. The child may initially refuse to eat with fingers if not accustomed to touching or handling food.
3. For the child with an oral-motor problem, consult a qualified specialist for teaching ideas.

Adap A

4. The child who is fed by gastrostomy or nasogastric tubes may also benefit from oral stimulation. Have a qualified specialist assess the child and program for appropriate oral activities.
5. For the child with a visual impairment, describe the foods as they are touched.
6. Consider safety with finger foods.

Objective 4.3   Accepts food presented on spoon

IMPORTANCE OF SKILL

Accepting food presented on a spoon increases the variety of foods the child can eat, allowing more active participation at mealtimes. This skill promotes attention to and interaction with the person who is presenting the spoon, which provides a positive and regular setting for building social skills.

PRECEDING OBJECTIVE

Adap A:1.4   Swallows liquids

CONCURRENT OBJECTIVES

Adap A:1.2   Uses lips to take food off spoon and/or fork
Cog C:2.1   Indicates desire to continue familiar game and/or action
Cog G:1.4   Uses sensory examination with objects
SC A:1.1   Turns and looks toward object and person speaking
SC A:3.1   Engages in vocal exchanges by cooing
Soc A:2.2   Responds to familiar adult's social behavior

TEACHING SUGGESTIONS
Activity-Based

■ Gain the child's attention before putting the filled spoon into the mouth. Help the child anticipate the utensil by playing lip smacking games while bringing the food to mouth.
■ Offer the child opportunities to play with a spoon during mealtimes. Use child-size spoons after the child's initial hunger is satisfied.
■ Provide the child many opportunities to observe others eating semisolid foods (applesauce, pudding, yogurt) from spoons. If the child opens and closes mouth, smacks lips, or sucks lips/tongue while watching someone else eat with a spoon, offer a very small bite.
■ Before presenting a utensil, allow the child to dip fingers into semisolid foods like cereal, applesauce, and yogurt and suck the food off the utensil.
■ Present food on a spoon during regular snack and mealtimes. Most children will open their mouth as the spoon approaches and use a suck-swallow pattern to remove the food from the spoon.
■ Use a small amount of favorite food on a spoon. Formula or breast milk thickened with cereal or fruit are often the earliest foods to be spoon-fed.

Environmental Arrangements

- Try different types of chairs (car seat, highchair, adaptive chair) to find the upright position most comfortable for introducing utensils.
- Begin introducing the spoon with only favorite foods. Choose a snack or mealtime with few distractions, ample time allotted, and multiple opportunities in a familiar and comfortable environment. Soft lights or music may be helpful.
- Lighting and position should permit the child to see the food on the spoon as it approaches the mouth. Establish the child's attention to the spoon before touching it to the mouth.
- Foods should be at the appropriate temperature—not too hot or too cold. Try spoons of various sizes and shapes. Offer semisolid foods first and move to solid foods.
- Put a dab of peanut butter on the child's lips and encourage the child to close lips and taste it. Once the child has begun to use lips, put the dab on fingers and wait for the child to remove it with lips.
- Systematically move from presenting food on the child's fingers to your finger, then to a spoon.
- Consult a qualified speech, occupational, or physical therapist for advice about lip control.

Instructional Sequence

- Model eating from a spoon, exaggerating opening your mouth to accept the spoon and closing your mouth to remove food. Have siblings and peers model eating from a spoon.
- Use verbal and facial cues to help the child anticipate the spoon and open mouth to take in food. Say "aaahh" while opening mouth wide and "mmmm" as you place the spoon in the mouth.
- Once the child is attending to the spoon, gently stroke or tap lips to encourage the child to open his or her mouth. Place the spoon on the tongue and slowly remove it, pulling straight out, to leave food in the mouth.

TEACHING CONSIDERATIONS

1. Seat the child in an upright position to avoid choking.
2. Use plastic-coated utensils for the child who tends to bite during feeding.
3. The child may prefer plastic or plastic-coated utensils that do not conduct the temperature of the food and are less harsh to the sensitive areas of the lips and tongue.
4. The child may initially refuse food from a spoon if accustomed to eating only from the breast, bottle, or with fingers.
5. For the child with an oral-motor problem, consult a qualified specialist for teaching ideas.
6. A child who is fed by gastrostomy or nasogastric tubes may also benefit from oral stimulation. Have a qualified specialist assess the child and program for appropriate oral activities.
7. For the child with a visual impairment, describe the food and have the child touch the spoon.
8. Consider safety with foods and utensils.

Adap A

GOAL 5   Transfers food and liquid

DEVELOPMENTAL PROGRAMMING STEPS

To achieve this goal, a child must perform Objectives 5.1–5.2 to criteria. Refer to the specific objective for Developmental Programming Steps to develop each skill.

IMPORTANCE OF SKILL

The skill of transferring food and liquid is an important step toward independent eating. It allows the child more opportunities to participate in group activities and interact with others.

PRECEDING OBJECTIVE

Adap A:5.1   Pours liquid

CONCURRENT GOALS AND OBJECTIVE

FM A:5.0   Places and releases object balanced on top of another object with either hand
Adap B:3.0 Brushes teeth
SC B:1.0   Gains person's attention and refers to an object, person, and/or event
SC B:2.0   Uses consistent word approximations
SC C:2.1   Carries out two-step direction *with* contextual cues
Soc A:3.0   Initiates and maintains communicative exchange with familiar adult
Soc B:2.0   Responds to established social routine
Soc C:2.0   Initiates and maintains communicative exchange with peer

TEACHING SUGGESTIONS

In order to achieve this goal, a child must perform Objectives 5.1–5.2 to criteria. Refer to the specific objective for Teaching Suggestions and Teaching Considerations to develop each skill.

Objective 5.1   Pours liquid

DEVELOPMENTAL PROGRAMMING STEP

PS5.1a   Child empties container of liquid or solids by dumping contents (child holds container and rotates wrists to empty it).

IMPORTANCE OF SKILL

The ability to pour liquid from one container into another is the basis for many leisure and daily living skills used throughout life. It involves the coordination of fine motor control, an understanding of spatial relations, and anticipation of the movement of the liquid. Pouring water is a form of play enjoyed by most children, providing recreational opportunities in addition to increased independence in meeting physical needs.

PRECEDING OBJECTIVE

FM B:1.1   Turns object over using wrist and arm rotation with each hand

CONCURRENT GOALS AND OBJECTIVES

FM B:2.0   Assembles toy and/or object that require(s) putting pieces together
Adap A:3.0 Drinks from cup and/or glass
Cog D:1.0   Imitates motor action that is not commonly used
SC B:1.0   Gains person's attention and refers to an object, person, and/or event
SC B:2.1   Uses consistent consonant–vowel combinations
SC C:2.2   Carries out one-step direction *without* contextual cues
Soc A:2.1   Initiates simple social game with familiar adult
Soc A:3.1   Initiates communication with familiar adult
Soc B:1.1   Meets physical needs of hunger and thirst
Soc B:2.0   Responds to established social routine
Soc C:2.0   Initiates and maintains communicative exchange with peer

TEACHING SUGGESTIONS
Activity-Based

- Provide regular opportunities for the child to practice pouring. Offer drinks during outside play, picnics, and regular snack and mealtimes, and have the child pour from a pitcher into individual glasses.
- Include the child in simple cooking chores. The child can pour water into a bowl for Jell-O, pour soup into a pan to heat, and pour milk into cake batter. Doing the dishes afterward provides more pouring opportunities.
- Include toy pitchers, cups, and tall containers of various sizes in the sink, bathtub, wading pool, or water table. Let the child practice filling and dumping from one container to another.
- Have a tea party for the child and peers, dolls, or stuffed animals. Have the child take turns pouring pretend drinks for guests, to practice the pouring motion without having to control actual liquids.
- Include the child in gardening activities and have child water plants using a small pitcher.

Environmental Arrangements

- Use pourable solids to introduce the pouring motion. Children can pour sand, cornmeal, macaroni, beans, rice, and cereal from one container to the other, using the same tipping motion with the wrist that is required to pour liquids. Start with larger items (cereal, beans) and systematically introduce smaller particles (rice, cornmeal, sand).
- Squeeze bottles are easy to control when first practicing pouring because they are lightweight and retain liquid when tipped.
- Begin pouring activities by using thick liquids (smoothies, milkshakes, ketchup) that

Adap A

pour slowly. As the child gains control over tipping the container to start and stop the flow of liquid, gradually introduce thinner liquids.
- Use a small container and fill it half full of liquid. A measuring cup with a handle and spout may be easiest for a child to first learn to pour.
- Use a heavy container with a sturdy base as a receptacle so the child will not tip it over when pouring.

Instructional Sequence

- Model pouring liquid into a container. Have peers and siblings demonstrate pouring in a group activity like filling a large pot with water.
- Verbally instruct the child to pour liquid from a small container to a cup by offering details ("Tip the cup down," "Pour slowly," "Tip it back up now").
- Help the child pick up the container and offer minimal physical assistance to guide the pouring movement. Try to prompt only the initial tipping of the container to pour or to stop pouring.

TEACHING CONSIDERATIONS

1. The child should be seated or standing in a supported, balanced position so that concentration is on the fine motor activity of pouring.
2. Avoid heavy or breakable containers and hot liquids.
3. Provide smock, bib, and floor covering; be prepared to mop up spills when the child is first learning this skill.
4. For the child with a motor impairment, consult a qualified specialist for teaching ideas.
5. Have the child with a visual impairment feel the pitcher and receptacle with hands before actually pouring solids or liquids. Describe what the child is feeling.
6. Consider safety with the selection and preparation of all liquids and utensils.

Objective 5.2   Transfers food

DEVELOPMENTAL PROGRAMMING STEP

PS5.2a   The child uses a utensil to remove food from a bowl or plate.

IMPORTANCE OF SKILL

This skill enables the child to function more independently during mealtime activities, increasing opportunities to interact with other people in socially appropriate ways. A similar skill is useful in cooking, gardening, and many leisure activities.

PRECEDING OBJECTIVE

FM B:1.1   Turns object over using wrist and arm rotation with each hand

CONCURRENT GOALS AND OBJECTIVES

FM B:2.1   Fits variety of shapes into corresponding spaces
Adap A:4.0   Eats with fork and/or spoon

Cog D:1.1   Imitates motor action that is commonly used
SC B:1.0   Gains person's attention and refers to an object, person, and/or event
SC B:2.1   Uses consistent consonant–vowel combinations
SC C:2.3   Carries out one-step direction *with* contextual cues
Soc A:3.1   Initiates communication with familiar adult
Soc B:1.1   Meets physical needs of hunger and thirst
Soc B:2.0   Responds to established social routine
Soc C:2.0   Initiates and maintains communicative exchange with peer

TEACHING SUGGESTIONS
Activity-Based

- Provide regular opportunities for the child to practice serving food. Offer food family style during outside play, picnics, and regular snack and mealtimes, and have the child transfer food from a large plate or bowl into individual servings.
- Include the child in simple cooking chores. The child can transfer cups of flour or sugar into bowls, scoop soup or juice concentrate into a pan or pitcher, or spread butter or jam on toast.
- Have a tea party for the child and peers, dolls, or stuffed animals. Have the child take turns serving pretend food to guests, to practice the serving motions without having to control real food.
- Ask the child to assist feeding pets; have the child scoop dog food into a dish.
- Include the child in gardening activities; have the child dig scoops of dirt and transfer them to a bucket.

Environmental Arrangements

- Include toy bowls, plates, and utensils of all types in the sandbox and garden and on the cornmeal table. Let the child practice transferring dirt, sand, and cornmeal from one container to another.
- Begin by letting the child transfer finger foods like toast and fruit chunks. Introduce spoon or fork after the child has established transferring food by hand.
- Bigger serving utensils may be easier for the child to use.
- Use foods like mashed potatoes, pudding, casseroles, applesauce, and yogurt that stick to the serving utensil. As the child becomes more proficient at transferring food, introduce drier and less sticky foods.
- Arrange special snacks that allow opportunities to transfer food. Cut bananas in chunks rather than offer them whole; cut strawberry or peach slices to spoon onto a dish one or two at a time.

Instructional Sequence

- Model or have peers and siblings model transferring food with utensils.
- Verbally instruct the child to use a spoon or fork to transfer food from a bowl to a plate by offering details ("Slide the spoon under the food," "Pick it up," "Put it on the other plate").
- Use minimal physical assistance to hold the child's hand around the utensil, then scoop and transfer the food. You may need to stabilize the bowl or plate that receives the food.

Adap A

TEACHING CONSIDERATIONS

1. The child should be seated or standing in a supported, balanced position so that concentration is on the fine motor activity of transferring from one container to the other.
2. Avoid bowls and plates that are easily broken and food that is too hot.
3. Provide smock, bib, and floor covering; be prepared for spills when the child is first learning this skill.
4. For the child with a motor impairment, consult a qualified specialist for teaching ideas.
5. Have the child with a visual impairment feel the utensils with hands before using them with food. Describe what the child is feeling.
6. Consider safety with the selection and preparation of all foods and utensils.

Adap A

Strand B

Personal Hygiene

GOAL 1   Initiates toileting

DEVELOPMENTAL PROGRAMMING STEPS

PS1.0a The child initiates toileting in unfamiliar and seldom-visited community settings (e.g., store, park, restaurant, doctor's office).

PS1.0b The child initiates toileting in familiar, frequently visited out-of-home settings
(e.g., car, grandparent's or neighbor's house, classroom).

PS1.0c The child initiates toileting in most familiar and frequent setting(s) with regular caregiver(s) (e.g., home with caregiver, daycare, classroom, extended family).

IMPORTANCE OF SKILL

Independence in toileting is viewed by parents and professionals as an important adaptive skill. It allows the child independence from the caregiver and it allows the caregiver
freedom from a frequent and messy chore. Along with allowing the child to function
more independently, being toilet trained decreases the behaviors that set the developmentally young child apart from other children and thus increases social acceptability.

PRECEDING OBJECTIVE

Adap B:1.1   Demonstrates bowel and bladder control

CONCURRENT GOALS AND OBJECTIVES

GM B:2.2   Maintains a sitting position in chair
Adap C:1.2 Takes off pants
SC B:2.0   Uses consistent word approximations
SC C:2.0   Carries out two-step direction *without* contextual cues
SC C:2.2   Carries out one-step direction *without* contextual cues
Soc A:3.1 Initiates communication with familiar adult
Soc B:2.0 Responds to established social routine

TEACHING SUGGESTIONS
Activity-Based

- Prior to taking the child to the toilet at established toileting times, ask if the child
  needs to use the toilet.

- When you take the child to a new place, indicate the location of the bathroom and tell the child to let you or another adult know if he or she needs to use the toilet.
- Encourage the child to indicate whenever he or she needs to use the toilet.
- At various times throughout the day, pair using the toilet with a regularly occurring activity. For example, before taking a nap, going for a ride in the car, going outside to play, or after waking from a nap or night's sleep, ask the child about using the bathroom.
- Whenever reasonable, make use of natural consequences for being wet or soiled. For example, require a change to dry clothes before allowing the child to sit on your lap, eat lunch, ride in the car, or play with peers.

☑ If your data indicate the child is not making progress toward the goal, provide additional structure within the suggested activities by incorporating the following *environmental arrangements:*

Environmental Arrangements

- Provide child-size potty chairs or toilet seats so that the child is secure and comfortable when going to the bathroom.
- At routine toileting times during the school day, have children line up to go to the bathroom.
- Dress the child in training pants during waking hours. Training pants are easier for the child to remove independently and are less absorbent than diapers. This may motivate the child to initiate toileting to avoid drippy, soaked clothes.
- Dress the child in easy-to-remove outer pants to avoid struggles with clothing and to allow easier undressing for the child who goes independently to the toilet.
- Provide opportunities for the child to observe other children initiating and going to the toilet.

☑ If this goal is particularly difficult for a child, it may be necessary, within activities, to use an *instructional sequence.*

Instructional Sequence

- Have an adult or peer model initiating and going to the toilet. Ask the child at the same time if he or she needs to go to the toilet.
- Remind the child (verbally or with timer) on a regular schedule that it is time to go to the bathroom.
- Physically direct the child to the toilet on a regular schedule. If child squirms or crosses legs at other times, ask, "Do you need to go to the bathroom?" and take the child to the toilet.

☑ Combining or pairing different levels of instructions may be helpful when beginning to teach a new and difficult skill. Fade to less intrusive instructions as soon as possible to encourage more independent performance.

TEACHING CONSIDERATIONS

1. Toilet training requires family involvement. Be sure toilet training is a priority at home before requiring the skill at school.
2. Consult with the family to determine how they refer to toileting needs (e.g., potty, toilet, bathroom). Use the same words when the child is practicing toileting.
3. Generally, a child gains bladder control before bowel control and becomes daytime trained before nighttime.

4. In order for the child to become toilet trained, he or she must have sphincter control. Consult with medical personnel if there are concerns about sphincter muscles or urological disorders.
5. Teach the child who is nonverbal a manual sign, signal, or gesture to use to initiate or request toileting.
6. Consult an occupational or physical therapist for adaptations and positions for the child with a motor impairment. Adaptive toileting equipment may be needed.
7. Be prepared to change pants and sometimes socks as the child learns to toilet independently.

Objective 1.1 Demonstrates bowel and bladder control

DEVELOPMENTAL PROGRAMMING STEPS

PS1.1a The child sits on a potty chair or toilet regularly and accomplishes bowel and bladder functions some of the time.
PS1.1b The child sits on a potty chair or toilet regularly, without necessarily accomplishing bowel or bladder function.

IMPORTANCE OF SKILL

The ability to control the bowel and bladder is essential for a child to independently take care of toileting needs. The child must be able to retain and release waste material at will in order to remain dry and unsoiled between trips to the toilet. This skill is of great value to parents and other caregivers who change and clean diapers. It is of obvious value to the child in social situations.

PRECEDING OBJECTIVE

Adap B:1.2 Indicates awareness of soiled and wet pants and/or diapers

CONCURRENT GOALS AND OBJECTIVES

GM B:2.2 Maintains a sitting position in chair
Adap A:2.0 Washes and dries hands
Adap B:2.0 Uses consistent word approximations
SC C:2.2 Carries out one-step direction *without* contextual cues
SC C:2.3 Carries out one-step direction *with* contextual cues
Soc A:3.1 Initiates communication with familiar adult
Soc B:2.1 Responds to routine event

TEACHING SUGGESTIONS
Activity-Based

- Take the child to the bathroom prior to activities that involve being away from a bathroom for 1 hour or more (e.g., bedtime, car ride, outside play).
- As soon as the child wakes from a nap or nighttime sleep, take the child to the bathroom.
- Take the child to the bathroom during established.toileting routines. For example,

after eating, before bedtime, upon arriving at school, or 20–30 minutes after drinking liquids.

■ Allow the child to follow adult or peer into the bathroom; let the child sit on the potty chair at the same time someone else is using the bathroom.

Environmental Arrangements

■ Provide child-size potty chairs or toilet seats so that the child is secure and comfortable when going to the bathroom.

■ Provide washable books or lap toys near the potty chair or toilet to occupy the child while sitting. Initially require a brief period of sitting and gradually increase the time as the child becomes accustomed to the activity.

■ Obtain a schedule of the child's regular elimination times. Record each time elimination occurs during the day. If the schedule shows a pattern of toilet times, sit the child on the toilet just prior to these times.

■ Dress the child in training pants during waking hours. This makes it easier to put the child on the toilet frequently. Training pants absorb less than diapers, making the child more aware of uncomfortable wet or soiled pants. This may motivate the child to use the toilet.

■ Increase the amount of liquids and fiber in the child's diet to increase the number of times the child will need to use the toilet.

■ Sit the child on a potty chair next to a peer who is using the toilet, allowing the child to observe what the peer is doing.

■ While the child is sitting on the potty chair, run water from the faucet. The sound of running water may trigger the child to urinate.

Instructional Sequence

■ Have an adult or peer model using the toilet.
■ Provide verbal direction for the child to use the toilet.
■ Place the child on the toilet for 5 minutes on a regular schedule (at least once every hour). Give the child a drink of water 10–20 minutes before this time.

TEACHING CONSIDERATIONS

1. Toilet training requires family involvement. Be sure toilet training is a priority at home before requiring the skill at school.
2. Consult with the family to determine how they refer to toileting needs (e.g., potty, toilet, bathroom). Use the same words when the child is practicing toileting.
3. Generally, a child gains bladder control before bowel control and becomes daytime trained before nighttime.
4. When training a male child, teach him to sit rather than stand to urinate. He can learn to urinate standing after he learns to distinguish between the need to urinate and to have a bowel movement.
5. In order for the child to become toilet trained, he or she must have sphincter control. Consult with medical personnel if there are concerns about sphincter muscles or urological disorders.
6. Teach the child who is nonverbal a manual sign, signal, or gesture to use to initiate or request toileting.
7. Consult an occupational or physical therapist for adaptations for a child with a motor impairment. Adaptive toileting equipment may be needed.

Adap B

Objective 1.2   Indicates awareness of soiled and wet pants and/or diapers

DEVELOPMENTAL PROGRAMMING STEPS

This objective is the most basic step for the goal, initiates toileting, to be taught. Most children will benefit from the activities outlined here that emphasize this skill. For children who need more instruction, consider designing programming steps from the *environmental arrangements* or from the *instructional sequence* outlined.

IMPORTANCE OF SKILL

Awareness of wet or soiled pants is important to learning independent toileting. When the child indicates this awareness, he or she is usually experiencing discomfort in wearing the soiled clothes. This can be a motivating factor for the child to become toilet trained. The child begins to sense that wet or soiled pants are not desirable, and that clean, dry pants are acceptable and comfortable.

CONCURRENT GOALS AND OBJECTIVES

Adap B:2.1   Washes hands
Adap C:1.2   Takes off pants
SC A:2.1   Follows person's pointing gesture to establish joint attention
SC B:1.0   Gains person's attention and refers to an object, person, and/or event
SC B:2.0   Uses consistent word approximations
Soc A:3.1   Initiates communication with familiar adult
Soc B:2.1   Responds to routine event

TEACHING SUGGESTIONS
Activity-Based

- If the child informs you verbally or by gesturing that his or her pants are wet or soiled, reinforce the child by changing his or her pants quickly.
- Establish a toileting routine. When you notice that the child has wet or soiled pants, ask what happened and then pause and wait for an indication that pants are wet or soiled. Provide gestures and facial expressions to indicate that being wet or soiled is unpleasant. Change the child's pants as soon as possible to prevent the child from becoming comfortable in soiled pants. Wash the child's hands as you wash yours after changing.
- As you change the child's diaper, clearly label it as wet or soiled. Have the child repeat the label with an appropriate sign, gesture, or word. After changing, label the diaper or pants as clean and dry. Use unpleasant and pleasant facial expressions and voice tone to emphasize wet or soiled and dry or clean, respectively.
- Use the labels clean, dry, dirty to describe objects and events throughout the day. For example, label muddy shoes as "dirty," washed and dried hands as "clean and dry," and bath sponge as "wet." Exposure to more examples of clean, dry, and dirty may assist the child in developing terms to describe diapers or pants.

Environmental Arrangements

- Use the child's schedule for urination and bowel movements to indicate when to ask the child about the dryness of his or her diapers or pants.
- Some children may find more discomfort in a soiled diaper than a wet diaper. Begin by verbally making the child aware of soiled diapers and then wet diapers.
- To help the child gain awareness, describe other indicators of wet or soiled diapers. Ask if the child smells something. Ask if the child sees wet pants in the mirror, hears the squish of a wet diaper when sitting, or hears the rattle of a wet plastic diaper. Combine multiple cues to help the child identify wet or soiled pants.
- Cloth diapers make it easier for the child to feel wetness and become aware of urinating. Whenever possible, use cloth diapers to work on this skill.
- Dress the child in training pants during waking hours. Training pants absorb less than diapers, making the child more aware of the discomfort of wet or soiled pants.

Instructional Sequence

- Acknowledge the child's wet or soiled diaper by labeling.
- Provide the child with a word, sign, or gesture as a cue that the diaper is wet or soiled. Model the cue and have the child imitate before changing pants.
- Physically direct the child to look at or touch the diaper and label it as wet or soiled. (A soiled diaper is usually also wet, so have the child touch the wet part only.) Wash child's hands immediately after changing.

TEACHING CONSIDERATIONS

1. Toilet training requires family involvement. Be sure toilet training is a priority at home before requiring it at school.
2. Some children do not become aware of wet or soiled pants until after gaining bowel and bladder control (Adap B:1.1). For these children, it is advisable to work on Objective 1.2 and Objective 1.1 simultaneously.
3. For the child who has no feeling in the genital area, teach awareness of a wet or soiled diaper by smell or vision.
4. After toileting (or diaper change) is a good time to practice the adaptive skill of washing hands.
5. Teach the child who is nonverbal a manual sign, signal, or gesture to indicate wet pants.

GOAL 2   Washes and dries hands

DEVELOPMENTAL PROGRAMMING STEPS

It may be necessary to break this skill down into the critical skills of the routine. If you are working on just one component of the skill (drying), teach it as part of the entire sequence, rather than as an isolated skill. It may also be necessary to continue giving more assistance on those components of the skill that you have not yet specifically taught.

PS2.0a   The child washes and rinses hands and dries effectively with a towel.
PS2.0b   The child washes hands with soap, rinses with water, and rubs hands on towel without necessarily drying them.

IMPORTANCE OF SKILL

As the child learns to wash and dry his or her own hands, the child begins to develop independence in grooming. This is important, as the child no longer depends on the caregiver to always be available to wash and dry hands. It is also important that the child develops good personal hygiene habits because washing hands helps stop the spread of germs. A clean appearance is socially acceptable and will help the child be more readily accepted by peers and adults.

PRECEDING OBJECTIVE

Adap B:2.1   Washes hands

CONCURRENT GOALS AND OBJECTIVES

FM A:5.1   Releases hand-held object onto and/or into a larger target with either hand
FM B:1.0   Rotates either wrist on horizontal plane
Adap B:1.0   Initiates toileting
Cog E:2.0   Uses an object to obtain another object
Cog E:4.0   Solves common problems
SC C:2.1   Carries out two-step direction *with* contextual cues
SC C:2.3   Carries out one-step direction *with* contextual cues
Soc B:1.0   Meets external physical needs in socially appropriate ways
Soc B:2.1   Responds to routine event

TEACHING SUGGESTIONS

Activity-Based

- As the child goes through the daily routine and encounters situations that require clean hands, pause and wait for the child to independently wash and dry hands. Ask, "What do we do to clean up?" This may be accompanied by the adult washing and drying hands, too.
- Provide opportunities for the child to wash and dry dishes, dolls, and toys. The child can practice washing and drying objects and his or her own hands.
- Establish hand washing as a part of regular daily activities, as in before and after eating, after toileting, before bedtime, and after engaging in a messy activity.
- Encourage activities that will get the child's hands messy and require them to be washed after the activity. Some fun messy activities are finger painting, playing in the dirt, spreading shaving cream over a table surface, making Play-Doh, and cooking.

Environmental Arrangements

- Water activities (e.g., washing dishes, washing dolls, water play) can be used to give the child opportunities to dry his or her own hands during and after the activity.
- Towels that are attached to a rack or holder may be easier for the child to manipulate.
- Colorful towels or towels with characters can be used to encourage hand drying.
- Some environmental adaptations can make the skill easier. Faucet knobs that turn are easier for a child to operate than those that pull.
- If the sink or towel is too high for the child to reach, have a sturdy stool available for the child to stand on.
- Soap in a pump dispenser may be easier to use than a large bar of soap or powdered

soap in a push-up dispenser. Also, small bars of soap (hotel size) are easier to handle than large ones.

Instructional Sequence

- Have an adult or peer model washing and drying hands, and have the child imitate the steps (e.g., turn on water, wash with soap, rinse, dry, throw away towel).
- Give the child verbal cues for the hand-washing routine (e.g., "Turn on the water," "Use the soap," "Rinse off the soap," "Dry your hands," "Put the towel away").
- Prompt the child by pointing to the next step in the routine. For example, if the child does not dry his or her hands, point to the towel.
- Physically assist the child as needed to help completely wash and dry hands.
- It may be necessary to break this skill down into its critical components. Complete the entire skill, even if you are teaching just one component of it, such as using soap.

    The child turns on the water, washes and rinses his or her own hands, and turns off the water.

    The child obtains a towel.

    The child rubs the towel on all sides of his or her hands until they are dry.

    The child returns the towel to the towel rack or throws it away in the trash can.

TEACHING CONSIDERATIONS

1. Ask the parent what type of faucet knobs the child uses most often at home. Begin teaching this skill with that type of knob, if possible.
2. Some children may not be able to regulate the water temperature when learning to wash hands. Check the water or teach the child to use just cold water. Use safety precautions.
3. The child may find it easier to dry hands on a soft hand towel rather than on paper towels. If using hand towels at school, each child will need his or her own to prevent the spread of germs.
4. Be sure adequate support is given to the child with a motor impairment to allow the child to perform the skills.
5. Teach the child who is nonverbal a manual sign, signal, or gesture to indicate a desire to wash his or her hands.

Objective 2.1   Washes hands

DEVELOPMENTAL PROGRAMMING STEPS

PS2.1a   The child makes attempts to rinse hands after washing with soap.
PS2.1b   The child grasps soap and rubs it on his or her hands.
PS2.1c   The child places his or her hands under running water or in a sink full of water.

IMPORTANCE OF SKILL

Washing hands is a skill that will lead to independence in grooming. Clean hands will give the child an attractive appearance and will help stop the spread of germs. Washing hands also helps the child develop motor control and is a functional activity for practicing many fine motor skills.

Adap B

CONCURRENT GOALS AND OBJECTIVES

FM A:3.3   Grasps hand-size object with either hand using whole hand
FM A:5.1   Releases hand-held object onto and/or into a larger target with either hand
FM B:1.0   Rotates either wrist on horizontal plane
GM C:3.3   Gets up and down from low structure
Adap A:4.0   Eats with fork and/or spoon
Adap B:1.1   Demonstrates bowel and bladder control
Cog D:1.0   Imitates motor action that is not commonly used
Cog E:4.0   Solves common problems
SC C:2.1   Carries out two-step direction *with* contextual cues
Soc B:1.0   Meets external physical needs in socially appropriate ways
Soc B:2.1   Responds to routine event

TEACHING SUGGESTIONS
Activity-Based

- Provide opportunities for the child to engage in water play and wash dishes, dolls, or toys.
- As the child goes through the daily routine and encounters situations that result in dirty or sticky hands, practice washing hands. An adult or peer may also model washing hands.
- Establish hand washing as part of regular daily activities, as in before and after eating, after toileting, before bedtime, and after engaging in a messy activity.
- Play imaginary games and sing songs such as "This is the way we wash our hands . . . ."
- Encourage activities that will get the child's hands messy and require them to be washed after the activity. Some fun messy activities are making cookies, planting seeds, finger painting with pudding, and playing with clay.
- Have the child practice washing hands while taking a bath.

Environmental Arrangements

- Set a dishpan of soapy water and a cloth at a table where the child can sit and leisurely wash hands and enjoy water play.
- Practice hand "rubbing" by allowing the child to apply hand lotion or baby powder after hands are clean. This gives a visual cue to "get all the spots" and is usually a pleasant treat.
- Some environmental adaptations can make the skill easier. Faucet handles that turn are easier for a child to operate than those that pull. If the sink is too high for the child to reach the faucet, have a sturdy stool available for the child.
- Soap in a pump dispenser may be easier to use than a large bar of soap or powdered soap in a push-up dispenser. Also, small bars of soap (hotel size) are easier to handle than large ones.

Instructional Sequence

- Have adult or peer model washing hands.
- Wash your hands and have the child imitate each step before going to the next. For example, wait to rinse your hands until the child has used soap.
- Verbally direct the child to wash hands. If necessary, give verbal directions to assist with the skill (e.g., "Rub your hands together").

Adap B

- Assist the child by pointing to the next step in the routine. For example, after the child wets hands, point to the soap.
- Physically assist the child as needed to help completely wash his or her hands.

TEACHING CONSIDERATIONS

1. Ask a parent what type of faucet knobs the child uses most often at home. Begin teaching this skill with that type of knob, if possible.
2. The child may not be able to regulate the water temperature when learning this skill. Check the water or teach the child to use just cold water. Use safety precautions.
3. Be sure adequate support is given to the child with a motor impairment to allow the child to perform the skill.
4. The child with a visual impairment may benefit from adaptive materials, such as soap-on-a-rope. Talk to the child as you assist with this skill (e.g., "The soap is slippery," "This water is warm"). Consult a specialist for recommendations.
5. Teach the child who is nonverbal a manual sign, signal, or gesture to indicate a desire to wash his or her hands.

GOAL 3   Brushes teeth

DEVELOPMENTAL PROGRAMMING STEPS

PS3.0a   The child makes a persistent attempt to brush in one spot.
PS3.0b   The child moves the toothbrush around in his or her mouth, briefly contacting the teeth.
PS3.0c   The child puts the toothbrush in his or her mouth and chews on the bristles.

IMPORTANCE OF SKILL

Good oral hygiene is essential to maintaining good health. It helps prevent cavities, gum disease, bad breath, and germs. A child with poor oral hygiene may develop tooth decay and swollen gums, and an unattractive appearance may separate the child from peers. As the child learns to brush teeth, the child becomes more independent in taking care of grooming needs.

PRECEDING OBJECTIVE

Adap B:3.1   Cooperates with teeth brushing

CONCURRENT GOALS AND OBJECTIVES

FM A:3.2   Grasps cylindrical object with either hand by closing fingers around it
FM B:1.1   Turns object over using wrist and arm rotation with each hand
FM B:2.2   Fits object into defined space
Adap A:3.0   Drinks from cup and/or glass
Adap A:4.1   Brings food to mouth using utensil
Cog B:3.1   Looks for object in usual location

Cog D:1.0   Imitates motor action that is not commonly used
Cog G:1.2   Uses functionally appropriate actions with objects
SC C:2.3   Carries out one-step direction *with* contextual cues
Soc A:3.1   Initiates communication with familiar adult
Soc B:1.1   Meets physical needs of hunger and thirst
Soc B:2.1   Responds to routine event

TEACHING SUGGESTIONS
Activity-Based

- Establish regular times during the day for the child to brush teeth. Incorporate brushing teeth into morning, evening, and going-out routines. Tell the child why brushing teeth is important and how to do it.
- Take advantage of opportunities in the community to expose a young child to dental information. Go to health fairs; have a dental hygienist speak at the preschool; and provide books about teeth and teeth brushing.
- Plan regular visits to the dentist for child age 3 or older. Use the type of brush recommended by the hygienist.
- Have the child brush teeth when other children or adults are doing the same.
- Assist the child in putting toothpaste on the brush, if necessary. While the child is learning this skill, you may need to complete brushing for the child.

Environmental Arrangements

- Stand behind the child with your arms around him or her, enabling the child to watch in the mirror. This is a good position to begin encouraging the child's participation through physical assistance.
- Specially flavored toothpaste encourages its use; however, toothpaste is not necessary for cleaning teeth and may be eliminated if the child does not tolerate it.
- Using colorful or character toothbrushes (e.g., Kermit, Mickey Mouse) adds interest to the task. Some brushes are available with chimes that sooth and divert the attention of the very defensive child.
- Let the child put the toothbrush in his or her mouth and suck off the water and a minimal amount of toothpaste. The child may also chew on the toothbrush.
- Give the child a carrot stick to suck on to practice grasping and putting something into his or her mouth. Encourage the child to rub the carrot over his or her teeth.
- Practice "spitting" drinking water in the sink.
- An electric toothbrush may be used if the child is not afraid of the noise; this brush does not have to be moved up and down.
- If the child has a neuromotor/oral-motor impairment, have a physical, occupational, or speech therapist evaluate to determine possible adaptive devices for teeth brushing.

Instructional Sequence

- Have an adult or peer model brushing teeth.
- Verbally direct the child to brush teeth. If necessary, give verbal directions for each step of the skill (e.g., "Brush the front teeth").
- Have the child brush teeth in front of a mirror.
- Give minimal physical assistance to start the child moving the toothbrush over the teeth.

Adap B

TEACHING CONSIDERATIONS

1. Use a child-size toothbrush with soft bristles.
2. When using toothpaste, use a very small amount.
3. Keep each child's toothbrush covered and separate from others to prevent spread of airborne germs.
4. An adult should complete the brushing to ensure the teeth are clean for a child who is developmentally 0–4 years old.
5. Certain medications may cause side effects that alter dental hygiene needs. Check with the child's doctor or dentist to coordinate care of teeth, gums, and mouth.
6. Be sure the child is positioned and supported so that the child does not fall and injure him- or herself with the toothbrush.
7. For the child with motor or oral-motor impairment, consult a qualified specialist for teaching ideas.
8. Teach the child who is nonverbal a manual sign, signal, or gesture to indicate a desire to brush teeth.

Objective 3.1 Cooperates with teeth brushing

DEVELOPMENTAL PROGRAMMING STEPS

PS3.1a The child tolerates an adult lightly brushing his or her teeth and gums.
PS3.1b The child tolerates the rubber tip of a toothbrush or an adult's finger covered with terry cloth moving along his or her gums and teeth.
PS3.1c The child tolerates an adult's finger moving along his or her gums and teeth.
PS3.1d The child opens his or her mouth on request.

IMPORTANCE OF SKILL

Good oral hygiene is essential to maintaining good health. It helps prevent cavities, gum disease, bad breath, and the spread of germs. Allowing an adult to brush the teeth establishes the habit and routine before the child is able to brush his or her own teeth.

CONCURRENT OBJECTIVES

Adap A:3.2 Drinks from cup and/or glass held by adult
Adap A:4.1 Brings food to mouth using utensil
Cog C:2.1 Indicates desire to continue familiar game and/or action
Cog D:1.1 Imitates motor action that is commonly used
SC C:1.3   Locates common objects, people, and/or events *with* contextual cues
Soc A:3.2 Responds to communication from familiar adult
Soc B:2.1 Responds to routine event

TEACHING SUGGESTIONS
Activity-Based

- When the child's teeth first begin to come in, clean them after the child eats and before bedtime by rubbing them with a washcloth.

- As the child gets more teeth, brush them after every meal and at bedtime. Initially, do not put toothpaste on the brush; as the child begins to tolerate brushing, add a small amount of toothpaste.
- Allow the child to suck on fingers, your finger, or pacifier to get used to having something in the mouth.

Environmental Arrangements

- Toothbrushes with chimes in the handles may divert the child's attention and facilitate cooperation.
- If toothpaste is used, use a very small amount. Toothpaste may be rinsed out by putting water on the toothbrush and rubbing it over the teeth.
- For the child who has a bite reflex or hypersensitive mouth, have a speech, physical, or occupational therapist evaluate and suggest ways to desensitize or adapt for dental hygiene.
- For the child who resists the toothbrush in his or her mouth, begin by introducing your finger with a dab of yogurt or applesauce into the mouth. Systematically introduce a washcloth on your finger and then a toothbrush.

Instructional Sequence

- Have an adult or peer model brushing teeth.
- Verbally prompt the child to keep his or her mouth open while the teeth are being brushed.
- For the child who does not have voluntary control of opening the mouth (or who resists opening), it may be necessary to physically assist in opening the mouth so that the teeth can be brushed. Place your thumb under the chin, your index finger along the side of the jaw, and your remaining fingers just below the bottom lip. Gently press down on the chin.
- For the tactilely defensive child, use other soft materials to clean the teeth before introducing a toothbrush.

TEACHING CONSIDERATIONS

1. Use a child-size toothbrush with soft bristles.
2. When using toothpaste, use a very small amount.
3. Keep each child's toothbrush covered and separate from others to prevent spread of airborne germs.
4. The child may be resistant to an adult brushing his or her teeth and will want to do it alone.
5. Certain medications may cause side effects that alter dental hygiene needs. Check with the child's doctor or dentist to coordinate care of teeth, gums, and mouth.
6. Be sure the child is appropriately positioned and supported to prevent gagging or choking on the toothbrush or saliva.
7. For a child with a motor or oral-motor impairment, consult a qualified specialist for teaching ideas.
8. For the child who has oral-tactile defensiveness, teeth brushing is a good way to help the child become more tolerant of food and objects that will be placed in the mouth.

Adap B

Strand C

Undressing

GOAL 1   Undresses self

DEVELOPMENTAL PROGRAMMING STEPS

In order to achieve this goal, a child must perform Objectives 1.1–1.6 to criteria. Refer to the specific objectives for Developmental Programming Steps to develop each skill.

The objectives in this strand are organized from easiest (1.6) to more difficult (1.1). However, many factors influence which articles of clothing the child learns to remove first (e.g., season of the year, interest, peers, and needs of individual children and families).

IMPORTANCE OF SKILL

Children gain independence by taking care of their own basic needs. Undressing represents one of the initial areas that allows a child independence from his or her caregiver. Undressing activities provide many opportunities for practicing fine and gross motor skills, learning concepts, and engaging in social interactions in a functional context. Learning adaptive skills also decreases the difference between developmentally young children and their peers.

PRECEDING OBJECTIVES

Adap C:1.1   Takes off coat and/or jacket
Adap C:1.2   Takes off pants
Adap C:1.3   Takes off shirt
Adap C:1.4   Takes off socks
Adap C:1.5   Takes off shoes
Adap C:1.6   Takes off hat

CONCURRENT GOALS AND OBJECTIVES

FM A:3.0   Grasps hand-size object with either hand using ends of thumb, index, and second fingers
FM B:1.0   Rotates either wrist on horizontal plane
GM B:1.2   Regains balanced, upright sitting position after *reaching* across the body to the right and to the left
GM B:2.0   Sits down in and gets out of chair

Adap B:1.0 Initiates toileting
Cog B:3.1   Looks for object in usual location
Cog D:1.0   Imitates motor action that is not commonly used
Cog E:4.1   Uses more than one strategy in attempt to solve common problem
Cog F:2.1   Groups functionally related objects
SC B:1.0   Gains person's attention and refers to an object, person, and/or event
SC B:2.0   Uses consistent word approximations
Soc A:3.1   Initiates communication with familiar adult
Soc B:1.0   Meets external physical needs in socially appropriate ways
Soc B:2.0   Responds to established social routine

TEACHING SUGGESTIONS

Activity-Based

In order to achieve this goal, a child must perform Objectives 1.1–1.6 to criteria. Refer to the specific objective for Teaching Suggestions and Teaching Considerations to develop each skill.

Objective 1.1 Takes off coat and/or jacket

DEVELOPMENTAL PROGRAMMING STEPS

PS1.1a   The child removes his or her coat part way. For example, the child removes a sleeve from one arm, removes the coat from one shoulder, or pulls off the coat that has been removed from one side.
PS1.1b   The child persists in pulling at sleeves, lapels, or collar in attempt to remove the coat or jacket.
PS1.1c   The child tugs briefly at a coat or jacket, points, or otherwise indicates to an adult a desire to have the coat removed.

IMPORTANCE OF SKILL

Taking off a coat is an important skill in becoming independent in undressing. It allows the child to become less dependent on other people for controlling body temperature. A child's self-concept may be influenced by his or her level of independent functioning in the adaptive area.

PRECEDING OBJECTIVE

FM A:3.3   Grasps hand-size object with either hand using whole hand

CONCURRENT GOALS AND OBJECTIVES

FM A:3.0   Grasps hand-size object with either hand using ends of thumb, index, and second fingers
FM B:1.0   Rotates either wrist on horizontal plane
GM B:1.2   Regains balanced, upright sitting position after *reaching* across the body to the right and to the left
Adap B:1.0 Initiates toileting

Adap C

Cog B:3.1	Looks for object in usual location
Cog D:1.0	Imitates motor action that is not commonly used
Cog E:4.1	Uses more than one strategy in attempt to solve common problem
Cog F:2.1	Groups functionally related objects
SC B:1.0	Gains person's attention and refers to an object, person, and/or event
SC B:2.0	Uses consistent word approximations
Soc A:3.1	Initiates communication with familiar adult
Soc B:1.0	Meets external physical needs in socially appropriate ways
Soc B:2.1	Responds to routine event

TEACHING SUGGESTIONS
Activity-Based

- This skill is best taught as a natural consequence to coming in from outside. A child might become confused or irritated if you try to teach this skill by putting on a coat and removing it without going outside.
- When a child arrives at a new destination (e.g., school, home, coming in from outside) wearing a coat or a jacket, encourage the child to remove it. If the child does not initiate removing the coat, offer a reminder (e.g., "Don't forget to take off your coat now that you're indoors").
- Whenever appropriate, have peers or siblings remove coats also.
- Provide various coats for the child to use in dress-up play (e.g., doctor coat, glamour coat, furry coat, explorer coat).
- During seasons that require the child to wear a coat or jacket, plan regular outdoor activities that provide opportunities to remove the coat when returning inside.

☑ If your data indicate the child is not making progress toward the objective, provide additional structure within the suggested activities by incorporating the following *environmental arrangements:*

Environmental Arrangements

- Plan activities that include dressing up as doctors, firefighters, animals, or other characters who wear distinctive coats.
- Play a hiding game by putting a special sticker or name tag on the back of the child's coat where it cannot be seen until the coat is taken off.
- Begin teaching this skill by using a cape. As the child demonstrates the intent and behavior of removing an outer garment, introduce loose-fitting coats and jackets.
- Use loose-fitting jackets. As the child learns to remove the loose jacket, teach the child to remove a jacket or coat that is the appropriate size for the child.
- Lightweight jackets are often easier to remove than heavy coats or sweaters. Coats with cuffs are slightly more difficult. Begin teaching with the easiest materials available and systematically introduce more difficult coats and jackets.
- Have a mirror by the door where the child takes off his or her coat, to allow the child to watch him- or herself remove the coat.

☑ If this objective is particularly difficult for a child, it may be necessary, within activities, to use an *instructional sequence.*

Instructional Sequence

- Give the child a general verbal or nonverbal cue to remove coat. Pause and wait for the child to begin taking off his or her coat.

Adap C

- Model taking off your coat or have a peer demonstrate removing the coat; then have the child imitate the behavior.
- Give the child specific verbal cues to remove the coat (e.g., "Grab the sleeve with your other hand," "Pull your arm out").
- Give the child visual or tactile cues. Pull on or point to the sleeve of the coat to prompt the child to remove an arm.
- Help the child remove the coat with minimal physical assistance as needed:
    The child takes off a coat that has been moved just off the shoulders.
    The child takes off a coat that has been moved just below the elbows.
    The child takes off a coat when the dominant arm is already out of the sleeve.
    The child takes off a coat that is partially off the nondominant arm and totally off the dominant arm.

☑ Combining or pairing different levels of instructions may be helpful when beginning to teach a new and difficult skill. Fade to less intrusive instructions as soon as possible to encourage more independent performance.

TEACHING CONSIDERATIONS

1. The child can learn different methods of taking off a coat or jacket. The child can remove one sleeve at a time, extend arms back and remove arms from sleeves from behind, or swing the coat or jacket over his or her head and pull off the sleeves from the front. Choose the method that is most appropriate for the child.
2. Consult a qualified specialist for adaptations and positions for a child with a motor impairment. Adaptive clothing (e.g., snaps, Velcro) may be necessary.
3. The child must be in a balanced or supported position that allows free use of arms.
4. The child with a visual impairment may need more manipulative, tactile, and auditory cues to replace models, gestures, and pointing.

Objective 1.2 Takes off pants

DEVELOPMENTAL PROGRAMMING STEPS

PS1.2a The child removes pants part way. (For example, the child takes off pants that have been pulled down to the knees, or the child pulls down pants to the knees.)

PS1.2b The child persists in pulling and pushing at legs, waist, or cuffs of pants in an attempt to remove them.

PS1.2c The child tugs at pants, vocalizes, points, or otherwise indicates to an adult a desire to remove pants.

IMPORTANCE OF SKILL

Taking off pants is an important skill in becoming independent in undressing. This one skill allows the child to take care of his or her own needs during toileting, swimming, bedtime, and morning routines.

PRECEDING OBJECTIVE

FM A:3.3   Grasps hand-size object with either hand using whole hand

CONCURRENT GOALS AND OBJECTIVES

FM A:3.0	Grasps hand-size object with either hand using ends of thumb, index, and second fingers
FM B:1.0	Rotates either wrist on horizontal plane
GM B:1.2	Regains balanced, upright sitting position after *reaching* across the body to the right and to the left
GM B:2.0	Sits down in and gets out of chair
Adap B:1.0	Initiates toileting
Cog D:1.0	Imitates motor action that is not commonly used
Cog E:4.1	Uses more than one strategy in attempt to solve common problem
Cog F:2.1	Groups functionally related objects
SC B:1.0	Gains person's attention and refers to an object, person, and/or event
SC B:2.0	Uses consistent word approximations
Soc A:3.1	Initiates communication with familiar adult
Soc B:1.0	Meets external physical needs in socially appropriate ways
Soc B:2.1	Responds to routine event

TEACHING SUGGESTIONS

Activity-Based

- Encourage the child to remove pants during daily caregiving routines such as undressing at bathtime, bedtime, or when changing into a clean pair of pants. If the child does not initiate taking off pants, offer a reminder (e.g., "Don't forget your pants").
- Whenever appropriate, have peers or siblings remove pants also. For example, when undressing for swimming, bedtime, or after dress-up, let children undress together. Only children who know each other well (e.g., siblings, regular playmates) should undress together, to promote learning about privacy.
- When changing the child's diaper or when helping the child use the toilet, encourage the child to assist in pulling down his or her own pants.
- A favorite time to remove pants is when they are replaced by a garment that symbolizes "fun," such as removing pajamas to get dressed for outside, removing clothes for a bath, or removing clothes to put on a swimsuit.
- Provide a dress-up box of clothes that are loose, fun, and representative of characters such as Superman, Mickey Mouse, or Smurfs. Use adult or sibling pants as part of the dress-up wardrobe. Encourage the child to take pants off independently at the end of dress-up time.

Environmental Arrangements

- Short pants are easier to remove than long pants. Begin teaching the removal of pants by using underpants and shorts. Introduce long pants once the child demonstrates the ability to remove short pants.
- Use loose or large pants at first. Drawstring sweatpants and elastic-waist pants are easy to remove. Begin teaching with these pants and introduce pants with zippers, buttons, and flies as the child becomes proficient at removing pants.
- Use "fun" and "wild" underwear or diapers beneath pants to motivate the child to remove outer pants. Have the child look for the characters on undergarments by taking off outer pants. A bandage on the knee is also a good hidden object to uncover.

- A child who needs support when taking off pants may be assisted by leaning against a wall or holding onto a chair or handrail. Some children find it easiest to pull pants down to the knees while standing and then sit to pull the legs out of the pants.

Instructional Sequence

- Give the child a general verbal or nonverbal cue to remove pants. Pause and wait for the child to begin taking off his or her pants.
- Model taking off your pants or have a peer demonstrate removing pants; then have the child imitate the behavior.
- Give the child specific verbal directions to remove pants (e.g., "Grab the waist," "Pull it down," "Pull it off your leg").
- Give the child visual or tactile cues. Pull on or point to the child's pant leg to show how to take it off.
- Help the child remove pants with minimal physical assistance as needed:
  While in a standing position, the child takes off pants that have been pulled down to the middle of the hips.
  While in a standing position, the child takes off pants that have been pulled down to the middle of the thighs.
  While sitting, the child will take off pants that have been pulled down to the ankles.
  While sitting, the child will pull pants off that are just around one ankle.

TEACHING CONSIDERATIONS

1. The child can learn different methods of taking off pants. The child can begin to take off pants by pushing down from the waist or by pulling down from below the waist. The child can remove the legs while sitting or lying down or by stepping out of pants while standing. Choose the method that is most appropriate for the child.
2. Consult a qualified specialist for adaptations and positions for the child with a motor impairment. Adaptive clothing (e.g., snaps, Velcro) may be necessary.
3. The child must be in a balanced or supported position that allows free use of arms.
4. The child with a visual impairment may need more manipulative, tactile, and auditory cues to replace models, gestures, and pointing.

Objective 1.3 Takes off shirt

DEVELOPMENTAL PROGRAMMING STEPS

PS1.3a The child removes the shirt part way. (e.g., the child removes a shirt from one arm by pulling it over his or her head.)

PS1.3b The child persists in pushing and pulling at arms, neck, and front of the shirt in an attempt to remove it.

PS1.3c The child tugs at the shirt, vocalizes, points, or otherwise indicates to an adult a desire to remove the shirt.

IMPORTANCE OF SKILL

Taking off a shirt is an important skill in becoming independent in undressing. It allows the child to become less dependent on other people for daily adaptive needs and uses a variety of gross and fine motor skills in a functional and frequent activity.

PRECEDING OBJECTIVE

FM A:3.3   Grasps hand-size object with either hand using whole hand

CONCURRENT GOALS AND OBJECTIVES

FM A:3.0   Grasps hand-size object with either hand using ends of thumb, index, and second fingers
FM B:1.0   Rotates either wrist on horizontal plane
GM B:1.2   Regains balanced, upright sitting position after *reaching* across the body to the right and to the left
Adap C:1.1   Takes off coat and/or jacket
Cog B:3.1   Looks for object in usual location
Cog D:1.0   Imitates motor action that is not commonly used
Cog E:4.1   Uses more than one strategy in attempt to solve common problem
Cog F:2.1   Groups functionally related objects
SC B:1.0   Gains person's attention and refers to an object, person, and/or event
SC B:2.0   Uses consistent word approximations
Soc A:3.1   Initiates communication with familiar adult
Soc B:1.0   Meets external physical needs in socially appropriate ways
Soc B:2.1   Responds to routine event

TEACHING SUGGESTIONS

Activity-Based

- Encourage the child to remove his or her shirt during daily caregiving routines such as undressing at bathtime, bedtime, or when changing shirts. If the child does not initiate, offer a reminder (e.g., "Don't forget your shirt").
- Whenever appropriate, have peers or siblings remove shirts also. For example, when undressing for swimming, bedtime, or after dress-up, let children undress together. Only children who know each other well (e.g., siblings, regular playmates) should undress together, to promote learning about privacy.
- A favorite time to remove shirts is when they are replaced by a garment that symbolizes "fun," such as removing pajamas to get dressed for outside, removing clothes for a bath, or removing a shirt to put on a swimsuit.
- Provide a dress-up box of clothes that are loose, fun, and representative of characters such as doctors, mail carriers, or firefighters. Use adult or sibling shirts as part of the dress-up wardrobe. Encourage the child to take shirts off independently at the end of dress-up time.
- When playing with paint, water, Play-Doh, or other messy substances, put a large shirt on the child to keep clothes clean. After the activity, ask the child to remove the shirt.
- When undressing the child, play a game of peekaboo by pulling the child's T-shirt off

to just above the nose, and let the child pull it the rest of the way. Gradually let the child take more of it off before you say peekaboo.

Environmental Arrangements

- Plan activities that require the child to use dress-up shirts such as painting, doctor, mail carrier, firefighter, or mommy/daddy.
- Front-opening shirts may be easiest for the child to remove. Begin teaching with these shirts and introduce pullover shirts once the child becomes proficient.
- Begin teaching with vests and short-sleeve shirts and systematically introduce long-sleeve shirts as the child demonstrates the intent and behaviors to remove shirts.
- When teaching the child to remove pullover shirts, let the child practice using sleeveless undershirts and large T-shirts. Gradually introduce shirts of an appropriate size and with longer sleeves.

Instructional Sequence

- Give the child a general verbal or nonverbal cue to remove shirt. Pause and wait for the child to begin taking off his or her shirt.
- Model taking off your shirt or have a peer demonstrate removing his or her shirt; then have the child imitate the behavior.
- Give the child specific verbal cues to remove his or her shirt (e.g., "Take your arm out").
- Give the child visual or tactile cues. Pull on or point to the sleeve of the shirt to prompt the child to remove his or her arm.
- Help the child remove his or her shirt with minimal physical assistance as needed:
    Front-opening shirt
    The child takes off a shirt that has been removed just off the shoulders.
    The child takes off a shirt that has been removed just below the elbows.
    The child takes off a shirt that has one arm already out of the sleeve.
    The child takes off a shirt that is on just the lower half of the nondominant arm.
    Pullover shirt
    The child takes off a shirt that has been pulled up to the chest.
    The child takes off a shirt that has one arm in and the other arm removed to just below the elbow.
    The child takes off a shirt that has one arm in and the other arm completely removed.
    The child takes off a shirt that has one arm removed and the other arm in just below the elbow.
    The child takes off a shirt that has been removed to around the neck.
    The child takes off a shirt that has been removed to above the nose.
    The child takes off a shirt that has been removed to crown of the head.

TEACHING CONSIDERATIONS

1. The child can learn different methods of taking off shirts. With pullover shirts, the child can remove sleeves first and pull the shirt over his or her head or simply pull the shirt over his or her head. With front-opening shirts, the child can remove one sleeve at a time, extend arms back and remove arms from sleeves, or swing shirt over his or her head and pull off sleeves from the front. Choose the method that is most appropriate for the child.

2. Supervise the child while removing a pullover shirt so that the child does not become "stuck" and frightened.
3. Consult a qualified specialist for adaptations and positions for a child with a motor impairment. Adaptive clothing (e.g., snaps, Velcro) may be necessary.
4. The child must be in a balanced or supported position that allows free use of arms.
5. A child with a visual impairment will need more manipulative, tactile, and auditory cues to replace models, gestures, and pointing.

Objective 1.4 Takes off socks

DEVELOPMENTAL PROGRAMMING STEPS

PS1.4a The child removes socks part way. For example, the child removes a sock that has been pulled over the heel, or pulls down a sock to the ankle.
PS1.4b The child persists in pushing and pulling at heel, toe, or foot of socks in an attempt to remove them.
PS1.4c The child tugs briefly at socks, vocalizes, points, or otherwise indicates to an adult a desire to remove socks.

IMPORTANCE OF SKILL

Taking off socks is an early step in becoming independent in undressing. The child learns that a fairly simple movement can result in the pleasure of being barefoot. Learning to take off socks also helps the child improve fine and gross motor skills of grasp, release, and voluntary movement of arms and legs.

PRECEDING OBJECTIVE

FM A:3.3   Grasps hand-size object with either hand using whole hand

CONCURRENT GOALS AND OBJECTIVES

FM A:3.0   Grasps hand-size object with either hand using ends of thumb, index, and second fingers
FM B:1.0   Rotates either wrist on horizontal plane
GM B:1.2   Regains balanced, upright sitting position after *reaching* across the body to the right and to the left
GM B:2.0   Sits down in and gets out of chair
Adap C:1.5   Takes off shoes
Cog B:3.1   Looks for object in usual location
Cog D:1.0   Imitates motor action that is not commonly used
Cog E:4.1   Uses more than one strategy in attempt to solve common problem
Cog F:2.1   Groups functionally related objects
SC B:1.0   Gains person's attention and refers to an object, person, and/or event
SC B:2.0   Uses consistent word approximations
Soc A:3.1   Initiates communication with familiar adult
Soc B:1.0   Meets external physical needs in socially appropriate ways
Soc B:2.1   Responds to routine event

TEACHING SUGGESTIONS
Activity-Based

- Encourage the child to remove socks during daily caregiving routines such as undressing at bathtime, bedtime, or when changing into a clean pair of socks. If the child does not initiate, offer a reminder (e.g., "Don't forget your socks").
- Engage the child in play activities that involve removing socks, such as washing socks and hanging them to dry, washing the child's feet, playing in the sandbox, or wading in water.
- Whenever appropriate, have peers or siblings remove socks also. For example, when undressing for swimming, bedtime, or after socks get wet, let the children undress together and help each other with their socks.
- A favorite time to remove socks is when the activity planned represents "fun," such as bathtime or swimming.
- When undressing the child at bathtime or bedtime, play a game of peekaboo with the child's socks and toes. Place the sock just over the tips of the child's toes and say, "Where are (Jenny's) toes?" After the child pulls off the sock, say, "peekaboo," and tickle the child's feet. This game can also be played with "This little piggy went to market."

Environmental Arrangements

- Plan activities that require removing socks, such as "This Little Piggy Went to Market" or a trip to the wading pool.
- Put adult-size socks on the child and let the child remove the socks after playing "Mommy" or "Daddy."
- Let the child pull off an adult's socks or a peer's socks. Once the child demonstrates the behavior and intent of taking off socks, introduce socks of the appropriate size.
- Put nail polish or tiny stickers on the child's toes to encourage the child to remove socks and find the "surprise."

Instructional Sequence

- Give the child a general verbal or nonverbal cue to remove socks. Pause and wait for the child to begin removing his or her socks.
- Model taking off your socks or have a peer demonstrate removing socks; then have the child imitate the behavior.
- Give the child specific verbal cues to remove socks (e.g., "Grab the heel and pull").
- Give the child visual or tactile cues. Pull on or point to socks.
- Help the child remove both socks with minimal physical assistance as needed:
  The child removes socks after being assisted to grasp the back of the cuff of the sock with the thumb and fingertips.
  The child removes the sock when the heel has been removed and the sock is positioned around the ankle.
  The child removes sock that is positioned on lower half of foot.
  The child removes sock that is positioned just over the tip of the toes.

TEACHING CONSIDERATIONS

1. The child can learn different methods of taking off socks. The child can pull from the toe or push from the top of the sock. Choose the method that is most appropriate for the child.

Adap C

2. The child must be in a balanced or supported position that allows free use of arms.
3. The child may find it easier to remove socks when sitting in a chair rather than on the floor.
4. Consult a qualified specialist for adaptations and positions for the child with a motor impairment.
5. A child with a visual impairment will need more manipulative, tactile, and auditory cues to replace models, gestures, and pointing.
6. Provide motivation and physical guidance when moving a child with a visual impairment to ensure the child's comfort and security.

Objective 1.5 Takes off shoes

DEVELOPMENTAL PROGRAMMING STEPS

PS1.5a The child removes shoes part way. For example, the child pulls shoe off from the heel or removes a shoe that has been pulled off of the heel.

PS1.5b The child persists in pushing and pulling at shoes in an attempt to remove them.

PS1.5c The child tugs briefly at shoes, vocalizes, points, or otherwise indicates to an adult a desire to remove shoes.

IMPORTANCE OF SKILL

Taking off shoes is an early step in becoming independent in undressing. It helps the child improve fine and gross motor skills of grasp, release, eye–hand coordination, and voluntary movement of arms and legs.

PRECEDING OBJECTIVE

FM A:3.3   Grasps hand-size object with either hand using whole hand

CONCURRENT GOALS AND OBJECTIVES

FM A:3.0   Grasps hand-size object with either hand using ends of thumb, index, and second fingers
FM B:1.0   Rotates either wrist on horizontal plane
GM B:1.2   Regains balanced, upright sitting position after *reaching* across the body to the right and to the left
GM B:2.0   Sits down in and gets out of chair
Cog B:3.1   Looks for object in usual location
Cog D:1.0   Imitates motor action that is not commonly used
Cog E:4.1   Uses more than one strategy in attempt to solve common problem
Cog F:2.1   Groups functionally related objects
SC B:1.0   Gains person's attention and refers to an object, person, and/or event
SC B:2.0   Uses consistent word approximations
Soc A:3.1   Initiates communication with familiar adult

Adap C

Soc B:1.0   Meets external physical needs in socially appropriate ways
Soc B:2.1   Responds to routine event

TEACHING SUGGESTIONS
Activity-Based

- Encourage the child to remove shoes during daily caregiving routines such as un-dressing at bathtime, bedtime, or when changing shoes. If the child does not initiate, offer a reminder (e.g., "Don't forget to take off your shoes first").
- Provide numerous opportunities for the child to remove shoes. For example, the sandbox, wading pool, and trampoline are fun and motivating barefoot activities.
- Whenever appropriate, have peers or siblings remove shoes also. For example, when undressing for swimming, bedtime, or after shoes get wet, let the children take off shoes together.
- A favorite time to remove shoes is when the activity planned represents "fun," such as bathtime, swimming, or sand play.
- Provide a variety of dress-up shoes to encourage the child to take off shoes and put them on. Use shoes that children associate with work, glamorous dress, the beach, or relaxation.
- Have the child wear shoes with no socks and play a game of peekaboo with the child's shoes and toes when undressing. Place the shoe just over the tips of the child's toes and say, "Where are (Jason's) toes?" After the child pulls off a shoe, say, "peekaboo," and tickle the child's feet. "This little piggy went to market" is also an appropriate game to play.
- Encourage the child to remove wet or muddy shoes after coming in from outdoors.
- Engage the child in dramatic play activities designed specifically to involve removing shoes. These could include playing dress-up, foot doctor, or shoe store.

Environmental Arrangements

- Shoes that are too large for the child (and are easily removed) can be used in dress-up activities.
- Plan activities for which removing shoes is appropriate. For example, trace the out-line of the child's foot or make finger paint footprints.
- Thongs and slip-on house slippers may be used as the child begins to learn to remove shoes. Shoes with Velcro straps, rather than shoestrings, will be easier for the child to remove when unfastened.

Instructional Sequence

- Give the child a general verbal or nonverbal cue to remove shoes. Pause and wait for the child to begin removing his or her shoes.
- Model taking off your shoes, or have a peer demonstrate removing shoes, and have the child imitate the behavior.
- Give the child verbal cues to take off shoes ("Grab the heel and pull").
- Give the child visual or tactile cues. Pull on or point to the shoe to prompt the child to remove it.
- Help the child remove shoes with minimal physical assistance as needed:
      The child takes off shoe when heel is slipped halfway off heel.
      The child takes off shoe when heel is slipped all the way off.
      The child takes off shoe when shoe is just covering lower half of foot.

Adap C

TEACHING CONSIDERATIONS

1. The child must be in a balanced or supported position that allows free use of arms.
2. The child may find it easier to remove shoes when sitting in a chair than when sitting on the floor.
3. The adult may unfasten shoes before the child removes them.
4. Consult a qualified specialist for adaptations and positions for the child with a motor impairment. Adaptive clothing (e.g., snaps, Velcro) may be necessary.
5. Adaptations will be made for the child who wears short leg braces with shoes connected.
6. A child with a visual impairment will need more auditory cues to replace models, gestures, and pointing.

Objective 1.6   Takes off hat

DEVELOPMENTAL PROGRAMMING STEPS

PS1.6a The child removes a hat part way. For example, the child pulls off a hat that has been removed from one side of his or her head.
PS1.6b The child persists in pushing and pulling at the hat in an attempt to remove it.
PS1.6c The child tugs briefly at the hat, vocalizes, points, or otherwise indicates to an adult a desire to remove the hat.

IMPORTANCE OF SKILL

Taking off a hat is an early step in becoming independent in undressing. It allows the child to demonstrate the functional use of reaching and grasping, independent use of arms, and intentional release of grasp. Removing a hat gives the child control of body temperature as the day becomes warmer or when the child comes indoors.

PRECEDING OBJECTIVE

FM A:3.3   Grasps hand-size object with either hand using whole hand

CONCURRENT GOALS AND OBJECTIVES

FM A:3.0   Grasps hand-size object with either hand using ends of thumb, index, and second fingers
FM A:5.2   Releases hand-held object with each hand
FM B:1.0   Rotates either wrist on horizontal plane
GM B:1.3   Regains balanced, upright sitting position after *leaning* to the left, to the right, and forward
Cog B:3.1 Looks for object in usual location
Cog D:1.0 Imitates motor action that is not commonly used
Cog E:4.1 Uses more than one strategy in attempt to solve common problem
Cog F:2.1 Groups functionally related objects
SC B:1.0   Gains person's attention and refers to an object, person, and/or event
SC B:2.0   Uses consistent word approximations
Soc A:3.1 Initiates communication with familiar adult

Soc B:1.0   Meets external physical needs in socially appropriate ways
Soc B:2.1   Responds to routine event

TEACHING SUGGESTIONS
Activity-Based

- When the child arrives at a new destination wearing a hat (e.g., school, home, coming in from outside play), encourage the child to remove the hat. If the child does not initiate removing the hat, offer a reminder (e.g., "Don't forget to take off your hat when you come indoors").
- During playtime, make a game of taking a hat off and on. Sit facing the child and play peekaboo by taking the hat off and on. Take turns taking off each other's hats.
- Allow the child to try on adult hats found in the home or school. Let the child look in the mirror to see how hats appear and practice taking them off and on.
- Provide a variety of hats for the child to use in play activities (e.g., cowboy, fire, silly, baseball hats).
- Plan activities that involve wearing hats as part of a costume (e.g., dress-up, cowboys, firefighters). Put a hat on the child as part of the activity and ask the child to remove the hat when finished. Some hats may need to be unfastened.

Environmental Arrangements

- Adapt materials by using a scarf or diaper as a hat that the child can remove. Once the child demonstrates the intent and behavior of removing the "hat," introduce loose-fitting caps and hats.
- Use loose-fitting hats initially, as they are easier for the child to remove. When the child has learned to remove loose-fitting hats, use hats that are the appropriate size for the child.
- Use a variety of styles of hats to ensure generalization (e.g., baseball caps, knitted hats, bonnets). Some of these may need to be unfastened.
- Have the child take hats and scarves off dolls or stuffed animals when playing dress-up with toys.

Instructional Sequence

- Give the child a general verbal or nonverbal cue to remove the hat. Pause and wait for the child to begin removing his or her hat.
- Model taking off your hat or have a peer demonstrate; then have the child imitate the behavior.
- Give the child specific verbal cues to remove the hat (e.g., "Reach for your hat," "Pull it off").
- Give the child visual and/or tactile cues. Pull on or point to the hat.
- Give minimal physical assistance as needed to help the child remove the hat.

TEACHING CONSIDERATIONS

1. The child must be in a balanced or supported position that allows free use of arms.
2. Consult a qualified specialist for adaptations and positions for the child with a motor impairment. Adaptive clothing (e.g., snaps, Velcro) may be necessary.
3. A child with a visual impairment will need more manipulative, tactile, and auditory cues to replace models, gestures, and pointing.

Adap C

COGNITIVE DOMAIN

Angela Notari, Juliann Cripe,
Kristine Slentz, and Betsy Ryan-Seth

The Cognitive Domain is the largest domain in the AEPS Curriculum, which indicates the scope and complexity of early cognitive development. Prior to the mid-1970s, the cognitive abilities of infants were rarely addressed in early intervention programs. The area of preacademic skills (e.g., shapes, colors, categories) was regarded as the earliest cognitive content relevant to special education students. The application of Piagetian theory of sensorimotor development to early intervention curricula has provided a valuable framework for the cognitive skills of infants and young children. The Cognitive Domain in the AEPS Curriculum is organized to reflect Piaget's theoretical framework, which incorporates sensory stimuli, object permanence, causality, imitation, problem solving, preacademic skills, and interaction with objects.

Newborn infants, with few exceptions, are perceptually equipped to respond to environmental stimuli. Sight, touch, and sound are important sources of sensation and information for the developing child. Initial responses may involve only a change in activity level, but the infant quickly learns to orient to the source of stimulation. Thus, a baby will snuggle into a parent's arms, look toward a mobile, and later reach toward a musical toy. The process of selecting certain stimuli out of the infinite variety of sights, sounds, and touches available provides the foundation for more sophisticated interactions with the environment.

Every interaction between caregivers and young children provides sensory stimulation. The human face holds special visual interest, and the human voice is a salient auditory stimulus for most infants. Many of the activities suggested in the AEPS Curriculum involve face-to-face interaction between adult and child. Saying an infant's name, making eye contact, and smiling when picking up a baby provide auditory, visual, and tactile stimulation in the space of seconds in a familiar and meaningful context.

Object permanence refers to the child's ability to form a mental representation of objects outside the immediate perceptual field. Initially, the child learns to control his or her own perceptual field by following objects visually and locating objects after seeing them hidden or covered. These skills culminate in the child's ability to look for missing or lost items.

The child who masters object permanence makes a significant cognitive leap from concrete and immediate experience to abstract experience. Object permanence is also a very practical skill to teach that promotes many related learning opportunities. The

243

child who has a firm concept of objects is likely to realize that the toy he or she plays with today is the same toy that a particular action activated yesterday. The child can immediately try that action again and move on to explore more sophisticated alternatives.

The notion of familiar adults is a specific case of object permanence, sometimes called "people permanence." The infant develops a mental representation of a caregiver and associates the caregiver with comfort. Once an infant develops a mental image of his or her mother, for example, crying becomes a means to an end, rather than just an expression of discomfort.

Causality refers to the child's ability to infer cause-and-effect relationships from action on objects or from interactions with people. A prerequisite to understanding cause and effect is the use of one means to achieve a specific end. For example, the infant uses vocalization as a means of soliciting adult attention or pushes a musical toy to produce a tinkling sound. The use of actions to accomplish a particular objective shows the child's intentional control over the immediate environment.

The repetitive use of specific actions with people and objects allows the child to develop means for achieving predictable ends. Young children can happily play peekaboo or manipulate a Busy Box many times, making sure that the same actions will produce similar results each time. These concrete experiences eventually culminate in the child's ability to mentally predict an outcome or infer the cause of a particular effect.

The development of cause-and-effect hypotheses is another example of the child's ability to move from concrete to abstract representations and from immediate to delayed associations. The child who purposely knocks a toy into the bathtub to create a splash has come a long way from the younger child who did not associate the toy falling with the water splashing.

Imitation is probably the single most valuable learning strategy available to infants and young children. Children observe and listen to adults and peers, learn from what they see and hear, and imitate. Children who can imitate are able to associate their own actions with those of others and then produce new behaviors. The efficiency of this strategy over trial and error learning is obvious.

Children begin to imitate by seeing their own actions performed by another person. Adults often mimic infant actions and vocalizations, and the infant responds by continuing the movement or sound. This game of mutual imitation is enjoyable and important for building imitative skills. Soon the child will follow an adult lead and imitate actions or sounds that are familiar and easy to produce. Eventually, the child makes use of imitation strategies to learn new and difficult skills.

Actions that children can see are generally easier to imitate than ones they cannot see. Patting the top of the head is more difficult than clapping hands because the child can see the hands and match the action to a model of the action. Similarly, vocal and/or verbal imitations are more difficult than other actions because the movements required to make sounds are often not visible, even with a mirror.

Imitation is an important component of successful problem solving. Faced with a problem at home, school, or in the community, a child's best strategy is often to see what peers or adults are doing in a similar situation. For example, the child who has too many blocks to carry may observe a peer using a wagon and find a wagon for the blocks. Parents and teachers typically show a young child how to do something, rather than do it for the child or explain a sequence of actions.

Problem solving requires the child to combine and use objects and people in novel ways to achieve certain ends. Skills developed in the areas of object permanence, causality, and imitation all come into play when the child successfully approaches and solves problems. The ability to solve common problems at play, in caring for self, and during interactions with adults and peers gives the young child a measure of independence and increases confidence in negotiating social and physical environments.

The young child initially approaches problems by persevering in one familiar strategy or solution. For example, the child who has used a low stool to reach the bathroom sink may try to use the same stool to reach the kitchen sink. As the ability to see the relationships between objects increases, the child will attempt alternative solutions. The child attempting to reach the counter may try to climb on an adult-size chair or may open a drawer and stand on the side of it. Gradually, the child develops the skills to evaluate the situation, compare it to others from previous experiences, and determine a workable solution.

Preacademic skills in this curriculum include the relationship of objects in space, categorization, and one-to-one correspondence. These skills are prerequisite to learning to use basic concept labels, perform precise manipulations of objects, and develop computational math skills.

A child learns to arrange objects in space by first aligning items on a horizontal plane and then stacking them vertically. Aligning is much easier because the toys or objects are supported and manipulated on a surface. The child needs only to arrange objects in a similar end-to-end fashion. Stacking requires a more precise coordination of fine motor skills and spatial awareness to successfully arrange objects in a vertical line. At first, only two items will be placed together in a horizontal or vertical arrangement. Gradually, the child adds more items to the vertical or horizontal plane.

The ability to categorize objects based on similar properties is an initial step in concept development. Matching similar objects or pictures and objects shows the child's ability to perceive similarities and differences between items. This skill is necessary for the identification of specific qualities such as size, shape, and color.

A child can sort objects into groups based on specific qualities long before the child can name the size, shape, or color of the objects. For example, a child might sort blocks into piles by shape or sort cars into containers by color. The same child, however, may not be able to label or even recognize circles, triangles, squares, or red, blue, or yellow.

Grouping functionally related objects requires the child to evaluate the use of each item and associate it with those of a similar function. For example, a child may put a fork and plate together because both are used for eating. A blanket and doll will go together because both are put into the crib for sleeping.

Ultimately, the young child develops conceptual classes such as vehicles, furniture, people, animals, and buildings. At this point, the child can start with the conceptual category and select items that represent it. For example, a child might take all the animals from a farm scene and put them in a different box than the buildings. Categorization and the development of concepts allow the child to organize people, objects, and events into a meaningful and interrelated mental framework. More sophisticated understanding of superordinate and subordinate concepts, and the relationships between levels, is dependent on early categorization skills.

The child also learns in the preacademic strand to match one, and only one, item to another. This skill has many functional and practical applications in daily living. For example, each foot gets one sock, each plate one fork, and each child one cracker. One-to-one correspondence is perhaps the earliest math skill. It is a necessary prerequisite to

Cog

understanding the concepts of more than, less than, and equality. Rational counting has as its basis the assignment of one numeral to each object, an obvious extension of the one-to-one concept.

The development of play in young children has social, motor, and cognitive components. It is included in the Cognitive Domain in the AEPS Curriculum because the sequence of play skills progresses from concrete to abstract, from simple to complex, and from unintentional to intentional. These simple-to-complex sequences are central to sensorimotor development and mark the way the child applies many of the skills delineated throughout the domain.

The earliest, object play, involves the infant holding and exploring objects. At first, all objects are explored with the same limited set of actions—sucking, banging, throwing. The child soon determines that certain actions are better suited for certain objects. At the same time, the schemes include increasingly complex actions. Dolls and stuffed animals are for hugging, cars and balls are for rolling, fingers and rubber toys are for sucking, and paper and fabric are for crumpling.

Once a child begins using objects in functionally appropriate ways, the stage is set for more abstract and symbolic play. The child who knows to talk into a toy telephone, rock a doll, comb hair with a brush, and sweep with a broom has a mental representation of each object and its function. When the correct object is not available, the child substitutes another object to perform the same function. A small box, for example, can serve as a shoe or as a bed for a doll. A block can be a telephone. The child's mental picture of the object and knowledge of its function allows one object to represent another.

Finally, the child can play without the benefit of object props. The child's imagination creates the object or event, and play becomes an abstract endeavor. The freedom and creativity available to children who can pretend is evident in imaginary play. No longer limited to available objects and events, or hindered by the immediate time frame of reality, children revel in imaginary scenes, perform feats of strength and daring, create new friends, and travel to the ends of the earth. Whether playing with superheroes, assuming exciting identities, creating new worlds, or simply doing something one cannot really do, imaginary play is a wonderful resource for entertainment and learning.

Cognitive skills for birth to 3-year-olds span the continuum from response to external stimulation to creation of imaginary play scenarios. The interventionist is constantly challenged not to underestimate the abilities of young children in the area of cognition. At the same time, it can be difficult to see the world from a concrete perspective. Our job is to detect the discrepancy between what children can already do and what skills they need to master next. We must design environments that encourage and interest children in problem solving while making certain that the problem is indeed solvable. Most important, we must try to see the world through the eyes of each child and find the excitement, challenges, and rewards that will motivate and maintain cognitive gains.

As we design learning environments, we must also consider the significance of cognitive development for all children, despite their levels of impairment. Our challenge is to facilitate cognitive development so that the child's disability does not impede progress. At times this will require consulting a qualified specialist for techniques for the child with a visual, auditory, or motor impairment.

Strand A

Sensory Stimuli

GOAL 1 Orients to auditory, visual, and tactile events

DEVELOPMENTAL PROGRAMMING STEPS

No standard developmental sequence appears to exist for orientation to different types of sensory events. Young children exhibit a range of individual differences in orientation to environmental events, and preferences of children may change over time. Certain sensory impairments also make orientation to some types of cues difficult. Careful observation of the child will help determine the sensory events the child orients to most and least easily. Begin teaching with the objective that the child is most likely to orient easily to, and then teach those modalities that initially elicit the least interest. Use multiple sensory cues and fade to each individual type (e.g., auditory, visual, tactile).

IMPORTANCE OF SKILL

Children actively construct knowledge through exploration of the environment. Locating, orienting, and responding to auditory, visual, and tactile events in the environment allow the child to exercise basic sensorimotor schemes on a variety of social and nonsocial objects.

CONCURRENT GOAL AND OBJECTIVES

FM A:1.2   Makes nondirected movements with each arm
GM A:1.0   Turns head, moves arms, and kicks legs independently of each other
Adap A:1.4 Swallows liquids
Cog B:1.2 Focuses on object and/or person
SC A:1.1   Turns and looks toward object and person speaking
SC A:2.2   Looks toward an object
Soc A:1.1 Responds appropriately to familiar adult's affective tone

TEACHING SUGGESTIONS

In order to achieve this goal, a child must perform the skills in Objectives 1.1–1.4 to criteria. Refer to the specific objective for Teaching Suggestions and Teaching Considerations to develop each skill.

Cog A

Objective 1.1　Orients to auditory events

DEVELOPMENTAL PROGRAMMING STEPS

☑ The objective above is the most basic step for the skill to be taught. Most children will benefit from the activities outlined here that emphasize this skill. For children who need more instruction, consider designing programming steps from the *environmental arrangements* suggestions or from the *instructional sequence* outlined.

IMPORTANCE OF SKILL

Orientation to auditory stimuli is essential for the acquisition of practical communication skills. A child needs to be attentive to sounds in the environment to comprehend and develop verbal language. The child establishes a socially appropriate nonverbal interaction by focusing on the person speaking.

PRECEDING OBJECTIVE

Cog A:1.4　　Responds to auditory, visual, and tactile events

CONCURRENT OBJECTIVES

FM A:1.2　　Makes nondirected movements with each arm
GM A:1.1　　Turns head past 45° to the right and left from midline position
Cog A:1.2　　Orients to visual events
Cog A:1.3　　Orients to tactile events
Cog B:1.2　　Focuses on object and/or person
SC A:1.2　　Turns and looks toward noise-producing object
Soc A:1.1　　Responds appropriately to familiar adult's affective tone

TEACHING SUGGESTIONS

Activity-Based

- Play with noise-producing objects (e.g., bells, rattle, crinkly paper, music box, squeeze-toy).
- Encourage the child to orient to sounds that occur near him or her by turning, looking, reaching, or moving in the direction of the sound.
- Expose the child to noises in the daily environment, such as vacuum cleaners, doorbell, garbage disposal, mixer, train, and animals.
- Talk to the child frequently during daily caregiving routines (bathing, dressing, feeding, play) and vary pitch, intonation, and intensity.
- Use a variety of sounds by varying the pitch of your voice, sounding bells or maracas, playing soft and loud music, to determine the cues to which the child most readily responds. Begin with auditory cues to which the child most readily responds and gradually present other cues until the skill is generalized across a variety of auditory cues.

Cog A

- Make funny sounds (tongue clicks, animal imitations) while interacting with the child.
- Call to the child from behind or the side; whisper in the child's ear.

☑ If your data indicate the child is not making progress toward the objective, provide additional structure within the suggested activities by incorporating the following *environmental arrangements:*

Environmental Arrangements

- Help the child differentiate between sounds and silence. Speak and then pause, turn on the radio and then shut it off and wait for the child to respond.
- Cease activity and listen to dogs barking, children shouting, airplanes, appliances; take the child to locate the noises.
- Alternate low tones (use wooden objects) and high tones (use plastic objects), and loud sounds (sing) and soft sounds (whisper).
- Give the child a noise-producing object to manipulate (e.g., rattle, crinkly paper).
- Attach noise-producing objects to child's arms or legs (e.g., jingle-bells on socks or wrist).
- Hide yourself or a toy and continue to speak or make a noise with the toy.

☑ If this objective is particularly difficult for a child, it may be necessary, within activities, to use *an instructional sequence.*

Instructional Sequence

- Increase intensity of auditory cues by using louder, more distinct sounds (e.g., drum, shout, larger bells) in place of speech and music.
- Pair auditory events with visual or tactile cues. For example, talk to the child while moving your face within the child's visual field.
- Gently assist the child to move, turn, or reach toward noise-producing objects or to touch the mouth of a person speaking.

☑ Combining or pairing different levels of instructions may be helpful when beginning to teach a new and difficult skill. Fade to less intrusive instructions as soon as possible to encourage more independent performance.

TEACHING CONSIDERATIONS

1. The child should be in a quiet and alert state.
2. The environment should be free of auditory, visual, or tactile events that compete with the auditory event presented.
3. When presenting paired cues to elicit a response to an auditory event, select those cues to which the child is most responsive (visual or tactile).
4. Be cautious about scaring the child or eliciting a startle with loud or sudden noises.
5. The child with a hearing impairment may require instructions that are more intense (louder) and are paired with tactile or visual cues.
6. Consult a qualified specialist for techniques for a child with a visual or motor impairment.
7. Consider safety with all objects that the child handles. Never leave the child unattended with potentially hazardous objects.

Cog A

Objective 1.2   Orients to visual events

DEVELOPMENTAL PROGRAMMING STEP

PS1.2a   The child uses reflexive pupillary and blinking responses. Present bright lights to elicit constriction of the pupils of the eyes or slowly approach the child's face with an object to elicit blinking.

IMPORTANCE OF SKILL

Orientation to visual events is a skill basic to development of both information processing and social interactions. Infants actively explore visual patterns, recognize familiar pictures of faces, and demonstrate depth perception. These skills serve as a basis for acquiring knowledge about the world, avoiding danger, establishing appropriate social interactions, and differentiating between familiar and unfamiliar people.

PRECEDING OBJECTIVE

Cog A:1.4   Responds to auditory, visual, and tactile events

CONCURRENT OBJECTIVES

FM A:1.2   Makes nondirected movements with each arm
GM A:1.1   Turns head past 45° to the right and left from midline position
Cog A:1.1   Orients to auditory events
Cog A:1.3   Orients to tactile events
Cog B:1.2   Focuses on object and/or person
SC A:2.2   Looks toward an object
Soc A:1.2   Smiles in response to familiar adult

TEACHING SUGGESTIONS
Activity-Based

- Vary facial expressions and engage in face-to-face interaction games such as peekaboo.
- Use a variety of objects, from social to nonsocial, with simple and complex patterns and with colors of varying brightness.
- When the child is lying on his or her back in the crib, activate a mobile.
- Provide sights in the daily environment, such as the child's own image in a mirror, colorful posters on the wall, and sunlight coming in a window.
- Present visual stimuli that do not produce a sound (e.g., colored ball, face of a doll, person smiling) within the child's visual field and encourage the child to turn, look, reach, or move toward the visual event.

Environmental Arrangements

- Hold objects directly in the child's visual field at a distance where accommodation is best (approximately 12 inches).
- Use large, bright-colored objects or objects that move (e.g., hand puppet, small balloon, mobile). Present objects or figures with patterned surfaces, curved lines, and

Cog A

bright colors. After playing with an object, maintain the child's interest by introducing new but visually similar objects.
- When the child focuses visually on an object, slowly move the object to elicit tracking, head turning, or reaching, and to maintain visual contact.
- Use a variety of colors and patterns over time to determine the cues to which the child most readily responds. Begin with those cues and gradually present others until the skill is generalized across a variety of visual cues.

Instructional Sequence

- Increase the intensity of visual cues by using contoured, bright-colored, large, or quickly moving stimuli.
- Pair visual events with auditory or tactile cues. Shake a bright-colored chime or bell rattle 8–12 inches from the child. Touch the child's cheek with a soft toy, or initiate face-to-face interaction while vocalizing and stroking the child.
- Gently assist the child to move, reach, or turn head toward visual stimuli.

TEACHING CONSIDERATIONS

1. The child should be in a quiet and alert state.
2. The environment should be free of auditory, visual, or tactile events that compete with the visual stimuli presented.
3. When presenting paired cues to elicit a response to a visual event, select those cues to which the child is most responsive (auditory or tactile).
4. The child with a visual impairment may require cues that are more intense (e.g., increased size or brightness).
5. Consult a qualified specialist for techniques for a child with a hearing or motor impairment.
6. Be cautious about balloons and consider safety when the child handles all objects. Never leave the child unattended with potentially hazardous objects.

Objective 1.3   Orients to tactile events

Cog A

DEVELOPMENTAL PROGRAMMING STEP

PS1.3a   The child displays reflexive responses, such as the rooting response, to tactile events. During feeding, stimulate the sides and upper and lower portions of the mouth to facilitate oral searching or head rotation prior to placing the nipple directly in the infant's mouth.

IMPORTANCE OF SKILL

Tactile sensitivity is important for a variety of reasons. Awareness of extreme temperatures and of pain is basic to maintaining good health and avoiding physical danger. Sensitivity to physical contact may play a role in enhancing nonverbal communication skills.

PRECEDING OBJECTIVE

Cog A:1.4   Responds to auditory, visual, and tactile events

CONCURRENT OBJECTIVES

FM A:1.2   Makes nondirected movements with each arm
GM A:1.2   Kicks legs
Adap A:1.4   Swallows liquids
Cog A:1.1   Orients to auditory events
Cog A:1.2   Orients to visual events
SC A:2.2   Looks toward an object

TEACHING SUGGESTIONS
Activity-Based

- Encourage the child to turn, look, reach, or move toward tactile events as they occur in the daily caregiving routine (e.g., gentle touch, stuffed animals, water, bottle or breast, adult or child's face, lotion).
- While bathing, gently splash the child or pour water over the child's back or side and observe whether the child turns his or her head toward the source of stimulation.
- Play nursery games that involve tactile stimuli, such as pat-a-cake or "Piggy Went to Market."
- Touch the child with warm or cold objects, such as a warm bottle, warm clothing just out of the dryer, or cold hands.

Environmental Arrangements

- Rub lotion, place sticky tape, or blow gently on different parts of the child's body.
- Provide materials that stick to the child's fingers, such as cereal, finger paint, or Play-Doh. Wipe off the materials with a cloth.
- Carefully pass balloons across the child's visual field and observe if the child orients to the balloons. (Pay special attention to the potential dangers of balloons.) Use bright, shiny Mylar balloons and banners of different colors and shapes to attract and hold the child's attention.
- Vary the texture of tactile cues over time to determine the cues to which the child most readily responds. Begin with those cues and gradually present others until the skill is generalized across a variety of tactile cues.

Instructional Sequence

- Increase the intensity of tactile cues. Use rough towels (gently), sand, soft feathers, or Jello.
- Pair tactile events with visual or auditory cues. Touch the child's leg with a bright-colored toy or a noise-producing object; talk and touch the child within the child's field of vision.
- Gently assist the child to touch materials of a variety of textures (e.g., water, towels, lotion, bottle or breast, stuffed animals).

Cog A

TEACHING CONSIDERATIONS

1. The child should be in a quiet and alert state.
2. The environment should be free of auditory, visual, or tactile events that compete with the tactile stimuli being presented.
3. When presenting paired cues to elicit a response to a tactile event, select those cues (visual or auditory) to which the child is most responsive.
4. If the child has a visual impairment, allow tactile exploration of the materials. Orientation to tactile events is especially important for the infant with a severe visual impairment because this child often identifies objects through exploration of tactile properties.
5. The child with a sensory impairment may respond differently to tactile events. If a child withdraws from tactile events, you may need to decrease the intensity of the stimulation. If a child does not respond to tactile events, you may need to increase the intensity of the stimulation.
6. Be aware of tactile defensiveness in the child with a visual or motor impairment.
7. Consult a qualified specialist for techniques for the child with a visual, hearing, or motor impairment.
8. Be cautious about balloons and consider safety when the child handles all objects. Never leave the child unattended with potentially hazardous objects.

Objective 1.4   Responds to auditory, visual, and tactile events

---

DEVELOPMENTAL PROGRAMMING STEPS

PS1.4a   Research to date has not shown a consistent developmental sequence among different sensory modalities. Soon after birth, infants are capable of detecting correspondences between different senses (internodal perception). Begin teaching with the sensory modality to which the child is most likely to respond and progress to those modalities that initially elicit the least interest.

PS1.4b   Use multiple sensory cues and fade to each individual type of cue (auditory, visual, tactile).

IMPORTANCE OF SKILL

Infants react to visual stimuli by scanning visual patterns, to auditory stimuli by localizing sounds, and to tactile stimuli with reflexive and voluntary responses. Observation of the infant's reactions will provide the observer with information about the infant's differential responses and preferential modes to specific sensory modalities. Development proceeds through ongoing interactions between the child and the environment. The child actively processes information in the environment, using auditory, visual, tactile, and olfactory modalities. This step represents the child's basic awareness of a variety of stimuli in the environment.

CONCURRENT OBJECTIVES

FM A:1.2   Makes nondirected movements with each arm
GM A:1.3   Waves arms

Cog A

Adap A:1.4   Swallows liquids
Cog B:1.2   Focuses on object and/or person
SC A:2.2   Looks toward an object

TEACHING SUGGESTIONS
Activity-Based

- Encourage the infant to respond by ceasing, increasing, or changing activity momentarily as events occur in the daily environment.
- During feeding, move the nipple gently in and around the mouth to stimulate response to tactile stimulation.
- When the child cries, rock, touch, stroke, or sing to elicit a quieting response.
- While bathing and dressing the child, encourage reactions to contact with the water, to rubbing lotion on the body, or to gentle stroking or tickling.
- Look for blinking responses when turning on a soft light in a dark room or when opening curtains.
- Watch for gaze direction or fixation when the infant is approached by a familiar person.
- Watch for cessation or increase of motor activity when a familiar person talks to the infant or when a noise occurs in the environment (e.g., door slams, radio is turned on).
- Play nursery games that involve tactile, auditory, or visual stimuli, such as "Piggy Went to Market," "Up We Go," or pat-a-cake.
- Throughout the daily routine (dressing, changing, bathing, feeding), present toys and/or objects within the child's visual field.
- When the child is on his or her back in the crib, activate a mobile.
- When dressing, changing, or bathing the child, present noise-producing toys and/or objects (e.g., rattle, squeak-toy).

Environmental Arrangements

Tactile Events

- Gently rub the infant's lips before placing the nipple in the mouth during feeding.
- Slightly vary the temperature of the bath water and encourage the infant to touch the water with hands and feet.
- Gently and briefly rub different objects (e.g., soft towel or diaper, cool plastic rattle) over the child's skin.
- Blow gently on the child's tummy, hair, and eyelids.
- Stick tape on the child's fingers and help the child move his or her thumb and fingers together to feel the tactile sensations. (Be cautious and remove the tape when finished so that the child does not put it in his or her mouth.)

Visual Events

- Elicit blinking responses by moving the child from a dark to a brightly lit room, or from indoors to outdoors on a sunny day.
- Present luminous objects such as a flashlight, mirrors, or crumpled aluminum foil.
- Engage in face-to-face interaction games. Put your face or hand close to the baby's face, cover and uncover your eyes, or exaggerate your facial expressions.
- Present bright-colored or contrasting objects within the child's visual field. Gradually move the objects closer to or farther from the child, horizontally from side to side, or in and out of the child's visual field.

Auditory Events

- Make sounds with noise-producing objects (e.g., soft rattle, squeeze-toy, musical toy) approximately 6 inches from the infant's ear. Gradually increase the loudness of the sounds if the child does not respond.
- While talking to the baby, vary and exaggerate vocal patterns (e.g., whisper, hum, sing, laugh).
- Present noise-producing objects (e.g., bells, rattle, musical toy) outside the child's visual field (to the child's side, behind the child).

Instructional Sequence

- Increase the intensity of the cues (size and brightness of visual cues, loudness of auditory cues, size and roughness of tactile cues).
- Pair cues and select events to which the infant is most responsive. For example, while stroking the infant's face, speak and use exaggerated facial expressions. Present a bright-colored noise-producing toy, such as a chime or rattle. Change your facial expression or turn your head toward the source of an auditory event in the environment.
- Physically turn the child's head toward a source of sound. Take the child to the location of the sound.

TEACHING CONSIDERATIONS

1. The child should be in a quiet and alert state.
2. The environment should be free of auditory, visual, or tactile events that compete with the stimuli presented.
3. The level of impairment is difficult to determine for a very young child with a sensory impairment. Try a variety of different events and cues over time to determine the ones to which the child most readily responds (e.g., vary pitch or types of sound of auditory cues, vary color and pattern of visual cues, vary texture of tactile cues).
4. For the child with a severe visual impairment, describe the object as you encourage the child to handle it.
5. Consult a qualified specialist for further techniques for the child with a visual, auditory, or motor impairment.
6. Consider safety with all materials or objects that the child handles. Never leave the child unattended with potentially hazardous objects.

Cog A

Strand B

Object Permanence

GOAL 1 Visually follows object and/or person to point of disappearance

---

DEVELOPMENTAL PROGRAMMING STEPS

☑ The goal above is the most basic step for the skill to be taught. Most children will benefit from the activities outlined here that emphasize this skill. For children who need more instruction, consider designing programming steps from the *environmental arrangements* suggestions or from the *instructional sequence* outlined.

IMPORTANCE OF SKILL

With this skill, the child begins to understand that objects are permanent and constant entities, even when moving through space. The child who is able to actively accommodate his or her own actions (e.g., looking, turning head) to maintain visual contact with moving objects demonstrates knowledge that objects have a certain permanence.

PRECEDING OBJECTIVE

Cog B:1.2   Focuses on object and/or person

CONCURRENT OBJECTIVES

FM A:1.1   Makes directed batting and/or swiping movements with each hand
GM A:1.1   Turns head past 45° to the right and left from midline position
Adap A:4.3   Accepts food presented on spoon
Cog C:1.2   Acts on mechanical and/or simple toy in some way
Cog G:1.4   Uses sensory examination with objects
SC A:1.2   Turns and looks toward noise-producing object
Soc A:1.2   Smiles in response to familiar adult

TEACHING SUGGESTIONS

Activity-Based

- Encourage the child to watch as people leave the room, as a car enters or leaves the garage, or as the dog goes into the doghouse. Make sure the child is focused on the person or object before it moves.

- Point out people crossing streets, going into buildings, and cars going down the street as you drive.
- While playing face-to-face games with the child, change location frequently by moving around the child or behind a barrier, such as a doorway. Watch for the child to follow as you slowly disappear from view. Reappear and play again.
- Move objects out of the child's visual field by having toys drop to the floor from your lap, a table, or a highchair.
- During meal or snack times, move the child's cup or spoon under the table or around and behind him or her, encouraging the child to follow the movement visually.

☑ If your data indicate the child is not making progress toward the goal, provide additional structure within the suggested activities by incorporating the following *environmental arrangements:*

Environmental Arrangements

- Use objects that are interesting or novel to the child. Cause a toy the child is playing with to drop to the floor, or slowly move the toy to another location.
- When the child's eyes are on the dog, ask the dog to come. Continue to speak to the dog so that the child's eyes will follow the dog.
- Pair visual with auditory cues. Speak to the child while moving out of sight. Use noisy, wind-up toys and let them drop off the table. Call the child's name if the child stops tracking before the person or the object disappears.
- Place objects on a high shelf or roll a ball under a bed. Repeat several times.

☑ If this goal is particularly difficult for a child, it may be necessary, within activities, to use an *instructional sequence.*

Instructional Sequence

- Verbally direct the child to follow an object to the point of disappearance, i.e., watch the dog until it disappears.
- Begin by having the child follow objects or people for short distances before disappearance. Systematically increase the distance.
- Begin by having the child follow an object or person with his or her eyes only. Then have the child turn his or her head to maintain visual contact. Finally, have the child turn his or her body to keep the object or person in sight until the point of disappearance. Physically direct the child if necessary.

☑ Combining or pairing different levels of instructions may be helpful when beginning to teach a new and difficult skill. Fade to less intrusive instructions as soon as possible to encourage more independent performance.

TEACHING CONSIDERATIONS

1. The child should be in a quiet, alert state.
2. The environment should be free of auditory, visual, or tactile events that compete with the stimuli presented.
3. If the child has a visual impairment, increase the intensity and variety of cues (increased size or brightness). For example, use noise-producing objects with the child who has a visual impairment; observe the child's ability to track the sound and/or object to the point where it disappears.
4. Consult a qualified specialist for further techniques for the child with a visual, auditory, or motor impairment.

Cog B

5. Consider safety with all objects that the child handles. Never leave a child unattended with potentially hazardous objects.

Objective 1.1   Visually follows object moving in horizontal, vertical, and circular directions

---

DEVELOPMENTAL PROGRAMMING STEPS

PS1.1a   The child visually follows an object moving in a circular direction.
PS1.1b   The child visually follows an object moving in a vertical direction.
PS1.1c   The child visually follows an object moving in a horizontal direction.

IMPORTANCE OF SKILL

Visual tracking plays an important role in cognitive development. It is an intermediate step between the mere perception of an object and the active search for an object that has disappeared from the visual field. Visual tracking constantly provides the foundation for learning from objects and interactions in a moving environment.

PRECEDING OBJECTIVE

Cog B:1.2   Focuses on object and/or person

CONCURRENT OBJECTIVES

FM A:1.1   Makes directed batting and/or swiping movements with each hand
GM A:1.1   Turns head past 45° to the right and left from midline position
Adap A:4.3   Accepts food presented on spoon
Cog C:1.3   Indicates interest in simple and/or mechanical toy
Cog G:1.4   Uses sensory examination with objects
SC A:1.2   Turns and looks toward noise-producing object
SC A:2.2   Looks toward an object

TEACHING SUGGESTIONS
Activity-Based

- Encourage the child to visually follow objects and people moving in horizontal, vertical, and circular directions within the child's visual field. Play with objects that can be rolled horizontally (e.g., balls, cars). Drop objects within the child's visual field. Turn toy dials and wheels in clockwise and counterclockwise directions. "Fly" toy birds or airplanes. Toss a balloon in the air several times.
- At snack time, pass food from one person to another in front of the child, bring food down from shelves, and move plates and cups from the counter to the table.
- When the child is lying on his or her back in the crib, activate a mobile.
- Play with toys that move in horizontal, vertical, or circular directions (e.g., roly-poly toy ball, toy car, or train on circular track).

Cog B

■ When feeding the child, present the spoon and move it in circular, horizontal, or vertical directions before bringing it to the child's mouth. Make airplane noises or similar sounds.

Environmental Arrangements

■ Use objects that are novel or especially interesting to the child. For example, move objects that the child is playing with or has touched. Make objects more interesting by attaching appealing stickers.

■ Begin by having the child focus on objects at midline. Vary the distance at which you present an object to determine the optimal distance for the child to focus. Hold the object until the child focuses on it before you move it.

■ Vary the direction in which objects move (left to right, right to left) in order to generalize the skill.

■ Over time, present objects with a variety of colors and patterns to determine the type of cues and objects to which the child most readily responds.

■ Dangle objects in front of the child (e.g., crib gym, toys tied to a rope) so that when the child bats at the object, it will move in horizontal, vertical, or circular directions.

Instructional Sequence

■ Verbally instruct the child to watch as you slide beads horizontally on an abacus.

■ Initially move objects very slowly and for short distances. Gradually and systematically increase both speed and distance.

■ Pair visual cues with auditory cues. Use noise-producing objects (e.g., clear ball with bells inside, noisy wind-up toys). Make airplane noises while pretending to make a plane fly. When the child begins to lose attention, increase auditory cues by shaking a bell or changing the tone of the airplane noise. Slowly fade the use of auditory cues in combination with visual cues.

■ Pair visual cues with tactile cues. Use gentle physical assistance to make the child move an object held in the hand. If the child loses sight of the object, bring the object back into the child's visual field. Once the child focuses on the object again, continue to move it.

TEACHING CONSIDERATIONS

1. The child should be in a quiet, alert state.
2. The environment should be free of auditory, visual, or tactile events that compete with the stimuli presented.
3. If the child has a visual impairment, increase the intensity and variety of cues (e.g., objects of increased size or brightness, noise-producing objects).
4. If the child has a hearing impairment, gain the child's interest in the object and/or person through visual or tactile means (e.g., use bright-colored objects, touch the child with the object).
5. If the child has a motor impairment, be aware of limitations and position the child to facilitate visual tracking.
6. Consult a qualified specialist for further techniques for the child with a visual, hearing, or motor impairment.
7. Consider safety with all materials or objects that the child handles. Never leave a child unattended with potentially hazardous objects.

Cog B

Objective 1.2 Focuses on object and/or person

IMPORTANCE OF SKILL

This skill represents the first step toward the active search for objects that have disappeared from sight. The ability to visually accommodate a stable object is basic to the subsequent skill of tracking a moving object. In addition, the ability to maintain a visual focus allows the child to explore the properties of objects in the immediate environment.

PRECEDING OBJECTIVE

Cog A:1.4   Responds to auditory, visual, and tactile events

CONCURRENT OBJECTIVES

FM A:1.2   Makes nondirected movements with each arm
GM A:1.2   Kicks legs
Cog A:1.2   Orients to visual events
Cog C:1.3   Indicates interest in simple and/or mechanical toy
SC A:1.2   Turns and looks toward noise-producing object
SC A:2.2   Looks toward an object

TEACHING SUGGESTIONS

Activity-Based

- Play face-to-face interaction games, such as gazing intently at the child before smiling. Vary your facial and vocal expression.
- During feedings, hold the bottle within the child's visual field momentarily before bringing it to the child's mouth.
- Place bold, colorful designs within the child's visual field when the child is in a crib, chair, or car seat. Allow the child to scan without distractions or interruptions.
- Throughout daily routines (e.g., when bathing, rocking, feeding, changing the child), move your face within 6 inches of the child's face. Look at and talk to the child.
- Encourage visual exploration of an object the child is manipulating.

Environmental Arrangements

- Present objects within the child's visual field at a distance where accommodation appears to be best (usually about 7–8 inches from the child). Move the object briefly to gain the child's attention. Keep the objects stationary for more than 4 seconds to allow the child to sustain focus.
- Introduce variations to maintain the child's focus. Sing, talk, and vary facial and vocal expressions.
- Use objects that move easily (e.g., wind chimes, mechanical toys, rocking clown, toy that rights itself when tipped over).
- Use lights and shiny surfaces to increase visual appeal.
- Use noise-producing objects. Activate the objects to maintain the child's interest.
- Hold a mirror in front of the child's face.

Cog B

- Use a variety of objects (e.g., bright- or different-colored, large, moving, or noise-producing objects).

Instructional Sequence

- Verbally instruct the child to look at a doll or other object.
- Make social, verbal, and tactile reinforcers contingent upon visual contact with a face or object. For example, wait until the child attends to your face before you talk or smile, or activate a mechanical toy after the child visually focuses upon it.
- Gradually increase the length of time (from immediate to 4 seconds) between the presentation of the object and the reinforcement.

TEACHING CONSIDERATIONS

1. The child should be in a quiet, alert state.
2. The environment should be free of auditory, visual, or tactile events that compete with the stimuli presented.
3. If the child has a visual impairment, increase the intensity and variety of the cues (e.g., objects of increased size or brightness, noise-producing objects). Encourage sustained tactile exploration of the object.
4. If the child has a hearing impairment, gain the child's interest in the object and/or person through visual or tactile means (e.g., move the object momentarily, touch the child with the object).
5. If the child has a motor impairment, be aware of limitations and position the child to facilitate focusing.
6. Consult a qualified specialist for further techniques for the child with a visual, hearing, or motor impairment.
7. Consider safety with all objects that the child handles. Never leave a child unattended with potentially hazardous objects.

GOAL 2   Locates object in latter of two successive hiding places

---

DEVELOPMENTAL PROGRAMMING STEPS

PS2.0a   After the child sees an object hidden first in one place, then another, the child searches for the object in the first hiding place, then in the next hiding place.

PS2.0b   After the child sees an object hidden first in one place, then another, the child searches for the object in the first hiding place.

IMPORTANCE OF SKILL

With this skill, the concept of an object becomes independent from the context. The object is no longer defined by a special position (the place where it is first placed and found). The child begins to understand that the same object can exist in many different places, and the child comprehends the order of hiding.

PRECEDING OBJECTIVE

Cog B:2.1   Locates object and/or person who hides while child is watching

Cog B

CONCURRENT GOALS AND OBJECTIVES

FM A:3.0   Grasps hand-size object with either hand using ends of thumb, index, and second fingers

FM B:3.1   Uses either hand to activate objects

GM B:1.2   Regains balanced, upright sitting position after *reaching* across the body to the right and to the left

Cog C:1.0   Correctly activates mechanical toy

Cog C:2.0   Reproduces part of interactive game and/or action in order to continue game and/or action

Cog E:3.1   Moves barrier or goes around barrier to obtain object

Cog E:4.1   Uses more than one strategy in attempt to solve common problem

Cog G:1.2   Uses functionally appropriate actions with objects

SC A:2.1   Follows person's pointing gesture to establish joint attention

SC C:1.3   Locates common objects, people, and/or events *with* contextual cues

Soc A:3.2   Responds to communication from familiar adult

TEACHING SUGGESTIONS

Activity-Based

- Place objects (e.g., toys, clothes, food) out of sight in dressers or cabinets that have similar drawers or doors.
- Hide objects in clothes with two or more pockets, or in bags with two or more compartments.
- Play guessing games by hiding objects in your hands or under boxes, cups, or sheets of paper. Objects serving as covers should be similar. Encourage the child to look in the second hiding place to find objects.
- Move toys, clothes, or household objects from their usual places to other hiding places. Encourage the child to look in the successive hiding places.

Environmental Arrangements

- Use objects that are of interest to the child to ensure the child's attention. Hide objects with which the child is playing. For example, cover an object held in the child's hand or lying in the child's lap, then slowly displace the object and hide it close to the child (e.g., under clothing, under a blanket the child is sitting on). Use covers of different color, size, or shape.
- Provide visual cues by using soft covers that make the contour of the hidden object visible.
- Begin by using transparent covers, such as drinking glasses, clear heavy plastic, or cupboards with glass doors.
- Use familiar opaque objects as covers and avoid bright, shiny covers so that the object remains more interesting than the cover.
- Use a lightweight lid, cloth, pillow, or your hand as a cover so that it is not too difficult for the child to remove. Avoid tight lids and heavy objects.

Instructional Sequence

- Model opening two successive cupboard doors to find the child's favorite toy.
- Verbally direct the child to look in two successive places for a favorite toy.

Cog B

- After placing the object in one hiding place, slowly move the object to another place where it is only partially hidden.
- After placing the object in one hiding place, slowly move the object to another position without hiding it. For example, move a toy onto a table within the child's visual field.
- Physically assist the child to open cupboards to find a toy.

TEACHING CONSIDERATIONS

1. If a cover (e.g., cup, blanket, paper, box, lid) is used to hide an object, it is important to differentiate the child's search for the object from pulling at the cover to play with the cover itself. In general, if the child removes the cover and immediately reaches for the object, it can be assumed that the child is looking for the hidden object.
2. If the child does not have the motor skills to reach for or grasp the object, the child may indicate awareness of its location by looking or pointing.
3. If the child has a visual impairment, increase the variety and intensity of cues (objects of increased size or brightness, noise-producing objects).
4. Consult a qualified specialist for further techniques for the child with a visual, hearing, or motor impairment.
5. Consider safety with all objects that the child handles. Never leave the child unattended with potentially hazardous objects.

Objective 2.1 Locates object and/or person who hides while child is watching

---

DEVELOPMENTAL PROGRAMMING STEPS

PS2.1a The child searches for the object by continuing to follow the object's path after it disappears. For example, the child looks for a toy train at the end of the tunnel through which the train has disappeared.

PS2.1b The child looks for a hidden object at the point where the object was last seen before it disappeared. For example, the adult takes a doll from the child's lap and covers it with a blanket. The child searches for the doll in his or her lap or in the adult's hand.

IMPORTANCE OF SKILL

The child becomes aware that objects have an existence that is permanent and independent from the child's actions. That is, the child learns that objects continue to exist even if they are not seen or manipulated directly. The child begins to understand that an object will disappear and can be found again. This skill is critical to the child's sense of control of the environment and sense of trust, and it affords the child more play opportunities.

PRECEDING OBJECTIVE

Cog B:2.2 Locates object and/or person who is partially hidden while child is watching

Cog B

CONCURRENT GOAL AND OBJECTIVES

FM A:3.1   Grasps hand-size object with either hand using the palm, with object placed toward the thumb and index finger

GM B:1.3   Regains balanced, upright sitting position after *leaning* to the left, to the right, and forward

Cog C:1.1   Correctly activates simple toy

Cog C:2.1   Indicates desire to continue familiar game and/or action

Cog E:2.1   Uses part of object and/or support to obtain another object

Cog E:3.1   Moves barrier or goes around barrier to obtain object

Cog G:1.2   Uses functionally appropriate actions with objects

SC A:1.0   Turns and looks toward person speaking

SC A:2.1   Follows person's pointing gesture to establish joint attention

SC C:1.3   Locates common objects, people, and/or events *with* contextual cues

Soc A:3.2   Responds to communication from familiar adult

Soc C:1.2   Responds appropriately to peer's social behavior

TEACHING SUGGESTIONS

Activity-Based

- During daily routines, pick up and place the child's favorite foods and toys in the refrigerator and cupboards while the child is still interested in them. Encourage the child to search for them.
- Intentionally make toys, cars, or balls roll out of sight. Place objects and food in boxes and paper bags and wait for the child to find them.
- Make toys disappear under sand or bubble bath. Cover floating toys with a washcloth.
- Hide small objects in your hand during interactive games.
- Play hide-and-seek. Hide while the child watches you.
- Say peekaboo and put towels or small blankets over your head or over other children. Encourage the child to find the people underneath. Say, "Where's Mama?" when the child's mother pulls a sweater over her head.
- When the child is playing with a toy, hide the toy (e.g., behind an adult's back, under a blanket, in a container) and encourage the child to find it.
- Present the child with toys that have parts that disappear and appear again, such as pop-up toys or jack-in-the-boxes. Activate the toy and encourage the child to find the part that disappeared (e.g., lift lid on jack-in-the-box).

Environmental Arrangements

- Use objects that are interesting to the child. As the child reaches toward an object, cover it with a cloth or your hand.
- Hide the object within easy reach of the child (e.g., under a blanket on which the child is sitting, to the side of the child's body).
- Hide and reveal objects repeatedly. For example, open and shut your hand while holding a small toy, or cover and uncover a cracker with a napkin.
- Pair visual with auditory cues (e.g., noise-producing toy). Hide a musical toy under a cloth while the toy is still playing music.
- Provide visual cues by using large objects and soft covers so that the contour of the object is visible under the cloth.

Cog B

- Pair visual with tactile cues by covering an object that the child is grasping or that is sitting in the child's lap.
- Use familiar, opaque objects as covers and avoid bright, shiny covers so that the object remains more interesting than the cover.
- Use a lightweight lid, cloth, pillow, or your hand as a cover so that it is not too difficult for the child to remove. Avoid tight lids and heavy objects.

Instructional Sequence

- Hide an object while the child is watching and then model finding it.
- Provide verbal or gestural cues by asking the child to find the object or point to its location.
- Gently guide and/or physically assist the child to remove the cloth cover on an object.

TEACHING CONSIDERATIONS

1. If a cover (e.g., cup, blanket, paper, lid) is used to hide an object, it is important to differentiate the child's search for the object from pulling at the cover to play with the cover itself. In general, if the child removes the cover and immediately reaches for the object, it can be assumed that the child is looking for the hidden object.
2. If the child does not have the motor skills to reach for and grasp the object, the child may indicate an awareness of its location by some other means (e.g., looking, pointing).
3. If the child has a visual impairment, increase the variety and intensity of cues (bright-colored or noise-producing objects).
4. Consult a qualified specialist for further techniques for the child with a visual, hearing, or motor impairment.
5. Consider safety with all objects that the child handles. Never leave the child unattended with potentially hazardous objects.

Objective 2.2   Locates object and/or person who is partially hidden while child is watching

---

DEVELOPMENTAL PROGRAMMING STEPS

PS2.2a   The child removes a cover from part of his or her body.
PS2.2b   The child removes a cover from his or her face.

IMPORTANCE OF SKILL

The ability to locate a partially hidden object implies that the child possesses an image of what the whole object is from seeing just a small component part. This skill opens up new possibilities in play and in exploring the environment.

PRECEDING OBJECTIVE

Cog B:2.3   Reacts when object and/or person hides from view

Cog B

CONCURRENT OBJECTIVES

FM A:2.3   Reaches toward and touches object with each hand
FM A:3.3   Grasps hand-size object with either hand using whole hand
GM A:3.5   Bears weight on one hand and/or arm while reaching with opposite hand
Cog C:1.2   Acts on mechanical and/or simple toy in some way
Cog E:2.1   Uses part of object and/or support to obtain another object
Cog E:3.1   Moves barrier or goes around barrier to obtain object
Cog G:1.3   Uses simple motor actions on different objects
SC A:2.1   Follows person's pointing gesture to establish joint attention
SC C:1.3   Locates common objects, people, and/or events *with* contextual cues
Soc A:3.2   Responds to communication from familiar adult

TEACHING SUGGESTIONS
Activity-Based

- Ask the child to find objects that are partially covered by blankets in the crib or by napkins at the table, objects that are partially hidden under furniture, or objects that are stacked upon one another in the toy box. Name objects and point to them if necessary. For example, say, "Where's your teddy bear?" when only the bear's legs are visible under a cover. If the child does not locate the bear, point to it and encourage the child to pull it out from under the cover.
- When giving an object to the child, hold the object in such a way that part of it is covered with your fingers, a cloth, or a paper bag.
- Offer objects that partially protrude from large pockets, paper bags, or boxes. Use objects such as necklaces and clothing so that they hang out of boxes or drawers.
- During water- and sand-play activities, partially hide objects under soap bubbles or in the sand.
- Play peekaboo and partially hide your face with a cloth.

Environmental Arrangements

- Use objects that are clearly interesting to the child. For example, partially cover an object that the child is trying to reach.
- Partially hide an object to the side or under the child's leg or arm.
- Pair visual cues with auditory cues by partially hiding noise-producing objects or by talking to the child if playing peekaboo.
- Pair visual cues with tactile cues by partially covering an object that the child is manipulating or by gently touching the child with an object that is partially covered.
- Use toys and/or objects that have strings attached (e.g., pull-toy, car with yarn attached) so that the child pulls the string to obtain the partially hidden toy.
- Use familiar, opaque objects as covers and avoid bright, shiny covers so that the object remains more interesting than the cover.
- Use a lightweight lid, cloth, pillow, or your hand as a cover so that it is not too difficult for the child to remove. Avoid tight lids and heavy objects.

Instructional Sequence

- Model finding an object that is partially hidden. Let the child know when you find it.
- Leave most of the object in full view of the child and cover only one segment. System-

Cog B

atically cover more of the object as the child's responses indicate that he or she can locate the object.

- Provide verbal and visual cues by asking the child to find the object or point toward it.
- Begin with objects that have component parts that are visually similar to the whole object, such as blocks, blankets, strings of beads, or a toy train. Introduce objects composed of parts that differ from one another, such as dolls, pots and pans, and clothing, as the child becomes more proficient.
- Physically assist the child to uncover a partially hidden object.

TEACHING CONSIDERATIONS

1. If a cover (e.g., cup, blanket, paper) is used to hide an object, it is important to differentiate the child's search for the object from pulling at the cover to play with the cover itself. In general, if the child removes the cover and immediately reaches for the object, one can assume that the child is looking for the hidden object.
2. If the child does not have the motor skills to reach for and grasp the object, the child may indicate awareness of its location by some other means (looking, pointing).
3. If the child has a visual impairment, increase the variety and intensity of cues (objects of increased size or brightness, noise-producing objects). Be sure that the cover contrasts with the object.
4. Consult a qualified specialist for further techniques for the child with a visual, hearing, or motor impairment.
5. Be cautious and consider safety with all objects that the child handles. Never leave the child unattended with potentially hazardous objects.

Objective 2.3   Reacts when object and/or person hides from view

---

IMPORTANCE OF SKILL

The reaction of the child to the disappearance of an object indicates that the child has acquired an elementary notion of the permanence of an object. The child reacts to the interruption of the visual perception and learns to expect that the object or person will reappear. This skill helps the child establish trust and build curiosity in exploring the environment.

PRECEDING OBJECTIVE

Cog B:1.2   Focuses on object and/or person

CONCURRENT GOAL AND OBJECTIVES

FM A:5.1   Releases hand-held object onto and/or into a larger target with either hand
Cog B:1.0   Visually follows object and/or person to point of disappearance
Cog C:2.1   Indicates desire to continue familiar game and/or action
SC B:1.4   Uses gestures and/or vocalizations to protest actions and/or reject objects or people

Cog B

Soc A:1.2   Smiles in response to familiar adult
Soc A:2.2   Responds to familiar adult's social behavior

TEACHING SUGGESTIONS

Activity-Based

- Play hiding games with the child, such as peekaboo. Cover face or parts of face with hands, a pillow, or a cloth. Hide behind furniture or in a doorway. Encourage the child to take turns hiding and act excited when you "find" the child.
- Make objects the child is playing with disappear from the child's visual field by dropping them on the floor, placing them on a high shelf, or covering them with a larger object.
- Observe the child's reactions when a person leaves the room, or when a toy or food is placed behind a cupboard door or in a drawer. Draw the child's attention to the object or person who disappears from sight.

Environmental Arrangements

- Hide toys or objects that the child is playing with under a blanket, towel, or box.
- Use objects that are clearly interesting and engaging for the child. Hide objects that the child is manipulating or is about to reach for.
- While the child is sitting on the adult's lap or in a highchair, hand the child a large, interesting toy that is likely to drop from the child's hands and visual field because of its size.
- Play with balls and other objects likely to roll out of view.
- Use objects such as wind-up toys that will continue to make noise while out of sight.
- Continue to talk to the child while moving behind the doorway, behind a large piece of furniture, or under a blanket.
- Use a variety of objects to keep the child's interest.

Instructional Sequence

- Model reacting when a ball or pet disappears from view.
- Provide verbal and visual direction by asking where an object is or by exaggerating a facial expression of surprise.
- Pair visual cues with auditory cues. Use noise-producing objects such as bells, a rattle, or a music box.
- Physically guide the child to react or search when an object disappears from view.

TEACHING CONSIDERATIONS

1. The environment should be free of auditory, visual, or tactile events that compete with the object presented.
2. If the child does not have the motor skills to turn his or her head toward the object, the child may indicate awareness of its location by some other means (e.g., blinking, pointing).
3. Consult a qualified specialist for further techniques for the child with a visual, hearing, or motor impairment.
4. Be cautious and consider safety with all objects that the child handles. Never leave the child unattended with potentially hazardous objects.

GOAL 3   Maintains search for object that is not in its usual location

DEVELOPMENTAL PROGRAMMING STEPS

PS3.0a   The child asks the adult for an object when the object is not found in its usual location.

PS3.0b   The child maintains a search for an object in its usual location. For example, the child searches a second time in a toy box for a favorite toy.

IMPORTANCE OF SKILL

This skill represents the beginning of an understanding of the permanence of objects. By maintaining the search for an object, the child demonstrates awareness that the object continues to exist somewhere. The existence of the object is disassociated from the child's direct perception and from the object's location in space. This skill enhances the child's exploration of the environment and increases opportunity for play.

PRECEDING OBJECTIVE

Cog B:3.1   Looks for object in usual location

CONCURRENT GOALS AND OBJECTIVES

Cog E:3.1   Moves barrier or goes around barrier to obtain object
Cog E:4.0   Solves common problems
SC C:1.0   Locates objects, people, and/or events *without* contextual cues
SC C:2.2   Carries out one-step direction *without* contextual cues
SC D:3.2   Asks questions
Soc B:2.1   Responds to routine event

TEACHING SUGGESTIONS
Activity-Based

- Ask the child to get bread out of the bread drawer when it is really in the refrigerator or in a grocery bag.
- Play a "You're getting warmer or colder" game and give the child clues as he or she searches for the missing object or peer.
- Ask the child to look for the dog inside when you know the dog is outside or in a closed room.
- Set up situations in which the child needs to search for objects. For example, give the child only one of two functionally related objects, such as a formboard without shapes or crayons without paper.
- Play games such as hide-and-seek with objects.

Environmental Arrangements

- Arrange the environment so that objects are not in their usual location. For example, tell the child to look in the cupboard for a particular color or shape of glass that is in the sink and not yet washed.

Cog B

- Place the object in another location similar to its usual location. For example, place the child's teddy bear, which usually rests on the child's bed, on the parent's bed.
- Arrange objects so that they are visible to the child when the child is searching for the object in its usual location. For example, place fish food on a nearby stool when the child goes to get the fish food in its usual location on a shelf.

Instructional Sequence

- Model searching for an object that is not in its usual location. Comment as you find it.
- Verbally encourage the child to continue looking for an object that is not in its usual location.
- Suggest places for the child to search. For example, as the child looks for the pet dog in the backyard suggest the child look on the front porch.
- Accompany the child in the search and physically assist the child to look in several places.

TEACHING CONSIDERATIONS

1. Be sure that the object and its usual location are familiar to the child.
2. The mastery of this skill does not require the child to find the object. If, however, the child appears to become upset about not finding the object after searching in more than one place, give the child the object or direct the child to it.
3. If the child has a severe visual or motor impairment, the child may indicate awareness of the object's location by some other means (e.g., vocalizing, blinking, pointing).
4. Consult a qualified specialist for further techniques for the child with a visual, hearing, or motor impairment.
5. Consider safety with all objects that the child handles. Never leave the child unattended with potentially hazardous objects.

Objective 3.1 Looks for object in usual location

DEVELOPMENTAL PROGRAMMING STEP

PS3.1a   The child looks for an object in the proximity of its usual location. For example, the child goes into the kitchen and requests a cracker or goes to the corner where the toys are kept to look for a ball.

IMPORTANCE OF SKILL

This skill represents the child's ability to generalize the notion of permanence of the object to situations in the daily environment. In addition, this skill requires the child to practice long-term memory skills and associate familiar objects with stable locations that are familiar reference points in the child's environment. This skill enhances the child's exploration of the environment and increases opportunity for play.

Cog B

CONCURRENT GOALS AND OBJECTIVES

Adap A:4.0 Eats with fork and/or spoon
Adap A:5.1 Pours liquid
Adap B:1.2 Indicates awareness of soiled and wet pants and/or diapers
Cog E:3.1   Moves barrier or goes around barrier to obtain object
Cog E:4.1   Uses more than one strategy in attempt to solve common problem
SC C:1.0   Locates objects, people, and/or events *without* contextual cues
SC C:2.2   Carries out one-step direction *without* contextual cues
SC D:3.2   Asks questions
Soc B:1.1   Meets physical needs of hunger and thirst
Soc B:2.1   Responds to routine event
Soc C:2.2   Responds to communication from peer

TEACHING SUGGESTIONS

Activity-Based

- Set up daily activities so that the child can independently search for familiar objects in their usual locations. For example, when it is time to go outside, ask the child to find his or her coat. When it is time for a change of clothes or diapers, ask the child to go get them. Announce bathtime and wait for the child to proceed to the bathroom.
- During play activities, avoid providing all necessary materials and have the child get some of them. For example, set out the people and animals, but not the barn; or bring out the strings without the beads. Encourage the child to look for the missing pieces.
- Give the child only one of two functionally related objects, such as a bowl of applesauce without a spoon or a cup without a pitcher of juice. Wait for the child to notice something is missing; encourage the child to look for it.

Environmental Arrangements

- Encourage the child to look for an object just after the child has placed it in its usual location. For example, the child places a box of crackers in the cupboard, the peer requests a cracker, and the child returns to the cupboard to get a cracker.
- Give the child one item of a pair, such as one shoe or sock, and ask the child to find the mate.
- Encourage the child to look for an object in its usual location when the object is within the child's visual field. For example, ask the child to get a book from an open bookshelf.
- Have the child look for the dog in its doghouse or bed.

Instructional Sequence

- Model looking for an object in its usual location. Comment as you find it.
- Give verbal directions to the child about the object's location.
- Have an adult or peer guide the child to the object's usual location. For example, the child follows the peer to the sink to get water to take to the sandbox.

TEACHING CONSIDERATIONS

1. Be sure the object and its usual location are familiar to the child.
2. Arrange objects systematically in the same locations within the child's reach.

Cog B

3. If the child has a visual or motor impairment, the child may indicate awareness of the location by some other means (e.g., vocalizing, blinking, pointing).
4. Consult a qualified specialist for further techniques for the child with a visual, hearing, or motor impairment.
5. Consider safety with any objects that the child handles. Never leave the child unattended with potentially hazardous objects.

Cog B

Strand C

Causality

GOAL 1   Correctly activates mechanical toy

DEVELOPMENTAL PROGRAMMING STEPS

PS1.0a   The child touches or attempts to manipulate a button, key, or switch to manipulate a mechanical toy.

PS1.0b   The child touches the part of the mechanical toy that produces a movement or a sound (e.g., the child touches the tail of a toy animal that wags when wound up).

IMPORTANCE OF SKILL

The child recognizes that effects can be attributed to causes other than direct sensori-motor actions. Causal links exist even though they are not perceived directly by the child. The child learns to produce effects that are not apparently connected to the child's action. This increases the child's play opportunities and exploration.

PRECEDING OBJECTIVE

Cog C:1.1   Correctly activates simple toy

CONCURRENT GOALS AND OBJECTIVES

FM B:1.0   Rotates either wrist on horizontal plane
FM B:3.0   Uses either index finger to activate objects
Cog D:1.1   Imitates motor action that is commonly used
Cog E:2.1   Uses part of object and/or support to obtain another object
Cog E:4.1   Uses more than one strategy in attempt to solve common problem
Cog G:1.2   Uses functionally appropriate actions with objects
SC C:2.3   Carries out one-step direction *with* contextual cues
Soc A:3.2   Responds to communication from familiar adult
Soc C:1.5   Entertains self by playing appropriately with toys

TEACHING SUGGESTIONS
Activity-Based

- Present the child with a variety of mechanical toys and objects that must be manipulated (e.g., push-button, knob, handle) to be activated.

Cog C

- Use many different examples of toys that are manipulated in a variety of ways. For example, a dump truck activated by pushing a button or pulling a lever, a musical toy activated by pulling on a string, wind-up toys activated by turning a key, or a toy piano played by hitting a key. Demonstrate the toy's correct action, if necessary.
- Select and offer toys that produce effects that are interesting to the child.

☑ If your data indicate that the child is not making progress toward the goal, provide additional structure within the suggested activities by incorporating the following *environmental arrangements:*

Environmental Arrangements

- Start by using toys that are easily activated (by pushing a button or lever, as opposed to turning a key or dial). Increase the complexity as the child's skills increase.
- Select toys that produce interesting effects that are tangible to the child (e.g., a water pistol that squirts water on the child, a flashlight or slide projector in a dark room). Demonstrate the toy or object's correct use, if necessary. Begin with simple, highly interesting items, such as a doorbell or light switch.
- Try demonstrating the use of a mechanical toy that the child is already acting upon in some way. Increase the complexity of the child's play by using similar toys with mechanical features. For example, for a child who enjoys doll play, introduce a doll that walks or talks when a button is pushed or a string is pulled.
- Many mechanical toys require considerable effort to produce an effect (e.g., a long pull string on a See-N-Say, a wind-up television or radio, many cranks of a jack-in-the-box handle). Assist the child by doing the initial pull or crank; let the child complete the task to produce the effect. Systematically reduce your input and require more participation by the child.

☑ If this goal is particularly difficult for a child, it may be necessary, within activities, to use an *instructional sequence.*

Instructional Sequence

- Model the correct use of a toy, then point to the part of the toy responsible for its activation.
- Verbally encourage the child to activate the toy (e.g., "Make it move") and provide instructions (e.g., "Push the button").
- Physically assist the child to touch the correct part of the toy to activate it.

☑ Combining or pairing different levels of instructions may be helpful when beginning to teach a new and difficult skill. Fade to less intrusive instructions as soon as possible, to encourage more independent performance.

TEACHING CONSIDERATIONS

1. Choose a toy that is appropriate for the child's motor skills (e.g., an electronic toy that can be activated with a light touch is helpful for a child with a motor impairment, toys with push buttons are easier to activate).
2. If the child has a severe visual impairment, allow tactile exploration of the toy before expecting the child to activate it. Provide verbal cues and describe what the child is touching. Use noise-producing toys.
3. Consult a qualified specialist for further techniques for the child with a visual, hearing, or motor impairment.
4. Consider safety with all objects that the child handles. Never leave the child unattended with potentially hazardous objects.

Objective 1.1 Correctly activates simple toy

DEVELOPMENTAL PROGRAMMING STEPS

☑ The objective above is the most basic step for the skill to be taught. Most children will benefit from the activities outlined here that emphasize this skill. For children who need more instruction, consider designing programming steps from the *environmental arrangements* suggestions or from the *instructional sequence* outlined.

IMPORTANCE OF SKILL

This skill represents the child's ability to produce actions that take into account the specific properties of the object. The child differentiates actions that activate specific objects from those that merely produce interesting results. Therefore, the child begins to identify the items that easily produce specific actions (e.g., balls roll and bounce, rattles shake).

PRECEDING OBJECTIVE

Cog C:1.2   Acts on mechanical and/or simple toy in some way

CONCURRENT OBJECTIVES

FM A:2.2   Holds an object in each hand
FM B:3.1   Uses either hand to activate objects
GM A:3.5   Bears weight on one hand and/or arm while reaching with opposite hand
GM B:1.4   Sits balanced without support
GM D:4.4   Rolls ball at target
Cog D:1.1   Imitates motor action that is commonly used
Cog G:1.3   Uses simple motor actions on different objects
SC A:1.1   Turns and looks toward object and person speaking
SC A:3.1   Engages in vocal exchanges by cooing
Soc A:2.2   Responds to familiar adult's social behavior
Soc C:1.5   Entertains self by playing appropriately with toys

TEACHING SUGGESTIONS

Activity-Based

- Provide the child with a variety of objects and toys that are activated directly by a simple action (e.g., shaking, banging, hitting, rolling, squeezing).
- Select toys that produce effects that are interesting to the child.
- Offer toys that are activated by different actions. For example, rattles and bells are activated by shaking; larger objects, such as a roly-poly toy, are activated by a push with the arm and hand; and squeeze-toys are activated by squeezing.
- Make sure the child has time to thoroughly explore and exercise a number of actions (e.g., mouthing, shaking, banging) on an object before you expect correct activation.
- Introduce objects within an interactive, turn-taking game and demonstrate the toys' correct use.

Environmental Arrangements

- Use toys that continue a movement after an initial activation (e.g., rocking horse, wobbly toy, wind chimes, toy with pendulum). Use toys that produce a sound (e.g., bell, drum) or a visual effect (e.g., a transparent rattle full of beads).
- Join in the child's play with the toy. Demonstrate the correct use of a toy the child is already using or manipulating. Encourage the child to incorporate new movements into play if he or she is holding a rattle with moving parts (demonstrate how to make other parts move).

Instructional Sequence

- Model or have a peer model activating a toy and then hand it to the child. If necessary, give specific instructions (e.g., say, "Shake the bells," "Kick the ball").
- If the child does not use a simple toy correctly, provide verbal directions to encourage the child and to focus the child's attention (e.g., say, "Look at this," "Something funny is going to happen").
- Physically assist the child to activate simple toys.

TEACHING CONSIDERATIONS

1. Adapt your choice of a toy to the sensory impairment of the child (e.g., use a wobbly toy that a child with a motor impairment can activate with a light touch, or use a noise-producing toy for a child with a visual impairment).
2. If the child has a severe visual impairment, allow tactile exploration of the toy before expecting the child to activate it. Provide verbal cues and describe the toy as the child touches it.
3. Consult a qualified specialist for further techniques for the child with a visual, hearing, or motor impairment.
4. Consider safety with all objects that the child handles. Never leave the child unattended with potentially hazardous objects.

Objective 1.2 Acts on mechanical and/or simple toy in some way

---

IMPORTANCE OF SKILL

The child begins to perceive his or her actions as the causes of interesting results. The child becomes aware of the contingency between personal actions and events and uses simple actions to produce effects on objects. This skill affords the child more interesting play opportunities.

PRECEDING OBJECTIVE

Cog C:1.3   Indicates interest in simple and/or mechanical toy

CONCURRENT GOALS AND OBJECTIVES

FM A:2.3   Reaches toward and touches object with each hand
GM A:3.6   Lifts head and chest off surface with weight on arms

GM B:1.6   Holds head in midline when in supported sitting position
Adap A:1.0 Uses tongue and lips to take in and swallow solid foods and liquids
Cog A:1.0   Orients to auditory, visual, and tactile events
Cog B:1.1   Visually follows object moving in horizontal, vertical, and circular directions
Cog G:1.4   Uses sensory examination with objects
SC A:1.2   Turns and looks toward noise-producing object

TEACHING SUGGESTIONS
Activity-Based

- Provide the child with a variety of mechanical and simple toys that produce an interesting effect as a result of the child's action on them (e.g., squeeze-toy, mobile, roly-poly toy, chime ball). Encourage the child to exercise simple actions on objects (e.g., swiping, banging, mouthing, shaking).
- Make your own pull-toy by threading yogurt cartons or spools on yarn.
- Wind a musical toy for the child. When it winds down, ask if the child would like to hear it again.

Environmental Arrangements

- Attach measuring spoons or jingle-bells to the car seat.
- Hang a rattle or chime toy on the side of the crib or hang a swing toy within swiping range when the child is lying on his or her back. Always be cautious of the danger of hanging objects in the crib.
- Place toys in close proximity to the child's hands or feet, so that the child might accidentally activate them. Encourage the child to repeat the movement.
- Use toys that are interesting to the child, such as large, bright-colored, and noise-producing toys.
- Attach mobiles or bells with a string to the child's wrist or ankle. Sew bells to the child's socks or sleeves.

Instructional Sequence

- Provide a model by activating the toy in some way. Observe the child for interest, and repeat activity.
- When the child purposely or accidentally activates a toy (e.g., sets a spinner in motion on a crib mobile), verbally acknowledge the movement by saying, "That's the way. Do it again."
- Place toys in the child's hands, on the child's lap, or by the child's feet. Assist the child to act on the toy by touching, kicking, moving, or swiping.

TEACHING CONSIDERATIONS

1. The child should be in a quiet, alert state.
2. The environment should be free of objects or events that compete with the toy presented to the child.
3. A child with a severe motor impairment may indicate awareness that a toy can be acted upon in ways other than manual exploration. For example, active visual exploration of an object may replace manipulation.
4. If the child has a severe visual impairment, allow tactile exploration before expecting

Cog C

the child to activate the toy. Provide verbal cues rather than a visual demonstration of the toy.

5. Consult a qualified specialist for further techniques for the child with a visual, hearing, or motor impairment.
6. Consider safety with all objects that the child handles. Never leave the child unattended with potentially hazardous objects.

Objective 1.3 Indicates interest in simple and/or mechanical toy

IMPORTANCE OF SKILL

The child indicates interest in an object by producing personal actions (e.g., waving, smiling, rocking) in response to specific events. This is the first step toward the recognition of the relationship between the child's actions and the production of interesting effects on objects. This skill is an important early step in the child's exploration of the environment.

PRECEDING OBJECTIVE

Cog A:1.4   Responds to auditory, visual, and tactile events

CONCURRENT OBJECTIVES

FM A:1.1   Makes directed batting and/or swiping movements with each hand
GM A:1.2   Kicks legs
Cog A:1.1   Orients to auditory events
Cog B:1.2   Focuses on object and/or person
SC A:1.2   Turns and looks toward noise-producing object
SC A:2.2   Looks toward an object
Soc A:1.2   Smiles in response to familiar adult

TEACHING SUGGESTIONS
Activity-Based

- Activate a variety of interesting simple or mechanical toys, such as a rattle, bell, squeeze-toy, wind-up radio, or jack-in-the-box.
- To stimulate the child's interest, use familiar objects in novel ways (e.g., bang a spoon on a metal or plastic bowl to produce a noise; use a hand puppet to shake a rattle; or make funny noises and exaggerated facial expressions).
- Routinely activate a mobile above the child's crib when you put the child down or get the child up from a nap.

Environmental Arrangements

- Create noises for toys that do not typically make noise (e.g., cry for the baby doll when you hold it, make "vroom" sound when you push a toy truck).
- Use objects that are likely to attract the child's attention, such as large, bright, or noise-producing toys.

Cog C

- Alternate activation of the toy with abrupt interruptions to maintain the child's interest.
- Model interest in the toy by exclaiming surprise when the toy activates.
- Introduce toys during face-to-face interactions when the child is showing interest in your behavior.

Instructional Sequence

- Pair presentation of the toy with visual or verbal cues by presenting the object in the child's visual field or by telling the child to look.
- Model a noise when you squeak a squeeze-toy.
- Provide tactile assistance by touching or tickling the child with the toy.

TEACHING CONSIDERATIONS

1. The child should be in a quiet, alert state.
2. The environment should be free of objects or events that compete with the toy presented to the child.
3. When the child indicates interest, continue activating the toy to reinforce the interest.
4. Toys should provide cues to which the child with a sensory impairment can respond (e.g., noise-producing toys for the child with a visual impairment, moving toys for the child with a hearing or motor impairment).
5. Consult a qualified specialist for further techniques for the child with a visual, hearing, or motor impairment.
6. Consider safety with all objects that the child handles. Never leave the child unattended with potentially hazardous objects.

GOAL 2 **Reproduces part of interactive game and/or action in order to continue game and/or action**

DEVELOPMENTAL PROGRAMMING STEP

PS2.0a The child indicates a desire for the adult to continue a game or action by touching a part of the adult's body used to produce the game or action. For example, the child touches the adult's hand or eyes to indicate the desire to continue playing peekaboo.

IMPORTANCE OF SKILL

The child learns how to reproduce an action or part of a game to cause others to repeat actions they have initiated. The child no longer uses random actions to make interesting events continue, but reproduces a precise action related to a specific type of interaction. The child also uses nonverbal communication, such as turn-taking and imitation, to cause a particular effect.

PRECEDING OBJECTIVE

Cog C:2.1   Indicates desire to continue familiar game and/or action

Cog C

CONCURRENT GOAL AND OBJECTIVES

FM B:3.1   Uses either hand to activate objects
Cog B:2.1   Locates object and/or person who hides while child is watching
Cog D:1.1   Imitates motor action that is commonly used
Cog D:2.2   Imitates words that are frequently used
SC A:3.0   Engages in vocal exchanges by babbling
Soc A:3.2   Responds to communication from familiar adult

TEACHING SUGGESTIONS

Activity-Based

- Engage the child in interactive games or actions with or without objects. Play games such as peekaboo, or pat-a-cake.
- Engage in simple motor activities that entertain the child and that the child can reproduce (e.g., bang or push objects, open and close hands, make funny noises, gesture good-bye, or splash water).
- Once the child's interest is gained (e.g., child looks, smiles, vocalizes, or moves part of body), cease the action and observe the child's ability to reproduce part of the game or action to continue it.
- Sing interactive songs or songs with motor actions such as "Row, Row, Row Your Boat," "Eency Weency Spider," and "Twinkle, Twinkle Little Star."

Environmental Arrangements

- Engage in actions, using unusual visual, auditory, and tactile stimuli. Play with shiny, noisy, or tactilely interesting objects (e.g., flashlight, aluminum foil, noise-producing toys, feathers, or soft stuffed animals).
- Play "Piggy Went to Market" on the child's bare foot; stop after the second toe.
- Pair actions with additional cues (e.g., vocalize, exaggerate facial expressions) to make the game or action interesting to the child.

Instructional Sequence

- Give the child verbal instructions ("It's your turn," or "More!").
- Integrate an action initiated by the child in an interactive game. For example, if the child bounces up and down while sitting on your lap, ask, "Do you want to play horsie?" Bounce the child up and down, making clicking noises with your tongue. Cease the activity and wait for the child to bounce again or make clicking noises.

TEACHING CONSIDERATIONS

1. Be sure the actions are developmentally appropriate for the child to reproduce.
2. Games and actions should provide cues to which the child with a sensory impairment can respond (e.g., noise-producing toys for a child with a visual impairment, moving toys for a child with a hearing or motor impairment).
3. If the child has a sensory impairment, make sure that the child is capable of reproducing the stimuli presented and the responses required.
4. Consult a qualified specialist for further techniques for the child with a visual, hearing, or motor impairment.
5. Consider safety with all objects that the child handles. Never leave the child unattended with potentially hazardous objects.

Cog C

Objective 2.1   Indicates desire to continue familiar game and/or action

DEVELOPMENTAL PROGRAMMING STEP

PS2.1a   The child reproduces an action (e.g., waves arms, vocalizes, smiles) after an adult is attentive to the child's initial behavior.

IMPORTANCE OF SKILL

This behavior indicates that the child is becoming aware of the effect of personal actions on people, objects, and events. The child learns to perceive the causal relationship between personal actions and their consequences. These behaviors also represent the first signals used intentionally by the child to communicate, which is an important first step in the communication process.

CONCURRENT GOALS AND OBJECTIVES

FM A:2.3   Reaches toward and touches object with each hand
FM A:3.3   Grasps hand-size object with either hand using whole hand
Adap A:4.3   Accepts food presented on spoon
Cog B:2.3   Reacts when object and/or person hides from view
SC A:1.0   Turns and looks toward person speaking
SC A:3.0   Engages in vocal exchanges by babbling
Soc A:2.2   Responds to familiar adult's social behavior

TEACHING SUGGESTIONS
Activity-Based

- Engage the child in interactive games or actions with or without objects. Observe the child's reactions (e.g., looking, smiling, body excitement, arm waving) to ascertain the child's interest in the game. Cease the activity and wait for the child to indicate a desire to continue the game or action. For example, play pat-a-cake or peekaboo; or play with hands (e.g., snap fingers, drum fingers on objects, knock on table top) to elicit the child's interest. Then pause and wait until the child vocalizes, waves arms, shakes head, arches, or rocks as a signal for you to continue.
- Throughout the daily routine, provide opportunities for interactive games or actions. For example, during diapering, place a diaper or cloth over the child's face or your face to play peekaboo. Play airplane while feeding the child with a spoon. While dressing the child, tickle his or her feet, tummy, or neck.
- Repeat the child's sounds or actions, pausing to allow the child to respond.

Environmental Arrangements

- Engage in actions that have a direct effect on the child's body (e.g., gently tickle the child's tummy, kiss and blow on the child's arm).
- Combine stimulations; for example, touch the child while vocalizing and exaggerating facial expressions.
- Play with objects that produce intense auditory, visual, and tactile stimuli (e.g., noisy

Cog C

mechanical toys, a radio set at increased volume, flashlight, soft and furry toys, feathers, or water).

■ Imitate a behavior initiated by the child and integrate it into a social game (e.g., if the child bangs an object, imitate the action). Ascertain the child's interest by observing the child's reaction. Cease imitating to allow the child an opportunity to indicate a desire to continue the action.

■ During feedings, stop offering the bottle or spoon and wait for the child to indicate desire for more.

Instructional Sequence

■ Model clapping your hands and pause for the child to do the same.
■ Provide verbal instructions by asking the child, "More?" or "Again?"
■ Physically clap the child's hands together and then exclaim, "Good job! You're clapping."

TEACHING CONSIDERATIONS

1. Make sure the interaction is familiar and interesting to the child. Try a variety of behaviors until the child manifests interest with a smile, look, or kick.

2. If a child has a sensory impairment, use games and actions to which the child can respond. Speak loudly and use gestures for the child with a hearing impairment; and play touching or tickling games with the child with a visual impairment.

3. Consult a qualified specialist for further techniques for the child with a visual, hearing, or motor impairment.

4. Consider safety with all objects that the child handles. Never leave the child unattended with potentially hazardous objects.

Cog C

Strand D

Imitation

GOAL 1   Imitates motor action that is not commonly used

DEVELOPMENTAL PROGRAMMING STEPS

PS1.0a   The child imitates an unfamiliar motor action demonstrated by the adult with an object the child is playing with or with parts of the body the child has just used. For example, the child claps his or her hands, the adult opens and closes his or her fingers, and the child imitates. Or the child places some beans in a container, the adult puts some beans in a row, and the child imitates.

PS1.0b   The child responds to a model of an unfamiliar motor action by performing a similar but different action involving the same body part(s). For example, the adult turns around and the child jumps up and down.

IMPORTANCE OF SKILL

The ability to reproduce an action the child does not yet use is important for the acquisition of new behaviors and skills. The child learns to modify familiar actions with respect to new models. Imitation of novel gestures requires the child to engage in problem-solving behaviors as the child tries different actions (means) to reproduce the modeled action (goal).

PRECEDING OBJECTIVE

Cog D:1.1   Imitates motor action that is commonly used

CONCURRENT GOALS AND OBJECTIVES

FM B:2.0   Assembles toy and/or object that require(s) putting pieces together
FM B:4.0   Copies simple written shapes after demonstration
GM D:1.0   Jumps forward
GM D:4.2   Kicks ball or similar object
Adap A:5.0 Transfers food and liquid
Adap B:2.0 Washes and dries hands
Adap B:3.0 Brushes teeth
Cog C:2.0   Reproduces part of interactive game and/or action in order to continue game and/or action

Cog E:4.0   Solves common problems
Cog F:1.1   Aligns objects
Cog G:1.2   Uses functionally appropriate actions with objects
SC C:2.3   Carries out one-step direction *with* contextual cues
Soc A:2.2   Responds to familiar adult's social behavior
Soc C:1.2   Responds appropriately to peer's social behavior

TEACHING SUGGESTIONS
Activity-Based

- As the child demonstrates interest during daily activities, seize the opportunity to demonstrate actions and the use of objects with which the child is not yet familiar. Show the child the functional use of objects (e.g., comb hair, brush teeth, scribble with a pencil), communicative gestures (e.g., shake someone's hand, blow a kiss, stroke a pet), or movement (e.g., step over an obstacle, kick a ball). Encourage the child to imitate the action.
- Engage the child in interactive activities (e.g., playing musical instruments, acting out and telling stories, playing with dolls and animals) and introduce a turn-taking interaction (e.g., the child imitates the adult hitting a bell with a drumstick; the adult tells a story about a bird and flaps his or her arms in the motion of wings, and the child imitates the motion).
- Play games such as "Simon says," introducing uncommon actions (e.g., rub feet, place hand under arm, touch forehead with one finger).
- Sing novel songs with motor actions (e.g., "Wheels on the Bus," "Open/Shut Them"). Encourage the child to join by imitating the novel motor actions.
- Encourage children to learn signs for a few basic words.

☑ If your data indicate that the child is not making progress toward the goal, provide additional structure within the suggested activities by incorporating the following *environmental arrangements:*

Environmental Arrangements

- Encourage the child to imitate less familiar actions within the child's visual range (e.g., swing a leg, put on a bracelet).
- Stand with the child in front of a mirror so that the child can see him- or herself. Demonstrate different actions (e.g., place an object on your head, try to touch the tip of your nose with your tongue). Encourage the child to imitate the action while observing him- or herself in the mirror.
- Exaggerate actions and pair them with auditory or tactile cues (e.g., make noises while kissing or blowing the child's ear or leg, hit your stomach and groan, wrinkle your nose or sniff at a strong-smelling substance and make an exclamation, pat your mouth while making sounds).
- Play imitative games beginning with imitation of commonly used, visible gestures. Gradually introduce gestures not commonly used. Make a desired event contingent on the child's imitation (e.g., demonstrate using your foot to obtain a desired object out of reach).
- Sing motor imitation songs such as "Head, Shoulder, Knees, and Toes" or "Put Your Left Foot In . . . ." Have another child demonstrate the action as a model.

☑ If this goal is particularly difficult for a child, it may be necessary, within activities, to use an *instructional sequence.*

Instructional Sequence

- Encourage the child to imitate the model in action. For example, during a magic show, continue to move your hand in a circular motion over a blanket and say, "Abracadabra" until the child imitates.
- Give verbal directions (e.g., "You do it," or "Your turn").
- Physically assist the child by gently touching the part of the body to be engaged in the action.
- If the child still does not imitate, physically guide the child through the action.

☑ Combining or pairing different levels of instructions may be helpful when beginning to teach a new and difficult skill. Fade to less intrusive instructions as soon as possible to encourage more independent performance.

TEACHING CONSIDERATIONS

1. Motor actions should be only slightly beyond the child's current abilities.
2. Select actions that the child has not yet performed, but that are functional and useful.
3. Do not provide the child with extra cues, such as verbal directions, unless intentionally used for assistance. The child needs to focus on the motor act, not the verbal direction.
4. The focus is on the ability to reproduce an unfamiliar and novel action, not on the complexity of the motor action.
5. If the child has a severe motor impairment, select motor actions not commonly used that are within the child's ability (e.g., pat knee, rub eyebrow).
6. The child with a visual impairment may need special adaptations such as verbal direction (e.g., say, "Jump up and down like me"). This goal may not be appropriate for a child with a severe visual impairment.
7. The child with a hearing impairment can learn new motor actions through total communication.

Cog D

Objective 1.1   Imitates motor action that is commonly used

DEVELOPMENTAL PROGRAMMING STEPS

PS1.1a   The child reproduces a motor action similar to, but different from, the adult's model. For example, the adult opens and closes his or her fingers and the child waves his or her hand.

PS1.1b   The child imitates a simple motor action that is commonly used after the adult imitates an action initiated by the child. For example, the child sticks out his or her tongue, the adult imitates, and the child repeats the action within a turn-taking interaction.

IMPORTANCE OF SKILL

Imitation enables the child to learn about people, objects, and events by reproducing behaviors and actions performed by models. At first, the child imitates only actions that he or she can already do. Imitation is important to the development of representation and language because the child uses gestures to indicate formerly perceived objects and events. Reciprocal imitation also represents a form of early communicative exchange.

PRECEDING OBJECTIVE

Cog B:1.2   Focuses on object and/or person

CONCURRENT GOALS AND OBJECTIVES

FM A:5.0   Places and releases object balanced on top of another object with either hand
GM D:1.1   Jumps up
GM D:4.0   Catches, kicks, throws, and rolls ball or similar object
Cog C:2.0   Reproduces part of interactive game and/or action in order to continue game and/or action
Cog F:1.2   Stacks objects
Cog G:1.3   Uses simple motor actions on different objects
SC B:1.1   Responds with a vocalization and gesture to simple questions
Soc A:2.2   Responds to familiar adult's social behavior
Soc C:1.2   Responds appropriately to peer's social behavior

TEACHING SUGGESTIONS
Activity-Based

- During daily routines and when the child is in a position that allows eye contact, smile, stick out your tongue, move your head from side to side or up and down, or produce any visible motor action and observe whether the child reproduces the same action.
- Bring a hand within the child's visual field, then move your fingers, wave bye-bye, open and close one hand, or move both hands together and apart. Encourage the child to imitate.
- When the child demonstrates interest in an object, act on the object, using actions that the child can perform. For example, shake a rattle, bang a spoon on the table, push a ball, or splash water.
- Engage the child in turn-taking activities, such as building a tower, in which each person takes a turn placing a block. Play games taking turns clapping each other's blocks, as in "Peas, Porridge, Hot."

Environmental Arrangements

- Encourage the child to imitate movements performed with parts of the body that the child can see on him- or herself. Use hands, arms, legs, or feet rather than parts of the face; shake hands rather than open and close eyes; or touch your knee rather than your nose.
- Perform actions that produce intense stimuli or interesting results for the child. For example, bang on a loud drum, bring a bottle to your mouth, splash water, or shake a flashlight.
- Pair visual, auditory, and tactile cues. Put sticky tape on the tips of your fingers and vocalize while gently drumming fingers on the child's arm or leg. Encourage the child to move his or her own fingers.

Cog D

- Make a desired event contingent on the child's imitation. For example, during meals, open and close your mouth and encourage the child to imitate before placing food in the child's mouth.
- Engage other children as models in interactive games of imitation.
- Encourage the child to imitate a model in action. While shaking a rattle, hand the child a similar rattle to shake.

Instructional Sequence

- Model common motor actions (i.e., kicking a ball).
- Give verbal instructions (e.g., say, "You do it," or "Your turn").
- Physically assist the child by gently touching the part of the body to be engaged in the action.
- If the child still does not imitate, physically guide the child through the action.

TEACHING CONSIDERATIONS

1. Motor actions should be developmentally appropriate for the child.
2. Select actions that the child has been observed to perform.
3. Do not provide the child with extra cues such as verbal directions (e.g., "Clap your hands") unless intentionally using them as instructions. The child needs to cue into the motor act and not the verbal direction.
4. The focus is on the ability to reproduce a previously performed action and not on the motor complexity of the action.
5. If the child has a severe motor impairment, select simple motor actions within the child's capabilities (e.g., blink eyes, open mouth, smile).
6. A child with a visual impairment will need special adaptations, such as verbal directions (e.g., "Jump up and down like me").
7. A child with a hearing impairment can learn new motor acts through sign language or total communication.
8. Consider safety with all objects that the child handles. Never leave the child unattended with potentially hazardous objects.

GOAL 2 Imitates words that are not frequently used

DEVELOPMENTAL PROGRAMMING STEP

PS2.0a The child imitates a word that he or she does not frequently use and that is a modification of a child-initiated sound or word. For example, the child says, "Ball." The adult says, "It looks like a ball, but this is a balloon." The child imitates and says, "Balloon."

IMPORTANCE OF SKILL

Through imitation of words that are not frequently used, the young child's basic vocabulary can be broadened to include words referring to both more general and more specific categories. In addition to modifying frequently used vocal patterns with respect to a new model, the child also learns to use a novel, meaningful speech sound to refer to an object or event.

Cog D

PRECEDING OBJECTIVE

Cog D:2.2   Imitates words that are frequently used

CONCURRENT GOALS AND OBJECTIVES

Cog E:4.0 Solves common problems
SC B:1.1   Responds with a vocalization and gesture to simple questions
SC C:1.2   Locates common objects, people, and/or events in familiar pictures
SC C:2.3   Carries out one-step direction *with* contextual cues
SC D:1.0   Uses 50 single words
Soc A:3.2 Responds to communication from familiar adult
Soc C:2.2 Responds to communication from peer

TEACHING SUGGESTIONS

Activity-Based

- If the child manifests an interest during daily activities, use the opportunity to refer to people, objects, or events with words the child does not yet use. For example, say the proper name of a relative (e.g., "Grandma Helen" if the child uses only "Grandma") and encourage the child to imitate the name.
- Respond to the child's questions of "What's that?" by labeling unfamiliar objects, people, or events; give the child a chance to imitate.
- Look at books with the child and label the pictures. Encourage the child to imitate the novel words.
- Point to and label novel body parts (e.g., knee, elbow, cheek). Encourage the child to imitate.
- During daily routines, label objects in the immediate environment that are of interest to the child. Label foods while eating meals.

Environmental Arrangements

- Name a more general or more specific category of an object or event for which the child uses a single term. For example, if the child labels all four-legged animals "doggie," tell the child, "That's a cow." If the child asks for an apple, tell the child that an apple is a fruit. If the child identifies a girl skipping as "jumping," tell the child the girl is skipping. Encourage the child to imitate the new word.
- Introduce objects similar to, but slightly different from, those that the child likes. If the child, for example, likes books, show the child a glossy, colorful magazine. Name the new object and encourage the child to imitate the new word.
- Place novel objects similar to highly desired objects out of reach but within the child's visual field. Make obtaining the object contingent upon the child's imitation. For example, the child sees yogurt in the refrigerator and asks for ice cream. Tell the child that it is yogurt; wait for the child to imitate before offering the yogurt. Make the novel object or event interesting to the child—tell the child yogurt is very good.
- Play interactive verbal imitation games and begin by having the child imitate frequently used words. For example, play guessing games. Hide an object under a cover and tell the child you will uncover the object only if the child imitates the correct word. Alternate familiar and unfamiliar words.
- Have other children demonstrate verbalization of words unfamiliar to the child.

Cog D

Instructional Sequence

- Repeat the word several times, pausing to allow the child to imitate.
- Give verbal directions (e.g., say, "You say milk ").
- Assist the child by gently touching his or her mouth.

TEACHING CONSIDERATIONS

1. Words should be phonologically and semantically appropriate for the developmental level of the child.
2. Words should be related to objects and events that are in the child's immediate environment (e.g., refer to a novel object with which the child is playing).
3. If the child has a hearing impairment, use total communication. Encourage the child to watch lip movements. Speak clearly and combine words with signs. Consult a communications specialist for further ideas for the child with a hearing impairment.
4. If the child has a motor impairment, proper positioning may facilitate sound production.
5. If the child has a visual impairment, provide descriptions of what the new words and labels represent. For example, "A teddy bear is furry and soft. It has four legs." Allow the child to feel your mouth while you speak new words.

Objective 2.1   Imitates speech sounds that are not frequently used

---

DEVELOPMENTAL PROGRAMMING STEP

PS2.1a   The child imitates an adult's modification of a child-initiated speech sound or word approximation. For example, the child says, "Baba"; the adult responds "Bobbie"; and the child imitates, "Bobbie."

IMPORTANCE OF SKILL

The child learns to reproduce new vocalizations to match the novel model by modifying vocal behaviors already in his or her repertoire. The child's increased flexibility in adapting behaviors with respect to an external model represents experimentation with different strategies to solve a problem.

PRECEDING OBJECTIVE

Cog A:1.1   Orients to auditory events

CONCURRENT GOALS AND OBJECTIVES

Cog C:2.0   Reproduces part of interactive game and/or action in order to continue game and/or action
Cog E:4.0   Solves common problems
SC B:2.2   Uses nonspecific consonant–vowel combinations and/or jargon
SC C:2.3   Carries out one-step direction *with* contextual cues
Soc A:3.2   Responds to communication from familiar adult

Cog D

TEACHING SUGGESTIONS
Activity-Based

- Engage the child in play with toys and other materials or social games where sound patterns can be easily integrated in the game. For example, play with toy animals and produce animal sounds. Say, "Moo" when playing with a cow and "Meow" when playing with a cat.
- Engage in pretend play or play with hand puppets. For example, pretend to be a magician and use magic words such as "poof."
- Engage in turn-taking interactive games by making "funny" sounds. Encourage the child to imitate unfamiliar speech sounds.

Environmental Arrangements

- Associate sounds with objects and events that are of particular interest to the child. Imitate the child's pet dog by saying, "Woof," or make the car noise, "Vroom," if the child wants to go for a ride.
- Captivate the child's attention during pretend play by imitating dangerous animals (e.g., growl like a bear, roar like a tiger). Encourage the child to imitate; ask the child to pretend to be an animal, a car, or a plane.
- Use picture books or sounds to stimulate imitation of animals, vehicles, and environmental sounds.
- Associate a speech sound with a motor action (e.g., say, "Sh, sh," while gesturing for quiet). Encourage the child to imitate both the action and the sound.
- Pair a speech sound to a child-initiated action (e.g., if the child pulls a string attached to a bell, say, "Ding-dong") and encourage the child to imitate the sound.
- Associate sounds to tactile-kinesthetic stimulation, such as tickling and bouncing. Hold the child in the air and say, "Boom," while rapidly bringing the child down. Repeat actions without vocalizing and observe whether the child repeats, "Boom."
- Engage other children as imitative models in verbal games.
- Repeat the sound or word often, speak slowly, and emphasize each syllable.

Instructional Sequence

- Repeat the sound several times, pausing to allow the child to imitate.
- Provide verbal directions by asking the child to imitate (e.g., "You say poof ").
- Assist the child by gently touching the child's mouth.

TEACHING CONSIDERATIONS

1. Sounds should be developmentally appropriate to the child's level of functioning but not frequently used by the child. The focus is not on the complexity of the speech sound but on the degree to which the sound differs from sounds already within the child's repertoire.
2. Integrate imitations within a game (e.g., peekaboo, "Simon says") and make them meaningful (e.g., animal sounds, onomatopoeic sounds associated with objects and motor actions).
3. If the child has a hearing impairment, use total communication. Encourage the child to watch lip movements. Speak clearly and combine words with signs.
4. If the child has a motor impairment, proper positioning may facilitate sound production.

Cog D

5. If the child has a visual impairment, provide descriptions of the new sounds and words (e.g., say, "When I blow the candle out, it goes poof"). Allow the child to feel your face and mouth while you speak new words.

Objective 2.2 Imitates words that are frequently used

DEVELOPMENTAL PROGRAMMING STEPS

PS2.2a The child imitates simple, familiar consonant-vowel words when the model is an imitation of a word the child has just used (e.g., the child says, "Go"; the adult says, "Go"; and the child imitates).

PS2.2b The child imitates the adult's expansion of a child-initiated word approximation (e.g., the child says, "Wa"; the adult says, "Water"; and the child imitates, "Wa wa").

PS2.2c The child imitates vocal sounds that are frequently used (e.g., the adult vocalizes, "Baba, ah-goo"; and the child imitates, "Baba, ah-goo").

PS2.2d The child responds to the adult's vocalization with a similar but different vocalization (e.g., the adult coos, "Gege"; and the child responds, "Ee").

PS2.2e The child responds vocally to the voice of others (e.g., the child coos when mother talks).

IMPORTANCE OF SKILL

The imitation of speech sounds and words plays an important role in the acquisition of language. By imitating familiar words, the child can learn to generalize newly acquired words over settings and to other objects. In addition, imitation is a form of turn-taking communication between the child and caregiver.

PRECEDING GOAL

SC B:2.0 Uses consistent word approximations

CONCURRENT GOALS AND OBJECTIVES

Cog C:2.0 Reproduces part of interactive game and/or action in order to continue game and/or action

SC B:1.1 Responds with a vocalization and gesture to simple questions

SC D:1.0 Uses 50 single words

Soc A:3.2 Responds to communication from familiar adult

Soc C:2.2 Responds to communication from peer

TEACHING SUGGESTIONS
Activity-Based

- Point to and label body parts (e.g., nose, eyes, hands). Encourage the child to imitate.
- During daily interactions, talk often to the child. Speak in short sentences about people, objects, and events that are in the immediate environment. Use words that the child frequently uses and observe whether the child imitates them.

Cog D

- While feeding, dressing, and playing with the child, comment on objects that are being used (e.g., the adult says, "Here's your shoe," and the child imitates, "Shoe"); people who are present (e.g., the adult says, "Look at Daddy," and the child imitates, "Daddy"); and actions that are performed (e.g., the mother says, "Mommy drinks juice," and the child imitates, "Drink").
- During daily routines, label objects in the immediate environment. For example, when eating, point to objects and say, "Spoon," "Apple," or "Cup." When dressing the child, point and say, "Shoe" or "Jacket."

Environmental Arrangements

- Comment on novel, changing objects or events (e.g., the adult says, "Mama's home," or "The doggie runs fast"); encourage the child to imitate part of the sentence (e.g., "Mama" or "Doggie").
- Refer to highly desired objects or events (e.g., when the child points to a cracker at mealtime, ask, "Do you want a cracker?" and encourage the child to imitate "Cracker"). Make the event contingent on the child's imitation (e.g., wait until the child imitates "cracker" before giving it to the child).
- Simplify sentences by using only one or two word utterances (e.g., if the child gestures to be picked up, ask the child, "Up?"; if the child wants to activate a mechanical toy, tell the child, "Push there"). Pair utterances with visual or tactile-kinesthetic cues. For example, bounce the child up and down while saying, "Up and down"; hide an object behind a screen and label the object while you slowly make it reappear; wave and say, "Bye-bye."
- Engage other children in conversation and have them provide a model for imitation.

Instructional Sequence

- Repeat a word often. For example, while playing with a doll, say, "Baby, baby sleep." If necessary, repeat until the child imitates.
- Provide verbal directions by asking the child to imitate (e.g., "You say, 'Hi' ").
- Physically assist the child by gently touching the child's mouth.

TEACHING CONSIDERATIONS

1. Integrate imitation in interactive games by introducing turn-taking activities.
2. Words should be ones that are frequently used by the child. Refer to objects and events that are meaningful to the child, such as an object the child is playing with.
3. Encourage the child with a hearing impairment to watch lip movements. Speak clearly and combine words with signs.
4. If the child has a motor impairment, proper positioning may facilitate sound production.
5. If the child has a visual impairment, provide descriptions of the sounds and words (e.g., say, "When the kitty cries, she closes her eyes and goes, 'Meow' "). Allow the child to feel your face and mouth while you speak new words.

Strand E

Problem Solving

GOAL 1 Retains objects when new object is obtained

DEVELOPMENTAL PROGRAMMING STEPS

PS1.0a The child retains two objects and acts upon a third. For example, the child holds a cracker and a spoon and bangs the highchair tray.

PS1.0b The child retains two objects while regarding a third object.

IMPORTANCE OF SKILL

When the child has two hands occupied, the presentation of a second or third object leads the child to search for a different strategy to retain all the objects. The child learns to plan, sequence, and coordinate different actions to attain a desired goal. This skill allows the child to engage in more interesting play activities by holding more than one toy or object.

PRECEDING OBJECTIVE

Cog E:1.1 Retains one object when second object is obtained

CONCURRENT GOALS AND OBJECTIVES

FM A:2.1 Transfers object from one hand to the other
FM B:2.0 Assembles toy and/or object that require(s) putting pieces together
GM A:3.0 Creeps forward using alternating arm and leg movements
Cog E:4.0 Solves common problems
Cog G:1.2 Uses functionally appropriate actions with objects
SC C:1.3 Locates common objects, people, and/or events *with* contextual cues
Soc A:3.2 Responds to communication from familiar adult

TEACHING SUGGESTIONS
Activity-Based

- While the child is manipulating or playing with two or more objects, present the child with an additional object. Make sure that the new object is of interest to the child and related to the activity in which the child is engaged. Encourage the child to retain all of the objects.

Cog E

293

- If the child is holding two toy cows, give the child a toy horse. The child may place the toy animals in his or her lap, freeing the hands to obtain the additional animal. If the child is shaking a rattle and a bell, hand the child a maraca; the child may transfer the rattle to the hand holding the bell and obtain the maraca with the free hand.
- Have the child hold one cracker in each hand. Offer a third cracker so that the child must place one cracker in his or her mouth or other hand to obtain the third.
- Follow the same routine with stuffed animals. The child has an animal in each hand and must place one somewhere to obtain the third.

☑ If your data indicate the child is not making progress toward the goal, provide additional structure within the suggested activities by incorporating the following *environmental arrangements:*

Environmental Arrangements

- Give the child objects that can be easily retained: clothing or small blankets that the child can drape over an arm; sheets of paper that the child can easily hold in one hand; small objects (e.g., raisins, crackers, small foam sponges, miniature toys) of which several fit in one hand; stickers that the child can stick on his or her body or on another object.
- Prior to presenting a third object, give the child two objects, one of which can retain the other. For example, a blanket can be draped over a doll, a sticker can be stuck on a sheet of paper, a spoon can be placed in a cup, and pop beads can be fitted together. Give the child two shoes and a third item to be carried to his or her bedroom.

☑ If this objective is particularly difficult for a child, it may be necessary, within activities, to use an *instructional sequence.*

Instructional Sequence

- Model retaining several objects. For example, place objects in your lap, hold several crayons in one hand, or place crackers in a cup. Encourage the child to imitate.
- Give the child verbal suggestions, such as "Put one of the crackers in your mouth," "Put the monkey under your arm," or "Put the spoon in the cup."
- Present a third object and physically assist the child to retain it. For example, when the child's hands are full with a bar of soap and bottle of shampoo, touch the child's arm with a washcloth. Assist the child to extend his or her arm to obtain the cloth. When the child's hands are full, touch the child's lips with a cookie and see if the child opens his or her mouth to obtain it.

☑ Combining or pairing different levels of instructions may be helpful when beginning to teach a new and difficult skill. Fade to less intrusive instructions as soon as possible to encourage more independent performance.

TEACHING CONSIDERATIONS

1. Objects should be interesting to the child so that the child will want to retain them all.
2. Make sure the child visually fixates upon the third object before offering it to him or her.
3. If the child has a visual impairment, provide an opportunity to tactilely explore the object so that the child can identify it before you expect him or her to retain it.
4. If the child has a motor impairment, observe the child's ability to attend simultaneously to all objects (e.g., the child visually explores one object after the other and then returns to explore the first object again).

Cog E

5. Consider safety with all objects that the child handles. Never leave the child unattended with potentially hazardous objects.

Objective 1.1 Retains one object when second object is obtained

DEVELOPMENTAL PROGRAMMING STEPS

PS1.1a The child retains an object with one hand while acting on a second object. For example, the child holds a block while banging another block with the other hand.

PS1.1b The child retains one object while regarding a second object.

IMPORTANCE OF SKILL

The child begins to interact with more than one object at a time. In order to attain a desired end (i.e., retain two objects), the child learns to coordinate two successive actions to maintain control of the first object while taking hold of the second. This skill allows the child to expand activities and engage in more interesting play.

PRECEDING OBJECTIVE

Cog E:1.2 Retains object

CONCURRENT GOALS AND OBJECTIVES

FM A:2.0 Brings two objects together at or near midline

FM A:3.0 Grasps hand-size object with either hand using ends of thumb, index, and second fingers

FM A:5.2 Releases hand-held object with each hand

GM B:1.2 Regains balanced, upright sitting position after *reaching* across the body to the right and to the left

Cog F:1.2 Stacks objects

Cog G:1.2 Uses functionally appropriate actions with objects

SC A:2.1 Follows person's pointing gesture to establish joint attention

SC C:1.3 Locates common objects, people, and/or events *with* contextual cues

Soc A:3.2 Responds to communication from familiar adult

TEACHING SUGGESTIONS

Activity-Based

- Place a variety of objects and toys of different sizes, colors, weights, and textures within the child's reach. Encourage the child to take two objects or hand the child two objects, one at a time.
- Observe the child's ability to take and hold both objects. If the child initially demonstrates interest in only one object, let the child manipulate or play with that object for a while before presenting a second object.
- Provide objects and toys that are similar or are functionally related so that the child can use two objects in a meaningful manner. For example, encourage the child to

bang two blocks together, fit two pop beads together, place an apple in a paper bag, or drop blocks in a bucket.
- When the child is holding one object, present a second object and encourage the child to hold both objects.

Environmental Arrangements

- Use toys and objects that can be easily retained, such as soft toys and sticky materials.
- Present one toy or object close to the child's hand or mouth. Once the child has secured the object, present a second object close to the other hand or arm.
- When the child is manipulating an object, present a second object that is functionally related to the first and will lead to an interesting result for the child. For example, hand the child a toy hammer or screwdriver when child is manipulating the nuts and bolts on a toy workbench.
- Place one object inside another, such as a sock inside a shoe, and give it to the child. Encourage the child to remove one object while holding the other.

Instructional Sequence

- Model an action that involves two objects. For example, bang two blocks together while the child is securing a second block.
- Remind the child verbally to hold onto the first object while securing the second. Say, "Hold your doll and take his bottle to feed him."
- Hold onto an object retained by the child while the child secures another object. Use objects large enough for you to hold onto without physically touching the child's hand (e.g., a rattle with a long handle, a big plastic ring, a blanket).
- Physically assist the child to select a second toy while holding one toy.

TEACHING CONSIDERATIONS

1. Make sure the child is in a posture that allows free use of at least two body parts to retain two objects.
2. Make sure the child visually fixates upon the second object before you offer it to the child.
3. Both objects should be interesting to the child so that the child will want to retain them.
4. If the child has a visual impairment, provide an opportunity for the child to tactilely explore the object and identify it before you expect him or her to retain it.
5. If the child's movements are limited, observe the child's ability to attend simultaneously to both objects (e.g., the child visually explores one object after the other and then returns to explore the first one again).
6. Consider safety with all objects that the child handles. Never leave the child unattended with potentially hazardous objects.

Objective 1.2   Retains object

DEVELOPMENTAL PROGRAMMING STEP

PS1.2a   The child momentarily grasps an object that is placed in his or her hand.

IMPORTANCE OF SKILL

The ability to voluntarily grasp an object is a first step toward the development of the use of a tool. The child learns that the hand and other body parts can be used as tools for obtaining and retaining objects. This behavior demands the use of means (body parts) to attain desired ends (objects).

PRECEDING OBJECTIVE

Cog B:1.2   Focuses on object and/or person

CONCURRENT OBJECTIVES

FM A:3.3   Grasps hand-size object with either hand using whole hand
GM B:1.4   Sits balanced without support
Adap A:4.2 Eats with fingers
Cog G:1.4   Uses sensory examination with objects
SC A:2.1   Follows person's pointing gesture to establish joint attention
Soc A:2.2   Responds to familiar adult's social behavior

TEACHING SUGGESTIONS
Activity-Based

- Make available to the child a variety of toys of different sizes, colors, weights, and textures. Place them easily within the child's reach and encourage the child to play. Observe the child's ability to retain toys in one hand, under one arm, in his or her mouth, or by any other means.
- During daily routines and play, give the child an object that the child looks toward. While the child is holding the toy or object, talk about it. Model using a similar toy or object to motivate the child to retain the object.
- While the child is holding a doll or similar large object, invite the child to follow you into another room and bring the doll along.
- Present the child with familiar objects that the child can manipulate.

Environmental Arrangements

- Give the child toys and objects that are easily retained because of their shape or texture (e.g., soft furry balls or animals, small blankets or clothing, rattles, spoons).
- Offer objects that are especially interesting to the child, such as noise-producing toys, bright-colored paper crumpled in a ball, or favorite foods.
- Use materials that stick easily, such as soft Play-Doh, sticky tape, or thick fingerpaint, to help the child retain them.
- Tie an object to a piece of yarn. Place the object in the child's hand and use the yarn to keep it in place.

Instructional Sequence

- Place part of an object in the child's hand, under the child's arm, or in the child's mouth, and continue to hold onto the object. Use objects of appropriate shapes and sizes, such as cloths, plastic rings, or rattles with long handles.
- Encourage the child to use more than one means simultaneously to retain an object.

Cog E

For example, while feeding, place the bottle in the child's mouth and encourage the child to grasp it.

■ Physically assist the child to hold objects by placing toys in the child's hand or under an arm; help the child retain the objects.

TEACHING CONSIDERATIONS

1. Make sure the child is in a posture that allows free use of body parts to retain objects. For example, hold the child upright rather than lying down.
2. Make sure the child visually fixates on the object before it is brought into contact with the child's body, hand, or mouth.
3. If the child has a visual impairment, allow sufficient time for tactile exploration (e.g., while the adult holds the object) so that the child can identify the object before you expect him or her to retain it.
4. If the child's movements are limited, accommodation of eye movements or head turning to a slowly moving object may be the child's way to maintain sight of the object.
5. Consider safety with all objects that the child handles. Never leave the child unattended with potentially hazardous objects.

GOAL 2   Uses an object to obtain another object

DEVELOPMENTAL PROGRAMMING STEPS

PS2.0a   The child uses a person to obtain an object. For example, the child asks for the object, looks at the person, and points toward the object; the child looks at the object, looks at the person, and returns the gaze to the object.

PS2.0b   The child uses an object to act upon another object. For example, the child hits a drum with a stick or draws a line with a stick in wet sand.

IMPORTANCE OF SKILL

The child learns to use tools, as well as direct actions, to produce desired effects or goals. The child combines a succession of different actions to find a strategy to solve a problem. First, the child has to search for and then use an object as a tool to obtain another object. In addition, the child has to spatially coordinate the two objects so that a contact occurs, enabling the child to obtain the desired object. This skill allows the child more independence in getting the things that he or she wants and needs.

PRECEDING OBJECTIVE

Cog E:2.1   Uses part of object and/or support to obtain another object

CONCURRENT GOALS AND OBJECTIVES

FM A:3.2   Grasps cylindrical object with either hand by closing fingers around it
GM C:3.3   Gets up and down from low structure
Adap A:4.1   Brings food to mouth using utensil

Cog B:3.0 Maintains search for object that is not in its usual location
Cog E:4.0 Solves common problems
Cog G:1.2 Uses functionally appropriate actions with objects
SC B:1.0 Gains person's attention and refers to an object, person, and/or event

TEACHING SUGGESTIONS

Activity-Based

- During daily routines and play activities, place objects and toys the child normally uses just out of reach. For example, place food on the far end of a table, favorite toys in a crib, or clothes on high shelves. Make available objects that the child can use as tools to obtain the desired object. For example, have a wooden spoon or rubber scraper for the child to obtain a cracker, a broom or plastic bat for the child to reach into the crib or behind a couch to obtain a toy, or a chair or stool for the child to climb on to obtain mittens before going outside.
- As the child colors at the table, have crayons just out of reach. Make available a ruler or rubber scraper for the child to use to obtain crayons.
- When playing outdoors, have the child use a toy rake to obtain a ball that has rolled away.
- Encourage the child to obtain objects that are functionally related to the objects used as tools by using a fork, for example, to obtain a piece of meat, or a paintbrush to transfer paint.

Environmental Arrangements

- Begin by providing tools that serve as an extension of the hand, such as a toy rake, broom, or long spoon. Encourage the child to reach for objects that are easily obtained. For example, use a toy rake to obtain a soft furry animal toy, a broom to obtain a ball or toy car that rolls easily, or a long spoon to obtain an apple or a box of raisins.
- Provide the child with a duster on a stick (not a feather duster, as this could be hazardous) to obtain a toy that has been pushed too far back on a shelf.
- Construct a situation that presents only one way to obtain the object the child desires.
- Place cooked macaroni on a fork and allow the child to eat it from the fork. Gradually require the child to spear macaroni pieces.
- Initially, have both the object and the tool close to the child and within the child's visual field. Gradually require the child to look around for the tool.
- Ask the child to dress a doll; have doll clothing on a shelf out of reach.

Instructional Sequence

- Model using an object to obtain another object. For example, poke the end of a paintbrush into a ball of Play-Doh to obtain the Play-Doh.
- Have the child begin to use a fork and spoon at mealtimes. Verbally direct the child to "Use your spoon to get some cereal," or "Use your fork to get a piece of meat."
- As the child tries to get a toy out of reach on a shelf, gesture toward a nearby stool.
- Give the child verbal instructions (e.g., say, "Climb on the chair," or "Reach with the spoon"). If the child is trying to obtain an object with another object but is not making contact, provide physical assistance by pushing the desired object toward the tool.
- Physically assist the child by guiding the use of the tool.

Cog E

TEACHING CONSIDERATIONS

1. Place the object where the child cannot obtain it without use of a tool. Be sure, however, that the object can be reached with the tool.
2. Be sure the actions required to obtain the object are developmentally appropriate for the child's level of functioning and are in the child's repertoire.
3. If the child has a visual impairment, give both objects to the child to explore tactilely before placing one out of reach.
4. If the child has a motor impairment, use tools that require a minimum of fine motor skills (e.g., attach a magnet to the end of a stick, use T-shaped tools).
5. Consider safety with all objects that the child handles. Never leave the child unattended with potentially hazardous objects.

Objective 2.1   Uses part of object and/or support to obtain another object

---

DEVELOPMENTAL PROGRAMMING STEPS

PS2.1a   The child acts on part of an object or support to produce a visible or auditory effect. For example, the child pulls a placemat and the dish rattles; or the child pulls a string and the toy moves.

PS2.1b   The child moves his or her own body parts to produce an effect on an object. For example, the child kicks a mobile.

IMPORTANCE OF SKILL

This skill represents a step toward the use of tools. The child learns that strings, handles, and supports, as well as direct actions, can serve to act upon other objects, and that spatial contacts between objects are necessary for this to happen. This skill aids the development of cause-and-effect relationships.

CONCURRENT GOAL AND OBJECTIVES

GM D:2.2   Sits on riding toy or in wagon while adult pushes
Adap A:4.1   Brings food to mouth using utensil
Cog B:2.1   Locates object and/or person who hides while child is watching
Cog C:1.0   Correctly activates mechanical toy
Cog E:4.1   Uses more than one strategy in attempt to solve common problem
Cog G:1.2   Uses functionally appropriate actions with objects
Soc C:1.5   Entertains self by playing appropriately with toys

TEACHING SUGGESTIONS

Activity-Based

- Give the child toys or objects that have parts the child could use to obtain the objects (e.g., pull-toy, toy with handle, toy telephone with cord).
- If the child shows an interest in having a toy or other object during play or daily caregiving activities, place the object out of immediate reach on various supports (e.g., pillow, blanket, towel, diaper). Verbally encourage the child to pull the support to obtain the object. Provide a demonstration.

Cog E

- Place a doll almost out of reach and observe whether the child pulls on the hair, ribbon, or dress to get the doll.

Environmental Arrangements

- Identify a number of objects in the child's environment that can be obtained by using part of the object (e.g., shoelace to get shoe, handle to pull wagon, string to pull toy) or by using a convenient support (e.g., placemat under a dish, book under a toy, pillow under a doll). Provide the child with these objects.
- Create a game by hiding or partially hiding an object with a string attached (e.g., under a blanket or low table, behind a chair). Present the string to the child.
- Tie strings on toys that produce auditory, visual, and other feedback when moved.
- Initially, shorten strings and place supports in close vicinity to the child so that accidental touching or pulling will produce an effect on the objects.

Instructional Sequence

- Model pulling a toy by a string or handle; give the child a turn to do the same.
- Show the child the support, string, or handle, and give a verbal direction to use it (e.g., say, "Pull the string," or "Pull the blanket").
- Use minimal physical assistance to help the child to pull a string or support to obtain an object. Reduce the assistance to give the child an opportunity to continue independently.
- Provide a direct connection between the child and an interesting toy by tying a soft string, ribbon, or yarn to the child's wrist so that moving the arm produces a visible or auditory effect on the toy. Start with shorter lengths of string and gradually lengthen. When the child has learned to move each arm to activate a toy, present the toy still attached to the string, but no longer tied to the child's wrist.

TEACHING CONSIDERATIONS

1. Objects should be interesting to the child (e.g., bright-colored and noisy toys for the child with a visual impairment).
2. If the child has a visual impairment, allow him or her to tactilely explore the toy and the string or support. Put the toy at a distance and place the string or part of the support in the child's hand. Talk about the toy.
3. If the child has a motor impairment, add a handle (e.g., a wooden bead to a string), use easily grasped supports, and assist the child in pulling.
4. In order to demonstrate that the child has used the support or part of the object to obtain it, the child should manipulate the object in some way.
5. Consider safety with all objects that the child handles. Never leave the child unattended with potentially hazardous objects.

GOAL 3   Navigates large object around barriers

DEVELOPMENTAL PROGRAMMING STEP

PS3.0a   The child moves a large object from one location to another without barriers in the pathway. For example, at mealtime the child pushes a chair from the corner of the room to the table nearby.

Cog E

IMPORTANCE OF SKILL

The child learns to coordinate his or her own movements and the movements of an object with respect to another object. The child has to simultaneously solve the problems of navigating an object and of moving around a barrier. This skill allows the child more independence of movement and more freedom in play.

PRECEDING OBJECTIVE

Cog E: 3.1   Moves barrier or goes around barrier to obtain object

CONCURRENT GOAL AND OBJECTIVES

GM C:1.0   Walks avoiding obstacles
GM D:2.1   Pushes riding toy with feet while steering
SC C:2.3   Carries out one-step direction *with* contextual cues
Soc A:3.2   Responds to communication from familiar adult
Soc C:1.3   Plays near one or two peers

TEACHING SUGGESTIONS

Activity-Based

- Provide the child with large objects that can be easily moved (e.g., toy wagon or truck, doll carriage, tricycle, small chair, stuffed animals). Encourage the child to move around pieces of furniture, toys on the floor, flower beds, or people while carrying, pushing, or pulling the object.
- Play with dolls that the child can place in a carriage; play grocery store so that the child can place groceries in a cart. Arrange the environment so that the child can move from one part of the room to another, moving around barriers. For example, pretend to visit a friend's house in another corner of the room, or place the cash register at the far end of the room for grocery store play.
- Set up and move through an obstacle course. Play "Follow the leader" on tricycles or while pulling wagons or carrying dolls.

Environmental Arrangements

- Begin with stationary barriers and then use moveable barriers as the child becomes more proficient.
- Call the child from the opposite end of the room or from behind a barrier, such as a door or couch. Remain visible to the child while the child moves around the barrier.
- Begin with objects that the child can move easily with him- or herself (e.g., push- or pull-toys).
- Have the child follow a peer as they both hold an object and navigate around barriers.
- As the child carries, pushes, or pulls objects, obstruct the child's path by standing so that the child must move around you.
- Arrange the situation so that there is no alternate path to the child's desired destination.

Instructional Sequence

- Model maneuvering a wagon around the flower bed.
- Give the child verbal directions to move around the barrier, to continue pushing or pulling the object. Direct the child which way to move the object.

- Give the child a small object to navigate and systematically increase the size of the object.
- Navigate a large object around a barrier and then physically assist the child in navigating the same object.

TEACHING CONSIDERATIONS

1. Physically assist the child who has a motor impairment to move the object while allowing the child to indicate the direction to move.
2. If the child has a hearing impairment, use gestures along with words to direct the child.
3. If the child has a visual impairment, use noise-producing objects. Allow tactile exploration of the barrier.
4. Ensure the child's safety by using barriers that are free from sharp corners and rough edges.
5. Consider safety with all objects that the child handles. Never leave the child unattended with potentially hazardous objects.

Objective 3.1 Moves barrier or goes around barrier to obtain object

---

DEVELOPMENTAL PROGRAMMING STEPS

PS3.1a The child moves a barrier to obtain an object.
PS3.1b The child goes around a barrier to obtain an object.

IMPORTANCE OF SKILL

The child learns to situate not only him- or herself in relation to a point in space, but also to situate objects in spatial relationship to each other. In order to obtain an object, the child modifies the position of the barrier in relation to the object, or the child readjusts his or her own movements as a function of the position of the barrier or the desired object. This skill is important for maneuvering in a desired direction.

PRECEDING OBJECTIVE

Cog E:3.2   Moves around barrier to change location

CONCURRENT GOALS AND OBJECTIVES

GM A:3.0   Creeps forward using alternating arm and leg movements
GM C:1.0   Walks avoiding obstacles
GM D:4.4   Rolls ball at target
Cog B:3.1   Looks for object in usual location
Cog E:4.0   Solves common problems
SC B:1.2   Points to an object, person, and/or event
SC C:1.3   Locates common objects, people, and/or events *with* contextual cues
Soc B:2.1   Responds to routine event

Cog E

TEACHING SUGGESTIONS
Activity-Based

- During daily activities, place objects that the child frequently uses behind barriers or slightly out of reach. Encourage the child to fetch objects normally used in daily routines that have been left in another room. At bedtime, let the child get a favorite toy left in the living room; at snack time, tell the child to find a favorite snack on a shelf behind the table. Observe whether the child moves around pieces of furniture to obtain the object.
- While playing with the child, place objects the child will want behind other objects. For example, place a small toy behind a larger toy and observe whether the child moves the larger toy to obtain the smaller toy.
- Have the child play with objects that roll away easily under barriers and behind pieces of furniture. For example, play ball near a sofa or bed so that the child can retrieve a ball that rolls away by moving around to the other side.

Environmental Arrangements

- Place a barrier between the child and an object or toy the child is playing with; observe whether the child moves or goes around the barrier to continue play. For example, when the child pushes a toy car across the table, make the car drop over the opposite side of the table and encourage the child to go around to retrieve it. Push a toy car or roll a ball slowly around a piece of furniture so that the child can visually follow the object and then follow the same path to retrieve the object.
- Devise a situation that provides no alternate way of obtaining the object except to remove the barrier or move around it.
- Use barriers that allow the object to remain at least partially visible to the child. For example, place a tricycle between the child and a large ball the child is rolling. Encourage the child to move the tricycle. Place a toy in a transparent plastic container or under a clear heavy plastic sheet so that the child will dump the container, remove a loose-fitting lid, or pull off the plastic sheet.
- Use lightweight barriers such as empty milk cartons that the child can easily move while reaching for an object. For example, partially hide the child's bottle behind an empty milk carton.

Instructional Sequence

- Model removing or going around a barrier.
- Give the child verbal directions to remove or go around the barrier.
- Give the child a small barrier to move or go around and gradually increase the size of the barrier.
- Physically assist the child to remove the barrier, or physically guide the child around the barrier to obtain the object.

TEACHING CONSIDERATIONS

1. If the child has a motor impairment, use barriers that the child can move with minimal physical effort, or ask the child to gesture or tell how to obtain the object.
2. If the child has a visual impairment, use noise-producing toys to help the child locate the object. Allow the child to tactilely explore the barrier; talk to the child to help identify the location.

3. If the child has a hearing impairment, use gestures along with words to direct the child.
4. Ensure the child's safety by using barriers that are free from sharp corners and rough edges.
5. Consider safety with all objects that the child handles. Never leave the child unattended with potentially hazardous objects.

Objective 3.2 Moves around barrier to change location

DEVELOPMENTAL PROGRAMMING STEPS

☑ The objective above is the most basic step for the skill to be taught. Most children will benefit from the activities outlined here that emphasize this skill. For children who need more instruction, consider designing programming steps from the *environmental arrangements* suggestions or from the *instructional sequence* outlined.

IMPORTANCE OF SKILL

The child learns strategies to solve detour problems. The child readjusts a planned route to move around a barrier and reach a location. This skill also develops the child's understanding of space as the child learns to situate his or her own position in relation to another point in space and to search for an alternate path when the direct path is obstructed by a barrier.

CONCURRENT GOALS AND OBJECTIVES

GM A:3.0   Creeps forward using alternating arm and leg movements
GM C:1.0   Walks avoiding obstacles
Cog: E:4.1   Uses more than one strategy in attempt to solve common problem
Soc B:2.1   Responds to routine event

TEACHING SUGGESTIONS
Activity-Based

- During daily inside and outside activities, have the child move around pieces of furniture, large toys, a fence, and flower beds in order to reach a designated location. At mealtime, observe the child's ability to move around a doll carriage to get to the table or to walk around a chair to join an adult or peer. Have the child help clean up after snack and move around furniture to take objects to the sink.
- Place a snack for the child on the far side of a table so that the child must walk around the table to get it.
- Ask the child to take objects to a person who is at the far end of a room or behind a piece of furniture.
- During pick-up time, ask the child to get a stuffed animal that has fallen on the other side of the bed.

Cog E

Environmental Arrangements

- When on the opposite side of a room or a barrier, call the child to participate in an activity. Place yourself close to the barrier so you are visible to the child. For example, situate yourself on the opposite side of a table from the child and ask the child to come around to join you for a snack or activity. When the child is on the other side of the sofa, sit down and call the child to come and look at a book.
- If the child hesitates or stops moving, call the child again.
- Choose barriers that do not obstruct the child's view of the destination he or she is moving toward.
- Have a peer call the child from the other side of a barrier and encourage the child to join the peer.
- Play "Follow the leader" and race games around obstacles and have the child follow peers.
- Walk and hold the child's hand or have the child follow a rope.
- Devise a situation that provides no alternate way of reaching the desired location except to move around a barrier.

Instructional Sequence

- Give the child verbal and gestural instructions (e.g., say, "Walk around the chair").
- Physically guide the child around the barrier.

TEACHING CONSIDERATIONS

1. Allow enough space for the child who uses a walker to maneuver around barriers.
2. If the child has a motor impairment, ask the child to gesture or tell how to change location.
3. If the child has a visual impairment, motivate the child to change location by calling the child. Keep talking to help the child identify your location.
4. If the child has a hearing impairment, use gestures and signs as well as words.
5. Ensure the child's safety by using barriers that are free from sharp corners and rough edges.
6. Consider safety with all objects that the child handles. Never leave the child unattended with potentially hazardous objects.

GOAL 4   Solves common problems

DEVELOPMENTAL PROGRAMMING STEP

PS4.0a   The child uses an adult to assist with solving a common problem. For example, the child hands a container to an adult to help open it.

IMPORTANCE OF SKILL

Finding a solution to common problems by trial-and-error represents the child's ability to modify actions as a function of their outcomes. After the first unsuccessful attempt, the child not only tries another strategy, but also adjusts successive strategies in response to outcomes of preceding strategies. In this way, the child attains the solution to the problem through gradual approximations and trial-and-error procedures. The child persists in trying until the problem is solved; this builds the child's self-esteem and confidence. Problem-solving skills will be used by the child throughout life.

PRECEDING OBJECTIVE

Cog E:4.1   Uses more than one strategy in attempt to solve common problem

CONCURRENT GOALS AND OBJECTIVE

FM B:2.0   Assembles toy and/or object that require(s) putting pieces together
GM D:2.0   Pedals and steers tricycle
Adap C:1.0   Undresses self
Cog D:1.0   Imitates motor action that is not commonly used
Cog D:2.0   Imitates words that are not frequently used
Cog E:1.0   Retains objects when new object is obtained
Cog E:2.0   Uses an object to obtain another object
Cog E:3.0   Navigates large object around barriers
Cog G:1.2   Uses functionally appropriate actions with objects
Soc B:1.0   Meets external physical needs in socially appropriate ways

TEACHING SUGGESTIONS
Activity-Based

- During daily routines and activities, observe the child's ability to use different strategies and appropriately modify each successive strategy to attain a solution to the problem by trial and error. For example, the child raises an arm in the direction of cookies that are out of reach, the child then stands on tip toes in attempt to reach the cookies, and finally the child moves a chair to stand on in order to obtain the cookies.
- Encourage the child to move a riding toy off the porch and down onto the sidewalk.
- Encourage the child to independently act on objects and to attempt different strategies when confronted with a problem. If necessary, provide a demonstration and encourage the child to imitate. For example, if the child begins to get upset after attempting to open a box by first shaking the box and then banging on the lid, demonstrate lifting the lid. Put the lid back in place and observe whether the child lifts off the lid.
- Allow the child independence to try activities such as dressing or undressing. If the child gets "stuck," wait before offering assistance and give the child the opportunity to solve the problem.
- Ask the child to get a toy from inside a toy box that is covered with several items.
- Have the child play a game of trying to gather all bath toys in a basket before the water drains out.

Environmental Arrangements

- Arrange the environment so that the solution to the problem is easily available; limit the number of alternative strategies. For example, if the child tries to eat applesauce with his or her fingers, have only a spoon available on the table. If the child tries to fit a square in a round hole, have several circles available.
- Use situations in which the solution can be found accidentally through manipula-

Cog E

tion, such as a mechanical toy the child can activate by accidentally touching a button, by banging on the toy, or by shaking it.

■ Set up materials close to the source of the problem. Have a step stool next to the cupboard, or put a string on a soft toy high on a shelf so it can be pulled down. Make the solutions obvious at first. Model if needed.

Instructional Sequence

■ Model taking the lid off a container to get a toy. Replace the lid.
■ Give the child verbal instructions (e.g., say, "Stand on the chair," "Push the button," or "Turn it around").
■ If the child becomes upset or bored after unsuccessful attempts, provide assistance by completing part of the action required to solve the problem. Encourage the child to complete the action (e.g., partially remove the lid from a container, partially push a button through the buttonhole).
■ Physically assist the child by helping the child's hand remove the lid.

TEACHING CONSIDERATIONS

1. Make sure the solution to the problem is meaningful and motivating for the child.
2. Problems should be slightly beyond the child's current abilities (principle of minimal discrepancy).
3. Make sure that the strategies required to solve the problem are within the child's repertoire (precise fine motor skills should not be required if the child's motor responses are limited).
4. Use materials that are safe for the child to manipulate and that lend themselves to a variety of uses. Never leave the child unattended with potentially hazardous objects.

Objective 4.1 Uses more than one strategy in attempt to solve common problem

---

DEVELOPMENTAL PROGRAMMING STEP

PS4.1a   The child repeats the same strategy to solve a common problem. For example, the child pulls on his or her mother's pants to get attention, the mother ignores the child, and the child pulls again.

IMPORTANCE OF SKILL

The child learns to modify actions as a result of the outcomes. If the child's first strategy is unsuccessful, the child searches for another strategy, instead of merely repeating the first attempt. This represents a first step in the development of trial-and-error strategies to solve problems.

CONCURRENT GOALS

FM B:2.0   Assembles toy and/or object that require(s) putting pieces together
GM D:2.0   Pedals and steers tricycle
Adap C:1.0   Undresses self

Cog B:3.0	Maintains search for object that is not in its usual location
Cog C:1.0	Correctly activates mechanical toy
Cog E:1.0	Retains objects when new object is obtained
Cog E:2.0	Uses an object to obtain another object
Cog E:3.0	Navigates large object around barriers
Cog F:2.0	Categorizes like objects
SC D:1.0	Uses 50 single words

TEACHING SUGGESTIONS
Activity-Based

- During daily activities and routines, a variety of common situations will occur in which the child is faced with problems he or she has not yet learned to solve. Observe the child's persistence and use of different strategies in an attempt to solve common problems.
- Observe the child's attempts to put on or take off clothing, to obtain objects out of reach, to open a paper bag or container with a favorite food, to turn on a water faucet, to open drawers or doors, or to gain attention.
- While playing with objects and toys, problems might occur when the child cannot open a book, fit an object into a defined space, or activate a mechanical toy. After trying a first unsuccessful strategy, encourage the child to try a different strategy. For example, the child first pushes on the water faucet, then bangs on it; the child tries to shake off a shoe, then taps his or her foot on the ground.
- Provide the child with the opportunity to discover and practice new strategies by not intervening and assisting too soon.

Environmental Arrangements

- While the child is engaged in an activity, introduce a problem for the child. For example, if the child reaches for an object, place it behind an obstacle, in a container, or on a shelf out of the child's reach.
- Give the child novel toys and objects (e.g., mechanical toys, kitchen gadgets) that the child does not yet know how to manipulate. Encourage the child to try different strategies to activate the object. If the child repeatedly uses only one strategy unsuccessfully, demonstrate how to activate the object. Observe whether the child modifies the first strategy to approximate the correct strategy modeled.
- If the child tries to get a jack-in-the-box to pop out by pounding on the lid or pulling the handle, model turning the crank until the "jack" pops out. Close the lid and offer the toy to the child.
- If the child twirls or hits a top to get it to spin, model pushing on the handle several times until the top spins on its own.
- Arrange situations so that a second strategy is readily available in the child's immediate environment. For example, place an object on a high shelf in a cupboard. Have a stool available so that after reaching for the object from the ground the child will use the stool to reach the object.

Instructional Sequence

- Show the child how a second strategy works after modeling a successful solution. Set up the situation for the child to try again.
- Give the child gestural or verbal cues, suggesting a second strategy after the child's

Cog E

first strategy was unsuccessful. After the child has tried unsuccessfully to sit on the floor while holding a book, point to a child-size chair nearby. Observe whether the child places the book on the chair and sits on the book. Tell the child to put the book down first; observe whether the child hands the book to an adult or sets it on the floor before sitting down.

■ Provide minimal physical assistance to help the child successfully solve the problem. For example, point to a stool and say, "Let's use this to reach the raisins." Assist the child, as necessary, to move the stool into position and stand on it to reach the raisins.

TEACHING CONSIDERATIONS

1. Arrange the environment so that the child will encounter interesting problems.
2. Arrange problems so that more than one strategy is available as a solution.
3. Assist the child with a sensory impairment to solve problems with an appropriate sensory modality.
4. Use materials that are safe for the child to manipulate and that lend themselves to a variety of uses. Never leave the child unattended with potentially hazardous objects.

Cog E

Strand F

Preacademic Skills

GOAL 1   Aligns and stacks objects

DEVELOPMENTAL PROGRAMMING STEPS

In order to achieve this goal, a child must perform the skills of Objectives 1.1–1.2 to criteria. Refer to the specific objective for Developmental Programming Steps to develop each skill.

IMPORTANCE OF SKILL

Aligning and stacking objects enables the child to discover spatial relationships among objects, such as "on top of" and "next to." The child becomes aware of the two basic directions (i.e., vertical and horizontal) within the spatial framework; the child puts objects in a simple order. This skill leads to the ability to arrange objects in a specified order (e.g., shortest to tallest), which is a prerequisite to sequencing numbers and letters.

Objective 1.1   Aligns objects

DEVELOPMENTAL PROGRAMMING STEP

PS1.1a The child places an object next to another. For example, the child places a spoon next to a bowl.

IMPORTANCE OF SKILL

The child learns to construct rows in the horizontal direction. By repeatedly adding objects one next to another, the child forms a horizontal line and learns about spatial relationships such as next to, in front of, behind, and left to right.

PRECEDING OBJECTIVE

Cog F:1.2   Stacks objects

Cog F

311

CONCURRENT GOALS AND OBJECTIVES

FM B:2.0   Assembles toy and/or object that require(s) putting pieces together
GM B:1.2   Regains balanced, upright sitting position after *reaching* across the body to the right and to the left
Cog G:1.1   Uses representational actions with objects
SC C:2.3   Carries out one-step direction *with* contextual cues
SC D:2.3   Uses two-word utterances to express location
Soc C:1.0   Initiates and maintains interaction with peer

TEACHING SUGGESTIONS
Activity-Based

- Use baskets to store toys on a shelf.
- During daily activities and routines, encourage the child to align at least three objects that are similar. While tidying the house, ask the child to align at least three pairs of shoes, to place books one against the other on the bookshelf, and to place boxes one next to the other in the cupboard.
- While playing, have the child align blocks or sticks to build fences, align toy animals to enter the barn, or align groceries for the cashier.
- Make trains of toy train cars, chairs, or boxes.
- Align blocks or books to build a road for cars, then park the cars along the road.

☑ If your data indicate the child is not making progress toward the objective, provide additional structure within the suggested activities by incorporating the following *environmental arrangements:*

Environmental Arrangements

- Make a parade or circus train by attaching milk cartons or boxes. Put toy animals or people inside for a ride.
- Provide the child with similar objects that can be fitted together in a horizontal direction (e.g., pop beads, magnets) or that are held together by some other means (e.g., beads the child can string to make a necklace).
- Line up plastic eggs in egg cartons.
- Have the child align objects by fitting them in defined spaces in a row (e.g., already dug holes to place tulip bulbs) or by placing them within a container (e.g., align crayons one next to another in a box).
- Encourage the child and a peer to take turns aligning objects such as cars, blocks, or books.

☑ If this objective is particularly difficult for a child, it may be necessary, within activities, to use an *instructional sequence.*

Instructional Sequence

- Model lining up objects (e.g., train cars in a row).
- Systematically decrease the space between objects in a line.
- Give the child verbal instructions to place objects one next to the other. Provide visual cues by pointing to where the child should place the object.
- Physically guide the child's hand to align objects.

☑ Combining or pairing different levels of instructions may be helpful when beginning to teach a new and difficult skill. Fade to less intrusive instructions as soon as possible, to encourage more independent performance.

TEACHING CONSIDERATIONS

1. Focus on spatial concepts and relationships rather than only on fine motor precision. While the child aligns objects, talk about next to, before, behind, beginning, and end.
2. If the child has a motor or visual impairment, align lightweight objects that are easy to manage. Use a flannel board or magnetic board to align objects.
3. If the child has a severe motor impairment, observe the child's understanding of the horizontal and vertical directions by asking the child to look up, down, and sideways.
4. If the child has a severe visual impairment, ask the child to move an arm or leg sideways, up, and down.
5. If the child has a hearing impairment, use a language modality such as total communication that ensures the child's understanding of your instructions.
6. Provide the child with flat, stable surfaces for aligning objects (e.g., table, floor boxes).
7. Consider safety with all objects that the child handles. Never leave the child unattended with potentially hazardous objects.

Objective 1.2 Stacks objects

DEVELOPMENTAL PROGRAMMING STEPS

PS1.2a The child places one object on top of another. For example, the child places a blanket over a doll, or a cracker on a plate.

PS1.2b The child touches one object to another in the vertical plane. For example, the child bangs a toy on a table without releasing the toy.

IMPORTANCE OF SKILL

Stacking objects can be considered constructing rows in a vertical direction. The child learns the spatial relation "on top of." The repetition of this relationship results in the construction of a vertical line. In addition, the child learns the differences between angles, edges, and flat surfaces, as the flat surface of one object must be placed on the flat surface of the other object to stack successfully. This skill fosters problem-solving as the child must learn to correctly place the objects so that the stack does not fall.

PRECEDING OBJECTIVE

FM A:5.1 Releases hand-held object onto and/or into a larger target with either hand

CONCURRENT GOALS AND OBJECTIVES

FM A:5.0 Places and releases object balanced on top of another object with either hand

FM B:2.2 Fits object into defined space

Cog F

GM B:1.2   Regains balanced, upright sitting position after *reaching* across the body to the right and to the left
Cog E:4.1   Uses more than one strategy in attempt to solve common problem
Cog G:1.1   Uses representational actions with objects
SC C:2.3   Carries out one-step direction *with* contextual cues
SC D:2.3   Uses two-word utterances to express location
Soc C:1.0   Initiates and maintains interaction with peer

TEACHING SUGGESTIONS

Activity-Based

- During daily activities and routines, encourage the child to stack at least three objects that are similar. Ask the child to help clean up after meals by stacking plates and cups to carry to the kitchen. Ask the child to stack groceries (e.g., lightweight boxes of crackers, cereals, small cans) in the cupboard or stack books when cleaning up the living room.
- Play construction games and suggest building towers, houses, and other vertical structures with blocks, books, cans, and boxes. Integrate the activity in a story so that it has meaning for the child. For example, ask the child to build a house for the toy dog.
- Play with and model building for the child. Build a barn for the toy horse and ask the child to build another barn for the cows.
- Play a game by encouraging the child to build a tower of blocks, knock down the tower, and then repeat building and knocking down the blocks. Encourage the child and a peer to take turns stacking a tower of blocks.

Environmental Arrangements

- Begin by requiring the child to stack small, hand-size objects, such as blocks. Move to larger objects as the child becomes more proficient.
- Provide the child with similar objects that can be easily stacked. Use objects with large flat surfaces (e.g., cartons, plates) or objects that can be partially contained in one another (e.g., cups, glasses). Soft objects such as foam blocks, bean bags, and pillows can be easily stacked.
- Hand the child objects one at a time so that smaller objects are always stacked on larger ones.
- Give the child objects that can be fitted one on top of another (e.g., nesting cups), that stick together (e.g., magnets), or that are held together vertically by some means (e.g., stacking rings over a stick, Ping-Pong balls in a transparent funnel, books in a narrow box).

Instructional Sequence

- Model stacking nesting cups for the child.
- Provide the child verbal encouragement to place an object on top of another. Provide visual cues by pointing to the surface of the object on which the child is to place another object.
- Hold the bottom object so that the construction will not fall, or push the top object toward the middle if the child has placed it too close to the edge.
- Physically guide the child to stack objects.

TEACHING CONSIDERATIONS

1. Focus on spatial concepts and relationships rather than only on fine motor precision. While the child is stacking objects, for example, tell the child that the building is "high" or "going up," or that one object is "on top of" or "under" the other.
2. If the child has a motor impairment, use large, lightweight objects that are easy to handle.
3. If the child has a severe motor impairment, observe the child's understanding of the vertical direction by asking the child to look up or down.
4. Help the child who has a visual impairment stack objects. Describe them as you do so.
5. If the child has a severe visual impairment, ask the child to move an arm or leg up or down.
6. If the child has a hearing impairment, use a language modality that ensures the child's understanding of your instructions.
7. Provide the child with flat, stable surfaces for stacking (e.g., table, floor without carpeting, box).
8. Consider safety with all objects that the child handles. Never leave the child unattended with potentially hazardous objects.

GOAL 2   Categorizes like objects

DEVELOPMENTAL PROGRAMMING STEP

PS2.0a The child acts successively upon objects belonging to a category. For example, when presented with a plate of apple slices and crackers, the child eats the crackers before the apples, or vice versa.

IMPORTANCE OF SKILL

The ability to categorize is essential to organizing and making sense of the environment. The grouping of new objects and events within a category allows the child some immediate knowledge about the new object or event. Categorization serves to organize perception of the environment and helps to organize familiar information and assimilate new information.

This skill enables the child to relate objects on the basis of conceptual equivalence. This allows the child to find similarities between objects based on social, conventional, and abstract properties. Categorizing objects broadens the child's awareness of likenesses and differences in the environment. Categorizing is important for understanding numbers and is fundamental to mathematical skills.

PRECEDING OBJECTIVE

Cog F:2.1   Groups functionally related objects

CONCURRENT GOALS AND OBJECTIVES

FM A:5.1   Releases hand-held object onto and/or into a larger target with either hand
FM B:2.0   Assembles toy and/or object that require(s) putting pieces together

Cog F

GM B:1.2   Regains balanced, upright sitting position after *reaching* across the body to the right and to the left
Cog B:3.1   Looks for object in usual location
Cog E:1.0   Retains objects when new object is obtained
Cog F:3.0   Demonstrates functional use of one-to-one correspondence
Cog G:1.2   Uses functionally appropriate actions with objects
SC C:2.3   Carries out one-step direction *with* contextual cues
Soc B:2.0   Responds to established social routine
Soc C:1.0   Initiates and maintains interaction with peer

TEACHING SUGGESTIONS
Activity-Based

- During daily activities and routines, give the child an opportunity to put together objects belonging to a broad-based category. Encourage the child to group toy animals, eating utensils, care items, and dolls during and after play.
- Encourage the child to help clean up. For example, put Legos in a container, books on a shelf, crayons and paper in a drawer, clothes in a dresser, or groceries on a shelf.
- When playing with peers, encourage the child to distribute a group of objects from one category to each peer. For example, the child gives all the toy cars to one peer and all the toy animals to another.
- Let the child help put paper in the trash, dirty clothes in the hamper, and dishes in the sink while cleaning up the house or classroom.
- Include the child in laundry chores (e.g., sort dad's from baby's clothes).

Environmental Arrangements

- Provide the child with containers for sorting objects into categories when cleaning up.
- Place at least three objects from a broad-based category that look, feel, and are used the same way into a group of completely dissimilar objects. For example, place mittens, a hat, and a scarf in a group of groceries.
- When putting away groceries, ask the child to put away all the canned goods.
- Present the child with sets of objects that can be fitted together, each differently. For example, have the child fit pop beads together, put beads on a string, and fit puzzle pieces.
- Place at least three identical objects in a group of different objects. For example, ask the child to take three identical cans of soup from the grocery cart that also contains large packages of diapers and gallon jugs of milk.

Instructional Sequence

- Model putting like objects together. Encourage the child to include additional like objects in the group one at a time.
- Give the child general verbal cues, such as "Put all the things to eat on this shelf."
- Provide verbal instructions by labeling the group in which to place the object (e.g., say, "That's a car; put it with the other cars").
- Indicate verbally or point to the location of the group in which the object belongs (e.g., "on the shelf," or "in the box"). Physically direct the child to the correct location.

Cog F

TEACHING CONSIDERATIONS

1. The activity should have a purpose. Cleaning up can be integrated in a game. For example, after playing grocery store, one child (sales clerk) picks up all the coins, and the other child (customer) picks up all the groceries.
2. If the child has a motor impairment, show the child an object and ask the child to point to a corresponding model to identify functional relationships.
3. If the child has a visual impairment, allow tactile exploration of the objects.
4. If the child has a hearing impairment, use a language modality that ensures the child's understanding of your instructions.
5. Consider safety with all objects that the child handles. Never leave the child unattended with potentially hazardous objects.

Objective 2.1 Groups functionally related objects

DEVELOPMENTAL PROGRAMMING STEPS

PS2.1a The child groups two functionally related objects, for example, a diaper and a pin or a doll and a blanket.

PS2.1b The child functionally relates one object to a succession of similar objects from another class. For example, the child gives each of three dolls a drink, in turn, from a toy cup.

IMPORTANCE OF SKILL

The child learns to relate a set of objects that look and feel different from one another by organizing them on the basis of a common function or use. This implies the ability to abstract a common *functional* similarity among perceptually different objects. In addition, this skill reflects the child's awareness of ways in which objects are interdependent through causal, spatial, and temporal relationships.

PRECEDING OBJECTIVE

Cog F:2.2 Groups objects according to size, shape, and/or color

CONCURRENT GOALS AND OBJECTIVES

FM B:1.0 Rotates either wrist on horizontal plane
GM B:1.2 Regains balanced, upright sitting position after *reaching* across the body to the right and to the left
Cog B:3.1 Looks for object in usual location
SC B:2.0 Uses consistent word approximations
SC C:2.1 Carries out two-step direction *with* contextual cues
SC D:3.0 Uses three-word utterances
Soc B:1.0 Meets external physical needs in socially appropriate ways
Soc B:2.0 Responds to established social routine
Soc C:1.5 Entertains self by playing appropriately with toys

Cog F

TEACHING SUGGESTIONS
Activity-Based

- Encourage the child to choose a play activity and observe whether the child selects toys that relate functionally. For example, when playing cars, the child obtains cars, a garage, and a road track; when playing house, the child obtains a dollhouse, furniture, and toy people; when feeding a baby, the child obtains a doll, bib, and toy bottle.
- During daily routines, provide the child with general verbal cues and observe whether the child groups functionally related objects. For example, you say, "Time to eat," and the child gets a bib and a spoon and goes to the highchair. The adult says, "Let's brush teeth," and the child gets the toothbrush and toothpaste and asks to turn on the water. The adult says, "Time to get dressed," and the child picks out pants, shirt, socks, and shoes.
- During daily activities and routines, make several sets of functionally related objects (e.g., shoes–socks, cups–bowls, washcloth–soap) available to the child. Encourage the child to put together functionally related objects of importance to the child and family.

Environmental Arrangements

- Use baskets or buckets to store personal items, such as a comb, brush, and mirror, or toys such as a road track and cars. Put a picture on the outside of the bucket to denote the objects to be stored.
- Put together sets of objects that present dissimilar functional characteristics. For example, when playing outdoors, place the child's book, paper, and crayons among gardening tools and observe whether the child gathers together the book, paper, and crayons to take indoors.
- Place a set of functionally related objects that are of interest to the child among other objects of less interest. For example, place a train, tunnel, and tracks among old newspapers or some cushions.
- Make available on the counter a cup, bowl, and spoon among papers, books, and pencils. Ask the child to set the table for lunch.

Instructional Sequence

- Model placing functionally related objects together. For example, set the child's place for lunch with a cup, plate, and spoon.
- Encourage the child with nonspecific verbal prompts (e.g., say, "What goes with this?" "You need something else," "The baby is hungry," "How will you dry your hands?").
- Give the child verbal instructions (e.g., say, "Go get your cup, plate, and spoon," "Cover the baby with a blanket and give the baby a bottle").
- Hand the child objects that are functionally related to the object the child is playing with. For example, give the child a blanket and toy bottle when the child is playing with a doll.
- Physically assist the child to place like objects together when cleaning up.

TEACHING CONSIDERATIONS

1. Arrange the situation so that objects the child needs are not readily available. Encourage the child to obtain the objects needed for the event. For example, at mealtime, do not set the table and wait for the child to get a spoon, plate, and cup.

2. If the child has a motor impairment, have the child point to the necessary objects to identify functional relationships.
3. If the child has a visual impairment, allow tactile exploration of the objects.
4. If the child has a hearing impairment, use a language modality that ensures the child's understanding of your instructions.
5. Consider safety with all objects that the child handles. Never leave the child unattended with potentially hazardous objects.

Objective 2.2   Groups objects according to size, shape, and/or color

DEVELOPMENTAL PROGRAMMING STEPS

PS2.2a   The child groups objects according to size.
PS2.2b   The child groups objects according to shape.
PS2.2c   The child groups objects according to color.

IMPORTANCE OF SKILL

The child learns to classify simple sets of objects by organizing them according to sensory and perceptual similarities and differences. This skill teaches the child to group objects consistently on different dimensions that are perceptually striking, such as size, shape, or color. This skill is fundamental to the understanding of numbers and mathematics skills.

PRECEDING OBJECTIVE

Cog F:2.3   Matches pictures and/or objects

CONCURRENT GOALS AND OBJECTIVES

FM A:5.1   Releases hand-held object onto and/or into a larger target with either hand
FM B:2.0   Assembles toy and/or object that require(s) putting pieces together
Cog E:4.0   Solves common problems
Cog F:1.0   Aligns and stacks objects
Cog G:1.2   Uses functionally appropriate actions with objects
SC C:2.3   Carries out one-step direction *with* contextual cues
SC D:1.1   Uses five descriptive words
Soc A:3.2   Responds to communication from familiar adult

TEACHING SUGGESTIONS
Activity-Based

- Allow the child to help clean up after mealtime and have available objects that can be grouped according to size, shape, or color. Provide a visual model by beginning to group the objects. For example, after meals, stack big plates, then small plates, and ask the child to continue.

Cog F

- When picking up after a play activity with Legos or blocks, begin to place the objects in different boxes, according to color, size, or shape, and have the child continue.
- Provide the child with several types of toys of different colors and set up a play activity in which the child groups by color. For example, child places blue blocks in blue trucks and red beads in red trucks.
- When preparing a snack, use crackers of different shapes and begin to place square crackers on one plate and round crackers on another. Encourage the child to continue placing crackers on plates.
- While folding laundry, have the child help group socks and pants by color or size. Make differences obvious, such as an adult's big socks and the child's little socks.
- During play, make two roads or two necklaces of two different colors by aligning blocks or stringing beads of the same color.
- While driving, point out different road signs by size, shape, and color.

Environmental Arrangements

- Have two groups of objects that differ on dimensions in addition to size, shape, and color. For example, after providing a visual model, have the child take the big cups to the kitchen and place the miniature cups in the doll house. Stick shiny star stickers on one sheet and opaque circles on another. Place big metal trucks in a toy garage and small wooden train cars on a railway track.
- Provide containers that match perceptually the objects to be grouped. For example, use two form boards, one with only square holes, the other with only round holes. Use a suitcase and a small box to group large toy animals and small animals. Use green and red paper bags for green and red apples or blocks.
- Make placemats that match the color of the child's cup and plate. Trace a small circle around the cup and a large circle around the plate on the placemat to give the child a size and color form to match when setting the table. Introduce contrasting placemats and dishes.
- Cut out different shapes in the lids of plastic containers. For example, cut a circle in one lid, a square in another, and a rectangle in a third lid. Encourage the child to drop blocks through the corresponding holes in the container lids.
- When playing with blocks, encourage the child to build towers of different colors or shapes, such as a red tower and blue tower, or a square tower and cylindrical tower.
- During art activities, encourage the child to group shapes, sizes, and colors. For example, use yarn to make different spaces to be filled with "big beans here" and "little beans there." Provide paper for the child to first "paste all the circles" and then "paste all the squares."

Instructional Sequence

- Model grouping objects in separate piles and have the child help you. Then have the child place the grouped objects in two different containers.
- Give verbal cues by systematically labeling the relevant dimension for the child. For example, while the child is sorting his or her own clothes from the father's clothes, say, "Big," or "Little."
- Provide verbal or visual assistance by indicating where to place an object (e.g., "in this box").
- Physically assist the child to stack large books in one pile and small books in another.

TEACHING CONSIDERATIONS

1. If the child has a motor impairment, ask the child to point or look at the corresponding visual model rather than place or move the object. Ask, "Where does this go?"
2. If the child has a visual impairment, allow the child to feel the objects. Use different textures and shapes.
3. If the child has a hearing impairment, use a language modality that ensures the child understands the task and directions. If necessary, demonstrate for the child.
4. Consider safety with all objects that the child handles. Never leave the child unattended with potentially hazardous objects.

Objective 2.3 Matches pictures and/or objects

DEVELOPMENTAL PROGRAMMING STEPS

PS2.3a The child groups together two or more similar objects. For example, the child plays with two toy airplanes or the child chooses two spoons from a drawer.
PS2.3b The child recognizes a familiar object, person, or event by responding the same way to a similar object, person, or event over time. For example, the child looks into all mirrors and smiles or pushes suspended objects to make them swing.

IMPORTANCE OF SKILL

A first step toward the ability to categorize objects is to recognize that two or more objects are the same. By matching objects, the child is learning to relate two objects on the basis of their similarity. This skill develops visual discrimination of objects and forms, which is necessary for the child to later recognize numbers and letters.

CONCURRENT GOAL AND OBJECTIVES

FM B:2.0   Assembles toy and/or object that require(s) putting pieces together
Cog G:1.2   Uses functionally appropriate actions with objects
SC B:1.2   Points to an object, person, and/or event
SC C:1.1   Locates common objects, people, and/or events in unfamiliar pictures
SC C:2.3   Carries out one-step direction *with* contextual cues
SC D:1.4   Uses 15 object and/or event labels

TEACHING SUGGESTIONS
Activity-Based

- During daily activities and games, provide the child with a variety of objects, at least two of which are the same. For example, while dressing, ask the child to select matching socks, a pair of shoes, or matching mittens.
- Participate in activities with the child by pointing out objects and pictures that are the same. Hold toy cars, beads, blocks, or animals next to each other and show the child

Cog F

that they match. Ask the child to find matching objects: "Find the one that matches," or "Give me the one that is the same."

- Show the child pairs of objects that match and pairs that do not match. Show how each pair is the same (matches) or not the same (does not match), that is, during dressing contrast mom's shoes, child's shoes; brother's pants, child's pants.
- Encourage the child to participate in routine tasks that involve matching objects, such as putting away silverware or folding socks.
- When looking at books, ask the child to point to or find similar objects (e.g., say, "Find more," or "Where's another one?").
- Play lotto games in which the child matches a picture to the same picture on a game board.

Environmental Arrangements

- Give the child a basket of two or three different types of interlocking toys (e.g., pop beads, Legos, Bristle Blocks). Encourage the child to match objects by finding and putting together the same type of interlocking toy (e.g., all the Legos).
- Present objects that are unlike the object to be matched in color, brightness, size, shape, and function. For example, have the child match a shiny red ball from an array of white toy cars and furry toy animals or a banana from an array of crayons and sheets of paper.
- Begin by having the child match objects to similar objects. Move to matching objects to pictures and finally pictures to pictures, as the child becomes more proficient.
- Limit the number of pictures or objects available so that only one distractor object is present. For example, when presenting a picture of a dog, have available only one picture of another animal in addition to a matching picture. Increase to three or four distractor pictures or objects as the child becomes more proficient in matching.
- Select matching objects that the child can act upon simultaneously and whose functional use differs from the other distractor objects. For example, have the child match blocks or pop beads that he or she can bang or pop together. Have these items available in an array of books or stuffed animals.

Instructional Sequence

- Model for the child by selecting three matching objects among others.
- Point to or verbally encourage the child to match objects or pictures (e.g., say, "What goes on top of this milk bottle?" or "Where is your other shoe?").
- Physically assist the child to place one matching sock on top of another.

TEACHING CONSIDERATIONS

1. Be sure the child understands the task and directions. If necessary, the adult may demonstrate with other objects.
2. When giving verbal instructions, such as "Show me the same," avoid giving a verbal cue by naming the object. For example, avoid saying, "Where's the horse?" as the child becomes proficient.
3. If the child has a visual impairment, use objects that are tactilely different, such as soft, furry animals and cold, metal cars. Also, use noise-producing objects. Allow tactile exploration of the objects.
4. If the child has a motor impairment, use alternate methods of matching objects or pictures, such as looking at similar objects or touching similar objects.

Cog F

5. If the child has a hearing impairment, use a language modality such as total communication that ensures the child's understanding of your instructions.
6. Consider safety with all objects that the child handles. Never leave the child unattended with potentially hazardous objects.

GOAL 3   Demonstrates functional use of one-to-one correspondence

---

DEVELOPMENTAL PROGRAMMING STEP

PS3.0a   The child demonstrates one-to-one correspondence by assigning one of two objects to another person and keeping the other object. For example, the child gives one of two daisies to the father and keeps the other.

IMPORTANCE OF SKILL

One-to-one correspondence is the simplest and most direct measure of the equivalence of two sets of objects. This skill is basic to the understanding of the numerical concepts of equal, more, and less. It also enables the child to make judgments of numerical equalities and differences, independent of how objects look, feel, or are arranged.

PRECEDING OBJECTIVE

Cog F:3.1   Demonstrates concept of *one*

CONCURRENT GOAL AND OBJECTIVES

FM A:5.1   Releases hand-held object onto and/or into a larger target with either hand
FM B:2.2   Fits object into defined space
Cog F:2.2   Groups objects according to size, shape, and/or color
Cog G:1.0   Uses imaginary objects in play
SC B:1.2   Points to an object, person, and/or event
SC C:1.3   Locates common objects, people, and/or events *with* contextual cues
SC C:2.3   Carries out one-step direction *with* contextual cues
Soc C:1.1   Initiates social behavior toward peer
Soc C:2.1   Initiates communication with peer

TEACHING SUGGESTIONS
Activity-Based

- During daily activities and routines, encourage the child to match functionally related objects to two or more other objects, using one-to-one correspondence. For example, when setting the table at mealtimes, provide opportunities for the child to place a cup or utensil next to each plate or give a cracker or piece of fruit to each peer.
- During group activities, have one child distribute materials to peers rather than having each child obtain his or her own materials.
- Encourage the child to engage in pretend play, such as a tea party or playing school with dolls, in which objects can be distributed to each doll. Have the child play grocery store and exchange a coin for each grocery item.

Cog F

- When assisting the child with dressing, be sure to point out, "One sock for each foot," "One mitten for each hand," and "One leg in each pant leg."

Environmental Arrangements

- Look at books with the child and count objects as you point to them. Encourage the child to assist by pointing to the objects while the adult counts.
- Have the child use one-to-one correspondence to fit parts of objects together. For example, encourage the child to fit covers on boxes or toy people into miniature cars.
- Provide arrays of objects in which the number of objects to be assigned is identical to the number of objects or people involved. For example, give the child four napkins to place beside four plates.
- Have the child match two or more objects that are members of a familiar pair. For example, while cleaning up the room, have the child place a glove next to the other glove, a sneaker next to the other sneaker, and a sock next to the other sock.

Instructional Sequence

- Model passing out napkins to each person at mealtime. Give the child the rest of the napkins to pass out.
- Give the child verbal instructions for each match. For example, say, "Give one crayon to Daddy," and "Give one crayon to Sally."
- Verbalize and point successively to each object to which the other object is being assigned. For example, point to each plate on which the child must place a cracker and say, "One cracker here."
- Physically assist the child to place one cup by each plate at the table.

TEACHING CONSIDERATIONS

1. The objects to be assigned should be functionally related to the objects or people involved.
2. If the child has a motor impairment, allow the child to use alternate means of demonstrating one-to-one correspondence (e.g., touching, looking).
3. If the child has a visual impairment, increase the intensity and variety of cues. Use bright-colored objects, tactilely different objects, or noise-producing objects.
4. If the child has a hearing impairment, use a language modality such as total communication that ensures the child's understanding of your instruction.
5. Consider safety with all objects that the child handles. Never leave the child unattended with potentially hazardous objects.

Objective 3.1 Demonstrates concept of *one*

DEVELOPMENTAL PROGRAMMING STEPS

☑ The objective above is the most basic step for the skill to be taught. Most children will benefit from the activities outlined here that emphasize this skill. For children who need more instruction, consider designing programming steps from the *environmental arrangements* suggestions or from the *instructional sequence* outlined.

IMPORTANCE OF SKILL

The development of quantitative knowledge is basic to the acquisition of a range of numerical and quantitative abilities, such as size discrimination, counting, and estimation of relative and equivalent numbers. The concept of *one* is fundamental to the understanding of numbers.

CONCURRENT GOALS AND OBJECTIVES

FM A:3.0   Grasps hand-size object with either hand using ends of thumb, index, and second fingers
FM B:2.2   Fits object into defined space
Adap A:5.0   Transfers food and liquid
Cog F:1.0   Aligns and stacks objects
SC B:1.2   Points to an object, person, and/or event
SC C:1.3   Locates common objects, people, and/or events *with* contextual cues
SC C:2.3   Carries out one-step direction *with* contextual cues
SC D:2.4   Uses two-word utterances to describe objects, people, and/or events
Soc A:3.2   Responds to communication from familiar adult
Soc C:1.0   Initiates and maintains interaction with peer

TEACHING SUGGESTIONS
Activity-Based

- During daily routines, ask the child to pick one book to read, one car to roll, one baby to rock to sleep.
- When several similar objects are present, ask the child to pick, show, or give only one object. For example, during meals ask the child to take only one cookie or give one cracker to a peer.
- During drawing activities, ask the child to take only one sheet of paper from a pile and one crayon from a box.
- Allow the child to help at a grocery store by placing one box of crackers in the grocery cart. Ask the child to select one loaf of bread.

Environmental Arrangements

- Encourage the child to select the one object out of several similar objects in a familiar situation that is customarily used for a purpose. For example, at changing time ask the child to get one diaper, or at mealtime ask the child to get one plate.
- Ask the child to place one object in a container that will hold only one, such as a doll in a doll bed or an egg in an egg cup.
- Ask the child to match an object to a visual model by selecting one from several dissimilar objects. For example, have the child search for a matching mitten from several assorted objects.
- Move the remaining objects after the child has selected one or have the child indicate an object when only one object is present. For example, ask the child to show one tricycle when only one tricycle is present.

Instructional Sequence

- Model showing, giving, or assigning one item for the child and encourage the child to imitate.

Cog F

- Provide the child with exaggerated examples of many and just one. For example, put large piles of blocks in a bucket and just one block in another bucket.
- Hand the child *one* object while verbally or visually emphasizing the numerical concept of *one*.
- Physically assist the child to select *one* block from several.

TEACHING CONSIDERATIONS

1. When asking the child to indicate *one*, verbally or visually emphasize *one* (e.g., by showing one finger) and avoid naming the object. If the object is named, the child may just locate the object rather than focus on the numerical concept.
2. If the child has a motor impairment, allow the child to use alternate means of demonstrating *one* (e.g., touching, looking).
3. If the child has a visual impairment, increase the intensity and variety of cues. Use bright-colored objects, objects that are tactilely different, or noise-producing objects. Allow tactile exploration of the objects.
4. If the child has a hearing impairment, use a language modality such as total communication that ensures the child's understanding of your instructions.
5. Consider safety with all objects that the child handles. Never leave the child unattended with potentially hazardous objects.

Cog F

Strand G

Interaction with Objects

GOAL 1 Uses imaginary objects in play

DEVELOPMENTAL PROGRAMMING STEPS

PS1.0a The child uses an action associated with a common object, but the object is absent. The focus of the child's play is on the action rather than the imaginary object. For example, the child kicks an imaginary ball, eats an imaginary cookie, or throws an imaginary ball.

PS1.0b The child enacts the typical action of a familiar character or animal by using a real object associated with the character or animal. For example, the child sits in baby brother's chair and pretends to cry or takes Mommy's keys and pretends to go bye-bye.

PS1.0c The child enacts imaginary events related to own daily routine activities. For example, the child pretends to sleep on the bed or drink from an empty cup.

IMPORTANCE OF SKILL

The ability to use imaginary objects in play demonstrates that the child's actions and thoughts no longer require the physical presence of objects. The child's interactions with objects and events become independent of time, space, and sensory perception as the child gains the ability to represent absent objects and mentally manipulate and interact with abstractions and representations. This skill leads the child into more complex play, which is important for social interactions with peers and greater exploration of the environment.

PRECEDING OBJECTIVE

Cog G:1.1 Uses representational actions with objects

CONCURRENT GOALS AND OBJECTIVE

GM D:5.0 Climbs up and down play equipment
Cog D:1.0 Imitates motor action that is not commonly used
Cog D:2.0 Imitates words that are not frequently used
Cog E:4.0 Solves common problems
SC C:1.2 Locates common objects, people, and/or events in familiar pictures
SC D:1.0 Uses 50 single words

Cog G

327

Soc A:2.0   Initiates and maintains interaction with familiar adult
Soc C:1.0   Initiates and maintains interaction with peer

TEACHING SUGGESTIONS
Activity-Based

- When playing with the child, talk about familiar activities such as going to the store, to bed, or in the car. Encourage the child to use imaginary objects to enact common situations. For example, ask the child to give you a bite of an imaginary cookie or help fasten an imaginary seatbelt.
- Throughout daily activities, provide the child with familiar toys or objects and encourage the child to use imaginary objects. For example, when dressing, put on imaginary boots and a hat. When going outside to play, take an imaginary dog for a walk. During mealtimes, pretend to eat imaginary food.
- When the child is playing with toys or objects, introduce an imaginary game. For example, when the child is playing with a stuffed animal, pretend to be in the jungle. When the child is climbing on an outdoor structure, pretend to be climbing a mountain.
- Encourage the child to assign roles to him- or herself and a peer or adult. For example, say, "You be the mama lion, and I'll be the baby lion."

☑ If your data indicate the child is not making progress toward the goal, provide additional structure within the suggested activities by incorporating the following *environmental arrangements:*

Environmental Arrangements

- Use mostly real objects in a particular situation but have one critical object be imaginary. For example, use a real pot, spoon, and bowl to cook and serve imaginary soup. Let the child swim in imaginary water after the tub has been drained. Feed the rocking horse imaginary hay from a real bucket.
- Use puppets or stuffed animals to perform imaginary actions.
- Sing familiar songs that require the child to use different actions, such as "Wheels on the Bus," "Baby Bumblebee," or "Row, Row, Row Your Boat."
- Plant a pretend garden, using a small shovel or spoon. Dig a hole in the sandbox, plant imaginary seeds, water the garden, and watch the "flowers" grow.

☑ If this objective is particularly difficult for a child, it may be necessary, within activities, to use an *instructional sequence.*

Instructional Sequence

- Model using an imaginary object and encourage the child to imitate.
- Provide verbal cues related to specific actions, such as "Let's go for a ride in the car: here's my seat and there's your seat," or "Let's paint this wall: here's my brush and here's yours."
- Physically assist child to work a puppet in imaginary play or stir imaginary soup.

☑ Combining or pairing different levels of instructions may be helpful when beginning to teach a new and difficult skill. Fade to less intrusive instructions as soon as possible to encourage more independent performance.

Cog G

TEACHING CONSIDERATIONS

1. Elicit use of imaginary objects within the context of dramatic play with peers. Encourage social interaction, communication, role-playing, and turn-taking among peers.
2. If the child has a motor impairment that restricts movement, engage the child in storytelling and relating of events. Observe the child's ability to relate stories and past events, tell stories about imaginary events, and create fictitious characters and objects.
3. If the child has a severe visual impairment, encourage play acting by describing actions the child should make on imaginary figures (e.g., say, "This is a very tall horse. Lift your leg high and jump on!").
4. If the child has a hearing impairment, model imaginary behaviors. Use total communication.
5. Consult a qualified specialist for further techniques for the child with a visual, hearing, or motor impairment.
6. Consider safety with all objects that the child handles. Never leave the child unattended with potentially hazardous objects.

Objective 1.1 Uses representational actions with objects

DEVELOPMENTAL PROGRAMMING STEPS

PS1.1a The child uses a picture or a toy to represent a real object. For example, the child pretends to peel and eat a plastic banana or makes a barking noise while holding a picture of a dog.

PS1.1b The child uses a functionally similar object as a substitute for another object to perform a game or action. For example, the child feeds the doll with a bottle and then takes a cup and gives the doll a drink.

IMPORTANCE OF SKILL

By using one object to represent another, the child's actions are no longer tied exclusively to the use of particular objects. The child becomes able to use one object for another. Using one thing to represent something else is a skill basic to using words to refer to objects and events. This skill increases the flexibility of the child's actions and thought so that the child is no longer restricted to the immediate environment. The child can use representational actions to refer to objects and events in the past, the future, or other contexts.

PRECEDING OBJECTIVE

Cog G:1.2 Uses functionally appropriate actions with objects

CONCURRENT GOALS AND OBJECTIVE

Cog C:2.0 Reproduces part of interactive game and/or action in order to continue game and/or action

Cog G

Cog D:1.0   Imitates motor action that is not commonly used
SC C:2.2   Carries out one-step direction *without* contextual cues
SC D:1.0   Uses 50 single words
Soc A:2.0   Initiates and maintains interaction with familiar adult
Soc C:1.0   Initiates and maintains interaction with peer

TEACHING SUGGESTIONS
Activity-Based

- Provide the child with a variety of objects that can be used for multiple purposes, such as blocks, sticks, cans, boxes, string, or cloth. Have a few defined objects available, but provide many objects that can serve multiple purposes. For example, give the child toy cars and encourage the child to use a box as a garage and blocks or string as a road.
- Have the child go "shopping" for food using blocks and cans for ingredients and string for spaghetti. Encourage the child to make lunch.
- During daily activities, encourage the child to use routine objects to represent something else, such as pretending that a cracker is an animal, a toothbrush is an airplane, or a plate of applesauce is a lake.

Environmental Arrangements

- Play interactive games. Have only one appropriate object available. Interact with the object and encourage the child to imitate, using another object. For example, pretend to talk to the child on the telephone, using the only telephone, and encourage the child to respond by using a block as a telephone.
- Have available other objects similar to the object to be represented. For example, while pretending to have a snack, substitute seashells for cups and observe whether the child pretends to drink from a shell.
- Take a ride using chairs or cushions to represent a car. Have the child close the door, buckle the seatbelt, and steer the car.
- During daily routines, arrange the situation so that key objects are missing. For example, at bedtime hide the child's pillow and ask the child to go to sleep on another "pillow."

Instructional Sequence

- Play interactive games and model representational actions with objects. Encourage the child to imitate. For example, pretend to eat a sandwich using a block, then offer the child a bite.
- Provide verbal cues, such as "Let's pretend this stick is a horse."
- Hand the child an object and instruct the child to use the object in a representational manner. For example, give the child a kitchen towel to cover a doll and say, "Pretend the towel is a blanket."
- Physically assist the child. For example, drink tea out of an imaginary cup.

TEACHING CONSIDERATIONS

1. Representational use of objects can be easily elicited in the context of pretend play. In pretend play, the child can practice a variety of social, communicative, and cognitive skills. The child gains a better understanding of the environment by reproducing and enacting familiar events.

2. If the child has a motor impairment restricting manipulation of objects, engage the child in verbal pretend games. For example, show the child an object such as a block, a stick, or a piece of cloth, and ask the child to verbally indicate what else the object could be.

3. If the child has a severe visual impairment, describe objects and verbally direct the child in representational actions with them.

4. If the child has a hearing impairment, model imaginary behaviors. Use total communication.

5. Consider safety with all objects that the child handles. Never leave the child unattended with potentially hazardous objects.

Objective 1.2 Uses functionally appropriate actions with objects

---

DEVELOPMENTAL PROGRAMMING STEP

PS1.2a   The child differentiates actions on objects according to the response of the object. For example, hard objects bang together, round objects roll, rattles shake, and soft objects are good to chew.

IMPORTANCE OF SKILL

The child's actions on objects begin to reflect socially approved modes of interacting with objects. The child recognizes the connection between the object and the intention of the object. The child discovers that objects differ in function, size, shape, weight, and texture, and the child no longer treats all objects in the same way. The functional use of objects is particularly important to the development of the child's independent movement in the daily environment.

PRECEDING OBJECTIVE

Cog G:1.3   Uses simple motor actions on different objects

CONCURRENT GOALS AND OBJECTIVES

FM A:5.0   Places and releases object balanced on top of another object with either hand
FM B:3.1   Uses either hand to activate objects
FM B:4.2   Scribbles
GM D:2.1   Pushes riding toy with feet while steering
GM D:4.3   Throws ball or similar object at target
Adap A:3.0 Drinks from cup and/or glass
Adap A:4.0 Eats with fork and/or spoon
Adap B:3.0 Brushes teeth
Cog C:1.0   Correctly activates mechanical toy
Cog C:2.0   Reproduces part of interactive game and/or action in order to continue game and/or action
Cog D:1.1   Imitates motor action that is commonly used
Cog F:1.2   Stacks objects

Cog G

SC C:1.3   Locates common objects, people, and/or events *with* contextual cues
Soc A:2.2   Responds to familiar adult's social behavior
Soc B:2.1   Responds to routine event
Soc C:1.5   Entertains self by playing appropriately with toys

TEACHING SUGGESTIONS
Activity-Based

- During daily activities and routines, encourage the child to independently perform actions with various objects rather than perform the action for the child. For example, encourage the child to put on clothing correctly, use feeding utensils correctly during mealtimes, and use toiletry objects (e.g., soap, towel, toothbrush, comb) during bathtime.
- Provide objects the child can use to imitate adult tasks or actions (e.g., toy broom, telephone, pitcher and cup, comb, toothbrush).
- Choose toys (e.g., rattles, balls, trucks, push- and pull-toys) with functional uses that involve simple motor actions.
- Provide a wide variety of situations in which the child can use functionally or socially appropriate actions on him- or herself (e.g., eats with a spoon, wipes washcloth over face), on others (e.g., feeds mother with a spoon), and on objects (e.g., pushes play button on a toy musical tape player).
- Observe the child's functional use of toys and objects. During pretend play, encourage the child to make a toy animal run or to give a doll a bath. During water and sand play, encourage the child to fill a bucket with water or dig a hole with a spoon. During art activities, give the child brushes to paint with, crayons to draw with, and scissors to cut paper. Have the child play musical instruments (e.g., drums, xylophone, bells, piano) by using the appropriate action with each instrument.

Environmental Arrangements

- Use objects with which the child is familiar and has had previous opportunity to explore and manipulate initially.
- Present objects that elicit functionally appropriate actions related to an activity that is reinforcing for the child, such as utensils for eating and drinking; hats or mittens to wear for outdoor play; and balls for rolling, kicking, and throwing.
- Begin with objects that the child can use to act on him- or herself, as compared to others (e.g., peers, adults) or objects (e.g., dolls, toy animals). For example, begin encouraging the functional use of bath and hygiene items, eating utensils, and clothing.
- Integrate activities within interactive games. Pretend to be hungry and ask the child to give you the bottle or cup. Take turns rolling a ball to each other.
- Use contextual language to elicit functional use of an object. For example, if the child is patting a doll with a bottle, encourage the child to feed the doll by saying, "The baby is hungry."
- Arrange situations that facilitate imitation. Use two toys or real telephones to talk to each other. Drive cars over a "racetrack" on the table. Get coats and put them on together when you are ready to go outside.

Cog G

Instructional Sequence

- Model the functional use of objects and encourage the child to imitate.
- Verbally instruct the child to "Give the baby the bottle," or "Comb your hair."
- Physically assist the child to brush his or her teeth or comb his or her hair.

TEACHING CONSIDERATIONS

1. Present a range of toys and objects that the child can use in functional ways (e.g., doll, car, blocks, paper and crayons, dishes).
2. If the child has a motor impairment, use objects and toys that are easy for the child to hold and activate.
3. If the child has a visual impairment, use large or bright objects or ones that can be easily recognized by tactile exploration.
4. If the child has a hearing impairment, model functionally appropriate actions. Use total communication.
5. Consider safety with all objects that the child handles. Never leave the child unattended with potentially hazardous objects.

Objective 1.3 Uses simple motor actions on different objects

DEVELOPMENTAL PROGRAMMING STEP

PS1.3a   The child produces a simple, undifferentiated action on all objects (e.g., drops or bangs).

IMPORTANCE OF SKILL

The child's interactions with objects are no longer centered only on the immediate sensory activities, such as mouthing, grasping, and looking, but they expand to include a variety of manipulations, such as shaking, striking, or dropping. These more advanced actions are directed at producing an external result on the object and the child learns that relationships exist between objects and the child's actions. Knowledge of object properties remains limited and the child's actions are applied to different objects randomly.

PRECEDING OBJECTIVE

Cog G:1.4   Uses sensory examination with objects

CONCURRENT GOAL AND OBJECTIVES

FM A:1.1   Makes directed batting and/or swiping movements with each hand
FM A:3.3   Grasps hand-size object with either hand using whole hand
FM B:3.1   Uses either hand to activate objects
GM A:1.0   Turns head, moves arms, and kicks legs independently of each other
Cog C:1.2   Acts on mechanical and/or simple toy in some way
Soc A:3.2   Responds to communication from familiar adult

Cog G

TEACHING SUGGESTIONS
Activity-Based

- Provide a variety of objects and encourage the child to use motor actions on different objects. Encourage the child to strike or kick hanging objects and mobiles, pat or bang toy animals and rattles, or tear or crumple paper and aluminum foil.
- Give the child measuring spoons and cups to bang on the floor and fit together.
- Provide musical toys such as cymbals, a tom-tom, or a wooden spoon and cake tin and allow the child to make music.

Environmental Arrangements

- Use objects that produce an interesting effect with minimal manipulation, such as noise-producing toys, balls and roly-poly toys that move easily when touched, and mirrors and bright-colored shiny objects that reflect the light when moved.
- Provide a Busy Box with bright dials, movable windows, and clicking parts. Allow the child to activate mechanisms on the box.
- Present objects with which the child has become familiar through sensory examination. Observe whether the child attempts to act differently on an object by using motor actions. For example, at bedtime the child sucks a favorite blanket then starts to stroke or rub it.
- If the child initiates a nondirected movement with hands, arms, or legs, introduce an object and observe whether the child continues the motor pattern. For example, if the child is making nondirected kicking movements, put a light blanket over the child's feet and encourage the child to continue to kick the blanket.

Instructional Sequence

- Model a simple motor pattern on an object the child is already exploring in a sensory manner. For example, if the child looks at a piece of aluminum foil, crumple the foil and encourage the child to imitate.
- Verbally encourage the child to bang a wooden spoon on a cake tin.
- Physically assist the child to contact and act on an object, such as a Busy Box.

TEACHING CONSIDERATIONS

1. Present a range of objects eliciting a variety of motor actions, such as squeeze-toys, dolls, balls, or cars.
2. If the child has a visual impairment, make sure the effect of the action on the object is interesting to the child, such as with a noise-producing object.
3. If the child has a motor impairment, use objects that can be easily activated, such as mobiles and balls.
4. Consider safety with all objects that the child handles. Never leave the child unattended with potentially hazardous objects.

Objective 1.4   Uses sensory examination with objects

DEVELOPMENTAL PROGRAMMING STEPS

PS1.4a   The child explores or plays with parts of his or her own body. For example, the child sucks fingers or watches hands and feet.

PS1.4b   The child explores or plays with objects that satisfy physical needs, such as the nipple on a bottle, a mother's breast or pacifier, or a blanket or clothing.

IMPORTANCE OF SKILL

The child acquires knowledge about the world through interactions with people and objects. Initially the child's interactions with the environment are based upon sensory and motor actions and gradually develop to include actions involving functional use of objects and symbolic representation. Sensory examination by looking, hearing, touching, smelling, and tasting constitutes the initial and most primitive means for the child to gain information about the physical properties of an object.

PRECEDING OBJECTIVE

Cog A:1.4   Responds to auditory, visual, and tactile events

CONCURRENT GOALS AND OBJECTIVES

FM A:2.3   Reaches toward and touches object with each hand
FM A:3.3   Grasps hand-size object with either hand using whole hand
GM A:1.1   Turns head past 45° to the right and left from midline position
GM A:3.6   Lifts head and chest off surface with weight on arms
Adap A:1.0 Uses tongue and lips to take in and swallow solid foods and liquids
Cog A:1.0   Orients to auditory, visual, and tactile events
Cog B:1.2   Focuses on object and/or person
Cog C:1.3   Indicates interest in simple and/or mechanical toy
Cog E:1.2   Retains object
SC A:1.0   Turns and looks toward person speaking
SC A:2.2   Looks toward an object
Soc A:1.2   Smiles in response to familiar adult

TEACHING SUGGESTIONS
Activity-Based

- Draw the child's attention to interesting objects that are familiar and used frequently in daily routines. Encourage the child to use sensory examination with the objects. For example, show the bottle to the child before placing it in the child's mouth, then encourage the child to pat the bottle during the feeding. Gently touch the child's face or body with a soft blanket at bedtime, then encourage the child to stroke the blanket.
- Place a safe object such as a furry musical bear with multiple sensory properties (i.e., an object that is interesting to look at, touch, smell, or listen to) within the child's reach in the crib or play area. Rotate objects occasionally to provide a variety of sensory explorations.
- Place an object such as a rattle in the child's hand. Observe whether the child takes the object into his or her mouth to explore by sucking.
- Make noises with objects to the side of the child and observe whether the child turns toward the sound, changes facial expression, or quiets to the sound. The child may look at the object or notice the sound it makes.
- Talk to the child from around the room. Watch to see if the child looks for you.
- Move a favorite object slowly across the child's visual field, up, down, and around in circles.

Cog G

Hold the object in the child's visual field and encourage the child to visually explore it.

- Place foods on the child's lips or tongue and observe whether the child moves the lips or tongue or swallows the food.

Environmental Arrangements

- Present strong-smelling foods or objects and observe whether the child moves to-ward or away from the odor.
- Play face-to-face interaction games with the child and gradually introduce objects within the game. For example, gently tickle the child, making the child laugh, then tickle the child with a soft toy and observe whether the child looks at or touches the toy.
- Play "gotcha" using a favorite stuffed animal or doll.
- Use objects that produce exaggerated stimulations, such as flashing lights or big, noisy, shiny toys.

Instructional Sequence

- Model a simple action with the object, then place the object within the child's prox-imity and observe whether the child acts on the object using sensory examination.
- Combine sensory explorations using a modality the child prefers, such as vision and sound, and then fade to one sensory modality.
- Give the child verbal assistance (e.g., say, "Look at this," "Can you smell it?" or "Touch the bear"). Use an exaggerated and captivating tone of voice and facial ex-pression to make the object interesting to the child.
- Physically assist the child to look by gently turning the child's face toward a visual or auditory stimulus. Touch the child's lips or hands with appropriate objects to taste or feel. Wait to see if the child repeats the action.
- Physically assist the child to play an interactive game with you that includes objects.

TEACHING CONSIDERATIONS

1. Present a range of objects likely to elicit a variety of behaviors.
2. If the child has a severe visual impairment, use noise-producing objects or objects with interesting textures.
3. If the child has a hearing impairment, use visually attractive objects or objects that can be easily activated.
4. If the child has a motor impairment that restricts movement, make sure the child can respond to the stimulation presented.
5. Consider safety with all objects that the child handles. Never leave the child unat-tended with potentially hazardous objects.

Cog G

SOCIAL-COMMUNICATION DOMAIN

Angela Losardo, Susan Janko, and Juliann Cripe

The Social-Communication Domain begins with prelinguistic communicative behaviors and culminates with three-word utterances. Early social-communication development is organized into four areas for this curriculum: prelinguistic communicative interactions; transition to words; comprehension of words and sentences; and production of social-communicative signals, words, and sentences. The title, social-communication, reflects the perspective that communication is primarily a social skill for young children. Communication occurs between people, and competence in communication represents more than the specific skills of production and comprehension (i.e., expression and reception). As the child learns to communicate, he or she becomes more independent of adults and other caregivers and is less likely to express frustration at being misunderstood, misrepresented, and overlooked.

Although the first communication skills seem to appear when the child starts to speak, in reality, the infant begins much earlier to engage in communicative interactions. An infant's earliest cries signal the caregiver to respond, and the cessation of crying communicates that a need has been met. Caregiving activities such as feeding, diapering, and bathing, as well as face-to-face play, provide valuable opportunities for early communication of preference, mood, comfort level, and affection.

Attending to sounds in the environment, and voices in particular, develops into more complex turn-taking interactions by the time a child begins to coo and babble. The production of sound becomes associated quickly with getting the caregiver's attention, showing attention to objects and people, and expressing likes and dislikes. Both the infant and young child send and receive an enormous amount of information long before they are able to produce speech.

The child uses a formal system of communication much earlier than he or she produces recognizable words. Concrete gestures and actions are combined with consistent vocalizations to form the earliest word approximations. Attention to the inflections of speech allows the child to respond appropriately to questions and statements before he or she can answer verbally. In this sense, early communication involves cognition, movement, and social development.

Because early communication is influenced by motor, cognitive, and social behaviors, there are times when a young child seems to emphasize one area at the expense of developing other skills. For example, it is common for the child to make few gains in language and communication skills while learning to walk. Once walking is mastered, development of communication skills accelerates.

SC

The rate of gaining skills in social-communication will vary over time in relation to development in other domains. More progress will ultimately be made by following the child's lead and encouraging mastery of new skills in the areas where the child is showing the most interest. The adage that "You can lead a horse to water, but you can't make him drink" has a parallel in teaching communication skills. The best intervention programs cannot be successful unless the child has a reason for communicating and is rewarded for the effort.

It is important to recognize that communication develops primarily in response to and with attention from the child's social environment. The child learns to ask for things by having someone respond to requests that are reasonable. A child learns to show interest in objects and people if the interest is reciprocated. Similarly, the child learns to follow directions by being encouraged and rewarded for doing so. Early communication in its many forms must obtain meaningful results or the child stops trying to communicate. This means that adults in the social environment must initiate often and respond quickly to the young child who is learning communication skills.

The prelinguistic interactions and comprehension skills addressed in this curriculum are designed to provide the foundations for communicative competence. Many of the activities suggested create the expectation that communication is a functional, generative, and reciprocal enterprise. The use of early caregiving and play routines in the AEPS Curriculum is a purposeful attempt to encourage this approach to teaching and learning communication.

The production of words demonstrates the child's ability to use abstract symbols to refer to concrete objects, events, and people in the immediate environment. The AEPS Test and Curriculum recognize signing and other formal symbol systems as both augmentative and alternative communication systems. Some children only use sign or other symbol systems when they begin to produce words and phrases. Many children quickly replace a gestural or pictorial system with speech after the notion of using symbolic communication is established. Other children continue to use alternative symbol systems as a primary method of communication. The curriculum activities suggested in the production strand are usually appropriate for any formal system of communication.

When the child begins to use words, he or she tends to talk about familiar topics. Early words usually refer to familiar people and favorite objects in the child's environment. Other early topics include familiar actions and favorite games, such as "go" and "peekaboo." Words that describe impressive events and objects, such as "hot" and "big," also appear early. The child learns to talk about the relationships between actions and objects that he or she has observed many times by using words such as "more," "mine," and "no."

The AEPS Curriculum does not select and sequence specific words because the words will vary from child to child. The child uses words that are important in play and in interactions with caregivers. The occupation and interests of a child's parents bring attention to certain events and objects. Some adults use expressions such as "whoops" and "uh-oh" when interacting with their infants. Other caregivers tend to label things in the environment, such as "milk," "baby," or "dog." The style of the caregiver's language is reflected in the early words the child uses; therefore, some children are more expressive and others are more referential.

When the young child begins to use words, he or she establishes meanings different from adult meanings. The child may use a word more narrowly than its true meaning, such as labeling only the family cat as "kitty." Conversely, the child may generalize words, such as calling any and all men "daddy." It is important to look for the concept behind the word that is misused rather than just correct the child's usage.

Several factors must be considered in identifying each child's communication needs. Words that serve multiple functions are good choices for early vocabulary because they quickly teach the child the usefulness of language. A word such as "help," for example, can be rewarded in many different situations for a child who needs assistance with dressing, eating, and operating toys. Many other words have this kind of broad usefulness: "more," "look," "go," "up," "down," and "want."

It is important to choose words that are used frequently because the child will have more opportunities to hear, learn, and use these words. The child who sees Kris the babysitter every day and his grandmother only twice a year, for example, will appropriately learn the word "Kris" before "Grandma." Because familiar objects, events, and people are often preferred by young children, it makes sense to choose labels for these favorites as initial language targets. Words such as "peek," "eat," "drink," "ball," and "go," that are common and frequently used, are most functional for young children.

The ease or difficulty of pronouncing words is another factor to consider in selecting early vocabulary. Usually, words that children use are short and easy to pronounce. A child will say "doll" or "baby" and "drink," but probably will not say "Cabbage Patch Kids" and "raspberry juice." If a word is important enough to a child, he or she will find a way to say it, even if it does not sound quite right. As a rule, however, it is wise to select words for the child that are easy to pronounce.

It is also important to identify words that will be rewarded by the child's social environment. Words such as "hi," "night-night," "bye-bye," and "please" are well received by caregivers and will bring a pleasant and affectionate response for the young child. Such social amenities are appropriate to many situations and offer opportunities for successful interactions with many different people.

Learning words that represent different parts of speech (e.g., nouns, verbs, adverbs, adjectives, pronouns) allows the child to combine words and become more specific about requests, comments, and directions. The ability to label people, objects, and actions allows the child to express who is doing what, or what happened to whom. Other parts of speech provide additional information about possession, description, and negation. Combining words into phrases and sentences provides opportunities to express many different things with the same labels; this is the first step in a generative repertoire.

Early attempts to combine words may require interpretation by the listener because the conventional rules of grammar are complex. The phrase "Juanita go" can mean "Juanita, let's go," "Juanita went somewhere," or "Juanita, go away!" The context is critical for understanding and responding appropriately to early utterances, and most children who expect a response will persist until the adult hits upon the correct meaning.

The AEPS Curriculum leaves selection of specific target words and phrases to caregivers and interventionists who are familiar with the child's environment, preferences, and interests. Careful selection of target words and phrases, creative and spontaneous use of the activities in the curriculum, and a constant sensitivity to the child's perspective should yield an environment that maximizes language learning. Communication can and should be taught all day and across all activities so that children learn the meaning, form, and function of word and phrase combinations in many settings.

SC

Strand A

Prelinguistic Communicative Interactions

GOAL 1 Turns and looks toward person speaking

DEVELOPMENTAL PROGRAMMING STEPS

☑ The goal above is the most basic step for the skill to be taught. Most children will benefit from the activities outlined here that emphasize this skill. For children who need more instruction, consider designing programming steps from the *environmental arrangements* suggestions or from the *instructional sequence* outlined.

IMPORTANCE OF SKILL

The ability to turn and look at people when they are speaking is an integral component of social-communication exchanges. It is an initial listening experience and it allows the child to attend to the speaker, be ready to take a turn, respond, and continue the exchange. Focusing on speakers offers numerous opportunities to learn the language system; a lot is learned by listening to and watching more mature users. Focusing is also a functional interaction of the visual, auditory, and motor skills that the child is developing.

PRECEDING OBJECTIVE

SC A:1.1 Turns and looks toward object and person speaking

CONCURRENT GOALS AND OBJECTIVES

GM A:1.0 Turns head, moves arms, and kicks legs independently of each other
Adap A:1.4 Swallows liquids
Cog A:1.0 Orients to auditory, visual, and tactile events
Cog B:1.0 Visually follows object and/or person to point of disappearance
Soc A:1.2 Smiles in response to familiar adult
Soc A:2.2 Responds to familiar adult's social behavior

TEACHING SUGGESTIONS

Activity-Based

■ Throughout the day, when the child is content and alert but is not attending to you, stand a few feet behind or to the side of the child. Call the child's name. When the child looks at you, smile and engage the child for several seconds by talking to him or her. Vary the pitch and melody of your voice as the child attends to help keep the child's interest.

340

- As you enter a room, greet the child by saying, "Hello, Andrea," or "Good morning, Thomas." Watch to see if the child turns and looks toward you.
- While the child is playing, provide opportunities for him or her to turn and attend to other children and other familiar and unfamiliar voices.

☑ If the child is not making progress toward this goal, provide additional structure within the suggested activity by incorporating the following *environmental arrangements:*

Environmental Arrangements

- Initially, the setting may need to be free of objects and events that compete for the child's attention. Let the child see you first and then move back and begin to speak.
- Build upon the child's ability to turn and look toward you by systematically varying your position in the room until the child can visually locate you when you are standing in back of, in front of, and beside the child. Gradually increase your distance from the child while remaining in the same room.
- Use exaggerated vocal and facial expressions to gain and maintain the child's attention. For example, sing a nursery song, a catchy phrase from a commercial, or a family favorite to gain the child's attention.
- Combine gestures with speech, such as a wave and "hello," or combine a pointing response with speech.
- Play a tactile and vocal game such as "goochy goo" by gently touching the child's face to orient him or her to the location of your voice.

☑ If this goal is particularly difficult for a child, it may be necessary, within activities, to use an *instructional sequence.*

Instructional Sequence

- Stand in front of the child and obtain a consistent response before moving a little farther to the child's side each time you speak. If your voice and interactions do not engage the child for more than a few seconds, present an interesting toy immediately *after* the child orients. Talk to the child as you present the toy. After the child consistently responds to your voice and the toy, use the toy intermittently to engage the child; then use your voice only.
- Systematically increase the distance from which the toy and your voice are presented to encourage the child to respond.
- Show the child an interesting toy or noise-producing object. After the child orients to the toy alone, present the toy close to your face and talk to the child at the same time. Gradually fade the use of the toy until the child orients to just your voice. Increase the distance from which the toy and your voice are presented to encourage the child to respond in a variety of situations.
- Gently guide the child's face toward you as you speak.

☑ Combining or pairing different levels of instructions may be helpful when beginning to teach a new and difficult skill. Fade to less intrusive instructions as soon as possible to encourage more independent performance.

TEACHING CONSIDERATIONS

1. A child with a hearing impairment may hear only selected frequencies (high- or low-pitched sounds) or may hear only loud sounds. The child may also be sensitive to certain sounds or intensities (sounds that seem normal to you may be uncomfortably loud to some children, certain frequencies may be painful, or combinations of sounds or too much noise may be uncomfortable).

SC A

2. A child with a visual impairment may orient his or her body toward the speaker rather than look at the speaker's face. If the child has some vision, the speaker should stand close enough for the child to see.
3. If a child has restricted range of motion in the head or trunk, objects should be presented in positions other than where the child is visually focused, but still within the child's field of vision. Observe the child's gaze to see if he or she consistently localizes to the speaker or noise-producing objects. Consult a qualified specialist for individualized teaching ideas.
4. Be alert to safety precautions for all materials used.

Objective 1.1   Turns and looks toward object and person speaking

---

IMPORTANCE OF SKILL

This objective is an intermediate skill that provides a transition from the child's ability to localize nonspeech sounds in the environment to the ability to localize speech sounds. The child is refining visual and auditory attention. The ability to turn and look at people when they are speaking is an integral component of social-communication exchanges.

PRECEDING OBJECTIVE

SC A:1.2   Turns and looks toward noise-producing object

CONCURRENT OBJECTIVES

GM A:1.1   Turns head past 45° to the right and left from midline position
Adap A:1.4   Swallows liquids
Cog B:1.1   Visually follows object moving in horizontal, vertical, and circular directions
Cog C:1.3   Indicates interest in simple and/or mechanical toy
Soc A:1.2   Smiles in response to familiar adult
Soc A:2.2   Responds to familiar adult's social behavior

TEACHING SUGGESTIONS
Activity-Based

- Throughout the day, when the child is content and alert but is not attending to you, stand a few feet behind or at the side of the child. Present an interesting toy or object close to your face while you call the child's name. Vary the pitch and melody of your voice. When the child looks at you or the toy, smile and engage the child for several seconds by talking to the child.
- As you enter a room, knock, call the child's name, and wave to get the child's attention.
- When the child consistently turns and looks toward you or an object, provide opportunities for the child to look for you by standing in back, in front, and to the side of the child from different positions around the room. Gradually increase your distance from the child.

SC A

- When feeding the child, use the bottle, spoon, or toy to direct the child's attention to your face while you speak.
- Provide a range of opportunities to practice listening and finding the source of the sound. Radio, television, vacuum cleaner, running water, falling rain, bird, and dog noises are everyday sounds that you can experience with your child. Whenever possible, combine the sound and your presence to help the child focus on both the sound and you.
- Objects such as jewelry (especially bright-colored beads and dangling earrings) and glasses can be moved to attract the child's attention to the speaker's face and voice.

Environmental Arrangements

- Use interesting bright, noisy, or novel objects and use exaggerated vocal and facial expressions to gain and maintain the child's attention.
- Manipulate bright-colored puppets next to your face while talking to the child. Move the puppets closer to the child to re-engage his or her attention as needed and then return the puppet next to your face.
- If the child does not readily respond to most objects, present objects that you are certain the child desires and then give the object to the child after the child looks at you. Be sure to talk to the child and say the child's name when you present the object. For example, present an interesting object near your face and talk to the child. After the child looks toward you, give the object to the child and comment about it or engage the child's attention with it.
- Be sure the person or the toy is the most interesting event for the child. The setting should be relatively free from objects and events that compete for the child's attention.
- Play a tactile and vocal game by gently touching the child with the object and talking to the child.

Instructional Sequence

- If the child does not respond to an object presented next to your face, present the object in front of the child (but not so close that it is offensive) and move it slowly toward your face before you smile and engage the child. Be sure to talk to the child and say the child's name as you present the object.
- Systematically increase the distance and alter the location from which the toy and your voice are presented to encourage the child to respond in a variety of locations.
- Gently guide the child's face toward you and the object as you speak to the child.

TEACHING CONSIDERATIONS

1. A child with a hearing impairment may hear only selected frequencies (high- or low-pitched sounds) or may hear only loud sounds. The child may also be sensitive to certain sounds or intensities (sounds that seem normal to you may be uncomfortably loud to some children, certain frequencies may be painful, combinations of sounds or too much noise may be uncomfortable).
2. A child with a visual impairment may orient his or her body toward the speaker rather than look at the speaker's face. If the child has some vision, the speaker should stand close enough for the child to see.
3. If a child has a restricted range of motion in the head or trunk, objects should be presented in positions other than where the child is visually focused, but still within the child's field of vision. Observe the child's gaze to see if he or she consis-

SC A

tently localizes the speaker or noise-producing objects. Consult a qualified specialist for individualized teaching ideas.

4. Be alert to safety precautions for all materials used.

Objective 1.2   Turns and looks toward noise-producing object

---

IMPORTANCE OF SKILL

Noisy objects such as rattles and bells are commonly used to attract a young child's attention. As the child develops, softer and more subtle sounds become easier to focus on and find. Early motor movements to search for the sound are often jerky and slow, but they improve with practice. Turning and looking for noise-producing objects offers the child opportunities to integrate motor movements and to use the eyes and ears together to explore new objects and events in the world. This provides a foundation for the desire to communicate.

PRECEDING OBJECTIVE

Cog B:1.2   Focuses on object and/or person

CONCURRENT OBJECTIVES

FM A:2.2   Holds an object in each hand
GM A:1.1   Turns head past 45° to the right and left from midline position
Cog B:1.1   Visually follows object moving in horizontal, vertical, and circular directions
Cog C:1.3   Indicates interest in simple and/or mechanical toy

TEACHING SUGGESTIONS

Activity-Based

- During daily routines such as bathing and changing, engage the child in play with noise-producing objects.
- Throughout the day, when the child is content and alert, but is not attending to you, stand a few feet behind or to the side of the child. Activate a toy (e.g., bell, squeak-toy) so that it produces a noise. Call the child's name. When the child orients to the sound, activate the toy again and try to engage the child's attention with the toy for several seconds.
- Use a variety of everyday objects and noises throughout the day. For example, pour water or splash it during bathtime or water play, crinkle paper before throwing it away, or turn on music during quiet times.
- As you encounter noises in the environment, observe the child's attention and encourage the child to notice. For example, observe the child when the doorbell rings, the television or radio is turned on, the dishwasher starts, or cars or trucks pass by, and comment on the event. Carefully expose the child to a variety of sounds to reduce startling the child.
- Use noise-producing objects when encouraging the child to grasp and hold objects.

SC A

Environmental Arrangements

- At first, the setting may need to be free of objects and events that compete for the child's attention. Let the child see and hear the noise-producing object first and then move it to the side before activating it.
- Place musical mobiles on a child's crib or playpen. Many different noise-producing toys can be attached to offer opportunities for independent engagement. Always consider safety with toys or dangling objects in a crib.
- When the child consistently turns and looks toward the noise-producing object, systematically vary your position in the room until the child can visually locate the object when it is activated behind, in front of, and beside the child. Gradually increase your distance from the child when you activate the object so that the child responds to sounds in a variety of locations.
- Use combs and toothbrushes with chimes. Put bells on shoes or socks, or attach bells to the sleeve of the child's shirt.
- Wind chimes are colorful and easy to activate when the child is near them. Let the child activate the chimes and then talk to the child about the noise and the chimes.
- Attractive objects such as bright-colored or patterned toys and objects with interesting shapes or sizes may be used to gain the child's attention. Wave or wiggle the objects to gain the child's attention.
- Play a tactile and auditory game by gently touching the child with the object and activating it to make noise.

Instructional Sequence

- Present an object in front of or close to the child (but not so close that it is offensive to the child). When the child consistently looks toward the object, present it at different angles.
- Systematically increase the distance and alter the location of the toy, from the easiest to the most difficult for the child to reach.
- Gently guide the child's face toward the object and activate it to make noise. You may also move the object slightly to engage the child's interest.

TEACHING CONSIDERATIONS

1. A child with a hearing impairment may hear only selected frequencies (high- or low-pitched sounds) or may hear only loud sounds. The child may also be sensitive to certain sounds or intensities (sounds that seem normal to you may be uncomfortably loud to some children, certain frequencies may be painful, combinations of sounds or too much noise may be uncomfortable).
2. A child with a visual impairment may orient his or her body toward the speaker rather than look at the speaker's face. If the child has some vision, the speaker should stand close enough for the child to see.
3. If a child has a restricted range of motion in the head or trunk, objects should be presented in positions other than where the child is visually focused, but still within the child's field of vision. Observe the child's gaze to see if he or she consistently localizes the speaker or noise-producing objects. Consult a qualified specialist for individualized teaching ideas.
4. Be alert to safety precautions for all materials used.

SCA

GOAL 2   Follows person's gaze to establish joint attention

IMPORTANCE OF SKILL

Attention to one topic or event by two or more people (joint attention) is an integral component of communication. Following a person's gaze to establish joint attention is a more developed skill than responding to a noise-producing object or person because the child no longer needs physical (e.g., toys, a pointed finger) or vocal cues to establish attention. Joint attention allows a common understanding between communicating partners and it precedes more sophisticated conversational behaviors, such as initiating and maintaining topics, switching topics, or following another person's conversational lead.

PRECEDING OBJECTIVE

Cog B:1.1   Visually follows object moving in horizontal, vertical, and circular directions

CONCURRENT GOALS AND OBJECTIVES

FM A:3.0   Grasps hand-size object with either hand using ends of thumb, index, and second fingers
GM A:2.1   Rolls from back to stomach
GM B:1.4   Sits balanced without support
Adap A:2.2 Munches soft and crisp foods
Adap A:3.2 Drinks from cup and/or glass held by adult
Cog B:1.0   Visually follows object and/or person to point of disappearance
Cog C:2.1   Indicates desire to continue familiar game and/or action
Cog E:4.1   Uses more than one strategy in attempt to solve common problem
Soc A:1.1   Responds appropriately to familiar adult's affective tone
Soc A:2.2   Responds to familiar adult's social behavior

TEACHING SUGGESTIONS
Activity-Based

- Throughout the day when you and the child are interacting, turn and look at another person, object, or event in the environment. When the child looks in the direction of your gaze, comment about the person, object, or event to confirm that the child is looking at the object of your attention.
- Look toward people or pets as they enter the area close to the child and comment. Encourage the child to look, too.
- Put frequently used and preferred items (e.g., child's ball, truck) in their usual location on a shelf. When it is time to play, look to the familiar location and wait for the child to follow your gaze. Tell the child to find the ball as you look at it.

SC A

Environmental Arrangements

- The setting should be free of objects and events that compete for the child's attention because it is difficult to follow a speaker's gaze in a crowded or confusing setting.
- Ask another person to produce an interesting visual or auditory event after you make an obvious shift in gaze. For example, look toward another person and have the person immediately activate an interesting action toy or musical instrument; or look toward a barrier and have another person immediately jump out and surprise the child.
- After the child responds consistently, make your gaze and physical movements less obvious. Be sure to comment about the object, person, or event after the child looks at it.
- Activate a musical toy on a table or bookcase. Engage the child in a game and then look to the toy.
- As you look toward an object of interest, change the tone of your voice, increase your volume, or use exaggerated facial expressions to help the child change the focus of attention.
- The child may not respond if a speaker or object is too far away. Check for an optimal distance and then vary the distance after the child responds consistently.

Instructional Sequence

- Look at objects and events within easy visual range as you activate them.
- Tell the child to look at the object or event. Use an item that the child is familiar with and desires, such as a bottle.
- Use auditory events as the source of your change in gazes. Look toward the phone as it rings, the door as it shuts, or the mobile as the music starts.
- Gently guide the child's face toward the object or action of interest.

☑ If this goal is particularly difficult for a child, it may be necessary to drop back to the previous objective.

TEACHING CONSIDERATIONS

1. A child with a hearing impairment may hear only selected frequencies (high- or low-pitched sounds) or may hear only loud sounds. The child may also be sensitive to certain sounds or intensities (sounds that seem normal to you may be uncomfortably loud to some children, certain frequencies may be painful, combinations of sounds or too much noise may be uncomfortable).
2. A child with a visual impairment may orient his or her body toward the speaker rather than look at the speaker's face. If the child has some vision, the speaker should stand close enough for the child to see. The object of interest must be within the child's visual range.
3. If the child has a severe visual impairment, use another sensory modality, such as sound, smell, or touch, to establish joint attention. For example, say, "I hear the music box playing. Do you hear it?"
4. If a child has a restricted range of motion in the head or trunk, objects should be presented in positions other than where the child is visually focused, but still within the child's field of vision. Position the child to reduce the amount of effort required to follow the speaker's gaze. Consult a qualified specialist for individualized teaching ideas.
5. Be alert to safety precautions for all materials used.

SC A

Objective 2.1   Follows person's pointing gesture to establish joint attention

IMPORTANCE OF SKILL

Joint attention to one topic or event by two or more people allows a common understanding between communicating partners and precedes more sophisticated communicative exchanges. Being able to follow a person's pointing gesture is a skill commonly used to attend with another person to an object, person, or event. This skill is a transition step for the child from attention toward a single object, person, or event to attention shared with another person toward an object, person, or event.

PRECEDING OBJECTIVE

SC A:2.2   Looks toward an object

CONCURRENT GOALS AND OBJECTIVES

FM A:2.3   Reaches toward and touches object with each hand
FM A:3.0   Grasps hand-size object with either hand using ends of thumb, index, and second fingers
GM A:2.2   Rolls from stomach to back
GM B:1.6   Holds head in midline when in supported sitting position
Adap A:2.2   Munches soft and crisp foods
Adap A:3.2   Drinks from cup and/or glass held by adult
Cog B:1.0   Visually follows object and/or person to point of disappearance
Cog E:4.1   Uses more than one strategy in attempt to solve common problem
Soc A:1.1   Responds appropriately to familiar adult's affective tone
Soc A:2.2   Responds to familiar adult's social behavior

TEACHING SUGGESTIONS
Activity-Based

- Throughout the day when you and the child are interacting, turn and point to another person, object, or event in the environment. When the child looks in the direction of your pointing gesture, comment about the person, object, or event to confirm that the child is looking at the object of your attention.
- When the child consistently follows your pointing gestures, systematically vary your distance from the child so that the child responds to you when you gesture from different places in the room. Systematically vary the position of the objects, people, or events to which you point so that the child will orient to a variety of points in space.
- Look through picture books together. Point to the pictures and name them for the child.
- While on walks or riding in the car, point out objects that the child is interested in, such as dogs, swings, big trucks, McDonald's, and flowers.
- Point to body parts while looking in the mirror or during bathtime.

Environmental Arrangements

- To assist the child in following the pointing gesture, the setting should be free of objects and events that compete for the child's attention.

SC A

- If the child does not readily follow your pointing gesture, follow the child's gaze, point to an object, person, or event within the child's field of vision, and comment on it. Point to objects in positions that become gradually more distant from the child's immediate focus of attention so that the child must follow your pointing gesture to a variety of objects. Be sure to comment on the object, person, or event after the child looks at it.
- If the child does not follow your pointing gesture alone, ask another person to produce an interesting visual or auditory event immediately after you point to that person. For example, point to the person and have him or her activate an interesting toy; or point to the person and have him or her engage the child in a social or communicative interaction.
- Sing songs that require the child to look for peers as you call their names and point.
- When the child is involved in an activity, gain the child's attention and then direct attention back to the activity by pointing.

Instructional Sequence

- When the child consistently follows your pointing gesture visually, present the objects to which you are pointing to the side of the child so that he or she must turn and look to follow your pointing gesture.
- Present new objects in front of the child by gradually increasing the distance between the child and the object. Point to the object each time before picking it up or giving it to the child to play with.
- Present directly in front of the child an object that you are certain the child desires. Point to the object, pick it up, and give it to the child.
- Touch the child as an attention-getting signal before you point. Gently guide the child's head to follow your point.

TEACHING CONSIDERATIONS

1. A child with a hearing impairment may hear only selected frequencies (high- or low-pitched sounds) or may hear only loud sounds. The child may also be sensitive to certain sounds or intensities (sounds that seem normal to you may be uncomfortably loud to some children, certain frequencies may be painful, combinations of sounds or too much noise may be uncomfortable).
2. A child with a visual impairment may orient his or her body toward the speaker rather than look at the speaker's face. Bring the item of interest to the child. If the child has some vision, the speaker should stand close enough for the child to see and feel the pointing gesture. The object of interest must also be within visual range.
3. If the child has a severe visual impairment, use another sensory modality, such as sound, smell, or touch, to establish joint attention. For example, direct the child's attention to the food you are serving by saying, "Oh, this is hot. Let's blow on it so that it doesn't burn you."
4. If a child has a restricted range of motion in the head or trunk, objects should be presented in positions other than where the child is visually focused, but still within the child's field of vision. Position the child to reduce the amount of effort required to follow the speaker's gesture. Consult a qualified specialist for individualized teaching ideas.
5. Be alert to safety precautions for all materials used.

SC A

Objective 2.2 Looks toward an object

IMPORTANCE OF SKILL

This skill allows the child to differentiate a single object, person, or event in the environment from the multiple objects, people, and events present. It is an important first step to identify the object of interest around which an interaction may occur.

PRECEDING OBJECTIVE

Cog B:1.2   Focuses on object and/or person

CONCURRENT GOAL AND OBJECTIVES

FM A:2.3   Reaches toward and touches object with each hand
GM A:1.1   Turns head past 45° to the right and left from midline position
GM B:1.6   Holds head in midline when in supported sitting position
Adap A:1.3 Swallows solid and semisolid foods
Cog A:1.0   Orients to auditory, visual, and tactile events
Cog B:1.1   Visually follows object moving in horizontal, vertical, and circular directions
Cog C:1.3   Indicates interest in simple and/or mechanical toy
Cog E:1.2   Retains object
Soc A:2.2   Responds to familiar adult's social behavior

TEACHING SUGGESTIONS

Activity-Based

- Throughout the day when you and the child are interacting, comment about objects, people, or events the child is looking at. Present some novel objects or events that are relevant to the situation. When the child looks in the direction of the object or event, comment about it so that the child knows he or she is looking at the object of your attention.
- When the child consistently looks at objects presented, systematically vary the objects and your position in relation to the child when you present the objects, so that the child will orient to a variety of points in space.
- Establish locations for preferred items to be routinely placed so the child can learn where to look for favorite, reinforcing objects that he or she may want to focus on. Allow the child time to look for objects before giving him or her a variety of entertaining toys.
- Throughout the day, watch for the child to attend to an object, person, or event. For example, if the child looks at a balloon, give it to the child and label it as you do so. (Exercise safety precautions when using balloons.)

Environmental Arrangements

- The setting should be free of objects and events that compete for the child's attention and distract the child.
- If the child does not readily look at objects presented, produce an interesting visual or auditory event. For example, activate a squeeze-toy or musical toy or blow on a pin-

wheel to set it in motion. When the child looks at the object, comment on it so that the child knows he or she is looking at the object of your attention.

- If the child does not look at objects you present, follow the child's gaze and manipulate an object at which the child is looking. For example, if the child looks at a toy bear, make the bear "dance" and "talk" to the child.
- The child may not respond if the object is too far away. Check for an optimal distance, then vary the distance after the child responds consistently.
- Place a toy within the child's visual range. Move the object and wait for the child to relocate it.
- Partially wind up a mechanical toy. Wait for the child to look at it before rewinding.

Instructional Sequence

- Verbally encourage the child to look at an object.
- Gain the child's attention by gently or playfully touching the child with the object, then move the object to a position where the child can easily view it.
- Gently guide the child's face to the object of interest.

TEACHING CONSIDERATIONS

1. A child with a hearing impairment may hear only selected frequencies (high- or low-pitched sounds) or may hear only loud sounds. The child may also be sensitive to certain sounds or intensities (sounds that seem normal to you may be uncomfortably loud to some children, certain frequencies may be painful, combinations of sounds or too much noise may be uncomfortable).
2. A child with a visual impairment may orient his or her body toward the speaker rather than look at the speaker's face. If the child has some vision, the speaker should stand close enough for the child to see and should bring the object of interest into the child's visual range.
3. If the child has a severe visual impairment, use another sensory modality, such as sound, smell, or touch, to direct the child's attention toward an object. For example, when the doorbell rings, say, "Someone's at the door. Let's open it."
4. If a child has a restricted range of motion in the head or trunk, objects should be presented in positions other than where the child is visually focused, but still within the child's field of vision. Observe the child's gaze to see if he or she consistently focuses on the speaker or noise-producing objects. Consult a qualified specialist for individualized teaching ideas.
5. Pay careful attention to the child's reaction to tactile cues. Some children may find them aversive or may be sensitive to the amount or type of touch.

GOAL 3 Engages in vocal exchanges by babbling

SC A

IMPORTANCE OF SKILL

The relationship between babbling and the child's later use of language is not clearly understood. The purpose of this goal is to establish give-and-take communication between the child and others, which is fundamental to the development of conversational behavior. A second purpose is to encourage the child to practice a variety of consonant and vowel sounds.

PRECEDING OBJECTIVE

SC A:3.1   Engages in vocal exchanges by cooing

CONCURRENT GOALS AND OBJECTIVES

FM A:2.0   Brings two objects together at or near midline
FM A:3.2   Grasps cylindrical object with either hand by closing fingers around it
GM B:1.4   Sits balanced without support
Adap A:2.1   Bites *and* chews soft and crisp foods
Adap A:4.3   Accepts food presented on spoon
Cog C:2.0   Reproduces part of interactive game and/or action in order to continue game and/or action
Cog G:1.3   Uses simple motor actions on different objects
Soc A:1.2   Smiles in response to familiar adult
Soc A:2.2   Responds to familiar adult's social behavior

TEACHING SUGGESTIONS

Activity-Based

- During daily caregiving routines (e.g., feeding, diapering, bathing) or when the child is content and alert, stand close to the child and talk. Use a varied pitch and melody. Make simple consonant–vowel combinations and repeat them for the child to hear.
- Pause repeatedly to give the child an opportunity to respond. The child may first respond by quieting, watching you, or increasing activity. Begin talking to the child again when you observe a response.
- The child may experiment with making sounds when playing quietly or when alone. Provide opportunities for privacy for the child to practice sounds; then join the child's activity.
- Join the child's sound play. Mimic the child's sounds rather than expect the child to make the sounds you want.
- Use consonant-vowel combinations as interjections in your speech when appropriate, such as "bye-bye" when leaving, "uh-oh" when something drops, "boo-boo" when an accident occurs, or "OK" when you are expressing affirmation.
- Provide opportunities for the child to be with other young children who babble or talk. Younger voices may be more interesting and initiate a response more readily.
- Identify the times or activities when the child vocalizes most. Use these times to engage in babbling or cooing activities.

Environmental Arrangements

- Use exaggerated vocal and facial expressions to gain and maintain the child's attention. Songs and rhymes can be used, too.
- Try different vowel and consonant noises and observe which sounds the child seems to prefer. Repeat what the child says or add a new syllable. It is not necessary for the child to imitate your sounds.
- Play tactile and vocal games to make the child laugh or produce a sound; reinforce the child with talking and cuddling. "Pop" and "boo" are good combinations to include in games.
- Try different visual and auditory stimuli (e.g., musical bear) to gain the child's attention. Talk to the child and remove the stimulus. Present it again when the child makes a sound and talk to the child as you do so.

- The child may not respond if the speaker is too far away. Check for an optimal distance, then vary the distance after the child responds consistently. It often helps the child to see your face and mouth movements.
- Include interesting objects in the sound-play activities. The child may vocalize when mouthing, banging, or shaking objects. Imitate the child's actions with objects and sounds.
- Sit behind the child looking into a mirror. Watch each other making sounds. Pat the child's mouth as the child makes sounds to show how to turn long vocalizations into intermittent sounds with pauses. Have the child pat your mouth to make the same "stop" sounds. Let the child feel your mouth as you babble.
- Make a tape recording of a young child babbling and intersperse the babbling with pauses to allow the child to respond. Play the tape for the child during quiet play times.

Instructional Sequence

- Imitate the child's sounds as the child babbles. Wait for the child to start again. It may be necessary to build turn-taking one turn at a time.
- Touch your fingers to your mouth and make a labial sound such as "ba" or "ma." Touch the child's mouth with your fingers as a cue that it is the child's turn.
- Touch the child's fingers to your mouth as you make sounds. Then touch the child's fingers to the child's mouth as a cue.

TEACHING CONSIDERATIONS

1. A child with a hearing impairment may hear only selected frequencies (high- or low-pitched sounds) or may hear only loud sounds. The child may also be sensitive to certain sounds or intensities (sounds that seem normal to you may be uncomfortably loud to some children, certain frequencies may be painful, combinations of sounds or too much noise may be uncomfortable).
2. A child with a visual impairment may orient his or her body toward the speaker rather than look at the speaker's face. If the child has some vision, the speaker should stand close enough for the child to see. Allow the child to use his or her hands to feel the speaker making sounds.
3. If the child has a severe visual impairment, allow the child to use his or her hands to feel the speaker making sounds. Encourage the child to babble in return. Consult a specialist for information on vocal skills for this child.
4. If a child has a restricted range of motion in the head or trunk, the speaker should stand close enough to facilitate visual contact with the child. Positioning is also critical to easy sound production. Latency of response may be noted. Consult a qualified specialist for recommendations for positioning and techniques to elicit sounds from a child with a motor impairment.

Objective 3.1 Engages in vocal exchanges by cooing

IMPORTANCE OF SKILL

The relationship between cooing and the child's later use of language is not clearly understood. The purpose of this objective is to establish give-and-take communication

SCA

between the child and other people, which is fundamental to the development of conversational behavior. A second purpose is to encourage the child to practice using a variety of vowel sounds.

CONCURRENT GOALS AND OBJECTIVES

FM A:2.0   Brings two objects together at or near midline
GM A:3.5   Bears weight on one hand and/or arm while reaching with opposite hand
GM B:1.6   Holds head in midline when in supported sitting position
Adap A:1.0 Uses tongue and lips to take in and swallow solid foods and liquids
Adap A:2.2 Munches soft and crisp foods
Cog C:2.1   Indicates desire to continue familiar game and/or action
Cog G:1.4   Uses sensory examination with objects
Soc A:1.2   Smiles in response to familiar adult
Soc A:2.2   Responds to familiar adult's social behavior

TEACHING SUGGESTIONS

Activity-Based

- During daily caregiving routines (e.g., feeding, diapering, bathing) and when the child is content and alert, stand close to the child and talk. Use a varied pitch and melody.
- Pause repeatedly to give the child an opportunity to respond. The child may first respond by quieting, watching you, or increasing activity. Begin talking to the child again when you observe a response.
- After a bath or diaper change, let the child talk to him- or herself in front of a mirror.
- While rocking the child, hum or sing softly, encouraging the child to participate. Wait for a response and reward the child for responding by singing more.
- Young children are often observed cooing quietly to themselves when they are content and alone; for example, after waking from a nap. Join the interaction and follow the child's lead.
- Identify the times or activities when the child vocalizes most. Use these times to engage in babbling or cooing.

Environmental Arrangements

- Use exaggerated vocal and facial expressions to gain and maintain the child's attention. "Mmm good" at mealtime or "ooh" and "ah" while applying lotion are examples of sounds that accompany events pleasurable to the child.
- Try different vowel and consonant noises and observe which sounds the child seems to prefer.
- Play tactile and vocal games to make the child laugh or produce any sound and then reinforce the child by talking and cuddling. "Goochy goo," "gotcha," and "Piggy Went to Market" are favorites.
- Try different visual and auditory stimuli (e.g., musical bear) to gain the child's attention. Talk to the child and remove the stimulus. Present it again when the child makes a sound and talk to the child as you do.
- The child may not respond if a speaker is too far away. Check for an optimal distance, then vary the distance after the child responds consistently. It is often easiest to start from a face-to-face position.

SC A

■ Include interesting objects in the sound-play activities. The child may vocalize when mouthing, banging, or shaking objects. Imitate the child's actions with objects and sounds.

Instructional Sequence

■ Imitate the child's vocalizations. Wait for the child to start again. It may be necessary to build turn-taking one turn at a time.
■ With the child lying on your legs, use touch cues such as gentle stroking to help initiate a vocalization. Take your turn and help the child again.
■ As the child makes sounds with an object or while eating, gently guide the object away, take your turn vocalizing, and return the object to the child to repeat sound play. Continue interrupting and taking your turn until the child begins to take turns without your physical guidance.

TEACHING CONSIDERATIONS

1. A child with a hearing impairment may hear only selected frequencies (high- or low-pitched sounds) or may hear only loud sounds. The child may also be sensitive to certain sounds or intensities (sounds that seem normal to you may be uncomfortably loud to some children, certain frequencies may be painful, combinations of sounds or too much noise may be uncomfortable).
2. A child with a visual impairment may orient his or her body toward the speaker rather than look at the speaker's face. If the child has some vision, the speaker should stand close enough for the child to see. Allow the child to feel you make sounds by holding his or her hands on your lips or throat.
3. If the child has a severe visual impairment, allow the child to use his or her hands to feel the speaker making sounds. Encourage the child to coo in return. Consult a specialist for information on vocal skills for this child.
4. If a child has a restricted range of motion in the head or trunk, the speaker should stand close enough to facilitate visual contact with the child. Positioning is also critical to easy sound production. Latency of response may be noted. Consult a qualified specialist for recommendations for positioning and techniques for eliciting sounds from a child with a motor impairment.

SC A

Strand B

Transition to Words

GOAL 1 Gains person's attention and refers to an object, person, and/or event

---

DEVELOPMENTAL PROGRAMMING STEPS

No standard developmental sequence appears to exist for the development of these pragmatic skills. Careful observation of the child will help determine the child's current skill level. Begin programming at the child's level of interest.

PS1.0a   The child gains a person's attention.

PS1.0b   The child establishes joint reference to an object, person, or event.

IMPORTANCE OF SKILL

Prior to comprehension and production of words, most children vocalize or gesture for a variety of communicative functions. Vocalizations and gestures are called prelinguistic communication signals because they precede symbolic language. It is important to establish a relationship between a vocalization or gesture from the child and some response from the environment. From this relationship, the child learns that communication signals serve a variety of functions and allow the child to gain a person's attention and refer to an object, person, or event. Eventually, vocalizations and gestures are shaped into more conventional language forms (i.e., first words).

PRECEDING OBJECTIVE

SC B:1.2   Points to an object, person, and/or event

CONCURRENT GOALS AND OBJECTIVE

FM A:2.3   Reaches toward and touches object with each hand

FM B:2.0   Assembles toy and/or object that require(s) putting pieces together

GM C:1.0   Walks avoiding obstacles

Adap A:3.0   Drinks from cup and/or glass

Adap A:4.0   Eats with fork and/or spoon

Adap B:1.0   Initiates toileting

Cog B:3.0   Maintains search for object that is not in its usual location

Cog C:2.0   Reproduces part of interactive game and/or action in order to continue game and/or action

Cog D:1.0   Imitates motor action that is not commonly used
SC A:2.0   Follows person's gaze to establish joint attention
SC A:3.0   Engages in vocal exchanges by babbling
Soc A:3.0   Initiates and maintains communicative exchange with familiar adult

TEACHING SUGGESTIONS
Activity-Based

- Encourage the child to draw your attention to objects and events by responding to the child and continuing the interaction.
- As events occur throughout the day, pretend not to notice immediately, giving the child an opportunity to direct your attention. For example, let the phone ring an extra ring or two, or use a kitchen timer, alarm clock, or doorbell to initiate a response.
- Use gestures with your words. For example, say, "Bye-bye," and wave or say, "Do you want up?" and hold out your hands. These frequent models are easily imitated by the child.
- Respond to the child's vocalizations and gestures in a variety of settings so that the child learns to gain attention in many situations. Watch for the child to indicate interest at the store, in the car, or at playtime with familiar and unfamiliar people. Respond consistently.

☑ If your data indicate the child is not making progress toward the goal, provide additional structure within the suggested activities by incorporating the following *environmental arrangements:*

Environmental Arrangements

- Arrange the play area so that desired toys are visible to the child but just out of reach. Wait for the child to use a vocalization or a gesture to gain your attention and refer to a desired toy. Then give the toy to the child.
- Show the child a noise-producing object such as a musical toy. Activate the toy and observe the child's response. If the child uses a vocalization or gesture, give the toy to the child. Wait for the child to use a vocalization or gesture to gain your attention and refer to the object, then reactivate the toy and give it to the child.
- When the child is consistently focusing on objects, people, or events of interest, refrain from offering the desired material until the child uses a gesture or vocalization to gain your attention and refers to the object, person, or event of interest. For example, when giving a snack to peers or siblings, wait until the child uses a vocalization or gesture to gain your attention and refers to the food or the other child eating. Then give the child the desired snack.
- The child may not attempt to gain your attention if you are too far away. Check for an optimal distance, then vary the distance after the child responds consistently.

☑ If this goal is particularly difficult for a child, it may be necessary, within activities, to use an *instructional sequence*.

Instructional Sequence

- Model gaining a person's attention to refer to an object. For example, say, "Ginny, would you like a cracker?"
- Systematically introduce the use of time delay and visual cues. For instance, during snack time, show the child a desired snack, establish eye contact, and give an expec-

tant look. Wait for the child to vocalize or use a gesture to refer to the desired food, then give it to the child.

■ Gestures are easy to model. Any looking, vocalizing, or motor gesture that can be shaped into a communicative signal should be encouraged and reinforced. Cues should be consistent and redundant, and all opportunities should be capitalized.

■ Show the child an interesting toy placed just out of reach and provide a verbal cue, "Show me what you want." Once the child is consistently vocalizing or gesturing to refer to the object, vary the distance between the object and the child.

■ When playing with the child, provide verbal and physical cues. For example, say, "Show me what you want." Then point to or move the desired toy closer to the child. Gently guide the child's hand toward the toy.

☑ Combining or pairing different levels of instructions may be helpful when beginning to teach a new and difficult skill. Fade to less intrusive instructions as soon as possible to encourage more independent performance.

TEACHING CONSIDERATIONS

1. The child's vocalizations need not approximate actual words.
2. Socially appropriate gestures and vocalizations should be modeled and encouraged to facilitate the child's acquisition of conventional and acceptable attention-getting behaviors.
3. A child with a visual impairment may orient his or her body toward the adult rather than look at the adult's face. Adaptations of conventional gestures may be necessary.
4. If the child has a restricted range of motion, the adult should stand in a position other than where the child is visually focused, but still within the child's field of vision. Adaptations of conventional gestures may be necessary.
5. A child with a hearing impairment may be acquiring an augmentative or alternative communication system such as a picture or sign system. Consult a qualified specialist for teaching techniques.

Objective 1.1	Responds with a vocalization and gesture to simple questions

---

DEVELOPMENTAL PROGRAMMING STEPS

No standard developmental sequence appears to exist for the development of prelinguistic or social-communicative signals. Careful observation of the child will help determine the function of early communicative vocalizations and gestures. Begin programming at the child's level of interest.

PS1.1a Confirmation function: For example, the adult asks, "May I have the doll?" The child vocalizes and uses "giving" gestures.

PS1.1b Comment/reply function: For example, the adult asks, "What did you do?" The child vocalizes and uses "showing" gestures.

PS1.1c Information function: For example, the adult asks, "Where is the ball?" The child vocalizes and uses "pointing" gestures.

PS1.1d Request function: For example, the adult asks, "Do you want toast?" The child vocalizes and uses "reaching" gestures.

IMPORTANCE OF SKILL

Communication signals serve a variety of functions and the child learns of the relationship between a vocalization or gesture and a response from the environment. This skill is an important step toward successful communication. For example, the adult asks, "Do you want up?" and the child raises his or her arms and vocalizes before the adult picks him or her up. This skill allows the child to respond to questions as well as make requests. Eventually, vocalizations and gestures are shaped into more conventional language forms (words).

PRECEDING GOAL

SC A:1.0   Turns and looks toward person speaking

CONCURRENT GOALS AND OBJECTIVE

FM A:2.3   Reaches toward and touches object with each hand
FM B:2.0   Assembles toy and/or object that require(s) putting pieces together
GM C:1.0   Walks avoiding obstacles
Adap A:3.0 Drinks from cup and/or glass
Adap A:4.0 Eats with fork and/or spoon
Adap B:1.0 Initiates toileting
Cog B:3.0   Maintains search for object that is not in its usual location
Cog C:2.0   Reproduces part of interactive game and/or action in order to continue game and/or action
Cog D:1.0   Imitates motor action that is not commonly used
SC A:2.0   Follows person's gaze to establish joint attention
SC A:3.0   Engages in vocal exchanges by babbling
Soc A:3.0   Initiates and maintains communicative exchange with familiar adult

TEACHING SUGGESTIONS
Activity-Based

- Throughout the day, talk to the child about routine activities and ask simple questions. For example, while filling the tub with water for a bath, talk to the child about the floating toys you put in the water. Ask the child, "What do you want?" and encourage the child to reach for the toys. Always pause to give the child time to vocalize or gesture before letting the child play with the toys. Ask what the child is playing with to encourage a showing gesture.
- When asking questions, use objects, people, or events with which the child is most familiar and readily responds. For example, when a sibling is walking through the door, ask, "Where's Billy?" and observe if the child vocalizes or looks toward the sibling. React by smiling and say, "That's right, there's Billy!"
- Ask questions and respond to the child's vocalizations and gestures in a variety of settings so that the child learns to respond in many situations. It is important to establish the child's interest in communicating with a variety of people, in different places, and at different times.

SC B

Environmental Arrangements

- Use exaggerated vocal and facial expressions when asking the child simple questions. For example, ask the child, "Where is teddy?" emphasizing the word teddy. Wait for the child to vocalize or gesture, then give the child the teddy bear.
- During snack time, give the child just one piece of a favorite finger food. Place the next piece of food outside the child's reach and ask, "What do you want?" When the child looks, vocalizes, and reaches, say, "Here's a pretzel," and give the child the pretzel to eat.
- Use questions paired with familiar games and activities. For example, cover the child's head with a diaper and say, "Where's baby?" Wait for the child to vocalize or gesture, then uncover and say, "There's baby." Repeat several times.

Instructional Sequence

- Model answering a simple question with both a vocalization and gesture.
- Systematically introduce the use of time delay and visual cues. For instance, during snack time, show the child a desired snack, establish eye contact, and give an expectant look. Wait for the child to vocalize or use a gesture to refer to the desired food, then give it to the child.
- Gestures are easy to model. Any looking, vocalizing, or motor gesture that can be shaped into a communicative signal should be encouraged and reinforced. Cues should be consistent and redundant and all opportunities should be used.
- Hold an interesting or bright-colored toy close to your face and ask the child, "What do you want?" When the child vocalizes or looks at the toy, smile and give the child the toy. Gradually vary the distance between the toy and your face until the toy is just outside of the child's reach.
- When the child is content and alert, hold out your arms and ask, "Do you want up?" If the child does not vocalize or gesture, gently put your hands under the child's arms and repeat the question. Wait for any slight movement or vocalization, then pick the child up. Systematically introduce vocal-gestural combinations.

TEACHING CONSIDERATIONS

1. The child's vocalizations do not need to approximate actual words.
2. Be consistent about requiring a response from the child before reinforcing the child in all contexts.
3. The child may not respond if the adult is too far away. Check for an optimal distance, then vary the distance after the child responds consistently.
4. A child with a visual impairment may orient his or her body toward the adult rather than look at the adult's face. Adaptations of conventional gestures may be necessary.
5. If the child has a restricted range of motion, the adult should stand in a position other than where the child is visually focused, but still within the child's field of vision. Adaptations of conventional gestures may be necessary.
6. A child with a hearing impairment may be acquiring an augmentative or alternative communication system such as a picture or sign system. Consult a qualified specialist for teaching techniques.

SC B

Objective 1.2 Points to an object, person, and/or event

DEVELOPMENTAL PROGRAMMING STEPS

No standard developmental sequence appears to exist for the development of prelinguistic or social-communicative signals. Careful observation of the child will help determine the function of early communicative vocalizations and gestures. Begin programming at the child's level of interest.

PS1.2a   Confirmation function: For example, the adult says, "There's the ball." The child points to the ball.

PS1.2b   Comment/reply function: For example, the adult asks, "What happened?" The child points to spilled milk.

PS1.2c   Information function: For example, the adult asks, "Where's your teddy?" The child points to the teddy bear.

PS1.2d   Request function: For example, the child points to a bottle. The adult asks, "Do you want your bottle?"

PS1.2e   Attention function: For example, the child points to a sibling jumping in a swimming pool. The adult says, "There's Billy."

PS1.2f   Question function: For example, the child points to a new stuffed animal. The adult says, "What's that?"

PS1.2g   Comment/describe function: For example, the child points to a truck. The adult says, "That's a truck."

IMPORTANCE OF SKILL

Communication signals serve a variety of functions and the child learns of the relationship between a vocalization or gesture and a response from the environment. This skill is an important step toward successful communication. For example, the child points to a desired object and the adult gives the object to the child to play with. Eventually, vocalizations and gestures are shaped into more conventional language forms (first words).

PRECEDING GOAL

SC A:1.0   Turns and looks toward person speaking

CONCURRENT GOALS AND OBJECTIVE

FM A:2.3   Reaches toward and touches object with each hand
FM B:2.0   Assembles toy and/or object that require(s) putting pieces together
GM C:1.0   Walks avoiding obstacles
Adap A:3.0 Drinks from cup and/or glass
Adap A:4.0 Eats with fork and/or spoon
Adap B:1.0 Initiates toileting
Cog B:3.0 Maintains search for object that is not in its usual location
Cog C:2.0 Reproduces part of interactive game and/or action in order to continue game and/or action

SC B

Cog D:1.0   Imitates motor action that is not commonly used
SC A:2.0   Follows person's gaze to establish joint attention
SC A:3.0   Engages in vocal exchanges by babbling
Soc A:3.0   Initiates and maintains communicative exchange with familiar adult

TEACHING SUGGESTIONS
Activity-Based

- While bathing, name body parts and ask the child to point to them. When the child touches a body part, say, "That's right! That's your foot." Repeat with different body parts.
- If the child is reaching for or pointing to a favorite toy, label it, talk about it, and give it to the child to play with.
- While reading a book, name the pictures that the child points to. Take turns pointing to favorite pictures and add new ones.
- During trips to new places, watch the child's gaze, name the objects and events the child looks at, and model pointing.

Environmental Arrangements

- Play "This Little Piggy Went to Market" and point to the child's toes. Then ask the child to point to your toes as you say the rhyme.
- During snack, give the child a small piece of cracker (or any favorite food). Put the next piece just out of the child's reach and ask, "Where's the cracker?" Wait for the child to reach for or point to the cracker and then give it to the child to eat.
- To encourage the child who does not point, offer two items (preferred and nonpreferred). Give the child the nonpreferred item while you hold the preferred item and wait for a gesture.
- Hold two objects, one a bright-colored or musical toy and the other a plain toy. Ask the child, "What do you want?" Wait for the child to reach for or point to the desired toy, then give it to the child.
- Use songs and finger plays that incorporate use of pointing.

Instructional Sequence

- Model pointing to an object or person and comment.
- Systematically introduce the use of time delay and visual cues. For instance, during snack time, show the child a desired snack, establish eye contact, and give an expectant look. Wait for the child to use a gesture to refer to the desired food, then give it to the child.
- Pointing is easy to model. Be consistent about requiring a response before reinforcing the child in all contexts. Cues should be consistent and redundant and all opportunities should be used.
- While looking at books, verbally instruct the child to find certain items in pictures. Encourage a single-finger pointing response.
- Show the child common objects around the house and hold them within the child's reach. Name them one at a time and ask the child, "Where's the ball?" Gently guide the child's hand toward the object. Repeat with different objects.
- While the child is bathing, name and touch the child's body parts. The child may relate to body parts more easily than objects at this stage of development. Ask the child to point to his or her own foot. If the child does not respond, gently guide the child's hand to the foot. Repeat with different body parts.

TEACHING CONSIDERATIONS

1. Respond to the child's vocalizations and gestures in a variety of settings so that the child learns to respond in many situations.
2. A child with a visual impairment may orient his or her body toward the adult rather than look at the adult's face. Adaptations of conventional gestures may be necessary.
3. If the child has a severe visual impairment, use another sensory modality, such as sound, smell, or touch, to direct the child's attention to an object, person, or event. Encourage the child to use the modality independently.
4. If the child has a restricted range of motion, the adult should stand in a position other than where the child is visually focused, but still within the child's field of vision. Adaptations of conventional gestures may be necessary.
5. A child with a hearing impairment may be acquiring an augmentative or alternative communication system such as a picture or sign system. Consult a qualified specialist for teaching techniques.

Objective 1.3 Gestures and/or vocalizes to greet others

DEVELOPMENTAL PROGRAMMING STEP

No standard developmental sequence appears to exist for the development of prelinguistic or social-communicative signals. Careful observation of the child will help determine the function of early communicative vocalizations and gestures. Begin programming at the child's level of interest.

PS1.3a Greet function: The child gestures or vocalizes to greet others. For example, when a sibling enters the room, the child vocalizes or uses a waving gesture. The adult enters the room and the child vocalizes or uses an "up" reaching gesture.

IMPORTANCE OF SKILL

Communication signals serve a variety of functions and the child learns the relationship between a vocalization and gesture and a response from the environment. This skill is an important step toward successful communication. For example, an adult enters the room and the child vocalizes and reaches toward the adult. The adult says, "Hello," and picks up the child. The child learns that the greeting function gains attention from the adult, and the child learns to acknowledge others. Eventually, vocalizations and gestures are shaped into more conventional language forms (first words).

PRECEDING GOAL

SC A:1.0 Turns and looks toward person speaking

CONCURRENT GOALS AND OBJECTIVE

FM A:2.3 Reaches toward and touches object with each hand
FM B:2.0 Assembles toy and/or object that require(s) putting pieces together
GM C:1.0 Walks avoiding obstacles

SC B

Adap B:1.0 Initiates toileting
Cog B:3.0 Maintains search for object that is not in its usual location
Cog C:2.0 Reproduces part of interactive game and/or action in order to continue game and/or action
Cog D:1.0 Imitates motor action that is not commonly used
SC A:2.0 Follows person's gaze to establish joint attention
SC A:3.0 Engages in vocal exchanges by babbling
Soc A:3.0 Initiates and maintains communicative exchange with familiar adult

TEACHING SUGGESTIONS
Activity-Based

- Throughout the day, when friends and family members enter or leave a room, wave and say, "Hi," or "Bye." Be consistent.
- When putting toys away, say, "Bye-bye," and wave to each one.
- Stand at the door or hold the child to look out the window at persons approaching or leaving. Say, "Wave bye-bye," or "Wave hello."
- Initially, it may be helpful to choose people to whom the child most readily responds. However, it is important to respond to the child's vocalizations or gestures in a variety of settings so that the child learns to respond in many situations.

Environmental Arrangements

- Sing hello and good-bye songs to friends in a group.
- Have a helper peek from behind a screen and say, "Hello," and wave. Say, "Hello," and wave back. Have the helper go behind the screen, come out again, and say, "Hello," with a wave.
- Put a blanket or cloth diaper over the child's head for a moment and say, "Bye-bye." Use exaggerated question intonation, "Where's baby?" Wait for the child to vocalize or gesture, remove the cover, and say, "Hello." Repeat several times, alternating between putting the cover over your head and the child's head.
- Use books such as *Hello, Kitty* and greet favorite pictures in stories.

Instructional Sequence

- Model using exaggerated waving gestures when someone enters or leaves the room. Gradually decrease to more appropriate waves. Wait to see if the child vocalizes or waves.
- Waving is easy to model. Be consistent about requiring a response before reinforcing the child in all contexts. Any looking, vocalizing, or motor gesture that can be shaped into a communicative signal should be encouraged and reinforced. Cues should be consistent and redundant, and all opportunities should be used.
- When a person leaves the room, wave and say, "Wave bye-bye." Be consistent about requiring a response before reinforcing the child in all contexts.
- Ask the child to wave to a person entering or leaving the room. If the child does not vocalize or gesture, say, "Wave bye-bye," and gently guide the child's hand to wave.

TEACHING CONSIDERATIONS

1. Teach skills in appropriate contexts.
2. Respond to the child's vocalizations or gestures in a variety of settings so that the child learns to respond in many situations.

SC B

3. A child may not respond if the adult is too far away. Check for an optimal distance, then vary the distance after the child responds consistently.
4. A child with a visual impairment may orient his or her body toward the adult rather than look at the adult's face. Adaptations of conventional gestures may be necessary.
5. The child with a severe visual impairment may need assistance to recognize the presence of another. For example, say, "Listen—Billy came in the door."
6. If the child has a restricted range of motion, the adult should stand in a position other than where the child is visually focused, but still within the child's field of vision. Adaptations of conventional gestures may be necessary.
7. A child with a hearing impairment may be acquiring an augmentative or alternative communication system such as a picture or sign system. Consult a qualified specialist for teaching techniques.

Objective 1.4   Uses gestures and/or vocalizations to protest actions and/or reject objects or people

---

DEVELOPMENTAL PROGRAMMING STEPS

No standard developmental sequence appears to exist for the development of prelinguistic or social-communicative signals. Careful observation of the child will help determine the function of early communicative vocalizations and gestures. Begin programming at the child's level of interest.

PS1.4a   Protest function: The child gestures or vocalizes displeasure. For example, the adult puts the child in a crib and the child expresses a negative vocalization (cries).

PS1.4b   Rejection function: The child gestures or vocalizes refusal. For example, the adult puts a bottle to the child's mouth; the child closes his or her mouth and turns away. The adult offers the child a toy; the child pushes the toy away. The adult gives the child a cracker; the child drops the cracker.

IMPORTANCE OF SKILL

Communication signals serve a variety of functions and the child learns the relationship between a vocalization and gesture and a response from the environment. This skill is an important step toward successful communication. It is valuable for the child to express preferences as a way to gain control over activities in the environment. For example, a clear "no" signal from the child that is respected by others helps the child learn the significance of communication and paves the way for making positive choices. Eventually, vocalizations and gestures are shaped into more conventional language forms (first words).

PRECEDING GOAL

SC A:1.0   Turns and looks toward person speaking

CONCURRENT GOALS AND OBJECTIVE

FM A:2.3   Reaches toward and touches object with each hand
FM B:2.0   Assembles toy and/or object that require(s) putting pieces together

SC B

GM C:1.0   Walks avoiding obstacles
Adap A:3.0 Drinks from cup and/or glass
Adap A:4.0 Eats with fork and/or spoon
Adap B:1.0 Initiates toileting
Cog B:3.0   Maintains search for object that is not in its usual location
Cog C:2.0   Reproduces part of interactive game and/or action in order to continue game and/or action
Cog D:1.0   Imitates motor action that is not commonly used
SC A:2.0   Follows person's gaze to establish joint attention
SC A:3.0   Engages in vocal exchanges by babbling
Soc A:3.0   Initiates and maintains communicative exchange with familiar adult

TEACHING SUGGESTIONS
Activity-Based

- Allow the child time to communicate his or her likes and dislikes by responding to people and objects before you introduce new ones. Try not to guess who or what the child prefers, but allow the child time to demonstrate preferences. It may be necessary to initially accept minimal responses from the child.
- When peers argue over sharing toys, taking turns, or choosing seats, give the child ample opportunity to protest or reject the peer's behavior before interfering.
- Give the child multiple opportunities to protest or reject by asking, "Do you want ___?" or "Do you like ___?" in situations where a rejection is reasonable. Give the child choices of food, clothing, and activities so that it is necessary to reject one option.
- If the child protests or rejects activities, food, toys, clothes, or people, make every effort to respect reasonable responses. For example, say, "Oh, you don't like that"; or stop tickling if a child says, "No," or squirms away.

Environmental Arrangements

- Observe the child throughout the day to determine which toys are of particular interest. Offer two objects, one that is known to be particularly desirable, such as a musical toy, and one that is not. Ask the child which object is preferred while offering the undesired object first. Both objects should be within the child's view.
- It may be helpful to have a sibling demonstrate preferences during snack time. Ask a sibling, "Do you want this?" and have the sibling say, "No," and shake his or her head. Repeat several times varying yes and no answers.
- During initial gestural training, practice action games such as "pat-a-cake" and "So big" to help the child learn to associate actions with words and events. These games also help the child learn to imitate your actions.
- Name a common object that the child consistently responds to, such as a cup. Provide the child with opportunities to express preferences by letting the child make simple decisions that you are willing to abide by. Ask, "Do you want a drink?", "Do you want to get up?", or "Do you want to rock?" Gesture and show objects, if possible, to give the child cues; then pretend to forget the object's name. Hold a cup and say, "Here's your nose." Observe to see if the child vocalizes or gestures, then laugh and say, "No, this isn't your nose. It's a cup!"
- Read or make up stories describing children who demonstrate protesting and refusing.

SC B

Instructional Sequence

- Model refusing food that you do not want by shaking your head and saying, "No, thank you."
- Cues should be consistent and redundant and all opportunities should be used. Systematically introduce the use of time delay and visual cues.
- Protesting or rejecting is easy to model. Verbally direct the child to say, "No, thank you" if he or she does not want a toy or food. Be consistent about requiring a response before reinforcing the child in all contexts.
- During snack time, offer the child a food that you know he or she dislikes. Wait for the child to show preferences. If the child does not respond, gently guide the child's hand to push the food aside.

TEACHING CONSIDERATIONS

1. Respond to the child's vocalizations and gestures in a variety of settings so that the child learns to gain attention in many situations.
2. The most conventional gestures are pushing objects away, shaking the head "no," turning away, and holding a hand up and out. Any vocalization or motor gesture that can be shaped into a communicative signal should be encouraged and reinforced.
3. The child's vocalizations do not need to approximate actual words.
4. The child may cease to vocalize and gesture if the adult is too far away. Check for an optimal distance. Do not leave before the child has an opportunity to respond.
5. A child with a visual impairment may orient his or her body toward the adult rather than look at the adult's face. Adaptations of conventional gestures may be necessary.
6. If the child has a restricted range of motion, the adult should stand in a position other than where the child is visually focused, but still within the child's field of vision. Adaptations of conventional gestures may be necessary.
7. For the child with a hearing impairment, make sure gestures are consistent, precise, and initially context-related. The child with a hearing impairment may be acquiring an augmentative or alternative communication system such as a picture or sign system. Consult a qualified specialist for teaching techniques.

GOAL 2   Uses consistent word approximations

DEVELOPMENTAL PROGRAMMING STEPS

☑ The goal above is the most basic step for the skill to be taught. Most children will benefit from the activities outlined here that emphasize this skill. For children who need more instruction, consider designing programming steps from the *environmental arrangements* suggestions or from the *instructional sequence* outlined.

IMPORTANCE OF SKILL

Prior to comprehension and production of words, most children use consistent speech sound combinations to refer to objects, people, or events. These communication sounds

SCB

precede symbolic language and are used to request, protest, inform, and direct attention. It is important to establish a relationship between communication sounds by the child and some response from the environment. From this relationship, the child learns that communication sounds serve a variety of functions. This skill is an important step toward successful communication. Over time, the child's sounds become word approximations, and the child uses them consistently to refer to the same object, person, or event. Eventually, the word approximations are shaped into more conventional language forms (first words).

PRECEDING OBJECTIVE

SC B:2.2   Uses nonspecific consonant–vowel combinations and/or jargon

CONCURRENT GOALS

Cog B:3.0   Maintains search for object that is not in its usual location
Cog C:2.0   Reproduces part of interactive game and/or action in order to continue game and/or action
Cog D:1.0   Imitates motor action that is not commonly used
Cog D:2.0   Imitates words that are not frequently used
Soc A:3.0   Initiates and maintains communicative exchange with familiar adult

TEACHING SUGGESTIONS

To achieve this goal, a child must perform the Objectives 2.1–2.2 to criteria. Refer to the specific objective for Teaching Suggestions and Teaching Considerations to develop each skill.

Objective 2.1   Uses consistent consonant–vowel combinations

IMPORTANCE OF SKILL

This skill is an important step toward successful communication, as consistent speech sound combinations are used to refer to objects, people, or events. Over time, the child's consonant–vowel sounds become word approximations and the child uses the same sound to refer to the same object, person, or event. For example, the child consistently points to a truck and says, "Da." Eventually, the child's consonant–vowel combinations are shaped into more conventional language forms (first words).

PRECEDING GOALS

SC A:1.0   Turns and looks toward person speaking
SC A:2.0   Follows person's gaze to establish joint attention
SC A:3.0   Engages in vocal exchanges by babbling

CONCURRENT GOALS

Cog B:3.0   Maintains search for object that is not in its usual location
Cog C:2.0   Reproduces part of interactive game and/or action in order to continue game and/or action

SC B

Cog D:1.0   Imitates motor action that is not commonly used
Cog D:2.0   Imitates words that are not frequently used
Soc A:3.0   Initiates and maintains communicative exchange with familiar adult

TEACHING SUGGESTIONS
Activity-Based

- When playing with, dressing, or feeding the child, imitate the sounds the child makes. Once reciprocal imitation is established, expand upon the child's repertoire by lengthening the sound sequence or adding new sounds.
- Maximize every opportunity to practice the consistent word approximations the child uses. Say, "Hi," and "Bye," when arriving or leaving. Wait for the child to request "more," not just at meals, but when reading books, stacking blocks, or playing games.
- Respond consistently to the child's verbalizations, even when those sounds bear little resemblance to words. Be persistent in attempting to identify objects, people, and events to pair with early word approximations. Repeat correct labels for the child.
- During routine activities, give the child many opportunities to vocalize and receive desired objects of interest. For example, while bathing, hold a desired float-toy and encourage the child to vocalize to receive the toy. The adult may model the appropriate response.
- Sit with the child and look at books. Point to pictures and name them and encourage the child to do the same.
- "Talk" to each other on toy telephones.
- Play repetitious nursery games such as "So big" and "Seek" to encourage approximation of common key words.

Environmental Arrangements

- Throughout the day, when playing with the child, place desired toys out of reach. For example, if stacking blocks, give the child one block, but place the others out of reach. Wait for the child to use the appropriate word approximation before giving the child another block.
- Play a naming game. Use the names of common objects and people throughout the day. Wait for the child to use the appropriate word combination, then imitate. If the child does not respond, repeat the model.
- Use exaggerated vocal expressions when naming interesting objects or pictures. For example, push a brightly painted train on a track and say, "Choo choo."
- Position the child so that your faces are close. Move your lips slowly and distinctly, varying pitch and intonation. Encourage all vocalizations.
- Set up a turn-taking game using word approximations and objects. For example, say, "block" and drop a block into a bucket, or say, "ball" and roll the ball to the child. Encourage the child to say the word approximation before performing the action.
- Throughout the day, observe the child's responses toward objects, people, and events to determine those to which the child most readily responds. When the child focuses on the desired object, person, or event, ask the child to vocalize. For example, as a sibling blows bubbles, ask the child, "What's that?" Wait for the child to respond, then model appropriate vocalization, "Pop, pop," if necessary.
- While bathing, encourage the child to touch and name his or her own body parts. For example, touch the child's foot and say, "What's this?" Give the child time to respond, then model appropriate vocalization if necessary.

SC B

Instructional Sequence

- Model using words that you want the child to imitate when you reach for food or toys.
- Systematically introduce the use of time delay and visual cues. For instance, during snack time, show the child a desired snack, establish eye contact, and give an expectant look. Wait for the child to vocalize to refer to the desired food, then give it to the child.
- Throughout the day, observe the child's responses toward objects, people, or events to determine those to which the child most readily responds. For example, when the child focuses on a desired object, ask the child, "What do you want?" Wait for the child to respond, then model an appropriate vocalization if necessary before giving the child the object to play with.
- Encourage the child to imitate. Use the initial sound of a consonant–vowel combination as a cue.
- Touch the child's lips as a cue to vocalize after you have modeled a consonant–vowel combination.

TEACHING CONSIDERATIONS

1. Words that are important to the family and are used throughout the child's environment are words that should be emphasized when practicing this skill.
2. Choose objects, people, and events to which the child most readily responds.
3. Be consistent about requiring a response from the child before reinforcing.
4. For the child with a visual impairment, touch cues are useful as a beginning step to learn to identify objects by their feel. Use sensory modalities other than visual whenever possible.
5. If the child has a restricted range of motion in the head or trunk, the speaker should be in a position that facilitates visual contact between the child and the speaker. Positioning will also be critical for easy sound production. Latency of response may be noted. Consult a qualified specialist for recommendations for positioning and techniques to elicit sounds from a child with a motor impairment.
6. A child with a hearing impairment may hear only selected frequencies (high- or low-pitched sounds) or may hear only loud sounds. The child may also be sensitive to certain sounds or intensities (sounds that seem normal to you may be uncomfortably loud to some children, certain frequencies may be painful, combinations of sounds or too much noise may be uncomfortable).
7. The child with a hearing impairment may be acquiring an augmentative or alternative communication system such as a picture or sign system. Consult a qualified specialist for teaching techniques.

Objective 2.2   Uses nonspecific consonant–vowel combinations and/or jargon

---

IMPORTANCE OF SKILL

Prior to comprehension and production of words, most children use consistent speech sound combinations with rising and falling intonation, such as, "ah-ba-ba-da," to relate to the environment in some way. Over time, the child's consonant–vowel sounds or jargon become specific to certain objects, people, or events. With practice, the sounds become word approximations, and eventually the child's consonant–vowel combinations are shaped into more conventional language forms (words).

PRECEDING GOAL

SC A:3.0   Engages in vocal exchanges by babbling

CONCURRENT GOALS

Cog B:3.0   Maintains search for object that is not in its usual location
Cog C:2.0   Reproduces part of interactive game and/or action in order to continue game and/or action
Cog D:1.0   Imitates motor action that is not commonly used
Cog D:2.0   Imitates words that are not frequently used
Soc A:3.0   Initiates and maintains communicative exchange with familiar adult

TEACHING SUGGESTIONS
Activity-Based

- When playing with, dressing, or feeding the child, imitate the sounds he or she makes. Once reciprocal imitation is established, expand upon the child's repertoire by lengthening the sound sequence or adding new sounds. For example, if the child says, "Ba," then you say, "Ba." If the child repeats, "Ba," try to expand the child's repertoire by saying, "Ba, ba" or by adding new sounds, "Ba, da."
- Play "touch and name" games. For example, while bathing the child, encourage the child to touch and name his or her own body parts. For example, touch the child's foot and say, "What's this?" Give the child time to respond, then model the appropriate vocalization if necessary.
- During routine activities such as feeding, place a desired object out of reach. For example, place a piece of cracker within the child's field of vision, but out of reach. Pause and give an expectant look. If the child vocalizes, imitate the response and give the child the cracker.
- Provide talking toys such as See-N-Say or stuffed animals that "talk."
- The child's vocalizations do not need to approximate actual words. For example, the adult gives a cracker to the child after the child points to the cracker and says, "Da."
- Allow the child to practice making sounds and sound combinations while playing quietly in private, such as before and after naps, after meals, and after baths or changing. When all physical needs are met, children are more often interested in learning.
- Play children's music with simple, repetitive lyrics.

Environmental Arrangements

- Use highly motivating objects, such as musical toys, to engage the child's attention. Activate the toy and pause to give the child an opportunity to vocalize. Ask the child, "What do you want?" and pause a second time. Encourage any vocalization before giving the child the toy to play with.
- Look through picture books. Point to pictures of common objects.
- Expand upon the single sounds the child makes to develop consonant-vowel combinations. For example, if the child says, "Rrr," when pushing a car or truck, expand

it to "rum-rum." If the child uses "mmm" as a request for food, expand on the single sound to develop the word "more."

■ Use exaggerated vocal expressions when naming objects or pictures in books. For example, say, "Moo moo," when playing with a toy cow or when you see a cow in a book.

■ Position the child so that your faces are close. Move your lips slowly and distinctly, varying pitch and intonation. Encourage all vocalizations.

■ Play peekaboo and wait for the child to say "peek" or "boo" before continuing the game.

Instructional Sequence

■ Model using words that you want the child to imitate when you reach for food or toys.

■ Systematically introduce the use of time delay and visual cues. For instance, during snack time, show the child a desired snack, establish eye contact, and give an expectant look. Wait for the child to vocalize to refer to the desired food, then give it to the child.

■ Throughout the day, observe the child's responses toward objects, people, or events to determine those to which the child most readily responds. For example, when the child focuses on a desired object, ask the child, "What do you want?" Wait for the child to respond, then model an appropriate vocalization if necessary before giving the child the object to play with.

■ Encourage the child to imitate. Use the initial sound of a consonant–vowel combination as a cue.

■ Touch the child's lips as a cue to vocalize after you have modeled a consonant–vowel combination.

TEACHING CONSIDERATIONS

1. Words that are important to the family and are used throughout the child's environment are words that should be emphasized when practicing this skill.

2. Choose objects, people, and events to which the child most readily responds.

3. Be consistent about requiring a response from the child before reinforcing.

4. For the child with a visual impairment, touch cues are useful as a beginning step to learn to identify objects by their feel. Use sensory modalities other than visual whenever possible.

5. A child with a hearing impairment may hear only selected frequencies (high- or low-pitched sounds) or may hear only loud sounds. The child may also be sensitive to certain sounds or intensities (sounds that seem normal to you may be uncomfortably loud to some children, certain frequencies may be painful, combinations of sounds or too much noise may be uncomfortable).

6. If the child has a restricted range of motion in the head or trunk, the speaker should be in a position that facilitates visual contact between the child and the speaker. Positioning will also be critical for easy sound production. Latency of response may be noted. Consult a qualified specialist for recommendations for positioning and techniques for eliciting sounds from the child with a motor impairment.

7. A child with a hearing impairment may be acquiring an augmentative or alternative communication system such as a picture or sign system. Consult a qualified specialist for teaching techniques.

SCB

Comprehension of Words and Sentences

GOAL 1 Locates objects, people, and/or events *without* contextual cues

---

DEVELOPMENTAL PROGRAMMING STEPS

☑ The goal above is the most basic step for the skill to be taught. Most children will benefit from the activities outlined here that emphasize this skill. For children who need more instruction, consider designing programming steps from the *environmental arrangements* suggestions or from the *instructional sequences* outlined.

IMPORTANCE OF SKILL

Children learn to associate words with objects, events, and people by repeatedly hearing the words while interacting with the environment. Eventually the child learns that certain words represent particular objects, people, and events, even if the child does not have the assistance of contextual cues.

This skill is important to children in understanding what other people say. Comprehending words and sentences permits the child to follow directions and interact with the environment. This skill helps develop social skills through conversation and an increased awareness of the environment.

PRECEDING OBJECTIVE

SC C:1.1 Locates common objects, people, and/or events in unfamiliar pictures

CONCURRENT GOALS AND OBJECTIVES

GM C:1.0 Walks avoiding obstacles
Cog B:3.0 Maintains search for object that is not in its usual location
Cog C:1.0 Correctly activates mechanical toy
Cog E:2.0 Uses an object to obtain another object
Cog F:1.0 Aligns and stacks objects
Cog G:1.1 Uses representational actions with objects
Soc A:3.0 Initiates and maintains communicative exchange with familiar adult
Soc C:1.3 Plays near one or two peers

TEACHING SUGGESTIONS
Activity-Based

- During routine activities such as bathing, ask the child to give you an object that is usually present, such as a washcloth. Then ask the child to give you an object that is not usually present, but is still relevant to the activity, such as a squeeze-toy.

373

- Ask the child to locate items or events not immediately present. For example, ask, "Where's Daddy?" when Daddy is in the backyard. Observe to see whether the child looks or moves toward the back door. Then take the child outside to see Daddy.
- Send the child on simple errands to other locations in the general vicinity. For example, ask the child to bring a toy to you, to take a cup to a table in the dining room, or to retrieve shoes from the closet.
- Make use of special or unusual events to develop the child's ability to comprehend without contextual cues. For example, say, "Your Aunt Janet is here!" If the child does not respond, go with the child to the front door, point to Aunt Janet, and repeat the statement.
- Recurring environmental events, such as the delivery of the mail, garbage pick-up, and sirens from fire trucks and police cars, offer opportunities to search for the source of the sound. Ask your child, "What do you hear?" "Where is it?"

☑ If your data indicate that the child is not making progress toward the goal, provide additional structure within the suggested activities by incorporating the following *environmental arrangements:*

Environmental Arrangements

- The words chosen should represent objects, persons, or events with which the child has frequent contact. Frequent opportunities to hear the word in relation to its referent will facilitate comprehension.
- The words chosen should refer to objects, persons, or events that are important to and are of functional value to the child. Learning names of common environmental items and events assists the child's adaptation to the environment and should have some intrinsically rewarding features.
- The words chosen should have sound combinations that are relatively easy to produce or are already used by the child. Although the objective of this goal is comprehension, production often follows or occurs simultaneously. Selection of easy-to-produce words may enhance production.
- When the child consistently locates common objects in usual locations, vary the locations so that the object is still within the child's view. For example, if a favorite toy is usually on the floor, place it in the toy box within the child's view and ask the child to locate it.

☑ If this goal is particularly difficult for a child, it may be necessary, within activities, to use an *instructional sequence*.

Instructional Sequence

- Model locating an object after searching for it.
- Use exaggerated facial and vocal expressions and verbally ask the child to locate objects, people, or events in the environment. Gradually reduce the number of extra-linguistic cues used to help the child.
- Systematically vary the distance the child is expected to travel. First, ask the child to locate a familiar object, person, or event that is within his or her field of vision. Then, ask the child to locate a familiar object, person, or event that is outside his or her field of vision.
- Point to or turn your body toward an object, person, or event while asking the child to locate the same.
- Gently guide the child's face or body while asking him or her to locate an object, person, or event.

☑ Combining or pairing different levels of instructions may be helpful when beginning to teach a new and difficult skill. Fade to less intrusive instructions as soon as possible, to encourage more independent performance.

TEACHING CONSIDERATIONS

1. Remember that the primary objective of this goal is comprehension or word recognition. Do not expect the child to produce words or sounds, but encourage any form of expression (e.g., vocalizations, gestures).
2. A child with a hearing impairment may hear only selected frequencies (high- or low-pitched sounds) or may hear only loud sounds. The child may also be sensitive to certain sounds or intensities (e.g., sounds that seem normal to you may be uncomfortably loud to some children, certain frequencies may be painful, combinations of sounds or too much noise may be uncomfortable).
3. A child with a hearing impairment may be acquiring an augmentative or alternative communication system such as a picture or sign system.
4. If the child has restricted range of motion in the head or trunk area, the speaker should be in a position that facilitates visual contact between the child and the speaker. Latency of response may be noted. Consult a qualified specialist for recommendations for positioning.
5. Consider safety with all objects that the child handles. Never leave the child unattended with potentially hazardous objects.

Objective 1.1 Locates common objects, people, and/or events in unfamiliar pictures

---

IMPORTANCE OF SKILL

Initially, contextual cues aid the child in comprehending the meaning of words. The word "cow" is easily understood if the child is looking at a toy cow in a play barn. Later, the child associates the word cow with an unfamiliar picture of a cow. The purpose of this skill is for the child to associate a referent with its word symbol while looking at unfamiliar pictures. This skill is important to children in understanding what others say and in developing social skills through conversation and an increased awareness of the environment.

PRECEDING OBJECTIVE

SC C:1.2   Locates common objects, people, and/or events in familiar pictures

CONCURRENT GOALS AND OBJECTIVES

Cog B:3.0   Maintains search for object that is not in its usual location
Cog C:1.0   Correctly activates mechanical toy
Cog F:1.0   Aligns and stacks objects
Cog F:2.3   Matches pictures and/or objects
Cog G:1.1   Uses representational actions with objects
SC D:1.0   Uses 50 single words
Soc A:3.1   Initiates communication with familiar adult

SC C

TEACHING SUGGESTIONS
Activity-Based

- Look at pictures in books. Name the objects, people, or events and point to them. Ask the child to point to the pictures that you label. Label the item or event several times.
- Look in the mirror and point to different body parts of the child and yourself. Ask the child to point to the body parts that you name. Label each body part several times.
- Introduce simple puzzles with pictures of objects. Ask the child to find the pieces as you name them.
- Look through catalogs and magazines to find variations on common objects such as shirts, shoes, tables, or cars.
- Go to a children's library and look at familiar and new books in another setting.
- Show the child pictures of favorite foods and label them several times. Then give the child the favorite food to eat. Offer the child variations of the food, such as a sliced banana, and compare it to the picture of a whole banana.
- When looking at unfamiliar pictures, show the child the object, person, or event the picture represents. For example, if looking at an unfamiliar picture of a shirt, point to the child's shirt.

Environmental Arrangements

- When the child consistently recognizes familiar pictures of objects, people, and events, introduce unfamiliar pictures. For example, if the child consistently points to a dog in a favorite picture book, introduce a picture of a different size or color dog and ask the child to point to the new picture.
- When the child consistently recognizes familiar pictures of objects, people, and events, introduce an unfamiliar picture along with the familiar one. For example, if the child consistently locates a dog in a favorite picture book, ask the child to point to a dog in an unfamiliar picture that shows the same dog and a cat.
- Use exaggerated vocal and facial expressions when naming an unfamiliar picture, to gain and maintain the child's attention.
- Introduce new characters to familiar stories in homemade books. Add new photos to an album or scrapbook.
- The words used should represent objects, persons, or events with which the child has frequent contact. Frequent opportunities to hear the word in relation to its referent should facilitate comprehension.
- The words chosen should refer to objects, persons, or events that are important to and are of functional value to the child. Learning names of common environmental items and events assists the child's adaptation to the environment and should have some intrinsically rewarding features.

Instructional Sequence

- Model finding a common object in an unfamiliar picture.
- Give the child a choice of two pictures, one familiar and one unfamiliar. Ask the child to point to the familiar one first, place it just out of reach, and ask the child to point to the unfamiliar picture.
- Combine familiar and unfamiliar pictures. First, ask the child to point to familiar pictures of objects, people, or events after you label them several times. Then, ask the child to point to unfamiliar pictures of objects, people, or events after you label them several times.

- Label and point to an unfamiliar picture, then ask the child to point to the picture.
- Gently guide the child's hand to point to an unfamiliar picture if the child fails to do so upon request.

TEACHING CONSIDERATIONS

1. Remember that the primary objective of this goal is comprehension or word recognition. Do not expect the child to produce words or sounds, but encourage any form of expression (e.g., vocalizations, gestures).
2. A child with a hearing impairment may hear only selected frequencies (high- or low-pitched sounds) or may hear only loud sounds. The child may also be sensitive to certain sounds or intensities (e.g., sounds that seem normal to you may be uncomfortably loud to some children, certain frequencies may be painful, combinations of sounds or too much noise may be uncomfortable).
3. A child with a hearing impairment may be acquiring an augmentative or alternative communication system such as a picture or sign system.
4. If the child has a restricted range of motion in the head or trunk area, the speaker should be in a position that facilitates visual contact between the child and the speaker. Latency of response may be noted. Consult a qualified specialist for recommendations for positioning.
5. Consider safety with all objects that the child handles. Never leave the child unattended with potentially hazardous objects.

Objective 1.2	Locates common objects, people, and/or events in familiar pictures

---

DEVELOPMENTAL PROGRAMMING STEPS

No single standard developmental sequence appears to exist for the recognition of objects, people, and events in pictures. Careful observation of the child will help determine the child's interests.

PS1.2a   Locates common actions and events in familiar books or pictures.
PS1.2b   Locates common objects and people in familiar books or pictures.

IMPORTANCE OF SKILL

Initially, contextual cues aid the child in comprehending the meaning of words. The word "bird" is understood if the child is looking at a real bird or a picture of a bird. The purpose of this skill is for the child to associate a referent with its word symbol while looking at familiar pictures. This skill is important to children in understanding what others say and in developing social skills through conversation and increased awareness of the environment.

PRECEDING OBJECTIVE

SC C:1.3   Locates common objects, people, and/or events *with* contextual cues

SCC

CONCURRENT GOALS AND OBJECTIVES

Cog B:3.0   Maintains search for object that is not in its usual location
Cog C:1.0   Correctly activates mechanical toy
Cog D:1.1   Imitates motor action that is commonly used
Cog F:2.3   Matches pictures and/or objects
Cog G:1.2   Uses functionally appropriate actions with objects
SC D:1.0   Uses 50 single words
Soc A:3.1   Initiates communication with familiar adult
Soc B:2.0   Responds to established social routine

TEACHING SUGGESTIONS

Activity-Based

- Read the same stories many times so that the child can become familiar with the pictures. Let the child choose favorite stories.
- Look at pictures of common objects in books. Name the objects, people, or events as you point to them. Ask the child to point to the pictures that you label. Label the item or event several times.
- Make a photo album or an "All About Me" book with photos of favorite people, toys, and events. Use it as a story or a schedule of activities.
- When on trips, point out common business logos such as the McDonald's golden arches, K-Mart, or Burger King. Watch for the same logos on TV commercials and in magazine ads and point out familiar ones to the child.
- When using boxes with pictures on them, such as cereal boxes, ask the child to locate familiar objects or events.
- When looking at familiar pictures, show the child the object, person, or event the pictures represent. For example, when looking at a picture of a cup, show the child an actual cup.

Environmental Arrangements

- Show the child two pictures: a bright-colored picture of an object and a black-and-white picture of the same object. Ask the child to point to the object. Repeat the activity several times with other sets of pictures to determine if the child has a preference for bright-colored or black-and-white pictures.
- Use exaggerated vocal expression when you show a picture and ask the child to point to it. Combine sounds and actions, as in animal sounds for pictures of animals, clapping for a picture of a child playing pat-a-cake, or hugging for a picture of a child with a doll.
- When the child consistently points to familiar pictures of objects, people, or events, introduce a new picture that shows a variation in color, shape, or size. For instance, if the child consistently points to a picture of a yellow flower, ask the child to point to a red flower.
- Put two familiar pictures on a table. Ask the child to give you one of them at a time.
- Make placemats with familiar pictures of the objects used at mealtime. Place a picture of a plate, cup, and spoon on construction paper and cover it with contact paper. Label items while the child matches objects and pictures.
- Put pictures of familiar objects next to their storage area to help the child locate where objects belong. Ask the child to find where the blocks go by finding the picture of blocks.

SC C

- The pictures chosen should represent objects, persons, or events with which the child has frequent contact. Frequent opportunities to hear the word in relation to its referent should facilitate comprehension.
- The pictures chosen should refer to objects, persons, or events that are important to and are of functional value to the child. Learning names of common environmental items and events assists the child's adaptation to the environment and should have some intrinsically rewarding features.

Instructional Sequence

- Model locating a familiar person in a photograph.
- When looking through picture books, ask the child to point to familiar pictures of objects, people, or events after you label them several times.
- Label and point to a familiar picture of an object, person, or event, then ask the child to point to the same picture.
- Label and point to a familiar picture of an object, person, or event, then gently guide the child's hand to point to the same picture.

TEACHING CONSIDERATIONS

1. The words chosen should have sound combinations that are relatively easy to produce or are already used by the child. Although the objective of this goal is comprehension, word production may follow or occur simultaneously. Selection of easy-to-produce words may enhance production.
2. Remember that the primary objective of this goal is comprehension or word recognition. Do not expect the child to produce words or sounds, but encourage any form of expression (e.g., vocalizations or gestures).
3. A child with a hearing impairment may be acquiring an augmentative or alternative communication system such as a picture or sign system. Consult a qualified specialist for teaching techniques.
4. A child with a hearing impairment may hear only selected frequencies (high- or low-pitched sounds) or may hear only loud sounds. The child may also be sensitive to certain sounds or intensities (e.g., sounds that seem normal to you may be uncomfortably loud to some children, certain frequencies may be painful, combinations of sounds or too much noise may be uncomfortable).
5. If the child has restricted range of motion in the head or trunk area, the speaker should be in a position that facilitates visual contact between the child and the speaker. Latency of response may be noted.
6. Consider safety with all objects that the child handles. Never leave the child unattended with potentially hazardous objects.

Objective 1.3 Locates common objects, people, and/or events *with contextual cues*

SC C

IMPORTANCE OF SKILL

Contextual cues aid the child in comprehending the meaning of words. The word "toe" is understood if an adult is touching the child's toe. The purpose of this skill is for the child to associate a referent to its word symbol with the help of a contextual cue. This skill is important to the child in understanding what others say and in developing social skills through conversation and an increased awareness of the environment.

CONCURRENT GOALS AND OBJECTIVES

FM A:5.0	Places and releases object balanced on top of another object with either hand
FM B:2.2	Fits object into defined space
GM C:1.0	Walks avoiding obstacles
Adap A:3.0	Drinks from cup and/or glass
Adap A:4.2	Eats with fingers
Adap B:2.0	Washes and dries hands
Adap C:1.0	Undresses self
Cog B:3.1	Looks for object in usual location
Cog C:1.0	Correctly activates mechanical toy
Cog D:1.1	Imitates motor action that is commonly used
Cog E:3.2	Moves around barrier to change location
Cog F:1.2	Stacks objects
Cog G:1.2	Uses functionally appropriate actions with objects
Soc B:2.0	Responds to established social routine
Soc C:1.5	Entertains self by playing appropriately with toys

TEACHING SUGGESTIONS

Activity-Based

- Throughout the day, talk to the child about what you are doing by labeling objects, people, or events in the child's environment. Show the child where objects are commonly located—coats in the closet, toys on the shelf, or snacks in the cupboard. Encourage the child to assist you in putting things away.
- Capitalize on interesting events by clearly labeling objects, actions, and people that capture the child's attention. For example, if the child drops a toy, say, "Where did the doll go? You dropped the doll."
- Use gestures with your words to help the child comprehend the meaning of words. For example, say, "Bye-bye," while waving your hand, or say, "Up," while extending your arms to the child.
- While playing with the child, ask him or her to hand you familiar toys. This is especially helpful when picking up toys to put them away.
- During daily routines such as dressing, washing, and eating, ask the child to find items integral to the activity. For example, ask the child to give you socks or a shirt from the clothes laid out, or ask the child to pick up the soap or washcloth.
- While bathing the child, touch and name different parts of his or her body. Ask the child to point to each body part after you label it.

Environmental Arrangements

- Observe the child throughout the day to determine which toys are of particular interest to him or her. Offer two objects, one that is known to be desirable and one that is not. Ask the child to point to the desirable toy and then give it to him or her.

SC C

- Use exaggerated facial and vocal expression when referring to common objects, people, or events in the child's environment.
- When the child consistently locates objects in familiar locations, vary the location of an object so that it is still within the child's field of vision. Then ask the child to locate the object.
- Imitate and identify sounds in the environment, such as the dog barking, the door shutting, the car running, fire sirens passing, and horns and whistles blowing. Find the source of the sound.
- Children's records are a good source of repetitive, familiar actions and sounds.
- The words chosen should represent objects, persons, or events with which the child has frequent contact. Frequent opportunities to hear the word in relation to its referent facilitates comprehension.
- The words chosen should refer to objects, persons, or events that are important to and are of functional value to the child. Learning names of common environmental items and events assists the child's adaptation to the environment and should have some intrinsically rewarding features.

Instructional Sequence

- Model locating a common object within its context. For example, open the refrigerator and say, "Oh, here's the juice."
- Ask the child to locate familiar objects, people, or events that are within his or her field of vision and relevant to the activity. For example, while bathing the child, ask him or her to give you the soap. Provide models. Give the soap to the child and then ask for it back. Take turns.
- Vary the positions of objects so that they are just outside the child's reach, but still within the child's field of vision. Ask the child to locate the objects.
- Point to or turn your body toward an object, person, or event while asking the child to locate the item or event.
- Gently guide the child's face, hand, or body while asking the child to locate an object, person, or event.

TEACHING CONSIDERATIONS

1. Remember that the primary objective of this goal is comprehension or word recognition. Do not expect the child to produce words or sounds, but encourage any form of expression (e.g., vocalizations, gestures).
2. A child with a hearing impairment may hear only selected frequencies (high- or low-pitched sounds) or may hear only loud sounds. The child may also be sensitive to certain sounds or intensities (e.g., sounds that seem normal to you may be uncomfortably loud to some children, certain frequencies may be painful, combinations of sounds or too much noise may be uncomfortable). Consult a qualified specialist for teaching techniques.
3. If the child has restricted range of motion in the head or trunk area, the speaker should be in a position that facilitates visual contact between the child and the speaker. Latency of response may be noted.
4. Consider safety with all objects that the child handles. Never leave the child unattended with potentially hazardous objects.

SC C

Goal 2   Carries out two-step direction *without* contextual cues

IMPORTANCE OF SKILL

Initially a child learns to follow one-step directions relying on contextual cues (e.g., one-step directions to get her coat when it is on a hook in front of her). A child then progresses to follow a one-step direction without contextual cues to retrieve the coat from the closet. Next, the child follows a two-step direction to get the coat and put it in a backpack. The purpose of this skill is to understand increasingly complex directions without immediate contextual cues. This skill allows the child to gain independence and participate in useful daily living activities. In addition, following directions is an important foundation for future academic activities.

PRECEDING GOAL

SC C:1.0   Locates objects, people, and/or events *without* contextual cues

CONCURRENT GOALS AND OBJECTIVES

FM B:4.1   Draws circles and lines
GM C:3.0   Walks up and down stairs
GM D:4.0   Catches, kicks, throws, and rolls ball or similar object
GM D:5.2   Moves under, over, and through obstacles
Adap A:5.0   Transfers food and liquid
Adap B:1.0   Initiates toileting
Adap B:2.0   Washes and dries hands
Adap B:3.0   Brushes teeth
Adap C:1.0   Undresses self
Cog B:3.0   Maintains search for object that is not in its usual location
Cog C:1.0   Correctly activates mechanical toy
Cog C:2.0   Reproduces part of interactive game and/or action in order to continue game and/or action
Cog D: 1.0   Imitates motor action that is not commonly used
Cog E: 2.0   Uses an object to obtain another object
Cog E:4.0   Solves common problems
Cog F:1.0   Aligns and stacks objects
Cog F:2.0   Categorizes like objects
Cog G:1.0   Uses imaginary objects in play
SC D:1.0   Uses 50 single words
Soc A:3.2   Responds to communication from familiar adult
Soc B:1.0   Meets external physical needs in socially appropriate ways
Soc C:1.2   Responds appropriately to peer's social behavior
Soc C:2.2   Responds to communication from peer

TEACHING SUGGESTIONS

Activity-Based

- During routine activities, talk about what you are doing. Label the materials used or the actions taking place. Periodically give the child simple requests to carry out that are related to the activity. For example, when playing with blocks, ask the child to get a storybook from another room to use as a platform for the blocks.

- Play telephone and give the child directions to carry out actions as a firefighter, grocer, pilot, or teacher.
- During adaptive routines, encourage the child to locate necessary objects and retrieve them for you. "Get your pajamas from the bedroom and bring them to the bathroom for your bath." Initiate independent activities, such as, "Go to the bathroom and go potty."
- At the playground, combine motor actions and direction skills while playing ball or climbing on equipment. Set up simple obstacle courses to go over, under, around, and through.

Environmental Arrangements

- Arrange the environment to help the child focus on the activity. The setting should be relatively quiet and free from objects and events that compete for the child's attention. The child might not respond if a speaker is too far away. Check for an optimal distance, then vary the distance after the child responds consistently.
- Use exaggerated facial and vocal expressions to gain and maintain the child's attention.
- Observe the child throughout the day to determine which toys are highly desirable. Ask the child to look for that toy when it is not present in the immediate environment. Say, "Go to your bedroom and get teddy."
- Play a hide-and-seek game. Hide particularly desirable objects out of immediate visual range and ask the child to find them. Give directions such as "It's in the kitchen, under the table."
- Give the child a two-step direction to carry out, using other children in the group as models. For example, during snack time, ask each child to get something needed for a snack and bring it to the table.

Instructional Sequence

- Model carrying out a two-step direction and comment as you do so.
- Include familiar actions and objects in directions. Then use new objects with old actions or old objects with new actions.
- Use exaggerated facial and vocal expressions when asking the child to locate objects, people, or events in the environment and gradually reduce the number of extralinguistic cues used to help the child.
- Systematically vary the distance the child is expected to travel. First, ask the child to locate a familiar object, person, or event that is within the child's field of vision. Then, ask the child to locate a familiar object, person, or event that is outside the child's field of vision.
- Point or use gestures when giving the child a direction to carry out.
- Gently guide the child toward a requested object. For example, guide the child toward the chairs and say, "Go get a chair and sit down for circle."

TEACHING CONSIDERATIONS

1. Carrying out directions should have functional value for the child, assist the child's adaptation to the environment, and have some intrinsically rewarding features.
2. A child with a hearing impairment may hear only selected frequencies (high- or low-pitched sounds), or may hear only loud sounds. The child may also be sensi-

SC C

tive to certain sounds or intensities (e.g., sounds that seem normal to you may be uncomfortably loud to some children, certain frequencies may be painful, combinations of sounds or too much noise may be uncomfortable).
3. A child with a hearing impairment may be acquiring an augmentative or alternative communication system such as a picture or sign system. Consult a qualified specialist for teaching techniques.
4. If the child has restricted a range of motion in the head or trunk area, the speaker should be in a position that facilitates visual contact between the child and the speaker. Latency of response may be noted.
5. Consider safety with all objects that the child handles. Never leave the child unattended with potentially hazardous objects.

Objective 2.1   Carries out two-step direction *with* contextual cues

---

IMPORTANCE OF SKILL

The purpose of this skill is to understand increasingly complex directions with the help of contextual cues. The child follows a one-step direction to put the cup on the table when an adult hands a cup to the child. Then the child progresses to following a two-step direction to take the cup and napkin from the counter and put them on the table. This skill allows the child to develop more sophisticated play and adaptive skills. In addition, following directions is an important foundation for future academic activities.

PRECEDING OBJECTIVE

SC C:2.2   Carries out one-step direction *without* contextual cues

CONCURRENT GOALS AND OBJECTIVES

FM B:4.1   Draws circles and lines
GM B:2.0   Sits down in and gets out of chair
GM C:3.0   Walks up and down stairs
GM D:4.0   Catches, kicks, throws, and rolls ball or similar object
Adap A:5.0 Transfers food and liquid
Adap B:1.0 Initiates toileting
Adap B:2.0 Washes and dries hands
Adap B:3.0 Brushes teeth
Adap C:1.0 Undresses self
Cog B:3.0   Maintains search for object that is not in its usual location
Cog C:1.0   Correctly activates mechanical toy
Cog D:1.0   Imitates motor action that is not commonly used
Cog E:2.0   Uses an object to obtain another object
Cog E:4.0   Solves common problems
Cog F:1.0   Aligns and stacks objects
Cog F:2.0   Categorizes like objects
Cog G:1.0   Uses imaginary objects in play
SC D:1.0   Uses 50 single words
Soc A:3.2   Responds to communication from familiar adult

SC
C

Soc B:1.0 Meets external physical needs in socially appropriate ways
Soc C:1.2 Responds appropriately to peer's social behavior
Soc C:2.2 Responds to communication from peer

TEACHING SUGGESTIONS
Activity-Based

- Watch children's television shows together. Encourage the child to participate in the actions and activities in programs such as "Picture Pages" and "You and Me, Kid."
- During routine activities, such as snack time, give the child simple requests to carry out that are related to the activity. For example, ask the child to go to the table and sit down.
- Throughout the day, when the child is playing, give the child simple directions to carry out, such as, "Feed your baby and put her to bed."
- During bathtime, direct the child to wash two body parts. For example, say, "Wash your hands and face."

Environmental Arrangements

- Use exaggerated facial and vocal expression to gain and maintain the child's attention.
- Read action stories and have the child participate along with the characters.
- Use flannel board characters to tell stories. Give directions to the child that match the story.
- Observe the child throughout the day to determine which toys are of particular interest to him or her. Put a desirable toy in an unusual location, but within the child's field of vision. Ask the child to find the toy and play with it.
- Play games and give directions on playground equipment that give cues to the action intended. For example, "Go *under* the tire and *around* the merry-go-round."

Instructional Sequence

- Model carrying out a two-step direction, such as brushing your teeth and taking a drink of water.
- Verbally direct the child to imitate the same two-step direction.
- Use gestures when giving the child directions to carry out. For example, say, "Go to the bedroom (point toward the bedroom) and get your hat (pat the top of the child's head)."
- Gently guide the child toward the requested object, person, or event. For example, turn the child toward the back door and say, "Go find Daddy and help him rake the leaves."

TEACHING CONSIDERATIONS

1. A child with a hearing impairment may hear only selected frequencies (high- or low-pitched sounds) or may hear only loud sounds. The child may also be sensitive to certain sounds or intensities (e.g., sounds that seem normal to you may be uncomfortably loud to some children, certain frequencies may be painful, combinations of sounds or too much noise may be uncomfortable).
2. If the child has a restricted range of motion in the head or trunk area, the speaker should be in a position that facilitates visual contact between the child and the speaker. Latency of response may be noted.

SC C

3. A child with a hearing impairment may be acquiring an augmentative or alternative communication system such as a picture or sign system. Consult a qualified specialist for teaching techniques.
4. Consider safety with all objects that the child handles. Never leave the child unattended with potentially hazardous objects.

Objective 2.2   Carries out one-step direction *without* contextual cues

---

IMPORTANCE OF SKILL

After depending on contextual cues to follow simple directions, a child then follows directions not related to the immediate environment or without contextual cues. This skill allows the child to expand vocabulary and memory and meet needs more independently (e.g., find toys, put on clothing without an immediate cue in the environment). Following directions is an important foundation for future academic activities.

PRECEDING OBJECTIVE

SC C:2.3   Carries out one-step direction *with* contextual cues

CONCURRENT GOALS AND OBJECTIVES

Cog B:3.0   Maintains search for object that is not in its usual location
Cog C:1.0   Correctly activates mechanical toy
Cog D:1.0   Imitates motor action that is not commonly used
Cog E:2.0   Uses an object to obtain another object
Cog G:1.1   Uses representational actions with objects
SC D:1.0   Uses 50 single words
Soc A:3.0   Initiates and maintains communicative exchange with familiar adult
Soc C:1.3   Plays near one or two peers

TEACHING SUGGESTIONS
Activity-Based

- Ask the child to help with simple errands such as taking Dad's shoes to the closet, getting a diaper from the bedroom, taking a towel to the bathroom or a cup to the kitchen.
- During routine activities such as dressing, talk about what you are doing. Label the materials being used or the actions taking place. Periodically, give the child simple requests to carry out that are unrelated to the activity, such as, "Give me a hug."
- Play hide-and-seek games. Hide objects and give the child directions to find them, or tell the child where to hide an object and ask another child to find it.
- When picking up toys after play, give the child directions for returning the toys to their proper location.
- Use a variety of objects and settings so that the child learns to respond in many situations. Have the child complete simple errands at Grandma's house, child care, or a friend's house.

SC C

Environmental Arrangements

- Read books such as *Pat the Bunny* and include actions.
- Listen to and sing songs in which the child can follow directions to perform motor actions. Use the tune "Here We Go 'Round the Mulberry Bush" and add your own lines, such as, "This is the way we eat our soup," ". . . comb our hair," or ". . . brush our teeth."
- Observe the child throughout the day to determine which toys are highly desirable to the child. Ask the child to look for the toy when it is not present in the immediate environment.
- Give the child a one-step direction to carry out, using other children in the group as models. For example, play "Simon says" and give each child directions such as "Clap your hands" and "Pat your head."
- Carrying out directions should have functional value for the child, assist the child's adaptation to the environment, and have some intrinsically rewarding features.

Instructional Sequence

- Model a one-step direction without contextual cues or have a peer model a direction.
- Verbally direct the child to follow a direction without a contextual cue. For example, say, "Go get your hairbrush."
- Point or use gestures when giving the child a direction to carry out.
- Gently guide the child toward a requested object. For example, the adult says, "Give me the book," while guiding the child's hand toward the book.

TEACHING CONSIDERATIONS

1. A child with a hearing impairment may hear only selected frequencies (high- or low-pitched sounds) or may hear only loud sounds. The child may also be sensitive to certain sounds or intensities (e.g., sounds that seem normal to you may be uncomfortably loud to some children, certain frequencies may be painful, combinations of sounds or too much noise may be uncomfortable).
2. If the child has a restricted range of motion in the head or trunk area, the speaker should be in a position that facilitates visual contact between the child and the speaker. Latency of response may be noted.
3. A child with a hearing impairment may be acquiring an augmentative or alternative communication system such as a picture or sign system. Consult a qualified specialist for teaching techniques.
4. Consider safety with all objects that the child handles. Never leave the child unattended with potentially hazardous objects.

Objective 2.3 Carries out one-step direction *with* contextual cues

---

DEVELOPMENTAL PROGRAMMING STEPS

PS2.3a The child participates in verbal and gestural regulatory social routines such as "Come here," "Sit down."

PS2.3b The child ceases action when told, "No."

SC C

IMPORTANCE OF SKILL

The child uses the situation or context to provide cues to the meaning of a simple one-step direction. For example, the child picks up a ball, and the adult says, "Throw the ball!" This skill allows the child to develop play and adaptive skills. Following directions is an important communication skill and a foundation for future academic activities.

PRECEDING GOAL

SC C:1.0   Locates objects, people, and/or events *without* contextual cues

CONCURRENT GOALS AND OBJECTIVE

FM B:2.2   Fits object into defined space
Adap A:3.0 Drinks from cup and/or glass
Adap B:2.0 Washes and dries hands
Adap C:1.0 Undresses self
Cog B:3.0   Maintains search for object that is not in its usual location
Cog C:1.0   Correctly activates mechanical toy
Cog D:1.0   Imitates motor action that is not commonly used
Cog E:2.0   Uses an object to obtain another object
SC D:1.0   Uses 50 single words
Soc B:2.0   Responds to established social routine

TEACHING SUGGESTIONS

Activity-Based

- Talk to your child throughout the day. Label the materials used and the actions occurring. Periodically, give the child simple requests to carry out that are related to the activity. For example, when cooking, ask the child to hand you a spoon.
- During routine activities, such as dressing, ask the child to cooperate by raising an arm or standing up straight.
- Play tea party together with real or toy dishes. Give simple directions for setting the table, passing snacks to friends, and cleaning up afterward.
- Play hide-and-seek with peers or toy animals. Games such as "Follow the leader" and "Simon says" are also good.
- Action records and tapes can be found in toy stores or bookstores or borrowed from the library. They provide many opportunities for following directions.

Environmental Arrangements

- Play "Give me" when the child extends toys to show you. For example, if the child extends a toy boat during bathtime, say, "Give me the boat." When the child releases the toy, say, "Thank you," and give it back.
- Place particularly desirable toys just out of reach, but within the child's field of vision. Ask the child to find the toy.
- Use exaggerated vocal and facial expressions to gain and maintain the child's attention.
- Use gestures when giving the child a direction. For example, point to the child's foot and say, "Get your socks."

- Hold two objects, one that is particularly desirable and one that is not. Tell the child to take the desirable object as you name it.
- Listen to and sing songs in which the child can follow directions to perform motor actions. Use the tune "Here We Go 'Round the Mulberry Bush" and add your own lines, such as, "This is the way we eat our soup," ". . . comb our hair," and ". . . brush our teeth." Use exaggerated facial and gestural expressions.
- Actions in finger plays or songs can be modeled and repeated for the child to imitate.

Instructional Sequence

- Model or have a peer model following a one-step direction in the presence of a contextual cue.
- Vary the position of objects so they are just outside the child's reach, but within his or her field of vision. Ask the child to locate the objects.
- Point to or turn your body toward an object, person, or event while asking the child to locate the item or event.
- Gently guide the child's hand toward a requested object. For example, say, "Give me the spoon" while placing the child's hand near the spoon.

TEACHING CONSIDERATIONS

1. Carrying out directions should have functional value for the child, assist the child's adaptation to the environment, and have some intrinsically rewarding features.
2. A child with a hearing impairment may hear only selected frequencies (high- or low-pitched sounds) or may hear only loud sounds. The child may also be sensitive to certain sounds or intensities (e.g., sounds that seem normal to you may be uncomfortably loud to some children, certain frequencies may be painful, combinations of sounds or too much noise may be uncomfortable).
3. A child with a hearing impairment may be acquiring an augmentative or alternative communication system such as a picture or sign system. Consult a qualified specialist for teaching techniques.
4. If the child has a restricted range of motion in the head or trunk area, the speaker should be in a position that facilitates visual contact between the child and the speaker. Latency of response may be noted.
5. Consider safety with all objects that the child handles. Never leave the child unattended with potentially hazardous objects.

SC C

Strand D

Production of Social-Communicative Signals, Words, and Sentences

Goal 1   Uses 50 single words

DEVELOPMENTAL PROGRAMMING STEPS

In order to achieve this goal, a child must perform the skills in Objectives 1.1–1.5 to criteria. Refer to the specific objective for Developmental Programming Steps to develop each skill.

IMPORTANCE OF SKILL

It is important that children learn to use words to control their environment. With words they can convey thoughts, wants, and needs. This skill also helps promote social skills and affords the child greater interaction with the environment. Before children produce their first words, they use consistent speech sound combinations to refer to objects, people, or events. A sound combination is considered a word if it is spontaneously produced by the child, is of consistent form, and consistently refers to the same object, person, or event.

PRECEDING GOAL

SC B:2.0   Uses consistent word approximations

CONCURRENT GOALS AND OBJECTIVES

FM A:5.0   Places and releases object balanced on top of another object with either hand
FM B:2.0   Assembles toy and/or object that require(s) putting pieces together
GM B:2.0   Sits down in and gets out of chair
GM C:3.0   Walks up and down stairs
GM D:4.0   Catches, kicks, throws, and rolls ball or similar object
Adap A:4.0 Eats with fork and/or spoon
Adap A:5.0 Transfers food and liquid
Adap B:2.0 Washes and dries hands
Adap B:3.0 Brushes teeth
Adap C:1.0 Undresses self
Cog B:3.0   Maintains search for object that is not in its usual location

Cog C:1.0 Correctly activates mechanical toy
Cog C:2.0 Reproduces part of interactive game and/or action in order to continue game and/or action
Cog D:1.0 Imitates motor action that is not commonly used
Cog D:2.0 Imitates words that are not frequently used
Cog E:2.0 Uses an object to obtain another object
Cog E:4.1 Uses more than one strategy in attempt to solve common problem
Cog F:2.2 Groups objects according to size, shape, and/or color
Cog G:1.1 Uses representational actions with objects
SC A:3.0 Engages in vocal exchanges by babbling
SC C:1.0 Locates objects, people, and/or events *without* contextual cues
Soc A:3.0 Initiates and maintains communicative exchange with familiar adult
Soc B:2.0 Responds to established social routine
Soc C:1.2 Responds appropriately to peer's social behavior
Soc C:2.2 Responds to communication from peer

TEACHING SUGGESTIONS

In order to achieve this goal, a child must perform the skills in Objectives 1.1–1.5 to criteria. Refer to the specific objective for Teaching Suggestions and Teaching Considerations to develop each skill.

Objective 1.1 Uses five descriptive words

DEVELOPMENTAL PROGRAMMING STEPS

☑ The objective above is the most basic step for the skill to be taught. Most children will benefit from the activities outlined here that emphasize this skill. For children who need more instruction, consider designing programming steps from the *environmental arrangements* suggestions or from the *instructional sequence* outlined.

IMPORTANCE OF SKILL

It is important for children to use a variety of words to convey thoughts, wants, and needs. The purpose of this skill is for the child to use descriptive words (other than names) that make a statement about an object, person, action, or event. For example, the child sees a steaming kettle on the stove and says, "Hot," or a large ball and says, "Big." These words provide a basis for future word combinations that are increasingly complex.

PRECEDING GOAL

SC B:2.0 Uses consistent word approximations

CONCURRENT GOALS AND OBJECTIVES

FM A:5.0 Places and releases object balanced on top of another object with either hand

SC D

FM B:2.1   Fits variety of shapes into corresponding spaces
FM B:3.0   Uses either index finger to activate objects
GM C:3.3   Gets up and down from low structure
GM D:3.2   Walks fast
GM D:4.0   Catches, kicks, throws, and rolls ball or similar object
Adap A:3.0   Drinks from cup and/or glass
Adap A:4.0   Eats with fork and/or spoon
Adap B:2.0   Washes and dries hands
Adap C:1.0   Undresses self
Cog B:3.0   Maintains search for object that is not in its usual location
Cog C:1.0   Correctly activates mechanical toy
Cog C:2.0   Reproduces part of interactive game and/or action in order to continue game and/or action
Cog D:1.0   Imitates motor action that is not commonly used
Cog D:2.0   Imitates words that are not frequently used
Cog E:2.0   Uses an object to obtain another object
Cog F:2.2   Groups objects according to size, shape, and/or color
Cog G:1.1   Uses representational actions with objects
SC C:1.0   Locates objects, people, and/or events *without* contextual cues
Soc A:3.0   Initiates and maintains communicative exchange with familiar adult
Soc B:1.0   Meets external physical needs in socially appropriate ways
Soc B:2.0   Responds to established social routine

TEACHING SUGGESTIONS

Activity-Based

- Provide frequent opportunities for the child to interact with peers who use descriptive words.
- Throughout the day, observe the child's responses toward objects, people, and events to determine those to which the child most readily vocalizes. Use descriptive words to expand on what the child says. For example, if the child touches his or her toe in the bathtub and says, "Toe," say, "Big toe, little toe," pointing to the different sizes.
- Clean out the toy box and sort items. Put the big balls together, red blocks together, and doll clothes together. Sorting and describing are activities that fit well with the daily routines of laundry, grocery shopping, and getting the mail.
- Throughout the day, during the child's daily routines, model developmentally appropriate descriptive words, such as big, little, hot, and dirty. For example, when changing the child's diaper, say, "Dirty diaper," or when cooking, tell the child, "Don't touch, hot!"
- Look at books with the child and describe the pictures. For example, point to a doll and say, "Sleepy baby," or point to a kitten and say, "Little kitty."

☑ If your data indicate the child is not making progress toward the objective, provide additional structure within the suggested activities by incorporating the following *environmental arrangements:*

Environmental Arrangements

- Arrange for the child to participate in small group activities with peers whose language is slightly advanced. Facilitate peer models of descriptive words during activities and encourage the child to imitate.

- Present two toys or stuffed animals, one plain and one brightly colored. Ask the child, "Which one do you want, this one or the *pretty* one?" Use an exaggerated pitch and intonation on the targeted word. If the child does not respond, model and present the bright-colored animal.
- Make or find a picture book with pairs of opposite words, one on each page. For example, look at one page and say, "This ball is *big*"; then turn the page and say, "This ball is ____." Pause and give the child an opportunity to respond. Model if necessary.
- Make a mailbox and sort letters by size and color.
- Hold several crayons or markers just out of the child's reach. Ask the child, "Which color do you want?" Pause, then model if necessary and give the child the marker.
- Watch television together. Programs such as "Sesame Street," "Captain Kangaroo," and "You and Me, Kid" are designed to encourage language development. Point out what is happening, talk about the action as it occurs, laugh and enjoy the entertainment, and ask questions about what you see.

☑ If this objective is particularly difficult for a child, it may be necessary, within activities, to use an *instructional sequence*.

Instructional Sequence

- Model using descriptive words. For example, when playing in a sandbox, hold the child's hand up and say, "Dirty." Pause and give an expectant look. Encourage the child to imitate.
- Give a partial sound (or word) cue. Say the first sound (or word) of the utterance. For example, while rolling a big ball to the child, say, "This ball is b__." Encourage the child to complete the utterance and then repeat.
- Ask a simple question and answer it. Repeat the question. Provide guidelines for the child. For example, when heating the child's food in a pan, say, "Don't touch, hot! What is it?" Encourage the child to answer the question with the delayed model.
- Give the child a model and a directive to repeat. For example, say, "Hot! Tell me 'hot.' "

☑ Combining or pairing different levels of instructions may be helpful when beginning to teach a new and difficult skill. Fade to less intrusive instructions as soon as possible to encourage more independent performance.

TEACHING CONSIDERATIONS

1. If sensory or motor difficulties interfere with normal speech development, augmentative or alternative systems (e.g., signing, communication boards) should be introduced. Consult a qualified specialist for teaching techniques.
2. A child with a hearing impairment may hear only selected frequencies (high- or low-pitched sounds) or may hear only loud sounds. The child may also be sensitive to certain sounds or intensities (e.g., sounds that seem normal to you may be uncomfortably loud to some children, certain frequencies may be painful, combinations of sounds or too much noise may be uncomfortable).
3. If the child has a restricted range of motion in the head or trunk area, the speaker should be in a position that facilitates visual contact between the child and the speaker. Positioning is also critical to easy sound production. Latency of response may be noted. Consult a qualified sepcialist for recommendations for positioning and techniques for eliciting sounds from the child with a motor impairment.
4. Consider safety with all objects that the child handles. Never leave the child unattended with potentially hazardous objects.

SCD

Objective 1.2 Uses five action words

IMPORTANCE OF SKILL

It is important for children to use a variety of words to convey thoughts, wants, and needs. The purpose of this skill is for the child to use action words that describe an action of the child or another. For example, the child hands a box of animal crackers to an adult and says, "Open," or throws a ball and says, "Catch." These words provide a basis for future word combinations that are increasingly complex.

PRECEDING GOAL

SC B:2.0   Uses consistent word approximations

CONCURRENT GOALS AND OBJECTIVES

FM B:2.0   Assembles toy and/or object that require(s) putting pieces together
FM B:3.0   Uses either index finger to activate objects
GM C:1.0   Walks avoiding obstacles
GM C:2.0   Stoops and regains balanced standing position without support
GM C:3.0   Walks up and down stairs
GM D:1.0   Jumps forward
GM D:2.0   Pedals and steers tricycle
GM D:3.0   Runs avoiding obstacles
GM D:4.0   Catches, kicks, throws, and rolls ball or similar object
GM D:5.0   Climbs up and down play equipment
Adap A:5.0   Transfers food and liquid
Adap B:2.0   Washes and dries hands
Adap C:1.0   Undresses self
Cog B:3.0   Maintains search for object that is not in its usual location
Cog C:1.0   Correctly activates mechanical toy
Cog C:2.0   Reproduces part of interactive game and/or action in order to continue game and/or action
Cog D:1.0   Imitates motor action that is not commonly used
Cog D:2.0   Imitates words that are not frequently used
Cog E:2.0   Uses an object to obtain another object
Cog E:3.0   Navigates large object around barriers
Cog E:4.0   Solves common problems
Cog F:1.0   Aligns and stacks objects
Cog G:1.1   Uses representational actions with objects
SC A:1.0   Turns and looks toward person speaking
SC B:1.0   Gains person's attention and refers to an object, person, and/or event
SC C:1.0   Locates objects, people, and/or events *without* contextual cues
Soc A:3.0   Initiates and maintains communicative exchange with familiar adult
Soc B:1.0   Meets external physical needs in socially appropriate ways
Soc B:2.0   Responds to established social routine
Soc C:1.3   Plays near one or two peers

SC D

TEACHING SUGGESTIONS

Activity-Based

- Provide frequent opportunities for the child to interact with peers who use action words.
- Allow the child to help take care of the family pet. Let the child feed the pet: open the box of food, pour the food, and give it to the pet to eat. Some pets can be combed, walked, rubbed, petted, chased, or tickled. Pets provide great action activities.
- Throughout the day, talk about what the child is doing and label the actions. For example, when the child is eating, say, "Eat," or when the child is drinking, say, "Drink." Encourage the child to imitate.
- If the child uses an action word spontaneously, respond immediately with an appropriate consequence. For example, if the child says, "help," and gestures toward a box of crackers, say, "Oh, you want a cracker," and give one to the child.
- When playing with push- or pull-toys, model the appropriate action word when the child is performing the action.
- Activities can be designed to help teach a related group of action words. Planting a garden (or pretending) provides opportunities to practice action words such as raking, digging, hoeing, planting, watering, or covering. Similar groups of words can be developed from cooking, art, exercise, and block activities.
- Playing ball games provides opportunities for practicing action words such as throwing, catching, passing, rolling, bouncing, hitting, and kicking.
- Playing "Simon says" includes many actions: jump up, sit down, clap your hands, shake your leg, wave, and roll.
- When the child is introduced to a new experience or environment, talk about it ahead of time. While you are in the new environment, point out both familiar and new objects and actions. Talk more about the activity, objects, and people when you return home.

Environmental Arrangements

- Arrange for the child to participate in small group activities with peers whose language is slightly advanced. Facilitate peer models of action words during activities and encourage the child to imitate.
- Play with dolls and stuffed animals. Have them perform common actions such as sitting, sleeping, or eating. Ask the child what the baby is doing.
- Bounce the child up and down on your knee and say, "Bounce, bounce." Pause and wait for the child to respond, then continue the action.
- Play ball with the child. Take turns kicking, throwing, catching, rolling, and hitting. Label the actions.
- When looking at a favorite picture book, comment and label familiar actions, using exaggerated pitch and intonation, as in, "The baby's *crying*."
- When pulling the child in a wagon, say, "Go," several times. Stop and wait for the child to say "Go" before continuing the action. Model if necessary. This activity also works well on swings at the playground.

Instructional Sequence

- Model using action words. For example, when playing with a ball, say, "Roll," and "Catch," each time it is your turn. Pause and give an expectant look. Encourage the child to imitate.

SCD

- Give a partial sound (or word) cue. Say the first sound (or word) of the utterance. For example, while watching a kitten eat, say, "Kitty e___." Encourage the child to complete the utterance and then repeat.
- Ask a simple question and answer it. Repeat the question. Provide guidelines for the child. For example, bounce the child on your knee and say, "Bounce, bounce." Pause and ask the child, "What do you want?" Encourage the child to answer the question with the delayed model.
- Give the child a model and a directive to repeat. For example, tell the child, "Say 'bounce' " before continuing the action.

TEACHING CONSIDERATIONS

1. If sensory or motor difficulties interfere with normal speech development, augmentative or alternative systems (e.g., signing, communication boards) should be introduced. Consult a qualified specialist for teaching techniques.
2. A child with a hearing impairment may hear only selected frequencies (high- or low-pitched sounds) or may hear only loud sounds. The child may also be sensitive to certain sounds or intensities (e.g., sounds that seem normal to you may be uncomfortably loud to some children, certain frequencies may be painful, combinations of sounds or too much noise may be uncomfortable).
3. If the child has a restricted range of motion in the head or trunk area, the speaker should be in a position that facilitates visual contact between the child and the speaker. Positioning is also critical to easy sound production. Latency of response may be noted. Consult a qualified specialist for recommendations for positioning and techniques for eliciting sounds from the child with a motor impairment.
4. Consider safety with all objects that the child handles. Never leave the child unattended with potentially hazardous objects.

Objective 1.3 Uses two pronouns

IMPORTANCE OF SKILL

It is important for children to learn a variety of words to convey thoughts, wants, and needs. The purpose of this skill is for the child to use pronouns that make reference to an object or person. For example, the child looks at a photograph and says, "Me," or points to another and says, "You." These pronouns provide a basis for future word combinations that are increasingly complex.

PRECEDING GOAL

SC B:2.0   Uses consistent word approximations

CONCURRENT GOALS AND OBJECTIVES

FM A:5.0   Places and releases object balanced on top of another object with either hand
FM B:2.0   Assembles toy and/or object that require(s) putting pieces together
GM B:2.0   Sits down in and gets out of chair

GM C:1.0   Walks avoiding obstacles
GM C:3.0   Walks up and down stairs
GM D:4.0   Catches, kicks, throws, and rolls ball or similar object
Adap A:4.0   Eats with fork and/or spoon
Adap A:5.0   Transfers food and liquid
Adap B:2.0   Washes and dries hands
Adap C:1.0   Undresses self
Cog B:3.0   Maintains search for object that is not in its usual location
Cog C:2.0   Reproduces part of interactive game and/or action in order to continue
game and/or action
Cog D:1.0   Imitates motor action that is not commonly used
Cog D:2.0   Imitates words that are not frequently used
Cog E:2.0   Uses an object to obtain another object
Cog E:4.1   Uses more than one strategy in attempt to solve common problem
Cog F:2.2   Groups objects according to size, shape, and/or color
Cog G:1.1   Uses representational actions with objects
Soc A:3.0   Initiates and maintains communicative exchange with familiar adult
Soc B:2.0   Responds to established social routine
Soc C:2.2   Responds to communication from peer

TEACHING SUGGESTIONS
Activity-Based

- Provide frequent opportunities for the child to interact with peers who use pronouns.
- Play with boy and girl puppets. Have them perform actions and ask questions such as, "Who did that?"
- While on outings or looking at picture books with the child, point to people or objects and say, "Look at this," or "He's funny." Model several times.
- Show the child a photograph of yourself and say, "Who's this?" Model if necessary.
- When the child comments on the activity or action of another child, rephrase the sentence. For example, if the child says, "Roll," the adult says, "That's right, *he* rolled the ball."
- Use both proper nouns and pronouns when looking through photos, books, and magazines.

Environmental Arrangements

- Arrange for the child to participate in small group activities with peers whose language is slightly advanced. Facilitate peer models of pronouns during activities and encourage the child to imitate.
- Present a plate of cookies to the child and hold it just out of reach. Ask the child, "Who wants one?" Offer praise when the child says, "Me," or "I do." Model if necessary, then give the child a cookie.
- Play games such as "Button button, who has the button?" or "Who's wearing . . .?"
- Play a "my turn, your turn" game with the child using a ball, beanbag, or similar toy.

Instructional Sequence

- Model using pronouns. For example, when offering the child a cookie from a plate of cookies, say, "*I* want *this* one." Pause and give an expectant look. Encourage the child to imitate.

SC D

- Give a partial sound (or word) cue. Say the first sound (or word) of the utterance. For example, while dressing the child, hold up his or her shoe and say, "Whose shoe is this? M___." Encourage the child to complete the utterance and then repeat.
- Ask a simple question and answer it. Repeat the question. Provide guidelines for the child. For example, sit in front of a mirror with the child and ask, "Who's that?" Encourage the child to answer the question with the delayed model.
- Give the child a model and a directive to repeat. For example, tell the child, "Say, 'me!'"

TEACHING CONSIDERATIONS

1. If sensory or motor difficulties interfere with normal speech development, augmentative or alternative systems (e.g., signing, communication boards) should be introduced. Consult a qualified specialist for teaching techniques.
2. A child with a hearing impairment may hear only selected frequencies (high- or low-pitched sounds) or may hear only loud sounds. The child may also be sensitive to certain sounds or intensities (e.g., sounds that seem normal to you may be uncomfortably loud to some children, certain frequencies may be painful, combinations of sounds or too much noise may be uncomfortable).
3. If the child has a restricted range of motion in the head or trunk area, the speaker should be in a position that facilitates visual contact between the child and the speaker. Positioning is also critical to easy sound production. Latency of response may be noted. Consult a qualified specialist for recommendations for positioning and techniques for eliciting sounds from the child with a motor impairment.
4. Consider safety with all objects that the child handles. Never leave the child unattended with potentially hazardous objects.

Objective 1.4   Uses 15 object and/or event labels

IMPORTANCE OF SKILL

It is important for children to use a variety of words to convey thoughts, wants, and needs. The purpose of this skill is for the child to use object and/or event labels. For example, the child sees a dog and says, "Didi," or sees a child swinging and says, "Swing." These labels provide a basis for future word combinations that are increasingly complex.

PRECEDING GOAL

SC B:2.0   Uses consistent word approximations

CONCURRENT GOALS AND OBJECTIVES

FM A:5.0   Places and releases object balanced on top of another object with either hand
FM B:2.0   Assembles toy and/or object that require(s) putting pieces together
GM B:2.0   Sits down in and gets out of chair
GM C:3.0   Walks up and down stairs

GM D:4.0   Catches, kicks, throws, and rolls ball or similar object

Adap A:4.0 Eats with fork and/or spoon

Adap A:5.0 Transfers food and liquid

Adap B:2.0 Washes and dries hands

Adap B:3.0 Brushes teeth

Adap C:1.0 Undresses self

Cog B:3.0   Maintains search for object that is not in its usual location

Cog C:1.0   Correctly activates mechanical toy

Cog C:2.0   Reproduces part of interactive game and/or action in order to continue game and/or action

Cog D:1.0   Imitates motor action that is not commonly used

Cog D:2.0   Imitates words that are not frequently used

Cog E:2.0   Uses an object to obtain another object

Cog E:4.1   Uses more than one strategy in attempt to solve common problem

Cog F:2.2   Groups objects according to size, shape, and/or color

Cog G:1.1   Uses representational actions with objects

SC A:3.0   Engages in vocal exchanges by babbling

SC C:1.0   Locates objects, people, and/or events *without* contextual cues

Soc A:3.0   Initiates and maintains communicative exchange with familiar adult

Soc B:2.0   Responds to established social routine

Soc C:1.2   Responds appropriately to peer's social behavior

Soc C:2.2   Responds to communication from peer

TEACHING SUGGESTIONS

Activity-Based

- Provide frequent opportunities for the child to interact with peers who use object and event labels.
- Play the naming game. Describe and comment on objects and events in the environment throughout the day. Talk to the child and label toys as the child plays with them or talk about what is happening around the house.
- Play a turn-taking game where you label an item and perform an action, and the child repeats it. For example, put a block on a stack for a tower and say, "block." Give the child a turn. Or put a cookie on a plate and say, "cookie." Give the child a turn.
- When interacting with the child during routine activities, imitate the child's words or word approximations.
- When bathing the child, talk about the parts of the body you are washing. "Let's wash your tummy. Now let's wash your foot. Oh, there's your nose!"
- Look in a mirror and take turns pointing out body parts.
- Play "Give me" and name items as you exchange with the child. For example, when the child extends the spoon during a meal, say, "Give me the *spoon.*"

Environmental Arrangements

- Arrange for the child to participate in small group activities with peers whose language is slightly advanced. Facilitate peer models of object and event labels during activities and encourage the child to imitate them.
- When looking at favorite books, comment and label the pictures, using exaggerated pitch and intonation: "Look at the *doggie.*"
- When looking at favorite books, label objects on one page, then turn the page and

SC D

pause to allow the child to respond. Encourage the child to point to pictures and name them.

■ Observe the objects the child interacts with frequently throughout the day. Model these labels and encourage the child to imitate.

■ Observe the child throughout the day to identify which toys the child most readily responds to. Hold a desired toy just out of reach and ask, "What do you want?" Pause and give the child an opportunity to respond, model if necessary, then give the child the desired toy.

■ Play "tickle" or "gonna get you" games. Ask the child what body part to tickle or get next. Make using words fun.

Instructional Sequence

■ Model labeling objects and events. For example, when a cat enters the room, say, "Kitty," or when the dog barks, say, "Bow-wow." Pause and give an expectant look. Encourage the child to imitate.

■ Give a partial sound (or word) cue. Say the first sound (or word) of the utterance. For example, when the child is looking at a picture of a pig, say, "Look, a p ___." Encourage the child to complete the utterance and then repeat.

■ Ask a simple question and answer it. Repeat the question. Provide guidelines for the child. For example, when it is time for a snack, say, "What do you want?" Encourage the child to answer the question with the delayed model.

■ Give the child a model and a directive to repeat. For example, tell the child, "Say, 'Cookie.' "

TEACHING CONSIDERATIONS

1. If sensory or motor difficulties interfere with normal speech development, augmentative or alternative systems (e.g., technological devices, signing) should be introduced. Consult a qualified specialist for teaching techniques.

2. A child with a hearing impairment may hear only selected frequencies (high- or low-pitched sounds) or may hear only loud sounds. The child may also be sensitive to certain sounds or intensities (e.g., sounds that seem normal to you may be uncomfortably loud to some children, certain frequencies may be painful, combinations of sounds or too much noise may be uncomfortable).

3. If the child has a restricted range of motion in the head or trunk area, the speaker should be in a position that facilitates visual contact between the child and the speaker. Positioning is also critical to easy sound production. Latency of response may be noted. Consult a qualified specialist for recommendations for positioning and techniques for eliciting sounds from the child with a motor impairment.

4. Consider safety with all objects that the child handles. Never leave the child unattended with potentially hazardous objects.

Objective 1.5   Uses three proper names

IMPORTANCE OF SKILL

It is important for children to use a variety of words to convey thoughts, wants, and needs. The purpose of this skill is for the child to use proper names that make reference to a specific person or to animals. For example, the child looks at a parent and says, "Mama," or at a photograph of the family dog and says, "Didi." These proper names provide a basis for future word combinations that are increasingly complex.

PRECEDING GOAL

SC B:2.0   Uses consistent word approximations

CONCURRENT GOALS AND OBJECTIVES

Cog B:3.0   Maintains search for object that is not in its usual location
Cog C:2.0   Reproduces part of interactive game and/or action in order to continue
            game and/or action
Cog D:1.0   Imitates motor action that is not commonly used
Cog D:2.0   Imitates words that are not frequently used
Cog E:2.0   Uses an object to obtain another object
Cog G:1.0   Uses imaginary objects in play
SC C:2.3   Carries out one-step direction *with* contextual cues
Soc A:3.0   Initiates and maintains communicative exchange with familiar adult
Soc B:2.0   Responds to established social routine
Soc C:1.2   Responds appropriately to peer's social behavior
Soc C:2.2   Responds to communication from peer

TEACHING SUGGESTIONS
Activity-Based

- Provide frequent opportunities for the child to interact with peers who use proper names.
- Throughout the day, use the names of siblings or neighborhood children several times. Call peers by their names and ask the child to "Go get Billy," "Come sit by Juan," or "Give Jenny a book."
- Look at photo albums while the child sits on your lap. If the child points to a picture, say, "There's Maria."
- Give names to the child's favorite stuffed animals. When the child is playing with one of them, refer to it by name.
- Have the child look in a mirror and ask, "Who is that?" Point to yourself, the child, or peers.

Environmental Arrangements

- Arrange for the child to participate in small group activities with peers whose language is slightly advanced. Facilitate peer models of proper names during activities and encourage the child to imitate.
- Make a family photo album. Name the person on one page, then turn the page and pause, giving the child an opportunity to name the next person. Model if necessary.
- Have more than one photo of the same sibling, parent, or peer. Label the first picture and ask the child to name subsequent pictures.
- Use exaggerated pitch and intonation when calling family members to dinner. "*Bobby*, time to eat." Ask the child to call to the family member. Model if necessary.

SC D

- Identify important people and pets in the child's life. Provide opportunities to see them. Call them on play telephones.

Instructional Sequence

- Model using proper names. For example, when a sibling enters the play area, say, "Hi, Ricardo!" Pause and give an expectant look. Encourage the child to imitate.
- Give a partial sound (or word) cue. Say the first sound (or word) of the utterance. For example, when the family dog, Didi, runs into the house, say, "Look, D ___!" Encourage the child to complete the utterance and then repeat.
- Ask a simple question and answer it. Repeat the question. Provide guidelines for the child. For example, when a parent enters the house, ask, "Who's that?" Encourage the child to answer the question with the delayed model.
- Give the child a model and a directive to repeat. For example, tell the child, "Say, 'Hi Daddy.' "

TEACHING CONSIDERATIONS

1. If sensory or motor difficulties interfere with normal speech development, augmentative or alternative systems (e.g., signing, communication boards) should be introduced. Consult a qualified specialist for teaching techniques.
2. A child with a hearing impairment may hear only selected frequencies (high- or low-pitched sounds) or may hear only loud sounds. The child may also be sensitive to certain sounds or intensities (e.g., sounds that seem normal to you may be uncomfortably loud to some children, certain frequencies may be painful, combinations of sounds or too much noise may be uncomfortable).
3. If the child has a restricted range of motion in the head or trunk area, the speaker should be in a position that facilitates visual contact between the child and the speaker. Positioning is also critical to easy sound production. Latency of response may be noted. Consult a qualified specialist for recommendations for positioning and techniques for eliciting sounds from the child with a motor impairment.
4. Consider safety with all objects that the child handles. Never leave the child unattended with potentially hazardous objects.

GOAL 2   Uses two-word utterances

DEVELOPMENTAL PROGRAMMING STEPS

In order to achieve this goal, a child must perform the skills in Objectives 2.1–2.6 to criteria. Refer to the specific objective for Developmental Programming Steps to develop each skill.

IMPORTANCE OF SKILL

Once the child has learned to produce single words that serve a variety of communicative functions, the child begins to combine words into two-word utterances or early phrases. This improves the child's ability to communicate and convey thoughts, wants,

SC D

and needs. It also promotes social skills and interaction with the environment. The purpose of this skill is for the child to use two-word utterances that express different meanings. For example, "baby bed" may refer to the child's doll in a bed, may denote ownership (baby's bed), or may be a directive (put the baby to bed). These two-word expressions provide a basis for future word communication that is increasingly complex.

PRECEDING GOAL

SC D:1.0   Uses 50 single words

CONCURRENT GOALS

FM B:2.0	Assembles toy and/or object that require(s) putting pieces together
FM B:3.0	Uses either index finger to activate objects
FM B:4.0	Copies simple written shapes after demonstration
GM C:2.0	Stoops and regains balanced standing position without support
GM C:3.0	Walks up and down stairs
GM D:1.0	Jumps forward
GM D:2.0	Pedals and steers tricycle
GM D:3.0	Runs avoiding obstacles
GM D:4.0	Catches, kicks, throws, and rolls ball or similar object
GM D:5.0	Climbs up and down play equipment
Adap A:5.0	Transfers food and liquid
Adap B:1.0	Initiates toileting
Adap B:2.0	Washes and dries hands
Adap B:3.0	Brushes teeth
Adap C:1.0	Undresses self
Cog B:3.0	Maintains search for object that is not in its usual location
Cog D:1.0	Imitates motor action that is not commonly used
Cog D:2.0	Imitates words that are not frequently used
Cog E:2.0	Uses an object to obtain another object
Cog E:3.0	Navigates large object around barriers
Cog E:4.0	Solves common problems
Cog F:2.0	Categorizes like objects
Cog F:3.0	Demonstrates functional use of one-to-one correspondence
Cog G:1.0	Uses imaginary objects in play
SC C:2.0	Carries out two-step direction *without* contextual cues
Soc A:3.0	Initiates and maintains communicative exchange with familiar adult
Soc B:1.0	Meets external physical needs in socially appropriate ways
Soc B:2.0	Responds to established social routine
Soc C:1.0	Initiates and maintains interaction with peer
Soc C:2.0	Initiates and maintains communicative exchange with peer

TEACHING SUGGESTIONS

In order to achieve this goal, a child must perform the skills in Objectives 2.1–2.6 to criteria. Refer to the specific objective for Teaching Suggestions and Teaching Considerations to develop each skill.

SC D

Objective 2.1   Uses two-word utterances to express agent–action, action–object, and agent–object

DEVELOPMENTAL PROGRAMMING STEPS

No standard developmental sequence appears to exist for the development of two-word phrases. Careful observation of the child will help determine the function(s) of two-word phrases.

PS2.1a   The child uses a two-word utterance to express agent–action.
PS2.1b   The child uses a two-word utterance to express action–object.
PS2.1c   The child uses a two-word utterance to express agent–object.

IMPORTANCE OF SKILL

The purpose of this skill is for the child to use two-word utterances that express agent–action, action–object, and agent–object to convey thoughts, wants, and needs. For example, the child sees the dog eating and says, "Doggie eat" (agent–action); the child holds out his or her arms and says, "Throw ball" (action–object); or the child watches the dog chewing a bone and says, "Doggie bone" (agent–object). These two-word expressions provide a basis for future communication that becomes increasingly complex.

PRECEDING GOAL

SC D:1.0   Uses 50 single words

CONCURRENT GOALS

FM B:2.0   Assembles toy and/or object that require(s) putting pieces together
FM B:3.0   Uses either index finger to activate objects
FM B:4.0   Copies simple written shapes after demonstration
GM C:2.0   Stoops and regains balanced standing position without support
GM C:3.0   Walks up and down stairs
GM D:1.0   Jumps forward
GM D:2.0   Pedals and steers tricycle
GM D:3.0   Runs avoiding obstacles
GM D:4.0   Catches, kicks, throws, and rolls ball or similar object
GM D:5.0   Climbs up and down play equipment
Adap A:5.0 Transfers food and liquid
Adap B:1.0 Initiates toileting
Adap B:2.0 Washes and dries hands
Adap B:3.0 Brushes teeth
Adap C:1.0 Undresses self
Cog B:3.0   Maintains search for object that is not in its usual location
Cog D:1.0   Imitates motor action that is not commonly used
Cog D:2.0   Imitates words that are not frequently used
Cog E:2.0   Uses an object to obtain another object
Cog E:3.0   Navigates large object around barriers
Cog E:4.0   Solves common problems
Cog F:2.0   Categorizes like objects

SC D

Cog F:3.0   Demonstrates functional use of one-to-one correspondence
Cog G:1.0   Uses imaginary objects in play
SC C:2.0   Carries out two-step direction *without* contextual cues
Soc A:3.0   Initiates and maintains communicative exchange with familiar adult
Soc B:1.0   Meets external physical needs in socially appropriate ways
Soc B:2.0   Responds to established social routine
Soc C:1.0   Initiates and maintains interaction with peer
Soc C:2.0   Initiates and maintains communicative exchange with peer

TEACHING SUGGESTIONS
Activity-Based

- Provide frequent opportunities for the child to interact with peers who use two-word or longer utterances.
- Comment on and describe what you are doing throughout the day. Whenever possible, use two-word combinations that the child can already say.
- When the child uses word approximations for labels and actions, expand on what he or she says. For example, if the child points to the family pet and says, "Doggie," say, "Doggie bark," or "Doggie sleeping," or "Pet doggie."
- Play with bubbles together. Blow, pop, step on, and wave at the bubbles. Label with two words, "Blow bubble," or "Bubble pop."
- While completing adaptive routines such as brushing teeth or washing hands, encourage the child to talk with you about what you are doing and to follow your directions.
- When the child is playing with a favorite stuffed animal, give the child directions. For example, say, "Make teddy sit," or "Feed teddy." Encourage the child to give the animal instructions while you manipulate the object.

Environmental Arrangements

- Arrange for the child to participate in small group activities with peers whose language is slightly advanced. Facilitate peer models of agent–action, action–object and agent–object utterances during activities and encourage the child to imitate them.
- Put the child's favorite toy just out of reach. Pause and wait for the child to request the toy, modeling if necessary, and then give the child the toy to play with.
- Toy sets such as a barnyard, garage, or circus train offer many opportunities to combine words while playing.
- Make a photo album and use pictures of the child and peers. Sit with the child in your lap and encourage the child to describe the pictures. Any two-word combinations should be encouraged.
- Tell a story using stuffed animals and have the animals act out the plot. If telling a familiar story, pause and encourage the child to tell what happens next. Then use the animals to act out the child's two-word utterances.
- When riding in the car, ask the child where he or she would like to go. Then ask what the child sees or hears.

Instructional Sequence

- Model using two-word expressions. For example, the child points to a cookie, and the adult says, "Want cookie." Pause and give an expectant look. Encourage the child to imitate.

- Give a partial sound (or word) cue. Say the first sound (or word) of the utterance. For example, when looking at a picture of a horse in a picture book, the adult says, "Ride ___," and pauses and waits for the child to respond. Encourage the child to complete the utterance and then repeat the phrase.
- Ask a simple question and answer it. Repeat the question. Provide guidelines for the child. For example, the adult asks, "What do you see?" Encourage the child to answer the question with the delayed model.
- Give the child a model and a directive to repeat. For example, tell the child, "Say, 'Kitty sleeping.'"

TEACHING CONSIDERATIONS

1. If sensory or motor difficulties interfere with normal speech development, augmentative or alternative systems (e.g., signing, communication boards) should be introduced. Consult a qualified specialist for teaching techniques.
2. A child with a hearing impairment may hear only selected frequencies (high- or low-pitched sounds) or may hear only loud sounds. The child may also be sensitive to certain sounds or intensities (e.g., sounds that seem normal to you may be uncomfortably loud to some children, certain frequencies may be painful, combinations of sounds or too much noise may be uncomfortable).
3. If the child has a restricted range of motion in the head or trunk area, the the speaker should be in a position that facilitates visual contact between the child and speaker. Positioning is also critical to easy sound production. Latency of the response may be noted. Consult a qualified specialist for recommendations for positioning and techniques for eliciting sounds from the child with a motor impairment.
4. Consider safety with all objects that the child handles. Never leave the child unattended with potentially hazardous objects.

Objective 2.2 Uses two-word utterances to express possession

IMPORTANCE OF SKILL

The purpose of this skill is for the child to use two-word utterances that express possession to convey thoughts, wants, and needs. For example, the child looks at his or her shoe and says, "My shoe," or gives a toy to a brother and says, "Jimmy's car." These two-word expressions of possession provide a basis for future communication that becomes increasingly complex.

PRECEDING GOAL

SC D:1.0   Uses 50 single words

CONCURRENT GOALS

FM B:2.0   Assembles toy and/or object that require(s) putting pieces together
FM B:3.0   Uses either index finger to activate objects

FM B:4.0   Copies simple written shapes after demonstration
GM C:2.0   Stoops and regains balanced standing position without support
GM C:3.0   Walks up and down stairs
GM D:1.0   Jumps forward
GM D:2.0   Pedals and steers tricycle
GM D:3.0   Runs avoiding obstacles
GM D:4.0   Catches, kicks, throws, and rolls ball or similar object
GM D:5.0   Climbs up and down play equipment
Adap A:5.0 Transfers food and liquid
Adap B:1.0 Initiates toileting
Adap B:2.0 Washes and dries hands
Adap B:3.0 Brushes teeth
Adap C:1.0 Undresses self
Cog B:3.0   Maintains search for object that is not in its usual location
Cog D:1.0   Imitates motor action that is not commonly used
Cog D:2.0   Imitates words that are not frequently used
Cog E:2.0   Uses an object to obtain another object
Cog E:3.0   Navigates large object around barriers
Cog E:4.0   Solves common problems
Cog F:2.0   Categorizes like objects
Cog F:3.0   Demonstrates functional use of one-to-one correspondence
Cog G:1.0   Uses imaginary objects in play
SC C:2.0   Carries out two-step direction *without* contextual cues
Soc A:3.0   Initiates and maintains communicative exchange with familiar adult
Soc B:1.0   Meets external physical needs in socially appropriate ways
Soc B:2.0   Responds to established social routine
Soc C:1.0   Initiates and maintains interaction with peer
Soc C:2.0   Initiates and maintains communicative exchange with peer

TEACHING SUGGESTIONS

Activity-Based

- Provide frequent opportunities for the child to interact with peers who use two-word utterances to express possession.
- Throughout the day, within the context of activities, ask occasional questions about ownership of objects. Say, "Whose __ is this?" Model by saying, "My __ " for your own things.
- During small group activities, comment about the materials being used by the child or those you are passing out. For example, say, "That's Tommy's paintbrush," or "Here's Cindy's crayon."
- While sorting laundry, categorize clothing by ownership—Joey's shirt, Mom's socks, and Susie's pants.
- Look through the family photo album and encourage the child to comment about who is doing what in the pictures. Ask questions.
- During a fingerpainting activity, encourage the child to make hand- or footprints. When they are dry, see if the child can find his or her print and tell peers about it.

SCD

Environmental Arrangements

- Arrange for the child to participate in small group activities with peers whose language is slightly advanced. Facilitate peer models of two-word utterances to express possession during activities and encourage the child to imitate.
- Make a little box or cubby that has the child's name on it and ask the child to put various materials in it throughout the day. Ask the child to label the activity while participating. Encourage the child to keep personal belongings.
- Use photos to label the cubbies so that children can describe what goes inside.
- Make a "Family Area" where pictures of the child's family members are hung. Ask the child to tell peers about the pictures.
- During an art activity, "accidentally" pick up something that the child is working on and say, "Here's *my* hat." (The "confused" adult is a great technique to use during any activity.)
- Hold up an object belonging to the child and ask, "Whose __ is this?" Withhold the object until the child verbally labels possession.
- Sing action songs or recite finger plays and poems that include "possession" words.

Instructional Sequence

- Model using two-word expressions for possession. For example, make a picture book with photos of some of the child's favorite toys and classroom items that belong to the adult. The adult says, "My book," or "My pencil," pointing to his or her own objects. Pause and give an expectant look. Encourage the child to imitate.
- Give a partial sound (or word) cue. Say the first sound (or word) of the utterance. For example, when the child comments about an article of clothing such as a shoe, the adult says, "That's right, my __." Encourage the child to complete the utterance and then repeat.
- Ask a simple question and answer it. Repeat the question. Provide guidelines for the child. For example, the adult asks, "Whose book is this?" and gestures to the child. Encourage the child to answer the question with the delayed model.
- Give the child a model and a directive to repeat. For example, "Whose sock is this? Mom's sock. Say, 'Mom's sock.' "

TEACHING CONSIDERATIONS

1. If sensory or motor difficulties interfere with normal speech development, augmentative or alternative systems (e.g., signing, technological devices) should be introduced. Consult a qualified specialist for teaching techniques.
2. A child with a hearing impairment may hear only selected frequencies (high- or low-pitched sounds) or may hear only loud sounds. The child may also be sensitive to certain sounds or intensities (e.g., sounds that seem normal to you may be uncomfortably loud to some children, certain frequencies may be painful, combinations of sounds or too much noise may be uncomfortable).
3. If the child has a restricted range of motion in the head or trunk area, the speaker should be in a position that facilitates visual contact between the child and the speaker. Positioning is also critical to easy sound production. Latency of response may be noted. Consult a qualified specialist for recommendations for positioning and techniques for eliciting sounds from the child with a motor impairment.
4. Consider safety with all objects that the child handles. Never leave the child unattended with potentially hazardous objects.

SC D

Objective 2.3   Uses two-word utterances to express location

IMPORTANCE OF SKILL

The purpose of this skill is for the child to use two-word utterances that express location to convey thoughts, wants, and needs. For example, the child points to his or her father and says, "There's Daddy," or puts a block in a toy truck and says, "In truck." These two-word expressions of location provide a basis for future communication that becomes increasingly complex.

PRECEDING GOALS

SC C:1.0   Locates objects, people, and/or events *without* contextual cues
SC D:1.0   Uses 50 single words

CONCURRENT GOALS

FM B:2.0   Assembles toy and/or object that require(s) putting pieces together
FM B:3.0   Uses either index finger to activate objects
FM B:4.0   Copies simple written shapes after demonstration
GM C:2.0   Stoops and regains balanced standing position without support
GM C:3.0   Walks up and down stairs
GM D:1.0   Jumps forward
GM D:2.0   Pedals and steers tricycle
GM D:3.0   Runs avoiding obstacles
GM D:4.0   Catches, kicks, throws, and rolls ball or similar object
GM D:5.0   Climbs up and down play equipment
Adap A:5.0 Transfers food and liquid
Adap B:1.0 Initiates toileting
Adap B:2.0 Washes and dries hands
Adap B:3.0 Brushes teeth
Adap C:1.0 Undresses self
Cog B:3.0   Maintains search for object that is not in its usual location
Cog D:1.0   Imitates motor action that is not commonly used
Cog D:2.0   Imitates words that are not frequently used
Cog E:2.0   Uses an object to obtain another object
Cog E:3.0   Navigates large object around barriers
Cog E:4.0   Solves common problems
Cog F:2.0   Categorizes like objects
Cog F:3.0   Demonstrates functional use of one-to-one correspondence
Cog G:1.0   Uses imaginary objects in play
SC C:2.0   Carries out two-step direction *without* contextual cues
Soc A:3.0   Initiates and maintains communicative exchange with familiar adult
Soc B:1.0   Meets external physical needs in socially appropriate ways
Soc B:2.0   Responds to established social routine
Soc C:1.0   Initiates and maintains interaction with peer
Soc C:2.0   Initiates and maintains communicative exchange with peer

SC D

TEACHING SUGGESTIONS
Activity-Based

- Provide frequent opportunities for the child to interact with peers who use two-word utterances to express location.
- Point out actions and locations while driving together in a car or van. "Where is the garbage truck?", "Can you see the park? Show me where," and "What is on that roof?"
- Throughout the day, within the context of activities, ask occasional questions about the location of specific objects or people. "What is *in* Susan's pocket?", "Where did you leave your lunch box?", and "Put this on the counter."
- Work on puzzles or shape-sorting activities together. Talk about where you are putting the pieces. "This one goes on the top," or "This piece goes with the flowers."
- Play with a farm set and set up a fence. Put chicks *on* the fence, cows *in* the barn, farmer *on* the tractor, and sheep *in* the pen.
- During small group activities, comment on the location of materials that the child is using. For example, when playing with toys in the sandbox, say, "Oops, the cow's buried *in* the sand," or "The shovel is *under* the pail."
- When looking through picture books, ask the child where certain objects or people are located. If the child points, say, "That's right. The ball is *under* the car."

Environmental Arrangements

- Arrange for the child to participate in small group activities with peers whose language is slightly advanced. Facilitate peer models of two-word utterances to express location during activities and encourage the child to imitate.
- During an art activity, put the box of crayons just out of reach, but within the child's field of vision. Pretend to have misplaced the crayons and say, "I wonder where I put the crayons."
- Play police and direct traffic by telling the child where to park a car.
- Play a "treasure hunt" game. Hide a favorite toy and give the child various directions on how to find it: "Look *under* the table," and "Now, look *in* the box." Then have the child hide a toy and give directions to another child. Model when necessary.
- When looking through picture books, use exaggerated pitch and intonation as you describe the locations of objects or people. For example, say, "Look at the kitty. He's hiding *under* the umbrella!"
- Play action games, such as "Simon says," on the playground. Use directives such as jump up, step over, climb in, and get on.

Instructional Sequence

- Model using two-word expressions for location. For example, arrange boxes and cans on the floor and hide little toys one at a time while the child is watching. Say, "In box," or "Behind can," while hiding toys. Pause and give an expectant look. Encourage the child to imitate.
- Give a partial sound (or word) cue. Say the first sound (or word) of the utterance. For example, as the child puts a block in a truck, the adult says, "In ___." Encourage the child to complete the utterance and then repeat.
- Ask a simple question and answer it. Repeat the question. Provide guidelines for the child. For example, when playing with the child, ask, "Where's kitty?" Encourage the child to answer the question with the delayed model.

■ Give the child a model and a directive to repeat. For example, tell the child, "Say, 'Kitty outside.'"

TEACHING CONSIDERATIONS

1. If sensory or motor difficulties interfere with normal speech development, augmentative or alternative systems (e.g., signing, communication boards) should be introduced. Consult a qualified specialist for teaching techniques.
2. A child with a hearing impairment may hear only selected frequencies (high- or low-pitched sounds) or may hear only loud sounds. The child may also be sensitive to certain sounds or intensities (e.g., sounds that seem normal to you may be uncomfortably loud to some children, certain frequencies may be painful, combinations of sounds or too much noise may be uncomfortable).
3. If the child has a restricted range of motion in the head or trunk area, the speaker should be in a position that facilitates visual contact between the child and the speaker. Positioning is also critical to easy sound production. Latency of response may be noted. Consult a qualified specialist for recommendations for positioning and techniques for eliciting sounds from the child with a motor impairment.
4. Consider safety with all objects that the child handles. Never leave the child unattended with potentially hazardous objects.

Objective 2.4   Uses two-word utterances to describe objects, people, and/or events

---

IMPORTANCE OF SKILL

The purpose of this skill is for the child to use two-word utterances that describe objects, people, or events as a way to convey thoughts, wants, and needs. For example, the child sees a favorite toy and says, "Red car" (object); the child takes a diaper off a doll and says, "Wet baby" (person); or the child sits on a swing and says, "Go fast" (event). These two-word expressions or description provide a basis for future communication that becomes increasingly complex.

PRECEDING GOAL

SC D:1.0   Uses 50 single words

CONCURRENT GOALS

FM B:2.0   Assembles toy and/or object that require(s) putting pieces together
FM B:3.0   Uses either index finger to activate objects
FM B:4.0   Copies simple written shapes after demonstration
GM C:2.0   Stoops and regains balanced standing position without support
GM C:3.0   Walks up and down stairs
GM D:1.0   Jumps forward
GM D:2.0   Pedals and steers tricycle
GM D:3.0   Runs avoiding obstacles
GM D:4.0   Catches, kicks, throws, and rolls ball or similar object
GM D:5.0   Climbs up and down play equipment

SC D

Adap A:5.0   Transfers food and liquid
Adap B:1.0   Initiates toileting
Adap B:2.0   Washes and dries hands
Adap B:3.0   Brushes teeth
Adap C:1.0   Undresses self
Cog B:3.0   Maintains search for object that is not in its usual location
Cog D:1.0   Imitates motor action that is not commonly used
Cog D:2.0   Imitates words that are not frequently used
Cog E:2.0   Uses an object to obtain another object
Cog E:3.0   Navigates large object around barriers
Cog E:4.0   Solves common problems
Cog F:2.0   Categorizes like objects
Cog F:3.0   Demonstrates functional use of one-to-one correspondence
Cog G:1.0   Uses imaginary objects in play
SC C:2.0   Carries out two-step direction *without* contextual cues
Soc A:3.0   Initiates and maintains communicative exchange with familiar adult
Soc B:1.0   Meets external physical needs in socially appropriate ways
Soc B:2.0   Responds to established social routine
Soc C:1.0   Initiates and maintains interaction with peer
Soc C:2.0   Initiates and maintains communicative exchange with peer

TEACHING SUGGESTIONS

Activity-Based

- Provide frequent opportunities for the child to interact with peers who use two-word descriptions
- Throughout the day, observe the child's response toward objects, people, and events to determine those to which the child most readily vocalizes. Use descriptive words to recast the child's utterance. For example, if the child says, "Truck go," say, "I see the red truck go."
- While drawing and coloring, use different colors to make big circles, long lines, fat marks, or happy faces.
- Throughout the day, during the child's daily routines, model developmentally appropriate descriptive words, such as words related to size, color, and temperature.
- Look at picture books with the child and describe the pictures. For example, point to a picture and say, "Look, it's cold outside," or "I see a baby chick."

Environmental Arrangements

- Arrange for the child to participate in small group activities with peers whose language is slightly advanced. Facilitate peer models of two-word descriptions during activities and encourage the child to imitate.
- Present two objects to the child that are the same except for one attribute, such as size or color. Say, "Which one do you want, the *big* cookie or the *little* cookie?" Use exaggerated pitch and intonation. If the child does not respond, model and present one of the items.
- Play a fishing game with cut-out fish of different colors, sizes, and textures. Have the child describe the catch.
- Make a picture book with pairs of opposite words on facing pages. Point to one page

and say, "Big boy," and point to the facing page and pause, giving the child the opportunity to respond with "Little boy." Model if necessary.

- Use songs and nursery rhymes to incorporate action with description, such as loud, soft, fat, thin, happy, and sad.
- Hold several color crayons or markers just out of the child's reach. Ask the child, "Which one do you want?" Pause, then model if necessary before giving the child the marker. Many objects can be within visual range, yet out of reach, making it necessary for the child to label and request them.

Instructional Sequence

- Model using a two-word expression to describe objects. For example, when looking at books with the child, say "red truck," "pretty baby," or "big circus." Pause and give an expectant look. Encourage the child to imitate.
- Give a partial sound (or word) cue. Say the first sound (or word) of the utterance. For example, when looking at a picture of a puppy, the adult says, "Dirty ___." Encourage the child to complete the utterances and then repeat.
- Ask a simple question and answer it. Repeat the question. Provide guidelines for the child. For example, when holding two objects, the adult asks, "Do you want the big ball?" Encourage the child to answer the question with the delayed model.
- Give the child a model and a directive to repeat. For example, tell the child, "Say 'Little ball.'"

TEACHING CONSIDERATIONS

1. If sensory or motor difficulties interfere with normal speech development, augmentative or alternative systems (e.g., signing, technological devices) should be introduced. Consult a qualified specialist for teaching techniques.
2. A child with a hearing impairment may hear only selected frequencies (high- or low-pitched sounds) or may hear only loud sounds. The child may also be sensitive to certain sounds or intensities (e.g., sounds that seem normal to you may be uncomfortably loud to some children, certain frequencies may be painful, combinations of sounds or too much noise may be uncomfortable).
3. If the child has a restricted range of motion in the head or trunk area, the speaker should be in a position that facilitates visual contact between the child and the speaker. Positioning is also critical to easy sound production. Latency of response may be noted. Consult a qualified specialist for recommendations for positioning and techniques for eliciting sounds from the child with a motor impairment.
4. Consider safety with all objects that the child handles. Never leave the child unattended with potentially hazardous objects.

Objective 2.5   Uses two-word utterances to express recurrence

---

IMPORTANCE OF SKILL

The purpose of this skill is for the child to use two-word utterances that express recurrence as a way to convey thoughts, wants, and needs. For example, the child holds up a cup and says, "More milk," or throws a ball and says, "Throw again." These two-word expressions of recurrence provide a basis for future communication that becomes increasingly complex.

PRECEDING GOAL

SC D:1.0   Uses 50 single words

CONCURRENT GOALS

FM B:2.0	Assembles toy and/or object that require(s) putting pieces together
FM B:3.0	Uses either index finger to activate objects
FM B:4.0	Copies simple written shapes after demonstration
GM C:2.0	Stoops and regains balanced standing position without support
GM C:3.0	Walks up and down stairs
GM D:1.0	Jumps forward
GM D:2.0	Pedals and steers tricycle
GM D:3.0	Runs avoiding obstacles
GM D:4.0	Catches, kicks, throws, and rolls ball or similar object
GM D:5.0	Climbs up and down play equipment
Adap A:5.0	Transfers food and liquid
Adap B:1.0	Initiates toileting
Adap B:2.0	Washes and dries hands
Adap B:3.0	Brushes teeth
Adap C:1.0	Undresses self
Cog B:3.0	Maintains search for object that is not in its usual location
Cog D:1.0	Imitates motor action that is not commonly used
Cog D:2.0	Imitates words that are not frequently used
Cog E:2.0	Uses an object to obtain another object
Cog E:3.0	Navigates large object around barriers
Cog E:4.0	Solves common problems
Cog F:2.0	Categorizes like objects
Cog F:3.0	Demonstrates functional use of one-to-one correspondence
Cog G:1.0	Uses imaginary objects in play
SC C:2.0	Carries out two-step direction *without* contextual cues
Soc A:3.0	Initiates and maintains communicative exchange with familiar adult
Soc B:1.0	Meets external physical needs in socially appropriate ways
Soc B:2.0	Responds to established social routine
Soc C:1.0	Initiates and maintains interaction with peer
Soc C:2.0	Initiates and maintains communicative exchange with peer

TEACHING SUGGESTIONS
Activity-Based

- Provide frequent opportunities for the child to interact with peers who use two-word utterances to express recurrence.
- Throughout the day, within the context of activities, make occasional comments about what you are doing. For example, when snacks are passed, say, "Cindy has more raisins," or "I think Kevin wants more juice."

- Play a tickle game or any rough-house activity that the child enjoys. Stop and wait for the child to ask for "more" or to do it "again."
- During snack time, when the child indicates a desire for an item, expand the sentence. For example, if the child holds up a cup and says, "Milk," say, "Oh, you want more milk."
- When looking through picture books, talk about objects you see more than once. For example, when looking at a farm animal book, say, "Look, more chicks!"

Environmental Arrangements

- Arrange for the child to participate in small group activities with peers whose language is slightly advanced. Facilitate peer models of two-word utterances to express recurrence during activities and encourage the child to imitate.
- Many toys can be manipulated so that the child asks for "more." Wind up the toy only a little so that it winds down quickly. Give only one piece of tape or a small amount of paint at a time. The child can ask for "More music," or to "Turn it again," or for "More paint."
- When playing with blocks, ask the child to build a tower like yours, but give the child only one block. Have more blocks just out of the child's reach, give an expectant look, and ask, "What do you need?"
- Play action games with the child, such as pulling the child in a wagon. Stop and wait for the child to say, "Go again," or "More wagon." Model if necessary before resuming action. Playground equipment (e.g., slides, swings, merry-go-rounds) are favorites for requesting "more."
- During snack time, give the child one cracker and put others just out of reach. Wait for the child to ask for more before giving the child another cracker. Model if necessary.

Instructional Sequence

- Model using two-word expressions of recurrence. For example, when pushing the child in a swing, stop, and say, "Push more," before resuming action. Pause and give an expectant look. Encourage the child to imitate.
- Give a partial sound (or word) cue. Say the first sound (or word) of the utterance. For example, at snack time when the child holds up his or her cup for juice, say, "More ___." Encourage the child to complete the utterance and then repeat the phrase.
- Ask a simple question and answer it. Repeat the question. Provide guidelines for the child. For example, when listening to music with the child, turn it down momentarily and ask, "What do you want?" Encourage the child to answer the question with the delayed model.
- Give the child a model and a directive to repeat. For example, tell the child, "Say, 'More music.'"

TEACHING CONSIDERATIONS

1. If sensory or motor difficulties interfere with normal speech development, augmentative or alternative systems (e.g., signing, communication boards) should be introduced. Consult a qualified specialist for teaching techniques.
2. A child with a hearing impairment may hear only selected frequencies (high- or low-pitched sounds) or may hear only loud sounds. The child may also be sensitive

SCD

to certain sounds or intensities (e.g., sounds that seem normal to you may be uncomfortably loud to some children, certain frequencies may be painful, combinations of sounds or too much noise may be uncomfortable).

3. If the child has a restricted range of motion in the head or trunk area, the speaker should be in a position that facilitates visual contact between the child and the speaker. Positioning is also critical to easy sound production. Latency of response may be noted. Consult a qualified specialist for recommendations for positioning and techniques for eliciting sounds from the child with a motor impairment.

4. Consider safety with all objects that the child handles. Never leave the child unattended with potentially hazardous objects.

Objective 2.6   Uses two-word utterances to express negation

IMPORTANCE OF SKILL

The purpose of this skill is for the child to use two-word utterances that express negation as a way to convey thoughts, wants, and needs. For example, the child holds up his or her hand and says, "No juice" (rejection); the child eats the last cookie and says, "All gone" (disappearance); or the child is given juice and says, "No milk" (denial). These two-word expressions of negation provide a basis for future communication that becomes increasingly complex.

PRECEDING GOAL

SC D:1.0   Uses 50 single words

CONCURRENT GOALS

FM B:2.0	Assembles toy and/or object that require(s) putting pieces together
FM B:3.0	Uses either index finger to activate objects
FM B:4.0	Copies simple written shapes after demonstration
GM C:2.0	Stoops and regains balanced standing position without support
GM C:3.0	Walks up and down stairs
GM D:1.0	Jumps forward
GM D:2.0	Pedals and steers tricycle
GM D:3.0	Runs avoiding obstacles
GM D:4.0	Catches, kicks, throws, and rolls ball or similar object
GM D:5.0	Climbs up and down play equipment
Adap A:5.0	Transfers food and liquid
Adap B:1.0	Initiates toileting
Adap B:2.0	Washes and dries hands
Adap B:3.0	Brushes teeth
Adap C:1.0	Undresses self
Cog B:3.0	Maintains search for object that is not in its usual location
Cog D:1.0	Imitates motor action that is not commonly used
Cog D:2.0	Imitates words that are not frequently used
Cog E:2.0	Uses an object to obtain another object

Cog E:3.0   Navigates large object around barriers
Cog E:4.0   Solves common problems
Cog F:2.0   Categorizes like objects
Cog F:3.0   Demonstrates functional use of one-to-one correspondence
Cog G:1.0   Uses imaginary objects in play
SC C:2.0   Carries out two-step direction *without* contextual cues
Soc A:3.0   Initiates and maintains communicative exchange with familiar adult
Soc B:1.0   Meets external physical needs in socially appropriate ways
Soc B:2.0   Responds to established social routine
Soc C:1.0   Initiates and maintains interaction with peer
Soc C:2.0   Initiates and maintains communicative exchange with peer

TEACHING SUGGESTIONS
Activity-Based

- Provide frequent opportunities for the child to interact with peers who use two-word utterances to express negation.
- During snack time, comment about what the child has eaten. For example, when the child finishes his or her juice, say, "No more," or when all the crackers have been eaten, say, "All gone."
- Ask yes and no questions whenever appropriate. Expand whenever possible. Allow the child to make choices and honor the child's preferences.
- Throughout the day, within the context of activities, model negative terms when appropriate, such as not, do not, and cannot. For example, when dressing the child, try to put the child's hat on his or her hand and say, "We don't put the hat on your hand."
- When the child uses a gesture or word to express negation, expand the child's utterance. For example, if the child holds up his or her hand to reject a cookie and says, "No," say, "No cookie."

Environmental Arrangements

- Arrange for the child to participate in small group activities with peers whose language is slightly advanced. Facilitate peer models of two-word utterances to express negation during activities and encourage the child to imitate.
- Make a picture book with pairs of pictures, one that denotes an action and one that does not. Point to the first picture and say, "Jumping," point to the next picture and say, "No jumping." Model several pairs, then give the child a turn, using action words that the child knows.
- When the child makes a choice, give the opposite object and wait for the child to reject it.
- Ask the child questions that are likely to elicit negative responses, such as, "Do you want to go to bed?"
- Occasionally, make absurd statements to the child during an activity. For example, when looking at a picture of a boy eating an ice cream cone, say, "Look, the horse is eating ice cream."

Instructional Sequence

- Model two-word expressions of negation. For example, when playing a hiding game with the child, the adult hides a toy and says, "All gone." Pause and give an expectant look. Encourage the child to imitate.

SC D

- Give a partial sound (or word) cue. Say the first sound (or word) of the utterance. For example, after snack time, hold up an empty plate of cookies and say, "No ___." Encourage the child to complete the utterance and then repeat.
- Ask a simple question and answer it. Repeat the question. Provide guidelines for the child. For example, offer the child something to eat that the child dislikes and ask, "Do you want this?" Encourage the child to answer the question with the delayed model.
- Give the child a model and a directive to repeat. For example, show the child an empty cup and say, "All gone. Tell me, 'All gone.'"

TEACHING CONSIDERATIONS

1. If sensory or motor difficulties interfere with normal speech development, augmentative or alternative systems (e.g., signing, communication boards) should be introduced. Consult a qualified specialist for teaching techniques.
2. A child with a hearing impairment may hear only selected frequencies (high- or low-pitched sounds) or may hear only loud sounds. The child may also be sensitive to certain sounds or intensities (e.g., sounds that seem normal to you may be uncomfortably loud to some children, certain frequencies may be painful, combinations of sounds or too much noise may be uncomfortable).
3. If the child has a restricted range of motion in the head or trunk area, the speaker should be in a position that facilitates visual contact between the child and the speaker. Positioning is also critical to easy sound production. Latency of response may be noted. Consult a qualified specialist for recommendations for positioning and techniques for eliciting sounds from the child with a motor impairment.
4. Consider safety with all objects that the child handles. Never leave the child unattended with potentially hazardous objects.

GOAL 3   Uses three-word utterances

DEVELOPMENTAL PROGRAMMING STEPS

In order to achieve this goal, a child must perform the skills in Objectives 3.1–3.4 to criteria. Refer to the specific objectives for Developmental Programming Steps to develop each skill.

IMPORTANCE OF SKILL

Shortly after two-word expressions are part of a young child's speech, three-word utterances develop. This skill is important for children to learn to control the environment with words and to help them cope more successfully with increasing social demands. The purpose of this skill is for the child to use three- or more word utterances that serve a variety of communicative functions.

PRECEDING GOAL

SC D:2.0   Uses two-word utterances

CONCURRENT GOALS

FM B:2.0 Assembles toy and/or object that require(s) putting pieces together
FM B:3.0 Uses either index finger to activate objects
FM B:4.0 Copies simple written shapes after demonstration
GM C:2.0 Stoops and regains balanced standing position without support
GM C:3.0 Walks up and down stairs
GM D:1.0 Jumps forward
GM D:2.0 Pedals and steers tricycle
GM D:3.0 Runs avoiding obstacles
GM D:4.0 Catches, kicks, throws, and rolls ball or similar object
GM D:5.0 Climbs up and down play equipment
Adap A:5.0 Transfers food and liquid
Adap B:1.0 Initiates toileting
Adap B:2.0 Washes and dries hands
Adap B:3.0 Brushes teeth
Adap C:1.0 Undresses self
Cog D:2.0 Imitates words that are not frequently used
Cog E:2.0 Uses an object to obtain another object
Cog E:3.0 Navigates large object around barriers
Cog E:4.0 Solves common problems
Cog F:2.0 Categorizes like objects
Cog F:3.0 Demonstrates functional use of one-to-one correspondence
Cog G:1.0 Uses imaginary objects in play
SC C:2.0 Carries out two-step direction *without* contextual cues
Soc A:3.0 Initiates and maintains communicative exchange with familiar adult
Soc B:1.0 Meets external physical needs in socially appropriate ways
Soc B:2.0 Responds to established social routine
Soc C:1.0 Initiates and maintains interaction with peer
Soc C:2.0 Initiates and maintains communicative exchange with peer

TEACHING SUGGESTIONS

In order to achieve this goal, a child must perform the skills in Objectives 3.1–3.4 to criteria. Refer to the specific objective for Teaching Suggestions and Teaching Considerations to develop each skill.

Objective 3.1 Uses three-word negative utterances

IMPORTANCE OF SKILL

In addition to increasing the child's control over the environment, the use of three-word negative utterances helps the child cope more successfully with increasing social demands. The purpose of this skill is for the child to use three- or more word utterances that contain negative terms. For example, the child hears a dog barking and says, "No do that," or tries to put a puzzle piece in place and says, "Don't go there." These negative expressions provide a basis for future communication that is increasingly complex.

SC D

PRECEDING OBJECTIVE

SC D:2.6   Uses two-word utterances to express negation

CONCURRENT GOALS

FM B:2.0   Assembles toy and/or object that require(s) putting pieces together
FM B:3.0   Uses either index finger to activate objects
FM B:4.0   Copies simple written shapes after demonstration
GM C:2.0   Stoops and regains balanced standing position without support
GM C:3.0   Walks up and down stairs
GM D:1.0   Jumps forward
GM D:2.0   Pedals and steers tricycle
GM D:3.0   Runs avoiding obstacles
GM D:4.0   Catches, kicks, throws, and rolls ball or similar object
GM D:5.0   Climbs up and down play equipment
Adap A:5.0 Transfers food and liquid
Adap B:1.0 Initiates toileting
Adap B:2.0 Washes and dries hands
Adap B:3.0 Brushes teeth
Adap C:1.0 Undresses self
Cog B:3.0   Maintains search for object that is not in its usual location
Cog D:1.0   Imitates motor action that is not commonly used
Cog D:2.0   Imitates words that are not frequently used
Cog E:2.0   Uses an object to obtain another object
Cog E:3.0   Navigates large object around barriers
Cog E:4.0   Solves common problems
Cog F:2.0   Categorizes like objects
Cog F:3.0   Demonstrates functional use of one-to-one correspondence
Cog G:1.0   Uses imaginary objects in play
SC C:2.0   Carries out two-step direction *without* contextual cues
Soc A:3.0   Initiates and maintains communicative exchange with familiar adult
Soc B:1.0   Meets external physical needs in socially appropriate ways
Soc B:2.0   Responds to established social routine
Soc C:1.0   Initiates and maintains interaction with peer
Soc C:2.0   Initiates and maintains communicative exchange with peer

TEACHING SUGGESTIONS
Activity-Based

- Provide frequent opportunities for the child to interact with peers who use three-word negative utterances.
- Provide the child opportunities to use negative terms throughout the day. Provide immediate consequences whenever applicable. For example, when the child indicates a dislike for a certain food by saying, "Don't want this," allow the child to choose another food.
- During small group activities, comment about the materials and describe the child's actions. For example, during art activities, say, "Mark's *not* putting a nose on his face" or "Mary *doesn't* like the blue hat."

SC D

- Play blindfold games in which the child must feel an object and guess what it is. Encourage comments such as "It's not hard," "It's not a book," or "It's not a shoe." You may need to give suggestions to help the child guess.
- Throughout the day, encourage the child to express likes and dislikes by offering many choices.

Environmental Arrangements

- Arrange for the child to participate in small group activities with peers whose language is slightly advanced. Facilitate peer models of three-word negative utterances during activities and encourage the child to imitate.
- Throughout the day, observe the child's responses toward objects, people, and events to determine those to which the child most readily responds. Choose two objects, one known to be particularly desirable and one that is not. Offer the object that is not particularly desirable to the child first, holding the desirable object just out of reach. Pause and give an expectant look. If the child does not respond, model a desired response and give the child the desired toy.
- When dressing the child, point to a body part and pretend to forget its name. For example, point to the child's head and say, "Okay, now put your sock on your tummy."
- Make absurd statements or give directions likely to elicit negative responses. For example, tell the child, "Climb inside the milk carton to see if it's all gone."
- During snack time, have a peer talk about food likes and dislikes. Model several times. Take turns naming preferred and nonpreferred items.

Instructional Sequence

- Model three-word negative expressions. For example, hide a familiar object and search for it with the child. Say, "Teddy's not here," or "Can't find teddy." Pause and give an expectant look. Encourage the child to imitate.
- Give a partial sound (or word) cue. Say the first sound (or word) of the utterance. For example, hide the teddy bear and say, "Teddy all ___." Encourage the child to complete the utterance and then repeat.
- Ask a simple question and answer it. Repeat the question. Provide guidelines for the child. For example, if the child does not like carrots, at snack time ask, "Do you want a carrot?" Encourage the child to answer the question with the delayed model.
- Give the child a model and a directive to repeat. For example, after bringing the cat indoors, say, "Don't go out. Tell the kitty, 'Don't go out.'"

TEACHING CONSIDERATIONS

1. If sensory or motor difficulties interfere with normal speech development, augmentative or alternative systems (e.g., signing, technological devices) should be introduced. Consult a qualified specialist for teaching techniques.
2. A child with a hearing impairment may hear only selected frequencies (high- or low-pitched sounds) or may hear only loud sounds. The child may also be sensitive to certain sounds or intensities (e.g., sounds that seem normal to you may be uncomfortably loud to some children, certain frequencies may be painful, combinations of sounds or too much noise may be uncomfortable).
3. If the child has a restricted range of motion in the head or trunk area, the speaker should be in a position that facilitates visual contact between the child and the

SC D

speaker. Positioning is also critical to easy sound production. Latency of response may be noted. Consult a qualified specialist for recommendations for positioning and techniques for eliciting sounds from the child with a motor impairment.

4. Consider safety with all objects that the child handles. Never leave the child unattended with potentially hazardous objects.

Objective 3.2   Asks questions

IMPORTANCE OF SKILL

In addition to increasing the child's control over the environment, the use of multiword utterances helps the child to cope more successfully with increasing social demands. The purpose of this skill is for the child to use three-word utterances that contain "Wh"-words, such as what and where, or use rising intonation that indicates a question. For example, the child sees a parent putting on a coat and says, "Where you going?", or sees a cookie and says, with rising intonation, "I have some?" Asking questions provides a basis for future communication that is increasingly complex.

PRECEDING GOAL

SC D:2.0   Uses two-word utterances

CONCURRENT GOALS

FM B:2.0 Assembles toy and/or object that require(s) putting pieces together
FM B:3.0 Uses either index finger to activate objects
FM B:4.0 Copies simple written shapes after demonstration
GM C:2.0 Stoops and regains balanced standing position without support
GM C:3.0 Walks up and down stairs
GM D:1.0 Jumps forward
GM D:2.0 Pedals and steers tricycle
GM D:3.0 Runs avoiding obstacles
GM D:4.0 Catches, kicks, throws, and rolls ball or similar object
GM D:5.0 Climbs up and down play equipment
Adap A:5.0 Transfers food and liquid
Adap B:1.0 Initiates toileting
Adap B:2.0 Washes and dries hands
Adap B:3.0 Brushes teeth
Adap C:1.0 Undresses self
Cog B:3.0 Maintains search for object that is not in its usual location
Cog D:1.0 Imitates motor action that is not commonly used
Cog D:2.0 Imitates words that are not frequently used
Cog E:2.0 Uses an object to obtain another object
Cog E:3.0 Navigates large object around barriers
Cog E:4.0 Solves common problems
Cog F:2.0 Categorizes like objects
Cog F:3.0 Demonstrates functional use of one-to-one correspondence

Cog G:1.0 Uses imaginary objects in play
SC C:2.0 Carries out two-step direction *without* contextual cues
Soc A:3.0 Initiates and maintains communicative exchange with familiar adult
Soc B:1.0 Meets external physical needs in socially appropriate ways
Soc B:2.0 Responds to established social routine
Soc C:1.0 Initiates and maintains interaction with peer
Soc C:2.0 Initiates and maintains communicative exchange with peer

TEACHING SUGGESTIONS
Activity-Based

- Provide frequent opportunities for the child to interact with peers who use questions.
- Several times throughout the day within the context of activities, ask the child simple questions that contain "Wh"-words, such as what and where.
- Observe the child's ability to ask simple questions or use rising intonation. Expand or recast the child's utterance. For example, if the child says, "Doggie go," using rising intonation, say, "Where did the doggie go?"
- Encourage the child to ask questions by introducing unique or novel objects and events. Have the child guess.
- Play question games, such as "20 Questions," or guessing games.

Environmental Arrangements

- Arrange for the child to participate in small group activities with peers whose language is slightly advanced. Facilitate peer models of questions during activities and encourage the child to imitate.
- During large or small group activities, encourage the child to ask questions by giving the child only some of the materials needed to complete a task. For example, offer the child a piece of paper, but do not offer a crayon or marker. Pause and give an expectant look.
- It might be helpful to use a peer to demonstrate questioning behavior during small group activities. For example, put several objects in a bag and ask the peer to feel the objects and ask simple questions.
- Set up a situation in which the child is given a direction to locate an object that is hidden or difficult to find. For example, hide the plastic spoons and ask the child to get them out of the drawer. Pause and give the child an opportunity to ask where to look.

Instructional Sequence

- Model asking questions. For example, when looking through picture books, take turns with the child playing "What's that?" Pause and give an expectant look. Encourage the child to imitate.
- Give the child a model and a directive to repeat. For example, "Ask Billy if he wants a cookie."
- Have the child repeat a question. Tell the child, "Say, 'Where's my coat?'"

TEACHING CONSIDERATIONS

1. If sensory or motor difficulties interfere with normal speech development, augmentative or alternative systems (e.g., signing, communication boards) should be introduced. Consult a qualified specialist for teaching techniques.

SCD

2. A child with a hearing impairment may hear only selected frequencies (high- or low-pitched sounds) or may hear only loud sounds. The child may also be sensitive to certain sounds or intensities (e.g., sounds that seem normal to you may be uncomfortably loud to some children, certain frequencies may be painful, combinations of sounds or too much noise may be uncomfortable).
3. If the child has a restricted range of motion in the head or trunk area, the speaker should be in a position that facilitates visual contact between the child and the speaker. Positioning is also critical to easy sound production. Latency of response may be noted. Consult a qualified specialist for recommendations for positioning and techniques for eliciting sounds from the child with a motor impairment.
4. Consider safety with all objects that the child handles. Never leave the child unattended with potentially hazardous objects.

Objective 3.3 Uses three-word action–object–location utterances

---

IMPORTANCE OF SKILL

Shortly after two-word utterances are heard in the young child's speech, longer utterances develop. In addition to increasing the child's control over the environment, the use of multiword utterances helps the child cope more successfully with increasing social demands. The purpose of this skill is for the child to use three-word action–object–location utterances. For example, the child says, "Put baby down," or "Pour juice here."

PRECEDING GOAL

SC D:2.0   Uses two-word utterances

CONCURRENT GOALS

FM B:2.0   Assembles toy and/or object that require(s) putting pieces together
FM B:3.0   Uses either index finger to activate objects
FM B:4.0   Copies simple written shapes after demonstration
GM C:2.0   Stoops and regains balanced standing position without support
GM C:3.0   Walks up and down stairs
GM D:1.0   Jumps forward
GM D:2.0   Pedals and steers tricycle
GM D:3.0   Runs avoiding obstacles
GM D:4.0   Catches, kicks, throws, and rolls ball or similar object
GM D:5.0   Climbs up and down play equipment
Adap A:5.0 Transfers food and liquid
Adap B:1.0 Initiates toileting
Adap B:2.0 Washes and dries hands
Adap B:3.0 Brushes teeth
Adap C:1.0 Undresses self
Cog B:3.0   Maintains search for object that is not in its usual location
Cog D:1.0   Imitates motor action that is not commonly used
Cog D:2.0   Imitates words that are not frequently used

Cog E:2.0	Uses an object to obtain another object
Cog E:3.0	Navigates large object around barriers
Cog E:4.0	Solves common problems
Cog F:2.0	Categorizes like objects
Cog F:3.0	Demonstrates functional use of one-to-one correspondence
Cog G:1.0	Uses imaginary objects in play
SC C:2.0	Carries out two-step direction *without* contextual cues
Soc A:3.0	Initiates and maintains communicative exchange with familiar adult
Soc B:1.0	Meets external physical needs in socially appropriate ways
Soc B:2.0	Responds to established social routine
Soc C:1.0	Initiates and maintains interaction with peer
Soc C:2.0	Initiates and maintains communicative exchange with peer

TEACHING SUGGESTIONS

Activity-Based

- Provide frequent opportunities for the child to interact with peers who use three-word action–object–location utterances.
- Play beside the child, commenting about or describing the location of play materials. For example, when playing with trucks and cars, say, "Drive under the bridge," or "Move that here."
- Throughout the day, within the context of activities, ask the child occasional questions about the location of specific objects.
- Play circus either with peers in a pretend situation or with toy animals and performers. Have the announcer give directions for the children and animals, such as "Stand lion up," or "Jump through hoop." Take turns being the announcer.
- When looking through picture books, comment about the location of objects and people. Pause and give the child an opportunity to comment. Expand the child's utterance when possible. For example, if the child points to a dog and says, "Doggie run," say, "That's right, the doggie runs into his house."

Environmental Arrangements

- Arrange for the child to participate in small group activities with peers whose language is slightly advanced. Facilitate peer models of three-word action–object–location utterances during activities and encourage the child to imitate.
- During snack time, put the container of juice just out of reach, but within the child's field of vision. Pretend to have misplaced the juice and say, "Where did I put the juice?" Pause and give the child an opportunity to respond, then model if necessary.
- Play "Treasure hunt." Hide an object and give the child directions on how to find it. For example, say, "Look under the blanket," or "Look in the box." Then have the child hide a toy and give directions to another child. Model when necessary.
- Use exaggerated pitch and intonation when commenting on the location of objects and people.
- Play "Pin the tail on the donkey." Tell where the tail was placed.

Instructional Sequence

- Model three-word expressions of action–object–location. For example, when playing ball, say, "Push ball here," or "Throw ball up." Pause and give an expectant look. Encourage the child to imitate.

SCD

- Give a partial sound (or word) cue. Say the first sound (or word) of the utterance. For example, when eating lunch, say, "Put cup down." Ask child where the cup is. Say, "Put _____." Encourage the child to complete the utterance and then repeat it.
- Ask a simple question and answer it. Repeat the question. Provide guidelines for the child. For example, after the child finishes playing with a toy, ask, "Where's your truck?" Encourage the child to answer the question with the delayed model.
- Give the child a model and a directive to repeat. For example, say, "Book on table. Tell me, 'Book on table.'"

TEACHING CONSIDERATIONS

1. If sensory or motor difficulties interfere with normal speech development, augmentative or alternative systems (e.g., signing, communication boards) should be introduced. Consult a qualified specialist for teaching techniques.
2. A child with a hearing impairment may hear only selected frequencies (high- or low-pitched sounds) or may hear only loud sounds. The child may also be sensitive to certain sounds or intensities (e.g., sounds that seem normal to you may be uncomfortably loud to some children, certain frequencies may be painful, combinations of sounds or too much noise may be uncomfortable).
3. If the child has a restricted range of motion in the head or trunk area, the speaker should be in a position that facilitates visual contact between the child and the speaker. Positioning is also critical to easy sound production. Latency of response may be noted. Consult a qualified specialist for recommendations for positioning and techniques for eliciting sounds from the child with a motor impairment.
4. Consider safety with all objects that the child handles. Never leave the child unattended with potentially hazardous objects.

Objective 3.4   Uses three-word agent–action–object utterances

IMPORTANCE OF SKILL

The purpose of this skill is for the child to use three-word agent–action–object utterances to express what the child sees in the environment. For example, the child says, "I make bubbles," while taking a bath or says, "Baby drink milk," while holding a bottle to a doll's mouth. These expressions provide a basis for future communication that becomes increasingly complex.

PRECEDING GOAL

SC D:2.0   Uses two-word utterances

CONCURRENT GOALS

FM B:2.0   Assembles toy and/or object that require(s) putting pieces together
FM B:3.0   Uses either index finger to activate objects
FM B:4.0   Copies simple written shapes after demonstration
GM C:2.0   Stoops and regains balanced standing position without support
GM C:3.0   Walks up and down stairs

GM D:1.0   Jumps forward
GM D:2.0   Pedals and steers tricycle
GM D:3.0   Runs avoiding obstacles
GM D:4.0   Catches, kicks, throws, and rolls ball or similar object
GM D:5.0   Climbs up and down play equipment
Adap A:5.0 Transfers food and liquid
Adap B:1.0 Initiates toileting
Adap B:2.0 Washes and dries hands
Adap B:3.0 Brushes teeth
Adap C:1.0 Undresses self
Cog B:3.0   Maintains search for object that is not in its usual location
Cog D:1.0   Imitates motor action that is not commonly used
Cog D:2.0   Imitates words that are not frequently used
Cog E:2.0   Uses an object to obtain another object
Cog E:3.0   Navigates large object around barriers
Cog E:4.0   Solves common problems
Cog F:2.0   Categorizes like objects
Cog F:3.0   Demonstrates functional use of one-to-one correspondence
Cog G:1.0   Uses imaginary objects in play
SC C:2.0   Carries out two-step direction *without* contextual cues
Soc A:3.0   Initiates and maintains communicative exchange with familiar adult
Soc B:1.0   Meets external physical needs in socially appropriate ways
Soc B:2.0   Responds to established social routine
Soc C:1.0   Initiates and maintains interaction with peer
Soc C:2.0   Initiates and maintains communicative exchange with peer

TEACHING SUGGESTIONS

Activity-Based

- Provide frequent opportunities for the child to interact with peers who use three-word agent–action–object utterances.
- Throughout the day when the child produces a one- or two-word utterance, expand the utterance. For example, if the child says, "Kitty eat," say, "That's right, the kitty's eating tuna," or "The kitty is hungry."
- Comment about and describe your activities throughout the day. Use three-word combinations that the child can already say whenever possible.
- When playing with dolls or stuffed animals, give the child directions, such as "Make the teddy bear go to sleep," or "Make teddy sing a song." Give the child the opportunity to give you directions.
- Plant a garden (real or pretend) and talk about the activity: "Mom digs holes," "Shovel fell down," and "Seeds lying on the dirt."
- At quiet time, encourage the child to recall the events of the day.

Environmental Arrangements

- Arrange for the child to participate in small group activities with peers whose language is slightly advanced. Facilitate peer models of three-word agent–action–object utterances during activities and encourage the child to imitate.
- Make a "Me Book" with the child, using photos of the child, family members, and peers. Sit with the child and encourage the child to describe the pictures. Any three-word utterance should be encouraged.

SCD

- Put the child's favorite toy just out of reach. Pause and wait for the child to request the object, modeling if necessary, and then give the child the toy.
- Call each other on a play telephone. Talk about who is doing what or what you want to do.
- Have on hand only part of the materials necessary to complete a task. Wait for the child to request other materials. For example, during an art activity, give the child a paper tree and scissors to cut out apples to paste on the tree, but do not put any glue on the table.

Instructional Sequence

- Model three-word agent–action–object expressions. For example, when playing beside the child, comment about and describe your play materials and actions. If playing with cars and trucks, say, "Truck bumps the car," or "Car climbs a hill." Pause and give an expectant look. Encourage the child to imitate.
- Give a partial sound (or word) cue. Say the first sound (or word) of the utterance. For example, while washing dishes together, say, "We wash cups. What do we do? We _____." Encourage the child to complete the utterance and then repeat the phrase.
- Ask a simple question and answer it. Repeat the question. Provide guidelines for the child. For example, when playing ball with the child, hold the ball, pause, and ask, "What should I do?" Encourage the child to answer the question with the delayed model.
- Give the child a model and a directive to repeat. For example, while watching television together, say, "We watch TV. Tell me, 'We watch TV.'"

TEACHING CONSIDERATIONS

1. If sensory or motor difficulties interfere with normal speech development, signing or augmentative systems (e.g., communication boards) should be introduced. Consult a qualified specialist for teaching techniques.
2. A child with a hearing impairment may hear only selected frequencies (high- or low-pitched sounds) or may hear only loud sounds. The child may also be sensitive to certain sounds or intensities (e.g., sounds that seem normal to you may be uncomfortably loud to some children, certain frequencies may be painful, combinations of sounds or too much noise may be uncomfortable).
3. If the child has a restricted range of motion in the head or trunk area, the speaker should be in a position that facilitates visual contact between the child and the speaker. Positioning is also critical to easy sound production. Latency of response may be noted. Consult a qualified specialist for recommendations for positioning and techniques for eliciting sounds from the child with a motor impairment.
4. Consider safety with all objects that the child handles. Never leave the child unattended with potentially hazardous objects.

SC D

SOCIAL DOMAIN

Angela Notari, Juliann Cripe,
Kristine Slentz, and Betsy Ryan-Seth

Social behaviors are so pervasive in the lives of infants and young children that it is difficult to imagine motor, adaptive, cognitive, or communication skills without a social component. The skills and behaviors included in the Social Domain focus on interactions that provide the context for developmental skills in other domains. This domain is organized into three areas of related social activity: interaction with adults, interaction with environment, and interaction with peers.

An infant is born totally dependent on a caregiving adult for health, safety, and sustenance. A relationship that begins as a physiological necessity soon develops into a social and emotional bond between parent and child. Most infants respond differently to familiar adults than strangers early in life. This is not surprising, as the familiar adult typically provides food, comfort, entertainment, and security for the young child.

It is in the context of this first relationship with a familiar adult that the infant is introduced to the rules of social response, initiation, and interaction. Babies are more attentive and responsive to features of the human face than to any other visual array in the first months of life. There is considerable evidence that the voice and smell of the primary caregiver are recognized by very young infants.

Babies learn early that crying will summon a caregiver to relieve discomfort. Soon the child learns more sophisticated methods of gaining the adult's attention, such as smiling or vocalizing. Developing mobility skills allows the child to seek proximity by crawling or walking after the familiar adult. Each developmental advance in the areas of cognition, motor control, and communication is used by the growing child as a means to a social end.

The importance of interactions with familiar adults, and the range of skills developed and perfected in this social arena, cannot be overstated. Many early childhood programs have developed curricula that capitalize on parent–infant interaction for both the content and context of intervention. The young child who has shared affection and mastered interaction with a familiar adult has a strong foundation for expanding social skills to peers and other adults.

Although parents and caregivers are usually the first and most salient, they are not the only familiar adults in the lives of young children. With the increase in two-career families, children age 3 and under are often in daycare situations. Daycare providers, babysitters, older siblings, neighbors, and extended family members may all be familiar adults for young children. When planning intervention and following curriculum suggestions in the Social Domain, it is helpful to begin by identifying all familiar adults and including them in the child's program.

The crux of a successful social interaction is a pleasurable activity; this will vary from child to child. It is important for interventionists to be thoroughly familiar with each child's sensory and object preferences, idiosyncratic response styles, and daily environments. The suggestions in the curriculum are general guidelines and they may be inappropriate for some children. For example, tickling to elicit social smiles will do more harm than good to an infant who is tactilely defensive. Interested involvement in the child by caregivers is the best insurance against creating stressful demands and making social intervention aversive for the child.

Routine events in the child's environment provide a ready source of opportunities for learning socially appropriate behaviors. The infant learns to associate specific events with caregiving and play routines. The sound of water, for instance, might alert the child to bathtime. Eventually, the child begins to anticipate the sequence of events that make up a routine. Putting on a jacket tells the child that it is time for a walk or drive; setting the table signals the beginning of a mealtime routine.

Many accepted social conventions are grounded in the simple, daily routine events learned in childhood. For example, "Wash your hands before coming to the table and after using the bathroom," "Take off muddy shoes at the door," "Go to the bathroom before you get in the car." Interventionists must be sensitive to the diversity in cultural practices when specifying appropriate social routines for mealtime, bedtime, outings, and family occasions. A thorough familiarity with each child's social and ethnic environment can help prevent culturally inappropriate expectations, conflicting demands, frustration, and confusion for family members and the child.

The child first masters the necessary adaptive skills and later becomes aware of the socially appropriate way of doing things. Before long, the expectation emerges that the child will recognize and conform to accepted social norms. This social requirement goes beyond simply performing an adaptive skill. Social expectations and feedback are generally conveyed through facial expressions and other subtle cues that the child may miss completely. Adults who care for the young child are responsible for making the child aware of proper behavior.

An adult's first response is often to tell the child that his or her behavior is not appropriate: "Don't grab your brother's glass," "Don't eat food from the floor," "Don't come in Grandma's house with wet bathing suits." This approach often stops the behavior in question but may leave the child wondering what to do instead. When instructing a child in socially appropriate ways to meet needs, it is important to be specific about acceptable alternatives to objectionable behavior: "If you are thirsty, get a glass from the counter," "If you are hungry, let's get a snack from the fridge," "If you are cold, dry off and come in to get dressed."

Interaction with peers is a constellation of skills that develops gradually in the first 3 years of life. The young infant seems not to notice the difference between peers and inanimate objects, but will clearly respond to an older child's voice. Two babies playing together may pull and grab at each other unintentionally at first; this behavior will evolve into social play as the babies get older.

It is an important step when a child becomes more independent and socially self-sufficient. The normal socialization process is a progressive movement away from the caregiver as a provider of social stimulation and regulation. The child develops resources for self-entertainment and sustained independent play in the presence of peers.

As the child grows, he or she begins to observe and imitate peers. The child uses his or her voice to gain another's attention, to play near peers, and to play with the same toys as peers. Eventually, the child maintains communicative interchanges with peers and engages in cooperative play. The young child exhibits the most sophisticated social skills in the presence of familiar peers and in familiar settings.

The range of social styles in young children is broad, and each child should be allowed to develop interaction skills that match temperament. One child will respond and initiate eagerly, even with unfamiliar peers, whereas another child will need to be more familiar to be comfortable and will require time to observe before interacting. By the time the child is 3 years old, the peer group usually becomes an important social arena, and the child seeks out playmates.

Social skills are inherent in almost all activities of early childhood. The lives of infants and young children are organized by adults and shared by peers. The routines of school, home, and community provide the setting for experiences that promote growth in all areas of development. Social competence can compensate for skill deficits in other domains, improve the quality of relationships among children and among the child and adults, and provide self-created learning opportunities for the young child.

Teaching in the Social Domain presents a valuable, if somewhat elusive, challenge for early interventionists. The interventionist's role is to provide appropriate and varied social opportunities and constant encouragement for each child to become a competent social participant.

Soc

Strand A

Interaction with Adults

GOAL 1   Initiates an affectionate response toward familiar adult

DEVELOPMENTAL PROGRAMMING STEPS

PS1.0a   The child responds to familiar adult's initiation of affection. For example, the child reaches up after his or her mother extends her arms to the child; the child hugs an adult after the adult initiates a hug.

PS1.0b   The child produces a behavior that has an effect on the adult. The behavior may or may not be intentional. For example, the child cries and the adult picks up the child to feed him or her; the child coos and the adult responds by cooing back.

IMPORTANCE OF SKILL

This skill demonstrates the child's awareness that certain behaviors indicate affection. The child's affectionate expressions are rewarding to the caregiver and serve to communicate attachment. The emphasis of this skill is on the child's ability to use socially appropriate signals of positive feelings toward a familiar adult. The item focuses specifically on the child's spontaneous expression of affection, rather than generally on the child's ability to initiate an interaction.

PRECEDING OBJECTIVE

Cog B:1.2   Focuses on object and/or person

CONCURRENT GOALS AND OBJECTIVES

Cog C:2.0   Reproduces part of interactive game and/or action in order to continue game and/or action

SC A:3.0   Engages in vocal exchanges by babbling

SC B:1.3   Gestures and/or vocalizes to greet others

Soc A:2.1   Initiates simple social game with familiar adult

TEACHING SUGGESTIONS

Activity-Based

- During daily routines and activities, engage in positive interactions with the child. Children learn to be affectionate through imitation. Talk to the child in an affection-

432

Soc A

ate tone and make positive comments about the child's appearance, activities, skills, interests, and qualities.

- Use feeding, dressing, bathing, and play to introduce affectionate verbal, tactile, and visual interactions. For example, offer a spoonful of food while saying, "Good food for a good boy," or "A big bite for a big girl." Count, kiss, and play "piggies" with toes and fingers while dressing; blow "raspberries" on the child's tummy. Wash or rub lotion on arms, legs, and tummy while naming body parts. Use terms of endearment with reference to the familiar adult: "Mama's good helper," or "Daddy's big boy."
- Pair affectionate interactions with consistent daily routines. For example, make a good-night kiss part of bedtime routine; use hugs for morning waking and after day-care. Once the routine is established, wait to see if the child will initiate.
- Engage in activities that involve affectionate physical contact. For example, read or tell stories with the child on the adult's lap. Snuggle during bottle or breast feeding, and before and after sleeping.
- Engage in games and activities that the adult also enjoys to ensure a positive give-and-take interaction between the child and the adult. Encourage the child to initiate affectionate responses toward the adult by hugging, kissing, patting, touching, and reaching toward the adult.
- Watch as a familiar adult enters the child's visual range. Encourage the child to reach to be picked up or to hug and kiss the adult after being picked up.
- Engage in activities that are rewarding to the child. For example, give the child favorite snacks, play with favorite toys, or tell favorite stories.
- Play simple games that require an interactive response; for example, roll balls back and forth between adult and child.
- Engage the child in caretaking games with dolls, stuffed animals, and pets—for example, feeding the doll, tucking Pooh Bear into bed, and brushing the dog.

☑ If your data indicate the child is not making progress toward the goal, provide additional structure within the suggested activities by incorporating the following *environmental arrangements:*

Environmental Arrangements

- Place a favorite object out of the child's reach so that the child asks the adult's help to obtain the object. Wait for the child to initiate an affectionate response as thanks for the help.
- Engage in body play, such as face-to-face interactions, rough and tumble play, bouncing the child on your lap, or running after and catching each other. Exaggerate facial expressions; laugh and talk in an affectionate tone to make the interaction lively and exciting to the child. Stop and wait for the child to initiate hugging, touching, or kissing, and then continue the game.

☑ If this goal is particularly difficult for a child, it may be necessary, within activities, to use an *instructional sequence.*

Instructional Sequence

- Model an affectionate response. For example, hug the child's sibling or pat the child's father on the arm.
- Tell the child to hug, kiss, or touch a familiar adult. For example, "Give Mommy a kiss good night."
- During play with dolls or stuffed animals, model giving a kiss, hug, backrub, or tickle. Ask the child to do the same, "Now give your baby a hug." Physically assist the child if necessary.

Soc A

☑ Combining or pairing different levels of instructions may be helpful when beginning to teach a new and difficult skill. Fade to less intrusive instructions as soon as possible to encourage more independent performance.

TEACHING CONSIDERATIONS

1. Cultural and individual differences may affect the appropriate frequency, intensity, and form of a child's expression of affection. In particular, the appreciation of physical contact varies greatly according to cultures and individuals.
2. Manifestations of affection may vary if a child has a sensory impairment. For example, a child with a visual impairment may respond affectionately with a whole body response.
3. A child with a hearing impairment may convey affection through facial expressions and gestures.
4. A child with a severe motor impairment may use verbal and visual modes, such as cooing and gazing, rather than motor and tactile modes of reaching and hugging.
5. Try not to reject the child's approximations of affection. Open-mouth or sloppy kisses are to be expected.
6. Provide overall body affection, being careful not to ignore body parts that are disabled.

Objective 1.1 **Responds appropriately to familiar adult's affective tone**

DEVELOPMENTAL PROGRAMMING STEPS

PS1.1a   The child responds with socially appropriate affect to familiar adult's negative affective tone. For example, the child cries and turns away from the loud voice when an adult says, "No."

PS1.1b   The child responds with socially appropriate affect to familiar adult's positive affective tone. For example, the child smiles when an adult laughs, or the child quiets when an adult speaks softly.

IMPORTANCE OF SKILL

The child's sensitivity to the adult's vocal, physical, and affective behaviors plays a crucial role in the active participation and regulation of human interactions. The interaction between the infant and adult is based on a pattern of dialogue in which each partner mutually influences and regulates the behavior of the other. This skill indicates the child's ability to perceive the emotional quality of adult behavior. (The tone of the interaction is an initial step toward reciprocation, or mutually enjoyable interactions, between an adult and a child.)

PRECEDING OBJECTIVE

Soc A:1.2   Smiles in response to familiar adult

CONCURRENT GOAL AND OBJECTIVES

Cog C:2.1   Indicates desire to continue familiar game and/or action
SC A:1.0   Turns and looks toward person speaking

Soc A

SC A:3.1   Engages in vocal exchanges by cooing
SC B:1.4   Uses gestures and/or vocalizations to protest actions and/or reject objects
             or people
Soc A:2.2   Responds to familiar adult's social behavior

TEACHING SUGGESTIONS
Activity-Based

- Talk to the child during feeding, diapering, and dressing. Comment on what the child is doing, on events that are occurring, or on objects that are present. Use short vocalizations, allowing time for pauses. Vary pitch, melody, and facial expressions to reflect a variety of affective tones.
- Use a clearly negative (but not harsh) tone and gesture when correcting or reprimanding the child. For example, if the child is reaching for a dangerous object, frown, shake your finger, and say, "No!" and note whether the child frowns or fusses and stops the behavior.
- Play interactive games such as peekaboo. Smile, laugh, and talk to the child. Encourage the child to respond with a similar socially appropriate affect (e.g., the child reproduces part of interactive game, smiles, coos).
- At quiet times, rock and sing with the child. Encourage the child to join in the activity by cooing and cuddling.
- Comfort the child quickly and consistently when he or she is in distress.

Environmental Arrangements

- Exaggerate expressions of affect (e.g., laugh, hug, and kiss the child; frown deeply and use a sharp voice if you must say, "No").
- Respond to and elaborate on the child's own affective tone and behaviors. For example, if the child smiles or initiates motor movements that indicate interest in the appearance of a pet dog, comment on the dog in a positive, excited tone and observe whether the child responds by laughing and waving arms. Observe the child when in proximity to other children who are crying and see if this causes the child to cry or express discomfort as well.
- Engage the child in activities that are likely to elicit a positive affect in the child. Observe whether the child responds accordingly. For example, when making funny faces or tickling the child, observe if the child smiles.
- Point out and label positive and negative affect in daily interactions with familiar adults.

Instructional Sequence

- Model pairing your own affective tone to strong pleasurable or negative events and stimuli. Tickle, pick up the child, and talk to the child in a positive tone. Observe if the child increases activity, smiles, or vocalizes. Cease interaction, put the child down, and quietly say, "All done." Observe if the child calms or fusses.
- Hug and kiss the child often. Describe what you are doing in a pleasant voice. Verbally encourage the child to respond.
- Repeat positive or negative affective cues if the child responds inappropriately.
- Lead the child into affectionate interactions by asking if the child wants a kiss or hug. Physically encourage the child to hug.

TEACHING CONSIDERATIONS

1. Make sure the child is responding to the affective quality of the social interaction and not to sensory stimulation or nonsocial events.
2. The child may present individual differences in arousal levels. Adapt the intensity of affective tone to each individual child to avoid over- or understimulation.
3. If the child has a sensory impairment, interact in a mode that is meaningful to the child. For example, if the child has a severe hearing impairment, convey affect through facial expressions and gestures.
4. If the child has a severe visual impairment, pair affective tone with tactile cues such as stroking, cuddling, or lightly tapping a finger.
5. Provide overall body affection, being careful not to ignore body parts that are disabled. A child with a severe motor impairment may respond to an adult's affection or affectionate tone with a quiver, a noise, or a gaze.
6. Use negative affect such as a sharp voice and corrections sparingly and with caution.

Objective 1.2   Smiles in response to familiar adult

DEVELOPMENTAL PROGRAMMING STEPS

PS1.2a   The child reacts differently to familiar versus unfamiliar adults. For example, the child looks at the familiar adult and ignores the stranger; the child vocalizes to the familiar adult and shies away from the stranger.

PS1.2b   The child stops crying in response to a familiar adult (e.g., approach, vocalization, smile, and/or appearance). For example, the child quiets when picked up by the primary caregiver.

IMPORTANCE OF SKILL

The smile is a basic social response. The child's smile in response to an adult tends to elicit further responses on the part of the adult. Selective social smiling in response to only certain individuals indicates that the child is able to recognize specific individuals as familiar. This ability is fundamental to the establishment of meaningful and lasting social relationships.

PRECEDING OBJECTIVE

Cog B:1.2   Focuses on object and/or person

CONCURRENT GOALS AND OBJECTIVES

FM A:1.2   Makes nondirected movements with each arm
GM A:1.0   Turns head, moves arms, and kicks legs independently of each other
Cog A:1.0   Orients to auditory, visual, and tactile events
SC A:1.0   Turns and looks toward person speaking
Soc A:2.2   Responds to familiar adult's social behavior

TEACHING SUGGESTIONS
Activity-Based

- Respond quickly and consistently to the child's bids for attention; vocalize and smile when the child does.
- During daily routines and activities, introduce moments of face-to-face interactions without objects between the child and a familiar adult. Have the adult smile and vocalize to the child.
- When a familiar adult enters the room, focus the child's attention on the person and talk positively about the person.
- Slowly move your face into the child's visual field. Smile and vocalize and wait for a response.

Environmental Arrangements

- Exaggerate facial expressions, move lips, change head orientation, and vary pitch and intensity of voice to evoke a smile from the child.
- Play an interactive game that elicits a response from the child. Interrupt the game briefly and leave the child's visual range. Observe whether the child smiles when you reappear.
- Gain the child's attention by various means, such as gently touching the child, calling the child's name, picking up the child, or showing an interesting object. After the child demonstrates interest, cease the interaction briefly, then smile or vocalize to the child. Encourage the child to smile back.
- Remove interesting objects from the child's immediate environment during face-to-face interactions so that the child focuses attention on social rather than nonsocial stimuli.

Instructional Sequence

- Model smiling at the child and be responsive (e.g., exaggerate facial expressions, vary pitch of voice) when the child attempts any change in facial expression that is positive and could lead to a smile.
- Verbally encourage the child to smile in response to a smile, vocalization, or approach by a familiar adult by simultaneously introducing other stimulations. Have the adult approach the child with a favorite toy or call the child by name.
- Gently stroke the child's face near his or her mouth to encourage a smile, being cautious not to elicit a rooting reflex.

TEACHING CONSIDERATIONS

1. Ideally, the child is in a quiet and alert state in order to attend to the external environment. Try to stimulate a young infant, if necessary, by providing varied tactile and physical stimuli to arouse the child; reduce stimulation or pick up and put the infant to your shoulder to soothe the child.
2. The child may present individual differences in social responsiveness and in preferences for specific stimulations. Vary the intensity, frequency, and type of social behaviors toward the child.
3. The child with a severe visual impairment or the child with low or high muscle tone may lack differentiation in facial expression. Be sensitive to subtle changes

in expression and to idiosyncratic manifestations of affect (e.g., finger or hand movements).
4. If the child has a sensory impairment, select social stimulations to which the child is most likely to respond. For example, if the child has a visual impairment, vocalize to the child and encourage the child to explore the adult's face with the hands.
5. If the child has a severe hearing impairment, convey affect through facial expressions and gestures combined with words.
6. A child with a severe motor impairment may respond with a bodily response other than a smile.

GOAL 2   Initiates and maintains interaction with familiar adult

DEVELOPMENTAL PROGRAMMING STEPS

PS2.0a   The child interacts with a familiar adult in a turn-taking pattern. For example, the child alternates gazing at and gazing away from an adult; the child waves his or her arms and kicks his or her legs while the adult is looking at the child and then quiets when the adult vocalizes to the child.

PS2.0b   The child responds to a familiar adult's social behavior by maintaining and/or continuing the interaction. For example, the child knocks down a block tower that the adult built and waits for or helps the adult rebuild the tower.

PS2.0c   The child responds in an attempt to prolong positive interaction. For example, the child protests when his or her mother leaves the room and reaches out his or her arms to be picked up again.

IMPORTANCE OF SKILL

The ability to participate in and maintain an interaction is important to the development of language, as it provides a basis for the turn-taking pattern underlying a number of conversational pragmatic skills. Also, learning to share, alternate, and reverse role relationships between partners plays a role in the development of empathy and social cognition.

PRECEDING OBJECTIVE

Soc A:2.1   Initiates simple social game with familiar adult

CONCURRENT GOALS AND OBJECTIVES

FM A:5.0   Places and releases object balanced on top of another object with either hand
GM D:4.0   Catches, kicks, throws, and rolls ball or similar object
Cog B:2.1   Locates object and/or person who hides while child is watching
Cog C:2.0   Reproduces part of interactive game and/or action in order to continue game and/or action
Cog D:1.1   Imitates motor action that is commonly used
Cog F:1.2   Stacks objects
Cog G:1.2   Uses functionally appropriate actions with objects

SC A:3.0   Engages in vocal exchanges by babbling
SC B:1.0   Gains person's attention and refers to an object, person, and/or event
Soc A:1.0   Initiates an affectionate response toward familiar adult
Soc B:1.0   Meets external physical needs in socially appropriate ways

TEACHING SUGGESTIONS
Activity-Based

- Engage in positive interactions with the child during daily activities and routines. Establish eye contact and joint attention and smile and talk to the child. The adult does not need to engage in direct interaction with the child, but must remain in close proximity while looking at the child or engaging in some other activity.
- Encourage the child to initiate an interaction with the adult and then respond for two or more exchanges. For example, the child shows the adult a dump truck, the adult fills the truck, the child dumps the load, and the adult looks surprised; the child throws a ball to the adult, the adult throws it back, the child kicks the ball, and the adult kicks it back.
- Present the child with toys and/or objects that are likely to elicit an interaction, such as a ball, toy telephone, or a cloth for peekaboo.
- When the child requests assistance with play or caregiving activities, respond by giving only partial assistance so that the child is likely to initiate a request for more help.

Environmental Arrangements

- In response to the child's initial behavior, have the adult provide a response that is likely to stimulate the child to maintain the interaction. For example, if the child puts a cloth over his or her head, the adult removes the cloth and says, "Peekaboo." The adult then puts the cloth over the child's head, the child removes the cloth, and the adult smiles and says, "Peekaboo"; or the child hands a bottle to the adult, the adult pretends to suck and hands the bottle back to the child, the child sucks the bottle, and the adult smiles and makes sucking movement with lips; or the child gives the adult a cracker, the adult places it out of the child's reach, the child gestures for the cracker, and the adult gives the cracker back to the child.
- Respond to the child by acting upon a shared object. For example, the child gives the adult a wind-up toy and the adult activates the toy. When the toy stops, the child tries to wind up the toy, and the adult smiles and claps his or her hands to praise the child.
- Provide a response that elaborates on the child's initial action. For example, the child sits in front of the adult and touches the adult's hands, and the adult sings and play acts "Row, Row, Row Your Boat." When the adult pauses, the child continues the game and the adult participates.
- Adapt toys to present problems that children must request help to solve. For example, present a clear tub of toys for which the child must request help to remove the lid.

Instructional Sequence

- Model repeating or elaborating on a response or pair the response with additional cues if the child does not continue the interaction. For example, the child raises his or her arms over head; the adult says, "So big"; the adult raises his or her own arms; and the child raises his or her arms again.
- Ask the child to continue an interaction by repeating the same behavior. For example, tell the child, "Your turn," or "Do it again."

■ Physically assist the child to continue the interaction. For example, the child claps hands, the adult says, "Pat-a-cake," and gently brings the child's hands together again.

TEACHING CONSIDERATIONS

1. Adapt the pace of the interaction to the individual child. Some children are stimulated by a fast pace, whereas others may need more time to process a response and to reinitiate an interaction.
2. A child with a severe sensory impairment may use signals that are difficult to read. For example, a child with a severe visual impairment may use hands to explore an adult's face or search for an object. Encourage sensory modalities other than visual, such as laughing or clapping, in your interaction with the child.
3. A child with a hearing impairment may interact with the adult through facial expressions and gestures.
4. A child with a severe motor impairment may interact with the adult through various facial and body responses.
5. Avoid continuous stimulation and interaction with the child. Allow for pauses and silences to give the child the opportunity to initiate or maintain the interaction.

Objective 2.1 Initiates simple social game with familiar adult

DEVELOPMENTAL PROGRAMMING STEPS

PS2.1a The child assumes an active role in drawing the attention of or getting close to a familiar adult to continue a social game. For example, the child crawls after father, tugs at grandma's clothes, or climbs into mother's lap.

PS2.1b When a familiar adult initiates a simple social game, the child responds by performing an action that is part of the game. For example, the adult says, "So big," and the child raises his or her arms; the adult places a blanket over the child's head, the child pulls the blanket off, and the adult says, "Peekaboo!"

IMPORTANCE OF SKILL

Simple social games, involving tactile and physical stimulation, are some of the earliest forms of social interaction between a child and an adult. The child learns the rules of social communication by participating in social interactions. The structure and repetition of simple rules provide a predictable, simple, and repetitive framework for the interaction, allowing the child to learn social behaviors and reverse role relationships between the adult and self.

PRECEDING OBJECTIVE

Soc A:2.2 Responds to familiar adult's social behavior

CONCURRENT GOALS AND OBJECTIVES

FM A:5.0 Places and releases object balanced on top of another object with either hand

Soc A

GM D:4.0 Catches, kicks, throws, and rolls ball or similar object
Cog B:2.1 Locates object and/or person who hides while child is watching
Cog F:1.2 Stacks objects
Cog G:1.2 Uses functionally appropriate actions with objects
SC A:3.0 Engages in vocal exchanges by babbling
SC B:1.0 Gains person's attention and refers to an object, person, and/or event
Soc A:1.0 Initiates an affectionate response toward familiar adult

TEACHING SUGGESTIONS
Activity-Based

- Provide the child opportunities to listen to records or tapes of nursery rhymes and simple social games.
- Engage in positive interactions with the child during daily activities and routines. Engage frequently in eye contact with the child; smile and talk often. Remain in close proximity to the child while engaging in other activities. Respond immediately if the child initiates simple social games.
- Whenever the child uses an action or vocalization from a social game, imitate the child and expand the game. For example, if the child claps hands, clap your hands and say, "Pat-a-cake."

Environmental Arrangements

- Lead or set the child up to initiate a social game. For example, during dressing, put a clean t-shirt over the child's head and wait for it to be pulled away. Say, "Oh, you want to play peekaboo?" Repeat the activity.
- Engage in face-to-face interaction with the child. Have available objects that are commonly used in social games, such as cloths to play peekaboo, a ball to roll back and forth, and hand-size objects to play give-and-take. Encourage the child to initiate a social game. If necessary, the adult may draw the child's attention to an object by pointing to or manipulating the object.
- Place the child in a situation or a position associated with the rules of a social game. For example, hold the child on your knees and encourage the child to play "horsy"; sit in front of the child on the floor and encourage the child to play pat-a-cake; run with the child and encourage the child to initiate "Gonna get you"; or sing a song related to finger games.

Instructional Sequence

- Model playing a game with the child's peer or another adult. Encourage the child to join in the game.
- Ask the child to initiate a simple social game (e.g., "Let's play pat-a-cake," "Roll the ball").
- Provide physical cues to the child. For example, hand the child a blanket to place over the head, push hands together to play pat-a-cake, push a hand to contact a ball to make it roll.

TEACHING CONSIDERATIONS

1. Make sure the child has the opportunity to engage in social games and knows the actions and rules of the games you want him or her to initiate.
2. Avoid continuous stimulation and interaction with the child. Allow pauses and silences to give the child the opportunity to initiate.

3. A child with a severe sensory impairment may use signals that are difficult to read. For example, a child with a hearing impairment may initiate a simple game with facial expressions and gestures.
4. A child with a severe visual impairment may initiate simple games by exploring with hands. Encourage touch and voice cues with this child.
5. A child with a severe motor impairment may move only one hand to initiate pat-a-cake or may move the head while gazing at a blanket to initiate peekaboo.
6. Engage in social games that are developmentally appropriate for the child. For example, younger children are more likely to initiate "peekaboo" or a give-and-take game, whereas older children may initiate playing with a ball.

Objective 2.2 Responds to familiar adult's social behavior

DEVELOPMENTAL PROGRAMMING STEP

PS2.2a The child shows interest in familiar adult's social behavior. For example, the child looks at the adult when the adult plays peekaboo, and smiles when the adult peeks around the corner.

IMPORTANCE OF SKILL

The participation of the child in social interactions is fundamental to social, emotional, and cognitive development. Through interactions with people, the child learns the rules of the social and cultural community. Also, it is within the context of interactions with people that the child learns about the properties of objects and actions in the physical world. The child's responsiveness reinforces the adult's initiations and stimulates the adult to maintain the interaction.

PRECEDING OBJECTIVE

Soc A:1.1 Responds appropriately to familiar adult's affective tone

CONCURRENT GOALS AND OBJECTIVES

FM A:3.0 Grasps hand-size object with either hand using ends of thumb, index, and second fingers
GM D:4.4 Rolls ball at target
Cog B:2.1 Locates object and/or person who hides while child is watching
Cog C:2.1 Indicates desire to continue familiar game and/or action
Cog D:1.1 Imitates motor action that is commonly used
SC A:1.0 Turns and looks toward person speaking
SC A:3.0 Engages in vocal exchanges by babbling
SC B:1.3 Gestures and/or vocalizes to greet others
Soc B:2.1 Responds to routine event

TEACHING SUGGESTIONS
Activity-Based

- Initiate social behaviors and encourage the child to respond. Social behaviors can vary a great deal from nonverbal facial expressions, such as smiling and frowning, to organized social action games with or without the use of objects, such as peekaboo, "Gonna get you," "So big," and build and bash.
- A number of opportunities exist for adults to engage in social behaviors during daily routines. Encourage the child to respond by using a socially appropriate and related behavior. For example, the child may laugh when the adult plays peekaboo, kick and squirm when the adult starts to tickle, or imitate adult's finger games.
- While changing and dressing the child, engage in tactile games such as tickling, making funny faces, or playing finger games.
- During outings, engage in gross motor games such as hide and seek or "Gonna get you."
- At bedtime play peekaboo, hug and kiss the child, and wave "bye-bye."
- When playing with a ball or cars, roll the ball or car toward the child and wait for the child to roll it back. Encourage the child if necessary.
- Engage in social behaviors appropriate to the context. Wave "bye-bye," hug the child during departures and arrivals, and play tickling games during changing and dressing routines.

Environmental Arrangements

- Initiate tactile and physical stimulation games likely to elicit a response, such as tickling, bouncing the child on a lap, moving the child quickly up and down, and walking fingers over the child's body.
- Introduce interesting objects within social interactions. Give the child favorite toys or snacks and encourage the child to smile or hand the objects back.
- To facilitate social behavior, expand and elaborate on the child's own behaviors. For example, if the child pats the table, pat the child's hand. Encourage the child to pat the table again or indicate an interest in continuing. If the child focuses attention on an object, get the object and hand it to the child.

Instructional Sequence

- Model social behaviors that involve a combination of auditory, visual, tactile, and physical cues. For example, play "horsy" with the child while singing a favorite song; play peekaboo using bright-colored cloth and calling the child's name.
- Use verbal cues to prompt the child to respond. For example, "Give me a kiss," "Push the ball," "Wave bye-bye."
- Gently assist the child physically. Touch the child's arm to make the child wave "bye-bye" or to prompt the child to pull off the blanket while you play peekaboo.

TEACHING CONSIDERATIONS

1. Engage in social behaviors that are developmentally appropriate for the child. For example, younger children are more likely to respond to tactile and physical stimulation, whereas older children may prefer more complex motor games, such as playing ball.

Soc A

2. Adapt the intensity of stimulation to the child's particular state. Avoid, for example, strong tactile and physical stimulation after feedings or when the child is sleepy or overstimulated.
3. If the child has a sensory impairment, provide stimulation that can be easily perceived by the child. For example, use tactile and auditory cues if the child has a visual impairment.
4. A child with a hearing impairment may respond better to facial expressions and gestures.
5. A child with a motor impairment may respond to an adult with sounds, facial expressions, and minimal or whole body movements. These responses may be subtle and/or hard to interpret.

GOAL 3 Initiates and maintains communicative exchange with familiar adult

---

DEVELOPMENTAL PROGRAMMING STEPS

PS3.0a The child responds to communication from a familiar adult and maintains the interaction. For example, the adult asks the child to tell about pictures in a book, and the child makes vocalizations about the pictures. Then the adult supplies words for the pictures, and the child vocalizes again or points to the picture.

PS3.0b The child interacts with a familiar adult in a vocally similar manner by matching the patterns of vocal exchanges. For example, the child gurgles when the adult stops vocalizing; the child varies the length of vocalizations as a function of the length of the adult's verbalizations; the child changes the rhythm of vocalizations when the adult sings to the child.

IMPORTANCE OF SKILL

The ability to actively engage in a sequence of communicative exchanges is basic to social, emotional, social-communicative, and cognitive development. By communicating with other people through a variety of gestural, facial, vocal, and physical means, the child learns about the social and cultural rules of the community, establishes relationships with others, expresses emotions and needs, and learns about properties of the physical environment.

PRECEDING OBJECTIVE

Soc A:3.1   Initiates communication with familiar adult

CONCURRENT GOALS AND OBJECTIVES

GM D:4.0   Catches, kicks, throws, and rolls ball or similar object
Cog C:2.1   Indicates desire to continue familiar game and/or action
Cog D:2.2   Imitates words that are frequently used
Cog E:4.0   Solves common problems
Cog G:1.2   Uses functionally appropriate actions with objects
SC A:3.0   Engages in vocal exchanges by babbling

Soc A

SC B:1.0   Gains person's attention and refers to an object, person, and/or event
SC B:2.0   Uses consistent word approximations
SC C:1.2   Locates common objects, people, and/or events in familiar pictures
SC C:2.3   Carries out one-step direction *with* contextual cues
SC D:1.0   Uses 50 single words
Soc A:2.0   Initiates and maintains interaction with familiar adult
Soc B:1.0   Meets external physical needs in socially appropriate ways

TEACHING SUGGESTIONS
Activity-Based

- Engage in positive interactions with the child during daily activities and routines. Establish eye contact frequently; smile and play with the child. Wait for the child to initiate or maintain a communicative exchange by directing gestures, signs, vocalizations, and verbalizations toward the adult for two or more consecutive exchanges. For example, the adult watches the child play in the sand, the child looks up at the adult and gestures, and the adult moves closer to the child and asks, "What's that?" The child answers by gesturing, verbalizing, or vocalizing.
- Arrange situations where communication is meaningful. For example, returning home after a walk with Daddy, the child runs toward his or her mother and says, "Quack, quack." The mother comments, "Did you see the ducks?" The child nods head, the mother smiles and comments, "Were the ducks at the park?"
- Seize the opportunity to elaborate and expand on the child's communication or knowledge. For example, respond with words to the child's word approximations or provide information on properties of objects so as to expand the exchange. Be sure not to preempt the interaction with your responses.

Environmental Arrangements

- In response to the child's initial communication, select a response that is likely to stimulate the child to maintain the interaction. For example, if the child points to a cracker, ask, "What do you want?" and wait for the child to gesture, vocalize, or verbalize.
- When playing interactive games with the child, interrupt the game and wait for the child to ask to continue the game or indicate a desire to continue. For example, the adult stops rolling the car, the child points to the car, the adult looks at the child and asks, "What do you want me to do?" The child answers, "Go," moves the adult's hand to the car, or makes car noises.
- Participate in sequential activities, such as getting dressed or making a sandwich. Interactions can follow the logical routine. If necessary, violate the logical sequence— put socks over shoes and wait for child to initiate and then continue.
- Use gestures and vocalizations from the child's repertoire or imitate the child's actions or vocalizations.
- Communicate about objects and events in the child's immediate environment.

Instructional Sequence

- Model repeating or elaborating on the child's response. Pair the response with additional cues if the child does not continue the communication. For example, the child points to the doll, and the adult says, "Baby." If the child does not respond, the adult

Soc A

repeats, "Baby, put the baby to bed." Wait for the child to repeat "baby" or follow the directions.

- Ask the child to continue the communication. For example, the child points to an object, and the adult labels the object. If the child does not respond, tell the child, "Your turn," "Show me again what you want," or ask, "Is this what you want?"
- Physically assist the child if an appropriate response can be given with a gesture. For example, the child holds up keys and says, "Ke-ke"; adult says, "Yes, those are your keys. Where do the keys go?" When the child does not respond, the adult moves the child's hand toward the keyhole.

TEACHING CONSIDERATIONS

1. Adapt the pace of the interaction to the individual child. Some children prefer a faster pace, whereas others need more time to process a response and reinitiate communication.
2. A child with a severe sensory impairment may use signals that are difficult to read. For example, a child with a motor impairment may have difficulty articulating words clearly and may use nonconventional gestures and signals, such as eye pointing or body orientation toward the object of communication.
3. A child with a severe hearing impairment may also use gestures and signals to communicate.
4. A child with a severe visual impairment may respond to tactile and auditory communication from the adult.
5. Expand upon other sensory modes to help the child with a severe sensory impairment.
6. Avoid continuous stimulation and interaction with the child. Allow pauses and silences to give the child the opportunity to initiate or maintain the communicative exchange.
7. Provide a stimulating environment and allow the child to actively explore objects and independently initiate actions so that the child will have reason and motivation to communicate.

Objective 3.1 Initiates communication with familiar adult

IMPORTANCE OF SKILL

The child gradually learns to communicate intentionally, using a conventional system of gestures or language. The child's first intentional communication may be a variety of gestures, vocalizations, and words used to achieve desired goals, such as requesting objects, actions, and attention. The child also comments on objects and actions and protests and rejects actions and events in the environment.

PRECEDING OBJECTIVE

Soc A:3.2   Responds to communication from familiar adult

CONCURRENT GOALS AND OBJECTIVES

Cog E:4.0   Solves common problems
Cog G:1.2   Uses functionally appropriate actions with objects
SC B:1.0   Gains person's attention and refers to an object, person, and/or event
SC B:2.1   Uses consistent consonant–vowel combinations
SC D:1.0   Uses 50 single words
Soc A:1.0   Initiates an affectionate response toward familiar adult
Soc A:2.1   Initiates simple social game with familiar adult
Soc B:1.1   Meets physical needs of hunger and thirst

TEACHING SUGGESTIONS
Activity-Based

- Engage in positive interactions with the child during daily activities and routines. Establish eye contact with the child; smile and provide tactile stimulation during feeding, dressing, and bathtime. Wait for the child to initiate a communicative behavior by calling for the adult, gesturing to continue a game or stimulation, or tugging at the adult to gain attention.
- Play games involving tactile and kinesthetic stimulation that may induce the child to vocalize. For example, play "Gonna get you" and observe whether the child protests when the adult suddenly stops chasing or hides.
- Play interactive games with and without objects. Encourage the child to label or point to objects. Ask for help in activating toys; hold up objects.
- Respond to the child's requests for interaction when he or she brings a book to look at, a shoe to put on, or a cup to put juice in. Label the child's request and your own actions.
- During familiar daily routines such as bathtime, story time, or snack, present objects such as apples and bananas and wait for him or her to initiate a choice.
- Encourage the child to greet familiar adults.
- Model conversations with other adults or peers. Wait for the child to initiate communication by participating in the conversation or by trying to gain the adult's attention.
- Walk away from the child and wait for him or her to call you.

Environmental Arrangements

- Place favorite toys and snacks out of the child's reach. Wait for the child to initiate a communicative behavior with a familiar adult in order to obtain the object.
- Put a desired object inside a difficult-to-open container, such as a clear plastic jar, and wait for child to request assistance.
- Introduce novel objects or unusual events. For example, while the child is placing blocks in a box, hand the child a toy animal and wait for the child to express surprise ("Oh") or label the animal.
- Interrupt a favorite activity by turning off the light or the radio. Wait for the child to verbalize, "Off" or "All gone," or point toward the switch or knob.
- Provide small amounts of materials such as only one or two blocks or just a swallow of juice to encourage the child to initiate a request for "more" before you provide more.
- Talk to the child, then pause and wait for the child to initiate a communicative behavior to reestablish the interaction.

Instructional Sequence

- Model initiating communications to familiar adults. Say, "Let's go tell your dad you're ready to go home," or "Let's go say 'Hello' to Aunt Molly." Initiate the interaction and then give the child a turn to initiate.
- Assist the child to initiate by saying, "Your turn to say 'Hi' to Aunt Molly." Encourage other adults to wait for the child to initiate.
- Give the child a verbal direction to initiate communication with a familiar adult. For example, say, "Your daddy is here. Tell him you're ready to go home," or "Mommy's home. Go say, 'Hello.' "
- Physically assist the child to move closer to Daddy and say, "Hello."

TEACHING CONSIDERATIONS

1. Children with severe sensory impairments may use signals that are difficult to read. For example, a child with a severe hearing impairment may ask a question about the missing pet cat by looking at the adult and then turning his or her head in various directions.
2. A child with a visual impairment may communicate by touching the adult and pulling toward an activity.
3. A child with a motor impairment may use gestures and signals to engage an adult in social interactions.
4. Expand upon other sensory modes to help the child with a severe sensory impairment.
5. Avoid continuous stimulation and interaction with the child. Allow for pauses and silences to give the child the opportunity to initiate communication.
6. Provide a stimulating environment and allow the child to actively explore objects and independently initiate actions so that the child will have reason and motivation to communicate.

Objective 3.2   **Responds to communication from familiar adult**

DEVELOPMENTAL PROGRAMMING STEP

PS3.2a   The child shows interest in communication from a familiar adult. For example, the child stops crying when the adult talks soothingly, increases motor action when the adult speaks playfully, looks at adult who is talking, and watches adult as he or she sings.

IMPORTANCE OF SKILL

In addition to being able to participate in a turn-taking interaction, this skill enables the child to learn about communication as a system of signals. Intentional communication includes gestures, vocalizations, and verbalizations. By responding to communication from an adult, the child indicates understanding of the communication.

PRECEDING OBJECTIVE

Cog B:1.2   Focuses on object and/or person

CONCURRENT GOALS AND OBJECTIVES

Cog C:2.1 Indicates desire to continue familiar game and/or action
Cog D:1.1 Imitates motor action that is commonly used
Cog D:2.2 Imitates words that are frequently used
SC A:1.0 Turns and looks toward person speaking
SC B:1.1 Responds with a vocalization and gesture to simple questions
SC B:2.1 Uses consistent consonant–vowel combinations
SC C:1.2 Locates common objects, people, and/or events in familiar pictures
SC C:2.3 Carries out one-step direction *with* contextual cues
SC D:1.0 Uses 50 single words
Soc A:2.2 Responds to familiar adult's social behavior
Soc B:2.1 Responds to routine event

TEACHING SUGGESTIONS

Activity-Based

- During daily activities and routines, talk with the child. Comment on your own activities and the child's. Ask questions; give directions. Verbalizations should be meaningful to the child and related to the immediate context. For example, the child is washing his or her hands and splashing water, and the adult comments, "Splashing looks like fun." The child splashes more enthusiastically. While helping the child dress, the adult comments, "I'm putting on your shoe." The child imitates, "Shoe."
- Ask the child questions about actions, events, and objects. For example, the child drops a spoon from the table; the adult asks, "What did you do?" The child answers by looking down to the floor and pointing.
- As opportunities occur, ask the child to label objects, call people by name, use gestures to greet others, look at people and objects, and locate objects and/or people by pointing.
- Talk to the child within the context of a social interactive game. For example, when the child puts a cover over his or her head to play peekaboo, the adult exclaims, "Where are you?" and the child answers, "Here," or uncovers his or her face.

Environmental Arrangements

- Comment only on objects the child is using or on aspects of the environment that are particularly important to the child. Ask, for example, the location of the child's pet dog and wait for the child to point toward the dog lying on the floor. Comment when the child lets go of a balloon and say, "It's flying away" and wait for the child to gesture bye-bye or say, "Gone" or "Up."
- Play "Where is the ___?" game. For example, the adult names an object and the child points to it. This game is easy to incorporate when looking at books or photos.
- Ask the child questions that can be answered using familiar words or gestures that have been recently produced by the child. For example, after observing the child point to an airplane, ask the child, "Where's the airplane?" or "What's that?"

Instructional Sequence

- Model pairing auditory, visual, and tactile cues with the communicative behavior. For example, tell the child to look at a raccoon while exaggerating the pitch of your voice and facial expression and pointing to the animal.
- Model the response and verbally encourage the child to imitate. For example, ask the

child the name of an object. Label the object if necessary and ask the child to repeat the name of the object.

■ Gently physically assist the child toward a gesture. For example, say, "Let's find the dog," and help the child point to the dog. Then say, "Find the dog again by yourself."

TEACHING CONSIDERATIONS

1. Use language and gestures that are developmentally appropriate for the child. If the child is young, use short phrases, raise and vary the pitch of your voice, and make large and visible gestures.

2. Adapt the type of stimulation to the child's mood. Talk soothingly to a child who is sleepy or nervous; speak in a lively manner to a child who is awake and alert. Adapt the pace to the individual child. Allow time for a slow-paced child to respond before using instructions.

3. Engage in communication that is appropriate to the context. For example, wave bye-bye when departing, talk about the object the child is playing with, and ask questions related to what the child is doing.

4. If the child has a sensory impairment, offer forms of communication that the child is able to perceive and understand. For example, use gestures if the child has a hearing impairment.

5. A child with a severe sensory impairment may use signals that are difficult to read. For example, a child with a severe motor impairment may not be able to clearly articulate a word, despite knowledge of the appropriate symbol.

6. A child with a visual impairment may respond to tactile and auditory communication from the adult and may offer the same kind of communication in return.

Strand B

Interaction with Environment

GOAL 1 Meets external physical needs in socially appropriate ways

---

DEVELOPMENTAL PROGRAMMING STEP

PS1.0a The child shows awareness of external physical needs such as being cold, hot, dirty, wet, or hurt. The child manifests discomfort by frowning or whining when wearing dirty or wet clothes.

IMPORTANCE OF SKILL

This skill is an important step in building the child's independent functioning in the daily environment. It also enhances the integration and acceptance of the child by other members of the social community. The child needs to learn to meet a variety of physical needs defined by the social group. The child develops a group identity by recognizing the social attitudes of other individuals and reproducing behaviors to meet standards set by the community.

PRECEDING OBJECTIVES

Soc B:1.1 Meets physical needs of hunger and thirst
Soc B:2.1 Responds to routine event

CONCURRENT GOALS AND OBJECTIVES

FM B:1.0 Rotates either wrist on horizontal plane
GM C:1.0 Walks avoiding obstacles
Adap B:1.0 Initiates toileting
Adap B:2.0 Washes and dries hands
Adap C:1.0 Undresses self
Cog E:4.0 Solves common problems
Cog G:1.2 Uses functionally appropriate actions with objects
SC B:1.0 Gains person's attention and refers to an object, person, and/or event
SC D:1.0 Uses 50 single words
Soc A:3.1 Initiates communication with familiar adult

TEACHING SUGGESTIONS
Activity-Based

- During daily activities and routines, encourage the child to use socially appropriate ways to meet a variety of external physical needs. When playing with water, sand, or paint, or when eating food, the child may soil hands or clothes. If the child shows discomfort or displeasure, assist in labeling the discomfort by asking, "What's wrong?" "What's the matter?" "What would make you feel better?" Give the child a chance to initiate hand washing or clothing change.
- If the child wets or soils his or her pants or diaper, wait briefly for the child to indicate the soiled garment to the adult, tug at pants, or go to the bathroom.
- Build hand and face washing and pants changing into daily routines, such as just before mealtime and bedtime.
- Wait briefly for the child to ask for additional clothes when cold or to take off clothes when hot.
- Encourage the child to ask for help to wipe a runny nose or to clean a scrape and put on a bandage. Use general cues and questions to draw the child's attention to solutions for meeting physical needs. For example, ask, "Do you need help?" or "What should you do now?"
- Establish "rules" for meeting needs appropriately, such as washing hands before a snack or going to the potty before leaving home. Maintain a consistent routine. Once the child is familiar with these rules, ask questions such as, "What do we need to do before __?"

☑ If your data indicate the child is not making progress toward the goal, provide additional structure within the suggested activities by incorporating the following *environmental arrangements:*

Environmental Arrangements

- Design activities with materials such as glue, sand, or water that are generally unappealing to have on hands or clothes.
- Leave the child's coat on briefly when entering a hot room or delay putting on coat and mittens in the cold to see if the child will ask for them.
- Practice washing after snacks with dolls during pretend tea parties.
- Make an appealing event contingent upon meeting a physical need in a socially appropriate way. For example, allow the child to eat only after hands have been washed or nose has been blown. Allow the child to get a favorite bedtime toy only after the child has sat on the potty or had his or her diaper changed. Allow the child to go outdoors only after putting on his or her coat and mittens.
- Make available objects the child might need. For example, place dry clothes on a nearby stool if the child is playing with water; go near if the child falls and scrapes his or her knee; and set out tissue for a child who has a runny nose.

☑ If this goal is particularly difficult for a child, it may be necessary, within activities, to use an *instructional sequence.*

Instructional Sequence

- Provide the child with a visual model or cue. Have a sibling model removing wet clothing. If the child needs to blow his or her nose, model blowing your nose with a tissue.

- Give verbal cues or directions that label needs: "Are your hands dirty?" or "Are you wet?"
- Give verbal cues or directions that propose ways to meet needs: "Get a diaper and I'll change your pants." or "Do you need a tissue/bandage/washcloth?"
- Physically assist the child to meet evident needs. Get dry clothes or assist the child to wash and dry hands.

☑ Combining or pairing different levels of instructions may be helpful when beginning to teach a new and difficult skill. Fade to less intrusive instructions as soon as possible to encourage more independent functioning.

TEACHING CONSIDERATIONS

1. Make sure the child is aware of the location of relevant objects.
2. If the child has a sensory impairment, make sure the child has the means to adequately meet needs. For example, if a child has a motor impairment and needs a walker, have clean clothes, tissues, and toys available within a reasonable distance. Encourage the child to request help.
3. If the child has a visual impairment, use appropriate means (e.g., tactile, auditory) to let the child know the location of relevant objects.
4. If the child has a hearing impairment, visually demonstrate the location of relevant objects.
5. Expand upon other sensory modes to help the child with a severe sensory impairment.
6. Consider safety with any objects the child handles. Never leave the child unattended with potentially hazardous objects.

Objective 1.1 Meets physical needs of hunger and thirst

DEVELOPMENTAL PROGRAMMING STEP

PS1.1a The child signals awareness of physical needs of hunger and thirst. The child grabs a bottle and starts to suck rapidly; the child smiles and waves arms when food is presented.

IMPORTANCE OF SKILL

The child recognizes the basic physical needs of hunger and thirst and learns to use socially appropriate ways to meet these needs. The recognition of basic physiological needs represents a first step in the development of a sense of self, taking place within the social context as the child adopts attitudes and behaviors of other individuals in order to meet needs. This skill also fosters independence as the child acts to take care of his or her own needs.

CONCURRENT GOALS AND OBJECTIVES

FM A:3.0 Grasps hand-size object with either hand using ends of thumb, index, and second fingers

Soc B

GM C:1.0   Walks avoiding obstacles
Adap A:3.0 Drinks from cup and/or glass
Adap A:4.0 Eats with fork and/or spoon
Cog D:1.1 Imitates motor action that is commonly used
Cog E:4.1 Uses more than one strategy in attempt to solve common problem
Cog G:1.2 Uses functionally appropriate actions with objects
SC B:1.0   Gains person's attention and refers to an object, person, and/or event
SC B:2.0   Uses consistent word approximations
SC C:1.3   Locates common objects, people, and/or events *with* contextual cues
SC D:1.4   Uses 15 object and/or event labels
Soc A:3.1 Initiates communication with familiar adult

TEACHING SUGGESTIONS
Activity-Based

- When the child is hungry or thirsty, wait to see if the child can use socially appropriate ways to meet those needs.
- At mealtimes, let the child help place food on the table. Do not place food directly on the child's plate, but wait for the child to request food or a drink before serving. Between meals, encourage the child to request food or a drink or go to the cupboard or refrigerator to get food or a drink. Use general questions such as, "What do you want?"
- Get food or a drink for yourself and wait for the child to indicate a desire for the same.
- Provide plastic cups and a stool at the sink or drinking fountain for the child to get a drink independently.

Environmental Arrangements

- Make the child's favorite foods and drink visible. For example, place cookies on open shelves near the snack table and place a bottle of juice on the sofa near the child's play area; cut up fruit and keep it on low shelves of the refrigerator.
- Take the child into settings related to meals and foods. For example, take the child to self-service restaurants and let the child go to a counter to get some food. In grocery stores, ask if the child wants anything available in displays.
- Plan for snacks or meals to take place later than usual. Wait for the child to request or obtain food or liquid at the regular time.

Instructional Sequence

- Model going to the refrigerator and taking out a bottle of juice. Give the child a turn to do the same.
- Give the child a verbal cue. For example, "There's fruit in the fridge," "You can pick some berries from the bush," "Tell me if you are thirsty."
- Physically assist the child by guiding the child to the cupboard or by touching a cup, indicating to the child to hold up the cup.

TEACHING CONSIDERATIONS

1. Make sure the child is aware of the location of food and drinks.
2. Place only appropriate foods and drinks within the child's reach.
3. If the child has a sensory impairment, make sure the child has the means to adequately meet needs. For example, if the child has a visual impairment, have avail-

able food and drinks that have a strong smell, such as fresh bread or steaming hot chocolate.

4. If the child has a hearing impairment, visually demonstrate the availability of food and drink.

5. Consider safety with hot foods or foods that lend themselves to choking.

GOAL 2   Responds to established social routine

DEVELOPMENTAL PROGRAMMING STEPS

☑ The goal above is the most basic step for the skill to be taught. Most children will benefit from the activities outlined here that emphasize this skill. For children who need more instruction, consider designing programming steps from the *environmental arrangements* suggestions or from the *instructional sequence* outlined.

IMPORTANCE OF SKILL

The ability to independently perform a sequence of responses to an established social routine demonstrates the child's awareness of a specific social structure. For example, the child gets his or her own jacket when he or she wants to go outside to play. The ability to produce and share in social events and routines enables the child to see him- or herself as part of a group and to gain control and independence by following socially approved rules.

PRECEDING OBJECTIVE

Soc B:2.1   Responds to routine event

CONCURRENT GOALS AND OBJECTIVES

FM B:1.0   Rotates either wrist on horizontal plane
Adap B:1.0 Initiates toileting
Adap B:2.0 Washes and dries hands
Adap B:3.0 Brushes teeth
Adap C:1.0 Undresses self
Cog E:4.0   Solves common problems
Cog F:3.0   Demonstrates functional use of one-to-one correspondence
SC C:1.3   Locates common objects, people, and/or events *with* contextual cues
SC C:2.3   Carries out one-step direction *with* contextual cues
Soc A:3.2   Responds to communication from familiar adult
Soc B:1.0   Meets external physical needs in socially appropriate ways

TEACHING SUGGESTIONS
Activity-Based

- During daily activities and routines, allow opportunities for the child to independently perform a series of responses to established social routines. Give the child one general verbal or contextual cue and wait for the child to perform actions to complete

a routine. For example, when the adult announces that it is time to leave the house, the child gets his or her coat, goes to the door, runs to the car, and gets in the car seat.
- When running bath water, wait for the child to get a towel and bath toys, remove his or her clothes, and climb into the bathtub.
- When it is time to dress the child, wait for the child to go to the bedroom and get clothes.
- At mealtime, give a general cue to indicate the start of the meal and wait for the child to come to the kitchen, sit at the table, and pick up a spoon.
- When playing, encourage the child to get materials, bring them to the play area, and begin an activity.
- At bedtime, wait for the child to get a favorite blanket, a book, a drink, and a kiss good night from the adult.
- Be sure the child has the opportunity to perform independently the series of responses associated with a social routine. Place relevant objects within the child's reach, use child-size furniture, and so forth.

Environmental Arrangements

- Provide general verbal or contextual cues for each step of the sequence of actions of the social routine. For example, begin to set the table for dinner and encourage the child to bring his or her favorite cup to the table. Then announce, "Dinner is ready," and encourage the child to sit at the table.
- Arrange for numerous social routines that are especially reinforcing to the child, such as favorite meals, outings to interesting locations, or favorite activities.
- Begin with social routines within which the sequence of actions can be performed in the same location or with the same objects. For example, give verbal or contextual cues for the child to take off pants and sit on the potty, to wash and dry hands, or to undress and go to bed.
- Make an event that is especially interesting to the child contingent upon the completion of a social routine. For example, have the child wash and dry hands before eating ice cream; or have the child undress and climb into bed before hearing a favorite bedtime story.
- Vary the type, length, and complexity of the social routines.

Instructional Sequence

- Have peers provide visual models of social routines for the child to follow.
- Demonstrate an entire routine and ask the child to imitate.
- Ask the child to continue the routine once you start it. For example, an adult gets out clean clothes, the child removes his or her pajamas, and the adult asks, "What do you do next?" The child then begins to dress.
- Give the child specific verbal instructions for each step of the routine. For example, when it is mealtime, tell the child, "Go to your chair." After the child arrives at the chair, say, "Put on your bib."
- Physically assist the child to the chair after saying, "It's time for dinner."

TEACHING CONSIDERATIONS

1. Allow enough time for the child to respond independently.
2. Make sure that verbal and contextual cues, as well as the responses required, are developmentally appropriate.

3. If the child has a sensory impairment, make sure the child has the means to respond to the routine event. For example, have relevant objects readily available for the child with a motor impairment.
4. Demonstrate the availability of relevant objects for the child with a hearing impairment. Direct the child with a visual impairment to the relevant objects.
5. Consider safety when the child handles foods and objects.

Objective 2.1 Responds to routine event

DEVELOPMENTAL PROGRAMMING STEP

PS2.1a The child cooperates during routine events. For example, the child extends his or her leg when the adult is putting on the child's shoes, or opens his or her mouth when being fed.

IMPORTANCE OF SKILL

Development is primarily social and takes place within a social and cultural context. Through interaction with others, the child becomes part of a culture and social system by learning the rules and conventions adopted by the community. Routine events embody the basic rules of everyday functioning. The child begins to systematically associate immediate experiences and actions to specific events of everyday life. Independent functioning increases as the child requires less assistance from others during routine events.

PRECEDING OBJECTIVE

Soc A:2.2 Responds to familiar adult's social behavior

CONCURRENT GOALS AND OBJECTIVES

FM B:1.0 Rotates either wrist on horizontal plane
GM C:1.0 Walks avoiding obstacles
Adap A:3.0 Drinks from cup and/or glass
Adap A:4.0 Eats with fork and/or spoon
Adap B:1.2 Indicates awareness of soiled and wet pants and/or diapers
Adap B:2.1 Washes hands
Adap B:3.0 Brushes teeth
Adap C:1.0 Undresses self
Cog B:3.1 Looks for object in usual location
Cog G:1.2 Uses functionally appropriate actions with objects
SC B:1.1 Responds with a vocalization and gesture to simple questions
SC C:1.3 Locates common objects, people, and/or events *with* contextual cues
SC C:2.3 Carries out one-step direction *with* contextual cues
SC D:1.0 Uses 50 single words
Soc A:3.2 Responds to communication from familiar adult

TEACHING SUGGESTIONS
Activity-Based

- During daily activities and routines, give the child general verbal or contextual cues associated with a routine event, rather than direct and specific instructions. Wait for the child to perform a single response associated with the routine event.
- At lunchtime, instead of telling the child to sit at the table, start setting the table, or say to the child, "It's lunchtime," and wait for the child to come and sit down.
- Before going outside, tell the child, "It's cold outside," and wait for the child to get a coat or other appropriate clothing.
- Before an art activity, remind the child not to soil clothes and wait for the child to put on an old shirt or apron.
- When dressing the child, say, "Shirt on," or "Pants on," and wait for the child to extend an arm or leg.
- Establish recognizable openings and closings to routines. "It's time for nap" becomes a signal to put away toys, get the favorite bear, or go toward the rest area.

Environmental Arrangements

- Engage the child frequently in social routines that are especially reinforcing, such as meals, art activities, or outings.
- Have objects associated with the routines visible to the child. For example, at snack time place crackers and juice on the table before announcing that it is time for a snack; at bathtime fill the tub with water and add soap bubbles and the child's favorite bath toys before expecting the child to remove clothes or climb in the tub.
- Perform initial events in a series of actions related to social routines so that the child will have to perform only the final event in the sequence. For example, at bedtime pull the curtains, dimly light the room, pull off the bed cover, place the child's favorite toy in the bed, and wait for the child to climb into bed.
- Set the table for lunch with food and all the tableware except the child's plate. Wait for the child to put a plate in place.
- Vary the type, length, and complexity of the routine event.

Instructional Sequence

- Have peers provide visual models for the child to follow in a social routine.
- Provide a demonstration and ask the child to imitate.
- Give the child specific verbal instructions. For example, "Eat your food," "Go to the potty," "Wave bye-bye."
- Physically assist the child. For example, take the child to the coat rack before letting the child go outside.

TEACHING CONSIDERATIONS

1. Provide the child with the opportunity to independently perform a response associated with a social routine. Place relevant objects within the child's reach, and provide child-size furniture, such as small chairs, that the child can climb onto independently.
2. Allow enough time for the child to respond independently to routine events.
3. Make sure that verbal and contextual cues, as well as the responses required, are developmentally appropriate.

4. Be consistent in conducting common daily routines so that the child can learn to anticipate the next action and therefore participate.
5. If the child has a sensory impairment, make sure the child has the means to respond to the routine event. For example, have objects relevant to the routine events readily available for a child with a motor or visual impairment. Use auditory and tactile cues to help the child with a severe visual impairment complete a routine event.
6. Demonstrate routines and the availability of objects for the child with a hearing impairment.
7. Consider safety when the child handles foods and objects.

Interaction with Peers

Initiates and maintains interaction with peer

DEVELOPMENTAL PROGRAMMING STEP

PS1.0a The child responds to and maintains interaction with peer. For example, the child is holding a ball, a peer takes the ball, and the child reaches for the ball until the peer hands it back.

IMPORTANCE OF SKILL

Initiating and maintaining a social interaction with a peer is a basic skill for the development of friendships. In a relationship, each person's behavior has an influence on the other. Friendships grow as children learn to understand each other and communicate and interact constructively. Initially, the focus in interactions is on the manipulation of objects or activities. Social behaviors such as exchanging objects, imitating actions, and building objects together are ways that children interact with each other.

PRECEDING OBJECTIVE

Soc C:1.1 Initiates social behavior toward peer

CONCURRENT GOALS AND OBJECTIVES

FM B:2.0 Assembles toy and/or object that require(s) putting pieces together
GM D:1.1 Jumps up
GM D:3.0 Runs avoiding obstacles
GM D:4.0 Catches, kicks, throws, and rolls ball or similar object
GM D:5.0 Climbs up and down play equipment
Cog C:2.0 Reproduces part of interactive game and/or action in order to continue game and/or action
Cog D:1.1 Imitates motor action that is commonly used
Cog E:3.0 Navigates large object around barriers
Cog F:1.0 Aligns and stacks objects
Cog F:3.0 Demonstrates functional use of one-to-one correspondence
Cog G:1.0 Uses imaginary objects in play
SC B:1.0 Gains person's attention and refers to an object, person, and/or event
Soc B:2.0 Responds to established social routine

TEACHING SUGGESTIONS
Activity-Based

- Provide settings where the child has the opportunity to interact with peers. For example, have the child go to daycare, take the child to playgrounds, and invite peers to the child's home.
- Provide toys that encourage interactions, such as balls, blocks, beanbags, puppets, musical toys, and doll houses. Encourage children to play together by directing interactions to peers. For example, if a child asks an adult for help or shows an object or activity, say, "Maybe Mara could help you," or "Jamal might like to see your doll."
- Allow the child to initiate social interactions with a peer and maintain two or more consecutive exchanges without interruption or assistance. For example, the child offers a toy cup to a peer, the peer takes the cup and puts it on a saucer, and pretends to pour some tea. The child takes the cup back, pretends to drink, and asks the peer for more. The peer pretends to pour more tea, but refuses to relinquish the cup.
- Encourage activities that require more than one step for completion, such as finishing large puzzles, building a tall tower with blocks, or preparing food.

☑ If your data indicate the child is not making progress toward the goal, provide additional structure within the suggested activities by incorporating the following *environmental arrangements:*

Environmental Arrangements

- Encourage the group of children to participate in activities that require collaboration, such as constructing with large blocks, painting on a large sheet of paper, or setting the table for meals.
- Encourage the child to play with familiar and preferred peers or peers who have been observed to be particularly friendly. Initially limit the size of the group of peers.
- Encourage the child to share or exchange objects. For example, children can paint together, exchanging colors with each other.
- Introduce one novel item for peers to play with and learn to manipulate, such as a turkey baster during water play.
- Give peers verbal cues to use in response to another child's initiation. For example, the child walks over and sits close to a peer and you tell the peer to offer a toy to the child.
- Comment on the peer's response to the child's initiation to encourage another exchange. For example, after the child puts a blanket over the peer and the peer takes it off, say, "Fred took off the blanket."
- Set up dramatic play roles that require the child to initiate and maintain interactions (e.g., bus driver, shop keeper, taxi driver).

☑ If this goal is particularly difficult for a child, it may be necessary, within activities, to use an *instructional sequence.*

Instructional Sequence

- Model maintaining an interaction. For example, the child places a block to build a tower and the peer places a second block. If the child does not continue, place a third block and hand the child another block.
- Give nonspecific verbal cues to encourage social behavior. For example, "Jason doesn't have anything to play with," or "Sarah's here!"
- Give the child specific verbal instructions to initiate or maintain the interaction. For

example, after the child approaches the peer and the peer greets the child, tell the child to say, "Hello."

■ Physically assist the child. For example, the child looks at the peer and claps his or her hands; the peer imitates. If the child does not continue clapping, gently press the child's hands together in a clapping motion.

☑ Combining or pairing different levels of instructions may be helpful when beginning to teach a new and difficult skill. Fade to less intrusive instructions as soon as possible to encourage more independent performance.

TEACHING CONSIDERATIONS

1. Ensure that the child feels at ease within the setting or activity. Some children might prefer quiet, sedentary activities; others might prefer noisy activities involving movement.
2. Provide the child the opportunity to initiate and maintain interactions. Avoid the presence of domineering peers or of too many adults. Activities should be child-directed rather than adult-directed.
3. A child with a severe sensory impairment might present social behaviors that are difficult for peers to read. Help peers interpret the child's initiations. For example, a child with a visual impairment sits close to a peer; the peer greets the child; and the child touches the peer's face. Explain to the peer that the child cannot see well and is exploring his or her face; this will help the peer feel comfortable with the tactile contact.
4. If the child has a hearing impairment, give visual and tactile cues as to appropriate interaction with peers. Use total communication.
5. Remember that sharing toys does not come easily to most toddlers. Many legitimate interactions may be initiated and maintained in conflicts over toys and materials. Encourage the child to negotiate with others, intervening only to avoid physical harm.
6. Consider safety with all objects that the child handles. Never leave the child unattended with potentially hazardous objects.

Objective 1.1   Initiates social behavior toward peer

DEVELOPMENTAL PROGRAMMING STEPS

☑ The objective above is the most basic step for the skill to be taught. Most children will benefit from the activities outlined here that emphasize this skill. For children who need more instruction, consider designing programming steps from the *environmental arrangements* suggestions or from the *instructional sequence* outlined.

IMPORTANCE OF SKILL

This skill is important because the child seeks the interaction with a peer. The child assumes an active role in interactions with peers. It is a skill that will be useful for establishing and maintaining relationships with peers. Initiating social behaviors is a step toward ongoing interactions with peers.

PRECEDING OBJECTIVE

Soc C:1.3   Plays near one or two peers

CONCURRENT GOALS AND OBJECTIVES

FM B:2.0   Assembles toy and/or object that require(s) putting pieces together
GM D:1.2   Jumps from low structure
GM D:3.1   Runs
GM D:4.2   Kicks ball or similar object
GM D:5.0   Climbs up and down play equipment
Cog F:3.1   Demonstrates concept of *one*
Cog G:1.1   Uses representational actions with objects
SC B:1.0   Gains person's attention and refers to an object, person, and/or event
Soc B:2.1   Responds to routine event

TEACHING SUGGESTIONS
Activity-Based

- Place the child in situations in which peers are present. Help the child have at least one or two consistent playmates to promote familiarity. Observe which peers the child prefers. Encourage the group of children to play interactive games, including interactive toys and rough and tumble play. Balls, cars, blocks, dolls, and dress-up all promote social behavior, as do running and jumping games.
- Have available objects that children can exchange and share. Have enough toys for children to use without conflict, but few enough toys to encourage interaction.
- Avoid the presence of too many adults and give the child freedom to direct the activity as much as possible. Wait for the child to initiate a social behavior toward a peer by looking and smiling, offering or showing a toy, and helping to complete a task.
- Encourage activities that stimulate collaboration, such as playing house, setting the table, building with blocks, painting on a large sheet of paper, or playing rhythm instruments.

Environmental Arrangements

- Arrange for the child to play with familiar and preferred peers.
- Keep the adult–child ratio low and encourage unstructured child-oriented activities, such as free play. A child is more likely to initiate interactions in a small group.
- Arrange a room in partitioned play areas to bring children into closer proximity for interaction.
- Provide materials that go together to stimulate the child to ask peers for objects. For example, give the peer all the dolls and the child all the doll clothes.
- Have the child play with slightly younger peers or participate in activities at which the child is proficient; this provides the opportunity for the child to help others.
- For quiet children, arrange quiet activities ahead of time to avoid too much noise or confusion, which may reduce peer interactions.
- Ask the child to assist a peer in washing hands, finding a toy, or picking up toys.

Instructional Sequence

- Ask more advanced peers to model initiating social behaviors toward others. Encourage the child to imitate.

Soc C

■ Give the child specific verbal directions to initiate. Have the child show an object or say, "Hello," or help another peer.

■ Physically assist the child to offer an object to another child.

TEACHING CONSIDERATIONS

1. Ensure that the child feels at ease within the setting or activity. Some children might prefer quiet, small group activities; others might enjoy large, noisy games.

2. Provide the child with the opportunity to initiate interactions. Avoid the presence of a domineering peer or too many adults. Activities should be child-directed, as opposed to adult-directed.

3. A child with a severe sensory impairment might present social behaviors difficult to read by peers. Help peers interpret the child's initiations. For example, if a child with a motor impairment looks at a peer, then looks at a cracker and leans toward it, tell the peer that the child is asking for the cracker.

4. If the child has a hearing impairment, provide visual and tactile cues as to appropriate interaction with peers. Use total communication.

5. Keep in mind that many social initiations by toddlers to peers are negative. Try not to discourage these initiations, but, instead, offer a constructive suggestion. For example, say, "Ask Alison for a turn," rather than, "Don't grab toys."

6. Do not expect very young children to share and take turns. Adult assistance and/or supervision will facilitate this.

7. Consider safety with all objects that the child handles. Never leave the child unattended with potentially hazardous objects.

Objective 1.2 Responds appropriately to peer's social behavior

---

DEVELOPMENTAL PROGRAMMING STEP

PS1.2a   The child shows interest in a peer's social behavior. For example, the child looks at a toy offered by the peer, or waves arms and smiles while watching a peer on a swing.

IMPORTANCE OF SKILL

Interactions with peers contribute to the acquisition of basic social and communicative skills in a manner that interactions with adults cannot. Peer interaction is an egalitarian experience, providing the child with the give-and-take essential to socialization, communication skills, and moral development. Responding appropriately to social approaches by peers plays an important role in the acceptance of the child by the peer group and in increasing the likelihood that the child will be approached again by peers.

PRECEDING OBJECTIVE

Soc C:1.3   Plays near one or two peers

CONCURRENT GOALS AND OBJECTIVES

FM A:5.0 Places and releases object balanced on top of another object with either hand
FM B:2.1 Fits variety of shapes into corresponding spaces
GM B:2.0 Sits down in and gets out of chair
GM D:4.4 Rolls ball at target
GM D:5.0 Climbs up and down play equipment
Cog C:2.0 Reproduces part of interactive game and/or action in order to continue game and/or action
Cog D:1.1 Imitates motor action that is commonly used
Cog E:1.1 Retains one object when second object is obtained
Cog F:1.2 Stacks objects
Cog G:1.2 Uses functionally appropriate actions with objects
SC A:1.1 Turns and looks toward object and person speaking
SC B:1.3 Gestures and/or vocalizes to greet others

TEACHING SUGGESTIONS

Activity-Based

- Take the child to settings with opportunities for peer interactions. For example, take the child to daycare centers or to playgrounds, or invite peers to the child's home.
- Encourage a peer to approach the child and wait for the child to respond to the peer's social behavior. Encourage the child to respond in a socially appropriate way. For example, ask a peer to hand out crackers at snack time and wait for the child to smile at the peer, or encourage the child to take the cracker and say, "Thank you."
- Encourage the child to participate in group activities and social interactive games with peers; facilitate interaction among peers by directing interactions to one another. For example, have children pass objects to each other, choose a partner to play ball with, and share a large toy or take turns at an activity with an object.
- Encourage the child to respond to peers in a socially appropriate way by pointing out positive aspects of peers' actions. For example, say, "That was nice of Evan to give everyone crackers."
- Have the child participate in interactive games such as "London Bridge," or "Duck, duck, goose."

Environmental Arrangements

- Have peers play with objects and toys of interest to the child to increase the child's response. Encourage a peer to offer a toy to the child and wait for the child to take it.
- Have the child participate in activities with select peers who are particularly sociable.
- Encourage activities that increase the likelihood that the child will be asked for help by peers. Ask a peer to ask the child for help in moving a small table.

Instructional Sequence

- Model responding to a peer's social behavior. For example, wave back to a peer.
- Provide the child with verbal instructions. For example, tell the child to accept a toy offered by a peer.
- Physically assist the child to respond to a peer. For example, gently place the child's

hand in the peer's hand after the peer extends his or her hand in an offer to take the child to the playground.

TEACHING CONSIDERATIONS

1. Take into account the child's individual differences when judging the appropriateness of a response. A child may not enjoy large group or noisy activities and may not respond to a peer's social behavior within such activities, but may adequately respond to a single peer's approach.
2. Appropriate responses also include reactions to negative social behaviors, such as moving away from a peer who is hitting or yelling, or shaking his or her head when a peer offers an object grabbed away from another child.
3. Children with severe impairments may have difficulties with the interpretation of a peer's social behavior. A child with a severe visual impairment may not be aware of a peer looking and smiling. Be sensitive to this and tell the child, for example, that the peer is smiling and wants to play.
4. If the child has a hearing impairment, give visual and tactile cues as to appropriate interaction with peers. Use total communication.
5. Young children often have difficulty sharing and taking turns. Adult assistance and/or supervision may facilitate sharing and turn-taking.
6. Consider safety with all objects that the child handles. Never leave the child unattended with potentially hazardous objects.

Objective 1.3 Plays near one or two peers

DEVELOPMENTAL PROGRAMMING STEP

PS1.3a The child plays near one or two peers in the presence of a familiar adult. For example, the child plays with Legos in the proximity of the teacher who is reading a story to a peer.

IMPORTANCE OF SKILL

Playing near peers is a step toward participation in a social activity. Although not interacting directly with peers, the child shares a common space and may engage in a similar activity. The child begins to acquire a collective identity as a member of the peer culture and begins to see him- or herself and other children as distinct from adults.

PRECEDING OBJECTIVE

Soc C:1.4 Observes peers

CONCURRENT GOALS AND OBJECTIVES

FM B:2.2 Fits object into defined space
FM B:3.0 Uses either index finger to activate objects
GM D:5.2 Moves under, over, and through obstacles
Cog C:1.0 Correctly activates mechanical toy

Cog D:1.1   Imitates motor action that is commonly used
Cog G:1.1   Uses representational actions with objects
SC B:1.2   Points to an object, person, and/or event
SC B:2.0   Uses consistent word approximations

TEACHING SUGGESTIONS
Activity-Based

- Give the child opportunities to be in the presence of peers. Invite children to play or take the child to the neighborhood park. Provide free play time in the classroom.
- Have the child go to a daycare center or a babysitter who has other children.
- Have objects available for the child to play with and explore. Provide farm and other play sets with multiple parts.
- Encourage the child to approach other children and remain near them when playing independently with a toy or object.
- At snack time, wait for the child to sit and eat at the same table as peers; during outdoor time, wait for the child to climb the same play equipment as other children; and encourage the child to ride a tricycle near peers.

Environmental Arrangements

- Place materials that interest the child close to where his or her peers are playing to encourage proximity.
- Give objects to the child to "deliver" to a peer. Say, "Give Bill a cup," or "Give Ann a spoon."
- Encourage older peers to talk to the child and offer objects to help the child maintain proximity.
- Arrange the environment so that peers and the child are within a restricted space. For example, have them all play in an activity center set off by a wall and three shelves. Encourage them to sit at the same table or play with water around the same basin.
- Have a sibling interact with the child and peers.

Instructional Sequence

- Model playing with a toy near a group of children. Hold out your hand and offer a toy to the child.
- Give the child verbal directions to play in proximity to peers.
- Assist the child by engaging him or her in exploring a toy near peers, then leave the child's presence.
- Have the child sit and play on the lap of an adult who is near one or two peers.

TEACHING CONSIDERATIONS

1. If possible, have the child play with peers whose developmental level is slightly above the child's. Their ages should be similar enough to allow the child to identify with a peer group, but the peers should have slightly advanced social skills to serve as models of constructive social interactions.
2. Take into account a child's individual differences and be aware that a child may not enjoy playing near a noisy group. Encourage two or three members of the group to pull away and play near the child.

Soc C

3. If the child has a hearing impairment, give visual and tactile cues to help direct the child to play near or with others. Use total communication.
4. If the child has a severe visual impairment, use tactile and auditory cues to orient the child to peer activities.
5. Consider safety with all objects that the child handles. Never leave the child unattended with potentially hazardous objects.

Objective 1.4   Observes peers

DEVELOPMENTAL PROGRAMMING STEP

PS1.4a   The child observes older peers, siblings, or a familiar peer. For example, the child watches older sibling playing with a friend.

IMPORTANCE OF SKILL

Observing is an early and distant form of peer-directed behavior. The child becomes aware of the presence of peers and manifests interest in their behaviors. The observation of peers is also important because peers can serve as models for the child in a variety of social and cognitive behaviors.

PRECEDING OBJECTIVE

Soc C:1.5   Entertains self by playing appropriately with toys

CONCURRENT GOALS AND OBJECTIVES

FM A:5.0   Places and releases object balanced on top of another object with either hand
GM B:1.4   Sits balanced without support
GM C:1.4   Stands unsupported
Cog B:1.0   Visually follows object and/or person to point of disappearance
Cog D:1.1   Imitates motor action that is commonly used
SC A:1.0   Turns and looks toward person speaking

TEACHING SUGGESTIONS
Activity-Based

- Take the child to places where peers are present, such as a daycare center, babysitter, park, or playground. Encourage the child to manifest an interest in peers by watching them play. For example, when on a playground take the child close to a group of children playing in the sandbox and point out peers and activities to the child.
- During free play at school, encourage the child to walk around the room to watch peers play. Say, "Let's go see what Jamie is doing." Stop near groups of children, observe activities, and comment on them.
- During daily activities, make sure the child has access to other peers and has free time to observe others during snack, toileting, dressing, or playing.

- Encourage peers to engage in activities that have an interesting outcome, such as baking cookies, dancing to music, or making masks or hats. Make sure that the child is aware of the meaning of the activity and encourage the child to stand by and observe peers engaged in the activity.

Environmental Arrangements

- Design activities so that a peer's action produces an interesting and immediate effect, such as pulling a chain or flipping a switch for lights, bouncing or rolling balls to knock blocks over, or sliding down a slide.
- Have peers engage in noisy activities involving movement or large, attractive objects. For example, take the child outside to observe peers climbing playground equipment or riding tricycles. Decorate a large sheet of paper on the classroom wall; play with large bright balloons; or listen to records.
- Give the child an object or toy similar to that used by peers and encourage the child to observe and imitate peers. For example, while peers are engaged in sand play, hand the child a bucket and shovel and ask, "Can you dig, too?"

Instructional Sequence

- Model observing peers in an interesting activity. Direct the child's attention to peers by pointing toward a group of children playing; describe their actions.
- Verbally encourage the child to watch peers, first by instructing the child to look at them and then by commenting on the peers. Ask the child to tell you what the peers are doing.
- Physically guide the child close to a group of peers so that the child cannot ignore them. For example, place the child in the middle of peers playing in the sandbox.

TEACHING CONSIDERATIONS

1. Make sure the child has access to peers.
2. Do not engage the child continuously in activities; allow the child some time to be an observer.
3. Differentiate a child whose cognitive style is to watch before becoming involved in an activity from a child who watches without becoming involved at all. Do not intervene for the child who becomes involved independently after initial observation.
4. If the child has a hearing impairment, provide visual and tactile cues that help orient the child to peer activities. Use total communication.
5. If the child has a severe visual impairment, use tactile and auditory cues to orient the child to peer activities.
6. Consider safety with all objects that the child handles. Never leave the child unattended with potentially hazardous objects.

Objective 1.5 Entertains self by playing appropriately with toys

---

DEVELOPMENTAL PROGRAMMING STEP

PS1.5a The child plays appropriately with toys with adult assistance.

Soc C

IMPORTANCE OF SKILL

Play is important to the child's acquisition of knowledge about the physical and social world. In particular, learning how to play facilitates the child's inclusion in the peer culture because it is the major activity that young children do together. A first step toward participation in social play with peers is solitary play, in which the child learns to play independently from the adult.

PRECEDING GOAL AND OBJECTIVE

Cog A:1.0   Orients to auditory, visual, and tactile events
Cog B:1.2   Focuses on object and/or person

CONCURRENT GOALS AND OBJECTIVES

FM A:3.0   Grasps hand-size object with either hand using ends of thumb, index, and second fingers
FM B:2.0   Assembles toy and/or object that require(s) putting pieces together
FM B:3.1   Uses either hand to activate objects
GM B:1.4   Sits balanced without support
GM D:2.1   Pushes riding toy with feet while steering
Cog C:1.0   Correctly activates mechanical toy
Cog E:4.0   Solves common problems
Cog F:1.0   Aligns and stacks objects
Cog F:2.0   Categorizes like objects
Cog G:1.2   Uses functionally appropriate actions with objects
SC B:1.0   Gains person's attention and refers to an object, person, and/or event
Soc B:2.1   Responds to routine event

TEACHING SUGGESTIONS

Activity-Based

- Provide the child with a variety of age-appropriate toys. Use both familiar and novel toys so that the child can play with favorite toys as well as explore new ones. Encourage the child to entertain self appropriately.
- Show the child an activity that produces a visible effect or has a purpose meaningful to the child. For example, ask the child to draw a picture for Grandma, or prepare a "snack" for Daddy with Play-Doh. Give the child objects that produce sounds and lights when activated.
- Set the child up with a toy or activity while an adult is nearby but otherwise engaged (e.g., on the telephone, conversing with another adult, washing dishes, reading).
- Encourage the child to entertain him- or herself by engaging in daily activities that the child especially enjoys. For example, let the child dig holes in the garden, sweep up the leaves, or play with soap bubbles and bath toys in the bathtub.

Environmental Arrangements

- Select a range of objects to allow the child to use a variety of modes of exploration: simple toys that are easily activated by motor actions and provide sensory stimulation (e.g., rattles, drums, bells); mechanical toys (e.g., dump trucks, wind-up toys); construction toys (e.g., Legos, blocks); miniature objects (e.g., dolls, animals); materials (e.g., paint, water, Play-Doh, sand); and books, paper, and crayons.

Soc C

- Provide the child with favorite activities, objects, and toys that the child can independently manipulate. Gradually increase the length of time between adult interactions with the child.
- Initiate an activity with the child then leave for a short period and encourage the child to continue to play alone. For example, build a house of Legos with the child and then ask the child to build a garage; take turns activating an object with the child and then allow the child to continue alone.

Instructional Sequence

- Encourage the child to entertain self by systematically increasing the amount of time the child plays independently and the distance the child plays from the adult.
- While at a distance from the child, verbally encourage him or her to play. From the opposite side of the room, observe the child and comment on the child's actions.
- Demonstrate the use of a toy and ask the child to imitate by acting independently on the toy. Physically assist the child to activate the toy.

TEACHING CONSIDERATIONS

1. Make sure that the toys and objects are interesting and developmentally appropriate for the child.
2. Avoid leaving the child alone for long periods. Check on the child regularly to ensure that the child continues to engage in constructive play or object exploration.
3. If the child has a visual impairment, provide bright, noisy objects or objects that have interesting tactile characteristics.
4. If the child has a hearing impairment, provide toys and/or objects that are colorful and visually appealing.
5. Consider safety with all objects that the child handles. Never leave the child unattended with potentially hazardous objects.

| GOAL 2 | Initiates and maintains communicative exchange with peer |

DEVELOPMENTAL PROGRAMMING STEP

PS2.0a   The child responds to communication from a peer and maintains the interaction for two or more turns. For example, a peer asks the child for an object, "Car?" The child answers, "No!" and the peer responds, "Mine!" The child insists, "My car."

IMPORTANCE OF SKILL

After playful interactions that gain a peer's attention, the child learns to use language to convey messages and meanings about objects, people, and events. The ability to initiate and maintain a communicative exchange with a peer demonstrates that the child can use basic conversational skills, focusing and expanding upon a topic and adjusting to topic changes.

PRECEDING OBJECTIVE

Soc C:2.1   Initiates communication with peer

CONCURRENT GOALS AND OBJECTIVES

FM B:2.0   Assembles toy and/or object that require(s) putting pieces together
GM D:3.0   Runs avoiding obstacles
GM D:4.0   Catches, kicks, throws, and rolls ball or similar object
GM D:5.0   Climbs up and down play equipment
Cog E:4.0   Solves common problems
Cog F:1.0   Aligns and stacks objects
Cog F:3.0   Demonstrates functional use of one-to-one correspondence
Cog G:1.0   Uses imaginary objects in play
SC B:1.0   Gains person's attention and refers to an object, person, and/or event
SC C:1.3   Locates common objects, people, and/or events *with* contextual cues
SC C:2.3   Carries out one-step direction *with* contextual cues
SC D:3.0   Uses three-word utterances
Soc B:2.0   Responds to established social routine
Soc C:1.0   Initiates and maintains interaction with peer

TEACHING SUGGESTIONS

Activity-Based

- Have the child engage in unstructured, child-directed activities with peers who have similar or slightly more advanced language and communication.
- Use dramatic play such as dress-up, playing house, or playing doctor to encourage communicative exchanges that are characteristic of common roles.
- Provide interesting toys and materials and wait for the child to initiate and maintain a communicative interaction with a peer for two or more consecutive exchanges. For example, take children on a field trip to pick strawberries and encourage interactions during the activity. The child might ask a peer, "Taste berry?" The peer responds, "Yum," the child looks at hands and says, "Yucky," and the peer responds, "Yucky."
- If the child engages in one communicative exchange, encourage more discussion on the same topic. For example, if the child says, "Me eat," and another child says, "Me, too," ask what they are eating and how it tastes.

Environmental Arrangements

- Design dramatic play such as shopping. Help the children arrange a clerk and customer setting where peers exchange objects and money. Practice with the children until they become familiar with the exchanges and then allow the children to interact independently.
- Have children engage in an activity involving two or more sequences of events to facilitate maintaining communication for two or more consecutive exchanges. For example, have two children share a book and take turns commenting about pictures. Encourage the child to comment about pictures; for example, the child may say, "Look, doggie," and the peer continues, "Doggie bark." The child turns a page and says, "Boy crying," and the peer answers, "Bad doggie." Ask children to describe what they see.
- Give peers verbal cues to respond to the child's initiation. For example, tell the peer, "Alex asked if you want a crayon; tell him if you do."
- Comment on the peer's response to encourage the child to maintain the interaction. For example, in response to the child's invitation to play, the peer nods his or her head. Say to the child, "Oh, Terry wants to play with you; he's glad you asked."

Instructional Sequence

- Provide visual or tactile cues to accompany communicative exchanges. For example, model identifying animals in pictures. Hand the pictures to the children. Pause and wait for the children to take turns identifying the pictures.
- Give the child verbal instructions and models to maintain the interaction. For example, after the peer accepts the child's invitation to go for a walk, instruct the child to "Tell Joy where we are going."
- Instruct the child or peer to initiate or maintain the communicative exchange. For example, after the child approaches and says, "Hello," encourage the peer to answer.
- Physically assist the child to go near a peer and offer a greeting.

TEACHING CONSIDERATIONS

1. Ensure that the child feels free to engage in communicative interactions. Provide an environment of stimulating language to foster interactions among children.
2. The child may have difficulty synchronizing communicative attempts with those of peers. Assist peers in allowing the child enough time to respond.
3. A child with a sensory impairment may present communicative behaviors that are difficult for peers to read. Help peers interpret the child's communication. For example, the child with a severe motor impairment might glance or nod toward a peer to initiate an interaction.
4. If the child has a hearing impairment, give visual and tactile cues that help orient the child to a peer's activities. Use total communication.
5. If necessary, translate for a peer the signs used by a child with a hearing impairment.
6. A child with a sensory impairment might have difficulty understanding a peer's response. Help the child interpret the peer's behavior. For example, a child with a severe visual impairment might not be aware that a peer responded to the child by coming near.

Objective 2.1 Initiates communication with peer

IMPORTANCE OF SKILL

The child uses language as a preferred way to convey meaning to a peer. The child learns to share feelings, ideas, and facts with peers. Communication with language is basic to social acceptance.

PRECEDING OBJECTIVE

Soc C:2.2   Responds to communication from peer

CONCURRENT GOALS AND OBJECTIVES

FM B:2.0   Assembles toy and/or object that require(s) putting pieces together
GM D:3.1   Runs
GM D:4.2   Kicks ball or similar object
GM D:5.1   Moves up and down inclines
Cog F:1.2   Stacks objects

Cog F:3.1   Demonstrates concept of *one*
Cog G:1.1   Uses representational actions with objects
SC B:1.0   Gains person's attention and refers to an object, person, and/or event
SC B:2.0   Uses consistent word approximations
SC D:1.0   Uses 50 single words
Soc B:2.1   Responds to routine event
Soc C:1.1   Initiates social behavior toward peer

TEACHING SUGGESTIONS

Activity-Based

- Encourage the child to engage in unstructured, child-directed activities with peers who have similar or slightly more advanced language and communication.
- Provide interesting toys and materials and encourage the child to initiate communication with a peer to obtain or offer materials, give instructions, ask questions, comment on an action, or refer to objects. For example, when the child plays in a sandbox, encourage the child to initiate communication with a peer by asking for a shovel. For example, say, "Ask Rosa," or "Tell Jamal."
- Encourage children to play verbal and/or vocal activities, such as telephone, house, school, store, or singing.

Environmental Arrangements

- Encourage a peer to play with objects or engage in activities of interest to the child to encourage the child to ask the peer for an object or to participate in the activity. For example, suggest that an older sibling go for a walk with the dog and wait for the child to ask to go along with the sibling.
- Assign the child the role of leader within a simple, familiar game or activity to encourage the child to initiate communication with peers by giving instructions. For example, have the child play the leader in "Follow the leader" or "Simon says." Encourage the child to "Tell them what to do."
- Introduce changes or novel elements and wait for the child to comment about them to a peer. For example, while the child and a peer are playing with a ball, make the ball roll out of sight. Make a surprised expression and shrug your shoulders; wait for the child to comment.

Instructional Sequence

- Have peers model communicative exchanges with other children. Ask the child to imitate. Say, "Show Alison how to ask for a cracker"; then tell Alison it is her turn to ask.
- Instruct the child to ask a question, greet a peer, or explain a behavior, describe an object or activity to a peer. For example, say, "Ask Jason for the block."
- Give the child a verbal model and ask the child to imitate it. For example, tell the child, "Say, 'Do you want a cookie?' "

TEACHING CONSIDERATIONS

1.   Ensure that the child feels free to initiate communicative interactions. Avoid activities that are led by a single adult or child. Encourage peers to interact equally.
2.   A child with a severe sensory impairment might present communicative behaviors

that are difficult for peers to read. Help peers interpret the child's communication. For example, translate into words the signs made by a child with a hearing impairment.

3. A child with a severe motor impairment might glance or nod toward a peer to initiate an interaction. Help the peer learn his or her signals.
4. A child with a severe visual impairment might not know that a peer is nearby and ready to receive a verbal initiation. Help the child locate peers.

Objective 2.2   Responds to communication from peer

DEVELOPMENTAL PROGRAMMING STEP

PS2.2a   The child shows interest in communication from peers. For example, the child looks at the peer when the peer asks a question.

IMPORTANCE OF SKILL

A child's early interactions with peers involve manipulation of objects and activities. Later the child receives verbal communication from a peer and responds. This reception of language is basic to the child's development of language.

PRECEDING OBJECTIVE

Cog B:1.2   Focuses on object and/or person

CONCURRENT GOALS AND OBJECTIVES

FM B:2.0   Assembles toy and/or object that require(s) putting pieces together
GM D:4.4   Rolls ball at target
GM D:5.2   Moves under, over, and through obstacles
Cog C:2.0   Reproduces part of interactive game and/or action in order to continue game and/or action
Cog D:2.2   Imitates words that are frequently used
Cog G:1.2   Uses functionally appropriate actions with objects
SC B:1.1   Responds with a vocalization and gesture to simple questions
SC B:2.0   Uses consistent word approximations
SC C:1.3   Locates common objects, people, and/or events *with* contextual cues
SC C:2.3   Carries out one-step direction *with* contextual cues
SC D:1.0   Uses 50 single words
Soc C:1.2   Responds appropriately to peer's social behavior

TEACHING SUGGESTIONS
Activity-Based

- Provide opportunities for the child to play with peers who communicate verbally or with gestures.
- Wait for the child to respond to the peer's communication by gesturing or verbalizing. For example, when playing dollhouse, the peer tells the child, "You're going to be the

baby," and the child answers, "No." Refrain from intervening unless the children are quarreling.

- Interpret the child's response to peers, if necessary, without pre-empting the interaction. Redirect the interaction back to the child. For example, say, "Maybe Patrick has an idea for who would like to be the baby, if he doesn't want to."
- Encourage children to play telephone, school, or store so that the primary interactions are verbal.
- Ask children to sing with you and continue singing without you.

Environmental Arrangements

- Encourage children to play games in which verbalizations are accompanied by kinesthetic or tactile components. Encourage the child to say, "Tickle, tickle," when playing a tickle game, or "Boom" when pretending to wrestle.
- Provide children with interesting toys and materials and allow them to play freely without adult intervention. Communication should occur as a result of wanting to obtain toys, exchange materials, collaborate on the construction of an object, or assign roles in pretend play.
- Sing songs and play games that require turn-taking and peer responses such as "Ring Around the Rosey."
- Encourage an older peer to assist the child to perform a task or activity by giving simple verbal instructions. Encourage the child to ask questions. Have the peer tell the child, "Put on your shoes," and observe whether the child asks for help.
- Encourage children to engage in activities that require collaboration. For example, place one child in a wagon and have a peer push the wagon. Wait for the peer to ask child, "Ready to go?" and for the child to answer, "Go."

Instructional Sequence

- If the child does not respond to the peer's communication, provide a model by answering the peer and asking the child to imitate.
- When a peer directs a communication to the child, verbally direct the child to answer.
- Interpret or comment on the peer's communication. For example, tell the child, "Jacob said, 'Hi!'" If the child does not respond, instruct the child, "Say, 'Hi,' to Jacob."

TEACHING CONSIDERATIONS

1. Create an environment stimulated by language in which peer modeling is provided.
2. Avoid the presence of adults or peers who tend to dominate the conversation.
3. Group children according to affinity in communication styles. Some children respond more to peers who have a quiet, economic style; others prefer louder, more talkative peers.
4. A child with a severe sensory impairment might have difficulty interpreting a peer's communication. Help the child interpret the peer's initiation. For example, translate words into signs for a child who has a hearing impairment.
5. A child with a severe motor impairment may offer gestures in response to communication from a peer. Help the peer interpret the gestures/signals.

Index

Page numbers followed by *f* indicate figures.